Clinical Assessment of Children's Intelligence

Clinical Assessment of Children's Intelligence

Randy W. Kamphaus, Ph.D.

THE UNIVERSITY OF GEORGIA

Allyn and Bacon
Boston   London   Toronto   Sydney   Tokyo   Singapore

Library of Congress Cataloging-in-Publication Data

Kamphaus, Randy W.
     Clinical assessment of children's intelligence / Randy W. Kamphaus.
       p.   cm.
     Includes bibliographical references and index.
     ISBN 0-205-13934-5 (casebound). — ISBN 0-205-14694-5 (prof.
version ; casebound)
     1. Children—Intelligence testing.   I. Title.
     [DNLM: 1. Intelligence Tests—in infancy & childhood.   BF 432.C48
K15c]
BF432.C48K36   1992
155.4'1393—dc20
DNLM/DLC
for Library of Congress   92-18063
                                                                 CIP

Printed in the United States of America
10 9 8 7 6 5 4 3 2 1   96 95 94 93 92

To Norma, Ashley, and Natalie—
Thanks for making life meaningful.
And to all of my former assessment students—
Thanks for teaching me how to teach.

CONTENTS

PREFACE

This book is born of necessity—my own necessity for a textbook to use for training psychology graduate students in the elementary principles of assessment and diagnostic practice with children and adolescents. I have struggled for years to teach the first graduate course in assessment at two universities. There are many good texts but none that suited my purposes specifically. Some assessment textbooks focus on only one measure. I needed a text that applied the same interpretive system across tests. Other texts and handbooks served my students well as a resource, but they did not provide them with enough "drill and practice" in interpretation.

Clinical assessment skills are difficult to teach, partly because of their esoteric nature and level of nuance and partly because the students do not have similar experiences to draw upon. Sometimes teaching intellectual assessment has seemed similar to teaching my children to read. The student begins "from scratch" and only through considerable toil and practice comes to master the basics. I wrote this text in the hope that it would aid in the assessment training process. I think of this as a *teaching text*, not a resource or reference text.

GOALS

I had the following goals in mind when preparing this book.

1. *Emphasize interpretation*. Intelligence test manuals are improving. New manuals are not only specific about administration and scoring procedures, but they also include generous interpretive information on every topic from significant profile fluctuations to ability/achievement discrepancy tables. The Binet-4 alone has three manuals and the WISC-III manual also meets high standards. Given the high quality of new manuals, it is no longer necessary to emphasize administration and scoring procedures in a textbook such as this one. Consequently, this book emphasizes the proper interpretation of intelligence tests in the context of all of the domains that may be assessed. I feel that interpretation is the crux of the assessment endeavor that is not addressed adequately in test manuals.

2. *Apply step-by-step interpretive methods*. New students of assessment need structure in their early attempts at test interpretation. This is undoubtably one of the reasons for the appeal of Kaufman's (1979b) now classic *Intelligent Testing with the WISC-R*. This book tries to capture a similar method of interpretation that can be applied to *all* measures of intelligence. Several devices are included to enhance the logical processes of assessment, beginning with test selection and concluding with the reporting of results. This is also one of the reasons why this text does not have sequential chapters on various tests. Rather, the student is taken through the entire process of assessment in Chapters 1 through 8 and then is exposed to the great variety of tests. This organization is intended to foster the ability of the student to grasp the

entire process of assessment regardless of the specific test(s) used.

3. *Maintain an emphasis on interpretive process over specific tests.* Related to the previous point is the goal to emphasize clear interpretive thinking rather than the use of a particular test. A truly suspect test can be useful in the hands of a gifted clinician. This approach is exemplified by Chapters 14 and 15, where research findings regarding the use of specific tests with groups of exceptional children are discussed by exceptionality not by test. This organization suggests that it is the diagnosis of the syndrome that takes priority over a preference for a particular measure. Besides, new tests are being produced at such a rapid rate that it is more important that clinicians have the interpretive skills necessary to adopt a new test and use it properly.

4. *Foster a deeper understanding of the intelligence construct.* Chapters 2 and 3 are devoted to theory and research findings separately in order to foster a deeper understanding of the nature of the construct that these tests purport to measure. Clinicians receive tough questions from parents and teachers about intelligence tests, and they must be able to respond in an enlightened fashion. Chapter 16 includes an expanded section on test bias to allow clinicians to speak to this topic with authority. If students simply study tests, they may think that Wechsler was famous among intelligence theorists. Not to take anything away from Wechsler, but he was a gifted clinician who made practical contributions to the field. The sophisticated clinician should be able to cite numerous individuals who have made less visible but nonetheless important theoretical contributions that may lead to tests of the future and important interpretations in the present.

5. *Enhance readability.* The text is written to communicate with *beginning* graduate students, not advanced students who have completed previous assessment coursework. One measure taken to enhance readability was to segregate formulas from Chapter 5 to a set of tables. I have found that students are distracted by formulas

and can comprehend them better after they have read the relevant text. I also attempted to write the copy in a more conversational style and limit "psychobabble" when possible. Drafts of the text were used in four assessment classes prior to publication in order to ensure readability.

6. *Maintain the interest of students.* Several measures were taken to improve student interest and comprehension. Case studies, anecdotes, research reports, and interviews are interspersed throughout the text to give students a respite from some of the difficult copy. In addition to enhancing interest, these breaks are intended to be instructive. In particular, the research reports are intended to give students a glimpse of state-of-the-art research related to intellectual assessment.

7. *Strive to communicate the state of the art.* While it is impossible to include every test and every new test as it is published, it is desirable to include newer techniques that apply to the interpretation of all tests including intelligence tests. Examples of such concepts include computerized adaptive testing and interpretation of confirmatory factor analysis fit indices. The research reports also meet this goal by giving students a glimpse of modern methods such as the effect of medical intervention on children's intelligence.

8. *Emphasize learning by example.* I have found it difficult to teach students about assessment without examples. My students have always forced me to "concretize" the process for them. They crave opportunities to see tests administered and review sample reports. My students seem to learn best by example. Hence, this text includes case after sample case. These cases provide students with numerous concrete models to emulate.

Uses of the Book

This book was written with several potential uses in mind. While its central purpose is to serve the instructor in a first graduate course in intellectual assessment, it will also be useful as a "refresher" for the clinician who was trained some time ago and seeks some updating. This book may also serve as a companion text in an assessment course. While the book is a teaching text, there is also a need for resource texts, so that the professor can emphasize specific tests or assessment procedures. Our (with Dr. Cecil Reynolds) (1990) two-volume *Handbook of Psychological and Educational Assessment of Children* is an example of a resource text that may supplement this book. This book may also be used with Dr. Alan Kaufman's (1990) new book, *Assessing Adolescent and Adult Intelligence*, for a course that covers both child and adult intellectual assessment.

Intended Audience

Psychologists have traditionally been charged with the assessment of children's intelligence. This book was intended to communicate to psychologists in training and assumes a certain amount of psychological background. This text may also be used with other trainees, such as educational diagnosticians, who have a similar educational background but are simply not called psychologists. This text may be useful to some educational policy makers and others who are charged with developing diagnostic guidelines for children and adolescents.

OUTLINE

Several aspects of the organization of the book require amplification.

1. *Boxes.* These are intended to enhance instruction by amplifying topics discussed in the text with more detailed information. The topics discussed in the boxes were also selected to enhance interest. Some of the boxes are merely anecdotes.

2. *Interviews.* These were included primarily to enhance reader interest by allowing the students to obtain a more personal glimpse of luminaries in the field of assessment. The responses to interview questions are thought-provoking and highly informative.

3. *Forms.* Several forms ranging from test review, interpretive, and report writing worksheets were included to help students structure their assessment work in a productive fashion.

4. *Research reports.* These summaries of research articles, theoretical articles, and chapters cover advanced topics not discussed in the text. These are intended to encourage the student to think more critically and deeply about various aspects of assessment.

5. *Chapter questions.* Two questions are included at the beginning of each chapter to serve as "advance organizers." If the student will keep these questions in mind when reading a chapter, he or she will be assured of not "missing the forest for the trees."

Alas, however, these prefacing comments are but hypotheses that require testing with students and psychologists.

ACKNOWLEDGMENTS

I had seen the acknowledgments section of other books and I knew that mine would be similarly long. I did not, however, intend for it to be *this* long, but I suppose that it is "normal" for a project this size.

Luckily I have had some of the best help "in the clutch" when I really needed it. Wanda Sanders put in countless hours preparing the final draft. I simply could not imagine how this project could have been finished in timely fashion without her assistance. Leslie Platt's devotion to the cause in the final stages is similarly legendary. Her competence and dedication are greatly appreciated. Susan Rast worked long hours assisting me with the onerous job of preparing the reference list. Numerous other graduate students at UGA helped with various parts of the project. Some of the more substantial contributions are noted elsewhere in the book. I especially appreciate the work of Kathy Smith, Dr. Marion Huettner, Carol Schmitt, Karen Pleiss, Lori Unruh, Kimberley Wells-Hatton, Dr. Alison Lorys, Dr. Pat Goodyear, Jose Gonzalez, Janna Dresden, Dr. Jerry Slotkin, Connie Silberman, and Brian Nicoll. Mary Cash worked tirelessly in the early stages to enter copy. Her modeling of her organizational skills was also invaluable.

Many colleagues provided assistance at various stages. Some contributed ideas for psychological reports, and others provided encouragement, feedback and advice on various aspects of the book. I especially appreciate the contributions of Dr. George Hynd, Dr. Paul Frick, Dr. Marion Ego, Dr. Gail Matazow, Dr. Jack Naglieri, Dr. Michael Shapiro, Dr. Janet Martin, Dr. Mary Shapiro, Dr. Roy Martin, Dr. Mark Daniel, and Dr. Ben Lahey.

Invaluable critical feedback came from numerous colleagues, who provided anonymous but skilled reviews. I am also grateful for the support of my scholarship by our Dean, Dr. Alphonse Buccino; Division Chair, Dr. George Gazda; and Department Chair, Dr. Joseph Wisenbaker.

Most importantly, this book would not have been possible without the intellectual leadership of colleagues and mentors. In this regard I owe a great debt to Dr. Alan S. Kaufman, Dr. Cecil R. Reynolds, Dr. Ronald Havens, Mr. Pete Prunkl, Mr. Dennis Campbell, Dr. Paul Caillier, and Dr. John Nolan.

Finally, the contributions of Mylan Jaixen of Allyn and Bacon to this volume are gratefully acknowledged. His editorial experience coupled with his considerable expertise served to encourage high-quality work at every step of the writing process.

History of Intelligence Testing

CHAPTER QUESTIONS

Why were intelligence tests invented?
Who invented intelligence tests?

Who were the first intelligence testers? They were parents, preschoolers, employers, teachers, spouses, grandparents, and philosophers. They were people like you and me who for whatever reason labeled an individual as intelligent or less than intelligent. The lexicon of intelligence and its assessment has been commonly used for centuries, long before the availability of intelligence tests. Individuals have always categorized others as "bright," "dull," "gifted," and the like. Even preschoolers "assess" their own intelligence and that of their peers. Parents of young children know that children make their own diagnoses of intelligence in the early school grades by saying such things as, "Suzie is smart—she's in the cardinals reading group." Teachers also know that the names they use to

deemphasize differences in instructional groups are usually decoded by children within minutes of their application. Children in early grades know full well if all the good readers are in one group that this is the "advanced" group. Actually, intelligence tests simply formalize a common practice used by people to identify individual differences between people—they assess intelligence. It is hoped that intelligence tests are more objective than people's armchair analyses!

Formal procedures for intellectual assessment have a long and colorful history, especially in western societies. While at first historical aspects of intellectual assessment may not appear striking, it is imperative that intelligence test users have a clear understanding of the roots of intellectual assessment. Much theoretical and research ground has already been plowed during at least a century of modern science. Unfortunately, some of these initiatives may have been forgotten by many. Thus, some researchers and theoreticians may consider some developments new when in fact they are not. A critical look at even "new" tests and theories sometimes shows them to be mirror images of previous work. In order to allow the psychologist who uses modern intelligence tests to avoid fads and trends and not misunderstand these as "breakthroughs," one must have a clear idea of the history of intellectual assessment.

An understanding of intelligence testing history is also practically useful for interacting with parents and teachers. These consumers of psychological test data can bring biases to the meeting with the psychologist who is charged with explaining intelligence test results and other findings. Parental and teacher biases may be a function of the historical context in which they were reared. In the 1970s intelligence tests were uniformly considered to be biased tools of those wishing to maintain societal inequities. In the 1980s, as in the early part of this century, there was considerably more appreciation for biological influences on intelligence. Understanding of these historical contexts may help a psychologist understand and react to parent or teacher questions.

The importance of historical knowledge for the modern use of intelligence tests and knowledge of research on intelligence and its measurement is stated most eloquently by Boring in his 1929 textbook:

> The experimental psychologist, so it has always seemed to me, needs historical sophistication within his own sphere of expertness. Without such knowledge he sees the present in distorted perspective, he mistakes old facts and old views for new, and he remains unable to evaluate the significance of new movements and new methods. In this manner I can hardly state my case too strongly. A psychological sophistication that contains no component of historical orientation seems to me to be no sophistication at all. (p. vii)

The history of research and development in intelligence testing is fraught with repeated missteps and failures. The several attempts to "raise" intelligence are among them (Glutting & McDermott, 1990). Many new tests will be

offered in the coming years, with some of them promising "breakthroughs." It is hoped that those psychologists who are well versed in history will be able to distinguish between true innovations, when they occur, and empty promises that have been tried before.

The remainder of this chapter presents a number of major events in the history of intellectual assessment. The reader is cautioned, however, that there are numerous other milestones that are not discussed due to space considerations. Discussion of other significant achievements can be found in sources such as Jenkins and Patterson (1961) and Thorndike and Lohman (1990).

EARLY HISTORY

While the roots of psychological testing cannot be traced to a particular culture, individual, or event (Anastasi, 1988), there is considerable agreement that the practice of assessing individual skills and abilities is an ancient one. The Chinese, for example, reportedly used civil service examinations as long as 3,000 years ago (DuBois, 1970). The idea of individual differences in performance was mentioned by great thinkers as diverse as Socrates, Plato, Mohammedan rulers, and Charles Darwin (French & Hale, 1990).

An early intelligence test, described by Sir Anthony Fitzherbert, was published in 1534. This first test was intended to differentiate between the "idiot" and the "lunatic." Fitzherbert described a crude measure of intelligence as follows (as cited by Pintner, 1923):

> And he who shall be said to be a sot and idiot from his birth, is such a person who cannot account or number 20 pence, nor can tell who was his father or mother, nor how old he is, etc., so as it may appear that he hath no understanding of reason what shall be for his profit, nor what for his loss. But if he hath such understanding, that he know and understand

his letters, and do read by teaching or information of another man, then it seemeth that he is not a sot nor a natural idiot. (p. 6)

While numerous authors and theoreticians throughout history have mentioned individual differences, it has been only during the last 100 years that formal procedures for the measurement of human abilities have been in widespread use. The relative recentness of the development of measures of intelligence may at least partially explain the considerable excitement and satisfaction on the part of early developers of psychometric measures. Emblematic of the excitement of the early test developers is the comment by Goddard (1912) describing the 1905 Binet-Simon scale, stating that "the scale would one day take a place in the history of science beside Darwin's theory of evolution and Mendel's laws of heredity" (p. 326). These individuals were true pioneers who changed dramatically the way people think about individual differences. Some might argue that the discoveries of early intelligence test developers are akin to modern discoveries such as the microcomputer. The introduction of intelligence tests spurred the development of hosts of measures of human abilities and skills, including academic achievement measures and employee selection tests in the 1920s.

Developments in Experimental Psychology

Wundt's Laboratory

The pioneering efforts of early intelligence test researchers were made possible in part by developments in experimental psychology (Anastasi, 1988). Students of psychology know that intelligence testing is about 100 years old. Not so coincidentally, experimental psychology also traces its roots back 100 years, to the opening of Wilhelm Wundt's lab in Leipzig, Germany in 1879. Many early efforts at measuring intelligence used tests that were developed in early experimental psychology laboratories. For example, Wundt and his first assistant, the American James McKeen Cattell, found numerous individual differences on measures of sensory abilities and reaction time. These types of measures were later incorporated into intelligence tests developed by Cattell and Sir Francis Galton.

Moreover, it became clear in early laboratory experiments that experimental conditions had to be carefully controlled in order to achieve reliable findings (Anastasi, 1988). The notion of "control" refers to the need to eliminate the effects of unwanted variables in the experiment. If one is interested in assessing individual differences in intelligence, then it would be wise to control for unwanted factors such as fatigue by ensuring that the examinee is well rested. Similarly, in Wundt's lab it was discovered that tests of physical skill, such as reaction time, had to be administered under consistent conditions in order to serve as reliable and valid measures of individual differences. Thus, the association of experimental control and mental measurement was established early. To this day, standardized (carefully controlled) procedures are a hallmark of individual intelligence testing.

Sir Francis Galton

Clearly, numerous early theorists and researchers were convinced that intelligence was an inherited trait. They considered the inheritance of intelligence to be so substantial that intelligence could be measured and studied in much the same way as other inherited characteristics such as height. The Englishman Sir Francis Galton was a contemporary of Cattell who was keenly interested in the inheritance of mental abilities. Galton (1869) strongly believed that intelligence was inherited and that it could be objectively measured, as is evident from the following quote:

I acknowledge freely the great power of education and social influences in developing the active powers of the mind, just as I acknowledge the effect of use in developing the muscles of the blacksmith's arm, and no further. Let the blacksmith labor as he will, he will find that there are certain feats beyond his power that are well within the strength of a man of herculean make, even although the latter may have led a sedentary life. (Jenkins & Patterson, 1961, p. 1)

Galton developed a battery of tests that he thought would allow him to study the inheritance of intelligence. His tests were similar in content to the tests of sensory and physical skill used by experimental psychologists such as Cattell. Galton viewed the use of these psychophysical measures as sensible because, he reasoned, if all information is obtained through the senses, then intelligent individuals must have very capable sensory abilities (Galton, 1883). Galton's tests were introduced to the public at the 1884 International Exhibition in London, where an individual could get his or her intelligence tested for three pence (Anastasi, 1988).

Galton made many other contributions to the study of individual differences, including laying the groundwork for the understanding of the normal curve. In 1869 he concluded, "Hence we arrive at the undeniable . . . that eminently gifted men are raised as much above mediocrity as idiots are depressed below it . . ." (Jenkins & Patterson, 1961, p. 16). This was an important insight into the nature of individual differences, as it operationalized what many people knew intuitively: There are many more people in the middle of the intelligence distribution than there are with either high or low scores. The properties of the normal curve are the foundation of what has been called "classical test theory." The normal curve is also the foundation for much of the interpretive work in intelligence assessment.

Early American Work

Shortly after Galton's original work on intelligence appeared, similar efforts were carried out in the United States. Cattell followed the tradition of the measurement of sensory and physical characteristics for the purposes of intellectual assessment when he returned to the United States, where he eventually joined the faculty of Columbia College (now Columbia University). The central problem with the use of psychophysical measures of intelligence, their *lack of correlation with school achievement*, became clear in the work at Columbia. Wissler (1901) reported that every student at Columbia College was required to take an annual psychological examination that was designed by Cattell and his colleagues. This exam included the following tests, some of which are direct descendants of measures developed in Wundt's lab:

Perception of Size	Size of Head
Strength of Hand	Fatigue
Eyesight	Color Vision
Hearing	Perception of Pitch
Sensation Areas	Sensitiveness to Pain
Color Preference	Reaction Time
Rate of Perception	Naming Colors
Rate of Movement	Accuracy of Movement
Association	Imagery

Rhythm and Perception of Time
Perception of Weight or Force of Movement
Memory (Auditory, Visual, Logical, Retrospective)

This was undoubtedly a more interesting test for college students than the SAT! Students must have reveled in the search for "sensation areas" and scorned the "sensitiveness to pain" tests! Some interesting results from Wissler's research that highlight the problem of the lack of correlation of early intelligence tests with school achievement are given in Table 1.1.

Inspection of the data from Table 1.1 leads inevitably to the conclusion that the best corre-

TABLE 1.1 Correlations of Psychology Clinic Measures with Measures of Academic Achievement from Wissler's (1901) Research

Strength of hand and class standing	−.08
Fatigue and class standing	+.23
Reaction time and class standing	−.02
Association time and class standing	+.08
Naming the colors and class standing	+.02
Logical memory and class standing	+.19
Auditory memory and class standing	+.16
Logical memory and mathematics	+.11
Logical memory and Latin	+.22
Latin and mathematics	+.58
Latin and rhetoric	+.55
Rhetoric and mathematics	+.51
German and mathematics	+.52

lates of achievement are measures that have item types similar to the achievement measures that they are intending to predict. Said another way, tests that are achievement-like, as opposed to tests of physical attributes, seem to be better predictors of achievement. For example, measures of sensory abilities (e.g., reaction time) and physical attributes have very weak correlations with achievement. On the other hand, proficiency in school subjects such as Latin has a considerably more positive relationship with other areas of achievement such as mathematics. Hence, the challenge remained in 1901 to develop a practical measure of intelligence that would correlate highly with important criterion variables (i.e., school achievement). A breakthrough that solved this problem was already in the making in France at this time.

The Societal Need

Like many other scientific breakthroughs, such as Salk's polio vaccine, the development of intelligence tests was carried out in response to a societal need. Modern intelligence testing can be traced most directly to the concern for the *humane treatment of mentally retarded individuals* that was exemplified by the work of pioneers such as Itard (1896–1962) and Sequin (1866–1907) during the nineteenth century. Prior to the work of Itard and Sequin, mentally retarded individuals were generally scorned and subjected to inhumane treatment. This lack of respect for the mentally retarded was evident during the Renaissance, when it was commonly believed that mentally retarded individuals were the children of Satan (Pintner, 1923). Since these individuals were presumed to be possessed by devils, severe forms of treatment were required to drive the evil from them. Frequently, mentally retarded and mentally ill individuals were whipped, bound with chains, and placed in dungeons until they changed their ways.

Itard and Sequin were primarily interested in developing cures for mental retardation. Common to all of their approaches was an emphasis on motor and sensory training to raise the intellectual levels of these individuals (Spitz, 1986b). It is interesting and perhaps not accidental that the emphasis on sensory ability as central to the treatment of mental retardation coincides with the common practice at the time of assessing sensory skills as measures of intelligence.

Of course, in order to first identify mentally retarded individuals for treatment, it was necessary to develop appropriate diagnostic criteria and procedures. As a result, the need for intelligence tests to diagnose mental retardation was clear. This need for accurate measures of intelligence, particularly measures of children's intelligence, provided an impetus for research and development in the field of intelligence testing.

THE BREAKTHROUGH OF BINET AND SIMON

Given the need expressed by European governments (particularly France) for the accurate diagnosis of children's intelligence and the failed efforts of Cattell and Galton at providing measures that correlated adequately with school achievement, the stage was set for some individual or group of individuals to overcome the predictive validity barrier and meet the societal need. In his 1901 presidential address to the American Psychological Association, Joseph Jastrow was optimistic about the prospects of a breakthrough in intelligence testing. He portrayed the future of intelligence testing as bright in the following passage from his speech:

> *The study of normal efficiency of that composite group of processes which contribute to our common humanity has, I confidently believe, an important and a practical future. Its progress is dependent upon careful analysis, upon systematic investigation, upon the cooperative and the coordinate labors of many, upon interpretive skill and psychological insight. An auspicious start has been made; the day of the production of works and fruit cannot be far off. (Jenkins & Patterson, 1961, p. 31)*

It was only a few years later that the breakthrough Jastrow envisioned occurred. Alfred Binet, along with his colleague Theophilius Simon, produced the first technological breakthrough in intelligence testing by developing the first practical intelligence test battery (Binet & Simon, 1905). (See Research Report for a history of Binet's earlier work in hypnosis and other areas.) It was practical in the sense that it assessed "higher"-level cognitive skills and, as a result, produced substantial correlations with measures of school achievement. As Boring (1929) observed, "Binet was seeking to measure the intellectual faculties, the complex mental processes, whereas Galton measured only simple capacities, hoping vainly that they might have some significance for the 'intellect.' Binet was right, Galton was wrong . . ." (p. 546).

The 1905 Scale

The 1905 scale consisted of 29 tests. It is notable that Binet and Simon retained some of the psy-chophysical measures of the past such as "comparing two weights." On the other hand, most of the "new" tests departed from past practice by measuring higher-level reasoning abilities. The inclusion of tests such as "reply to an abstract question" and "defining abstract terms" was intended to measure more complex cognitive activities.

The tests on the 1905 scale were as follows:

1. Following a moving object with one's eyes
2. Grasping a small object that is touched
3. Grasping a small object that is seen
4. Recognizing the difference between a square of chocolate and a square of wood
5. Finding and eating a square of chocolate wrapped in paper
6. Executing simple commands and imitating simple gestures
7. Pointing to familiar named objects
8. Pointing to objects' representation in pictures
9. Naming objects in pictures
10. Comparing two lines of markedly unequal length
11. Repeating three spoken digits
12. Comparing two weights
13. Susceptibility to suggestion
14. Defining common words by function
15. Repeating a sentence of 15 words
16. Telling how two common objects are different
17. Memory for pictures
18. Drawing a design from memory
19. Telling how two common objects are alike
20. Comparing two lines of slightly unequal length
21. Placing five weights in order
22. Discovering which of the five weights has been removed
23. Making rhymes

RESEARCH REPORT

Binet's biography

In a series of articles published in the early 1960s, Theta Wolf (1961, 1964, 1966) documents some of the less well-known aspects of Binet's career and personal life. Through interviews with Binet's faithful colleague Simon and reviews of Binet's papers, she gives some valuable insight into the nature of Binet's persona and the early beginnings of intelligence test development. This set of papers must be read by any serious student of Binet's work.

Binet was in some ways a late bloomer and merely happened upon the area of intellectual assessment. He published his first paper in 1880 at the age of 23. The first 10 years of his career were tumultuous. He began as an "armchair" psychologist who used techniques such as hypnosis to study hysterics. By 1891 his career had reached a low point, as is described aptly by Wolf (1964).

He had become a man almost bereft of theoretical underpinnings, and, what was worse, even of the "facts" on which he had been so sure he could count, whatever theories might be built out of them. . . . They were years in which his own studies and controversies led him into blind alleys and humiliating defeats. (p. 702)

The birth of Binet's children, Madeleine in 1885 and Alice in 1887, may have helped him sharpen his interests in individual differences. First, he noted continuing temperamental differences between his daughters. He described Madeleine as "silent, cool, concentrated, while Alice was a laugher, gay, thoughtless, giddy, and turbulent" (cited in Wolf, 1966). Binet began experimenting with his daughters, studying changes such as dominance (e.g., handedness) and reaction time. He concluded early on that higher-level cognitive tasks would be necessary to differentiate child and adult intelligence. He demonstrated this using a task where the subject was asked to discriminate lines of different lengths—two lines of differing lengths on five cards (Wolf, 1966). He found that his two daughters could discriminate the lines on all of the cards except the last one, and, when he showed the cards to two adults, they had the same success rate as the children. This important experiment, showing a lack of age differentiation for a sensory task, led him to depart from his contemporaries who were using psychophysical measures of intelligence.

What was Binet like? Wolf (1966) describes him as shy and somewhat uncomfortable in social situations. Some of his colleagues described him as demanding and difficult to work with. He was also very selective about his colleagues. Simon apparently worked diligently to endear himself to Binet in order to get a chance to work in his laboratory. Simon also hypothesized that Binet would not tolerate teaching well, as he would likely have had little patience for students. Simon's perseverance, however, was rewarded with the admiration of his mentor. Binet said of Simon:

I have had many students and collaborators, but I have never had any as sincere and as loyal as Simon. And another thing, never would he say "yes" to me when he thought "no." (cited by Wolf, 1961, p. 247)

24. Sentence completion
25. Using three words in a sentence
26. Replying to an abstract question
27. Reversal of the hands of a clock
28. Paper cutting
29. Defining abstract terms

Binet validated his tests by administering them to groups of normal and mentally retarded children and determining the ability of each measure to differentiate these two distinct groups. An interesting fact is that Binet used the common-sense judgment of parents and teachers in order to form his groups of normal and mentally retarded youngsters (Pintner, 1923). As such, society's informal conceptions of who was or was not intelligent played a central role in the validation of this most important measure.

Content Validity

Binet also recognized that if verbal tests were to be used, they should not be too closely related to school tasks. If his tests were too similar to classroom tasks, then they could be said to measure academic achievement and not intelligence. Consistent with his idea that his test had to be obviously different from achievement tests, he proposed the following three methods of studying intelligence and showed how intelligence testing differed from other types of assessment:

> 1. *The medical method*, which aims to appreciate the anatomical, physiological, and pathological signs of inferior intelligence.
>
> 2. *The pedagogical method*, which aims to judge the intelligence according to the sum of acquired knowledge.
>
> 3. *The psychological method*, which makes direct observations and measurements of the degree of intelligence. (Binet & Simon, 1905)

Binet and Simon (1905) stated further:

> *Our purpose is to evaluate a level of intelligence. It is understood that we here separate natural intelligence and instruction. It is the intelligence alone that we seek to measure, by disregarding, insofar as possible, the degree of instruction the subject possesses. He should, indeed, be considered by the examiner as a complete ignoramus knowing neither how to read nor write. This necessity forces us to forego a great many exercises having verbal, literary or scholastic character. These belong to a pedagogical examination. (p. 93)*

Binet and Simon, then, placed considerable emphasis on the establishment of content validity for their scale, an emphasis that has been lacking in many subsequent measures. Many modern tests such as the WISC-III and the latest edition of the Binet, the Binet 4, include arithmetic and other school-related items, whereas the original Binet scale tried to avoid such items.

Binet and Simon proposed the purposes outlined below for their test battery in 1905. These purposes have important implications for the interpretation and use of modern tests of intelligence. This is the case because, in many ways, intelligence testing has not changed much since the time of Binet (Kaufman, 1979a).

> *Our purpose is to be able to measure the intellectual capacity of a child who is brought to us in order to know whether he is normal or retarded. We should, therefore, study his condition at the time and that only. We have nothing to do either with his history or with his future; consequently we shall neglect his etiology, and we shall make no attempt to distinguish between acquired and congenital idiocy; for a stronger reason we shall set aside all consideration of pathological anatomy which might explain his intellectual deficiency. So much for his past. As to that which concerns his future, we shall exercise the same abstinence; we do not attempt to establish or prepare a prognosis and we leave unanswered the question of whether this retardation is curable, or even improvable. We shall limit ourselves to ascertaining the truth in regard to his present mental state. (Jenkins & Patterson, 1961, p. 90)*

Binet and Simon elaborated on their earlier work in a 1908 paper where they propose that one purpose of their measuring scale of intelligence is to be ". . . useful in formulating a course of instruction really adapted to their aptitudes" (Jenkins & Patterson, 1961, p. 103).

THE CONTRIBUTIONS OF TERMAN

Lewis Terman (1916) gave one of the first rationales for the use of intelligence tests. He was evidently very optimistic about the value of intellectual assessment. He proposed the use of intelligence tests for individual child study by saying:

> *Every child who fails in his school work or is in danger of failing should be given a mental examination. The examination takes less than one hour, and the result will contribute more to a real understanding of the case than anything else that could be done.*

It is necessary to determine whether a given child is unsuccessful in school because of poor native ability, or because of poor instruction, lack of interest, or some other removable cause. (p. 5)

Evidently Terman believed, as did many of his day, that intelligence tests were the best measures available of "innate intelligence." He also believed that if a trait like intelligence was inherited, then it was not malleable. It is important to be aware of the views of early intelligence researchers—that intelligence tests measured an unchangeable and inherited trait—because those views have shaped the opinions of some scientists and society at large.

Terman (1916) produced the most successful of the English translations of Binet's work. His scale, the Stanford-Binet, met high psychometric standards for the time. He took great pains, for example, to collect a United States norming sample. He also introduced the concept of the *intelligence quotient (IQ)*, which was originally the invention of a German scientist named William Stern (Boring, 1929). Hence, the IQ score is one of Terman's contributions to intelligence testing and not a contribution of Binet. In fact, Simon stood in opposition to the use of the intelligence quotient (Wolf, 1961). This original IQ was called a Ratio IQ, using the formula $IQ = 100 \times MA/CA$, where MA equals the child's mental age (as typically determined by the number of tests a child passed that were designated for a particular age group of children) and CA equals the child's chronological age in years and months. When this formula was used, a child who passed few of the tests designated for his or her age group would have a lower MA than CA, which would result in an IQ less than 100. Conversely, the child who passed all of the tests designated for his or her age group and perhaps some for an older age group would obtain an IQ higher than 100. Unfortunately, this Ratio IQ metric has some rather severe psychometric limitations (Davis, 1964). It was soon replaced by Wechsler's so-called Deviation IQ (actually a standard score; see Chapter 5).

Terman participated in the development of several subsequent revisions of the Stanford-Binet. The various editions of the Stanford-Binet are listed below.

Year	Test	Authors
1916	Stanford-Binet Intelligence Scale This was the version that popularized the term "IQ."	L. Terman
1937	Stanford-Binet Intelligence Scale This version of the Binet had two forms (versions), L and M.	L. Terman, M. Merrill
1960	Stanford-Binet Intelligence Scale Form L-M For this scale the two 1937 forms were combined into one again.	L. Terman, M. Merrill
1972	Stanford-Binet Intelligence Scale Form L-M This version was revised under the direction of Robert L. Thorndike.	L. Terman, M. Merrill
1986	Stanford-Binet Intelligence Scale Fourth Edition	R. L. Thorndike, R. Hagen, J. M. Sattler

Early workers in intelligence testing were also keenly aware of the limitations of the popular tests of the day. Terman called for intelligence tests that gave more than just global estimates of ability. He noted the need for tests of specific abilities. Terman (1916) compared the need for more specific tests of ability to medical diagnosis by proposing:

It is necessary to have a definite and accurate diagnosis, one which will differentiate more finely the many degrees and qualities of intelligence. Just as in the case of physical illness, we need to know not merely that the patient is sick, but also why he is sick, what organs are involved, what course the illness will run, what physical work the patient can readily undertake. . . . (p. 23)

Terman stated further that Binet also agreed with this point of view. Terman (1916) believed that "Binet fully appreciated the fact that intelligence is not homogeneous, that it has many aspects, and that no one kind of test will display it adequately" (p. 36). It is interesting that one of the "modern" trends in intelligence theory today is to speak of multiple intelligences (e.g., Sternberg, 1987). Terman argued this same point of the multifaceted nature of intelligence over a half century ago!

Terman also agreed with other intellectual assessment pioneers, such as Binet and Simon, who emphasized the importance of devising tests that limit the impact of formal schooling on the results. Terman (1916), in describing the development of verbal comprehension items, stated, "In developing tests of this kind we should, of course, have to look out for the influences of formal instruction" (p. 337). This problem of the overlap of the assessment of school achievement and intelligence remains as a nagging interpretive dilemma for users of these tests even today.

THE WORLD WAR I YEARS

Intelligence testing received considerable attention in the United States during World War I. During the war, Robert Yerkes directed an assessment committee of the American Psychological Association that was eventually charged with the screening of about a million and a half potential soldiers (Anastasi, 1988). It was this group of psychologists that developed the first group-administered tests of intelligence.

A Graduate Student's Insight

As it turns out, this group of researchers benefitted greatly from the pioneering work of a student of Lewis Terman's by the name of Arthur Otis (Lennon, 1985). Otis began as an engineering student who switched majors to psychology and became intrigued with the work of Terman. While Otis was convinced that Terman was correct in arguing that every schoolchild should receive an individual evaluation in order to understand him or her better, Otis wondered if this was truly practical. He reasoned that if children could be tested in groups that they could, in fact, all receive an evaluation of their intelligence. In a 1959 television interview with Walter Durost Otis describes how he became involved in this undertaking. Otis discusses his involvement in a response to a question by Durost as follows (as cited by Lennon, 1985):

Otis: Yes. Well, when World War I began, Major Yerkes, a psychologist at Yale University, conceived the idea that it would be very desirable to test the intelligence of the draftees as soon as they came into the Army so that the superior officers could pick out officer material and could place the men in the various functions of the Army to the best advantage. So he invited some other psychologists, Drs. Whipple, Terman, and Haggerty, to form with him a committee to consider the possibility of doing this testing. It was Major Yerkes' idea at the time that they would have to train a lot of psychologists to give the Binet. He didn't know anything about any group tests. . . . So, fortunately perhaps, Dr. Terman presumably had a copy of my test in his pocket with him at the time. You see this incident occurred, this incident of World War I—just at the time that I was finishing my doctor's degree, and I had this manuscript of the test and it was pretty well standardized. Dr. Terman had been convinced that it was fairly sound and workable, and so he probably told him that they needn't bother with giving the Binet to everybody because there's a young fellow out at the University in my class who has made up a group test. He presumably convinced them that

they should send for me and make up some group tests which, of course, was done. They enlisted the help of perhaps 100 or so psychologists from all over the country and we got together and made up as many items as we could. They just followed my group test. They said, "Wess, he made up opposites, we'll do that, and he made up analogies, we'll do that," and they made up groups of tests just of personnel of the Army. Very much to the surprise of everyone, including our psychologists, we found that the privates did the most poorly, and the corporals did better, and the sergeants did better, and the second lieutenants did better, and the first lieutenants did better, and the captains did better, and the majors did better, and the lieutenant colonels did better, and the colonels did better, and the majors, and the generals did the best of all. Well, that sold intelligence testing to the Army completely, of course.
. . .

The Army Alpha was used for the screening of most recruits, while the Army Beta, a nonverbal test, was used with nonreaders and those who did not speak English. Among other things, these tests highlighted the practical and cost-efficient nature of multiple-choice item types. As a result, these first group intelligence tests spawned the creation of similar tests for a variety of age groups and populations. Group intelligence testing soon became standard fare in American classrooms. The army recruit screening effort was seen as being so successful that the invention of these tests was cited as one of many factors that contributed to the winning of the war (French & Hale, 1990).

Controversy has surrounded intelligence testing since its inception. The use of tests to screen recruits led to some of the first controversial stances taken based on intelligence test results. It was found, for example, after the test results from the recruits were analyzed, that there were distinct group differences. After the war, it was reported that the recruits with the highest scores were from England, Scotland, Canada, and Scandinavia, and those with the lowest scores were from Russia, Italy, and Poland (Eysenck & Kamin, 1981). Consequently, it was concluded

that "Nordics" were genetically superior to their counterparts from "Alpine" and "Mediterranean" races (Eysenck & Kamin, 1981). In these early years it was a commonly held belief that intelligence tests measured genetic potential—a position not held by all psychologists of the day, including Binet (Eysenck & Kamin, 1981). Evidently, the stage was set early on for the nature/nurture debate regarding the determination of intelligence.

The Second 50 Years

The 1920s

One of the most influential early theories of intelligence was popularized by Spearman in the 1920s (1927). In his frequently cited 1927 text, *The Abilities of Man*, Spearman defined his hierarchical model of intelligence. This model emanates largely from Spearman's pioneering work in factor analysis. At the top of Spearman's hierarchy is the *general factor* (general intelligence or *g*), the factor that explains most of the variance in the factor analytic solutions conducted by Spearman. While *g* is frequently the most important determinant of an individual's performance on a particular test, every test also required a *specific factor* (*s*) or mental ability for the particular test. In Spearman's (1927) own words, the concepts of *g* and *s* are explained thusly:

The one part has been called the general factor and denoted by the letter g; *it is so named because, although varying freely from individual to individual, it remains the same for any one individual in respect of all the correlated abilities. The second factor has been called the "specific factor" and denoted by the letter* s. *It not only varies from individual to individual, but even for any one individual from each ability to another. . . . Although, however, both of these factors occur in every ability, they need not be equally influential in all. . . . At one extreme lay the talents for classics, where the ratio of the influence of g to s was rated to be as high as 15 to 1. At the other extreme was the talent for music, where the ratio was only 1 to 4. (p. 75)*

The notion of intellectual abilities being hierarchically organized is an alluring one that has been embraced by a number of influential intelligence theorists. Spearman's influence can also be found in the everyday practice of assessing intelligence, where psychologists may be observed discussing the g-loading of a particular subtest from an intelligence test battery. In addition, Spearman's introduction of factor analytic methods into intelligence research has resulted in a continuing emphasis on factor analytic procedures for, among other things, establishing the validity of intelligence measures. A final example of the enduring influence of Spearman's theorizing is the continuing research into the nature of g (Jensen, 1986).

It was also at about this time that scientists were expressing a great deal of doubt about the practice of intelligence testing. Respected scientists such as E. L. Thorndike (Thorndike et al., 1927) questioned whether anyone knew what intelligence tests measured. Furthermore, writers such as Pintner (1923) were wholly dissatisfied with vague concepts of general intelligence. In fact, Pintner (1923) argued the following:

We may say rather that the psychologist borrowed from everyday life a vague term implying all-round ability and knowledge, and in the process of trying to measure this trait, he has been and still is attempting to define it more sharply and endow it with a stricter scientific connotation. (p. 53)

Wechsler's Tests

David Wechsler was a clinical psychologist at Bellevue Psychiatric Hospital in New York. He was to adult intelligence testing what Binet was to children's intelligence testing (see Box 1.1).

He used some of the same tests as Binet, and he introduced and adapted other tasks for the purpose of assessing adult intelligence.

Most importantly, Wechsler was the beneficiary of the World War I testing experience. In many ways his tests mimic the methods used in the war effort. One of the contributions of his scale was the inclusion of separate verbal and performance scales akin to the Army Alpha/Beta measures that he used in the war. Wechsler popularized other innovations in individual intelligence testing, including the use of the Deviation IQ (standard score) in lieu of the old Ratio IQ and the provision of subtest scores in addition to composite scores. His children's test batteries differed substantially from Binet's test. Wechsler did not order his subtests sequentially by developmental age as Binet did. Instead, Wechsler created subtests that possessed enough range of item difficulty to span the entire age range of the scale. Hence, there was much less switching from one subtest to another when administering the Wechsler scales, making them easier for examiners to master. The Wechsler-Bellevue I, an adult intelligence test published in 1939, was Wechsler's first test. The chronology of Wechsler's prolific test development career is given below.

YEAR	TEST
1939	Wechsler-Bellevue I
1946	Wechsler-Bellevue II
1949	Wechsler Intelligence Scale for Children (WISC)
1955	Wechsler Adult Intelligence Scale (WAIS)
1967	Wechsler Preschool and Primary Scale of Intelligence (WPPSI)
1974	Wechsler Intelligence Scale for Children-Revised (WISC-R)
1981	Wechsler Adult Intelligence Scale-Revised (WAIS-R)

Box 1.1

Dr. Matarazzo on Dr. Wechsler

Dr. Joseph D. Matarazzo is one of the most notable psychologists of today. He is widely recognized as an accomplished clinician and researcher. He recently served as president of the American Psychological Association. Dr. Matarazzo also had the opportunity to work with Dr. David Wechsler on joint research and writing projects. Dr. Matarazzo described David Wechsler in an interview for this book. He said of Wechsler:

Briefly put, David Wechsler was a thoroughly genial individual and hard working psychologist who enjoyed his work. Psychologists who worked with him, as well as colleagues and students, always gave him lavish praise—both for his contributions as a clinician and for his warm, human qualities.

1989 Wechsler Preschool and Primary Scale of Intelligence—Revised (WPPSI-R)

1991 Wechsler Intelligence Scale for Children—Third Edition (WISC-III)

(The latter two scales were published without the benefit of Wechsler's involvement in the project.)

One aspect of the Wechsler tradition that has resulted in considerable misunderstanding is the offering of the Verbal and Performance scales. Wechsler (1974) ascribed to a notion of general intelligence. He states that "intelligence is the overall capacity of the individual to understand and cope with the world around him" (p. 5). What is often misunderstood is that the Verbal and Performance scales were constructed not to represent distinct abilities but as "two languages" through which the underlying general intelligence may express itself. Stated in Wechsler's own words, "This dichotomy is primarily a way of identifying two principal modes by which human abilities express themselves" (p. 9).

The Age of Theory

It was in the 1950s that many psychologists turned to the development of theories that explained the concept of intelligence. Up until this time, intelligence testing was more empirical than theoretical in nature. Binet and Simon recognized the independence of theory and practice by stating their view on the nature of the intelligence testing controversy in this excerpt from a 1908 paper.

> *Some psychologists affirm that intelligence can be measured; others declare that it is impossible to measure intelligence. But there are still others, better informed, who ignore these theoretical discussions and apply themselves to the actual solving of the problem. (p. 96)*

Similarly, in his APA presidential address of 1946, Henry Garrett made the following statement showing his recognition of the separation of intelligence testing and theory:

> *. . . it may be well to recall that the measurement of intelligent behavior began as a practical enterprise and that theory has in general followed rather than preceded application. Perhaps, had theory come first, we might have been saved much argument and many intelligence tests. (1946/1961, p. 573)*

It is this lack of theory that has led to the common criticism that intelligence is defined as "what the test measures." This criticism is understandable when one reads the manuals of older tests and finds no explicit theory behind the selection of items or subtests. The gap between theory and intelligence testing began to close in the 1950s, when many theories were offered to explain intelligence. Some of the most influential theories of the day included Cattell's (1971) theory of Fluid and Crystallized intelligence, Guilford's (1967) Structure of Intellect Model, and Vernon's (1950) Hierarchical Model of Intelligence. Unfortunately, while these numerous theories spawned a great deal of research, they have not yet produced popular intelligence tests that could compete with the Binet and Wechsler scales. These theories have been used primarily to interpret tests such as the Wechsler scales (Kaufman, 1979b) that were based on practical and clinical rather than theoretical concerns. The true merger of intelligence testing and theory did not occur until the 1980s.

Intelligent Testing

The 1960s were another era of concern about intelligence tests. There were questions about test bias and test misuse. In 1968, an article by Alexander Wesman, "Intelligent Testing" appeared in *American Psychologist*. Among other things, Wesman pointed out the need for psychologists to be very clear about the nature of intelligence tests and what they measure. Wesman stated unequivocally that intelligence tests measured "previous learnings," not ability to learn. He offered the following conclusions regarding intelligence that he described as "obvious":

1. Intelligence is an attribute, not an entity.
2. Intelligence is the summation of the learning experiences of the individual.

Given these conclusions, he then argued that the separation of intelligence, ability, and achievement measures was more artificial than real. This is a dramatic departure from the early part of the century, when many psychologists were convinced that some sort of innate intellectual ability could be measured.

Wesman's article has also proven to be so

influential because of the adoption of many of his tenets by Alan Kaufman (1979b) in his book *Intelligent Testing with the WISC-R*. In this very popular text, Kaufman emphasizes flexibility in WISC-R interpretation. He provides a logical and systematic approach to test interpretation and many alternative theories to the Wechsler Verbal/Performance model for WISC-R interpretation. In this way interpretation is fit to the child rather than the child being forced to fit the theoretical model of a particular test. Anastasi (1988) lauds Kaufman's approach to WISC-R interpretation by saying:

> *The basic approach described by Kaufman undoubtedly represents a major contribution to the clinical use of intelligence tests. Nevertheless, it should be recognized that its implementation requires a sophisticated clinician who is well informed in several fields of psychology. (p. 484)*

Kaufman's approach to interpretation has proven popular, as aspects of it have been incorporated into modern tests such as the Vineland Adaptive Behavior Scales (Sparrow, Balla, & Cicchetti, 1984), the Kaufman Assessment Battery for Children (Kaufman & Kaufman, 1983b), and the Stanford-Binet Fourth Edition (Delaney & Hopkins, 1988).

The Contributions of Dorothea McCarthy

The McCarthy Scales of Children's Abilities was published in 1972. The McCarthy was a welcome change in the assessment of young children. The scale was more sensitive to the needs of young children than tests such as the WPPSI. It included full color art work and tasks such as a bean bag toss that were appealing to young children. The examiner directions for the McCarthy were also hailed as an improvement because their simple wording did not require preschoolers to understand basic concepts that were beyond their comprehension (Kaufman & Kaufman, 1977).

McCarthy also took a very bold move with her scale by eschewing the term *IQ*. It was the first popular test not to call the overall composite score an IQ. Instead, it used the term *general cognitive index (GCI)*. This was a risk in that it made some potential users question whether or not the McCarthy was an intelligence test. It appears now that McCarthy was ushering in a new era, as many popular tests of today do not use the term *IQ*.

RECENT HISTORY

The Demise of the IQ

The term "intelligence quotient" has been outdated for some time. Once the use of standard scores became widespread, the IQ was no longer descriptive; the score from an intelligence test was not a "quotient" but rather a standard score. Yet the IQ was retained on popular tests such as the Wechsler scales. Several writers have also proposed that the IQ fostered misunderstanding and misuse of intelligence tests. Plotkin (1974), for example, observed, "In a sense there is a certain personal worth interpretation that is put on the results of an IQ test," and furthermore, "the IQ, however, has much more of a final, unquestioned, and innate sort of sound to it. . . ." The IQ score has even been found to have a substantial impact on family relationships (Dirks, Bushkuhl, & Marzano, 1983). Dirks et al. (1983) found that parents who were told that their child had an average IQ were less accurate in their memory of the test results and reported few positive consequences from the testing. The parents of above-average children, on the other hand, reported that they experienced considerable pride and self-confidence as a result of finding out about their child's high IQ.

Today, most modern intelligence tests no longer use the term IQ to describe an overall intelligence test score. The Wechsler Scales still do. The Stanford-Binet Fourth Edition, which was a substantial revision of previous editions, now calls the overall score a Composite Standard Score. The Kaufman Assessment Battery for Children (K-ABC) calls its overall score a Mental Processing Composite (MPC). Only a few group-administered tests retain names such as "intelligence" or "mental ability" (Lennon, 1985). The days of the use of the term "IQ" appear numbered. While renaming the composite scores of intelligence tests is not revolutionary, it is symptomatic of the changing intellectual assessment scene.

It is also conceivable that the term "intelligence test" may fall into disuse. Long ago, group-administered tests of intelligence dropped the term "intelligence" from their titles, using other terms such as "cognitive skills" or "scholastic ability" instead. It would not be surprising to see tests of the future opting for alternate terms to intelligence.

Public Law 94-142

In 1975, the Education for all Handicapped Children Act (PL 94-142) was passed by Congress. This federal law mandated that school districts provide a "free and appropriate" public education for all handicapped children living in their jurisdiction. Public Law 94-142 mandated the identification of all children eligible for special education services. This "child find" effort created a great need for examiners of children and enhanced the demand for intelligence testing of children.

This law also carried with it some explicit guidelines for the use of tests, including intelligence tests, in the diagnostic process. The important aspect of these regulations for intelligence testing was that, in many ways, this was the first time that federal standards for the use of intelligence tests in the schools were instituted.

The PL 94-142 standards, for example, make it clear that intelligence test results should not outweigh other test results in making diagnostic decisions. They should be viewed as but one piece of evidence to be considered when making diagnoses. This is an important point to remember when interpreting intelligence tests to parents and others who may focus almost exclusively on intelligence test data in order to gauge their child's needs. Public Law 94-142 emphasizes the point that other tests may be equally or more important in making decisions and that they should not be undervalued because of the presence of intelligence test scores. Furthermore, PL 94-142 also created a need for translations and modifications of popular intelligence tests. This occurred because of the standard indicating that a test should be administered in the child's native language or "other means" should be used to assess intelligence without undue influence from linguistic difference.

Larry P. v. Riles

The case of *Larry P. v. Riles* is of significance in the annals of intellectual assessment. As a result of the testimony at this trial, intelligence tests were found to be biased against African American children, and the San Francisco public schools were enjoined from using intelligence tests when evaluating such children (Elliott, 1987). In 1986, the Larry P. decision was reiterated and clarified (Landers, APA Monitor, 1986). Judge Peckham, who presided over the original Larry P. trial, made his decision quite clear in this most recent statement. He said, "School districts are not to use intelligence tests in the assessment of Black pupils who have been referred for special education services" (Landers, APA Monitor, 1986, p. 18).

This trial and the associated testimony brought into clear focus all of the data, and the lack of data, on issues of test bias. As a result, this case provided the impetus for considerable research and discussion of issues of test bias that may not have taken place otherwise. This is a landmark case also because it is the only one where intelligence tests were found to be invalid for use with a particular cultural group (see Chapter 16).

Mergers of Theory and Intelligence Testing

The marriage between intelligence testing and psychological theory has always been a tenuous one. In fact, intelligence testing began primarily as an empirical effort relatively uninfluenced by theory. The separation of test development and theory was recognized by many psychologists and is reflected in the following quote by Henry Garrett (1946/1961) in his presidential address to the American Psychological Association in 1946:

> *The trial and error period in mental measurement is, I believe, drawing to a close. Much progress has been made over the war years in the construction and use of mental tests. I think that we can anticipate a bright future for psychometrics, and by no means the smallest achievement will be an increase in the number of valid tests capable of measuring precisely defined aptitudes and traits. (p. 581)*

It appears that Garrett's prediction was accurate but its fulfillment belated. Up to this point it has been difficult to argue that intelligence tests are measures of precisely defined traits. The traits being measured by the Wechsler scales and older editions of the Binet scales have not been clearly delineated in the tests' manuals. The Kaufman Assessment Battery for Children (K-ABC) ushered in a new era with its publication in 1983 by devoting much space in its manual to discussing the theory underlying the test development process and interpretation of results. More recently, the Stanford-Binet Fourth Edition devotes considerable attention in its various manuals to discussing the theory underlying this most recent version. New measures of intelligence are promising to continue the trend of measuring intelligence from a stronger theoretical basis.

Intelligence Tests of the 1990s

The major breakthroughs of the 1990s are likely to be an increase in the number of available tests and a further rapprochement between theory and intelligence testing. New tests are likely to expand on the precedents of the 1980s set by the Kaufman Assessment Battery for Children (K-ABC) and the Stanford-Binet Fourth Edition, which have more clear-cut theoretical foundations. There are likely to be a variety of tests available because of the increasing diversity of theories of intelligence. Some of this diversity is reflected in Table 1.2, where a sampling of definitions of intelligence is given.

It is also important to consider that it may not be necessary, or even desirable, to achieve unanimity on the definition of intelligence. Jensen (1987) likened the term "intelligence" to other broadly defined scientific terms. He said, "Scientists don't actually try to define 'nature' or to construct 'theories of nature.' 'Intelligence' ought to be regarded like 'nature' in this respect" (p. 196). This school of thought suggests that intelligence should be viewed as a field of study with many potentially appropriate lines of inquiry.

It is unlikely, and probably undesirable, that one definition of intelligence will be found. It is probable, however, that new intelligence tests, based on a variety of theoretical approaches, will measure more precisely defined intellectual skills, abilities, traits, styles, or behaviors. Intelligence and cognition researchers frequently call for future tests to assess very precisely defined cognitive activities (Pellegrino, 1986; Richardson & Bynner, 1984). Richardson and Bynner (1984), for example, suggest that intelligence researchers ". . . follow in the footsteps of more rigorous sciences by seeking precise definitions of the different elements of cognitive functions and processes . . ." (p. 521). We will wait with eager anticipation to see the new tests offered and their associated theories. It appears that, regardless of the theories that will be favored, the criticism that intelligence is "what the test measures" will no longer apply as we move from the empirical to the theoretical age of intellectual assessment.

TABLE 1.2 Definitions of Intelligence from the Distant Past to the Present

Rudolf Pintner (1923): "It includes the capacity for getting along well in all sorts of situations. This implies ease and rapidity in making adjustments and, hence, ease in breaking old habits and in forming new ones. . . . The intelligent person has a multiplicity of responses; the unintelligent few. The intelligent organism responds to a great number of situations; the unintelligent few. Intelligent behavior leads one from one thing to another in ever-widening circles; unintelligent behavior is narrow and restricted, and leads to repetition or cessation."

C. Spearman (1927): "This is to regard 'g' as measuring something analogous to an 'energy'; that is to say, it is some force capable of being transformed from one mental operation to another different one. Even on the physiological side, there are some grounds for hoping that some such energy will sooner or later be discovered in the nervous system, especially the cerebral cortex."

Henry E. Garrett (1946/1961): ". . . intelligence as I shall use the term in this paper includes at least the abilities demanded in the solution of problems which require the comprehension and use of symbols. By symbols I mean words, numbers, diagrams, equations, formulas, which represent ideas and relationships ranging from the fairly simple to the very complex. For simplicity we may call the ability to deal with such stimuli *symbol or abstract intelligence*."

Frederick B. Davis (1964): "From time immemorial, men have observed that their fellows differ greatly in the ease and accuracy with which they perceive facts and ideas, remember them, draw logical conclusions and inferences from them, and benefit or learn from experiences."

Alexander G. Wesman (1968): "Intelligence as here defined is a summation of learning experiences. The instances in which intelligent behavior is observed may be classified in various ways that appear to be logical or homogeneous, but they are individual instances all the same. Each instance represents a response the organism has learned; each learned response in turn predisposes the organism for learning additional responses which permit the organism to display new acts of intelligent behavior."

(continued)

TABLE 1.2   *(Continued)*

J. P. Guilford (1979): ". . . intelligence is defined as a systematic collection of abilities or functions for processing different kinds of information in various ways. Intelligence is thus concerned both with kinds of information and kinds of operations performed with information. Regarding the brain as 'that computer between our ears' is a useful conception, at least by analogy. Like computers, brains also possess information in storage and programs for dealing with that information."

Robert J. Sternberg (1984): "I view intelligence as consisting of purposive selection and shaping of and adaptation to real-world environments relevant to one's life."

Jaan Valsiner (1984): ". . . We can operationalize it in terms of the process structure—the dynamic organization of the actor's goal-directed actions in the particular (possibly dynamic) ecological niche. . . ."

Phillip A. Vernon (1985)": ". . . individual differences in mental ability can be thought of as being a function of what appears to be a rather general factor of neural efficiency. At one level, neural efficiency allows information to be processed quickly, preventing an overload of the limited capacity of working memory. At another level, the factor is expressed as neural adaptability, again relating to an efficient use of limited neural resources. At still a third level, neural efficiency will at some time undoubtedly be identified with some sort of neuronal biochemical processes. . . ."

CONCLUSIONS

The development of intelligence tests remains a major technological advance in psychological assessment. These measures provided a means for assessing a particularly intriguing construct (Davis, 1964). While there may be natural curiosity about measuring intelligence, there is also great societal concern about the use of these measures for diagnostic or placement decisions. Because intelligence tests have been used to make very important decisions about children's lives, such as the diagnoses and services they receive and the educational opportunities they are afforded, these tests are likely to continue to be controversial. Hence, any discussion of the history of intelligence testing must consider not only the scientific aspects of these measures, but the sociopolitical aspects as well (Elliott, 1987). The last century of intelligence assessment has been marked by considerable change in the tests themselves, theoretical approaches, and guidelines for test use. There is no indication from history that this pace of change is slowing. The pool of available measures and theories (see Chapter 2) continues to expand rapidly. The next century of intelligence assessment should be very different from the first 100 years.

CHAPTER SUMMARY

1. The first intelligence testers were parents, preschoolers, employers, teachers, spouses, grandparents, and philosophers, among others.

2. There is considerable agreement that the practice of assessing individual skills and abilities is an ancient one.

3. Many early efforts at measuring intelligence used tests that were developed in early experimental psychology laboratories.

4. Galton viewed the use of psychophysical measures to assess intelligence as sensible because, he reasoned, if all information is obtained through the senses, then intelligent individuals must have very capable sensory abilities.

5. The central problem with the use of psychophysical measures of intelligence was their lack of correlation with school achievement.

6. The development of intelligence tests was carried out in response to a societal need. Modern intelligence testing can be traced to the concern for the humane treatment of mentally retarded individuals that was exemplified by the work of pioneers such as Itard (1896–1962) and Sequin (1866–1907) during the nineteenth century.

7. Alfred Binet (1905), along with his colleague Theophilius Simon, produced the first technological breakthrough in intelligence testing by developing the first practical intelligence test battery.

8. The Binet-Simon scale assessed "higher"-level cognitive skills and, as a result, produced substantial correlations with measures of school achievement.

9. Binet and Simon placed considerable emphasis on the establishment of content validity for their scale, an emphasis that has been lacking in many subsequent measures.

10. Terman (1916) produced the most successful of the English translations of Binet's work. His scale, the Stanford-Binet, met high psychometric standards for the time.

11. Terman also introduced the concept of the intelligence quotient (IQ), which was originally the invention of a German scientist named William Stern.

12. There were four editions of the Stanford-Binet. The 1972 version was simply a renorming.

13. During the war, Robert Yerkes directed an assessment committee of the American Psychological Association that was eventually charged with the screening of about a million and a half potential soldiers (Anastasi, 1988). It was this group of psychologists that developed the first group-administered tests of intelligence. The Army Alpha was used for the screening of most recruits, while the Army Beta, a nonverbal test, was used with nonreaders and those who did not speak English.

14. In 1927, Spearman introduced an influential hierarchical theory of intelligence. At the top of Spearman's hierarchy is the "general factor" (general intelligence or "g"), the factor that explains most of the variance in the factor analytic solutions conducted by Spearman.

15. David Wechsler was a clinical psychologist at Bellevue Psychiatric Hospital in New York who developed adult and children's intelligence tests. He used some of the same tests as Binet, and he introduced and adapted other tasks for the purpose of assessing adult intelligence.

16. In the 1950s, many psychologists turned to the development of theories that explained the concept of intelligence. Some of the most influential theories of the day included Cattell's (1971) theory of Fluid and Crystallized intelligence, Guilford's (1967) Structure of Intellect Model, and Vernon's (1950) Hierarchical Model of Intelligence.

17. Wesman (1968) stated unequivocally that intelligence tests measured "previous learnings," not ability to learn. He offered the following conclusions regarding intelligence that he described as "obvious":

    1. Intelligence is an attribute, not an entity.
    2. Intelligence is the summation of the learning experiences of the individual.

18. The McCarthy Scales of Children's Abilities is a preschool intelligence test that was published in 1972.

19. The term *intelligence quotient* is outdated. Once the use of standard scores became widespread, the IQ was no longer descriptive; the score from an intelligence test was not a "quotient" but rather a standard score.

20. In 1975, the Education for all Handicapped Children Act (PL 94-142) was passed by Congress. This law also carried with it some

explicit guidelines for the use of tests, including intelligence tests, in the diagnostic process.

21. The case of *Larry P. v. Riles* is of significance in the annals of intellectual assessment. As a result of the testimony at this trial, intelligence tests were found to be biased against African American children, and the San Francisco public schools were enjoined from using intelligence tests when evaluating African American children.

22. New measures of intelligence are promising to continue the trend of measuring intelligence from a stronger theoretical basis.

CHAPTER 2

Theories of Intelligence

CHAPTER QUESTIONS

What is intelligence?
Is there one type of intelligence or are there many?

Why is theoretical knowledge important? It is important because it can affect behavior—in this case the interpretive behavior of the clinician using an intelligence test. Our interpretations of test results, either in writing or orally in a parent conference or other venue, are expressions of our theoretical knowledge or biases. Similarly, a person's reaction to being called into the boss's office is influenced by theory, depending on whether one thinks that the boss is calling the meeting to offer congratulations or a reprimand. So, too, in intellectual assessment, a psychologist may offer either a dismal prognosis for a child or a favorable one depending on the examiner's theories of intelligence. This is one crucial reason why psychologists should have a clear understanding of intelligence theory.

Another reason is to allow implementation of the "intelligent testing" approach to interpretation (Kaufman, 1990, 1979b). This interpretive method is highly sophisticated and individualized, requiring substantial theoretical knowledge on the part of examiners. Take, for example, the case of a child who is referred for an evaluation subsequent to receiving a head injury in a car wreck. If this child's intelligence test score is considerably lower than premorbid estimates (estimates of the child's intelligence before the injury), a psychologist would be hard pressed to argue that the child's scores are now lower due to changes in reinforcement contingencies (behavioral theory). More than likely a neuropsychological model of intelligence would best explain the score decrement in this case. The variety of problems and circumstances presented by children call for a clinician who is well versed in a variety of disciplines and possesses knowledge of several theories if interpretation is going to be truly "intelligent."

A psychologist who does not individualize interpretation is easily "found out" by referral sources. If all children are found to have brain damage, or task-intrinsic motivation deficits, or long-term memory problems, the consumers of reports, such as teachers, psychiatrists, and parents, will soon realize the limited knowledge of the psychologist and stop referring cases or only refer those that fit the psychologist's theoretical bent. Perhaps the worst eventuality that can befall a psychologist bereft of theory is to simply report scores without any interpretation. This practice will not satisfy parents and others, and it poses a great danger to the well-being of children. The mere "tester" of children offers no advice for helping a child and, perhaps more dangerously, produces scores that can be misunderstood by others since they are not connected to useful interpretation.

The remainder of this chapter is designed to help foster the theoretical sophistication necessary to be a capable interpreter of scores. This chapter provides overviews of various theories of intelligence. These brief descriptions of theories are intended to give the reader a very general sense of the meaning of a theory. They are also intended to serve as retrieval cues to help the reader remember the basics of theories learned in previous courses. These descriptions of theories are simplified and incomplete. After all, entire chapters and books have been written about most of these theories. Reading this chapter, therefore, is no substitute for strong graduate level course work in areas such as cognitive psychology and developmental psychology. If these vignettes do not serve as adequate retrieval cues, the reader is advised to consult the original sources cited in this section.

SPECIFIC THEORIES

The Public's Theory

We all have our own implicit theories of what constitutes intelligent individuals and intelligent behavior (Weinberg, 1988). When commuters waiting for a train, shoppers in a supermarket, and university students were asked, "What is intelligence?", there were three general areas of agreement: (1) practical problem-solving ability, (2) verbal ability, and (3) social intelligence (Weinberg, 1988). It has also been found that adults consider problem solving and reasoning to become increasingly important markers of intelligence with increasing developmental age. In addition, perceptual and motor abilities are seen as measures of intelligence for infants and younger children, whereas verbal ability is perceived as important from age 2 through adulthood (Weinberg, 1988). Weinberg (1988) also makes the point that these public conceptions of the nature of intelligence are quite similar to the conceptualizations commonly held by professionals such as psychologists.

The idea that something such as intelligence exists appears to be universal. Neisser (1979) made the following observations about African conceptions of intelligence and their similarity to Western definitions.

The notion that some people are intelligent (or clever, or cunning, or bright, or smart, or wise, or insightful, or brilliant, or intellectual, or . . .) is widespread indeed. I suspect that every language must have some such galaxy of cognitive terms. It is at least certain that the existence of intelligence-related words does not depend on technology or education, or testing. E. F. Dube (1977) recently conducted an inquiry into the meaning of such concepts among non-literate traditional villagers in Botswana. He used 13 Setswana words which had been suggested by translators as possible equivalents of "intelligent" and other related words in English. The elders of the villages were easily able to "define" these terms, by giving examples of the behaviors and characteristics that justify using a given word. Moreover, their attributions were genuinely predictive of behavior. At Dube's request, the elders pointed out which of the children were definitely "botlhale" (the Setswana word closest to "intelligent") and which ones were not. These attributions were powerful predictors of the children's subsequent performance in an experiment on memory for stories. (p. 222)

The universality of the concept of intelligence, not just intelligence testing, perhaps explains why the tests are viewed with such reverence by some and disdain by others. The idea that the construct of intelligence can be measured is intriguing to many. The search for a definitive theory of intelligence is equally alluring.

Binet's Theory

Though Binet's efforts in developing the first intelligence test were mostly practical and empirical, he did theorize about the nature of intelligence. His theoretical stance, however, seems to vary from citation to citation (Thorndike & Lohman, 1989). By most accounts, he did seem to ascribe to the notion of intelligence as a single entity. One of his most recognized statements on his views of the nature of intelligence is given in this excerpt:

> It seems to us that in intelligence there is a fundamental faculty, the alteration or lack of which, is of the utmost importance for practical life. This faculty is judgment, otherwise called good sense, practical sense, initiative, the faculty of adapting one's self to circumstances. To judge well, to comprehend well, to reason well, these are the essential activities of intelligence. A person may be a moron or an imbecile if he is lacking in judgment; but with good judgment he can never be either. Indeed the rest of the intellectual faculties seem of little importance in comparison with judgment. (Binet & Simon, 1905, pp. 42-43)

Even in this statement, Binet seems to waver. While emphasizing the preeminence of judgment, he then begins to retreat and mention that this is but one of many faculties. This retreat suggests that he considers other abilities or skills as aspects of intelligence. This lack of precise definition, however, is not only a characteristic of Binet's work but also of Wechsler's (1958) and others' definitions of intelligence. Binet's emphasis on a single global entity is consistent with the *zeitgeist* of the times in which numerous workers emphasized an "intelligence" as opposed to distinct intelligences, abilities, or faculties. Additional theories that emphasized a global ability are exemplified by the work of the British.

The British Approach and "g"

Spearman's theory exemplifies an approach to conceptualizing intelligence that has sometimes been called the "British approach" (Minton & Schneider, 1980). This approach is exemplified by the work of Spearman (1927), Burt (1950), and Vernon (1950). Weinberg (1988) describes these theorists as "lumpers," or those who tend to focus on a single general intelligence as the major concept. Spearman is usually credited as the first to offer a hierarchical theory of intelligence. In his theory, "g," or general intelligence, is placed at the top of the hierarchy because this is the underlying "mental energy" that is central to all intelligent problem solving. While all cognitive tasks also require a specific factor, or "s," it is the general ability that is clearly viewed as most important for intelligent performance.

Vernon (1950) expanded on the hierarchical model proposed by Spearman by offering a more detailed hierarchy of intellectual abilities, as shown in Figure 2.1. At the top of this hierarchy is the major group factor, general intelligence, which is highly consistent with the theorizing of Spearman. Next in the hierarchy are the minor group factors, which are of two varieties: verbal/educational *(v:ed)* and spatial/mechanical *(k:m)* types of intelligence. Within these two group factors, then, are several specific factors of intelligence.

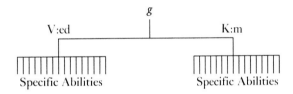

FIGURE 2.1

Vernon's (1950) hierarchical model

Vernon (1984) supports the further division of "g" into the verbal/educational and spatial/mechanical dimensions primarily with factor analysis. His studies have shown that when overall "g" is held constant, verbal tests intercorrelate and visual/spatial tests intercorrelate, but the correlation between the two types is usually negative. Vernon, however, finds little evidence to support focusing on particular cognitive styles, including the verbal/spatial dichotomy as most of the variance in intelligence tests is still attributable to the major group factor—"g."

Vernon's theory is of greater interest today than perhaps at any time because a very similar theory was used to design the Stanford-Binet Fourth Edition (Binet 4) (Thorndike, Hagen, & Sattler, 1986). The Binet 4 factor model (see Chapter 10) is strikingly similar, with "g" at the top of the model and secondary and tertiary group factors beneath it.

Another well-known proponent of the British hierarchical approach to the study of intelligence is the American researcher Arthur Jensen. Jensen (1969) proposed a hierarchical theory of intelligence that hypothesized the existence of two mental processes. Level I processing (associative ability) typically does not require manipulation or transformation of the stimulus input prior to producing a response. Level I ability is tapped by rote learning tasks such as digit recall and paired associate learning. Level II processing (conceptual ability), on the other hand, requires considerable manipulation and elaboration of the stimulus input in order to produce a response. Level II processing is tapped by tests such as concept learning and spatial problem solving. Level II processing is clearly the higher level of processing in Jensen's hierarchy of intelligence, whereas Level I processing does not require very complex problem solving. While only hypothesizing two mental processes, Jensen's theorizing clearly resembles the hierarchical approach to understanding intelligence that has its roots in the early work of eminent British psychologists.

More recently, Jensen has turned his attention to "g" and its definition. He has responded to the criticism that psychometric "g," the positive correlation among mental tests, is a statistical artifact. After a careful review of research studies, he concludes:

> *Evidence is summarized showing that g is correlated more highly than any other factor with a number of phenomena that are wholly independent of both psychometrics and factor analysis. Relationships have been found between g and the heritability of test scores, the effects of inbreeding depression on test scores, reaction times to elementary cognitive tasks which have virtually no intellectual content, evoked electrical potentials of the cerebral cortex, and other physical correlates. This evidence of biological correlates of g supports the view that g is not a biological artifact but is a fact of nature. However, the causal nature of g itself is not yet scientifically understood. That goal awaits further advances in neuroscience. (p. 157)*

Detterman (1987) takes issue with the concept of "g," using the modern large university as an analogy. He proposes that intelligence tests currently in use are made up of complex tasks that when summed or averaged produce an estimate of overall system (intellectual) functioning. This estimate is similar to the size of a university's endowment or library holdings in that it is a gross estimate of the quality of a university (Detterman, 1987). This information is helpful to the high school senior who intends to select among various colleges so long as the student is interested in the overall quality of the institution. But what if a high school student is interested in a specific program at the university, say the Journalism school? It is conceivable that the university is excellent overall but the Journalism school for some reason is in turmoil. In this case the overall university rating or "g" is of no value. So, too, is the case with intelligence testing, where a child may receive a particularly high or low composite score. A child may have a rather unique skill or weakness that is masked because the focus is on the composite score.

Taking this argument one step further, this point of view suggests that both Galton and Binet were wrong! Galton had the right idea by measuring very discrete basic cognitive skills, but he erred by not demonstrating how combining these skills can be used to solve certain problems. Binet, too, erred by using only complex tasks, making it difficult to determine how cognitive skills may interact to solve problems.

Vandenberg and Vogler (1985) take issue with the concept of "g" from a different vantage point by concluding:

Against the argument that all ability tests correlate positively and therefore measure the same ability, one can point out that height and weight also correlate, and rather substantially, yet we consider them to be separate characteristics. (p. 6)

Detterman's ideas are provocative in that they are one way of reconciling the differences between Weinberg's "lumpers" and "splitters." He suggests that both points have something to contribute to our understanding of intelligence that may be greater than the sum of their parts.

Thurstone's Primary Mental Abilities

In direct opposition to Spearman was the factor analysis–based theory of Thurstone. While Spearman used factor analysis to "prove" the existence of "g," Thurstone used factor analytic techniques to prove the opposite, that intelligence was made up of a rather large number of faculties, the so-called *primary mental abilities*. Performance of an individual on a particular cognitive task was not then a function of "g" and the "s," or specific cognitive ability, required for the task; rather, performance was dictated by the primary mental abilities required for successful completion of the cognitive task. As such, Thurstone's theory was not hierarchical in nature as was Spearman's.

Thurstone (1938) first identified nine, then

seven (Thurstone & Thurstone, 1941), then six (Thurstone, 1951/1941) primary mental abilities through factor analytic investigations. The seven abilities most frequently attributed to Thurstone include those listed below (Minton & Schneider, 1980).

Space (S)	Facility in spatial or visual imagery
Perceptual Speed (P)	Quick and accurate noting of visual details
Number (N)	Speed and accuracy in making arithmetic computations
Verbal Meaning (V)	Understanding ideas and meanings of words
Word Fluency (W)	Speed in manipulating single and isolated words
Memory (M)	Facility in rote memory of words, numbers, letters, and other materials
Inductive Reasoning (I)	Ability to abstract a rule common to a set of particulars

Wechsler's Views

David Wechsler placed a great deal of emphasis on the assessment of general intelligence even though his test offers the Verbal and Performance scales (see Chapter 1). Wechsler (1958) views intelligence as a complex interaction of abilities that produce intelligent behavior that reflects "g." He explains:

But Vocabulary is a better test of intelligence than a Form Board, primarily because people can express themselves more meaningfully in verbal than in geometric symbols. This, of course, would not hold in the case of deaf-mutes or individuals who are in the habit of thinking spatially, manipulatively or in any other way. Hence, as a general principle, an effective test of intelligence should be made up of tasks calling upon as many "abilities" as possible. This was intuitively perceived by Binet, who was the first to devise an effective test of general intelligence. (p. 16)

Wechsler (1958) also takes a stand on the issue of the localization of intelligence. He says that essentially intelligence will never be localized in a particular area of the brain. Since intelligence, in Wechsler's view, is basically the "perception of relations" among stimuli, then the modality of neural representation of these stimuli is unimportant. The perception of relations, then, will be independent of the localization of specific stimuli.

Just as it is important to understand the history and original purposes of the Binet scale, it is equally important to understand Wechsler's purposes in order to use his tests appropriately. Binet's test was designed solely for the purpose of diagnosing mental retardation, yet it and other intelligence measures have become centerpieces of neuropsychological and learning disability diagnosis, purposes for which they were not specifically designed. In similar fashion there is much discussion in the literature about verbal and nonverbal (or performance) intelligence, yet these scales were formed based on practical considerations, not theoretical ones (see Chapter 1). The Verbal and Performance scales of the Wechsler series were similarly not designed to assess laterality of cerebral function (see Chapter 15). With these points of view in mind, it is probably best for modern psychologists to use the Wechsler scales as they were originally intended, as measures of general intelligence designed primarily for use with adults.

Cattell's Fluid and Crystallized Abilities

Another intelligence theory of both historical and practical import is Cattell's dichotomy (Cattell, 1940). Cattell, as is seemingly common for intelligence theorists, hypothesized two types of intelligence. Essentially, Cattell found that the ideas of Spearman's "g" and Thurstone's Primary Mental Abilities were not irreconcilable (Cattell, 1979). He proposed reconciling the two approaches by designating two types of "g." The first type is "g_f," or fluid intelligence. This is similar to Spearman's "g" in that it affects all types of problem solving. As Cattell (1979) states, "It flows with unrestricted expression into all fields of relation perception." Fluid intelligence has been found to develop rapidly to about age 15 (regardless of education) and to decline thereafter. It is also more related to physiological factors and more highly influenced by genetic factors (Cattell, 1979). Crystallized intelligence, "g_c," by contrast is related to some particular area of expertise that an individual has specifically learned or experienced (e.g., arithmetic, vocabulary, general information, etc.).

Presumably a culture-free intelligence test could be devised using only "g_f" tests. This has proved difficult in practice, and some expert academicians such as Anastasi (1988) have advised against it, saying it is not possible to separate the two.

Horn (1979), a colleague of Cattell's, has expanded on the "g_f" and "g_c" dimensions by adding second-order factors. He has identified further factors, including "g_v," *visualization.* Abilities that are part of this factor include visualization, spatial orientation, flexibility of closure, and speed of closure. Another factor, "g_a," *general auditory organization,* includes abilities such as speech perception under distraction/distortion, auditory cognition of relationships, and temporal tracking. The *short-term acquisition and retrieval (SAR)* factor measures the ability of the individual to learn and retain information over the span of a few seconds or minutes. A final factor is labeled *tertiary storage and retrieval (TSR)*, and abilities it assesses include associational fluency, ideational fluency, and expressional fluency. This factor assesses the ability to make associations with material recalled from the distant past. Horn's (1979) approach to the study of individual differences may receive more attention since it is serving as the basis for the cognitive assessment portion of the Woodcock-Johnson Psychoeducational Test Battery—Revised.

J. P. Guilford

Guilford's (1967) book *The Nature of Human Intelligence* outlined a comprehensive and complex theory of intelligence designed to explain the great variety of human cognition. According to Guilford's (1979) "structure of intellect" (SI) model, intelligence is

a systematic collection of abilities or functions for processing different kinds of information in different ways. Intelligence is thus concerned both with kinds of information and kinds of operations performed with information. Regarding the brain as "that computer between our ears" is a useful conception, at least by analogy. Like computers, brains also possess information in storage and programs for dealing with that information. (p.33)

The three components of the SI model are contents, operations, and products. *Content* refers to a kind of information. The five kinds of content are shown in Table 2.1. *Products* are items of information from the same content category (see Table 2.1). Guilford (1979) proposes that humans are constantly striving to organize related content for more efficient search and processing. As an example, it is much easier to retrieve information about hieroglyphics, a question that has been included on intelligence tests for some time, if one has a

category for "languages" that can be systematically searched for the information. *Operations* are rules of logic or mental procedures that act on content to solve problems.

Two of the more well-known operations from Guilford's theory are convergent and divergent production. *Convergent production* is a "focused search for a particular item of information that satisfies well-defined specifications" (Guilford, 1979, p. 35). *Divergent production* differs substantially in that it is "a broad search of the memory store, scanning it for alternative items of information all of which could possibly satisfy the same need" (Guilford, 1979, p. 35). A convergent question might be something like, "Who sells the brand X mousetrap?" versus a more divergent question, "How does one catch mice?" Divergent production has been used as the basis for the assessment of creativity (Torrance, 1965).

DEVELOPMENTAL PERSPECTIVES

Jean Piaget

Piaget's theory of cognitive development has had a profound influence on the way professionals view the thinking of young children. Most undergraduate students are at least somewhat familiar with his insightful observations of young children's thinking. Perhaps his most famous contribution is his delineation of a series of stages of cognitive development.

Piaget also theorized about the nature of intelligence. He proposed that children progress to successively higher stages of intellectual development through the use of two intellectual functions that promote cognitive growth. One of these processes is called *assimilation*. The process of assimilation is used by a child to incorporate a stimulus into an existing cognitive representation or schema. This is the process whereby a young child may take a piece of candy

TABLE 2.1 Categories of the structure of intellect model

Operations	Contents	Products
Cognitive	Visual	Units
Memory	Auditory	Classes
Divergent Production	Symbolic	Relations
Convergent Production	Semantic	Systems
Evaluation	Behavioral	Transformations Implications

SOURCE: Adapted from Guilford (1979).

that she has never seen before and unwrap it and eat it. This child was able to fit the new stimulus, a new type of candy, into an existing schema and eat it, as opposed to fitting the new stimulus to an inappropriate schema, such as ball, and trying to bounce it. So what is a child to do when a new stimulus cannot be incorporated into an existing schema? In this case the child uses the other intellectual process called *accommodation*. Accommodation is said to occur when a child has to create a new schema or significantly alter an existing schema in order to incorporate a new stimulus. Say an infant is given a book for the first time. The infant is likely to first try to use assimilation to incorporate the stimulus into an existing schema. The child would put the book in his mouth. Should he be unsuccessful at ingesting the book, he will likely form a new schema for "book" through the process of accommodation. It is easy to see how the use of assimilation and accommodation produces cognitive growth allowing the child to move through the cognitive stages of Piaget.

Piaget's theory has only infrequently been used as a model for the development of intelligence tests. An attempt was made by Uzgiris (1989) to develop an intelligence measure based on Piaget's theory of cognitive development. Other attempts to measure intelligence with Piagetian tasks depended heavily on conservation tasks. This approach resulted in considerable disagreement as to whether or not Piagetian intelligence differs significantly from so-called "psychometric" intelligence as measured by the Wechsler or Binet scales (Carroll, Kohlberg, & DeVries, 1984). In one large-scale investigation it was concluded that traditional intelligence tests and tests based on Piagetian tasks measure the same construct (Humphreys & Parsons, 1979). The logical extension of this conclusion is that Piagetian tasks offer nothing new for measuring intelligence or cognitive development and, therefore, are not needed. Carroll et. al. (1984) countered that Piagetian intelligence is somewhat distinct from psychometric intelligence, but their results were not considered conclusive.

A recent investigation used Piagetian theory as a basis for an intervention program with low socioeconomic children (Campbell & Ramey, 1990). The Concept Assessment Kit-Conservation (CAK) was used to assess the conservation skills of eighty-six 5-, 6-, and 7-year-olds in a longitudinal investigation. The low SES children did show a favorable response to conservation training. More germane to this discussion, however, were the findings of significant relationships between CAK scores and WISC-R and mathematics achievement scores. CAK scores correlated .49 with the Full Scale and Verbal scores of the WISC-R and .37 with the Performance Scale. Similarly, the CAK scores correlated .46 with a measure of mathematics achievement (Campbell & Ramey, 1990). These results provide empirical support for the continued study of Piaget's theory in order to assess its contribution to intelligence theory and measurement. On a practical level, it appears that despite the profound influence of Piaget's theorizing on education, his views have had relatively little influence on the day-to-day practice of intellectual assessment.

Transactional Theory

Transactional theory as proposed by Haywood and Switzky (1986) presents a theory of intelligence that attempts to explain the nature of the genetic/environmental interaction that produces various levels of performance on intelligence tests. A central premise of this theory, which is the same as other transactional notions of intelligence offered long ago, is that current intelligence tests, such as the Wechsler scales, are confounded measures in that they measure two constructs. One of the constructs measured by the Wechsler scales is intelligence, or native ability, which Haywood and Switzky attribute almost exclusively to genetic factors. The other construct is cognitive functions, or "learned cognitive operations, principles, processes, and strategies, as well as a host of 'non-intellective' variables such as attitude toward learning, work

RESEARCH REPORT

Piagetian intelligence and Binet's test

Carroll, Kohlberg, and DeVries (1984) tried to discern the difference, of lack of it, between the intelligence measured by practical tests such as the Binet and Wechsler scales and intelligence as measured by tasks inspired by Piaget's theory and used in his clinical method. Carroll et al. (1984) reanalyzed data from two samples that were administered the Stanford-Binet form LM and a variety of Piagetian tasks in order to assess the degree of overlap in the measures. The Piagetian tasks included Magic, Class Inclusion, Dream Concepts, L-R Perspectives, Number Conservation, Conservation—Liquid, Conservation—Length, Mass Conservation, Ring Segment, Generic Identity, Sibling Egocentrism, Length Transitivity, Guessing Game, and Object Sorting.

Scores on these various measures were then submitted, along with the Binet, to a series of factor analyses where age was partialed out. The loadings of the measures on a two factor solution are shown below.

Test	Factor A	Factor B
Stanford-Binet	.78	.01
Magic	.49	.06
Class Inclusion	.58	−.12
Dream Concepts	.44	.20
L-R Perspectives	.51	−.19
Number Conservation	.06	.68
Conservation—Liquid	.04	.69
Conservation—Length	.07	.60
Mass Conservation	−.07	.62
Ring Segment	.37	.41
Generic Identity	.28	.24
Sibling Egocentrism	.15	.14
Length Transitivity	.37	−.09
Guessing Game	.41	.07
Object Sorting	.08	.00

The authors observed that since the conservation tasks have their highest loadings on a separate factor from the Binet, these tests measure something that is not part of traditional test batteries. Carroll et al. (1984) likened this conservation factor to other group factors that have been identified for cognitive tests, such as spatial, verbal, or numerical abilities. They also concluded, however, that the majority of the Piagetian tests are like other tasks on intelligence measures in that there is a significant correlation among the measures or "g" factor. Based on these results the authors offered the proposition that Piagetian and traditional "psychometric" intelligences were similar and yet distinct, and that current intelligence tests did not assess some of the important milestones of cognitive development such as conservation.

---

habits, and motives" (Haywood & Switzky, 1986).

Haywood and Switzky's ideas build upon the writings of McCall (1983). One central feature of this theory is the concept of *canalization*, which McCall (1983) describes as follows:

Canalization . . . postulates a species typical path, called a creod, along which nearly all members of the species tend to develop. However, a given characteristic follows the creod only so as long as the organism is exposed to species-typical, appropriate environments. In the presence of such environments, development proceeds "normally"; when the environment deviates markedly from the typical, development may stray from the creod. (pp. 113–114)

Davis (1964) also agrees with the transactional viewpoint. He gives a more practical application of the notion of deviation from a genetically determined path (or creod): "Of course, the predictive accuracy of an aptitude test is poorest for individuals of high native ability who have had exceptionally barren or stultifying environments and for individuals of low native ability who have had exceptionally rich and stimulating environments" (p. 130).

In a simplified way, transactional theory stipulates that everyone has a creod for intelligence. If, for example, a child's genetic endowment includes a creod for high intelligence, this may or may not be evident in the child's scores. If the child has had a minimally supportive environment (e.g., adequate parental stimulation and schooling), then high intelligence will be expressed on the intelligence test. If, however, the child has been reared in a harsh and unstimulating environment, then the child may obtain lower scores on the intelligence test. In this latter situation a child's creod for high intelligence is "masked." Haywood and Switzky (1986) cite this idea of the masking of intelligence as the reason why current intelligence tests are seriously flawed in that in many cases they underestimate the intelligence of children from nonsupportive environments.

Some of the basic tenets of the way intelligence is conceptualized by transactional theory are given below.

1. Intelligence is largely transmitted genetically through a polygenic inheritance system.
2. Certain genetic and environmental characteristics occur fairly consistently together. Thus, children who inherit polygenes for high IQ from their parents are often reared in psychologically stimulating environments, and the reverse is often true of children who inherit polygenes associated with low IQ.
3. Persons differ in the extent to which their intellectual functioning is affected by more or less standard environmental variations. Thus, some children gain many IQ points from participation in a preschool education program, while other children in the same classes gain very little.
4. Other biological events such as clinical (and even subclinical) malnutrition and anomalies of the nervous and metabolic systems often produce dramatic effects on intellectual development.
5. These biological events often are correlated with specific environmental circumstances that alter their effects on intellectual development. A child's response to malnutrition and premature birth are dependent on the qualities of the rearing environment.
6. The greatest intellectual deficits can be expected to occur among children who have the combination of poor nutrition, poor biomedical history, and poor environment (Haywood, 1986, pp. 5–6)

Haywood and Switzky (1986) hypothesize further that there are equally important factors that should be considered when evaluating children and their intelligence test scores. The most important of these are environmentally determined cognition and task-intrinsic motivation. It is these latter two constructs that Haywood has attempted to modify in his experimental preschool programs.

Transactional theory gives psychologists a way of conceptualizing the relationship between environmental and genetic factors and intelligence test scores. Often a parent of a young child will ask a psychologist to offer a prognosis for a child's future test scores. Transactional theory may be one model to draw on in responding to such a difficult parental request.

Neuropsychological Theory

The body of literature on neuropsychological theory and research is large enough to consider this area a separate specialty. The reader is thus cautioned that the nuances of the findings in this area are so substantial that this cursory treatment of the topic is certainly simplistic and perhaps not representative. The most publicized of research findings in neuropsychology are those emanating from cerebral specialization research.

Hemispheric Specialization

Since the 1860s when Broca first implicated the left hemisphere as specialized for language functions, there has been considerable interest in determining which behaviors and skills are subserved by which cerebral hemisphere. This search for cerebral lateralization or specialization was pursued with particular vigor again in the 1960s. Sperry (1968, 1970), Gazzaniga (1970), and their colleagues discovered the best methodology to date for studying the functions of the cerebral hemispheres in isolation when they began to work with split-brain patients.

These were patients with severe epilepsy that could not be controlled by medication. If epilepsy is the result of the random spread of electrical activity across the brain, perhaps severe epilepsy could be controlled by limiting the area of the brain available for the spread of this electrical activity. If the corpus callosum, the large bundle of nerve fibers connecting the two hemispheres, were severed, then when a seizure occurred the activity would not be able to spread to the other hemisphere. This situation should result in less severe seizures. As it turns out, the surgery worked rather well in that the seizures were less severe after the preparation. An unanticipated opportunity was provided by the surgery in that the differences between the two hemispheres became obvious when psychological and experimental tasks were solved by the respective

hemispheres. Researchers could now see how the hemispheres responded to stimuli relatively independent of one another, and some striking findings resulted.

The less verbal nature of the right hemisphere became apparent in several experiments. In one task an object would be shown briefly to the left visual field and the patient would be allowed to grasp the object with his or her left hand (both of which are connected to the right hemisphere), and yet, when asked what the object was, patients were not able to name it. Similarly, patients were more adept at assembling blocks into designs using their left hand (which is connected to the right hemisphere). In some cases patients would shove the right hand out of the way in order to correct its faulty work. There are numerous caveats to these findings, including the fact that these results are most applicable to right-handed individuals (Vernon, 1984).

As a result of findings such as these, various intellectual functions have been attributed to the two hemispheres. The left hemisphere has been said to be specialized for linguistic, analytic, sequential, and temporal mental skills, whereas the right hemisphere performs holistic, synthetic, creative, and spatial operations (Kaufman, 1979b). Levy (1974) identified two types of intellectual processes located in the cerebral hemispheres. She concluded that the left hemisphere was specialized for analytic processing and the right hemisphere for holistic processing. The various processes identified in the two hemispheres have piqued the interest of researchers and theoreticians because they are so similar to other dichotomous theories, only some of which come from neuropsychology (see Kaufman & Kaufman, 1983).

Das and Colleagues

In like manner, Das, Kirby, and Jarman (1979) proposed a neuropsychological model of intelligence based on the illustrious career of the Soviet neuropsychologist A. R. Luria. Part of the theory of Das et al. (1979) is a "coding" dichotomy postulating two major mental processes: successive and simultaneous processing. *Successive processing* is characterized by serial and temporal handling of stimulus input. A prototypical successive task is digit recall, where the number stimuli are presented to the child one at a time. Hence, the child has to process the incoming stimuli one at a time and then hold them in correct sequence in order to reproduce them. In contrast, *simultaneous processing* is more suited to "wholes," or large chunks of information that have some common theme or unifying quality. Simultaneous processing may be involved in puzzle-solving tasks where a child has to see how all of the stimuli fit together at one point in time. Das et al. (1979), however, emphasize that processing is more important than the type of content (e.g., verbal versus nonverbal content). Simultaneous processing may be involved in some verbal tasks (e.g., analogies) and sequential processing may be used to solve some spatial tasks (e.g., map reading). This theory has proved quite influential and has produced a large body of related research over the last decade.

Recently, Das and his colleagues (Naglieri & Das, 1990) have investigated a third component of the Luria model, planning. This component assesses primarily frontal lobe functions having to do with planning and carrying out problem solving. These types of skills have also shown significant correlations with achievement measures (Naglieri, 1990; Naglieri & Das, 1988).

INFORMATION PROCESSING THEORY

Information processing approaches to the study of human cognition burst onto the scene in the late 1960s and early 1970s. A central characteristic of information processing theories is the use of the computer, and the way it processes information, as a metaphor for human cognition. A classic information processing model that may

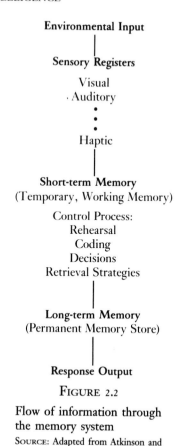

FIGURE 2.2

Flow of information through the memory system
SOURCE: Adapted from Atkinson and Shiffrin (1971).

be used for understanding performance on intelligence tests is depicted in Figure 2.2.

A simplified description of how the system works is as follows. The processing begins in response to an environmental stimulus, which could be a test question. The question, asked of the child by the examiner, must first be correctly encoded by the sensory register. Note that the sensory register must be capable of encoding a variety of types of stimuli. In this case, auditory sensory capabilities are most important. The sensory register holds the stimuli intact, but only for a short period of time—milliseconds (Bjorklund, 1989). At this point the question is transferred to the short-term memory store for further processing. Here there is a limited capacity, but the stimulus trace is more durable, lasting for seconds (Bjorklund, 1989). It is in short-term memory that a great deal of "thinking" is done. Perhaps this is why it is sometimes called "working memory." It is also in short-term memory where a number of strategies can be used to process information efficiently. In the case of an intelligence test item, it will probably be necessary for retrieval strategies to be generated in order to find the answer to the question. A retrieval cue such as a related concept or mental image may be used to search for information related to the item. In order to carry out this search one has to go to the last component of the system, long-term memory. It is here where memory traces are placed for extended periods of time—hours, days, or years. Surely the answer is in there somewhere! Once the answer to the test item is found in long-term memory, it is transferred back to short-term memory and given in a vocal response to the examiner.

Kyllonen and Alluisi

The basic information processing model has been expanded by a number of researchers. Kyllonen and Alluisi (1987), for example, break long-term memory into two components, declarative memory and procedural memory. *Declarative memory* is similar to traditional notions of long-term memory in that it is characterized by long-term storage and slow decay of memory traces and it stores acquired facts. More of the characteristics of this type of memory are given in Table 2.2. *Procedural memory* differs in a number of ways, but most importantly in that it stores rules for problem solving or production of knowledge. Procedural memory stores knowledge about how to solve problems or apply information (Kyllonen & Alluisi, 1987). These two types of long-term storage then work in concert with working (short-term) memory to solve problems. Currently there are no well-developed tests of these two types of long-term storage. Having these kinds of instruments at hand for research and everyday assessment practice would be interesting. Much needs to be learned about these and other aspects of memory, including how procedural memory develops (Kyllonen & Alluisi, 1987).

Flavell and Colleagues

The basic human information processing system has been expanded by others. Flavell and Wellman (1977) offered the idea of *metacognition*. As the name implies, metacognition is knowledge about how thinking works. Metacognition may include knowledge about one's own cognitive strengths and weaknesses, about how to keep memory working efficiently, or about how to size up the demands of a cognitive task (Bjorklund, 1989). An important finding for understanding children's intelligence test performance is that metacognitive knowledge increases with age.

More recently the focus of information processing research has begun to shift from process to knowledge and its organization and use (Curtis & Glaser, 1984). Some researchers have proposed that knowledge may even be prerequisite to the use of some strategies (Bjorklund, 1989). This intermingling of the concepts of knowledge and process in the study of children's intelligence is described in the following excerpt from Curtis and Glaser (1984).

> . . . *individual differences in the ability to learn can be attributed to differences in the content and structure of the knowledge base, and to differences in the way that knowledge is accessed, applied, and modified. It must be noted that this view is in sharp contrast to one in which skilled learners are thought to differ from those who are less-skilled simply because of superior mental ability. Instead, cognitive models view intellectual competence as a much more complex function of the knowledge that has been acquired and the processes that act on that knowledge.* (p. 481)

This point of view is not an isolated one. It suggests that the difference between intelligence and achievement is illusory, at least as these two constructs are currently assessed.

TABLE 2.2   Characteristics of declarative and working memories

	Declarative	**Procedural**
PRIMARY FUNCTION	Stores meaning of inputs	Stores how-to knowledge
CAPACITY	Unlimited	Unlimited
CONTENTS	Semantic codes	Semantic codes
	Spatial codes	Spatial codes
	Acoustic codes	Acoustic codes
	Motor codes	Motor codes
	Temporal codes	Temporal codes
INFORMATION UNITS	Concepts	Productions (if-then rules)
	Propositions	Specific to general
	Schemata/frames/scripts	

SOURCE: Adapted from Kyllonen and Alluisi (1987).

A Cognitive-Developmental Model

Borkowski (1985) has elaborated on the work of Campione and Brown (1978) and drawn heavily from information processing research to propose a theory of intelligence and methods for its assessment. This is a hierarchical model with two levels, as shown below (Borkowski, 1985).

1. The *architectural system*, which might include capacity for memory span, durability of stimulus traces, and efficiency or speed of encoding/decoding information

2. The *executive system*, which includes retrieval of knowledge from long-term memory, Piagetian schemes, control processes (e.g., rehearsal strategies), and metacognitive states

One of the interesting aspects of this theory is its emphasis on the development of these systems and their components over the life span. This makes this theory potentially useful for conceptualizing children's intelligence. The developmental trajectories for several components of the architectural and executive systems are shown in Figure 2.3. Efficiency, for example, peaks very early, perhaps by age 5, and declines

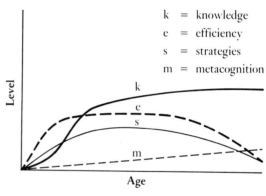

FIGURE 2.3

Borkowski's hypothetical development of intellectual skills

SOURCE: Adapted from Borkowski (1987).

in old age. Knowledge, on the other hand, increases throughout the life span.

Triarchic Theory

As proposed by Robert Sternberg, triarchic theory is an attempt to produce an integrative theory of intelligence (Sternberg, 1987). Sternberg (see Box 2.1) has thoroughly reviewed the

Box 2.1

An interview with Dr. Robert J. Sternberg

How do you view the current relationship between intelligence theory and everyday assessment practice as embodied in our current tests?

I view the relationship between intelligence theory and everyday assessment practice as embodied in our current tests in about the same way as I view the relationship between flour and a cake. Flour is an important ingredient of a cake. You certainly wouldn't want to have a cake without it, except on special occasions, perhaps. But flour does not make the whole cake (especially if it is only half-baked!).

I think present tests, such as the WISC-III and the Stanford-Binet, do a creditable job of measuring a part of children's intelligence, especially their memory, analytic, and spatial skills. To the extent that my goal was to predict performance in elementary or secondary school, and nothing more, I would be fairly comfortable with either of these tests. But I would not be happy with either test if I wanted to probe more deeply into a child's intelligence, broadly defined. Neither test gives a reading on children's creative-intellectual or practical-intellectual skills. And we know from our own research, as well as from that of others, that these skills are far from perfectly correlated with the skills we are now measuring on conventional intelligence tests.

Do we really want to continue to determine children's futures on the basis of their ability to think in conventional ways? Certainly, such abilities are important. But doesn't the future of our society, as well as of each individual child, depend at least as much on the child's ability to generate new and useful ideas, and to adapt to as well as shape the environments in which he or she lives? I would like to see us broaden our emphasis in testing to include the creative and practical parts of intelligence that are currently so widely ignored.

What is the current status of triarchic theory? Do you anticipate making any substantive changes to the theory?

The triarchic theory was first presented in published form in 1984, and it seems to have made some inroads in affecting people's thinking about intelligence. With time, I do hope the theory will evolve, as all good theories do. In particular, it needs to spell out more explicitly what is involved in adapting to, shaping, and selecting environments, and in coping with novelty. Those parts of the theory are less well specified than I would like, and we are doing ongoing research in each of these areas.

Since the publication of the triarchic theory, I have developed theories of intellectual styles (how we *use* our intelligence). The theory of styles is based on a notion of mental self-government: that in using our intelligence, we need to govern ourselves, much as governments do for countries. The theory of creativity is an investment model, based on the notion that creative people are ones who "invest" themselves in ideas that are often unconventional and even out of favor, and then make these ideas conventional and favored by others. So my own path has been to expand the domains about which I theorize, and to try to understand phenomena that go beyond intelligence.

---

so-called "psychometric" and other approaches to the study of intelligence in the process of proposing his model. His theory has a distinctly information processing flavor to it, making it resemble various aspects of cognitive theories. Perhaps the greatest contribution of Sternberg is his attempt to "decompose" intellectual performance into the various strategies, procedures, and processes used to solve a problem. In a sense it could be said that his theory allows for a detailed task analysis of problem solving, fostering better understanding of the reasons *why* a child may perform well or poorly on a problem.

This theory hypothesizes three types of information processing components that are necessary for competent problem solving. One type of process consists of *metacomponents*. These are executive processes that plan, monitor, and evaluate problem solving. Clearly, there is some relationship here to the cognitive term "meta-cognition." Metacomponential processes include the following (Sternberg, 1987):

1. Deciding on the nature of the problem
2. Selecting a set of lower-order processes to use to solve a problem
3. Selecting a strategy for combining processes to solve a problem
4. Selecting a mental representation upon which the processes and strategy can act
5. Allocating mental resources
6. Monitoring problem solving

Performance components are a second level of cognition that consists of lower-order mental processes that are controlled by metacomponents. Inductive reasoning is one type of performance component. The third part of Sternberg's theory involves *knowledge acquisition components* that are used to learn the metacomponents and components processes. According to Sternberg, these skills are not well researched at this point, but they are crucial for acquiring important factual information needed for problem solving. Knowledge acquisition components include selective encoding, selective combination, and selective comparison.

Another part of triarchic theory, *experiential subtheory*, has two characteristics. It deals with the effects of experience on the expression of intelligent behavior. As Sternberg (1987) and others have correctly observed, all tasks used to assess intelligence have some level of familiarity to the individual being tested. As such, the ability to deal with novelty becomes a factor in intelligence test performance. Sternberg (1987) proposes that one reason why cultural groups may have different mean scores on intelligence tests is due to the cultural group's experiences, or lack of same, with novel stimuli.

The second ability that is central to this ex-

periential subtheory is the ability to automatize information processing. This ability refers to the common finding that problem solving occurs more expeditiously with repeated trials.

The *contextual subtheory* of triarchic theory states that intelligent behavior is directed toward the achievement of three behavioral goals: adaptation to an environment, shaping of an environment, and selection of an environment (Sternberg, 1987). The idea that intelligence has to be understood in relationship to environmental context makes this and other recent theories of intelligence (e.g., Valsiner, 1984) very distant cousins to early intelligence theories in that the vast majority of early intelligence theories emphasize the internal world of the person being tested. An example of how intelligent behavior can be defined differently based on culture or context is provided by Cole, Gay, Glick, and Sharp (1971) as described by Sternberg (1987) in the following quote:

> These investigators asked adult Kpelle tribesmen to sort 20 familiar objects into groups of things that belong together. Their subjects separated the objects into functional groupings (e.g., a knife with an orange), as children in western societies would do. This pattern of sorting surprised investigators, who had expected to see taxonomic groupings, (e.g., tools sorted together and food sorted together) of a kind that would be found in the sortings of western adults. Had investigators used the sorting task as a measure of intelligence in the traditional way, they might well have labeled the Kpelle tribesmen as intellectually inferior to western adults. However, through persistent exploration of why the Kpelle were sorting in this way, they found that the Kpelle considered functional sorting to be the intelligent form of sorting. When the tribesmen were asked to sort the way a stupid person would do so, they had no trouble sorting taxonomically. In short, they differed on this test not in their intellectual competence vis-a-vis western adults, but in their conception of what was functionally adaptive. Indeed, it takes little thought to see the practicality of sorting functionally: people do, after all, use utensils in conjunction with foods of a given category (e.g., fruits) on a frequent basis. (p. 159)

Another example of the application of this subtheory in interpreting the profile of a college student can be found in Box 2.2. The notion of the contextualist nature of intelligence is receiving increasing attention by recent theorists. The theorizing of Jaan Valsiner (1984) may place the greatest premium on understanding intelligence in context.

THE ECOLOGY OF INTELLIGENCE

Valsiner

Jaan Valsiner (1984) takes an interesting approach to conceptualizing intelligence by disavowing the vast majority of approaches to understanding intelligence. Valsiner (1984) observes, as did Sternberg, that definitions of intelligence and intelligent behavior are frequently culture-specific (remember the Kpelle). Many western cultures, for example, refer to intelligence as a stable property of the individual (e.g., "she's intelligent"). According to Valsiner (1984), this traditional approach assumes that intelligence is an internal characteristic of the individual. The traditional view also conceptualized intelligence as static, with a level of intelligence for any one individual that is relatively stable.

Valsiner (1984) argues that in order for an intelligence theory to be relevant to a host of cultures, it must be set in an ecological framework. In other words, intelligence theory

Box 2.2

Application of Sternberg's theory to interpretation of a young adult's WAIS-R results

---

The various theories described in this chapter may seem somewhat removed from the realm of everyday intelligence test interpretation. I beg to differ. On the contrary, I find myself labeling children as little Jensens, Sternbergs, Cattells, or the like. One of the clearest cases of the application of a theory comes from a college student who volunteered to take the WAIS-R for a student in my graduate level assessment course.

The student who tested the young woman brought the results to my class for presentation and discussion. My student's concern about the examinee was obvious shortly after the case was presented. The woman had achieved a WAIS-R Full Scale of *only* 86. We then launched into a discussion of whether or not we should tell this person about her "low IQ" despite our policy to the contrary and commitment to confidentiality. I then interrogated my student to produce the following profile of the woman.

She had a B college GPA, she was well liked by all, her major was recreation studies, she planned to open a health club after graduation, she was engaged and looking forward to getting married, and she was an elected member of student government. It then struck me that this student's profile was a perfect example of one of Sternberg's contextual notions of adult intelligence. Namely, intelligent people shape and adapt to their environments by making maximum use of their strengths and deemphasizing their weaknesses.

By traditional measures of intelligence, the WAIS-R, this student had "problems," was "below average — dull" or "at risk" to say the least. However, when broadening the concept of intelligence to include adaptation, this woman was clearly clever, and, I thought to myself, she will definitely be physically healthier, if not happier and wealthier than myself! She was clearly behaving quite adaptively, as was indicated by her choice of major field of study. She must have some strengths in this area to have a good GPA, and she avoided majors that could have perhaps highlighted whatever cognitive limitations she may possess. My suggestion to the class was to review Sternberg's ideas, to continue to strive to integrate theory and practice so as to avoid being merely a producer of intelligence test scores, and to *not attempt to seek this young lady out and tell her that she has a low IQ*.

---

must move from being internal/static in nature to being relationship/dynamic. Viewed in this way, intelligence cannot be attributed to the individual *or* to the environment, but to the relationship between the two. Valsiner (1984) cites the mother–child relationship as an example. If two mothers are observed trying to calm their crying children and one mother is much more successful more quickly, is she the intelligent one (an internal/static attribution)? As mothers know, however, frequently the key to calming a crying child is determined by cues given by the child that allow the mother to ascertain if the child is tired, is hungry, or has soiled pants. Perhaps the mother who calmed her child first was more successful not because *she* is intelligent, but because her child has very distinct cries that allow her to easily discern the source of the child's discomfort. Valsiner (1984) argues for this latter viewpoint, that it is the ecology of this relationship that needs to be studied if we are going to be able to define intelligence in a cross-culturally meaningful way.

Vygotsky

Recently, Valsiner and others (Belmont, 1989) have cited Vygotsky's (1978) theory regarding the *zone of proximal development (ZPD)* as the theoretical basis for the ecological point of view. Briefly, the ZPD is the difference between how a child may perform on an intelligence test in isolation and how the child would perform given some hints, clues, and suggestions by the examiner. Some children, then, may have identical IQs but very different ZPDs based on how they benefit from social interaction with a competent adult. Characteristics of the ZPD include the notion that all learning is interpersonal and ecological in nature. A child does not have a ZPD per se, but rather a ZPD exists between the adult and child in an interpersonal interaction (Belmont, 1989).

The concept of the ZPD has been used to support the development and use of dynamic

assessment models (Belmont, 1989). These models (see Chapter 12) hold out the promise of a strong link between cognitive assessment and intervention planning since "teaching" is an integral part of the assessment process.

Ecological models are also better able to capture the full range of intelligent behavior (Frederiksen, 1986). Group-administered measures of intelligence are most limited in the range of behavior they assess. Three major limitations of these measures include (Frederiksen, 1986):

1. The basic format of intelligence tests is unable to access the full range of real-life behavior, especially when multiple-choice formats are used.

2. A particular problem with intelligence tests is their inability to diagnose the various processes that underlie a person's performance on a test. Individual children may use a host of different strategies for responding to the same stimuli. A child may respond to a puzzle-solving item nonverbally and use spatial skills to solve it or a child may speak out loud while solving the item and use verbal mediation to assemble the puzzle.

3. There is little variation in the situations in which intelligence test data are collected, thus precluding the possibility of novel responses to problem solving. In a sense, the standardized procedures that enhance reliability may force a limited range of intellectual assessment. In less structured settings a child may respond to a challenge very differently than in an academic-like setting.

In ecological fashion, Frederiksen (1986) has also proposed numerous alternatives to group tests of intelligence that use different formats, including tests of hypothesis testing using real-life types of problems, interviewing to assess intelligence, and "in-basket" tests. An "in-basket" test, for example, might require an individual to solve problems presented in written form much in the same way an executive solves problems by delegating, prioritizing, and making decisions based on the requests of others. The facility with which an individual solves problems in the "in-basket" in an appropriate and timely fashion could be an indication of intelligence.

INTELLIGENCE AS A TYPE OF ACHIEVEMENT

One point of view that has been offered is that intelligence tests are specialized types of academic achievement measures (Wesman, 1968). This viewpoint is very practical in that it obviates the nature/nurture issue. Intelligence test results merely reflect what an individual has learned due to a variety of interacting forces affecting development.

Anastasi's View

Anastasi (1986; see Box 2.3) defines intelligence as "a quality of behavior. Such behavior is adaptive and highly influenced by cultural/environmental factors." Anastasi (1988; see Chapter 1) offers the viewpoint that intelligence should be viewed as a type of developed ability, similar to academic achievement. In fact, she describes intelligence tests currently in vogue as measures of "academic intelligence" or "scholastic aptitude." She also proposes that instead of attempting to develop methods of assessing intelligence that would apply to all cultures, as Valsiner suggests, intelligence tests be devised to be culture-specific.

Anastasi's theory stands in direct contrast to that of Valsiner and, to a lesser extent, that of Sternberg. Be assured that her theory is *not* being introduced so as to confuse the reader of this text. Anastasi's theory is offered here because it appears to be practical for the interpretation of current intelligence tests (as will be shown later in this text). Intelligence tests currently in use tend to correlate highly with measures of academic achievement and many have academic content such as mathematics items.

REACTION TIME AND "G"

Jensen (1982; see Box 2.4) has declared a revival for theories of reaction time as measures of general intelligence. Previously, reaction time and simple psychophysical measures were found not to correlate highly with criterion measures, especially academic achievement. Jensen, however, has concluded that Galton was in fact correct but that he lacked the technology necessary to assess reaction time adequately. He also observes that much of the reaction time research suffered from other problems, such as not using enough trials to get reliable estimates of reaction time. Jensen (1982) cites numerous recent studies and research paradigms as indicative of renewed interest in reaction time as a measure of general intelligence. More recently, Jensen (1987) has shown correlations as high as .98 between dual reaction time measures and the "g" (general intelligence) factor of an aptitude battery.

There are also studies that have not found high correlations between reaction time measures and intelligence tests. Ruchala, Schalt, and Vogel (1985) found only a complex reaction time task to correlate somewhat with a German test of intelligence, the "Intelligenz-Struktur-test." However, even the correlation of the complex reaction time task with the intelligence test was significant, but unimpressive. The highest correlation found was only .164.

THE CLINICIAN'S THEORY

The examiner's theories may, in fact, prove to be the theories commonly used by the examiner in drawing conclusions about a child's performance. It is important for the trainee to un-

Box 2.3

An interview with Dr. Anne Anastasi

You have been an observer of changes in intellectual assessment, and the tests used for this purpose, for the greater part of this century. Given this unique perspective, could you tell me what noteworthy changes have occurred in this field in approximately the past 50 years?

Much has happened during those years. I see first the movement away from single, global indexes of "intelligence" and toward the assessment of more clearly defined competencies. This trend has been stimulated, on the one hand, by the identification of multiple abilities through factor analyses of intelligence and, on the other hand, by the practical demands for more specific information in such areas as education, career counseling, personnel selection and classification, and other rapidly developing applications of psychological knowledge.

I see also the gradual dissolution of the artificial distinction between traditional aptitude and achievement tests and the substitution of the concept of developed abilities that vary in the degree to which they are linked to specific learning contexts.

Still another significant change is an increasing recognition of the contribution of the individual's interests, attitudes, motivation, and value system, not only to his or her immediate task performance (and test scores), but also to the long-term development of different ability patterns.

Again, given your special perspective, what recent work in intelligence theory or the assessment devices do you find particularly exciting and potentially rewarding right now?

With regard to intelligence theory, I would say the hierarchical model of intelligence, whereby intelligence can be effectively described and assessed at different levels, from broad "general" factors such as scholastic aptitude or mechanical intelligence, through group factors of successively diminishing breadth, to highly specific skills. Within this hierarchy, different levels are appropriate for different testing purposes and contexts. Second, I would cite the increasing trend toward comprehensive orientations that incorporate, for example, the traditional correlational and trait approach with the approach of cognitive psychology which focuses on process analyses of *what* the individual does in solving problems and in responding to test items.

With regard to assessment devices, there is no question in my mind that the most exciting event is the development of computerized adaptive testing (CAT), whereby each test can be custom-built for the individual while he or she is taking the test.

What do you think should be the focus of research in intellectual assessment: new theories, new tests, litigation, or other priorities?

As for litigation, it is my hope that we shall soon work out the major problems that have arisen as both society and tests have undergone dramatic and significant changes. We can then concentrate on exploring the various innovative types of tests that have been appearing on the horizon, as well as new and more effective ways of using tests so as to aid the individual in making his or her best contribution both to society and to personal fulfillment. These developments should themselves arise from and contribute to the formulation and testing of more scientifically powerful theories of human abilities.

---

derstand his or her informal theoretical notions of intelligence and be able to differentiate them from the aforementioned theories. In addition, it is crucial that the trainee keep an open mind in order to consider the various empirical findings on intelligence that are discussed in the next chapter. The findings presented in Chapter 3 are likely to cast doubt on some of the trainee's implicit theories and on some of the formal conceptualizations reviewed earlier in the chapter.

Box 2.4

An interview with Dr. Arthur Jensen

Can you give us a glimpse of some of the exciting findings emanating from research on speed of information processing?

Items in conventional tests of mental ability, of course, reflect in part individual differences in the speed or efficiency of cognitive processes. But they do so rather indirectly, because successful performance on typical test items usually depends on some acquired intellectual *content or skill*, which may be confounded with the cognitive processes involved in their acquisition and effective use. If we wish to study mainly the *information processing* aspect of mental ability and minimize its confounding with content or skill, we must use *chronometric* techniques, or the measurement of response times (RTs) to a variety of *elementary cognitive tasks* (ECTs).

One important feature of ECTs is that they are so simple to perform that the only reliable source of individual differences is the subject's RT. This is often less than 2 seconds and usually less than 1 second, and error rates on these ECTs are very low, so you can see these tasks are exceedingly simple. The important point is that they do measure the speed or efficiency of the particular processes involved in a given ECT. Each ECT reflects just one or two, or very few, elementary information processes, such as the time needed to apprehend and respond to the onset of an external stimulus (for example, simple RT to a light or a sound), or the time needed to make a single discrimination (choice or discrimination RT), or to scan one's short-term memory in order to respond whether a given single "target" digit had or had not been displayed just 2 or 3 seconds previously, or the time needed to retrieve from one's long-term memory some highly overlearned common item of information, such as recognition of whether or not the symbols "A" and "a" represent the same letter of the alphabet. These are just a few ECTs that reflect basic processes. The average RTs to simple ECTs amount to only fractions of a second and can be measured accurately in milliseconds.

Now the really interesting fact is that these RTs show highly reliable individual differences, and each different ECT shows some correlation (usually about .30) with the IQ obtained from conventional intelligence tests; the correlation is somewhat higher with just the general ability factor, "g," common to all so-called intelligence tests. Multiple correlations, based on a number of different ECTs, are often much higher, generally in the .50 to .70 range, depending on the number and diversity of ECTs that enter into the multiple correlation coefficient. This demonstrates the possibility, which however has not yet been fully developed, of measuring individual differences in mental ability by means that are virtually independent of acquired intellectual contents and skills, and of localizing relative strengths and weaknesses in the various components of the information processing system reflected in the different ECTs. A whole new science, with an already large literature, has already developed along these lines and I believe it will advance our understanding of the nature of individual differences in mental abilities more than anything else that has happened in psychometric science in the last half-century.

What do you see as the practical applications of research on speed of processing?

My interest in this subject, and that of many other researchers, so far has been mainly theoretical. We are trying to explain why RTs to such simple tasks share variance in common with psychometric *g* derived from performance on complex tests of reasoning. The explanation of *g* remains one of the main theoretical challenges in differential psychology. It is now quite clear that speed of information processing, or perhaps some even more fundamental variable that is manifested in part as processing speed, is strongly implicated in the explanation of *g*.

If *g* and other ability factors reflect individual differences in the speed of operation of a number of different elementary processing components, such as stimulus discrimination, encoding, and memory retrieval, then the practical implications for psychological diagnosis seem fairly obvious. We should be able to measure and describe individual differences in *g* (or other abilities) in terms of the relative efficiency of the various component information processes. We are just now beginning to study children with special learning disabilities in these

(continued)

Box 2.4 *(continued)*

terms. Our studies of academically gifted children show clearly that they are far above the general average of their age peers in speed of processing on every ECT we have tried. Mentally retarded persons generally show much slower processing—just the opposite of the gifted children. Children who have at least average IQ but who have specific learning disabilities, however, may be expected to show unusual inefficiency in only one or two of the elementary processes. We are just now investigating this hypothesis. Whether any psychological techniques might be able to remedy a particular processing deficiency has not yet been adequately investigated.

Two important features of mental chronometry suggest other practical uses: (1) Exactly the same ECTs can be used to measure processing speed throughout the entire age range from preschool to maturity and old age. This is not true of any conventional tests, in which the items must differ in order to be appropriate for different ages and different levels of mental ability. And (2) chronometric measures of performance of ECTs represent real time, and hence they constitute a true ratio scale, which permits us to plot meaningful frequency distributions of population parameters and growth curves showing the rates of development of the various elementary processes. Scores on conventional tests are not true ratio scales and therefore do not permit either of these scientific advantages of absolute measurement scales. Children's mental development, as reflected in ECTs, thus can be measured just as are differences in physical growth rates. Similarly, the rate of decline in mental efficiency during later maturity and old age can be studied chronometrically with respect to various information processes. We have already found that speed of processing decreases gradually with increasing age. No one who lives long enough escapes this, apparently, but we find that there are large individual differences in the rate of decline. Also, pathological conditions, such as Alzheimer's disease, could probably be detected much earlier than usual by means of chronometric techniques.

How would an intelligence test that assesses speed of processing be different from current intelligence tests in vogue?

A composite (or average) measure of speed of processing on several diverse ECTs, each one taking about 10 minutes of testing time, would be substantially correlated with the general factor, or *g*, measured by the Full Scale IQ on tests such as the Wechsler and Stanford-Binet scales. It would differ only in that it would be a relatively pure *process* measure of *g*, not dependent on the specific knowledge and skill contents, such as vocabulary, arithmetic, and general factual information, which serve as the vehicles for reflecting individual differences in *g* in standard psychometric tests. A "profile" of subtest "scores" on a battery of processing tests would indicate the person's absolute and relative standing on a number of different ECTs designed to reflect particular elementary cognitive processes that contribute to the person's overall mental efficiency that is reflected in what we refer to in psychometrics as general mental ability, or *g*. Conventional tests, like the Wechsler, analyze mental abilities in terms of performance on various subtests, each of which reflects a certain ability *factor* (in the sense of *factor analysis,* such as Verbal, Numerical, Spatial, and Memory) more than it reflects other factors. A proper set of ECTs would analyze general ability in terms of elementary cognitive processes. Both the traditional psychometric view and the speed-of-processing view of a person's abilities should be complementary and diagnostically revealing. It is something like taking pictures of a complex natural phenomenon, say the Grand Canyon, from two quite different perspectives. Each reveals different facets and we then have a more telling analytic view of the phenomenon.

Modern microcomputers with millisecond timing devices now make it quite easy to obtain chronometric assessments of information processes. The test stimuli appear on the standard monitor, and we have special response consoles with large, well-spaced push buttons interfaced with the computer that minimize the perceptual-motor skill requirements of the person's responses. A reactive subject-paced computer program controls the entire test administration, records all of the person's RTs (and response errors), and, at the conclusion of the test, prints out various summary statistics on the person's performance. I expect that within a decade or so we will see something resembling our present computerized laboratory set-up in use in many psychological clinics, for assessing the mental abilities of children and adults in terms of basic information processes.

CONCLUSIONS

Recent intelligence theorists such as Jensen (1987) and Baltes (1986) propose that intelligence should not be viewed as an elusive construct that requires one definition upon which everyone agrees. They propose that intelligence be a more global construct that defines a field of study. Jensen (1987) argues that the term "intelligence" should be treated in the same way as the term "nature," in that it can be viewed as a broadly descriptive term of an area of inquiry. Intelligence, like nature, includes a variety of different phenomena to be studied. Baltes (1986) eloquently describes this view of intelligence as an area of investigation.

First, intelligence should not be used as a "theoretical" construct, but as the label for a field of scholarship. . . . Second, if one is interested in formulating theoretical accounts of facets of the field, then it is necessary to introduce qualifiers to be added to the term intelligence. *Otherwise, surplus meaning and metatheoretical discord will continue to be paramount. For example, rather than speak of intelligence per se, my preference is to speak of constructs such as innate intellectual capacity (Anlage), intellectual reserve capacity, learning capacity, intellectual abilities, intelligent systems, problem-solving ability, and knowledge systems. Each of these compound terms permits the generation of more theoretical specificity and precision. (Sternberg & Detterman, 1986, p. 24)*

While there is an emerging consensus that a single theory of intelligence will not in the near future be deemed the "correct" one (Eysenck, 1986), current data suggest problems and promise for some theories. A study of empirical findings regarding intelligence (see next chapter) will aid in developing an even deeper understanding of the constructs assessed by the various tests in use.

CHAPTER SUMMARY

1. A psychologist's interpretations of test results, either written in a report or orally presented in a parent conference or other venue, are expressions of the psychologist's theoretical knowledge or biases.

2. The idea that something such as "intelligence" exists appears to be universal.

3. Binet seemed to ascribe to the notion of intelligence as a single entity.

4. Spearman is usually credited as the first to offer a hierarchical theory of intelligence. In his theory, "g," or general intelligence, is placed at the top of the hierarchy because this is the underlying "mental energy" that is central to all intelligent problem solving. There are also specific, or "s," factors at the bottom of the hierarchy.

5. Vernon (1950) offered a more detailed hierarchy of intellectual abilities where general intelligence is at the top of the hierarchy. Next in the hierarchy are the major group factors, which are of two varieties; verbal/educational (v:ed) and spatial/mechanical (k:m) types of intelligence.

6. Jensen (1969) proposed a hierarchical theory of intelligence that hypothesized the existence of two mental processes. Level I processing (associative ability) typically does not require manipulation or transformation of the stimulus input prior to producing a response. Level II processing (conceptual ability) requires considerable manipulation and elaboration of the stimulus input in order to produce a response.

7. Thurstone (1938) first identified nine, then seven (Thurstone & Thurstone, 1941), then six (Thurstone, 1941) primary mental abilities through factor analytic investigations.

8. Weinberg (1989) offered the broad categories of "lumpers" and "splitters"—those who propose that intelligence is a general ability and those who prefer to consider it as a set of abilities, respectively.

9. Piaget's theory has only infrequently been used as a model for the development of intelligence tests (e.g., Uzgiris & Hunt, 1974).

10. David Wechsler views intelligence as a complex interaction of abilities that produce intelligent behavior that reflects "g."

11. Cattell proposed two types of intelligence: Fluid and Crystallized. His follower, John Horn, has expanded the model to include other factors such as visualization and short-term memory.

12. Transactional theory, as proposed by Haywood and Switzky (1986), presents a theory of intelligence that attempts to explain the nature of the genetic/environment interaction that produces various levels of performance on intelligence tests.

13. Transactional theory stipulates that everyone has a creod, a species specific developmental path, for intelligence.

14. Levy (1974) identified two types of intellectual processes located in the cerebral hemispheres. She concluded that the left hemisphere was specialized for analytic processing and the right hemisphere for holistic processing.

15. Das et al. (1979) postulated a "coding" dichotomy that included two major mental processes: successive and simultaneous processing.

16. Jensen (1987) has shown correlations as high as .98 between dual reaction time measures and the "g" factor of an aptitude battery.

17. The three components of Guilford's structure of intellect model are contents, operations, and products.

18. A central characteristic of information processing theories is the use of the computer, and the way it processes information, as a metaphor for human cognition.

19. Declarative memory is similar to traditional notions of long-term memory in that it is characterized by long-term storage and slow decay of memory traces and it stores acquired facts. Procedural memory stores rules for problem solving or production knowledge.

20. Robert Sternberg proposed his triarchic theory in an attempt to produce an integrative theory of intelligence.

21. Valsiner argues that intelligence theory must move from being internal/static in nature to being relationship/dynamic.

22. Frederiksen (1986) proposed numerous alternative methods for assessing intelligence, including tests of hypothesis testing using real-life types of problems, interviewing to assess intelligence, and "in-basket" tests.

23. Anastasi (1987) views intelligence as a type of developed ability similar to academic achievement.

24. Intelligence can be conceptualized as a global construct that defines a field of study.

Chapter 3

Research Findings

Can we "cure" low intelligence?

Why are there ethnic group differences in intelligence?

What about research findings regarding intelligence? Is there substantial evidence of genetic inheritance? Are there large differences between boys and girls? Can intelligence be changed significantly? These, fortunately, are well-researched areas that can be discussed with data as support. There remains much to be done, however. This chapter summarizes the available research on these and other important topics.

Like knowledge of theories of intelligence, intelligence research findings can be invaluable to the new clinician struggling to explain test results to parents and teachers, and perhaps such knowledge is equally prized by some experienced psychologists. Research findings can help clinicians answer questions such as:

1. Will Sam's intelligence improve if I send him to a competitive preschool?
2. Will Bobby outgrow his low intelligence test score?
3. Isn't that test biased against my little girl?
4. How did my child get a low score—was it my fault?

Some of these are also incorrect questions that have to be reframed by the psychologist. Regardless, questions such as these arise regularly, and the psychologist who is not aware of relevant research may have considerable difficulty responding.

I have also found intelligence test research to be helpful for gauging the accuracy of intelligence test scores. I am occasionally presented with a set of intelligence test scores that my students have had difficulty interpreting. I was recently asked about a case in which there was a huge difference between Verbal and Performance scores on the WISC-III (about 50 standard score points). Since the profile did not fit

45

with any research I had ever seen, I asked if the student checked the scores. Much to the chagrin of the student, after checking the profile, an addition error was found. I wish that I had a nickel for the number of times I have found computation errors because the scores were unlawful from a research standpoint! A concrete (and perhaps unrealistic) example of such a case would be a child who was born to well-educated and well-meaning parents, had a negative medical history, had met all developmental milestones early, went to the most prestigious schools, and had won academic honors, and yet the new psychologist obtained a WISC-III Full Scale of 85 (16th percentile and below average). This result is highly suspicious based on the current knowledge of factors affecting intelligence test scores and beckons the psychologist to recheck the obtained scores.

Throughout this chapter, I will refer to *changes in intelligence test scores as opposed to changes in intelligence.* I think that this distinction is important because there is scientific debate regarding whether or not current intelligence tests measure "intelligence." Just as the original Roentgen Ray (X-ray) machines may have been difficult to read because of "shadows" and other factors, so, too, modern intelligence tests may in some cases not measure intelligence well because of socioeconomic, motivational, and other factors. Breakthroughs in intelligence testing and other assessment areas lie ahead. Hence, all of the findings in this chapter refer to results obtained with the current technology, which likely is not the ultimate measure of the intelligence construct. In those cases where I do use the word "intelligence," I am only doing so as a short form for "intelligence test score."

STABILITY OF INTELLIGENCE TEST SCORES

Age and Test Interval

There are two major findings of importance on this topic. First, intelligence test scores are less stable for infants and preschoolers than for older children (Goodman, 1990; Anastasi, 1988). Secondly, the longer the interval between tests the greater the instability (Schuerger & Witt, 1989; Anastasi, 1988).

Infant intellectual assessment is a special problem area. The instability of infant intelligence test scores has led some to question the continued practice (Goodman, 1990). The lack of stability for infant intelligence test scores is most apparent for samples of "nonhandicapped" children. Some typical results are shown in Table 3.1. These results clearly demonstrate that the stability of the obtained scores increases dramatically as a result of the child being older at the time of the initial assessment.

The stability of scores for developmentally handicapped infants and preschoolers, however, is considerably better than for nondelayed children (Goodman, 1990) (see also Chapter 13). Whereas the stability coefficients in Table 3.1 are only in the .30 to .50 range at best, coefficients for delayed samples of this same age range are generally above .50 when retested at 5 to 7 years of age. Some studies have found stability coefficients as high as .80 and .90 (Goodman, 1990).

Given this contrast in findings, a single statement cannot be made about the stability of intelligence test scores for infant and preschool

TABLE 3.1 Average Correlations Between Infant and Later Intelligence Test Scores for Non-Handicapped Children

Age in Months at Initial Test	Age in Years at Childhood Test		
	3–4	5–7	8–18
1–6	.21	.09	.06
7–12	.32	.20	.25
13–18	.50	.34	.32
19–30	.59	.39	.49

Correlations of .30 and above are in boldface.
SOURCE: Adapted from McCall (1979).

children. Therefore, two statements are in order.

1. Intelligence test scores should be considered as unstable for nonreferred, otherwise "normal" preschool and even seemingly precocious children.
2. Intelligence test scores are fairly stable for handicapped, particularly mentally retarded, infants and preschoolers.

What about the stability of scores for older children? Here the results are much less interesting. Intelligence test scores seem to stabilize at about age 6. Schuerger and Witt (1989) reviewed 34 studies of test-retest reliability for the WAIS, WAIS-R, WISC, WISC-R, and several editions of the Stanford-Binet, exclusive of the Binet 4. Using multiple regression procedures they found that age and interval between tests were the two variables most predictive of changes in intelligence test scores. Gender was not a significant variable, nor was treatment status (i.e., patient versus nonpa-

tient). These results reinforce the previous findings of studies regarding age, but they also show clearly the relationship between age and test interval for elementary grade samples and samples of adults.

Schuerger and Witt (1989) found stability coefficients to be high, even for 6-year-olds. The coefficients for 6-year-olds ranged from .85 for a 1-week interval to .67 for a 20-year interval! Stability was better for 39-year-olds, where coefficients ranged from .99 for 1 week to .82 for 20 years. This relationship between age and interval and stability of test scores is depicted graphically in Figures 3.1 and 3.2. Stability is maximized as age increases and interval between tests decreases.

We cannot, however, simply commit a single rule to memory. The results shown in Figures 3.1 and 3.2 are based on group data, not single case data. These results may or may not apply to individual children (Anastasi, 1988). Schuerger and Witt (1989) also calculated the percentage of each sample that would show a change in intelligence test score of 15 points or more. They found that of 6-year-olds evaluated

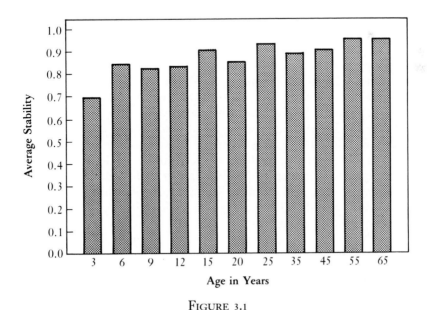

FIGURE 3.1

Graph depicting the relationship between age and stability
Adapted from Schuerger and Witt (1989).

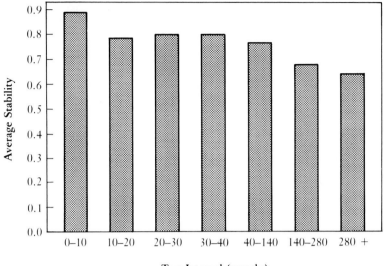

Test Interval (months)

FIGURE 3.2

Graph depicting the relationship between test interval and stability
Adapted from Schuerger and Witt (1989).

1 year apart, fully 13% of the sample changed scores by at least 1 standard deviation—a big change by any standard! Even 7% of the 30-year-olds changed their scores by more than 15 standard score points. In another study of changes in intelligence test scores from age 6 to 18 years, stability coefficients were high, but considerable changes in the *magnitude* of scores was noted (Anastasi, 1988). One study found 59% of the children to change by 15 or more standard score points, 37% by 20 or more points, and 9% by 30 or more points (Honzik, Macfarlane, & Allen, 1948). In a recent investigation of 170 learning-disabled children who were tested 3 years apart, the changes were less dramatic than in the studies just cited (Oakman & Wilson, 1988). However, 4% of the sample experienced changes of at least 15 points on the WISC-R. The hard part for the psychologist is to figure out who the "changers" are. It is up to the experience and acumen of the psychologist to figure out who these children are. The following discussion will help.

The Growth and Decline of Intelligence

What is the trajectory of intellectual development? Early research and theory gave a pessimistic view of intellectual development beyond adolescence. Pintner (1923) reviewed the research on the intelligence test scores of World War I recruits in order to determine when intelligence test scores reached an asymptote in adulthood. As far as the maximum level of mental development, he concluded that "[a]t present, it is customary to assume the fourteen-year-old level in view of the general results of the mental testing in the army, where it was found that the average recruit had a mentality about equal to a mental age of 13.8 on the Stanford Revision" (p. 67). Since the early days of testing the outlook for adult intelligence has become more optimistic.

The pessimistic views regarding the growth and decline of intelligence were in ascendance in the 1940s and 1950s. At that time a number of research investigations using cross-sectional methods made the claim that intelligence test scores declined, in some cases dramatically, in old age (Dixon, Kramer, & Baltes, 1985). This finding generated much controversy and resulted in a number of longitudinal investigations of intellectual growth. These longitudinal investigations did not produce such pessimistic outcomes (Dixon, Kramer, & Baltes, 1985). One study using a longitudinal research design found that one of the few reliable decrements before age 60 was in word fluency. There was a reliable *increment* in verbal meaning to the age of 39 years (Schaie & Parham, 1977). Why, then, is there a seeming disagreement between longitudinal and cross-sectional studies? The most likely hypothesis is that differences in educational attainment are a potent factor in cross-sectional investigations. The average level of education for the American population has increased over the generations, resulting in older individuals in a cross-sectional design having lower levels of educational attainment than younger individuals. Of course, the effect of educational attainment can be more easily controlled in a longitudinal investigation.

There are, however, some reliable decrements in intelligence (Schaie & Hertzog, 1983). Schaie and Hertzog (1983) found a reliable decrement in overall intelligence between the ages of 60 and 80 years of about 1 standard deviation. In addition, when these same individuals were placed in an intervention program, their intelligence test scores gained by about the same amount, 1 standard deviation. They returned to pre-decline levels. The decrement in intelligence test scores in late adulthood has been attributed to both biological and social factors. It has been attributed, for example, to effects of cardiovascular disease (Hertzog, Schaie, & Gribbin, 1978) and social deprivation (Gribbin, Schaie, & Parham, 1975).

The application of the fluid/crystallized dichotomy still seems to be useful for conceptualizing the rise and fall of specific cognitive skills. Recent investigations have replicated previous findings regarding the decline of WAIS-R IQs (Kaufman, Reynolds, & McClean, 1989). Verbal scores, typically considered to be measures of crystallized ability, tend to show little decline over the course of adulthood, while Performance scores, considered to be measures of fluid abilities, decline precipitously (see Figure 3.3). These data do support the relationship between fluid ability and physical well-being. Kaufman (1990) provides a very detailed analysis of this issue and summarizes relevant research on changes in adult intelligence.

These findings have resulted in reframing the question, do intelligence test scores decline in late adulthood? There are now a host of questions about which intelligence test scores decline, the causes of the decline, and its permanence. Similarly, why do some scores show great resistance to decline? Some of these findings may have relevance for understanding the declining scores of some children. If, for example, physical well-being is associated with intelligence test scores in adulthood, then this may also be the case for children. (See Chapter 14 for related research on the effects of brain injury on children's intelligence test scores.)

Cumulative Deficits

The cumulative deficit is a more distressing type of instability that psychologists have to face all too often. There is a tendency for children from low SES environments to have their intelligence test score gradually decrease over the course of development in relationship to the normative mean (Anastasi, 1988; Saco-Pollitt, Pollitt, & Greenfield, 1985). Jensen (1974, 1977) has defined cumulative deficits as the tendency for the effects of an unfavorable environment to compound with time. Jensen explains that new learning is dependent on previous learning. When initial learning is inadequate, considerable effort must be expended in order to reverse the inadequate course of cognitive development. This conceptualization is consistent with Piaget's and

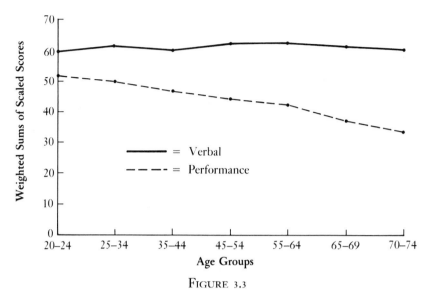

FIGURE 3.3

Data from the Kaufman, McClean, and Reynolds (1989) investigation on changes in intelligence in adulthood

other developmental theories. A lack of early stimulation may inhibit opportunities for accommodation and stunt cognitive growth. Haywood (1986) has noted this phenomenon with mentally retarded children and labeled it the MA (mental age) deficit.

Evidence for the existence of the cumulative deficit phenomenon comes from a variety of sources. One of the first studies was conducted with impoverished mountain children in Appalachia (Sherman & Key, 1932). Cumulative deficits in performance have also been identified for low SES children in India (Misra, 1983), low SES African-American children (Jensen, 1977), and disadvantaged children from England and Wales (Cox, 1983).

The cumulative deficit is often explained based on environmental variables. It has been documented that low SES children who have not participated in a preschool intervention program are at higher risk for special education placement, and, "as a result, their parents, their teachers, and they themselves come to expect less of themselves, and thus the twig is bent" (Bouchard & Segal, 1985, p. 451). This in turn

creates a spiral of decelerating school performance resulting in cumulative deficits in test scores.

This type of instability in test scores is of particular importance for psychologists given that in a number of settings the primary type of referral will be "high-risk" children from impoverished environments. When these children are retested by psychologists, the cumulative deficit phenomenon may be observed. Unfortunately, the cure for this distressing phenomenon is not yet readily apparent (see upcoming section on schooling and environment).

NATURE VERSUS NURTURE

Environmental Determinants

Sometimes research merely confirms conventional wisdom. The idea that good care leads to better development of children is intuitive. Proper child care, including being affectionate and meeting the social and physical needs of

RESEARCH REPORT

Nature versus nurture

A study by Rice, Fulker, DeFries, and Plomin (1988) made an effort to understand better the environmental and genetic contributions to intelligence. Rice et al. (1988) used causal modeling procedures to partition parental environmental influence into genetic and environmental components. In other words, their model assumed that parents create environments for their offspring and that parents create these environments based on their own genetic makeup and their environment.

The subjects for the study were taken from the Colorado Adoption Project data base. Adopted children were separated from their biological parents shortly after birth. Most children were adopted within a month or two. Nonadoptive families were matched to the adoptive families based on child gender, family size, age, parental occupational status, and father's educational attainment. There was considerable data missing from biological fathers of adopted children.

Children were administered the Bayley scales of infant development at ages 1 and 2 and the Stanford-Binet Form L-M at ages 3 and 5. Parents' intelligence was assessed by 13 tests of cognitive abilities that were developed for the project. The first factor of these tests correlated highly with WAIS-R IQ. Environment was measured using the Home Observation for Measurement of the Environment (HOME) scale.

Generally, the authors found their initial model to fit the data well at ages 1, 2, and 4, and marginally at age 3. The authors tested numerous additional models to try to partial out environmental and genetic effects on intelligence. One model found that there was a significant relationship (path) between environment and intelligence test scores at ages 1 and 2 but not at ages 3 and 4.

The authors drew several conclusions from their results. Most notable was their conclusion that parental mediation (environmental effects) are actually due to parental genetic effects. There was also a trend toward larger genetic effects with increasing age. Environmental effects alone were only significant at age 1. These results suggest, then, that genetic influences on children's intelligence become *stronger* with increasing age, at least during the preschool years.

---

children, is associated with positive developmental outcomes (Horney, 1939). Research on the relationship between environmental effects and intelligence dates back to the 1930s, with numerous studies producing evidence of environmental effects.

Skodak and Skeels

A classic study was conducted by Skodak and Skeels and reported in 1949 (reprinted in Jenkins & Paterson, 1961). This study suggested that environmental effects might be important by conducting follow-up evaluations of children who were adopted in infancy. In its day it was one of very few studies reporting longitudinal data. This study does have methodological flaws,

since it was conducted as a service project as opposed to a research study. Regardless, the data were intriguing then and are now.

The children who were placed (adopted) were generally from low SES backgrounds, whereas the adoptive parents were "above the average of their communities in economic security and educational and cultural status" (p. 633). The children were tested at five intervals ranging from an average age at the first evaluation of 2 years, 2 months to an average at the fifth follow-up evaluation of 13 years, 6 months. The major finding of the study was that the average IQ score of this group remained remarkably stable across development from a mean of 117 at the first test to a mean of 117 at the last follow-up. Based on these findings the authors concluded:

The intellectual level of the children has remained consistently higher than would have been predicted from the intellectual, educational, or socioeconomic level of the true parents, and is equal to or surpasses the mental level of children in environments similar to those which have been provided by the foster parents. (p. 650)

Other Studies of Environmental Effects

One could easily attack this study on methodological bases. Other more recent studies, however, have produced consistent results. A well-known study by Scarr and Weinberg (1976) investigated groups of African-American and "inter-racial" children who were adopted at a young age by upper-middle-class families who were white. These authors found that the adopted children performed well above average in intelligence tests and on school achievement measures, and considerably better than African-American and inter-racial children from similar genetic backgrounds who were not adopted.

Using a different approach, Hanson (1975) found significant correlations between a number of environmental factors and intelligence test scores. Significant variables produced correlations of .26 and higher, and these included freedom to engage in verbal expression, direct teaching of language behavior, parental involvement with the child, emphasis on school achievement, emphasis on performing independently, models of intellectual interests, and models of language development. Nonsignificant variables included emphasis on female sex role development, freedom to explore the environment, and models of task orientation. It is also noteworthy that correlations were higher for girls than for boys in many cases.

Harnqvist (1968) investigated the results of tracking in Swedish schools. He concluded that when variables such as initial estimates of ability were held equal, pupils who chose a more challenging academic track gained as much as two-thirds of a standard deviation more than students who chose a vocationally oriented track. These results suggest that the greater intellectual demands of the college preparatory curriculum promoted intellectual development. Flynn (1984) studied changes in intelligence test scores across generations and found a 14 standard score point increase from 1932 to 1978. He concluded that a change in the gene pool of the American population is not a plausible explanation for this gain in the intelligence of a population. Rather, he asserts that these data support the hypothesis that intelligence test scores are clearly affected by environmental influences, saying, "The period in question shows the radical malleability of IQ during a time of normal environmental change; other times and other trends cannot erase that fact" (p. 48).

Researchers who are interested in environmental effects assert that there is a technological vacuum that is hindering the study of environmental factors on intelligence and other traits (Horowitz & O'Brien, 1989; Bouchard & Segal, 1985; Bloom, 1964). There are not well-developed and normed measures of "environment" that are as respected as those used to measure intelligence. There may be many unexplored aspects of environmental effects that are awaiting the development of interviews, observational systems, or tests. The use of sophisticated measures of environments may reveal "traits" of families as opposed to individuals.

Genetic Effects

The evidence for the heritability of intelligence is weighty. More and more researchers are willing to attribute at least some of the variance in intelligence tests scores to genetic factors (Snyderman & Rothman, 1987). Much of the evidence rests on the evaluation of correlations between biologically related relatives. The first studies to point to the likelihood of a strong genetic effect on intelligence test performance were twin studies.

Bouchard and McGue (1981) reviewed all of the research comparing monozygotic and dizygotic twins. Monozygotic twins are the so-called "identical twins" that emanate from one fertilized ovum. Dizygotic twins, better known to the public as "fraternal twins," are those that are the result of two fertilized ova. In behavior genetics research, it is important to note that correlation coefficients are described in particular ways. The two words that are used to describe correlational relationships are *concordant* and *discordant*. A concordant relationship means that there is a high correlation between relatives, and discordant means that there is a low or perhaps even negative correlation between relatives. Twins tend to be concordant for intelligence with monozygotic twins having higher concordance rates than dizygotic twins. As Bouchard and McGue (1981) reported, the average correlation for monozygotic twins between their intelligence test scores is .86, whereas for dizygotic twins the correlation is only .60. These values show the tendency for intelligence test performance to be related to degree of genetic similarity among individuals.

Another large-scale analysis of twin studies again showed a substantial relationship between genetic similarity and intellectual similarity (Osborne, 1980). Osborne (1980) also separated the twin correlations for various specific types of abilities. Skills with greater heritability included spatial visualization, reasoning, and clerical speed and accuracy. Skills that are least affected by hereditary factors are verbal fluency and divergent thinking. Vandenberg and Vogler (1985) suggest cautious interpretation of these data by noting that if all of the variance was due to genetic factors, the correlation for monozygotic twins would be near 1.0., which is clearly not the case.

Twin studies, however, have frequently been criticized because twins not only share genetics, but frequently they also share environmental influence. This situation is changing, however, as more and more data are becoming available on twins that have been reared apart. These data also show a strong genetic component in the inheritance of intelligence, since the correlations between twins and their adoptive parents tend to be smaller than those between twins and their biological parents with whom they do not share any environmental circumstances. Studies of this nature and their results are shown in Table 3.2. In a study by Bouchard at the University of Minnesota (as cited by Vandenberg & Vogler, 1985) the correlation between twins reared apart on the Wechsler Adult Intelligence Scale was .66.

As the state of science currently stands, it appears that there is considerable evidence of the heritability of intelligence from a host of

TABLE 3.2 Parent-Child IQ Correlations in Four Adoption Studies

Study		Adoptive		Biological	
		r	N	r	N
Scarr & Weinberg (1976)	Fathers	.27	170	**.39**	142
	Mothers	.23	174	**.34**	141
Scarr & Weinberg (1978)	Fathers	.15	150	**.39**	237
	Mothers	.04	150	**.39**	237
Horn (1979)	Fathres	.17	457	**.42**	162
	Mothers	.19	455	.23	162
Labuda et al. (1986)	Fathers	.16	133	**.46**	133
	Mothers	.16	133	.23	133

Correlations above .30 are in **boldface**.

different types of investigations. Based on numerous twin studies, Vandenberg and Vogler (1985) estimate that 30% to 40% of the variance in intelligence test scores is due to hereditary factors.

Plomin (1989) notes further that there is not only a strong relationship between genetic inheritance and intelligence, but that this relationship becomes stronger with increasing age. In some of his own investigations he has found that the correlation between biological parents and their adopted away infants increases with increasing age of the child (Plomin, 1989). This tendency was demonstrated in a study by LaBuda, DeFries, Plomin, & Fulker (1986). In this study 133 adopted children were followed and their intelligence test scores correlated with those of their biological and adoptive mothers and fathers (see Table 3.3).

The results of the Labuda et al. (1986) study suggest a strong hereditary component to intelligence. With the exception of year 3, the correlations are significantly higher between biological parents and offspring than between adoptive parents and offspring (see Table 3.3).

Another convincing bit of evidence for the genetic point of view is the lack of correlation of intelligence test results and other scores for individuals in the same environment. Plomin (1989) summarizes the research on the correlations between children who are adopted into the same family (shared environment, not shared inheritance).

Results are clear in showing little influence of shared environment. For personality, adoptive sibling environments are about .05 on the average. Genetically unrelated individuals adopted together show no-greater-than-chance resemblance for psychopathology. For cognitive abilities, although adoptive siblings are similar in childhood (correlations of .25), by adolescence, their correlations are near zero, suggesting that the long-term impact of shared family environment is slight. . . . (p. 109)

There is a potential problem with the increased willingness on the part of the scientific community to consider genetic determinants of intellectual abilities (Plomin, 1988; Weinberg, 1988). Some may search for a single gene that mediates the inheritance of intelligence. A single gene is an unlikely explanation. According to at least one well-known researcher in the area of behavior genetics, this is misguided (Plomin, 1989). Plomin (1989) notes, for example, that early reports of a single gene determining spatial ability have turned out to be unfounded. He asserts, furthermore, that researchers have not been able to find a single gene that is associated with susceptibility to disorders such as schizophrenia and depression. Intelligence is a very complex construct, and the search for a single

TABLE 3.3   Relationship between Intelligence Test Scores of Biological and Adaptive Parents and Offspring

Age in years	Adaptive Mother	Adaptive Father	Biological Mother	Biological Father
1	.11	.10	.18	.48
2	.02	.08	.11	.49
3	.16	.21	.15	.25
4	.16	.16	.23	.46

Source: These correlations are pooled estimates adapted from Labuda et al. (1986).

gene that determines intellectual abilities is likely to prove fruitless. As such, intelligence is likely determined polygenetically (by a number of genes) (Plomin, 1989). In addition, genetic effects on intelligence are likely to be probabilistic, as opposed to deterministic (Plomin, 1989). In comparison, diseases such as sickle cell anemia are determined by a single gene and express themselves regardless of environment or genetic background of the individual. Intelligence is not likely to follow this pattern because of the complexity of intellectual behaviors that are assessed. Environmental factors will still be considered to play an important role in affecting the expression of the genetic potential of the individual. As Plomin (1989) notes:

> *As the pendulum swings from environmentalism, it is important that the pendulum be caught mid swing before its momentum carries it to biological determinism. Behavioral genetic research clearly demonstrates that both nature and nurture are important in development.* (p. 110)

Anastasi (1988) gives additional caveats regarding research on the heritability of intelligence, citing specific problems with the use of heritability coefficients. Heritability estimates, the percentage of variance in a trait that is due to genetic factors, are affected by the nature of the sample on which the index was calculated. More importantly, heritability indices are based on group, not individual, data, and the psychologist is most concerned with the individual client. One child with mild mental retardation could suffer from Down's syndrome, a genetic disorder, whereas another mildly retarded child may have been adversely affected by an extremely stultifying environment. For these two cases the heritability index in the population is irrelevant; of greatest importance to the psychologist seeking to understand these cases is the "heritability index" *for each case.* As is the situation with other aspects of clinical assessment, group-based research aids primarily in giving a set of probabilities for the case, but the psychologist has to decide if these probabilities apply.

CONFUSING MALLEABILITY AND GENETIC DETERMINATION

The conventional wisdom, and perhaps one of the causes for the polemics associated with intellectual assessment, is that if a trait such as intelligence is at least partly genetically determined then the trait is affected very little by environmental factors. This viewpoint is a fallacy. A number of authors have shown convincingly that the relationship between genetic determination of a characteristic, such as intelligence, to its malleability is a tenuous one (Anastasi, 1988; Angoff, 1988; Horowitz & O'Brien, 1989; Plomin, 1989).

Angoff (1988) observes, for example, that even characteristics that are thought to have heritability coefficients near 1.0 can be malleable. He uses height as an example of a trait that is considered by most people to be 100% genetically determined. Yet a number of studies have shown remarkable changes in height due to environmental variation. As an example, some research has shown that American and British adolescents are about six inches taller today than their peers of a century ago (Angoff, 1988). Other data are cited showing that Japanese children born in California are taller, heavier, and more long-legged than children born in Japan (Angoff, 1988). It is also important to remember that some of these changes noted in a characteristic over time are masked by correlation coefficients. This is the case because a correlation coefficient between two groups of related individuals, such as twins, indicates only the rank ordering of the individuals on the characteristic being studied (see Chapter 5). Angoff (1988) observes that "the correlations between heights of fathers and heights of their sons would be unaffected whether the sons were two, three, or five inches taller, or shorter, than their fathers" (p. 714). Hence, since correlation coefficients between biologically related individuals do not assess mean differences, they may mask important changes in a characteristic under study. In other words, correlation coefficients can be high as well and yet mean differences between groups can be large.

Statistical caveats aside, the important notion regarding heritability is that the construct for the most part should be considered separately from the issue of malleability. An excellent example of this distinction is the genetic disorder phenylketonuria (PKU) (see Chapter 14). PKU is 100% caused by genetic factors and yet 100% cured or controlled by environmental factors (proper diet). The next section, however, shows that intelligence may be rather difficult to change with the current instructional technology.

Can We Cure Low Intelligence?

The early workers such as Seguin and Itard were hoping to be able to identify and "cure" low intelligence. This is akin to today's researcher's search for a cure for AIDS, diabetes, and other debilitating illnesses.

Many pioneers in mental retardation treatment tried a variety of sensory and motor training tasks to improve intelligence. In this century the movement to train intelligence continues in various theoretical guises. The work of Feuerstein, Rand, and Hoffman (1979) on dynamic assessment (see Chapter 13) has garnered a great deal of attention in this regard. Feuerstein's theory of cognitive modifiability assumes that intelligence is a highly malleable trait. After intellectual assessment, he advises that pupils receive his instrumental enrichment program to improve their intelligence and, hence, their academic success in school.

Despite these seemingly sensible theories, research does not show that intelligence, as measured by current intelligence tests, is highly trainable. Glutting and McDermott (1990) elucidate several statistical problems with research on the training of intelligence. For example, some of the positive results shown for the training of intelligence may be explained by regression to the mean. Since the subjects of these investigations tend to be individuals with test scores far below the mean, it may be that gains in performance over time are not the result of a training program such as instrumental enrichment, but rather simply regression to the mean (see Chapter 5 for a discussion of regression effects). Given that intelligence tests are not perfectly reliable measures, the amount of the regression effect can be predicted based upon a test's reliability coefficient. Glutting and McDermott (1990) have done just this. They conclude that the vast majority of gains in performance shown in intelligence training studies are within the range of improvement that could be explained by regression effects alone.

One of the most disconcerting aspects of the intelligence training movement is the lack of generalization of improvements in intelligence to improvements in academic performance (Glutting & McDermott, 1990). Perhaps the focus of this type of research is misguided in that it emphasizes intelligence (the predictor variable), when the real question of import is how well the child is doing in school (the criterion variable). A similarly illogical situation would occur when an individual does perfectly well in college when admitted on a probationary basis without test scores and later obtains an admission test score that is so low that it results in the individual's suspension from school.

This same confounding of predictor and criterion variables may be evident in intelligence training research, suggesting that the focus of research should be on developing new instructional technologies for improving the achievement test scores of individuals with low intelligence test scores rather than on improving intelligence per se. There is also a remarkable lack of data on the Feuerstein methodology. It may be that there is simply not yet enough data available on the Feuerstein approach to evaluate its validity (Brody, 1985).

Lidz and Mearig (1989) take issue with criticisms of Feuerstein's so-called "dynamic assessment" by emphasizing the differing emphasis that this approach embodies. They argue that the virtues of Feuerstein's approach are numerous, including:

1. An emphasis on the link between assessment and intervention
2. A deemphasis on passive placement and prediction

They cite disillusionment with current approaches by saying, "It is historical fact that many children have been misclassified by static, 'objective,' standardized tests, and on this basis have been assigned to programs with minimal content, low expectations, and restricted (rather than enriched) teaching approaches" (p. 83). This point may be argued, but it is emblematic of the concern over the use of intelligence tests and their association with special education programs of dubious value. While reforms in special education are underway, changes in intellectual assessment should also be sought. Though Feuerstein's Learning Potential Assessment Device (LPAD) method lacks empirical support, a cure for low intelligence should still be pursued earnestly (Spitz, 1986b).

Head Start Research

Another important evaluation of the malleability of intelligence concerns the evaluation of Head Start programs designed for impoverished preschool-age children. After a careful review, Haskins (1989) has drawn the following four conclusions regarding research on the effectiveness of Head Start programs in improving intelligence and academic achievement. He concludes:

1. Both model programs and Head Start produce significant and meaningful gains in intellectual performance and socioemotional development by the end of a year of intervention.
2. For both types of programs, gains on standardized IQ and achievement tests as well as on tests of socioemotional development decline within a few years (or even less in the case of Head Start programs).
3. On categorical variables of school performance such as special education placement and grade retention, there is very strong evidence of positive effects for the model programs and modest evidence of the effects for Head Start programs.
4. On measures of life-success such as teen pregnancy, delinquency, welfare participation, and employment, there is modest evidence of positive impacts for model programs but virtually no evidence for Head Start. (p. 278)

To some readers of this text these research findings on the early positive effects and later disappointing effects of Head Start types of intervention may be surprising or disconcerting. There are essentially enough data surrounding the malleability of Head Start children's intelligence and academic achievement test scores to support the arguments of proponents *and* opponents of Head Start and other types of intervention studies. There are, however, potential confusions to keep in mind when evaluating this research. Haskins (1989) has noted that in the comparison between Head Start and control-group children, the Head Start sample seemed to be a more high-risk sample than the control groups. It consisted of children with mothers with fewer years of schooling, homes that were more crowded, bigger families, and other characteristics that have been associated with at-risk children.

In a previous review, Bouchard and Segal (1985) provide the following summary of the effects of preschool intervention as studied by the Consortium for Longitudinal Studies founded in 1975. This group combined data from 11 major preschool projects and reached the following conclusions. Program children scored higher than control children at immediate posttesting (7.42 points), 1 year follow-up (4.32), 2 year follow-up (4.62), and 3–4 year follow-up (3.04). By the time the children were followed at 10 to 19 years of age, however, there were no significant differences in WISC scores between control and program children (Bouchard & Segal, 1985). Even at these older ages, however, there were differences in favor of the program children, but they were not IQ variables. Bouchard and Segal (1985) describe these other program outcomes.

> Some superiority in achievement test scores was maintained by program children, especially in mathematics, in grades three through six. Some other benefits were in the areas of achievement orientation, school competence, educational attainment, and career accomplishments. For example, at age 15 years, program participants cited a school-related activity when asked to name something that makes them proud (achievement orientation). Parents of these children voiced high aspirations for these children. Furthermore, only 13% of the program children, compared with 31% of the nonprogram children, were eventually enrolled in special education classes. (p. 451)

Bouchard and Segal (1985) present considerable data to show that while school accounts for some of the variance in intelligence test scores, the effects of family are as potent or more potent. These findings are consistent, then, with the Head Start results showing school effects primarily during the phases of intensive intervention.

There is also some relationship (Bouchard & Segal, 1985) between the amount of schooling and intelligence test scores. Correlations in the .60s and .70s between the intelligence test scores of adult males and number of years of schooling are typical. The effect of education, however, may not be as dramatic as the correlations indicate, since the typical effect of a year of education is to produce 1 standard score point improvement in general intellectual level (Bouchard & Segal, 1985).

Perhaps the conclusion drawn by the Coleman report (Coleman et al., 1966) on the relationship between schooling and outcomes for a child speaks most clearly to this issue. The report concluded:

> Taking all these results together, one implication stands out above all: the schools bring little influence to bear on a child's achievement that is independent of his background and general social context; and that this very lack of an independent effect means that the inequalities imposed on children by their home, neighborhood, and peer environment are carried along to become the inequalities which control life at the end of school. For equality of educational opportunity through the schools to be effective, one must imply a strong effect of schools that is independent of the child's immediate social environment, and that strong independent effect is not present in American schools. (Coleman et al., 1966, p. 325)

In addition to the influence of family factors—and this point is frequently overlooked—it may be that Head Start intervention is too brief, as it is primarily focused on the preschool years. It may be necessary to continue intervention throughout a child's lifetime of schooling in order to produce positive outcomes. This point of view is eloquently stated in the following quotation (Horowitz & O'Brien, 1989):

> Development is not a disease to be treated. It is a process that needs constant nurturance. There is not reason to expect that an intensive program of early stimulation is an inoculation against all further developmental problems. No one would predict that a child given an adequate amount of Vitamin C at two years of age will not have Vitamin C deficiency at 10 years of age. Currently, according to the most viable model of development that applies to both at-risk and normal children, developmentally functional stimulation is desirable at every period of development and not only in early years. (p. 444)

Identifying
Environmental Influences

Unfortunately for practicing examiners, the research aimed at identifying environmental factors that affect intelligence is at about the same stage as the search for specific genes that may play a role in intellectual development. Now that it is clearly recognized that genetic and environmental factors are crucially important in affecting intellectual development, the call is out for researchers to determine the exact interplay of these factors (Horowitz & O'Brien, 1989). Bouchard and Segal (1985) have listed a number of specific environmental variables that require investigation, including, among others: early separation from parents; physical illness; prenatal and postnatal trauma; differential treatment by siblings; sibling spacing; interactions of parent and child characteristics; and the effects of teachers, television, peer groups, and relatives. While all of these factors are believed to be important, the contribution of each factor is a long way from being understood completely.

Given the current state of knowledge, it is incumbent upon the psychologist to use his or her clinical acumen to decipher the possible biological and environmental effects that may be influencing a child's current measured intelligence. A clinician on a daily basis will encounter children where these issues must be considered. Psychologists will encounter preschoolers from dysfunctional families who when placed in a supportive family and exposed to good teachers will blossom academically. Similarly, children who receive traumatic head injuries may show disheartening intellectual deficits compared to premorbid levels (as will be discussed in Chapter 15). Psychologists are well advised to keep abreast of the current research findings in this area and to learn from their clinical experience, in order to guide their test interpretation and the recommendations they make for the treatment of individual children.

OTHER FACTORS
AFFECTING INTELLIGENCE

Race Differences
and Intelligence

Since the time of Galton there has been theorizing about the differences observed between various racial/ethnic/linguistic groups. For example, the results of the Army Alpha and Beta examinations after World War I were used to construct a hierarchy of various ethnic groups, with Scandinavian groups being considered more intellectually competent (see Box 3.1).

In a 1922 study there was great concern about the genetic differences between the various "stocks" found in different areas of the United States (see Box 3.1). In 1923 (Pintner) there was great concern about the genetic inferiority of farmers' children, African-Americans, and American Indians. Cautions about these findings were also delineated in these early days, although these were often ignored. One such caution regarding the lower intelligence test scores of rural children was that "Lincolns come from rural districts, but they never go back" (Pintner, 1923, p. 250). Polemics arise when the difference between various racial groups is attributed to genetic factors alone. This position, however, is nonsensical because of the wealth of data to show that intelligence test scores do not have a heritability coefficient of 1.0. They are also changeable, as several research investigations have demonstrated. Also, the relationship of heritability to malleability is not one to one. Traits that are totally inherited can be changed. Over the years there have been many hypotheses offered about the genetic inferiority of various racial and ethnic groups. The only change has been the targets of the hypotheses (see Box 3.1). After World War I, one of the first targets were the Italians. Later, in the 1920s, there was great concern about the inferiority of rural children (Pintner, 1923). Also in the 1920s there was concern about the genetic inferiority of Amer-

Box 3.1

The beginnings of controversy over genetic differences

After World War I, Alexander (1922, reprinted in Jenkins & Paterson, 1961) published the results of the Army Alpha testing program. This article is an excellent example of the type of report that engenders polemics regarding intelligence testing. One can imagine the consternation of politicians over such an article. Alexander drew several controversial conclusions after reviewing the average Alpha scores of the states' recruits, including the following: "It may be argued that the best blood tends to be attracted to the cities, that good endowment assures success in economic advancement, and that states having the better stocks build the better schools" (p. 183). The rankings of the top five and bottom five states are given below.

STATE	RANK (HIGHEST TO LOWEST)
Oregon	1
Washington	2
California	3
Connecticut	4
Idaho	5
North Carolina	37
Georgia (my home)	38
Arkansas	39
Kentucky	40
Mississippi	41

---

ican Indians (Pintner, 1923), and there have been continuing hypotheses offered about African-Americans (Jensen, 1969).

Now new cultural differences in intelligence are of interest. Comparisons between American children as a group, American white children, and various Asian groups are getting considerable attention. This controversy asserted itself in a study by Lynn (1977) who compared the standardization data for older versions of the Wechsler scale that were normed in both the United States and in Japan. The Japanese outperformed the American children consistently, leading the author to conclude that the Japanese were genetically superior in intelligence.

Stevenson and colleagues (Stevenson et al., 1985) tried to eliminate potential methodolog-

ical problems by developing cognitive and academic tests specifically for cross-cultural study. The tests were constructed to be as comparable as possible for Taiwanese, Japanese, and American children. In contrast to Lynn (1977), Stevenson et al. (1985) found no significant differences in overall cognitive (intelligence) test scores for the two groups. The most striking difference was the American children's inferiority in mathematics achievement. These findings essentially rule out genetic differences in intelligence in favor of other factors that may give some Asian groups an advantage in quantitative skills.

Sue and Okazaki (1990) propose a theory of relative functionalism to explain Asian and American differences in achievement. They note the consistent finding that Asian children show higher educational attainment than other American minority groups, and they propose that this is true because it is more "functional" for Asians. Their theory of relative functionalism has three premises:

1. Every cultural group has a drive for upward mobility that is shaped by environmental factors.

2. When opportunities for a cultural group are limited in most areas but educational attainment, a cultural group will choose educational attainment as a goal.

3. Having other cultural groups adopt Asian educational values will likely be unsuccessful since other cultural groups have outlets for attainment other than education.

Sue and Okazaki (1990) conclude that Asian-American children seek educational attainment in part because of premise 2. Unlike other cultural groups that have opportunities in areas such as politics, government, entertainment, sports, and the like, Asian-American children do not have such opportunities readily available to them, leaving education and the professions as avenues for realizing their strivings. This is an especially interesting theory since it serves to enlighten the murky area of environmental factors and how they may affect achievement above and beyond the influence of intelligence.

Given our current knowledge of research on the nature/nurture question, these hypotheses about racial and ethnic group differences should be clearly identified as such, hypotheses as opposed to conclusions that can be strongly reinforced by research data. The only conclusion that can be drawn is that there are mean differences between various ethnic groups worldwide and in the United States. Even on newer intelligence tests that have virtually eliminated individually biased items, mean differences persist. Kaufman and Kaufman (1983) note that on the WISC-R the commonly found difference between black and white children is about 15 standard score points. On the K-ABC, the difference was somewhat less, about 7 to 9 standard score points (Kamphaus & Reynolds, 1987). Though we know that this difference exists, we are still far from understanding the phenomenon. The different cultural rates of teratogens, family factors and values, poverty, social status, societal opportunities, and a long list of other factors must be studied in order to understand group differences. Hence, to say that the difference between groups of children (and just defining the group members is not an easy task) is due to genetic or environmental factors is likely a gross oversimplification of the complex factors that may produce an intelligence test score. Furthermore, general conclusions are frequently going to be useless to psychologists who must strive to understand the complex interplay of biological and environmental factors affecting children's cognitive development. What conclusions can be drawn, for example, for the case where a child's mother and father are both products of multiracial backgrounds? The "dual ocular test of race" (what they look like) frequently is not of great help in understanding the case (see Chapter 16). The knowledge that is going to be of most importance for understanding the child is knowledge of theories such as Piaget's and research findings such as those from cognitive psychology and attribution research.

More recently Zuckerman (1990) has challenged much of the work on group differences as being based on flawed research studies. He suggests that the difficulties involved in diagnosing race for research purposes are not appreciated by many researchers and are not recognized as a confounding variable in many investigations on group differences. Zuckerman (1990) observes,

> *Studying distributions of blood types shows that some groups with common blood-type frequencies do not resemble each other in classical racial features, whereas others, like Africans and Oceanic Negroids, who have common features of color and hair form, differ in blood types. Australoid aborigines resemble American Indians far more than they do Africans,*

Asians, or Europeans in their low frequencies of the type B gene even though they are markedly different in physical type. The modern anthropology of population genetics raises serious questions about the old concepts of race based on phenotypes. (p. 1298)

So how do most researchers assess race for research purposes? They usually make a judgment of the subject's phenotype, or they ask the subject to evaluate his or her own phenotype. Zuckerman (1990) also cites data to show that within-group variability is larger than between-group variability for some traits, which further calls into question some findings on racial group differences. There is a continuing need to identify the biological and environmental variables that affect cognitive development so that treatment and preventive measures can be taken. This research agenda is a more important endeavor than studying group differences (Zuckerman, 1990).

Gender Differences

Boys and girls show consistent differences on children's intelligence measures, and again psychologists disagree over the attribution of these differences to genetic factors. The differences, however, are extremely small in comparison to racial/ethnic group differences. As an example, Kaufman (1979b) found that girls outperform boys by about 1 1/2 scaled score points on the Coding subtest of the WISC-R (this is a 1/2 standard deviation difference). On all other WISC-R Performance scale subtests, boys scored slightly higher than girls, about a half scale score point for each subtest (this is only a 1/6 standard deviation difference). As a result, the girls' advantage on the Coding subtest and the boys' slighter advantage on the other Performance subtests result in approximately equal Performance IQs for boys and girls.

Vandenberg and Vogler (1985) have investigated the possibility of genetic differences existing in the performance of females and males on spatial subtests. They agree with the con-

clusions of Plomin (1989) that the data do not quite give adequate support for a genetic explanation for the relative superiority of boys on spatial tests. Jacklin (1989) offers the point of view that sex differences on various measures of intelligence, especially measures of verbal ability, have shown a closing of the gap between girls and boys over the years. Perhaps another reason why there are only a few sex differences between boys and girls on intelligence measures is that as far back as the 1916 version of the Stanford Binet, attempts were made to search out and eliminate items that appeared to be gender-biased. The most reasonable conclusion is that a child's gender is not likely to be a worthwhile explanation for a child's profile of scores. The differences between boys and girls on tests such as the WISC-R, while statistically significant (primarily due to large sample sizes), are not clinically significant or meaningful. The gender issue seems to be of more theoretical than practical importance.

Socioeconomic Status and Intelligence

During the long history of the development of intelligence tests, there has been a consistent and robust relationship noted between measures of socioeconomic status—such as parental occupation, levels of parental educational attainment, and median family income—and intelligence test scores. As far back as 1942, McNemar found that the average intelligence test score of 15–18-year-old children whose parents were classified as professionals was 116.4, while that of children whose parents were classified as day labor urban and rural workers was 97.6. These results have been found for other intelligence tests such as the WISC-R (Kaufman & Doppelt, 1976) and the K-ABC (Kaufman & Kaufman, 1983).

Intelligence and SES are so intertwined that they cannot be separated, much like genetic and environmental influences (Brody, 1985). Individuals with higher intelligence test scores obtain more schooling, and educational attainment is the most potent predictor of occupational status (Brody, 1985). This fact suggests that SES can be viewed as a proxy variable for intelligence and vice versa.

The intermingling of SES and intelligence is most important for interpretive purposes. It should cause clinicians to consider statements emphasizing the differences between these variables very carefully before making them orally or in written reports.

Birth Order and Intelligence

Birth order is another variable related to intelligence test scores. Apparently, if one has a choice it is best to be born first. Bouchard and Segal (1985) draw the following conclusions regarding this field of research:

1. IQ declines with increasing family size.

2. Within each family size, IQ declines with increasing birth order.

3. Excluding last-borns, the data assume the form of a quadratic function. This means that, until the last-born child, there is a progressive reduction in IQ decrement, and an eventual upswing for families of eight and nine children.

4. Within each family size, last-borns show a greater decline than do children of any other birth rank.

5. Only children score at about the same level as second-borns in two-child families, or first-borns in four-child families. (p. 438)

The theories as to why this association between birth order and intelligence test scores occurs are numerous—and none is widely accepted. The confluence model of Zajonc and Markus (1975) has been frequently cited as one explanation for the decline in intelligence test scores with increasing family size. Presumably, as family size increases, parents have less and less time to devote to each child. Thus, while the first-born child receives a great deal of parental attention and interaction with competent adult models, second and later born children have less access to more competent models and more access to their siblings, who are presumably not maximally intellectually developed. The finding of an eighth or ninth child having a higher intelligence score than some of the earlier children is also explained by this model.

Regardless of the theories offered, the "pecking order" of siblings for intelligence test scores has been a fairly robust finding. Given that it requires a certain intellectual level to be using a graduate level text such as this one, it may be interesting to know the number of first-borns that are in the intellectual assessment course using this textbook. If more intellectually capable individuals enroll for graduate coursework, there should be a large number of first-borns in the class using this text.

The effects of birth order, however, typically do not warrant interpretation for intelligence tests. This is a phenomenon similar to gender differences, where the findings are more provocative for theory building than for clinical assessment practice. This is because the changes from child to child in a family are relatively small, only a standard score point or two. The only reason that the phenomenon is worth mentioning is that the finding of small differences between siblings is so consistent across studies.

Teratogens and Trauma

Malnutrition

Malnutrition may be a powerful teratogen (a factor that adversely affects development). There are, however, dramatic differences in the way malnutrition affects the development of various organs. Naeye and colleagues (1969) compared the organ weights of 445 consecutive stillbirths for poor and nonpoor children. They found that all major organs were smaller for the malnourished children. Of those affected the thymus was only 66% of normal size for these offspring and the adrenal gland was 77% of normal. Of particular interest was the finding that the only organ that was expected size was the brain (101% of normal for the poor group and 107% of normal for the nonpoor group). This surprising finding is consistent with research on the intellectual development of malnourished children, suggesting that children seem to be resilient.

An investigation of Korean children who experienced severe malnutrition during their first two or three years of life and were later adopted into relatively prosperous American families before the age of 3 showed a reversal of the effects of malnutrition. They showed dramatic gains in height and weight and in intelligence and achievement test performance (Winick, Meyer, & Harris, 1975). This finding was cross-validated by a study of nutritionally deprived children from Colombian families (McKay et al., 1978). Malnutrition and other potential teratogens may be responsible for the lower than average intelligence test scores seen in samples of homeless children (Rafferty & Shinn, 1991).

Low Birth Weight

The relationship between low birth weight and intelligence test scores is also not as permanent and immutable as was initially hypothesized. Bouchard and Segal (1985) conclude, based upon an exhaustive review of the research, that the correlation between IQ and birth weight is due to differences between families, such as socioeconomic status, not to birth weight per se. Children from impoverished families who are of low birth weight tend to have lower than average intelligence test and other scores. The lower scores, however, are more likely due to the multiple effects of impoverishment rather than the low birth weight or, for that matter, malnutrition, specifically.

Anoxia

Similarly, children suffering anoxia (a significant lack of oxygen) shortly after birth have been hypothesized to have a higher incidence of men-

tal retardation (Gottfried, 1973). However, on further analysis of longitudinal data it was found that while there was an intelligence test score decrement for anoxic children, the decrement had all but disappeared by the age of 7 years (Bouchard & Segal, 1985).

Findings regarding the relationship between prenatal and perinatal insults, malnutrition, and intelligence suggest a great deal of resilience on the part of children. If an insult, such as anoxia, occurs at a fairly young age and is not of a sufficient nature to be particularly life threatening or result in easily documented physical damage, the prognosis for recovery of intelligence test performance in the early elementary grade years is remarkably good. These results should not, however, rule out the possible effects of early trauma on obtained intelligence test scores. When the trauma is fairly substantial or occurs later in life than infancy, there may be a substantial impact on scores.

Fetal Alcohol Exposure

Two recent studies highlight the detrimental effects of maternal alcohol use during pregnancy on cognitive (Coles et al., 1991) and behavioral outcomes (Brown et al., 1991). The Coles et al. (1991) investigation followed three groups of high-risk mothers from an impoverished inner city environment. One group of 21 mothers reported never drinking alcohol during pregnancy. A group of 22 mothers drank during part of the pregnancy but quit after being advised of the risk to the fetus. This group averaged 11 1/2 ounces of alcohol per week up until the time they quit drinking. The third group of 25 mothers continued drinking an average of 12 ounces of alcohol per week in spite of being advised not to. Numerous measures were taken on the offspring.

The results revealed a direct relationship between maternal alcohol use and cognitive function, with the never drank and stopped drinking groups being similar and the continued drinking group showing significant cognitive impairment. The composite intelligence test scores (the composite for the K-ABC is called the Mental Processing Composite or MPC) for the K-ABC taken at follow-up for the three groups were significantly different. The mean MPC for the no drinking and stopped drinking groups were similar at 92 and 89, whereas the mean MPC for the continued drinking group was 84. These results show the clear teratogenic effects of alcohol use during pregnancy.

Implications for Clinicians

Other traumas and physical problems may adversely affect intelligence test scores. The above research suggests that child clinicians should be alert for any such conditions that may affect current performance. Among other things, the child clinician should simply inquire about the current health status of a child during the administration of an intelligence test. In a study of adults, Field, Schaie, and Leino (1988) found a significant relationship between the adults' self-reported health and intelligence test scores.

Clinicians should also try to apply research on these and related issues from their graduate-level coursework in child development, pediatric psychology, and physiological psychology. Research findings from these disciplines can be extremely useful for interpreting intelligence test results.

Motivation, Temperament, and Intelligence

Research that addresses the relationship between motivational and temperament variables and intelligence test scores is minimal (Brody, 1985). Anastasi (1988) cites some research showing a relationship between personality characteristics and intelligence test performance. She notes that some studies show that when personality test scores are added to intelligence test scores in order to predict a person's subsequent academic achievement, they do add a significant amount of variance to the prediction.

Martin (1988) reports some studies assessing the relationship between his Temperament Assessment Battery for Children (TABC) and cognitive criterion variables such as school grades and achievement tests that are good correlates of intelligence measures. In one sample of 43 first-grade children, some TABC scales were stronger correlates of achievement than others. Emotional intensity was a relatively low correlate of reading grades, whereas adaptability and persistence had strong positive correlations in the .60s and distractibility had a negative correlation of .63. A similar pattern was found for mathematics grades. These findings were cross-validated in a second study of 104 first-grade children where reading and mathematics achievement test scores and grades were used as criterion variables. These findings suggest that certain temperament variables may be related to intelligence test scores. Adaptability and persistence may be positively related and distractibility may be negatively related. This does appear, however, to be a remarkably understudied topic that requires further research.

Intelligence and Academic Achievement

If, as transactional theory dictates, psychologists are trying to measure intelligence as opposed to achievement, then intelligence tests should be substantially different from measures of academic achievement, or, as Binet called achievement, "the pedagogical method." Generally, there is a significant overlap in variance between the two types of measures (Anastasi, 1988).

This overlap in variance has led Anastasi (1988) and others (Kaufman, 1990) to propose that intelligence and achievement are not unique and, therefore, intelligence tests should be interpreted as specialized types of achievement measures. Correlations between the two measures, however, cannot be used as sole evidence that these measures are redundant. In another, virtually identical context, Vandenburg and Vogler (1985) eschew the substantial correlation argument as evidence for "g" by pointing out,

"Against the argument that all ability tests correlate positively and therefore measure the same ability, one can point out that height and weight also correlate, and rather substantially, yet we consider them to be separate characteristics" (p. 6). Similarly, measures of reading and mathematics achievement also correlate highly, and we do not consider reading and mathematics to be the same construct.

The problem with the relationship between intelligence and scholastic achievement is the "chicken and egg" phenomenon. Since intelligence is called such, people often assume that it is the causative agent for academic achievement. It is equally likely that poor achievement "causes" poor intelligence test scores, since intelligence tests, especially the more verbal ones, have vocabulary, mathematical, and other achievement item types (see Chapter 14 regarding the effects that a learning disability may have on intelligence test scores). Given the substantial overlap in the measurement of these constructs, it appears that the savvy psychologist should discard the intelligence/achievement dichotomy as it is portrayed by the test scores provided. The psychologist would be wise to focus on *all* of the child's test scores, from intelligence, achievement, visual/motor tests, and so forth, and try to interpret patterns in light of theory and research.

It is therefore up to the skill of the practicing psychologist to determine the factors that may be influencing intelligence test performance. In summary, while in the abstract, intelligence and achievement are easily separated constructs, in everyday assessment practice, the division is not clear-cut, and yet it is crucial for interpreting some individual cases.

Intelligence and Adaptive Behavior

There are numerous similarities in definitions of adaptive behavior. Edgar Doll, an illustrious psychologist at the Vineland State Training School in New Jersey, introduced the construct

in the 1930s as central to the process of assessing mental retardation. He believed that "social maturity" (an older term for adaptive behavior) was as important in the assessment of mentally retarded individuals as was intelligence. He published the first edition of what is now called the Vineland Adaptive Behavior Scales (Sparrow et al., 1984). His definition of adaptive behavior is similar to modern ones. He states: "Social competence is the functional ability of the human organism for exercising personal independence and social responsibility" (Doll, 1953, p. 10).

Doll's test and subsequent scales measure a host of skills needed for personal independence. The Vineland, for example, includes scales that assess communication, daily living skills, socialization, and motor skills.

The relationship between intelligence and adaptive behavior measures is well researched, although there is considerable variability among studies (Destefano & Thompson, 1990). Over all, though, the evidence reveals modest relationships (correlations in the .30 to .60 range) with adaptive behavior scales (Kamphaus, 1987; Keith et al., 1987).

Keith et al. (1987) conducted an exhaustive study of the relationship between the Vineland and the K-ABC involving 556 children in grades one through eight from a variety of locations around the United States. Three confirmatory factor models were fit to the data. Model 1 was constrained so that the relationship was assumed to be low (r = .39). Model 2 assumed no correlation between intelligence and adaptive behavior. This model assumes that the two constructs are completely independent. Model 3 hypothesized a perfect relationship between the two constructs, which assumes that both constructs are subserved by the same general ability. The various fit statistics for the models are given in Table 3.4. The fit statistics show Model 1 to be the best fit to the data. This model had the smallest Chi-square, the largest fit index, and the smallest root mean square residual, all indications of better fit to the model. This study exemplifies a more sophisticated approach than

TABLE 3.4   Fit statistics for the three factor models compared in the Keith et al. (1987) study

	Model 1	Model 2	Model 3
Chi-Square	83.01	134.36	379.91
Adjusted Fit Index	.876	.843	.521
Root Mean Square Residual	.072	.160	.153

comparing simple zero order correlations between the two variables, but the results are the same—intelligence tests are separate but related constructs (Keith et al., 1987).

This relationship is notable in that it differs significantly from the relationship between intelligence and academic achievement, in which correlations tend to range from .55 to .90 depending on the study and achievement domain (e.g., reading, writing, etc.). This modest relationship does leave considerable room for variability between intelligence and adaptive behavior scores for a particular child, making interpretation a challenge.

One of the reasons for variability among studies is the nature of the adaptive behavior scale being used. Some scales use teachers as informants, and these produce larger correlations between intelligence and adaptive behavior (Kamphaus, 1987). Also, scales that assess academic types of adaptive behavior tend to produce more overlap between intelligence and achievement measures (Destefano & Thompson, 1990). Hence, the agreement between intelligence and adaptive behavior scales, or lack thereof, depends on the nature of the adaptive behavior test's item content as well as the informant. Psychologists are likely to find adaptive behavior to differ from intelligence test scores when the items pertain to nonschool behavior and parents serve as the informant. Even though the correlations of intelligence with adaptive behavior are lower than for achievement, they will often be statistically significant and moderate in magnitude. This fact begs psychologists not to consider these measures as independent and

calls for interpretation of intelligence test scores and adaptive behavior scores in combination. Psychologists should, for example, look for integration of results between verbal intelligence test scores and communication domains of adaptive behavior. Use of these multiple measures is most likely to produce the greatest insight into the child's referral problems.

CONCLUSIONS

Intelligence test scores have been shown to be influenced by numerous background and other factors. While these findings are theoretically interesting and scientifically meaningful, they are also immediately important for everyday assessment practice. Research findings can provide the clinician with invaluable explanations for test scores that are necessary for reasonable and helpful interpretations of scores. Hence, clinicians are advised to return to this chapter and refresh their memories when struggling with intelligence test interpretation.

CHAPTER SUMMARY

1. Intelligence test scores are more stable for handicapped than nonhandicapped preschoolers.

2. Intelligence test scores are less stable for preschoolers than for school-age children and adults.

3. Intelligence test scores are fairly stable for adults, yielding coefficients in the .60s over a 20-year time span.

4. In some cases, intelligence test scores can change by a standard deviation or more, even in adulthood.

5. Early researchers believed that intelligence test scores peaked in adolescence and declined together. Recent research suggests that intelligence test scores peak in adulthood and some scores do not show substantial decline in the late adult years.

6. The term "cumulative deficit" refers to the theory that the ill effects of an impoverished early environment accumulate over the course of development to reveal decreasing intelligence test scores with increasing age. There is some research to support the phenomenon.

7. Early adoption studies suggested that environment factors played a very important role in intellectual development. Recent studies have shown that genetic endowment is a more important determinant of intelligence test scores.

8. Intelligence is likely determined polygenetically, as opposed to being linked to a single gene.

9. The issues of the genetic causation and malleability are often confused. It is often assumed that if intelligence is genetically determined it is not malleable.

10. Research to date shows that intelligence test scores are not highly malleable, at least with short-term intervention. There is not yet a "cure" for low intelligence, although there may be some day.

11. Race/cultural group differences in intelligence test scores persist. Traditionally these differences have been attributed to genetic differences, and this has caused great controversy. Today it is recognized that these differences are so intertwined with SES, values, family constellation, and other factors that it is difficult to determine the extent of the differences due to genetic factors.

12. Gender differences in intelligence test scores are small and not clinically meaningful.

13. SES differences in intelligence test scores are large and clinically significant.

14. The effects of birth order on intelligence test scores are consistent but small. Oldest children tend to have slightly higher scores.

15. Prenatal and postnatal teratogens adversely affect intelligence test scores. There is evidence of resiliency whereby the effects of teratogens such as low birth weight can be overcome by the time a child reaches elementary school.

16. The relationship of personality to intelligence test scores is not yet well understood.

17. Intelligence and academic achievement tests show substantial intercorrelations. These measures covary a great deal in clinical assessment practice.

18. Intelligence and adaptive behavior scales correlate moderately at best.

The Assessment Process

CHAPTER QUESTIONS

How do examiners test infants and young children?

What is "standardized procedure"?

The clinical skill required to properly administer an intelligence test cannot be overemphasized. Clinical skill is especially needed when assessing children, since they are highly influenced by adult behavior. The psychologist who acquires the necessary knowledge to use intelligence tests but not the requisite clinical skill is ill prepared. This individual will find intelligence testing to be arduous and unrewarding, and perhaps punishing. The clinician who is skilled in interacting with children will be capable of making the often stilted test directions used by some intelligence tests seem like ordinary conversation to a child. She will make the intellectual evaluation a pleasant experience for the child rather than an onerous one.

Acquiring Clinical Skill

It is also not possible to acquire clinical skill by reading a book chapter. Clinical skill may be a personality-related factor leading to the old question, are clinicians born or are they trained? While this debate is far from settled, there are steps in addition to reading chapters that trainees can take to enhance their clinical skill. Useful activities include the following:

1.   Observe a variety of children in a variety of settings. Trainees in intellectual assessment should be keenly aware of the developmental characteristics of children. Such awareness can be gained by observing children in preschool and other school settings, on playgrounds, and in other public settings such as shopping centers. Trainees should also notice how children interact with parents and other adults in these settings.

2.   Observe master teachers interacting with children. This will allow the trainee to acquire a host of skills for interacting effectively with chil-

dren and adolescents. Experienced teachers can model a number of important skills for establishing and maintaining rapport with children.

3.   Observe experienced psychologists administering tests to normal and handicapped children when possible. Clinicians may also see the differences, and lack of them, between normal and handicapped children and adolescents.

4.   Observe a special education teacher administering tests to handicapped children. Special education teachers have to work with children intensively for long time periods and develop an exhaustive repertoire of skills for dealing effectively with them.

5.   Practice administering intelligence tests to cooperative individuals before giving a test for clinical or course grading purposes. This practice will allow the new examiner to work out minor problems in a nonthreatening atmosphere prior to testing a "real" case.

6.   If videotape equipment is available, it can serve as an important self-evaluation tool. If such equipment is not available, audiotapes of several testing sessions can also be helpful. Using these methods, examiners frequently find that they are using repetitive wording, or they can discover why a session was so difficult when the reasons were not apparent at the time.

These exercises and others will go a long way toward supplementing this text in order to develop necessary clinical assessment skills. One key to acquiring good assessment skills, which has little to do with the personal qualities of the examiner, is to know the test well before testing. While this seems to be an obvious statement, it requires stating because I have found many students to overlook this basic premise.

COLLECTING BACKGROUND INFORMATION

A number of psychological, social, and medical factors are either related to or have an effect on

intelligence test scores. These variables include SES, ethnicity, dominant language, low birth weight, head trauma, and others, and examiners must collect information regarding these variables when gathering background information. A lack of such background information puts the evaluator at a disadvantage when it is time to interpret the obtained scores. Hence, it is important to conduct a thorough interview of a child's or adolescent's parents or caregivers in order to understand the meaning of her scores.

The importance of even minimal background information for interpreting a child's scores is evident in the following example. I once had a case where there seemed to be little resemblance between parent and child. The parents brought their 10-year-old daughter to be evaluated for academic problems. The parents were high-achieving individuals both holding Ph.D. degrees. The daughter obtained an average score on the K-ABC and had little interest in academic endeavors. In addition, the daughter did not look like her parents. She had red hair and fair skin in contrast to her parents, who had brown hair and darker complexion. The differences in intellectual level and physical appearance between parents and child did not seem readily understandable given the background information obtained using a standard form, until I asked if they had adopted their daughter. They indicated that they had adopted her a couple of years prior to the evaluation. This case was very puzzling until I had complete background information. Prior to uncovering the child's complete history, I questioned the validity of my obtained scores because they seemed at odds with the scores one would expect given parental characteristics.

Now the question is, which pieces of background information are important to obtain? The clinician should collect information on all of the relevant variables that are known to affect intelligence test scores. In addition to these variables, however, it is also important to collect information on variables that may be specific to the clientele that the clinician usually assesses.

RESEARCH REPORT

Validity of test session behavior

A study by Glutting, Oakland, and McDermott (1989) studied the validity of clinicians' observations and ratings of children's behavior during a test session. The purposes of the study were stated as follows:

> *Empirical inquiry is needed concerning both the intra- and exosession validity of observations, where* intrasession validity *refers to the degree of concurrence between conclusions derived from observations and from the formal tests they accompany and* exosession validity *represents the degree of generality of test observations to conditions outside the test situation. (p. 156)*

Subjects for the study were 311 children ranging in age from 7 years 6 months to 14 years 4 months with a mean of 10.5 years. Each child was administered the WISC-R, the Adaptive Behavior Inventory for Children (ABIC) (administered to parents), and the California Achievement Test (CAT). The Test Behavior Observation Guide (TBOG) was used as the measure of test session behavior. The items of interest from the TBOG included performance rate, orientation to examination, initial adjustment, interest, cooperation, expressive ability, attention, self-confidence, motivation, effort, persistence, ability to shift, reaction to praise and encouragement, reaction to failure, and self-criticism. Each item was rated by examiners on a 5-point scale where 1 represents optimal behavior.

The TBOG was submitted to an exploratory factor analysis procedure and three factors were identified as the most parsimonious explanation of the item set. The first factor was labeled *Task Attentiveness*, the second *Task Confidence*, and the third as *Cooperative Disposition*. These three factors of the TBOG were used in all subsequent analyses.

The correlations between the TBOG and the WISC-R were moderate (.40 to .50 range). The TBOG correlations with the ABIC and CAT were generally smaller. The correlations of the TBOG with the ABIC ranged from .08 to .29, and with the CAT .04 to .36. Canonical correlation analyses were then used to study further the overlap in variance between these variables.

The higher correlations of the TBOG with the WISC-R were interpreted as supportive of the intrasession validity of observations during testing. The lower correlations of the TBOG with the ABIC in particular were taken as evidence of a lack of exosession validity of test session observations. The authors caution that these findings suggest that test session behaviors may not generalize to other settings, thus limiting the ability of the clinician to confidently draw hypotheses about exosession behavior. These results also argue for the importance of taking samples of behavior from multiple environments as standard operating procedure for child examiners.

For example, in a rehabilitation facility for brain-injured children, it will be vitally important to gather detailed information on the nature of the trauma that caused the injury, including such things as the recency of the insult and the medical interventions carried out to treat the condition. Often examiners will use a two-stage process for obtaining background information: the first stage involving collecting general information about the child's background and the second stage involving collecting very detailed information about a specific episode or condition that may be especially germane to the testing. The latter type of information usually centers around the referring problem.

There are numerous forms and interview formats for use with children and their families for obtaining background information. Some topics that are often part of questionnaire/interview schedules are shown in Figure 4.1. It is probably

FIGURE 4.1

Topics/content that are typically part of background information questionnaires

Demographic Information
Name, birthdate, address, parents' names, educational attainment, occupation, etc.

Referral Information
Source and nature of referral

Family Structure and History
Siblings, parenting style, history of medical/psychiatric illnesses, dwelling, family activities, etc.

Pre- and Perinatal History
Conception, maternal care or problems, type of delivery, complications, etc.

Child's Medical History
Respiratory, gastrointestinal, neuropsychiatric, vision, hearing, etc.

Developmental History
Motor and language milestones, toilet training, sleep habits, etc.

Social History
Hobbies, friends, behavior, etc.

School History
Preschool, elementary, high school, retentions, special education, etc.

wise for the new examiner to use standard forms or outlines for collecting information to ensure that important aspects of behavior are not missed. This information will prove crucial in the final stages of test interpretation.

THE TESTING ENVIRONMENT

Test Setting

The importance of environmental variables to the intelligence testing process was recognized long ago by Sarason (1954), who asserted that there exists an

unstated but oft made assumption that a test measures something independent of the conditions or

time of measurement. In these terms a test presumably is like an x-ray: regardless of the conditions external to the patient (the immediate environment) the "thing" being studied (e.g., a bone, intelligence, fantasy) can be observed in splendid isolation—a statement which is true neither for a test nor for an x-ray. (p. 59)

There are many treatises on the desirable characteristics of the testing environment that are helpful for guiding examiner practice (Kamphaus, Dresden, & Kamphaus, in press; Anastasi, 1988; Paget, 1983; Sattler, 1988).

To provide an optimal testing environment: (1) The testing room should

- Be free from interruptions.

- Be pleasantly, but minimally, decorated so as not to distract the child.

- Be well lit, without being too bright and with no glare.

- Have adequate ventilation.
- Be quiet with no noise from adjoining rooms.
- Be a few degrees cooler than a room meant for adults, as children have higher body temperatures than adults.
- Be sparsely furnished to minimize possible distractions.

(2) The furniture should

- Be comfortable.
- Be child-sized—a table 36'' long and 20–24'' wide and adjustable in height is best. The child's elbows should rest on the table and his feet on the floor—if his feet do not touch the floor, put a box under the feet to avoid a restless feeling.

(3) The materials should

- Be child-sized (i.e., large crayons).
- Be well-organized and accessible to the examiner.
- Be set up so that the child can only reach the materials needed for the current task. These materials should be directly in front of the child.
- Be set up so that the examiner can effectively use the manual without it becoming a barrier between the child and the examiner.
- Be set up so that the examiner can efficiently use the scoring sheet, but so the child cannot see it.

Timing

Another important environmental variable is the timing of the assessment. Young children may still take naps and show fatigue quickly in an assessment situation. For most purposes it is best to test children and adolescents when they can give their optimal performance. In most in-

stances this is going to be in the morning, the same time when the most demanding work is offered in schools. If a young child does need to take a break because of fatigue or for toileting needs, *it is important to break in between tests or subtests in order not to spoil a test.*

One common pitfall that I have seen a number of trainees encounter is not recognizing when a young child needs a break. Usually my students will ask a child about halfway through the testing session if they need a break, and many children who are very compliant will deny the offer. The examiner then pays a price for the child's compliance by having to help the child clean his soiled pants.

In order to avoid this embarrassment it is important for examiners to develop the skills to "read" a child's behavior. One way of doing this is to observe the child's behavior closely and take a break if the child's behavior changes from being calm to fidgety, or from being alert to yawning. It is also helpful for the examiner to monitor her own behavior. If the examiner feels that the room is getting stuffy or finds herself yawning, the child may also be experiencing these problems, and a break will be in order. In other words, examiners should not always make the decision to take a break in the testing based on the verbal report of the child.

In addition to considering sleeping and eating routines, examiners need to consider the possible impact of activities that precede the assessment (Anastasi, 1988). Children are likely to behave differently in an assessment situation if the preceding activity has been a boisterous outdoor time or a quiet story time (Kamphaus, Dresden, & Kaufman, in press).

Other Participants

A final environmental variable involves the presence of other people, particularly parents, in the testing room. Psychologists generally agree that having parents present is not advisable for children, especially those over the age of 3 (Paget, 1983). There is some suggestion, however, that for very young children parental presence may, in fact, be beneficial (Sattler, 1988). With young children an examiner must weigh the potential distraction caused by an additional person in the testing room against the problems caused by separation anxiety. More valid assessments of young children may be obtained when a parent is with the child in the testing room but is sitting quietly out of the child's line of vision (Kamphaus, Dresden, & Kaufman, in press). Most importantly, when addressing the issue of parental presence, examiners must treat parents with respect, not as unwanted intruders. If a parent wants to observe the testing session, an examiner must take the time necessary to explain fully the pros and cons of observing. It may be helpful, for example, to explain how difficult it is for parents to observe their child being tested. Parents who are allowed to observe may find the experience very stress-provoking. Parents want their children to do well, and when they do not, it can be extremely punishing to a parent, especially when they know that their child is taking an intelligence test. To some parents it is helpful to simply be aware that such stress is universal.

Physical Arrangements

Examiners are typically well advised to keep test materials out of sight from the child so as to avoid distracting the child from the task at hand and to keep the young or obstreperous child from destroying the organization of the materials. Examiners should also have all of the materials arranged prior to the child's entering the testing room. This preparation will allow the examiner to focus on his interaction with the child when he enters the testing room as opposed to arranging materials.

For some examiners the choice of seating arrangements is influenced by their personal preference. Some examiners, for example, prefer to sit across the table from the child. This allows the examiner to easily keep the materials and the record form out of the child's view. For many examiners who work with children, it is either necessary and/or preferable to sit next to the child. For young children this allows the examiner to monitor the child more closely during testing (in other words, this allows the examiner to grab the child if he starts to run) and direct his attention as necessary.

One advantage of sitting across the table from the child is that it makes it more likely that the examiner will orient materials correctly for the child's viewing or manipulation. I have seen many anxious novices who are so concerned about reading instructions correctly that they pay little attention to the child. Therefore, they sometimes do not place materials in the correct orientation, which is usually parallel to the child. Note, also, that examiners can also produce a psychological barrier between themselves and the child by placing a test manual between themselves and the child. In such a circumstance, the test manual appears to be protecting the examiner from intrusion by the child. This situation should be avoided as it hinders working comfortably with the child and perhaps also hinders rapport.

Finally, and perhaps most importantly, it is important for the child to be seated comfortably regardless of the examiner's physical stature. Young children should be seated in chairs and at tables that are appropriate to their size. This arrangement is necessary to ensure that the child can easily see and manipulate the test materials.

ESTABLISHING RAPPORT

Rapport is the process of establishing a comfortable working relationship with a child (Anastasi, 1988). More than anything else, the practical advice given earlier in this chapter on familiarizing oneself with the developmental characteristics of children will be most helpful to the new examiner in learning how to establish rapport. This section will also provide some sage wisdom on the topic. Binet and Simon (1905) give recommendations on the establishment of rapport. As the inventors of modern intelligence testing, their words are worthy of our attention.

> The examination should take place in a quiet room, quite isolated, and the child should be called in alone without other children. It is important that when a child sees the experimenter for the first time, he should be reassured by the presence of someone he knows, a relative, an attendant, or a school superintendent. The witness should be instructed to remain passive and mute, and not to intervene in the examination by either word or gesture. The experimenter should receive each child with a friendly familiarity to dispel the timidity of early years. Greet him the moment he enters, shake hands with him and seat him comfortably. If he is intelligent enough to understand certain words, awaken his curiosity, his pride. If he refuses to reply to a test, pass to the next one, or perhaps offer him a piece of candy; if his silence continues, send him away until another time. These are little incidents that frequently occur in an examination of the mental state, because in its last analysis, an examination of this kind is based upon the good will of the subject. (Jenkins & Patterson, 1961, p. 94)

Binet and Simon (1908) give additional recommendations on the conduct of an intellectual assessment:

> The subject to be examined should be kindly received; if he seems timid he should be reassured at once, not only by a kind tone but also by giving him first the tests which seem most like play, for example—giving change for 20 sou., constantly encourage him during the tests in a gentle voice; one should show satisfaction with his answers whatever they may be. One should never criticize nor lose time by attempting to teach him the test; there is a time for everything. The child is here that his mental capacity may be judged, not that he may be instructed. Never help him by supplementary explanation which may suggest the answer. Often one is tempted to do so, but it is wrong. (Jenkins & Patterson, 1961, p. 97)

It has also been argued that the intelligence test itself (Glasser & Zimmerman, 1967) is often effective at building rapport for the school-age

child. This comment highlights a major difference between establishing rapport and establishing a therapeutic relationship. Some students confuse the two. Perhaps because of their therapeutic training and good intentions, they try to develop something more akin to a therapeutic relationship in lieu of a working relationship. For the purposes of assessing a child's intelligence, a therapeutic relationship is not necessary unless the testing session is a prelude to or occurs in the context of psychotherapy. Many of my students have found that trying too hard to establish a relationship has proved counterproductive. They have found that after spending a half hour trying to develop a relationship, the child may then be too weary to take the test.

Young Children

Kamphaus, Dresden, and Kaufman (in press) delineate several characteristics of young children that make them more of a challenge in the assessment setting. These include the following characteristics.

1. Young children view the world differently from adults and older children and so have a different view of the assessment process (Goldman, Stein, & Querry, 1983). More specifically, children under the age of 5 or 6 tend to be egocentric and are unable to take the perspective of another person. Because young children are only able to understand their own feelings and needs they are less likely to be motivated by extrinsic rewards, and are often less compliant than older children (Goldman, Stein, & Querry, 1983; Lidz, 1983).

2. The physical development of young children requires a high level of activity, and they may have trouble sitting still for long periods of time (Lidz, 1983). Dealing with this problem may require considerable ingenuity on the part of the examiner.

3. Many children of this age require naps (Pa-

get, 1983) and/or frequent snacks, so testing sessions must be scheduled to accommodate these needs.

4. One of the major developmental tasks of the preschool years is the ability to separate successfully from significant adults. As many children continue to struggle with this issue, the assessment process will be complicated by the difficulties involved in being away from a parent or trusted teacher (Lidz, 1983).

5. The cognitive capabilities of young children also differ from those of older children and create challenges for the examiner. Preschool-age children are beset with several cognitive limitations: (1) they are only able to perceive or focus on one dimension of an object at a time (e.g., height *or* width); (2) they are only able to remember a few pieces of information at a time (and don't know how to use mnemonic strategies to increase their memory capacity); (3) they do not understand the principle of transitivity (knowing that A > B, and B > C does not, to them, imply that A > C); (4) they may not understand concepts of time, or even such relational terms as alike or different; and (5) they often do not have well-developed verbal expressive skills (Goldman, Stein, & Querry, 1983; Lidz, 1983).

6. The behavior of young children is simply more variable than that of older children (Lidz,

Box 4.1

Testing children or friends

Remember the old saying, "No good deed goes unpunished"? I remember it all too well. The year was 1975 and I was taking my first graduate-level course in intellectual assessment. I learned the meaning of this old saying on two occasions that summer.

The first mistake I made was to volunteer to take a 5-year-old to the university for testing in order to meet course requirements. The child's mother was perfectly willing to bring the young boy into the university, but I was sure that I could handle it. I was wrong. I did not have children of my own at the time and knew precious little about the small creatures. I picked up the boy at home. He was well scrubbed and polite. I drove him to the university amid sweltering summer heat. Since "parking on campus" is a true oxymoron, we had to walk several blocks in the heat to reach the building. Immediately upon entering the building, I offered the lad a soft drink (a Coke), and those who know young children can imagine what happened next. He quaffed the Coke and proceeded to have an emesis (i.e., "vomit"). Of course, I panicked and took him home immediately.

There was, however, an important lesson to be learned from this. Clinicians who test children have to have more than academic knowledge of their intended victims. They also have to have practical experience with children. I recommend to my students without extensive childrearing experience that they spend a few hours a week volunteering in schools, preschools, or churches in order to acquire more experience with children. I had to learn the hard way so that my students will not.

The second lesson that I learned in this first course was to never test a friend, spouse, relative of any sort, or other significant other who wants to know his or her IQ. I had a friend, who was a fellow psychology student, who wanted to know his IQ. Despite my professor's admonitions regarding this issue, I decided to test him with the 1955 WAIS. Well, I knew that I was in trouble before we even finished the Information (the first) subtest. His response to "What is the Vatican?" was, "I think it's a big bird, isn't it?" Well, needless to say his scores were not as high as he had hoped, and I had to break the news.

I also admonish my students not to test significant others because of their own preconceptions of the IQ score, but they often do it anyway. If I didn't know better I would say that some students in my class last term were testing potential spouses for their fitness!

1983), and, in addition, young children are much more susceptible to the influence of extraneous variables. The characteristics of the examiner and of the environment exert more control over the performance of children, especially young children, than they do on the performance of adults (Anastasi, 1988).

In addition to child characteristics, it is also important to consider the effects of examiner characteristics on children's behavior, especially the more variable behavior of young children. Unfortunately, while opinions abound on the potential effects of examiner characteristics on a child's intelligence test performance (Anastasi, 1988; Barber, 1973; Epps, 1974; Sarason, 1954), the research literature provides very little guidance on the impact of examiner variables. Concern has been voiced on the effects of a mismatch between examiner and child on characteristics such as race (Epps, 1974) and linguistic background (Figueroa, 1990). There appears to be a consensus, even without research data, that it is desirable for examiner and child to share as many background characteristics as possible in order to establish rapport.

Several suggestions have been offered for developing a personality style that is optimal for the development of rapport, especially with young children. Kamphaus, Dresden, and Kaufman (in press) have gleaned the following suggestions from the literature on this topic.

- 1. Examiners should be friendly, cheerful, relaxed, warm and natural (Anastasi, 1988).

- 2. Examiners should be reassuring and encouraging (Anastasi, 1988; Epps, 1974).

- 3. Examiners should be patient with the child's efforts (Paget, 1983).

In addition to the style used by the examiner to interact with the child, the appearance of the examiner may even come into play. Exceedingly elaborate clothing or jewelry may receive more interest from the child than the test materials. All of this information is not intended to make the new trainee obsess unduly about his personality style or appearance prior to his first testing session. Examiners will find that most children and adolescents will respond to any adult who is sincerely interested in their well-being.

Establishing Rapport with Young Children

Some specific suggestions for examiner behaviors that may be helpful for establishing rapport with particularly young children include the following (Kamphaus, Dresden, & Kaufman, in press).

1. Place yourself at the child's eye level before you begin talking to her (Sattler, 1988); squatting is preferable to bending over because you are then truly at her level.

2. Introduce yourself to the child, avoiding use of the title "Dr.," and ask what you should call him or her (Kaufman & Kaufman, 1983).

3. Do not be overly demonstrative or intrusive; allow the child to make the first move (Anastasi, 1988).

4. Be honest and direct; explain to the child exactly what will happen during the session.

5. Speak clearly—avoid both a "cutesy," high-pitched approach and an overly technical, adult style of conversation (Paget, 1983).

The astute examiner will notice that there are basically two methods for establishing rapport, talking and doing. For many school-age children and adolescents, talking will suffice. The examiner may be able to develop rapport satisfactorily by asking her about her family, hobbies, toys, friends, and school. For the younger child, on the other hand, doing may be more important than talking. Many preschool and early elementary grade children may present themselves as mutes when initially greeted by the examiner. Often it is difficult to counteract their reticence by asking them questions. I have a "magic wand" given to me by a colleague. I have found that many young children overcome their reticence when they are given the wand and its uses are explained to them. The point is that the examiner should have at his or her disposal objects such as toys, puppets, or even pencil and paper that may be used to draw out the reticent child.

CONDUCTING AN ASSESSMENT

The process of conducting an assessment is complex, requiring all of the clinical and interpersonal skill an examiner can muster. Several practical aspects of the skills required and process of conducting an effective intellectual assessment will be discussed in this section.

Children should not be asked to leave in the middle of a classroom activity or at the beginning of a preferred activity (Kamphaus, Dresden, & Kaufman, in press). To the extent possible, the examiner should spend some time in the classroom just watching the child. This observation time will facilitate the familiarization process *and* will likely add a great deal to the examiner's understanding of the assessment results. When it is time to begin the session, the child should not be asked if he or she is "ready to go"—this violates the old adage of never giving a child a choice unless they do, in fact, have a choice (Kamphaus, Dresden, & Kaufman, in press). Instead, the examiner should approach the child with positive, confident anticipation and simply state that now it is time to go (Paget, 1983), play some "games," or "help" the examiner gather some information. Specific words are not particularly important; it is the way the examiner approaches the child that will make a difference.

If the child is brought to the examiner, it is helpful to begin the conversation with a neutral or "easy" topic such as the weather. Especially useful for starting conversations in these situations are concrete objects like fish tanks or appealing toys.

Creating Interest and Motivation

Motivating the child requires the examiner to understand how the child perceives the assessment and how the child feels about being assessed. This knowledge will enable the examiner to present the various tasks in a manner that is both interesting and nonthreatening.

In addition, the attitude of the examiner toward the assessment process will have an impact on the child's level of interest and motivation. An examiner with a cheerful and friendly attitude will convey to the child the message that the assessment process will be enjoyable for both of them (Kaufman & Kaufman, 1983).

The plan for the entire session and the requirements of each task as it is presented should be thoroughly explained to the child. Testing should begin as soon as the child seems ready, in order to maximize the time before the child gets tired (Kaufman & Kaufman, 1983). Tasks should be presented as shared activities, and it is generally useful to begin with subtests that are appealing and relatively easy (Anastasi, 1988).

How to Start

One of the most frequent questions of new examiners is how to start. Glasser and Zimmerman (1967) provide an introduction to the WISC that can be used to introduce any test of intelligence. They advise beginning the session by saying the following:

I will be giving you this test which, as you see, is divided into eleven parts (here demonstrate this by showing the selections on the blank). Each part starts out with easy questions which then get harder as we go along. This is because the test is made up to test children from the first grade on, up through high school. Don't worry if you can't get all the questions right—I don't expect you to. But I do want you to do the best you can. (p. 11)

I use a similar statement to introduce intelligence tests. My little speech is as follows:

I will be administering you this test to determine how you think and solve problems. Your job in taking this test is to try as hard as you can. You will probably find some of the items easy and others to be hard. This is to be expected since this test has items for both very young and older children. The important thing is that you just give your best effort. Let me know if you get tired or for whatever reason you need to take a break.

I do recommend that the examiner be flexible in the wording she uses to introduce the test. Some children require considerable assurance, while others do not. As children differ, so should the introduction.

Using Praise

In attempting to encourage children, examiners should praise effort instead of correctness. This advice is awkward to follow. I have found that new students have an extremely difficult time avoiding the use of phrases such as "that's right" or "you got it." This temptation to praise correctness is particularly difficult after a child has worked very hard on a demanding item. This situation may tempt the examiner to stand up and cheer, let alone praise correctness. Of course, the reason why it is desirable for the examiner not to praise correctness is because the child may then become demoralized when his behavior is not praised.

There are some steps that the new examiner can take to avoid the temptation to praise correctness. These include the following.

1. Make a point to praise effort on items that the child *did not get correct* as well as on items that the child did get correct.

2. Use phrases such as the following to praise effort.
   "You are working very hard."
   "Keep up the good effort."
   "I really appreciate the hard work you are doing on this."
   "Thanks for your hard work."
   "You are really concentrating well."
   "That was a tricky one—thanks for sticking with it."

3. Avoid praising effort by not using the following phrases.
   "You got it right."
   "Good answer."
   "Right."
   "That's correct."

It is also important not to give "faint praise" (undeserved praise). Even the youngest examinees can detect false praise, and the examiner risks the possibility of rewarding uncooperative behavior. I was recently reminded again of the savvy of young children when my 5-year-old brought home her first report card from school. She pointed to the "excellent" that she received in reading and said, "That's an A."

New examiners can gauge their skill at praising effort in lieu of correctness by observing the reactions of young elementary-grade children to the testing session. If the trainee uses praise appropriately, most young children will speak positively or at least not negatively of the testing session. If many children are demoralized and apparently upset at the end of a testing session, then the examiner is likely doing something wrong that may have something to do with the appropriate use of praise.

Keeping the Child on Task

The primary tool for keeping children on task is simply the reinforcement of on-task behavior. Social approval or praise may be used liberally, but, again, praise should be directed at process, *not* the product (Anastasi, 1988). Such comments

---

Reinforcement and testing

A 1988 article by Joseph M. Fish reviewed the issue of reinforcement in testing. The review assessed the research findings regarding the assumption a child's intelligence test performance can be changed by enhancing motivation. Clinicians generally assume that a child is giving maximum effort when taking an intelligence test. If substantial reinforcement effects could be shown then clinicians would have to question the accuracy of their obtained scores more frequently and evaluate examiner, rapport, and other environmental effects on intelligence test scores more carefully.

Fish's review of the literature included a total of 35 studies. Studies were included only for nonhandicapped samples and data on children with intelligence test scores below a standard score of 70 were omitted. The studies included an ample representation of boys, girls, ethnic groups, and SES levels. All studies used control groups, and children were randomly assigned to experimental groups. Some studies used reinforcers, including verbal praise with words such as "good," "you're smart," and "excellent," and tangible rewards included candy and toys. All rewards were given in response to correct responses on various editions of the Binet and Wechsler scales.

Of the 35 studies, 18 showed some effect for reinforcement and 17 did not. Two of these 18 studies showed effects for only one experimental group. The effect sizes for the 18 supportive studies were relatively small. A Chi-square of .47 for the overall effects was not significant. The author concluded that: "Considering the number of studies conducted to date, tests administered, and subject variables, the findings are not substantial. The literature does not lend itself to an adequate determination of whether rewards influence performance, under what conditions, and for whom" (p. 214).

Fish (1988) recognized that individual children may not be putting forth maximum effort and proposed the use of reinforcement as a procedure for "testing the limits." An examiner could retest a child on portions or all of an intelligence test if the child's motivation on the first test is suspect. If scores obtained under reinforcement conditions are significantly higher (higher than one would expect by chance) than previous scores, the examiner will be able to more confidently interpret a child's profile and how it may be affected by motivational factors.

---

as "I see you're really thinking hard" or "I can tell you're really trying" can be valuable reinforcers. Praise of this type, however, should be spontaneous and genuine, not redundant or perfunctory. Physical contact, used appropriately, can also be reinforcing and motivating to a child. A pat on the arm, or even a hug, can show children that their efforts are appreciated.

Keeping children on task will be easier if the testing sessions are brief (Anastasi, 1988) and if the examiner makes allowances for different needs wherever possible. Some subtests can be administered on the floor or in a different part of the room, and the order of the tasks can be varied to suit the individual needs of the child. For example, shy or anxious children are likely to perform best when the initial tasks are un-

structured, play-type procedures that do not have obvious right and wrong answers, while highly active children benefit from beginning with structured activities that help them to focus their attention. For most children, however, alternating tasks demanding close attention with those that are more play-like and/or emphasize motor skills makes good sense (Paget, 1983).

Another area where testing sessions can be modified to suit the needs of individual children is in the area of the pacing or tempo of the assessment. Some children do best with a slow and relaxed pace, while other children need to move very swiftly from one subtest to the next in order to keep their attention on the tasks. Examiners should be attentive to signs of boredom, fatigue, or overstimulation and should adjust the tempo or length of the testing session accordingly.

Children should also be allowed to respond in their own way and at their own pace. It takes much sensitivity to know how to handle children who are very slow to respond or who frequently say that they don't know the answer (Paget, 1983). On the one hand, children should not be urged to respond before they are ready, but, on the other hand, children who respond that they don't know should generally be encouraged to try again. It is sometimes difficult to know what to do, but when children hesitate or say, "I don't know," it is usually a good idea to make sure that they have understood the directions and then encourage them to try again.

A final technique for keeping children on task is the judicious use of breaks. Some children will be refreshed by a chance to get up and stretch for a moment; others will lose their concentration and have difficulty getting back to work. It is the examiner's job to use breaks in such a way that they maximize the child's ability to perform well on the tests. Although it is advisable to let children work steadily if they seem to be doing fine, the examiner should watch for any signs of discomfort and offer the shy child an opportunity to use the bathroom or get a drink of water. Active or restless children will frequently request breaks or the opportunity to play again with some favorite materials. These requests can be granted upon completion of other tests, thus serving as rewards for appropriate behavior — for example, "You may have another drink of water as soon as we finish this game." In this way the examiner maintains control while being responsive to the needs of the child.

Cuing Responses

Examiners are not permitted to query responses in such a way as to give hints as to the correct response. As with the use of praise, examiners are again forced to respond to children in the assessment setting in an unusual and awkward manner. Examiners have to elicit more information regarding a child's response by asking the child for elaboration without giving hints as to the correct response.

The need for cuing responses usually comes into play in the following circumstances:

1. When a child responds to an item very quickly by saying, "I don't know"
2. When a child refuses to respond to an item and communicates this nonverbally (by perhaps shaking his head no), or by saying something like, "That's too hard for me" or "I can't do it"
3. When the child asks for help with the problem
4. When the child responds in a matter that is not clearly correct or incorrect, but is ambiguous

In the first two situations, when a child does not seem to be giving her best effort or even some effort, the child may be masking her own intelligence by not responding at a level that she may be capable of. This behavior does not allow the examiner to view the child's maximum performance and may result in scores that are invalid in the sense that they do not reflect the child's ability. Hence, the examiner should help the child put forth maximum effort by cuing responses. Examiners should use neutral phrases such as the following that do not give hints as to the correct response.

- "Tell me more about it."
- "Explain what you mean."
- "Explain more fully."
- "Tell me more."

None of these statements is given in the form of a question, so as not to allow the child to respond to a query by saying "no" (Wechsler, 1974). Questions such as "Can you tell me more about it" are thus discouraged.

The queries suggested can be used to elicit more complete explanations of verbal responses. This situation is particularly germane to the

Wechsler scales, which use a multipoint scoring system for many verbal subtests. Examples of responses to items that would require cuing include the following.

> *Item*: Tooth
>
> *Unclear Response*: Mouth.
>
> *Item*: Who was the first United States president?
>
> *Incomplete Response*: He was a Virginian.

In these situations the examiner would use one of the cues given above to get the child to elaborate. As Wechsler (1974) recognized, cuing responses requires considerable skill since it is important that the cuing be nonthreatening and nonevaluative. Examiners should constantly evaluate their cuing and nonverbal behavior, which to some children may seem punitive.

Following Standardized Procedures

Perhaps the most difficult and awkward set of skills that new examiners must acquire is that of adhering to standardized procedures. The importance of adhering to standardized procedures cannot be overemphasized, however, since it is one of the hallmarks of intelligence testing. Why are standardized procedures important? They are crucial because they ensure that the testing was conducted under similar circumstances for both the child currently being tested and the children tested in order to develop the norm tables. The examiner can then feel confident that comparing the child's scores to the norm (referenced scores of children the same age) is justified. *If an examiner does not use standardized procedures, then the norm tables should not be used.*

A recent study highlights the importance of using standardized procedures. Hutchens and Thomas (1990) administered the same digit span test to 82 undergraduate students under two conditions. In the first condition the examiner administered the stimuli monotonically without dropping his voice at the end of the stimulus string. In the second condition the same examiner (actually test administration was done by audiotape for better control) administered the items while dropping his voice after the last stimulus digit was given. The scores on the digit span test differed significantly across the conditions, with the monotonic administration being significantly more difficult. This finding shows how even seemingly minor changes in administration procedure can affect test results (Hutchens & Thomas, 1990).

One of the best ways for new examiners to understand the importance of standardized procedures is to think of their own experience taking tests. Most examiners recall taking a college and/or graduate school entrance exam. They also recall that there was a great deal of time at the beginning of the test session that was devoted to explaining the "rules" to be followed in taking the test. Examiners probably also remember that the proctor read instructions word for word from an instruction sheet and that they may have sounded stilted and uninteresting. These instructions that were read verbatim were an important part of the standardized method for the test, in addition to other procedures such as time limits, the number of proctors, and the seating arrangements of examinees.

This same level of rigid adherence to standardized procedures has to be followed by a user of intelligence tests. The critical difference for intelligence test users is that they have to achieve the difficult balance of rigid adherence to procedure and yet *not sound stilted or rigid.* This is a difficult task indeed! One suggestion I give my students is to try to smile as they read instructions. I hope that this will force them to think about having to portray a warm and friendly attitude when administering a test. I think, however, that the ability to be rigid and yet warm develops only after considerable practice. New examiners should practice as if they were actors preparing for a performance.

GENERAL ADMINISTRATION PROCEDURES

There are also some administration procedures that apply to most tests. One of the common prohibitions is not to repeat memory items. Whether it be digit, sentence, or object recall, if the goal is to assess memory, it is not sensible to repeat the stimuli for the child.

A frequent situation encountered by examiners is the child who asks, "Did I get it right?" The examiner is not allowed to answer this question, as it effectively gives away too much information about the test's content, an act prohibited by the Ethical Principles of Psychologists (American Psychological Association [APA], 1981). Releasing test content is prohibited by principle 8, which states: ". . . Psychologists make every effort to maintain the security of tests and other assessment techniques within the limits of legal mandates . . ." (p. 637).

Another nuance of test administration that can be problematic for trainees is the use of a stopwatch. New examiners are advised to handle the stopwatch as they do a wristwatch, as if it is a very normal tool to use. Unfortunately, I have seen many new examiners attempt to hide the stopwatch. This makes use of the watch seem nefarious.

Testing the Limits

Now I would like to contradict everything that I just said in the previous section, or a least it will seem that way to the reader, because this section deals with using nonstandardized procedures to assess intelligence. In common usage this procedure is called "testing the limits." More than anything else, testing the limits allows the professional examiner to, test hypotheses. An example would be a fire alarm interrupting the testing session at the end of a subtest where a child had missed several items in a row and was near to meeting the discontinue criterion. The null hypothesis that the examiner may want to test here is that the interruption caused by the fire alarm did not adversely affect the child's performance.

In this case the examiner would go back and readminister these items in order to test this hypothesis. This will allow the sophisticated examiner to qualify test results appropriately in written and verbal reports. If the child were to get several of the previously missed items correct during limit testing, then the null hypothesis would be disproved. If this occurred the examiner would have to carefully describe the potential detrimental impact of the interruption on the child's performance. If the impact were such that the child's intelligence were severely underestimated by the test, then limit testing may provide enough evidence to discard the entire test. In this situation the examiner would likely administer a new intelligence test to the child.

The examiner who readministers items for the purposes of testing limits should, however, follow these guidelines.

1. Items should be readministered *only after the entire intelligence test has been administered.*

2. Items that are readministered using nonstandardized procedures or for the purposes of limits testing *should not be counted in any way in the scoring of the test.*

One important point that a new examiner should take from this discussion is that testing the limits is a very powerful procedure in the hands of an experienced and sophisticated examiner. Limit testing is not likely to be as valuable a method for the new examiner.

General Scoring Principles

There are a few principles of item scoring that apply to virtually all major intelligence tests. One of these is the importance of adherence to time limits. Generally speaking, a correct response given after the time limit allowed for the item has expired is scored as a failure. Examiners may not reason that the response was given "close enough" to the time limit and give credit, as this would be a violation of standardized scoring procedures.

A more difficult scoring dilemma occurs when a child gives multiple verbal responses to an item. The question in the examiner's mind then is which item to score, and what to do if a child gives an incorrect *and* a correct response. It is generally agreed that in the case of multiple verbal responses to an item the examiner should score the response that the child clearly identifies as the "final" response. Consider the following example.

Vocabulary Item: Bird

Response: "A small animal with fur; no it has feathers and can fly."

In this case the child clearly intended that the last response replace the first. This situation, however, is relatively clear-cut. In some cases it is not clear at all if a child intends a later response to replace an earlier one. If a child gives a laundry list of responses with no clear indication of which one is preferred, then the examiner may have to ask something like, "Which one is it?" (Wechsler, 1974; Kaufman & Kaufman, 1983).

It is also possible for a child to spoil a response by replacing a correct response with an incorrect response. This event may occur on both verbal and nonverbal items. An examiner can get very frustrated watching a child construct something like a Wechsler Block Design item correctly and then dismantle it. If the child indicates that an incorrect Block Design construction is intended to replace the previous correct construction, then it is the incorrect one that is scored. Similarly, if a child responds correctly to a verbal item but replaces this response with an incorrect one, credit for the item is not given. The following example illustrates this point.

Vocabulary Item: Roach

Response: "An insect; no, a style of clothing."

Examiners often have difficulty reading a child's intentions. They can develop a better sense for this with training and experience.

Recording Responses

To the extent that it is practical, a detailed written record of the child's responses to the individual items needs to be kept. This record is important for a number of reasons. A written record is invaluable for use by the examiner in interpretation and report writing. Moreover, the written record will provide valuable details to enhance the examiner's memory of the child's performance for the purposes of report writing. Unfortunately, there is frequently a time delay between testing a child and writing a report. This delay of hours, days, or even weeks can cause the memory of a child's performance to fade.

A written record of responses is also important when an examiner needs to report on the child's performance at some time in the future. For example, an examiner may be asked to give considerable detail about a child's performance at a court proceeding that is called years after the child was originally tested. A written record also serves as proof that services were in fact delivered, should this ever be questioned.

The examiner needs to take the process of recording responses seriously. While this endeavor may seem an arduous one for the trainee, it is in the long-term interest of the child and the examiner to do so. Fortunately, some time can be saved by using a "shorthand" system for recording the child's responses. A sample system is shown next.

1. All of the child's verbal responses to items should be recorded verbatim.

2. If a response is unclear or incomplete and is

cued by the examiner, he or she should enter a "*Q*" *(Query)* and record the child's response to the cue.

3. Many tests require an examiner to model correct responses, especially on easy items. If, for example, a child responds to the question, "Who discovered the north pole" incorrectly, the examiner may be instructed to give the child a correct response to this question before proceeding to the next question. When an examiner models a response per standardized procedure, an "*M*" *(model)* should be entered by the item on the record form.

4. If a child exceeds the time limit allowed for an item, the examiner should enter a "*T*" *(time)* on the record form.

5. If the examiner repeats an item at the child's request (note that this is not allowed on a number of subtests, especially memory tests—this is typically allowed on arithmetic and vocabulary tests), then an "*R*" *(repeat)* should be entered on the record form.

6. If a child points to indicate a correct response in lieu of a verbal response (this is allowed on the Picture Completion subtest of the WISC-III and the Expressive Vocabulary subtest of the K-ABC), the examiner should enter "*pts*" *(points)* on the record form.

7. A "*Ro*" *(rotation)* is noted when a child constructs a design correctly but rotates it significantly (about 30 to 40 degrees or more). This notation is used on tests such as WISC-III Block Design and Stanford-Binet Fourth Edition Pattern Analysis.

8. The notation "*OT*" *(over time)* is used to signify when a child solved an item correctly but did so after the time limit for the item had expired.

9. The letters "*DK*" *(don't know)* are written to signify when a child said something like "I don't know" in response to an item.

Making and Recording Observations

The child's behavior during testing is frequently a crucial variable for testing hypotheses that may explain a child's performance. Hence, making relatively detailed behavioral observations eases somewhat the interpretive work of the examiner by providing a considerable amount of data against which to test hypotheses. The richness of interpretive information yielded by detailed observations is shown in the psychological report excerpts given in Figures 4.2 and 4.3. Note that like a good novel the detailed description of the child yields a vivid portrayal in the reader's mind. The lucidness of the portrayal assists the reader in understanding the child's results more fully.

A variety of informal procedures for recording behavioral observations have been offered (e.g., Aylward & MacGruder, 1986). Guides such as the *Test Behavior Checklist* are particularly helpful to the new examiner because they provide a framework for observing behavior during the session. Among other possibilities, some of the typical aspects of child test-taking behavior that are observed by examiners include the following.

- A description of the examinee, which may include aspects such as appearance, physical handicaps and posture
- Speech, including quality of the individual's voice, amount and quality of verbalization, and a general impression of the ability of the child to express himself verbally
- Vision and hearing, including any signs of deficiencies in these areas, such as squinting or asking that questions be repeated frequently
- Attitude toward the testing, including observations of a lack of cooperation
- Gross and fine motor skills, including the individual's gait, the presence or absence of motor tics
- Activity level, ranging from high activity

FIGURE 4.2

Behavioral observation—WISC-III

Brad, an 8-year-old, was eager to be tested. He met the examiner at the door of the clinic room and enthusiastically escorted her into the room. He was ready immediately to begin testing.

It was apparent early on that Brad is a highly verbal child. He chattered incessantly before, during, and after testing, and he particularly enjoyed the tests that required verbal responses. He occasionally bragged about how much he knew, and commented on how easy some of the questions were. However, his thoughts often became tangential and he had to be directed back onto task frequently. For example, when asked to answer questions that required comprehension of certain concepts, he would answer the question and then start telling a story either about the question or about something that had nothing to do with the question at all. He was particularly excited over the stopwatch, and many of his stories revolved around how fast he could run, how fast he could ride his bike, and how fast the race cars would be going at the Talladega 500.

Brad's behavior was marked by drastic changes from one subtest to the other, a change that was usually brought about by moving from a Verbal subtest to a Performance test. On the Verbal items he appeared comfortable and at ease, and when confronted with an item he did not know, he simply said he forgot or he had not done that in school yet. When presented with Performance tasks, he became irritated and frustrated. On an item on which he was asked to assemble pieces of a puzzle together, he accused the examiner of not giving him all of the pieces. He continually insisted that he could not do what was being asked and that the tasks were not fair. However, he eventually did complete the puzzles, only giving up completely when the task clearly was too difficult for him. He grew frustrated at another subtest that required him to assemble blocks to match a picture, and at one point he stood up and pushed the pieces across the table. This mood did not seem to spill over onto the immediately succeeding test, however, as Brad became calm again with the introduction of a more verbally oriented task.

One final note—Brad went on four self-imposed breaks. The examiner felt these were necessary in order to get optimal performance for the remaining test items. It was clear that he could not stick to the testing for prolonged periods of time, as during testing he occasionally got out of his chair and began walking around. His conversation became most tangential at these times, and it was relatively easy for the examiner to predict when his next break would be.

---

levels to very low levels of energy or activity
- Self-confidence, including any self-deprecating statements made by the child
- Attention, concentration, achievement motivation, and effort
- Persistence, tenacity, and the child's reaction to praise or encouragement

These are just a few of the variables that examiners typically note about the child's behavior during testing. More structured behavioral observation systems are also available, such as the *Test Behavior Checklist* (Aylward & MacGruder, 1986).

Whether the examiner chooses to use one of the systems mentioned or not, the new examiner should use some sort of system for recording observations during testing. This forces the new examiner to think more critically about a variety of aspects of child behavior that may affect children's obtained scores.

PROBLEMS IN THE ASSESSMENT PROCESS

Most problems in the assessment process can be avoided by following the guidelines outlined thus far, providing clear limits and redirecting any inappropriate behavior. When a child is uncooperative and is clearly not putting forth adequate effort, the examiner should confront the child directly, but not angrily, and verbally acknowledge the situation (Paget, 1983). The examiner should attempt to discuss the situation

FIGURE 4.3

Behavioral Observation/K-ABC

Observation and Interview Results

Sharon is an attractive and friendly 9-year-old female who was tested in her home. Throughout the assessment session, she was cooperative and helpful. For example, she offered the examiner a soft drink several times during the assessment session. In addition, she offered to help transport testing material from the examiner's car into her home. Sharon maintained excellent eye contact during the course of the assessment, and excellent rapport was established.

Prior to testing, Sharon appeared concerned that she would not do well on the test. She asked the examiner several questions such as, "What grade do most kids get on the test?" and "If I don't do very good, can I take it again?" Consequently, Sharon appeared to work hard on each test item. Before answering a question, she often spent several seconds thinking intently. While contemplating an answer, Sharon would wrinkle her forehead and repeat the question to herself before answering. On several items, she asked the examiner to repeat the question. During the Number Recall subtest, a test that requires the examinee to repeat a string of numbers back in a certain sequence, and the Word Order subtest, a test that requires the examinee to identify a series of pictures from memory, Sharon demonstrated rehearsal strategies. She repeated items softly to herself several times before answering. At one point during the Word Order subtest, Sharon stated, "I'm trying to figure out the best way to remember these." She appeared to work especially hard during the Triangles subtest, in which the examinee uses triangles to reproduce abstract designs. On most of the items, Sharon would not give up until she was able to reproduce the appropriate design. For example, after working for several minutes on a particular design, the examiner suggested that Sharon try another pattern. Sharon would not agree to move on to the next item until she was told that she would be allowed to come back to the item on which she was working. After the Triangles subtest was completed, Sharon stated that she had enjoyed the subtest. She said, "It's kind of fun doing this to see how well you can match the picture (copy the abstract design with the blocks)."

with the child but should not try to change the child's behavior through negative comments or comparisons with other children (Sattler, 1988).

If an assessment is proving totally unproductive, the examiner may want to terminate the session before the child is completely miserable or before the examiner has lost control. However, the examiner's offer to terminate a session and reschedule may have a variety of results. The offer to end the current session and reschedule may cause the child to begin to cooperate more fully; the child may accept the offer and a subsequent session may prove more productive; or the termination may simply reinforce the child's uncooperative behavior and cause future testing sessions to be even more difficult (Goldman, Stein, & Querry, 1983; Paget, 1983). Thus the examiner must evaluate the situation very carefully before offering to terminate a session.

Debriefing

At the close of the assessment, the examiner should discuss the testing session with the child and elicit feedback about it (Goldman, Stein, & Querry, 1983). The examiner might ask how the child felt about participating in the assessment, whether or not it was enjoyable, which parts the child liked best, and so forth. The examiner should also honestly acknowledge the way the child behaved during the session by saying something like, "I realize that you were a little unhappy about being here today, but you tried hard to do what I asked and I really appreciate that." Such a discussion will provide a sense of closure for what has probably been an intense, if not difficult, experience for the child. It also may help the child gain a better understanding of the experience and place it in some kind of context.

Testing Infants

The assessment of children under 24 months of age typically involves different psychometric instruments (as is discussed in Chapter 14) and some further modifications in the standard assessment procedure. The most notable difference in the assessment of infants is that their mothers are typically present during the testing session and are an integral part of the process. Parents are crucial in the assessment of infants because of their ability to translate the "baby talk" of their children. Thus, infant assessment requires that the examiner develop a good rapport with the mother (or father!) as well as with the baby. In fact, rapport with the mother is probably more important. Rapport with the mother will be facilitated by making eye contact, smiling, and approaching her in a direct and friendly manner. The reason for the assessment and/or more neutral topics such as the weather and parking difficulties may provide good material for an opening conversation. It is also important to explain the testing procedures thoroughly to the mother and to continue to explain them as the testing progresses.

The examiner should be aware of the context surrounding the individual testing session. This awareness is particularly important when testing infants because the examiner has the opportunity to provide the parent with some information about the child. For example, the examiner may use the session to model appropriate interaction with an infant for a parent whose parenting skills need strengthening, or may highlight the child's capabilities in order to reassure an overly anxious parent.

Scheduling, an important consideration with preschoolers, is crucial with infants. Infants may have only an hour or two of alert time each day, and it is imperative that examiners attempt to schedule testing for this time. Unfortunately, predicting these alert times is often very difficult, making the testing of infants very tricky indeed. In any case, a testing session should not be scheduled during a regular nap or feeding time.

Recommendations regarding the environment are essentially the same for infants as for preschoolers, with the addition of several suggestions. The floor should be carpeted, and there should be comfortable places for the infant—a quilt on the floor and an infant seat, for example. If infant seats are not available, the mother can be asked to bring the infant to the testing session in a car seat and the car seat can be used instead.

Because infants generally have such brief periods when they are happy and alert, the examiner must pace the session carefully and be extremely flexible. The pace of the session must be rapid in order to catch as much optimal behavior as possible, *and* very calm and gentle in order not to overstimulate the baby. Too many repetitions of an item or too many items in too little time can cause the baby to be overwhelmed. Flexibility is also necessary—the examiner may have to follow a toddler around the room administering whatever item seems most likely to attract the child's attention. The key to flexible, swift, yet relaxed administration of a test is a very thorough knowledge of the test and total familiarity with the materials. This preparedness enables the examiner to move rapidly from one item to another while focusing on the child and maximizing the likelihood that the child will perform optimally.

CONCLUSIONS

Acquiring clinical assessment skills can be a daunting task, especially for the new clinician who has little experience with children. A lack of experience with children, however, is easily remedied through experiential means. It behooves the new examiner to seek out these experiences in order to ease the process of testing.

Strong clinical interaction skills are also important to parents who are seeking evaluations for their children. A clinician without strong interpersonal skills has the same difficulties as a physician without "bedside manner." Parents are also especially sensitive to how a child responds to a professional, and they may become dissatisfied if a clinician cannot develop a good working relationship with their child.

Chapter Summary

1. Substantial clinical skill is required to administer an intelligence test properly.

2. Observing other child professionals can be a useful activity for acquiring clinical skills for assessing young children.

3. It is important to conduct a thorough interview of a child's or adolescent's parents or caregivers in order to collect relevant background information.

4. It is helpful for the new examiner to use a standard form for collecting background information in order to ensure that no important aspects of behavior are missed.

5. Environmental variables can be crucial for determining the success or failure of an intelligence testing session.

6. If a parent wants to observe the testing session, an examiner must take the time necessary to fully explain the pros and cons of observing.

7. Rapport refers to the process of establishing a comfortable working relationship with a child.

8. Examiners should have at their disposal objects such as toys, puppets, or even pencil and paper that can be used to draw out the reticent child.

9. If the child is brought to the examiner, it is helpful to begin the conversation with a neutral or "easy" topic such as the weather. Especially useful for starting conversations in these situations are concrete objects like fish tanks or appealing toys.

10. Motivating the child requires the examiner to understand how the child perceives the assessment and how the child feels about being assessed.

11. Examiners should praise the child's effort instead of the correctness of the child's response.

12. The primary tool for keeping children on task is simply the reinforcement of on-task behavior.

13. It is not permissible for examiners to query responses in such a way as to give hints as to the correct response.

14. Examiners must adhere to standardized procedures.

15. Testing the limits allows the professional examiner to test hypotheses.

16. A correct response given after the time limit allowed for the item has expired is scored as a failure.

17. A detailed written record of the child's responses to the individual items should be kept.

18. Making detailed behavioral observations eases somewhat the interpretive work of the examiner by providing a considerable amount of data against which to test hypotheses.

19. At the close of the assessment the examiner should discuss the testing session with the child and elicit his or her feelings about it.

20. Mothers, fathers, and other caretakers are crucial in the assessment of infants because of their ability to translate the "baby talk" of their children.

Psychometric Principles and Issues

CHAPTER QUESTIONS

How do scientists assess the reliability of intelligence tests?

How are intelligence tests validated?

Users of intelligence tests should have a thorough understanding of statistics, scaling, and measurement principles. The discussion to follow, however, would hardly qualify as "thorough." This chapter is merely a reminder of what students have already covered in previous coursework that is central to the use of intelligence tests. It is assumed that the user of this text has had, at a minimum, undergraduate courses in statistics and tests and measurement. If a user of this text is not acquainted with some of the principles discussed here, then a statistics and/or measurement textbook should be consulted. There are a number of excellent measurement textbooks available, including Nitko (1983) and Anastasi (1988).

This chapter begins with a review of basic principles of statistics and measurement, including topics ranging from measures of central tendency to factor analysis. The last portion of the chapter introduces measurement issues that are more specific to the use and interpretation of intelligence tests.

MEASURES OF CENTRAL TENDENCY

Mode

Measures of central tendency are useful for describing the performance of a group of individuals. Everyone is interested in the "average" obtained for a particular group of individuals. Examples are the average SAT score for a particular high school or the typical size of the modern family unit. One such measure of

Box 5.1

Interview with Gary J. Robertson, Ph.D. (American Guidance Service)

As an experienced developer of assessment devices you have to come face to face with a number of statistical and technical problems. What is a major technical problem facing the development of intelligence tests? How do you see this problem being resolved?

There are two problems that I would like to mention, one of which is specific to intelligence tests, the other to norm-referenced tests in general.

First, with respect to intelligence tests, test developers and authors have not, in some cases, adequately clarified the construct(s) assessed by a particular intelligence test. Newer tests that are more explicitly theory-based than their older counterparts can be validated vis-a-vis the theory guiding test development. Much work still needs to be done, however, to improve the test validation process. Imprecise definition of the underlying construct of intelligence tests has caused much confusion when the tests are used and interpreted within the context of practical day-to-day decision making in school or other settings. Numerous examples of incorrect assumptions about what intelligence tests measure attest to such misunderstandings. One solution to this problem relies upon a more thorough, rigorous test validation program undertaken before a test is released for operational use. Such validation efforts require the application of appropriate statistical analyses to test results obtained from carefully selected samples of examinees representative of the desired age, ethnic, and socioeconomic groups.

A second and related problem common to all norm-referenced tests is the lack of understanding by test users of the most basic measurement principles needed for proper test use and interpretation; for example, the meaning and use of such terms as standard scores, percentile ranks, age equivalents, and standard error of measurement are adequately understood by altogether too few test users. More concerted efforts to educate test users are needed by professional organizations, graduate training programs, school systems, and test publishers. Authors of applied measurement textbooks need to go much farther than most presently do in providing more good examples of the proper use and interpretation of test results.

What advice do you have for a would be test author?

My advice to those individuals who aspire to become test authors is this:

1. Make certain that the test instrument you have developed and want to publish is clearly different from other instruments that are already available. Is there a distinct competitive advantage that will place your test ahead of others in the field? If not, reconsider your plans to seek publication.

2. Test publishers have different target markets for their test products. Analyze carefully the types of test publications and target markets of test publishers before contacting a specific publisher. Identify the appropriate publisher.

3. Contact the prospective publisher to obtain submission guidelines. Most publishers require compliance with an established set of specifications before a publication proposal will be evaluated.

central tendency is the *mode (Mo)*, the most frequently occurring score in a distribution of scores (see Figure 5.1 for an example of its calculation). This most frequently occurring score is, however, not what most consumers of test data want in terms of the "average." As a result, the mode is not a frequently used test statistic in psychological measurement.

Median

An alternative measure of central tendency is the *median (Md)*, the midpoint of a distribution of scores (again, see Figure 5.1 for a computational example). The Md is the point in a distribution that divides it into equal halves, with 50% of the cases falling below the Md and 50% of the cases above the Md.

FIGURE 5.1

Examples of formulas and statistical computations

Example
A group of students takes two tests designed to measure vocabulary knowledge. The scores are:

STUDENT	TEST 1	TEST 2
Jeff	150	75
Mary	100	55
Abbi	125	50
Todd	95	55
Steve	100	65

MODE
Formula: Most frequent score
Example:

Test 1	Test 2
100	55

MEDIAN (MD)
Formula:

1. Arrange scores from highest to lowest.
2. $n/2 + .5 = n$th score

If n is even, take the midpoint of the two middle scores.
Example:

Test 1	Test 2
150	75
125	65
100	55
100	55
95	50
$5/2 + .5 = $ 3rd score $ = 100$	$5/2 + .5 = $ 3rd score $ = 55$

MEAN ($\overline{X}$, M)
Formula: $\Sigma X / N$
Example:

Test 1
$\Sigma X = 150 + 100 + 125 + 95 + 100 = 570$
$N = 5$
$\overline{X} = 570/5$
$\overline{X} = 114$

Test 2
$\Sigma X = 75 + 55 + 50 + 55 + 65 = 300$
$N = 5$
$\overline{X} = 300/5$
$\overline{X} = 60$

RANGE (R)
Formula: R = highest score – lowest score
Example:

Test 1
R = 150 – 95
R = 55

Test 2
R = 75 – 50
R = 25

FIGURE 5.1 (continued)

VARIANCE (s^2)

Formula: $s^2 = \dfrac{\Sigma x_i^2}{N} - \bar{X}^2$

Example:

Test 1	Test 2
$\Sigma x_i^2 = 150^2 + 100^2 + 125^2 + 95^2 + 100^2$	$\Sigma x_i^2 = 75^2 + 55^2 + 50^2 + 55^2 + 65^2$
$\bar{X}^2 = 114^2 = 12996$	$\bar{X}^2 = 60^2 = 3600 \ N = 5$
$N = 5$	
$s^2 = (67150/5) - 12996$	$s^2 = (18400/5) - 3600 = 80$
$s^2 = 434$	

STANDARD DEVIATION

Formula: $s = \sqrt{\dfrac{\Sigma x_i^2}{N} - \bar{X}^2}$ or $\sqrt{s^2}$

Example:

Test 1	Test 2
$\Sigma x_i^2 = 67150$ (computed for variance)	$\Sigma x_i^2 = 18400$
$\bar{X}^2 = 12996 \ N = 5$	$\bar{X}^2 = 3600 \ N = 5$
$s^2 = 434$	$s^2 = 80$
$s = 20.83$	$s = 8.94$

P-VALUES

Formula: P = # of successes/# of trials

P = proportion of successes

Example:

Test 1	Test 2
success if score is above 110	success if score is above 52
p = 2/5	p = 4/5
p = .40	p = .80

STANDARD SCORE (SS)

Linear $(\bar{X} = 100, s = 15)$

Formula: $SS = [(X - \bar{X})/s]15 + 100$

Example: Todd's Scores

Test 1	Test 2
$SS = [(95 - 114)/20.83]15 + 100$	$SS = [(55 - 60)/8.94]15 + 100$
$= 86.32$	$= 91.61$

Mary's Scores

$SS = [(100 - 114)/20.83]15 + 100$	$SS = [(55 - 60)/8.94]15 + 100$
$= 89.92$	$= 91.61$

PERCENTILE RANK

Formula: Percentile Rank $= \dfrac{[(X - lrl)/i]fw + sfb \times 100]}{N}$

lrl = lower real limit

i = width of target interval

fw = frequency in target interval or score

fb = cumulative frequency below interval

FIGURE 5.1 *(continued)*

Example:

Test 1

lrl	=	124.5
i	=	1
fw	=	1
Σfb	=	3
N	=	5

%ile Rank = $[(125 - 124.5)/1] \times 1 + 3 \times 100$
$$\frac{}{N}$$

%ile Rank = 70

Test 2

lrl	=	49.5
i	=	1
fw	=	1
Σfb	=	0
N	=	5

$[(50 - 49.5)/1] \times 1 + 0 \times 100$
$$\frac{}{N}$$

%ile Rank = 10

STANDARD ERROR OF MEASUREMENT (SE$_m$)

Formula: $SE_m = s\sqrt{1 - r_{tt}}$

Example:

Test 1

SE_m = 20.83(1 – .97)

    = 3.61

s   = 20.83

r_{tt} = .97

CONFIDENCE INTERVALS OR CONFIDENCE BANDS (CI)

Formula: $CI = X \pm Z(SE_m)$

Z = score associated with % level of confidence; e.g., at 95% level, Z = 1.96

Example:

    95% confidence interval for Test 1 for Jeff's score:

    CI = 150 ± 1.96(3.61)

    CI = 142.92–157.07

CORRELATION
(Pearson product-moment correlation coefficient [r])

Formula: $r_{xy} = [N\Sigma xy - (\Sigma x)(\Sigma y)]/[N\Sigma x^2 - (\Sigma x)^2][N\Sigma y^2 - (\Sigma y)^2]$

Example:

    $\Sigma xy = (150 \times 75) + (100 \times 55) + (125 \times 50) + (95 \times 55) + (100 \times 65)$

        = 34725

    $\Sigma x = 570$ $(\Sigma x)^2 = 570^2 = 324900$

    $\Sigma y = 300$ $(\Sigma y)^2 = 90000$

    $\Sigma x^2 = 67150$

    $\Sigma y^2 = 18400$

    $N = 5$

r_{xy} = $[(5)(34725) - (570)(300)]/[5(67150) - 324900][5(18400) - 90000]$

r_{xy} = .56

SPLIT-HALF RELIABILITY (r_{tt})
Sperman-Brown correction formula

Formula: $r_{tt} = (Zr_{hh})/(1 + r_{hh})$

Split test into two halves (usually odd and even items)

r_{hh} = correction between halves

FIGURE 5.1 *(continued)*

Example:

Test 1

	odd score	even score
150	76	74
100	54	46
125	62	63
95	50	45
100	49	51

$r_{hh} = [(5)(16763) - (291)(279)]/[\ 5(17437) - 84681][5(16187) - 77841]$

$\Sigma xy = (76 \times 74) + (54 \times 46) + (62 \times 63) + (50 \times 45) + (49 \times 51) = 16763$

$\Sigma x = 291 \quad \Sigma y = 279 \quad (\Sigma x)^2 = 84681 \quad (\Sigma y)^2 = 77841$

$\Sigma x^2 = 17437 \quad \Sigma y^2 = 16187 \quad N = 5$

REGRESSION TOWARD THE MEAN

Regression for the standard score on Test 2 from standard score on Test 1 (prediction is relatively closer on Test 2 to the mean than on Test 1)

Formula: $Z'_y = r_{xy}Z_{xi}$

Example:

$r_{xy} = .56$

Abbi's standard score on Test 1 $= (125 - 114)/20.83$

$$Z = .53$$

$Z'_y = .56 \times .53$

$Z'_y = .30$ (z score)

Conversion from z score $= (Y - 60)/8.94 = .30$

$X = 62.68$ (predicted score on Test 2)

SUBTEST SPECIFICITY

Formula: $r_{tt} - R^2$

Variance due to a particular subtest

Example:

r_{tt} for Test 1 $= .97$

$R =$ the multiple correlation (.92)

Specificity $= .97 - .92^2$

Specificity $= .12$

DIFFERENCE SCORES

Formula: $SE_{diff} = s\sqrt{2 - r_{11} - r_{22}}$

Example:

s for test 2 $= 8.94$

given: split half for two of Abbi's subtests of .92 and .90

$SE_{diff} = 8.94\sqrt{2 - .92 - .90}$

$SE_{diff} = 3.79$

at $\alpha = .05$ (95% confidence level or z = 1.96)

$3.79 \times 1.96 = 7.42$

   The scores of these two subtests have to differ by approximately 8 points to be significant.

FIGURE 5.1 *(continued)*

SIGNIFICANT PROFILE DEVIATION

$D = CR \times SE_{m[(T/M) - Zt]}$

$SE_{m[(T/m)-Zt]} = \sqrt{(SE^2_{mT}/m^2) + [(m-2)/m] \times SE^2_{mZt}}$

D = deviation from average

CR = critical ratio

$SE_{m[(T/M)-Zt]}$ = standard error of measurement of the difference between an average subtest scaled score and any of the subtest in that average.

SE_{mZt} = squared standard error of measurement of any one of the subtest scaled scores

m = number of subtests

SE^2_{mT} = sum of the squared standard error of measurement of subtests

Example:

Jeff's scores on subtests of Test 1	*SE_m of subtests*
1. 28	1.29
2. 29	1.18
3. 29	1.01
4. 30	1.32
5. *34*	1.15

Total 150 $\bar{X} = 29$ $SE_{mZi} = 1.15$ (Test 5)

1. $SE^2_{mT} = (1.29)^2 + (1.18)^2 + (1.01)^2 + (1.32)^2 + (1.15)^2$
         $= 7.14$
2. $SE^2_{mZi} = 1.15^2 = 1.32$
3. $m = 5$
4. $SE_{m[(T/m)-Zt]} = \sqrt{(7.14/25) + (3/2) \times 1.32}$
         $= 1.5$

$CR = 2.58$

5. $D = 2.58 \times 1.50 = 3.88$

$X = 29$

$29 + 3.88 = 32.88$ = minimum score of deviation

e.g. $34 > 32.88$ or significant deviation

NOTE: I appreciate the assistance of Kathryn Smith with the preparation of this table.

Mean

The Md, however, is also not the statistic that most consumers have in mind when inquiring about average test scores. Most people want to know the arithmetic average of the distribution of scores, the *mean (M)* (see Figure 5.1 for a computational example). Most people frequently compute means as part of their everyday work. Professors frequently compute mean test scores for students in their classes. Students in these same classes compute their mean test score in order to decide whether or not they want to drop the professor's class. Meteorologists may compute mean temperatures. Doctors compute the mean number of patients they see in a week.

Farmers compute the mean amount of feed consumed by their livestock. The mean, then, is the most widely used measure of central tendency, as will be the case in this textbook.

MEASURES OF VARIABILITY

Range

While the public is interested in the average test score, they are also sometimes interested in more specific information. Similarly, parents may inquire about how their child compares to the average for an age group, but, most importantly, they want to know *how far below or above average* their child performed. This latter question has to do with the variability of a distribution of scores. A rather crude measure of variability is the *range*, the difference between the highest and lowest scores in a distribution (see Figure 5.1). The range is an imprecise measure of variability in that it rarely pinpoints exactly where a child's score lies (unless a child's score is extremely high or low).

Standard Deviation

The preferred statistic for measuring variability is the *standard deviation (SD)*, the square root of the average squared deviation from the mean in a group of scores (Nitko, 1983; see also Figure 5.1 for the formula for the standard deviation and variance). The SD is large when there is much variability (a large range) of scores, and small when there is little variability.

If, for example, a researcher collects a sample of all children living in Alaska, the intelligence test scores are likely to be very heterogeneous, or highly variable. If, however, an intelligence test researcher collects test scores for a sample of 30 gifted children from the same classroom, then the standard deviation is likely to become more homogeneous, less variable, smaller. The SD is useful for intelligence test interpretation since it pinpoints more exactly how far a child's score falls from the center of a distribution. The SD is also important because it helps in understanding the normal curve.

THE NORMAL CURVE

The normal curve refers to the graphic depiction of distributions of test scores that is symmetrical (normal), resembling a bell (hence, the term "bell-shaped"). Sometimes researchers do not obtain normal distributions of scores in their samples, but when large samples of intelligence test performance are collected and there is little sampling error, the distributions approximate normality very closely (see Figure 5.2). In a normal distribution there are a few people with very low scores (these people are represented by the tail of the curve on the left), a few with very high scores (the tail on the right), and many individuals with scores about the average (the highest point in the curve).

When a distribution is normal or bell-shaped, as is the case in Figure 5.2., the SD always divides up the same proportion of the distribution. More specifically, ± 1 SD always includes approximately 68% of the cases in a normal distribution, and ± 2 SD always includes approximately 95% of the cases, as is shown in Figure 5.2. The normal curve is also sometimes referred to as the *normal probability* or *Gaussian curve*.

NORM-REFERENCED SCORES

Intelligence test interpretation focuses on *norm-referenced interpretation*, the comparison of children's scores to some standard or norm. For the

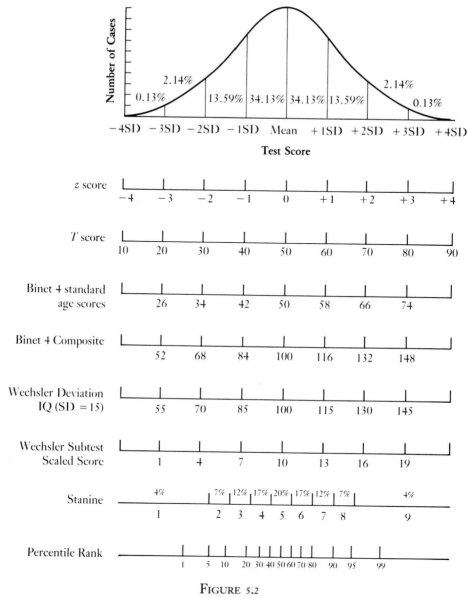

FIGURE 5.2

The normal curve and various derived scores

purposes of intelligence test interpretation, scores are usually compared to those of children the same age. Achievement tests may compare children's scores to those of others in the same grade. College admission counselors may compare an incoming student's GPA to that of fresh- men who entered the year before. Just as people frequently compute means, they also engage in norm-referenced interpretation. Students may compare their performance to others in the same class or compare their professors to others they have had in the past.

TYPES OF SCORES

Intelligence tests yield a great variety of scores, most of which are norm-referenced.

Raw Scores

The first score that the clinician encounters after summing item scores is usually called a *raw score*. Raw scores on most tests of intelligence are simply made of the number of items correct, or they are a summation of the number of points earned on individual items. The term "raw" is probably apropos for these scores in that they give little information about the child's performance as compared to his or her peers. As such, raw scores are not helpful for norm-referenced interpretation.

Standard Scores

The most popular type of score for intelligence tests is the *standard score*. Standard scores convert raw scores to a distribution with a set mean and standard deviation, with equal units along the scale. The typical standard score scale used for intelligence tests is what Wechsler termed the *Deviation IQ*, where the mean is set at 100 and the standard deviation is set at 15 (see Figure 5.1 for examples of the computation of Deviation IQs). Because there are equal units along the scale, standard scores are very powerful for statistical analyses and useful for making comparisons across tests. The equal units (or intervals) that are characteristic of standard scores are shown in Figure 5.2 for the various Deviation IQ scores, where the distance between 55 and 70 is the same as that between 70 and 85, which is the same as between 85 and 100, and so on.

Standard scores are also particularly useful for intelligence test interpretation because they allow comparisons among various subtests or composites yielded by the same intelligence test.

In other words, they facilitate profile analysis. Most modern intelligence tests use for their composites standard scores that have a mean of 100 and a standard deviation of 15. This is true of popular tests such as the WISC-III, K-ABC, and WAIS-R. The notable exception to this standard score scale is the Binet 4, which yields a standard score scale with a mean of 100 and standard deviation of 16 for its composite scores (see Figure 5.2). Fortunately, a number of tables (see Table 5.1) are available for equating one scale to another.

There are other popular standard score scales. Wechsler also popularized the *scaled score* metric for intelligence test subtest scores. Scaled scores have a mean of 10 and a standard deviation of 3 (see Figure 5.2). A standard score scale that is commonly used in personality assessment is the *T-score* scale (see Figure 5.2). The T-score scale has a mean of 50 and standard deviation of 10. The Binet 4 Standard Age Scores are a variant of the T-score scale having the same mean of 50, but a standard deviation of only 8 (Thorndike, Hagen, & Sattler, 1986) (see Figure 5.2).

A more unusual type of standard score scale is the *normal curve equivalent*, better known as the *NCE*. The NCE was developed to produce a standard score that ranges from 1 to 99. In order to achieve this end, the NCE scale has a mean of 50 and a rather unusual standard deviation of 21.06 (Nitko, 1983)!

A less popular type of standard score is referred to as *stanines*, which stands for "standard nines." This scale was used heavily by the armed forces and was rather convenient because it is the lone standard score scale that uses only one digit and ranges from a low of 1 to a high of 9. (The stanine scale is also shown in Figure 5.2.) Stanines are rarely used in modern intelligence test interpretation.

The important thing to remember about this great variety of standard scores is that they are simply different ways of doing the same thing, expressing children's scores in terms of their distance from the mean or average. All standard scores that reflect a normal distribution divide

TABLE 5.1 Standard score and percentile rank conversion table

Standard Score M = 100 SD = 15	Standard Score M = 100 SD = 16	T-score M = 50 SD = 10	Binet Subtest Score M = 50 SD = 8	Subtest "Scaled Score" M = 10 SD = 3	Percentile Ranks
160	164	90	82		99.99
159	163	89			99.99
158	162	89	81		99.99
157	161	88			99.99
156	160	87	80		99.99
155	159	87			99.99
154	158	86	79		99.99
153	157	85			99.98
153	156	85	78		99.98
152	155	85			99.97
151	154	84	77		99.96
150	153	83			99.95
149	152	83	76		99.94
148	151	82			99.93
147	150	81	75		99.91
146	149	81			99.89
145	148	80	74	19	99.87
144	147	79			99.84
143	146	79	73		99.80
142	145	78			99.75
141	144	77	72		99.70
140	143	77		18	99.64
139	142	76	71		99.57
138	141	75			99
138	140	75	70		99
137	139	75			99
136	138	74	69		99
135	137	73		17	99
134	136	73	68		99
133	135	72			99
132	134	71	67		98
131	133	71			98
130	132	70	66	16	98
129	131	69			97
128	130	69	65		97
127	129	68			97
126	128	67	64		96
125	127	67		15	95
124	126	66	63		95
123	125	65			94
123	124	65	62		93
122	123	65			92
121	122	64	61		92

TABLE 5.1   *(continued)*

120	121	63		14	91
119	120	63	60		89
118	119	62			88
117	118	61	59		87
116	117	61			86
115	116	60	58	13	84
114	115	59			83
113	114	59	57		81
112	113	58			79
111	112	57	56		77
110	111	57		12	75
109	110	56	55		73
108	109	55			71
108	108	55	54		69
107	107	55			67
106	106	54	53		65
105	105	53		11	65
104	104	53	52		62
103	103	52			57
102	102	51	51		55
101	101	51			52
100	100	50	50	10	50
99	99	49			48
98	98	49	49		45
97	97	48			43
96	96	47	48		40
95	95	47		9	38
94	94	46	47		35
93	93	45			33
93	92	45	46		31
92	91	45			29
91	90	44	45		27
90	89	43		8	25
89	88	43	44		23
88	87	42			21
87	86	41	43		19
86	85	41			17
85	84	40	42	7	16
84	83	39			14
83	82	39	41		13
82	81	38			12
81	80	37	40		11
80	79	37		6	9
79	78	36	39		8
78	77	35			8
78	76	35	38		7
77	75	35			6

(continued)

TABLE 5.1   (continued)

Standard Score M = 100 SD = 15	Standard Score M = 100 SD = 16	T-score M = 50 SD = 10	Binet Subtest Score M = 50 SD = 8	Subtest "Scaled Score" M = 10 SD = 3	Percentile Ranks
76	74	34	37		5
75	73	33		5	5
74	72	33	36		4
73	71	32			3
72	70	31	35		3
71	69	31			3
70	68	30	34	4	2
69	67	29			2
68	66	29	33		2
67	65	28			1
66	64	27	32		1
65	63	27		3	1
64	62	26	31		1
63	61	25			1
63	60	25	30		1
62	59	25			1
61	58	24	29		.49
60	57	23		2	.36
59	56	23	28		.30
58	55	22			.25
57	54	21	27		.20
56	53	21			.16
55	52	20	26	1	.13
54	51	19			.11
53	50	19	25		.09
52	49	18			.07
51	48	17	24		.06
50	47	17			.05
49	46	16	23		.04
48	45	15			.03
48	44	15	22		.02
47	43	15			.02
46	42	14	21		.01
45	41	13			.01
44	40	13	20		.01
43	39	12			.01
42	38	11	19		.01
41	37	11			.01
40	36	10	18		.01

NOTE: I appreciate the assistance of Dr. Gary Robertson with obtaining some of the raw data for this table.

up the same proportions of the normal curve. As can be seen in Figure 5.2, a Deviation IQ of 85, a T-score of 40, a scaled score of 7, and a Standard Age Score of 42 all represent the same level of performance! These scores are also all at the 16th percentile rank (see Figure 5.2).

Percentile Ranks

A score that is particularly useful for intelligence test interpretation is the *percentile rank* (see Figure 5.1 for the computation of percentile ranks). A percentile rank gives an individual's relative position within the norm group (Lyman, 1965). Percentile ranks are very useful for communicating with parents, administrators, educators, and others who do not have an extensive background in scaling methods (Lyman, 1965). It is easy for parents to understand that if their child received a percentile rank of 50 he or she scored better than approximately 50% of the norm group and worse than approximately 50% of the norm group. This type of interpretation works well so long as the parent understands the difference between percentile rank and percent of items passed.

As can be seen from inspection of Figure 5.2, percentile ranks have one major disadvantage in comparison to standard scores: percentile ranks have unequal units along their scale. Note in Figure 5.2 that the difference between the 1st and 5th percentile rank is *larger* than the difference between the 40th and 50th percentile ranks. In other words, percentile ranks in the middle of the distribution tend to *overemphasize* differences between standard scores, whereas percentile ranks at the tails of the distribution tend to *underemphasize* differences in performance.

Here is an example of how confusing this property of having unequal units can be. Every time I teach my intellectual assessment course, I ask my students the following question: "How would you describe a child who obtained a percentile rank of 25 on an intelligence test: well above average, above average, average, below average, or well below average?" Most often the majority of the class responds with "below average." Then I ask, "How would you rate the intelligence of a child with a standard score of 90 using the same classification system?" In this latter case most students describe the child as being "average" or "below average." Usually, however, one or two students are not fooled, and they correctly point out that a *percentile rank of 25 equals a standard score of 90* (see Figure 5.2). This is one graphic method of portraying one of the interpretive problems with percentile ranks, their unequal scale units. An average standard score, for example, can be made to sound much worse when converted to a percentile rank. As a result, if percentile ranks may be misleading when used to describe a child's performance, they should not be used, despite some of their obvious advantages.

Age Equivalents

Individual intelligence tests have a long history of the use of *age equivalents (AE)*, *developmental ages*, or *mental ages (MA)*. These terms all refer to the same type of score. Age equivalents are computed based upon the performance of every age group used in the norming of the test. For example, if the average raw score for 7-year-olds on an intelligence test is 24, then 24 becomes the raw score that yields an age equivalent of 7 years. If the average raw score on the same intelligence test for 10-year-olds is 32, then 32 becomes the raw score corresponding to an age equivalent of 10 years. If a 7-year-old obtains a raw score on an intelligence test of 32, the child's age equivalent on this intelligence test is 10 years, and he is considered above average for his age group. The 10-year-old who obtains a raw score of 24 is assigned an age equivalent of 7 years and is deemed as being below average in comparison to other 10-year-olds. The important thing to remember about the derivation of age equivalents is that they describe nothing more than the number of raw score points obtained by a particular age group.

Since age equivalents merely reflect whether or not a child obtained a high or low raw score, they are typically prone to overinterpretation (Lyman, 1965). A frequent scenario would be for the 7-year-old who obtained an age equivalent of 10 years to be considered to have the "mind of a 10-year-old." This, in fact, may or may not be the case. What is true is that the 7-year-old has certainly obtained *more items correct* than the average 7-year-old. Whether or not he or she has the "mind" of a 10-year-old is open to debate and is not measured directly by the mental age score.

Perhaps a more extreme case would better illustrate this point. Say an 18-year-old moderately mentally retarded individual is working in a sheltered workshop setting and living in a group home for retarded individuals. This person is responsible for some of his own cooking and all of his housekeeping duties. He maintains his own room and laundry, and he is responsible for taking public transportation to and from the sheltered workshop every day. He is currently dating another resident of the group home and plans to get married. This individual is tested with an intelligence test and obtains an age equivalent of 7-4 (7 years-4 months). This score indicates that he obtained a relatively low score on the intelligence test in comparison to other 18-year-olds. This score does not, however, mean that this 18-year-old has the "mind" of a 7-year-old. He is involved in a host of activities that may or may not even occur to a 7-year-old child. This tendency to ascribe superfluous psychological meaning to age equivalents is a major reason for their deemphasis in test interpretation.

On a technical level, age equivalents are also problematic since they have different standard deviations at each age level, with a trend for larger standard deviations with increasing age (Anastasi, 1988). As such, age equivalents have unequal units along their scale and, just as is the case with percentile ranks, powerful statistical methods cannot be used with them.

Grade Equivalents

Grade equivalents (GE) are another type of developmental norm. These were derived specifically for plotting growth through the academic curriculum. Unfortunately, grade equivalents may not be the best score for this purpose as they share all of the interpretive and technical weaknesses of age equivalents. Grade equivalents are computed in identical fashion to age equivalents and have the same central interpretive problem in that they do not indicate a particular level of curricular knowledge. They simply indicate whether or not a child obtained a higher or lower raw score than her particular grade-reference group. The following example illustrates the problem with grade equivalents.

Suzie is a student in the first grade who is very intelligent. She obtained a grade equivalent of 3-4 (third grade-fourth month) on the mathematics portion of an academic achievement test. Her performance on every item is shown below.

Item	Score
1	1
2	1
3	1
4	1
5	1
6	0
7	0
8	0

Raw score = 5

Amy is a student in the third grade who is of about average intelligence, and she also obtained a grade equivalent of 3-4 (third grade-fourth month) on the same mathematics test. Her performance is shown below.

ITEM	SCORE
1	1
2	0
3	0
4	1
5	0
6	1
7	1
8	1

Raw score = 5

Note that Suzie and Amy obtained the same raw scores on the achievement test and, consequently, the same grade equivalents. Suzie's parents, however, may easily misinterpret her grade equivalent by thinking that, if she has a third-grade equivalent, then perhaps she should be advanced to that grade level in mathematics. This course of action, however, does not appear to be warranted because although the two children received the same raw score and grade equivalents, they achieved them in very different ways, with Amy showing considerably more mathematical knowledge (albeit with a tendency to make some "silly" errors) than Suzie. Suzie has also clearly not mastered the higher-level skills. Grade equivalents thus do not necessarily indicate the level of curricular knowledge or expertise that an individual child possesses. They simply indicate a level of performance. In addition, as was the case with age equivalents, grade equivalents do not have equal units along their scale.

Latent Trait Scores

A proposed solution to the problems of age equivalents and grade equivalents is *latent trait*

methodology, also referred to as *item response theory* (Anastasi, 1988). The terms most frequently used to describe these scores are *scaled scores, latent trait scores, Rasch scaling techniques, one-, two-, or three-parameter scaling techniques,* or *item response theory scaling methods.* Latent trait scores are developmental norms like grade equivalents and age equivalents with one exception: these scores have equal units along their scale. These scores, frequently referred to as "scaled scores" on academic achievement tests, are designed for the same purposes as GEs, tracking growth through the curriculum. At this point in their development, they do not solve the interpretive problems of grade equivalents or age equivalents as far as providing an estimate of curricular knowledge goes. They do, however, solve one interpretive problem in that obtaining the same difference between scaled scores from year to year indicates a similar level of growth. Again, an example is in order here. Say that Jimmy obtained the grade equivalents and scaled scores shown below:

	FIRST GRADE	SECOND GRADE	THIRD GRADE	FOURTH GRADE
Grade Equivalent	1-7	2-7	3-7	4-7
Scaled Score	240	260	280	300

One can say, based upon scaled score information, that Jimmy does seem to be progressing at about the same rate from year to year. This statement can be made since scaled scores have equal units along the scale. A teacher, however, cannot say that Jimmy is making the same gains every year based on GEs because GEs have unequal units along their scale.

Another notable characteristic of scaled scores is that they are not useful for making comparisons across subtests or composites. If a child, for example, obtains a scaled score of 392 in mathematics and 377 in reading, it does not necessarily follow that he or she is better in mathematics than in reading.

Latent trait derived scores are creeping onto the clinical assessment scene. Users of individually administered intelligence tests and other clinical measures will soon have to become more familiar with their properties.

CORRELATION

Correlation Coefficients

A *correlation coefficient* ($r_{x,y}$) expresses the degree to which two variables, in this case test scores, covary, or go together. The formula and an example of the computation of a correlation coefficient are shown in Figure 5.1. The range of values for expressing this covariance is from –1 to +1. The value –1 is a perfect negative correlation in that as one test score increases the other decreases, and +1 is a perfect positive correlation in that as one variable increases so does the other. In addition to being expressed numerically, the correlation between two variables can also be expressed graphically with a scatterplot. A scatterplot is a graph of a group of children's scores in which each child's scores on the two variables being correlated are plotted as shown in Figures 5.3, 5.4, and 5.5.

An example of a negative correlation between two tests is shown in Figure 5.3, in which the relationship between psychoticism and intelligence is depicted in a scatterplot. In this case, higher levels of intelligence are associated with lower levels of psychoticism and vice versa. (The correlation coefficient will approximate 1.0.)

In the second example, shown in Figure 5.4, the opposite situation is displayed—a strong positive correlation between intelligence and mathematics achievement. Here the correlation coefficient will approximate +1.0. The third example, shown in Figure 5.5, is of a poor correlation between hair length and intelligence, where the resulting coefficient will be near 0.

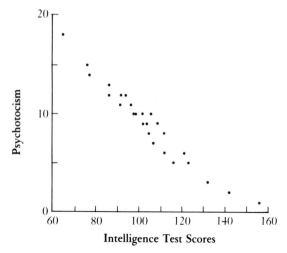

FIGURE 5.3

A strong negative correlation

Correlations between two variables occur because two variables share some common variance. Correlations can be squared to calculate the exact amount of variance shared by the two tests or variables being correlated. If, for example, tests A and B correlate .70 with each other, the amount of shared variance equals 49% ($.70^2$).

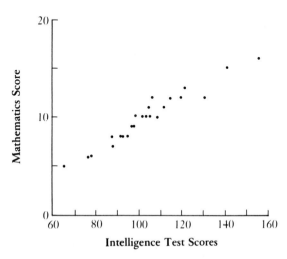

FIGURE 5.4

A strong positive correlation

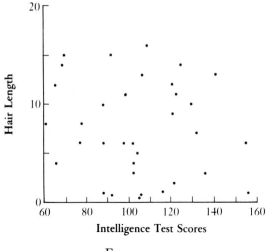

FIGURE 5.5

A poor correlation

correlation can only be computed when scores on three or more scores are available on the same sample of children. An example is the correlation of SAT score (variable 1) *and* high school GPA (variable 2) with college GPA (variable 3). This multiple correlation serves as the basis for formulas using SAT scores and high school GPA to predict college GPA. Multiple correlations are otherwise similar to other correlations in that they range from –1 to +1, and the amount of variance shared between one variable and two or more others is computed by squaring the coefficient (R^2). Using the example above, R^2 indicates the amount of variance shared by the predictors (SAT and high school GPA) and the criterion (college GPA).

In this book, as in most others, the plus sign (+) is assumed for correlation coefficients when it is not present. An important understanding is that correlation coefficients assess rank ordering, not agreement (Lyman, 1965). For example, the correlation between two sets of scores may be high, and yet the means of the two sets of scores can be very different. The comparison of the concepts of correlation and agreement can be better appreciated by computing an example. If a correlation was computed between the numbers 2, 4, 6, 8, 10, and the squares of these numbers, the resulting correlation is .95, and yet the means are 6 and 44 respectively. Since correlations do not necessarily reflect agreement, a high correlation between two scores does not suggest that a child will obtain highly similar scores on the two measures.

Multiple Correlation

A *multiple correlation* ($R_{x.yz...}$) is the correlation between one variable and two or more other variables (Nitko, 1983). In contrast to the correlation just described (in which scores were obtained for only two variables), a multiple

RELIABILITY

The *reliability* of a test refers to the degree to which its scores are free from errors of measurement (Test Standards, APA, 1985). The type of reliability that is of particular interest to intelligence test users is stability, or the degree to which a child's intelligence test scores are likely to be similar from one measurement to the next. The various theories of intelligence all suggest that it is a fairly stable trait over the course of development. If an individual has an extremely high level of intelligence, it is likely to remain this way barring any unusual circumstances.

The Reliability Coefficient

The reliability of an intelligence test is expressed by the computation of a *reliability coefficient*, which is a special type of correlation coefficient (Anastasi, 1988). One essential difference between a reliability coefficient and a correlation coefficient is that reliability coefficients are typically not negative, while negative correlation coefficients are eminently possible. Reliability coefficients range, then, from 0 to +1. Reliability coefficients represent the amount of reliable variance associated with a test. In other words, a reliability coefficient is not squared, as is the case with correlation coefficients, to calculate the amount of reliable variance (Anastasi, 1988). For example, the reliable variance of a test with a reliability coefficient of .90 is 90%, an unusually easy computation (Anastasi, 1988)!

The error variance associated with a test is also easy to calculate. It is done by subtracting the reliability coefficient from 1 *(perfect reliability)*. Taking the previous example, the error variance for a test with a reliability coefficient of .90 is 10% (1 − .90).

Test-Retest Method

The most popular method for computing the stability of intelligence test scores is the *test-retest method*. In this method the same test, for example the WISC-III, is administered to the same group of individuals under the same or similar conditions over a brief period of time (typically 2 to 4 weeks). The correlation between the first and second administrations of the test is then computed, yielding a test-retest reliability coefficient that is typically very close to 1.0, usually somewhere between .90 and .98.

Internal Consistency Coefficients

Another type of reliability coefficient that is typically reported in intelligence test manuals is an *internal consistency coefficient*. This is very different from test-retest or stability coefficients in that it does not assess directly the stability of the measure of intelligence over time. Internal consistency coefficients assess what the name implies—the average correlation among the items in an intelligence test, or, in other words, the homogeneity of the test item pool. Internal consistency coefficients are primarily valuable because they are inexpensively produced, since they only require one administration of the test,

and serve as good *estimates* of test-retest or stability coefficients. Typical formulae used for the computation of internal consistency coefficients include split-half coefficients (see Figure 5.1 for a computational example), Kuder Richardson 20, and Coefficient Alpha (Anastasi, 1988).

On occasion there are differences between internal consistency and test-retest coefficients that can affect intelligence test interpretation. A test may, for example, have a relatively poor internal consistency coefficient and yet have a strong test-retest coefficient. An example is the Gestalt Closure subtest of the K-ABC, which has a very heterogeneous item pool. Its internal consistency coefficients are in the .60 to .70 range, but its test-retest coefficient is in the .80 range. Because internal consistency coefficients are imperfect estimates of stability coefficients, both types of coefficients should be recorded in the manual for an intelligence test (see also the Test Standards, APA, 1985).

Variables That Affect Reliability

Clinicians who use intelligence tests should be especially cognizant of factors that can affect reliability. Foremost among these is test length (Nitko, 1983). The longer the test, the more likely the clinician is to obtain an accurate assessment of a child's intelligence. For this reason, short forms of intelligence tests are generally frowned upon. Other factors that the clinician should keep in mind when estimating the reliability of a test for a particular child include the following:

1. Reliability is affected by homogeneous ability levels. Differentiating among the very gifted or severely impaired may be difficult since these individuals represent a very small range of scores (Nitko, 1983).

2. Reliability can change for different ability levels. A test that is very reliable for gifted students is not necessarily as reliable for men-

tally retarded students without research evidence to support its use (Nitko, 1983).

3. Reliability can suffer when there is a long interval between assessments (Nitko, 1983).

4. Reliability can be affected by characteristics of the child, including age, fatigue, and other factors. Reliability of intelligence measurement drops precipitously at preschool-age levels.

Reliable Specific Variance

Another reliability coefficient that has become more popular in recent years is the estimate of *reliable specific variance*, more commonly referred to as *subtest specificity* (Kaufman, 1979b). Subtest specificity is the amount of reliable specific variance that can be attributed to a single subtest. Kaufman (1979b) popularized the use of subtest specificity in clinical assessment as a way of gauging the amount of confidence a clinician should have in conclusions that are based on a single subtest. In effect, knowledge of subtest specificity makes clinicians more cautious about drawing conclusions based on single subtest scores.

A reliability coefficient represents the amount of reliable variance associated with a test. An example would be a quantitative reasoning test taken from a larger battery of 13 tests, all of which are part of a major intelligence test battery. The quantitative reasoning test has a test-retest reliability coefficient of .82. On the surface this test looks reliable. If this test produces the child's lowest score, the examiner may wish to say that the child has a problem with quantitative reasoning. The examiner can then make this statement with confidence because the test is relatively reliable, right? Not necessarily. As Kaufman (1979b) points out, the conclusion being drawn by the clinician is about some skill or ability (in this case quantitative reasoning) that is specific or *measured only by this one subtest*. The reliability coefficient, on the other hand, reflects not just reliable specific variance but also reliable

shared variance. As such, Kaufman (1979b) presents revised reliability estimates for the WISC-R that reflect only subtest specificity. He computes and evaluates subtest specificity in the following way:

1. Compute the multiple correlation (R) between the test in question and all other tests in the battery and square it (R^2). This computation yields the amount of reliable shared variance between the test in question, in this case quantitative reasoning, and the other tests in the battery.

2. Subtract the squared multiple correlation coefficient from the reliability coefficient or r_{tt}. If $R^2 = .30$, $.82 - .30 = .52$. This formula yields the reliable specific variance (see Figure 5.1).

3. Compare the amount of reliable specific variance (.52) to the amount of error variance (1 – .82 = .18). If the reliable specific variance exceeds the error variance by .20 or more, then the test is considered to have adequate specificity for interpretive purposes. If the reliable specific variance exceeds the error variance by .19 or less, then the test lacks specificity, and it should be cautiously interpreted. If the reliable specific variance does not exceed the error variance, then very cautious interpretation of the subtest is advised.

Fortunately, subtest specificity values are already computed for most tests, and summary tables are provided. New clinicians should remember that the observed reliability coefficients for a subtest are not adequate for gauging the reliable specific variance of a subtest.

Standard Error of Measurement

The *standard error of measurement (SEM)* gives an indication of the amount of error associated with test scores. In more technical terms, the SEM is the standard deviation of the error distribution of scores (see Figure 5.1 for the formula for the SEM). The reliability coefficient of an intelligence test is one way of expressing the amount of error associated with an intelligence test score in order to allow the user to gauge the level of confidence that she should place in the obtained scores. An examiner may report an intelligence test score for a child as being 113 with a test reliability coefficient of .95. This practice, however, is unorthodox and clumsy. The typical practice is to report an intelligence test score along with the test's standard error of measurement. This procedure is frequently done for opinion polls that are conducted by the popular media. In a poll a national sample may be surveyed to determine what percentage of the population eats rutabagas on a daily basis. A news reporter may report the results of the poll by saying, "Rutabagas are a less than popular vegetable in that only 5% of the respondents to our poll indicate that they eat rutabagas at any time. The error rate of this poll is 3%." The error rate reported by newscasters is typically the standard error of measurement for the poll that was taken. The standard error of measurement simply is another way of reflecting the amount of error associated with a test score.

In theory, if a child were administered an intelligence test 100 times under identical conditions, he or she would not get the same composite score on all 100 administrations. The child would not obtain the same composite score because the reliability of an intelligence test is imperfect. Rather, the child would obtain a distribution of scores that approximates a normal curve. Hence, in theory, *error is also normally distributed.* This error distribution would have a mean. The mean of this theoretical distribution of scores is the child's "true score." *A true score is a theoretical construct that can only be estimated.* This error distribution, like other normal distributions, not only has a mean, it also can be divided into standard deviations. In an error distribution, however, instead of being called a standard deviation it is called the SEM. As one would predict then, in this error distribution of scores ± 1 SEM divides up the same portion of

the normal curve (68%) as does a standard deviation and ±2 SEMs divides up the same proportion of the error distribution (95%) as ±2 standard deviations does for a normal distribution of obtained scores.

Confidence Bands

A *confidence band* is a probability statement about the likelihood that a particular range of scores includes a child's true score (see Figure 5.1 for an example of the computation of a confidence band). Just as is done with the televised opinion polls, clinicians use the SEM to show the amount of error, or unreliability, associated with obtained scores on intelligence tests. Obtained scores are banded with error. Banding is accomplished by subtracting 1 SEM from and adding 1 SEM to the obtained score. If, for example, the child obtained a standard score of 103 on the WISC-III, one could apply the theory of standard error of measurement to band this score with error. With most age groups the standard error of measurement for the WISC-III Full Scale Score rounds to about three standard score points (Wechsler, 1991). Given that ± 1 SEM includes approximately 68% of the error distribution of scores, the clinician could then say that there is a 68% likelihood that the child's true score lies somewhere in the range of 100 to 106. Or, if an examiner wanted to use a more conservative ± 2 SEMs, he or she could say that there is a 95% probability that the child's true score lies somewhere between 97 and 109. Confidence bands may be obtained for a variety of levels. Most manuals include confidence bands for the 68%, 85%, 90%, 95%, and 99% levels of confidence.

Regression Effects

Regression effects refer to the well-known phenomenon of discrepant scores tending to regress toward the mean upon retesting (see Figure 5.1 for the formula). Using the obtained score to make a probability statement about the child's true score is probably a very reasonable practice for scores in the middle of the distribution—that is, for those children with scores near the average. However, at the tails of the distribution for the developmentally delayed or the exceedingly precocious, use of the obtained score with its associated confidence band is more questionable because of regression effects. In theory and in everyday practice, scores at the tails of the distribution are less reliable, and, as such, they are more likely to regress (move) toward the mean upon retesting. This regression can be seen very clearly in the examples of computations of true scores shown in Figure 5.6.

If, for example, a child has an obtained score of 103 on a test with a reliability coefficient of .95, there is little regression to the mean when a theoretical true score is computed. The resulting true score is 102.85, which rounds to 103 (see Figure 5.6). On the other hand, for a child who has a standard score of 65, when the true

FIGURE 5.6

Examples of computations of true scores

The formula for a true score is:
   True Score $= X + r_{xx}(X-\bar{X})$
Examples:
1. Obtained score is 103 and the test's reliability is .95.
    True Score $= 100 + .95(103-100)$
    True Score $= 102.85$ (103)
    If the test's SEM $= 3$, then the symmetrical confidence band for the *obtained score* would be 100–106.
    If the test's SEM $= 3$, then the asymmetrical confidence band for the *true score* would also be 100–106.
2. Obtained score is 65 and the test's reliability is .95.
    True Score $= 100 + .95(65-100)$
    True Score $= 66.75$ (67)
    If the test's SEM $= 3$, then the symmetrical confidence band for the *obtained score* would be 62–68.
    If the test's SEM $= 3$, then the asymmetrical confidence band for the *true score* would be 64–70.

score is computed there is considerable regression toward the mean (see Figure 5.6).

Most test manuals ignore the fact of regression and simply use what are called *symmetrical confidence bands*, where the *obtained score* is assigned a confidence band. This practice has become customary for at least two reasons. First, many clinicians are accustomed to using symmetrical bands and have not been introduced to the computation of true scores and their underlying theory. Secondly, some children upon retesting violate what would be predicted based upon test theory and obtain scores that are even further from the mean! This has been the frequently noted case with data associated with the cumulative deficit hypothesis (see Chapter 3).

A few tests such as the Peabody Picture Vocabulary Test (PPVT-R) and the Wechsler Intelligence Test for Children-Third Edition (WISC-III) use *asymmetrical confidence bands*. When true score confidence bands are used, the obtained score is not banded with error; rather, the child's estimated true score is banded with error. This procedure takes into account regression effects, which results in confidence bands about the obtained score that are asymmetrical, especially at the tails of the distribution (see Figure 5.6). Clinicians should understand the difference between symmetrical and asymmetrical confidence bands, because some tests do prefer the latter, most notably the PPVT-R and WISC-III. In addition, many more computer programs offer true scores and/or asymmetrical confidence bands as output.

VALIDITY

Validity is the foundation upon which the use of modern tests of intelligence is based. *Validity* is defined as *the degree to which tests measure what they purport to measure.* There are a number of different ways of evaluating the validity of a test. A variety of the more common types of validity evidence will be discussed in this section. Validity is the most important psychometric characteristic that an intelligence test must possess. A test can be extremely well normed and extremely reliable and yet have no validity for the assessment of intelligence. One could, for example, develop a very good test of algebra knowledge, but if one were to try to call this a test of general intelligence, there would likely be a number of opponents to this point of view.

Content Validity

One of the reasons that many people would disagree with using a test of algebra knowledge as a measure of intelligence is that it does not appear to possess valid content. *Content validity* refers to the appropriate sampling of a particular content domain (Anastasi, 1988). Content validity has been most closely associated with the development of tests of academic achievement for use in school settings (Anastasi, 1988). Typically, procedures for the establishment of content validity are judgmental in nature (Petersen, Kolen, & Hoover, 1989). In the process of developing an academic achievement test, a test publisher will hire a number of consulting editors to define the appropriate content for reading, mathematics, spelling, and other areas included in the battery. This board of editors will define the content and, in addition to that, determine the agreement between the content used in the test and the curricula typically used in the schools.

Unfortunately, intelligence test developers until recently have paid little or no attention to the establishment of content validity (Kamphaus, 1988). This oversight is perhaps why the construct of intelligence has been criticized as being "what the test measures." Intelligence tests were first developed for empirical purposes. More recently, attention has been given to the content validity issue.

The K-ABC, for example, took a very strong theoretical stand in the test's manuals and then selected the content for individual subtests based upon this theoretical model. As such, the authors attempted to define content domains and select subtests and items to assess the domains. For older tests, however, very little information regarding the theory behind the test was given in the test manuals. Consequently, the purposes behind the selection of items and subtests were never clearly explained. It is hoped that new tests and revisions of older tests will now pay more attention to the establishment of content validity.

Criterion-Related Validity

Criterion-related validity assesses the degree to which intelligence tests relate to other tests in a theoretically appropriate manner. There are two kinds of criterion-related validity, concurrent and predictive validity.

Concurrent Validity

Concurrent validity stipulates that intelligence tests should show substantial correlations with other measures to which they are theoretically related. One of the important criteria for the evaluation of intelligence measures since their inception was that they show a substantial correlation with measures of academic achievement. The typical concurrent validity investigation involves administering a new intelligence test and an academic achievement test to a group of students. If a correlation of .20 was obtained, then the concurrent validity of the intelligence test would be in question. A .75 correlation, on the other hand, would be supportive of the validity of the intelligence test. Other possible criterion measures that may be used in concurrent validity studies include measures of psychomotor skills, speech/language tests, and tests of information processing.

Predictive Validity

The other important type of criterion-related validity is *predictive validity*—the ability of an intelligence test to predict (as shown by its correlation) some later criterion of success. This type of research investigation is conducted very similarly to a concurrent validity study, with one important exception. The important difference is that in a predictive validity study the intelligence test is first administered to a group of children, and then sometime in the future, perhaps 2 months, 3 months, or even 2 years, a criterion measure is administered to the same group of children. Usually some measure of academic achievement is administered as the criterion measure since this is the criterion variable that is frequently of interest. With regard to measures of academic achievement, correlations have typically been found to be in the .50 to .75 range (Anastasi, 1988). Of course, correlations tend to be higher the closer the interval between the administration of the intelligence and achievement measures.

Construct Validity

Virtually every aspect of an intelligence test either contributes to or detracts from its ability to measure the construct of intelligence, or its *construct validity*. Construct validity is the degree to which a test measures some hypothetical construct such as intelligence. As such, the construct validity of an intelligence test cannot be established based upon a single research investigation or the study of only one type of validity (e.g., factor analysis). Construct validity is based upon the long-term accumulation of research evidence about a particular instrument, using a variety of procedures for the assessment of validity.

Age Differentiation Validity

One aspect of the construct validity of an intelligence test is the degree to which raw scores show theoretically lawful increases or decreases with age, or *age differentiation validity*. Intelligence test raw scores tend to increase with

age, especially in childhood and adolescence. One aspect of the validity of an intelligence test would be for it to show increases in mean raw scores for the age groups for which the test is designed. In the example shown in Figure 5.7, Test A shows good evidence of age differentiation validity, whereas Test B does not.

Correlations with Other Tests

One can use correlations with other tests in order to evaluate the validity of an intelligence test. In a sense this method is a special type of concurrent validity study. The difference here is that the correlation is not between an intelligence measure and some criterion variable, such as academic achievement, but between an intelligence test and a measure of the same construct, another intelligence measure. If a new intelligence test comes onto the scene, it should show a substantial relationship with previous measures, but not an extremely high relationship (Anastasi, 1988). If a new intelligence test correlates .99 with a previous intelligence test, then it is not needed as it is simply another form of an

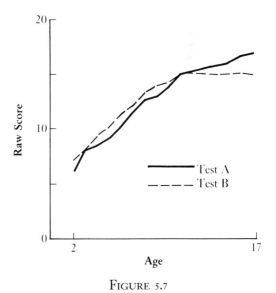

FIGURE 5.7

A distribution of intelligence test raw scores

existing test and does not contribute any to increasing our understanding of what is, at times, the seemingly nebulous construct of intelligence (Anastasi, 1988). If a new intelligence test correlates only .15 with existing intelligence tests, it is likely also to not be a good measure of intelligence. New intelligence tests should show a moderate to strong relationship with existing tests of intelligence, yet contribute something new to our understanding of the intelligence construct.

Convergent/Discriminant Validity

Convergent validity is established when an intelligence test construct correlates with constructs with which it is hypothesized to have a strong relationship. *Discriminant validity* is supported when an intelligence measure has a poor correlation with constructs with which it is hypothesized to be unrelated. This type of assessment of validity is shown clearly in Table 5.2, taken from an investigation from the K-ABC *Interpretive Manual* (Kaufman & Kaufman, 1983).

It is evident from Table 5.2 that the Simultaneous and Sequential scales of the K-ABC show evidence of convergent/discriminant validity. To show evidence of convergent/discriminant validity the following pattern of correlations should hold:

1. The K-ABC Simultaneous scale should correlate highly with the Das Simultaneous scale and poorly with the K-ABC Sequential and Das Successive scales.

2. The K-ABC Sequential scale should correlate highly with the Das Successive scale and poorly with the Simultaneous scales of both tests.

The results are generally consistent with these predictions. The Simultaneous scale of the K-ABC correlates with a measure of the same construct on the other test battery substantially,

which is indicative of evidence of convergent validity. Yet, the Simultaneous scale of the K-ABC did not correlate as highly with measures of dissimilar constructs, including the Sequential scale of the K-ABC and the successive scale of the other test battery. The predicted pattern also emerged for the K-ABC Sequential scale. Table 5-2 shows an excellent example of the establishment of convergent and discriminant validation, a type of validity evidence that is all too frequently missing from test manuals.

Factor Analysis

Factor analysis is a popular technique used in the process of validating modern tests of intelligence that traces its roots to the work of the eminent statistician Karl Pearson (1901). Factor analysis has become increasingly popular as a technique for test validation because of the onset of high-speed computers that greatly facilitate what was formerly a very laborious statistical procedure. Hence, there are a wealth of factor analytic studies beginning with the widespread availability of computer systems in the 1960s.

Factor analysis is a difficult topic to broach in only a few paragraphs. Those readers who are interested in learning factor analysis require a separate course on this particular technique and much independent reading and experience. A very thorough discussion of factor analytic techniques can be found in Gorsuch (1988). An introductory-level discussion can be found in Anastasi (1988).

Factor analysis is a data reduction technique[1] that attempts to explain the variance in an intelligence test in a parsimonious fashion (Anastasi, 1988). Most subtests included in a larger battery of intelligence tests correlate with one another. As such, it is theorized that this correlation between subtests is the result of one or more common factors. The purpose of factor

---

1. Thorndike (1990) argues the contrary—that factor analysis is more than a data reduction technique but also a method for identifying latent variables (underlying constructs). See Thorndike (1990) for this alternative point of view.

TABLE 5.2   Correlations between K-ABC scores and factor scores on the Das-Kirby-Jarman Successive-Simultaneous Battery

Correlations with Das-Kirby-Jarman Factors for Learning Disabilities Referrals (N = 53)

	Successive	Simultaneous
Global Scales		
Sequential Processing	**.50**	.32
Simultaneous Processing	.12	**.54**
Sequential Processing Subtests		
3. Hand Movements	**.30**	.31
5. Number Recall	**.46**	.27
7. Word Order	**.48**	.33
Simultaneous Processing Subtests		
1. Magic Window		
2. Face Recognition		
4. Gestalt Closure	-.10	**.43**
6. Triangles	.27	**.51**
8. Matrix Analogies	.03	**.52**
9. Spatial Memory	.37	**.47**
10. Photo Series	.23	**.42**

Adapted from Kaufman & Kaufman (1983).
Correlations of .30 and above are in **boldface.**

analysis is to reduce the correlations between all subtests in an intelligence test to a smaller set of common factors. This smaller set of factors will presumably be more interpretable than all of the subtests in an intelligence test battery considered as individual entities.

Factor analysis begins with the computation of an intercorrelation matrix showing the correlations among all of the items or subtests in an intelligence test battery (most studies of intelligence tests use subtest intercorrelations as input). These intercorrelations then serve as the input to a factor analytic program that is part of a popular statistical analysis package. The factor analytic program calculations take the intercorrelations and reduce the number of subtests entered to a smaller number of factors—hence, the term "data reduction technique." Factor analyses of the WISC-R have resulted in

the 12 subtests being reduced to three primary factors. This reduction allows the subtests contributing to these factors to be combined to produce composite scores for the test (Anastasi, 1988). Similarly, subtests that are not contributing to the factors are typically removed from the test battery.

The output from a factor analysis, which is frequently reported test validation research, is a factor matrix showing the factor loading of each subtest on each factor. A *factor loading* is in some cases the correlation between a subtest and a factor.[2] Factor loadings in many cases range from −1 to +1 just as do correlation coefficients.

2. When orthogonal (independent or uncorrelated) rotation techniques are used (and these techniques are very frequently used in test validation research), the factor loading represents the correlation between the subtest and a factor. This is not the case when oblique or correlated methods of factor analysis are used (Anastasi, 1988).

The factor loadings for a seminal WISC-R factor analysis of the standardization sample (Kaufman, 1975b) are shown in Table 5.3. A high positive correlation between a subtest and a factor means the same thing as a high positive correlation between two subtests in that they tend to covary to a great extent. Therefore, one can see from Table 5.3 that the Vocabulary subtest is highly correlated with Factor 1, and Block Design is not highly correlated with Factor 1 but it is rather highly correlated with Factor 2. In general, the Verbal subtests of the Wechsler scales tend to have higher loadings on (correlations with) Factor 1, the Performance subtests on Factor 2, and Factor 3 is a combination of both Verbal and Performance tests.

Once the factor matrix is obtained, as is shown in Table 5.3, the researcher must provide a label for the obtained factors. This labeling is done not based upon statistical procedures but based upon theoretical considerations on the part of the individual researcher (Anastasi,

1988). For the WISC-R there is general agreement as to the names of the first two factors. The first factor is typically referred to as Verbal Comprehension, and the second is Perceptual Organization. The debate regarding the WISC-R has been in the naming of the third factor (Kaufman, 1979b). For many tests such as the K-ABC and Binet 4 there is considerable disagreement as to the names of the obtained factors (Kamphaus, 1990; Thorndike, 1990).

Test developers usually eliminate subtests based upon factor analyses or design their composite scores based upon factor analytic results. This process was not done in the development of the Wechsler scales, as this test was developed long before the ready availability of factor analytic procedures. Although the WISC-R appears to be a three-factor test, it produces only two composite scores. This decision is defensible in that the third factor is by far the smallest factor (Kaufman, 1979b). The WISC-III (see Chapter 6), by contrast, did benefit substantially from the

TABLE 5.3 Average WISC-R factor loadings for the standardization sample

WISC-R Subtest	Verbal Comprehension	Perceptual Organization	Third Factor
VERBAL			
Information	63	25	41
Similarities	64	34	28
Arithmetic	37	20	58
Vocabulary	72	24	33
Comprehension	64	30	24
Digit Span	18	12	56
PERFORMANCE			
Picture Completion	35	57	11
Picture Arrangement	33	41	12
Block Design	27	66	28
Object Assembly	21	65	12
Coding	15	20	42
Mazes	12	47	22

Adapted from Kaufman (1975).

Decimal points were omitted.

use of factor analytic procedures during the test development process, which resulted in clearer definition of the obtained factors.

Consumers of factor analytic research and users of individually administered intelligence tests may be interested in the agreement between the factor structure of intelligence tests and the composite scores produced by the test. If there is a one-to-one relationship between the number of factors found and the number of composite scores produced, then the validity of the composite scores is likely enhanced.

"g" Loadings

A commonly encountered term in the factor analytic literature on intelligence is "g" *loading*. The "g" loading is simply a special type of factor loading—the factor loading of a subtest on the first factor yielded by the factor analysis. (This first factor, however, is unrotated. In other words, the first factor yielded after a rotation technique such as varimax is not considered a "g" factor.) The term "g" stands for "general intelligence" in the tradition of Spearman (see Chapter 2). Spearman noted that all collections of subtests produce a first factor that explains most of the variance in a test battery (it is the largest factor). As a result, he and his followers have argued strenuously for focusing on the first factor yielded by intelligence tests as the most important one for understanding the construct of intelligence. The typical procedure in factor analyses of intelligence tests is to first examine the "unrotated factor structure" produced by a factor analytic program. This first factor matrix maximizes the loading of each subtest on one (the first) factor. The "g" loadings of subtests in a battery are then the loadings of the subtests on this first factor. First-factor, or "g," loadings can also be obtained by using confirmatory factor analytic procedures where one factor is identified (see next section).

The "g" loadings for the Differential Ability Scales (DAS) (Elliott, 1990) subtests are shown in Table 5.4. Verbal, quantitative, and spatial

TABLE 5.4   DAS subtest "g" loadings

Subtests	"g" Loading
Word Definitions	.68
Similarities	.69
Matrices	.71
Sequential and Quantitative Reasoning	.76
Pattern Construction	.70
Speed of Information Processing	.28
Recognition of Pictures	.42
Recall of Designs	.63
Recall of Digits	.36
Recall of Objects	.35

Adapted from Elliott (1990).

reasoning subtests are the better measures of "g." As such, these tests can be expected to be more consistent with the overall composite General Conceptualization Ability (GCA, analogous to the Wechsler Full Scale IQ) score. DAS short-term memory and processing speed tests, on the other hand, are poorer measures of "g." Interpretation of "g" loadings, however, depends on how much one agrees with Spearman's theory.

Confirmatory Factor Analysis

The procedures discussed thus far are generally referred to as "exploratory factor analytic procedures." A newer factor analytic technique that is receiving increasing attention is often referred to as "confirmatory factor analysis" (Joreskog & Sorbom, 1987). These two factor analytic procedures differ in some very important ways. In exploratory factor analysis the number of factors to be yielded is typically dictated by the characteristics of the intercorrelation matrix; that is, the number of factors selected is based upon the amount of variance that each factor explains in the correlation matrix. If a factor, for example, explains 70% of the variance in the correlation matrix, then it is typically included as a viable factor in further aspects of the factor analysis. If, on the other hand, the factor only accounts for 2% of the variance in a factor matrix, then it may not be included as a viable factor.

In direct contrast, in confirmatory factor analysis the number of factors is not dictated by data, but rather by the theory underlying the test under investigation. In confirmatory factor analysis the number of factors is selected a priori, and the factor loadings of each subtest on the designated number of factors is then analyzed. In addition, the general fit between the factor structure dictated a priori and the obtained data are assessed. If there is a great deal of correspondence between the hypothesized structure and the obtained factor structure, then the validity of the intelligence test is supported (hence the term "confirmatory"), and the theory is confirmed. If, for example, a researcher hypothesized the existence of four factors in a particular intelligence test, the confirmatory factor analysis will, in fact, yield four factors. Statistics assessing the fit of these four factors to the data (i.e., diagnostics) may, however, indicate a lack of congruence (correlation) between the hypothesized four factors and the obtained four factors.

Confirmatory factor analytic studies use a variety of statistics to assess the fit of the hypothesized factor structure to the data. These include a Chi-square statistic, goodness-of-fit index (GFI), adjusted goodness-of-fit index (AGFI), and root mean square residual (RMR) among others. Several statistics are desirable for checking the fit of a confirmatory factor analysis because all of these statistics have strengths and weaknesses. The Chi-square statistic, for example, is highly influenced by sample size (Glutting & Kaplan, 1990). Some general guidelines for assessing the fit of a confirmatory factor analysis include the following (Kline, 1989):

1. Nonsignificant Chi-square statistic
2. Goodness-of-fit index > .90
3. Adjusted goodness-of-fit index > .80
4. Root mean square residual < .10

Consequently, confirmatory factor analytic procedures may yield the number of factors hypothesized by the test developer, which in exploratory factor analysis would lend support to the theory and structure of the test. In confirmatory factor analysis, however, consumers of the research have to evaluate the statistics that assess the fit between the hypothesized and the obtained factor structure. These statistics will indicate whether or not the evidence is strong or weak for the validity of the scores yielded by the test under study.

Another issue in confirmatory factor analysis is that many researchers use it in an exploratory factor analytic manner (Thorndike, 1990). Some authors specify a model a priori and then modify that model numerous times until adequate fit statistics are obtained. Thorndike (1990) contends that this is a misuse of the methodology that dilutes the theoretical importance of the obtained results. Ideally, researchers should conduct studies comparing competing theoretical models (see Kline, 1989, for such an example) in order to evaluate the theoretical structure of a test (Thorndike, 1990). An excellent nonmathematical introduction to confirmatory factor analytic procedures can be found in Kline (in press).

STANDARDIZATION SAMPLING

Intelligence test scores are rather meaningless without the use of norm groups. Generally speaking, individuals are to be compared to norm groups of their peers. Intelligence test developers thus strive to collect norm samples that are reflective of a child's peers.

The ideal for developing intelligence test norms for an American test would be to test all children in the United States in order to compare individual children with the norm. This procedure would be used for any country that would be using a particular intelligence test. Unfortunately, this process is not possible, so test developers collect samples of children that are representative of the national population, much in the same way that pollsters collect samples of the population in order to gauge the political will of voters prior to an election.

Stratification Variables

In order to select a representative sample of the national population for any country, test developers typically use what are called *stratification variables*. These stratification variables are assumed to have important effects upon intelligence test scores. One of the most important stratification variables is some indication of socioeconomic status. Differences in SES relate to large differences in intelligence test scores. Some stratification variables such as gender and geographic region are included based more upon tradition, since they do not produce substantial differences in intelligence test scores. A good example is the gender of the child. While boys and girls differ very little in their overall intelligence test scores, most standardization samples still include approximately half boys and half girls.

In the United States the stratification variables are based on U.S. Census Bureau statistics. If the census, for example, says that 75% of the U.S. population is made up of white children, then test developers will typically try to include 75% white children in the norming sample. Some typical stratification variables are age, gender, parental socioeconomic status (tests have traditionally used either parental educational attainment or occupation), race or ethnic group, community size, and geographic region.

Local Norms

Occasionally a clinician may want to have local norms available (Kamphaus & Lozano, 1981). *Local norms* are those based on some subset of the national population. Say, for example, a child was transferring from an impoverished area of a city to a school system in a high-SES area. The child from the impoverished environment may have obtained an intelligence test composite score of 100. This child, however, may be at considerable risk for school problems if she is moved to a highly competitive school system where the average intelligence test composite score is 117. In this case the national norms are of some benefit in that they indicate that the child has average intelligence, but local norms based upon a sample from a high-SES school district may be even more enlightening and might assist with planning the transition of this child from one school system to another. Local norms, however, are rarely available for clinical tests because they are time-consuming and somewhat expensive to develop. Local norms are readily available for group-administered multilevel survey achievement batteries.

WHY TEST SCORES DIFFER

A frequently perplexing problem for clinicians is having to explain why two or more sets of intelligence test scores for the same child differ, sometimes substantially. There are a number of psychometric reasons for changes in scores, including the age of the norms, floor and ceiling effects, selection bias/regression effects, age at which the child was first tested, item content differences, and reliability of gain/difference scores.

Age of Norms

One of the most important characteristics of norm tables is the necessity that they be recent. A comprehensive analysis of changes in Stanford-Binet and Wechsler norms from the years 1932 to 1978 by James Flynn (1984) highlights the problem of using antiquated norms. Flynn's conclusion was that the American population became about one standard deviation (15 standard score points) "smarter" over an approximately 50-year period. In other words, the norm tables became "tougher" with each succeeding decade in the sense that a child had to obtain a higher raw score every time a test was renormed to obtain the same standard score that he had obtained previously. If a child, for example, took the WISC (normed in the 1940s) in 1956 and correctly answered 13 Vocabulary items, she may obtain a scaled score of 10. If a child took the Vocabulary test on the WISC-R (normed in the early 1970s) and answered 13 items correctly, her scaled score may be only 8 or 9.

One of the most interesting aspects of the Flynn investigation is that he provides a rule of thumb for this change in the difficulty of American intelligence test norms. He concludes that intelligence test norms for the United States increase in difficulty by about three standard score points every decade. A test, for example, that was normed in 1980 would have "softer" or easier norms. This test would yield standard scores that, on the average, are about three standard score points (based upon a mean of 100 and a standard deviation of 15) higher than for a comparable or the same test with norms collected in 1990. This statement assumes, of course, that the norm samples for both tests are representative of the national population.

Based upon data other than Flynn's, it is striking how aptly this rule of thumb of a change of three standard score points applies. A perusal of the WISC-III manual shows that it produced scores about five points lower than the 1974 WISC-R. Similarly, the 1981 edition of the WAIS-R produces standard scores about six points lower than the 1955 WAIS. Finally, the Binet-4 and K-ABC, both normed in the 1980s, produce standard scores in a number of investigations anywhere from about two to four points lower than the WISC-R, which was normed in the 1970s (Kamphaus & Reynolds, 1987).

Though this rule of thumb may not be in effect forever, at this time when a clinician selects an intelligence test for use, one of the first things to look for is the date of the data collection for the sample. *If the standardization sample is 10 years old or more, then the clinician has to be wary of the accuracy of the norms for current use.* This psychometric hypothesis is one of the first to entertain when a difference is observed between intelligence test scores gathered on separated occasions.

Floor and Ceiling Effects

Floor effects occur when the test being administered to a child lacks enough easy items to allow the child to obtain a raw score (i.e., the child gets all of the items wrong). Conversely, *ceiling effects* occur when a test lacks difficult items, resulting in the child obtaining a perfect score. These problems of a lack of an adequate range of difficulty are frequently encountered in clinical assessment. Floor and ceiling effects are problematic in that if a child obtains either a perfect score or a zero raw score his intelligence has not been measured adequately. The examiner then does not know how far his ability lies below the lowest item or how far he is above the last item.

Clinicians are most likely to encounter problems with insufficient floor and ceiling near the extremes of a test's age range. The WISC-R age range, for example, is 6 to 16 years. The WISC-R is likely to exhibit ceiling effects for 15-year-olds of average to above-average ability and floor effects for 6- and 7-year-olds who are developmentally delayed. Some tests, however, may be more prone to floor effects than others. The clinician can identify these problems through experience with a particular test.

Another way to identify the presence of floor and ceiling effects, however, is to inspect P-values for a particular test. A *P-value* is the percent of children passing an item (e.g., 45% of 2-year olds passed the first item on a test) (see Figure 5.1 for a sample calculation of P-values). Unfortunately, publishers usually do not include P-values in their test manuals (P-values for the

K-ABC are available in Kamphaus & Reynolds, 1987). Publishers are, however, likely to publish raw score descriptive statistics by age group, including means and standard deviations. Floor effects can be gauged by reviewing the relationships of the mean to the standard deviation for the younger age ranges of a test. If the standard deviation exceeds the mean at an age group, this suggests that the test is too difficult (Kamphaus & Reynolds, 1987).

Similarly, the age differentiation validity of a test can indicate whether or not ceiling effects are present. If the mean raw score for the oldest age group is very similar to or less than the preceding age group, the test has poor age differentiation validity and an associated ceiling effect. Ceiling effects are a problem for all tests at their extreme age ranges. The best way to avoid ceiling effects if little is known about the nature of the referral is to not use a test with an age range that will increase the likelihood of a lack of item difficulty. For example, for a 14-year-old child (adolescent) use a test with an upper age limit of 23, instead of using a test that has an upper age limit of only 16.

Correlations Between Tests

Certainly one of the most straightforward reasons for test score differences is the possibility that the two tests are not highly correlated. Intelligence test composite scores typically have reliability coefficients in the .90 range. As a result, when a child is tested with the same test twice, his or her scores are likely to be similar. If, on the other hand, a child is administered two different intelligence tests, his scores are likely to differ more, simply because an intelligence test typically correlates more with itself than it does with other intelligence tests.

Selection Bias

The regression effect for extreme scores is frequently compounded by selection bias, which is also a plausible explanation for score differences. *Selection bias*, as coined by Richard Woodcock (1984), occurs when the regression effect is compounded for the second test administered to a child who is at the extremes of the normal distribution. Say, for example, that children are selected for mental retardation classes using the WISC-R and these children are reevaluated with the new Differential Ability Scales (DAS). Selection bias predicts that the mean score for the DAS will be higher (closer to the mean) than for the WISC-R since the WISC-R was used as the selection test.

The selection bias phenomenon for this scenario is shown graphically in Figure 5.8. This figure is a scatterplot, divided into four quadrants approximating the relationship between the WISC-R and DAS. If the sample of mentally retarded children is selected based on having WISC-R scores less than 70 (these are the children whose scores are represented in quadrants 1 and 2), then some children with DAS composite scores of less than 70 (and WISC-R scores greater than 70) were not diagnosed as mentally retarded and not included in the sample (these cases are in quadrant 4). The use of the WISC-

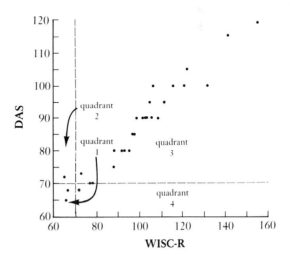

FIGURE 5.8

Scatterplot showing selection bias

R as the selection test therefore lowers the mean of the WISC-R for the sample and raises the mean of the DAS since the children's scores in quadrant 4 with DAS composites below 70 and WISC-R scores above 70 were excluded from the sample. The phenomenon of selection bias suggests that the scores of children who are diagnosed because of being at the tails of the normal distribution can be quite discrepant on two tests of intelligence.

Reliability, Age, and Test Length

Generally, intelligence tests are less reliable for preschool-age children (Anastasi, 1988). This unreliability is a plausible hypothesis for differences between intelligence test scores for a preschool child and for differences between scores when a child is tested in the preschool years and again at a later date.

Test length can also be a plausible hypothesis for differences between intelligence tests. The K-ABC, for example, is shorter than either the WISC-III or Binet-4 by about two subtests. Similarly, short forms of intelligence tests can produce differences between tests.

Item Content Differences

Intelligence tests can be based on a variety of theories that dictate item and subtest selection. Some tests may place a premium on verbal skills, others on motor skills. The child suffering from cerebral palsy, for example, may perform very differently on two intelligence measures depending on the content of the items—verbal versus nonverbal.

Reliability of Gain/ Difference Scores

Gain scores are computed by subtracting a child's first score on an intelligence test from his or her second score. They are commonly re-ferred to as "gain scores" because scores tend to be slightly higher on the second testing (a gain) in test-retest reliability studies. Difference scores subsume gain scores. The term "difference score," however, is usually used in conjunction with comparing composite scores within a test or across tests (see Figure 5.1 for the formula and an example). An example of a difference score would be the difference between Verbal and Performance scores on the WISC-III. It is important when interpreting score differences to keep in mind that difference scores and gain scores are inherently less reliable than composite or subtest scores (Anastasi, 1985). Specifically, a gain or loss from one test administration to another is a difference score. *Difference scores possess the error variance of both tests used* in producing the difference. If, for example, each test has a reliability coefficient of .90, then the error variance associated with the difference score is .20 (.10 + .10). Being aware of the increased error associated with difference scores, clinicians frequently attribute small differences between composite scores to chance variation.

Practice Effects

Practice effects may explain small differences in scores between intelligence tests. *Practice effects* are observed when scores improve (a gain score) due to familiarity with the test items. The size of practice effects is usually less than 10 standard score points (2/3 SD).

Interpreting Score Differences

Based on the previous discussion, the following list of psychometric hypotheses should be considered when differences between intelligence tests occur.

- Age of norms
- Floor and ceiling effects
- Correlations between tests
- Selection bias

- Reliability and age
- Reliability and test length
- Content differences
- Reliability of difference (gain) scores
- Practice effects

These hypotheses are primarily psychometric. Scores may differ due to other factors. Say, for example, a child is tested on two occasions, once when she is taking medication and once when she is not. This situation could have a dramatic impact on the two test scores that is independent of psychometric reasons.

CONCLUSIONS

Knowledge of psychometric principles is becoming an increasingly important issue since this type of coursework has been deemphasized in many psychology programs. Yet psychologists have a continuing reputation for assessment expertise that is well known to the public and other professions. This chapter is just one more psychometrics resource that serves as a supplement to coursework on psychometric theory. A strong background in psychometrics is as important in the assessment process as knowledge of specific tests and clinical skill.

CHAPTER SUMMARY

1. The mode (Mo) is the most frequently occurring score in a distribution of scores.
2. The median (Md) is the midpoint of a distribution of scores.
3. The mean (M) is the arithmetic average of the distribution of scores.
4. The range is the difference between the highest and lowest scores in a distribution.
5. The standard deviation (SD) is the square root of the average squared deviation in a group of scores. The SD is large when there is a great deal of variability (a large range) of scores, and it is very small when there is little variability.

6. Raw scores on most tests of intelligence are simply made up of the number of items correct, or they are a summation of the number of points earned on individual items.
7. The most popular type of score for intelligence tests is the standard score. Standard scores convert raw scores to a distribution with a set mean and standard deviation, with equal units along the scale.
8. Scaled scores are standard scores that have a mean of 10 and a standard deviation of 3.
9. A T-score is a standard score that has a mean of 50 and standard deviation of 10.
10. A normal curve equivalent (NCE) is a standard score that has a mean of 50 and a rather unusual standard deviation of 21.06.
11. Stanines, which stands for "standard nines," were used heavily by the armed forces and were rather convenient because they represent the lone standard score scale that uses only one digit and ranges from a low of 1 to a high of 9.
12. A percentile rank gives an individual's relative position within the norm group.
13. Age and grade equivalents are computed based upon the performance of every age/grade group used in the norming of the test.
14. Latent trait scores are developmental norms like GEs and AEs with one exception: these scores have equal units along their scale.
15. A correlation coefficient ($r_{x.y}$) expresses the degree to which two variables (test scores) covary.
16. A multiple correlation ($R_{x.yz...}$) is the correlation between one variable and two or more other variables.
17. The "reliability" of a test refers to the degree to which its scores are free from errors of measurement.

18. Subtest specificity is the amount of reliable specific variance that can be attributed to a single subtest.

19. The standard error of measurement (SEM) is the standard deviation of the error distribution of scores.

20. A confidence band is a probability statement about the likelihood that a particular range of scores includes a child's true score.

21. "Regression effects" refer to the well-known phenomenon of discrepant scores tending to regress toward the mean upon retesting.

22. Validity is defined as the degree to which tests measure what they purport to measure.

23. Content validity refers to the appropriate sampling of a particular content domain.

24. Concurrent validity stipulates that an intelligence test should show substantial correlations with other measures that should theoretically correlate with intelligence tests.

25. "Predictive validity" refers to the ability of an intelligence test to predict (as shown by its correlation) some criterion of success.

26. The age differentiation validity of an intelligence test is the degree to which raw scores show theoretically lawful increases or decreases with age.

27. Convergent validity is established when an intelligence test construct correlates with constructs with which it is hypothesized to have a strong relationship. Discriminant validity is supported when an intelligence measure has a poor correlation with a construct with which it is supposed to have a poor correlation.

28. Factor analysis is a data reduction technique that attempts to explain the variance in an intelligence test in a parsimonious fashion.

29. A factor loading is in some cases the correlation between a subtest and a factor.[3]

3. See footnote 2.

30. The "g" loading is simply a special type of factor loading—the factor loading of a subtest on the first factor yielded by the factor analysis.

31. A newer factor analytic technique that is receiving increasing attention is referred to as "confirmatory factor analysis."

32. In confirmatory factor analysis, however, consumers of the research have to evaluate the statistics that assess the fit between the hypothesized and the obtained factor structure.

33. In order to select a representative sample of the national population for any country, test developers typically use what are called "stratification variables."

34. Local norms are those based on some subset of the national population.

35. One of the most important characteristics of norm tables is the necessity that they be based on recent data.

36. Floor effects occur when the test being administered to a child lacks enough easy items to allow the child to obtain a raw score (i.e., the child gets all of the items wrong). Conversely, ceiling effects occur when a test lacks difficult items, resulting in the child obtaining a perfect score.

37. A P-value is the percent of children passing an item (e.g., 45% of 2-year-olds passed the first item on a test).

38. Selection bias occurs when the regression effect is compounded for the second test administered to a child who is at the extremes of the normal distribution.

39. Gain scores are computed by subtracting a child's first score on an intelligence test from his or her second score.

40. Practice effects are observed when scores improve (a gain score) due to familiarity with the test items.

The Wechsler Intelligence Scale for Children, Third Edition (WISC-III)

CHAPTER QUESTIONS

What features made the Wechsler scales so popular?

What are the strengths and weaknesses of the WISC-III?

A necessary condition for competent test interpretation is detailed knowledge of the test instruments being used. Therefore, it is necessary to introduce the most popular intelligence scale today, the WISC, before presenting an interpretive system. This chapter, then, serves as an important prelude to Chapter 7, which will discuss a detailed interpretive system that can be applied to the WISC-III or any other intelligence test.

The Wechsler scales enjoy unprecedented popularity and have a rich clinical and research tradition. The publication of the Wechsler/Bellevue in 1939 was a bold stroke on the part of David Wechsler in even attempting to challenge

the hallowed Binet scales (Reynolds & Kaufman, 1990). Somewhat surprisingly, from the outset the Wechsler scales were welcomed. The Wechsler/Bellevue offered a number of features that were not available in previous editions of the Binet scales, including separate norms for children and adults; the provision of subtest standard scores, which made the test more amenable to profile interpretation; the inclusion of a separate Performance scale to allow for the assessment of linguistic and cultural minorities; and a Standard Score (Deviation IQ) that solved many of the psychometric problems associated with Ratio IQ scales (Zimmerman & Woo-Sam, 1985).

The Wechsler scales also enjoyed immediate credibility because of the reputation of David Wechsler himself. In contrast to Binet, who was known as a researcher, Wechsler was a clinical psychologist who had a wealth of experience in the individual study of psychiatric patients at the Bellevue Psychiatric Hospital (Zimmerman & Woo-Sam, 1985). For many reasons, at the time the Wechsler/Bellevue was published, it was clearly differentiated from the Binet scales and offered a number of advantages that were attractive to practicing psychologists.

This extensive popularity has led to the publication of a variety of scales by Wechsler, including his most famous children's scale, the Wechsler Intelligence Scale for Children-Revised (WISC-R). The original WISC was published in 1949 and its revision, the WISC-R, was published in 1974. The WISC-R has also enjoyed a great deal of popularity with researchers. As a result, it is a very well-known test both clinically and empirically, with over 1,100 publications that assess various aspects of its clinical utility and validity (Reynolds & Kaufman, 1990). The Wechsler scales promise to be popular for the foreseeable future, especially with the publication of the WISC-III. Through all of these revisions, the structure of the Wechsler scales has not changed appreciably. The most daring changes in the WISC were made in the WISC-III when a new subtest, Symbol Search, was added.

Detterman (1985) attributes the popularity of the WISC to its ease of administration. This ease of administration is fostered by the organization of the tests into subtests that are brief yet long enough to be reliable and have long clinical histories (Detterman, 1985). Detterman's (1985) major complaint about the WISC is that it clings to the tradition of offering "only one interpretable score." He acknowledges the need for an intelligence test that assesses more specific skills so that it will lend itself better to treatment planning.

Opinions about the WISC run the gamut from ebullient praise to condemnation. A review by Witt and Gresham (1985) of the WISC-R concluded that the WISC-R was overrated. Specifically, they suggested that the WISC is outdated and that it lacks treatment validity. Regarding its outdated nature, they described the WISC-R as, "an anachronistic albatross which hangs gamely around the necks of applied psychologists." Regarding its lack of a direct link to treatment, they conclude: "The test was not designed for such purposes . . . it is a kind of idiocy which stands in the way of the advancement of the science of assessment."

WECHSLER'S VIEW OF INTELLIGENCE

David Wechsler's conceptualization of intelligence is consistent with that of other well-known theorists of his day. He, as well as Spearman, Galton, and others, emphasized the concept of general intelligence. An excerpt from Wechsler's WISC-R manual (1974) best describes his view:

> *Intelligence is the overall capacity of an individual to understand and cope with the world around him. Stated in these general terms, this definition may impress the reader perhaps as not too radically different from any other definitions that might be cited. A careful comparison with these, however, would reveal that it differs from most of them in two important respects: (1) it conceives of intelligence as an overall or* global *entity; that is, a multidetermined and multifaceted entity rather than an independent, uniquely-defined trait. (2) It avoids singling out any ability, however esteemed (e.g., abstract reasoning), as crucial or overwhelmingly important. In particular, it avoids equating general intelligence with intellectual ability. (p. 5)*

Wechsler designed his scale with subtests in order to give numerous opportunities for the clinician to assess this global entity. He spoke of these subtests as different "languages" that can be used to assess the expression of intelligence. He also points out that *he does not consider the Verbal and Performance scales to represent separate abilities*, but, rather, he considers them as two additional "languages" through which the underlying general intelligence may express itself.

STRUCTURE OF
THE WISC-III

The primary test development goals for the WISC-III included, (a) enhancing, and perhaps clarifying, the WISC factor structure; (b) improving the subtests; (c) minimization of test bias; and (d) developing supplementary materials such as a conormed achievement test (Roid, 1990). An overriding goal, however, was to keep the basic structure of the WISC intact.

The WISC-III comprises 10 mandatory and 3 supplementary subtests, all of which span the age range of 6 through 16 years. The 5 mandatory subtests on the Verbal Scale include Information, Similarities, Arithmetic, Vocabulary, and Comprehension. The supplementary subtest on the Verbal Scale is Digit Span. Traditionally, Digit Span is administered with the remainder of the Verbal subtests, although it is not included in the computation of the Verbal IQ unless one of the Verbal subtests is spoiled or invalidated, at which point it may be substituted in the computation of the Verbal IQ. Wechsler (1974) points out clearly, however, that the Digit Span score may not be substituted for a Verbal Scale subtest simply because a Verbal Scale subtest score may be low.

Similarly, the Performance scale of the WISC-III comprises five subtests: Picture Completion, Picture Arrangement, Block Design, Object Assembly, and Coding. The two supplementary subtests on the Performance scale are Mazes and Symbol Search, which (as was the case with Digit Span) are not included in the computation of the Performance IQ. The Symbol Search subtest, however, is somewhat unique in that it may only be substituted for the Coding subtest (Wechsler, 1991). The Mazes subtest, however, may be substituted for any Performance scale subtest.

The Verbal and Performance IQs are then combined in order to compute the Full Scale IQ. In the computation of the composite scores of the WISC-III, all subtests and composites are weighted equally, reflecting Wechsler's belief that all of the Wechsler subtests and scales have an equal opportunity of uncovering an individual's intelligence. The WISC-III uses standard scores for interpretation. The subtest scaled (standard) scores have a mean of 10 and standard deviation of 3, whereas the IQs have a mean of 100 and standard deviation of 15.

The WISC-III offers a new set of composites referred to as Index Scores. These are essentially factor scores which combine subtests identified by a prepublication factor analytic study that supported the existence of four factors (see later section of this chapter on factor analytic validity). The Verbal Comprehension Index score is made up of the Information, Similarities, Vocabulary, and Comprehension subtests. The Perceptual Organization Index includes Picture Completion, Picture Arrangement, Block Design, and Object Assembly. Two of the Index scores include only two subtests each. Arithmetic and Digit Span form the Freedom from Distractibility Index, and Coding and Symbol Search comprise the Processing Speed Index.

Enhancements to Subtests

The subtests of the WISC-III were targeted for substantial revision. Efforts were made to modernize artwork, reduce biased or offensive content, ease administration and scoring, and add items so as to allow the tests more range of item difficulty for the assessment of 6- and 16-year-olds (Wechsler, 1991).

The great variety of item and administration and scoring changes for the subtests is discussed in detail in the WISC-III manual (Wechsler, 1991). One of the more substantial administration changes is the placement of Picture Completion as the first test. This is a much needed reorganization, particularly for young children, who no longer will be queried in a manner that seems like an onerous inquisition to many children. The Picture Completion subtest is more innocuous and more interesting to youngsters.

Symbol Search

This new subtest was added in an attempt to clarify the controversial WISC-R third factor, often called "freedom from distractibility" (Wechsler, 1991). The WISC-R third factor included the Arithmetic, Digit Span, and Coding subtests (Kaufman, 1979b). The controversy surrounding the labeling of this third factor in a manner that best describes the major abilities assessed by the factor is legendary (this controversy will be discussed in detail in later sections). The rationale for adding the Symbol Search test was that this addition might clarify the nature of the third factor by determining whether or not attention/distractibility, short-term memory, or some other ability is central to successful performance on the third factor subtests (Wechsler, 1991). To some extent the addition of this new test clarifies the third factor; however, it also produced a new fourth factor. A proposed answer to the third factor puzzle is provided later.

Other enhancements to the WISC included modernizing artwork, collecting a new national standardization sample, and providing a more comprehensive manual.

Psychometric Properties of the WISC-III

Item and Subtest Development

Item Tryout 1

The WISC-III was first pilot-tested with a sample of 119 children. One of the goals of this first data collection effort was to test the value of the Symbol Search subtest as a measure of memory or attention that could clarify the nature of the WISC-III third factor (Wechsler, 1991).

Item Tryout 2

The second field testing of the WISC-III was conducted in 1988 with a sample of 450 children (Wechsler, 1991).

Norming

The WISC-III was normed in early 1989 using a stratified sampling procedure. The stratification variables used included age, sex, race/ethnicity, geographic region, occupation of head of household, and urban-rural residence. The sample included 200 children in each of 11 age groups from 6 through 16 years. This sampling plan produced a total of 2,200 cases in the standardization sample.

The stratification percentages for the WISC-R sample are based on 1988 U.S. Census Bureau data. There is a very close match between the standardization sample and Census Bureau statistics on all of the stratification variables.

Reliability

The internal consistency of the WISC-III is exemplary. The average internal consistency coefficient for the Full Scale IQ is .96; the Verbal IQ, .95; and the Performance IQ, .91. Average subtest coefficients range from .70 for Mazes to .87 for Vocabulary and Block Design. Mazes has particular problems at older age levels, where its internal consistency coefficient falls to .61 at age 15 and .67 at age 16. The internal consistency of Index scores is also adequate, varying from .94 for the Verbal Comprehension Index to .85 for Processing Speed.

Test-Retest Reliability

The test-retest studies described in the WISC-III manual produce stability coefficients very close to the internal consistency coefficients. However, some estimates of reliability drop precipitously. The reliability of the Performance IQ drops to .87 and the Freedom from Distractibility Index drops to .82. Several subtest coefficients drop considerably, including Picture Arrangement to .64, Object Assembly to .66, and Mazes to .57. These subtest stability coefficients are worrisome in that they suggest that many of the subtest scores are likely to be unstable. These findings should make clinicians appropriately cautious in interpreting WISC-III subtest scores.

Gain Scores

An instructive aspect of the research on the test-retest reliability of the WISC-III is the information that it provides on practice effects. The WISC-III manual shows the changes in test scores for individuals who were tested on two different occasions (an average of 23 days apart) with the WISC-III. These data suggest that the Verbal IQ changes relatively little from the first to second administration. For the study for ages 6 and 7 the Verbal IQ changed from 100.8 on the first testing to 102.5 on the second test. The Verbal IQ changes for the 10- to 11-year-olds and 14- to 15-year-olds were 100.3 to 102.2 and 99.4 to 102.7 respectively. A gain of 2 to 3 points is the typical practice effect for the Verbal IQ over the short term.

In contrast, experience with Performance scale subtests is more advantageous, as the gain from first to second testing on the Performance scale is more in the range of 11 to 13 points. The changes in the Performance IQ from first to second testing for the 6–7, 10–11, and 14–15-year-old age groups was 102.7 to 114.2, 99.0 to 112.0, and 99.6 to 112.1 respectively (see tables 5.3 through 5.5 in Wechsler, 1991). These data suggest that if a child's scores are higher by only a few points from one administration of the WISC-III to the next, the gain is likely attributable to familiarity with the test materials, or practice effects. It is also more sensible to attribute small gains in performance to practice effects since gain scores are like difference scores in one very important respect—they are more

unreliable than the composite scores themselves (see Chapter 5).

Coding and Picture Arrangement appear to be "driving" the Performance IQ gain upon retest. These tests gained anywhere from 2/3 to a full standard deviation upon retest. If these scores were expressed in the traditional IQ metric of mean = 100 and SD = 15 the gains could be as much as a change of 100 to 115. This gain is impressive. These results indicate that a child's performance could change substantially upon retest, which can be crucial for some diagnostic decisions. A child with a WISC-III profile where Verbal = 73, Performance = 73, and Full Scale = 71 is very close to the criteria for the diagnosis of mental retardation. The results of the test-retest studies portend that this child's Performance score upon retest could easily change to 84, which, in turn, could change the Full Scale to 77. This prediction also assumes that the Verbal scale would not change, which is not an accurate assumption. This child's first set of scores is very close to the mental retardation range (usually considered as a Full Scale of about 70 or below), but the second set of scores is clearly outside this range. In fact, the child's second Performance score is only somewhat below average. The Performance scale gain scores suggest that while the first score obtained is reliable, the second score may be significantly higher. This is an important distinction to draw because it makes the examiner more cautious when interpreting the Performance score the first time it is administered.

The Performance scale gain scores are only rivaled by the Perceptual Organization and Processing Speed Index scores. These composites produce gains ranging from about 9 to 11 points in the three test-retest studies (see tables 5.3 through 5.5 in Wechsler, 1991). These scores should also be expected to improve, perhaps significantly, on a second test.

Standard Error of Measurement

The standard error of measurement (SEM) is simply another way of expressing the amount of error associated with a test score (see Chapter 5). The average standard error of measurement for the Full Scale IQ across all age groups for the WISC-III is 3.20 (Wechsler, 1991). The standard error of measurement is larger for the Performance IQ (4.54) than for the Verbal IQ (3.53). A value of 3 standard score points for the SEM of the Full Scale IQ is a good rule of thumb to keep in mind when reporting scores from the WISC-III.

WISC-III SEMs for the Index scores are somewhat higher (table 5.2, Wechsler, 1991). These SEM values range from 3.78 for the Verbal Comprehension Index to 5.83 for the Processing Speed Index.

Validity

Item Bias

The manual reports that efforts were made to eliminate item bias using both statistical and judgmental methods (Wechsler, 1991). Tryout and standardization data were both analyzed to detect items that were exceedingly difficult for one group of children despite controlling for overall ability level. Analyses were conducted to assess ethnic, gender, and regional bias. This procedure resulted in the elimination and modification of items primarily on the Information, Vocabulary, and Comprehension subtests (Wechsler, 1991).

The actual results of these bias analyses and reviews are not presented in the manual. Nor is there any indication that they are available upon request. Presumably independent studies of bias will soon become available that can help clinicians evaluate a child's responses to individual items.

Age Differentiation

Mean raw scores by age group are not provided in the WISC-III manual. Hence, age differentiation validity has to be inferred from the norm tables. The norm tables do provide a good range of scores for each subtest, and the IQ scores produce a range of 40 to 160. The index scores, however, do not produce much differentiation at low- and high-score levels, with scores ranging from 50 to 150.

Concurrent Validity

Correlations between the WISC-III and other intelligence tests are high. Concurrent validity studies reported in the manual show the WISC-III Full Scale to correlate .89 with the WISC-R, .86 with the WAIS-R, .85 with the WPPSI-R, and .92 with the Differential Ability Scales.

While the rank orders of these scores for various tests are likely to be similar, there are consistent mean score differences. In these same studies the Full Scale score of the WISC-III was 5 points lower than for the WISC-R, 4 points lower than WAIS-R, 4 points higher than WPPSI-R, and 2 points higher than the DAS. Weiss (1991) explains that the WISC-III should produce lower scores than the WISC-R because of the out of date standardization sample of the latter. Weiss (1991) provides a sample explanation for parents about the changes in norms, which may also be helpful to others trying to conceptualize the issue:

> *Often the pediatrician will tell the parent that their child's height or weight is in a certain percentile for children his/her age. These charts are (or should be) based on a contemporary sample. Using older charts, the same child would have a higher percentile ranking. This is because children are generally taller now than they were 20 years ago, so an average child today will appear tall when compared to average children 20 years ago. The same is true of intelligence. Children are generally smarter now than they were 20 years ago. So, children need to do better than before just to get an average score. (p. 8)*

This point of view is highly consistent with the research cited in Chapter 5 showing the generational changes in norms. Moreover, the differences between the two sets of Wechsler scale norms are mostly due to changes in the difficulty of Performance scale items. WISC-III Performance scale scores were found to be about 8 points lower than for WISC-R, whereas Verbal scores were only about 3 points lower than their WISC-R counterpart.

On the other hand, why would the WAIS-R score so much higher than the WISC-III? And why would the WPPSI-R, published in 1989, score lower than the WISC-III? These differences are likely due to differences in content, ceiling and floor effects, and other factors. Such routine differences between the WISC-III and other test scores should be taken into account when making diagnostic decisions, in addition to considering the SEM of the WISC-III and other measures.

The manual data for exceptional samples are also revealing. The WISC-III produced a Full Scale score approximately 9 points lower than the WISC-R for a sample of 43 children diagnosed as mentally retarded. In direct contrast, the WISC-III produced a Full Scale IQ approximately 5 points lower than the WISC-R for a sample of 23 children who were identified as gifted. These results suggest that while on the average WISC-III scores may be 5 points lower than on the WISC-R, the differences may be more substantial for children diagnosed as mentally retarded. Further research with exceptional samples is needed.

Predictive Validity

A central issue in intellectual assessment is the importance of showing that intelligence measurement is highly related to some important criterion, which in most cases is school achievement. The WISC-III follows in the tradition of other intelligence tests by showing substantial correlations between its IQ scores and measures of academic achievement. A number of investigations have shown that the WISC-R is predictive of future school achievement as measured by achievement tests (Kaufman,

1979b; Reilly et al., 1985; McGrew & Pehl, 1988). Typically, predictive validity coefficients are in the range of .50 to .65. While these correlations are not overwhelming, they are significant and stable over a number of investigations (Kaufman, 1979b). More recently, Figueroa and Sassenrath (1989) found the WISC-R Full Scale IQ to have predictive validity coefficients ranging from .49 to .64 when predicting reading and mathematics scores over a *10-year period*. A study of 358 children cited in the WISC-III manual produced significant correlations with a variety of group-administered achievement tests. Correlations of WISC-III scores with total achievement were .74 for the Full Scale and .74 for the Verbal scale. The Performance scale correlation with achievement was considerably lower at .57.

An important finding from concurrent and predictive validity studies is that the Verbal scale of the WISC-R and WISC-III is more highly correlated with school achievement than the Performance scale (Figueroa & Sassenrath, 1989). This relationship is sensible from a number of vantage points, especially considering the content that is included in the Verbal scale subtests. The Arithmetic subtest, for example, includes items that are highly related to school instruction. Similarly, Information and Vocabulary contain items that are likely influenced by various aspects of school instruction. These findings give further credence to Anastasi's (1988) conceptualization of intelligence tests (see Chapter 2). The Verbal IQ of the WISC-III in particular should be regarded as a specialized type of achievement measure. Kaufman (1979b) argues that the Performance IQ should be conceptualized similarly—that is, as a measure of what a child has learned.

These relationships with academic achievement are clarified somewhat by the correlations of the WISC-III Index scores with achievement. In the aforementioned investigation of 358 youngsters the Verbal Comprehension Index (VCI) correlated highest with total achievement at .70. The Freedom from Distractibility Index (FDI) was next at .63. The Perceptual Organization Index (POI) and the Processing Speed Index (PSI) were the poorest correlates with achievement with coefficients of .56 and .50. In another study with the Wide Range Achievement Test-Revised (WRAT-R), the VCI and FDI were again higher correlates with achievement than the POI and PSI. There was an exception to this rule in that the PSI was a high correlate of mathematics scores on the WRAT (.73) (Wechsler, 1991).

VERBAL COMPREHENSION	PERCEPTUAL ORGANIZATION	FREEDOM FROM DISTRACTIBILITY
Information	Picture Completion	Arithmetic
Similarities	Picture Arrangement	Digit Span
Vocabulary	Block Design	Coding
Comprehension	Object Assembly	
	Mazes	

Factor Analysis: WISC-R

The factor structure of the WISC-R is important to understand as a backdrop to factor studies of the WISC-III. There are many studies, using many samples, that have evaluated the factor structure of the 1949 WISC and WISC-R (Reynolds & Kaufman, 1990).

Like many intelligence tests, the WISC-R produced a large first or general intelligence "g" factor (see Chapter 5). The large WISC-R "g" factor also supported the WISC-R, yielding an overall composite score, or, to use WISC-R terminology, the Full Scale IQ (the combination of the Verbal and Performance IQs) (Wallbrown et al., 1975). The results of studies of "g" loadings suggest that tests such as Digit Span, Coding, and Mazes prove to be interpretive challenges, as they may frequently be deviant from the overall trend in a child's scores.

One of the consistent findings in the WISC-R factor analytic literature was the robust nature of its three-factor structure (Reynolds & Kaufman, 1990). Kaufman's (1975) seminal investigation showed the WISC-R to have a very comparable factor structure to its predecessor, the 1949 WISC, including three factors that are easily labeled Verbal Comprehension, Perceptual Organization, and Freedom from Distractibility. The 12 subtests of the WISC-R correspond to the three factors, as shown below.

The three-factor structure of the WISC-R has been shown to be consistent for a variety of populations. These same three factors have emerged for learning-disabled children (Naglieri, 1981b), learning-disabled children tested on two occasions 3 years apart (Juliano, Haddad, & Carroll, 1988), and mildly mentally retarded children (Cummins & Das, 1980). Another consistent finding in these investigations is that the Freedom from Distractibility factor is small. It accounts for a small proportion of variance in comparison to the first two factors. As a result, the Verbal and Performance scales of the WISC-R have long been considered to have adequate construct validity as assessed by factor analysis. The third factor, or Freedom from Distractibility factor, was the only blemish on this otherwise favorable picture of validity for the Verbal and Performance scales. The "Freedom from Distractibility" label comes from the work of Cohen (1959) on the original WISC. The Freedom from Distractibility factor (hereafter referred to as the WISC-R "third factor") has been enigmatic (Kaufman, 1979b), with a number of alternative names for this factor being proposed including attention/distractibility, anxiety, symbolic ability, sequential processing, and memory (Reynolds & Kaufman, 1990).

Some researchers voiced dissenting opinions on the labels applied to the WISC-R factors. Most notably, Wallbrown et al. (1975) proposed application of Vernon's (1950) hierarchical model (see Chapter 2) of intelligence to the WISC-R. At the top of the hierarchy is "g" or general intelligence. The two lower levels in the hierarchy, the major group factors according to Vernon, are Verbal-Educational-Numerical (V:ed) and Spatial-Practical-Manual-Mechanical (K:m). In the Wallbrown et al. (1975) investigation, the Verbal Conceptualization and Perceptual Organization factors were renamed Verbal-Educational and Spatial-Mechanical, consistent with Vernon's theory. Silverstein (1982a) concluded that there was only a slight advantage for three- versus two-factor WISC-R solutions.

The label of Verbal-Educational for the first WISC-R factor was also supported by a recent investigation by Kaufman and McClean (1987). These researchers performed a joint factor analysis for 212 nonhandicapped children on the WISC-R and the K-ABC. The Verbal subtests of the WISC-R and the Achievement subtests of the K-ABC showed a great deal of congruence; all loaded on the same first factor (see Chapter 9). The term "educational" from Vernon's theory seems comparable to the term "achievement" from Kaufman's conceptualization for the K-ABC, implying that there is a heavy emphasis on the assessment of academic skills for the Verbal subtests. These findings are also consistent with the aforementioned predictive validity data on the WISC-R showing that the Verbal scale is considerably more predictive of future school success than the Performance scale.

In summary, there are several important lessons to be learned from the factor analytic research on the WISC-R. The more pertinent of these findings include:

1. There was strong factor analytic support for the Full Scale IQ.

2. There was strong factor analytic support for the Verbal and Performance IQs.

3. There was strong support for the third factor, but little agreement as to what it measures. The third factor was also smaller in comparison to the Verbal and Performance factors.

4. Some subtests such as the Coding, Picture Arrangement, and Digit Span subtests more frequently emerged as deviant subtests that are difficult to interpret.

Factor Analysis: WISC-III

The factor analysis of the WISC-III reported in the manual produces some interesting findings (Wechsler, 1991) in that there are numerous points of agreement with tradition and yet some disagreement. Findings of agreement will be considered first.

Points of Agreement

The WISC-III produces two factors that correspond fairly well to the Verbal and Performance scales. The verbal factor has strong average loadings for the Information (.72), Similarities (.72), Vocabulary (.79), and Comprehension (.65) subtests. The Arithmetic subtest also loads on this factor at .41.

The perceptual organization factor remains intact, but it is less well supported, consisting primarily of three subtests. This factor is defined by strong loadings for Picture Completion (.53), Block Design (.70), and Object Assembly (.69). As was the case with the WISC-R, Picture Arrangement has a mediocre loading on this factor (.37), as does Mazes (.36).

Picture Arrangement (PA) not only loads poorly on the perceptual organization factor; it does not affiliate itself with any WISC-III factor. Picture Arrangement loaded .33 on the verbal factor, .37 on the performance factor, .08 on the third factor, and .25 on the processing speed factor (Wechsler, 1991). These data suggest that PA will continue to be difficult to interpret because of its allegiance to numerous factors and composites.

Digit Span (DS) is similar to PA in that it is not strongly linked with a particular factor. This test loads .26 on verbal, .19 on performance, .34 on the third factor, and .18 on the processing speed factor (Wechsler, 1991). Digit

Span is also not likely to consistently align itself with a particular composite.

Points of Disagreement

The addition of the Symbol Search subtest did not strengthen the "distractibility" factor as was anticipated. The Symbol Search subtest helped create a new fourth factor (based on an exploratory factor analysis with varimax rotation) labeled "processing speed," which is marked by high loadings for Coding (.79) and Symbol Search (.46). No other subtests have substantial loadings on this factor. This finding of a new fourth factor raises the question of the clarity of the third factor.

The WISC-III third factor differs substantially from that of the WISC-R. This factor is now marked by only two subtests—Arithmetic (.73) and Digit Span (34). The label now assigned to this factor is "freedom from distractibility." This label is questionable at best given the history of controversy surrounding the identification of the unifying ability underlying it (Kaufman, 1979b; see also Chapter 15). One recent writer argued for dropping the "freedom from distractibility" label by commenting, "Would it not therefore make more sense to abandon this terminology now so that individuals would be less likely to make faulty assumptions?" (Little, 1991, p. 24). The WISC-III third factor seems even more difficult to label because of the pattern of loadings of its two subtests. The loadings for the Arithmetic subtest are consistently high, ranging from .54 for 8- to 10-year-olds to .85 for ages 14–16. The Arithmetic subtest also has consistent secondary loadings on the verbal factor (average = .41). As was previously cited, the Digit Span loadings show no particular allegiance to a factor. While its mean loading on the third factor is .34, its average loading on the verbal factor is .26, which is not a substantial difference. There is no early evidence that the WISC-III third factor is any more interpretable than the third factor for the WISC-R. Researchers can still argue for previous interpretations ranging from distractibility, to numerical facility, to auditory short-term memory. Further studies are needed comparing the third factor to measures of numerical facility, distractibility, and so on to assist the clinician in interpretation of this factor. Some studies have suggested that distractibility is not the most appropriate label for this set of tests (see Chapter 15).

Similarly, the labeling of the new fourth factor as processing speed should be considered as tentative pending the outcome of future studies of the relationship of this factor to other measures of processing speed. There is the potential for irony here in that the new fourth factor may turn out to be more interpretable and meaningful than the new third factor.

Interpretive Implications of Factor Analysis

The implications of these findings for interpretive purposes are myriad. My experience has shown me that many a case will agree with factor analytic findings. The clinician who understands these findings has a clear sense of how the WISC-III subtests are likely to covary for most children. This allows the clinician to know when test results are likely attributed to normal variation and when they are anomalous and therefore clinically meaningful. At a minimum the WISC-III factor analyses teach us the following lessons about expected covariation on the WISC-III.

1. The Verbal and Performance scales remain interpretable for the most part. The PA subtest, however, does not appear to belong on the Performance scale. Alternate subtests such as Digit Span and Mazes also do not load well on the Verbal and Performance scales respectively. These subtests at least do not dilute the meaning of their scales because they are typically not included in the computation of the composite as is PA.

2. The third factor should not be routinely

referred to as "distractibility." Clinicians are left to their own devices in interpreting this factor. They will only be able to interpret the factor in light of other data. If, for example, a child with a mathematics disability has a depressed third-factor score, then numerical facility may be a plausible reason for the low score. This type of case-by-case interpretation is the only reasonable course until convincing concurrent and predictive validation studies are conducted.

3.   The fourth factor possesses evidence of factorial validity but not evidence of criterion-related or predictive validity. Pending such research this factor should also be considered as supplementary and only interpreted in the context of case data that are compelling.

4.   Arithmetic is the marker task for the third factor, yet it has a substantial secondary loading on the verbal comprehension factor. The Arithmetic subtest is therefore only slightly more likely to align itself with the third factor than with the Verbal IQ. As such, clinicians evaluating the profile for a particular child should not be surprised to see the Arithmetic subtest align itself with either the Verbal IQ or the third-factor subtests Digit Span and Coding.

5.   Also noteworthy from these factor analytic results is that Digit Span bears little relationship to the Verbal IQ, despite the fact that it is placed on this scale. The Digit Span subtest, therefore, is not a good substitute for other verbal tests that have been spoiled or have somehow been invalidated. Perhaps *prorating*, the process of computing an estimated IQ when one or more subtests are missing for either the Verbal or Performance IQ, is a better option than substituting a Digit Span score (see the WISC-III manual for discussion of prorating procedures).

6.   Clearly, Block Design and Object Assembly are the marker Perceptual Organization tasks contributing to the Performance IQ. Picture Arrangement, on the other hand, has a mediocre loading on the perceptual organization factor (.37). Picture Arrangement is less likely than other Performance subtests to align itself with

the Performance IQ. In addition, the Picture Arrangement subtest has slightly smaller secondary loadings on the fourth factor and on the verbal comprehension factor. Consequently, *the Picture Arrangement subtest score is more likely than most WISC-III subtests to be a maverick or outlier* in the profile for an individual child.

7.   The Coding subtest, despite its placement as an alternative Performance scale test, is not a strong member of the Performance IQ, similar to the way Digit Span shares little variance with the Verbal IQ making it a poor substitute if one of the Performance scale subtests is spoiled. Coding, then, may frequently be found to be deviant from the remainder of the Performance subtests.

8.   The new Symbol Search test actually has a better perceptual organization factor loading (.35 versus .13) than the Coding subtest. This subtest may be an equally suitable Performance scale alternate as Coding.

9.   Given the preliminary nature of the processing speed factor and the controversial nature of the third factor, these factors are only advised for use by experienced WISC-III examiners, and only by these individuals if future validity studies are supportive of these factors.

ADMINISTRATION

The WISC-III administration procedures are consistent with the history of psychological assessment. For example, while many newer tests such as the K-ABC, Woodcock-Johnson, and Binet-4 use an easel format where the various stimuli and instructions are self-contained, the WISC-III test stimuli and manual are separate from one another. The WISC-III, in contrast to the WISC-R, obviates the need for purchasing a bookstand because of the "crack back" manual that stands on its own. Administration of the WISC-III can be rather awkward for the new examiner, since both the manual and the test stimuli have to be manipulated separately.

The WISC-III also places a premium on the use of a stopwatch. The stopwatch has also been supplanted by newer tests that place more emphasis on power than speed. Since the WISC-III makes heavy use of a stopwatch, it is incumbent on the examiner to develop skill in its use. Examiners should not expect use of the stopwatch to come naturally, as it takes a great deal of practice for most.

Some of the examiner instructions on the WISC-III are wordy. Examiners therefore have to do their best to make the testing seem less contrived in spite of this. Examiners have to achieve this, however, without shortcutting or modifying the standardized wording. *The standardized wording must be used* (see Chapter 4).

The new examiner must also study the starting points and discontinue rules for each subtest carefully. On the WISC-III these rules differ considerably for each subtest. On Information, for example, there are four different starting points depending on a child's age. By contrast, on Comprehension every child begins with Item 1.

SCORING

For the most part the WISC-III is easy and objective to score. The scoring of some subtests can still be tricky for new examiners. While the scoring of Mazes is objective, it does take some time and practice. Similarly, awarding partial credit for the Object Assembly items can be tricky. For partially complete items the raw score is equal to the "number of correct junctures." New examiners would benefit from practice in giving partial credit for various arrangements of puzzle pieces.

Scoring Verbal Responses

The Similarities, Vocabulary, and Comprehension tests were particularly difficult for new ex-

aminers to score correctly (Slate & Chick, 1989). It is not clear how much easier the scoring of these verbal tests will be for the WISC-III. These tests are unusual because of their use of a trichotomous scoring system (scores of 2, 1, 0). Most modern tests eschew such a system and use dichotomous scoring for vocabulary and similar tests. The WISC-III tries to ease scoring of these tests by placing scoring criteria adjacent to the item. The advantage of such a trichotomous system is that it requires more verbal expression on the part of the child, which provides the examiner with rich observations of the child's verbal skills.

In order to use the discontinue rules for each of these tests appropriately, one should commit the scoring criteria for each item to memory. This task, however, is difficult to accomplish. A frequent error made by my students is to score a questionable response from memory when the exact response given by the child is listed verbatim in the scoring criteria accompanying the item. I suggest that for a questionable response, new examiners should *read every response given in the scoring criteria for the item before assigning a score to the response.*

Computing Derived Scores

The computation of WISC-III raw and derived scores is simple. Clinicians do have to be careful when adding item scores to obtain a raw score. A frequently made mistake is to fail to give a child credit for items not administered *prior* to the starting point for a particular subtest.

Subtest scaled scores (standard scores with a mean of 10 and SD of 3) are easily obtained from table A.1 of the WISC-III manual. The Wechsler IQ equivalents (standard scores with a mean of 100 and SD of 15) are then computed based on the sums of scaled scores using tables A.2 through A.4. Index scores are provided in tables A.5 through A.7. The Index scores are the alternative "IQ equivalents" for the four factor scores. These standard scores also use the mean = 100 and SD = 15 metric.

One oft made mistake of new examiners is to pick raw scores off the front of the record form when writing a report. New examiners may want to highlight the standard scores to avoid this frequent and embarrassing mistake.

Confidence bands for the WISC-III are included with the composite score norm tables in the manual. Examiners will note that the WISC-III form offers asymmetrical confidence bands (see Chapter 5). For most cases a 90% confidence level is reasonable to use (Kaufman, 1979b).

Age equivalents and prorating tables are also given in the WISC-III manual. The numerous WISC-III interpretive tables will be discussed in Chapter 7.

THE WECHSLER SUBTESTS

This section discusses some of the distinctive aspects of each subtest. Most of the WISC-III subtests have a long and rich clinical history. Understanding the origins of the item types and formats of the individual subtests is crucial to an integrative approach to interpretation. The description of each subtest will begin with an overview of the nature of the task, its history, and any distinctive aspects. Any noteworthy characteristics having to do with administration and scoring will then be addressed. Common problems and tips for beginners are also delineated. This section, however, is not a substitute but a supplement to the WISC-III manual.

Next some important psychometric characteristics for each test that have implications for interpretation are listed. The reliability coefficients reported are median internal consistency coefficients from the WISC-III manual (Wechsler, 1991). The factor analytic results are median loadings taken from the factor analysis of the WISC-III standardization sample cited in the manual (Wechsler, 1991). The "g" loadings and reliable specific variance (subtest specificity) estimates were computed based on the in-

tercorrelation matrix of the WISC-III subtests for all ages combined[1] (Wechsler, 1991).

A list of noteworthy behaviors for examiners to observe during testing is also provided. These behaviors can be helpful for testing hypotheses about a child's performance. Finally, hypotheses regarding variables that may influence subtest performance are provided. The interpretive process that is used to test these hypotheses will be discussed in detail in the following chapter. These lists are offered in this chapter to help the examiner better understand the range of possible skills and behaviors that influence each WISC-III subtest.

Picture Completion

On Picture Completion the child has to identify the missing part in a picture. This test is an analog of a similar test from the Army examinations from World War I (Reynolds & Kaufman, 1990). Picture Completion is a nonthreatening introduction to the Performance scale (Zimmerman & Woo-Sam, 1985) and to the WISC-III as a whole. This test has a sample item that allows the child ample opportunity to understand the nature of the test demands. Similarly, for young children, beginning with item 1 the examiner may model the correct response for the child who misses either items 1 or 2.

A stopwatch or other timing device is used on the Picture Completion subtest to time the 20-second maximum response time, resulting in associated anxiety on the part of some children and adolescents. Children sometimes approach the task impulsively by giving a response before taking the time to survey the picture. The examiner should note whether or not a child tends to respond verbally or prefers pointing, for which credit is also given.

---

[1] The "g" loadings used for this chapter represent the loading for each subtest on the unrotated first principal component. The subtest specificities were computed in the same fashion as in Kaufman (1979b). These values were computed by subtracting the squared multiple correlation of each subtest from its average internal consistency coefficient. I am indebted to Dr. Leslie Oliver Platt for her expeditious computation of these values.

A child's negativism may also be observed on this subtest (Zimmerman & Woo-Sam, 1985). This tendency is reflected for some children with comments such as "nothing is missing." This comment results in the examiner having to practice the art of encouraging the child to try without giving clues or pushing the child to respond to the point of frustration.

Some students of mine have substituted verbal bludgeoning for encouragement in this situation. The examiner has to "read" carefully the child's reaction to encouragement, and discontinue prodding when it is clear that the child is becoming frustrated.

Administration and Scoring Pointers

1. Practice using a stopwatch for timing short intervals (20 seconds).
2. Practice the verbal cues used to follow up responses.

Psychometric Properties

Average reliability = .77

"g" loading = .60

Loading on verbal comprehension factor = .38

Loading on perceptual organization factor = .53

Loading on third factor = .10

Loading on fourth factor = .08

Subtest specificity = .39 (ample)

Behaviors to Note

1. Squinting or other behavior suggesting difficulty seeing the stimuli
2. Excessive concern and interest in turning the cards
3. Excessive attention to the timing device

Cognitive Hypotheses to Investigate

1. Knowledge base

2. Holistic (simultaneous) processing (Luria, Das)
3. Coping with novelty (Sternberg)
4. Perceptual organization (factor analysis)
5. Spatial ability
6. Part-whole relationships
7. Perceptual speed (Thurstone)
8. Executive system (Borkowski)

Biographical and Behavioral Hypotheses to Investigate

1. Anxiety related to the timing device
2. Willingness to venture a response or guess when uncertain
3. Attention span/impulsivity
4. Visual acuity and discrimination

Information

The Information subtest requires the child to answer factual questions presented by the examiner. This test is an adaptation of tests developed by the Army to screen recruits for World War I (Reynolds & Kaufman, 1990).

The Information subtest gives the examiner a sense of the child's cultural, linguistic, and educational background. A foreign-born child, for example, may be unable to identify Christopher Columbus (Item 13). Similarly, a child whose primary language is Spanish may have difficulty articulating some of the responses such as months and seasons of the year in English. A child who is the product of an impoverished family or a poor educational experience may show substantial gaps in his or her knowledge base.

The Information items for the most part are perceived as being innocuous. Accordingly, a child's indignant response or refusal to complete the task is highly significant (Zimmerman & Woo-Sam, 1985).

Administration and Scoring Pointers

1. Be prepared to give the supplemental queries associated with some items (e.g., Item 26).

Psychometric Properties

Average reliability = .84

"g" loading = .78

Loading on verbal comprehension factor = .72

Loading on perceptual organization factor = .29

Loading on third factor = .25

Loading on fourth factor = .09

Subtest specificity = .25 (adequate)

Behaviors to Note

1. Seeming familiarity with the item but struggle to remember the specific response
2. Self-deprecating statements
3. Comments about schooling
4. Comments about the difficulty of the items
5. Long response latency
6. Unwillingness to respond or guess when uncertain
7. Strong desire to know the correct answer
8. Requesting repetitions from examiner

Cognitive Hypotheses to Investigate

1. Knowledge base (acquired knowledge or fund of information)
2. Verbal expressive skill
3. Long-term memory
4. Knowledge acquisition components (Sternberg)
5. Verbal comprehension (factor analysis)
6. General intelligence (factor analysis)
7. Verbal meaning (Thurstone)
8. Crystallized ability (Cattell)
9. Executive system (Borkowski)
10. Social science knowledge

Biographical and Behavioral Hypotheses to Investigate

1. Quality of schooling
2. English language proficiency
3. Acculturation (familiarity with American culture)
4. Parental cognitive stimulation
5. Achievement motivation
6. Interest in reading

Coding

The Coding subtest requires a child to copy letter and number-like symbols according to a specified pattern as quickly as possible. This test measures a great deal of motor skill akin to clerical aptitude tests that have been used in military and employment testing for generations. It requires some visual perception skill to recognize the code, and the ability to remember the code can be quite advantageous to success. Some fine motor skill is also required to complete the items expeditiously. This test has unnecessarily long instructions. Examiners will find it very difficult to read the instructions verbatim when a child obviously understands what to do. The examiner must persevere nonetheless.

Administration and Scoring Pointers

1. Be sure to use a pencil without an eraser.
2. Use only the standardized instructions given.

Psychometric Properties

Average reliability = .79

"g" loading = .41

Loading on verbal comprehension factor = .11

Loading on perceptual organization factor = .13

Loading on third factor = .09

Loading on fourth factor = .79

Subtest specificity = .49 (ample)

Behaviors to Note

1. Rechecking the code indicating that it is not memorized

2. Squinting or other evidence of difficulty seeing

3. Poor motor control

Cognitive Hypotheses to Investigate

1. Fluid ability (Cattell)

2. Clerical speed and accuracy

3. Sequencing or successive processing (Luria, Das)

4. Coping with novelty (Sternberg)

5. Pencil and paper skill

6. Short-term memory (information processing theory)

7. Following instructions

8. Level I processing (Jensen)

9. Visual-Motor coordination

Biographical and Behavioral Hypotheses to Investigate

1. Visual acuity and discrimination

2. Anxiety related to the stopwatch

3. Attention span/impulsivity

4. Achievement motivation

5. Fatigue or boredom

Similarities

On this test the child has to orally identify a unifying attribute for two verbal concepts. Similarities can trace its roots to the work of Binet, who used similar tasks at the turn of the century (Reynolds & Kaufman, 1990). This subtest is a rather unusual test of concept formation in that all of the verbal stimuli used, even on the more difficult items, are familiar to most children. As such, vocabulary knowledge is not as much of a factor on this test as it may first appear. The crucial issue for the child to grasp is the notion of "sameness." Some young children never fully grasp this concept.

Administration and Scoring Pointers

1. Become extremely familiar with the trichotomous scoring system prior to administration.

Psychometric Properties

Average reliability = .81

"g" loading = .77

Loading on verbal comprehension factor = .72

Loading on perceptual organization factor = .29

Loading on third factor = .23

Loading on fourth factor = .09

Subtest specificity = .23 (adequate)

Behaviors to Note

1. Preponderance of 1-point responses indicative of more concrete thinking

2. A tendency to "talk around" the issue

Cognitive Hypotheses to Investigate

1. Verbal expression

2. Categorical thinking

3. Level II processing (Jensen)

4. Knowledge base

5. Verbal comprehension (factor analysis)

6. Inductive reasoning (Thurstone)

7. Verbal meaning (Thurstone)

8. Executive system (Borkowski)

Biographical and Behavioral Hypotheses to Investigate

1. Quality of schooling

2. English language proficiency

3. Achievement motivation

4. Interest in reading

5. Parental cognitive stimulation

Picture Arrangement

This test requires the child to arrange cards depicting a scene from a story in their correct sequence. Picture Arrangement was also originally developed during the World War I screening effort (Reynolds & Kaufman, 1990). This test assesses whether or not the child can follow a story line given in pictures. This component is probably one of the reasons why this test has a significant factor loading on the verbal comprehension factor in some investigations. Clearly, children will be helped if they are able to verbally identify the plot (although this is usually done subvocally by children taking the test) and to explain the order of the pictures. Generally, however, this test can be difficult to interpret as it has mediocre loadings on three of the four WISC-III factors (save factor 3). In fact, when five-factor exploratory factor analysis solutions were computed for the WISC-III, the Picture Arrangement subtest occasionally produced its own factor, particularly at younger age groups (Weschler, 1991). This failure to align itself clearly with a factor makes it enigmatic.

Administration and Scoring Pointers

1. Always replace pictures in the box *in layout order* so that they are ready for the next administration.

2. Practice the procedures for modeling and giving second trials.

Psychometric Properties

Average reliability = .76

"g" loading = .53

Loading on verbal comprehension factor = .33

Loading on perceptual organization factor = .37

Loading on third factor = .08

Loading on fourth factor = .25

Subtest specificity = .48 (ample)

Behaviors to Note

1. Gives several responses in reverse sequence

2. Does not survey the cards before responding

Cognitive Hypotheses to Investigate

1. Social judgment

2. Knowledge base

3. Inferring cause and effect relationships

4. Executive system (Borkowski)

5. Fine motor skill

6. Sequential processing (Luria, Das)

Biographical and Behavioral Hypotheses to Investigate

1. Anxiety related to the stopwatch

2. Experience with comic strips

3. Experiences with social interaction

4. Attention span/impulsivity

5. Visual acuity and discrimination

Arithmetic

The Arithmetic subtest requires the child to answer applied mathematical questions that are, for the most part, presented orally by the examiner. This subtest is probably the most school-like of any subtest on the WISC-III. It is essentially a test made of "word problems." Arithmetic, however, does differ from mathematics testing in school in a number of ways. This test has a distinct speed component. Rarely is a child's mathematics problem solving clocked by a stopwatch. For the child who is insecure about his or her mathematics ability, the timing of performance may be especially threatening.

This test is also rather unusual in that the child is not allowed to use aids such as pencil and paper or a calculator. This format makes the task unrealistic in comparison to everyday mathematics calculation tests.

Finally, the Arithmetic test is not a comprehensive test of mathematics knowledge, and in some cases it may not even serve well as a screener. This situation is primarily due to the fact that the Arithmetic test lacks evidence of content validity. Evidence has not been presented to support the item selection for Arithmetic or to assess the degree to which the items reflect the content domain of mathematics. This lack of content validity is most clearly seen for adolescents. Adolescents are not asked to use estimation, measurement, graphing, or many other skills that they have been taught. Hence, while the Arithmetic test is school-like, performance depends primarily on whether or not the child has acquired basic skills. It does differ enough from the arithmetic tests that children encounter in school that clinicians should not expect scores from this test to always agree with mathematics scores from the child's school, or even with parents' or teachers' report of a child's mathematics performance in school. I have often evaluated adolescents who are failing mathematics coursework and yet achieve an average score on the Arithmetic subtest.

The Arithmetic subtest also has a significant and consistent secondary factor loading on the verbal comprehension factor (see below). Hence, although this test marks the third factor, it may also be influenced to some extent by verbal skills, perhaps above and beyond mental calculation skills.

Administration and Scoring Pointers

1. Be sure to time each item.

Psychometric Properties

Average reliability = .78

"g" loading = .76

Loading on verbal comprehension factor = .41

Loading on perceptual organization factor = .27

Loading on third factor = .73

Loading on fourth factor = .15

Subtest specificity = .30 (adequate)

Behaviors to Note

1. Self-deprecating statements about mathematics skills

2. Comments about schooling

3. "Rushes" to beat the stopwatch

Cognitive Hypotheses to Investigate

1. Mathematics knowledge

2. Number (Thurstone)

3. Crystallized ability (Cattell)

4. Short-term memory (information processing)

5. Long-term memory (information processing)

6. Knowledge acquisition components (Sternberg)

7. Level II processing (Jensen)

8. Architectural system (Borkowski)

Biographical and Behavioral Hypotheses to Investigate

1. Anxiety related to mathematics or stopwatch

2. Quality of schooling

3. Attention span/impulsivity

4. Achievement motivation

5. Auditory acuity and discrimination

6. Attitude toward mathematics

7. English language proficiency

Block Design

On this task the child is required to construct designs out of blocks to match a model. Block Design is a variant of a test developed in the early part of this century by Kohs (1923). Block Design has a distinctly spatial component and requires a minimal level of fine motor skill to make the necessary constructions. The spatial aspects of the task are emphasized in the scoring, in which rotations of greater than 30 degrees are scored as incorrect. Scoring rotations suggest that they are pathological (possibly indicative of something like a brain insult), although there are no data to document this. Again, speed becomes an important factor on this test, as additional points are awarded for quick responses. Consequently, it is crucial to use the standardized procedures, which make it clear that a child should not dawdle. Some very intelligent children may obtain average scores on this test because they were more concerned with accuracy than speed. Two children can obtain average scores on this test in very different ways. A child can achieve a scaled score of 10 by working quickly and getting a few items wrong. A child can also work slowly, get all of the items correct, and still get a 10.

This test has been raised to preeminence by research on split-brain patients (Springer & Deutsch, 1981) (see Chapter 2). In a number of studies, Block Design was used as a marker task of right brain (holistic) processing. In contrast, Schorr, Bower, and Kiernan (1982) tested two strategies for solving Block Design items: "an analytic strategy in which subjects mentally segment each block in the design to be constructed and a synthetic strategy, which involves wholistic pattern matching" (p. 479). These authors found that the analytic strategy was dominant in a series of four experiments. Schorr, Bower, and Kiernan (1982) also theorize that it is the inability to employ an analytic strategy that adversely affects the Block Design performance of brain-injured individuals.

Administration and Scoring Pointers

1. Practice modeling and administering second trials.
2. Practice scoring rotations.

Psychometric Properties

Average reliability = .87

"g" loading = .71

Loading on verbal comprehension factor = .29

Loading on perceptual organization factor = .70

Loading on third factor = .24

Loading on fourth factor = .17

Subtest specificity = .34 (ample)

Behaviors to Note

1. Attempts to align the sides of the blocks in addition to the tops
2. Excessive frustration over failures on difficult items

Cognitive Hypotheses to Investigate

1. General intelligence (factor analysis)
2. Spatial ability
3. Holistic (simultaneous) processing (Luria, Das)
4. Coping with novelty (Sternberg)
5. Fine motor coordination
6. Visual-motor coordination
7. Fluid ability (Cattell)
8. Executive system (Borkowski)
9. Perceptual organization (factor analysis)
10. Right hemisphere processing (split-brain research)

Biographical and Behavioral Hypotheses to Investigate

1. Attention span/impulsivity

2. Anxiety related to the stopwatch

3. Achievement motivation

4. Visual acuity and discrimination

Vocabulary

The Vocabulary test requires a child to orally define words presented by the examiner. The Vocabulary test follows in the tradition of Binet's emphasis on the assessment of higher-level cognitive skills. This format creates the opportunity for the examiner to assess how eloquently a child expresses his or her thoughts. The open-ended response format of the test also allows the child to express information of great clinical importance (e.g., "a knife is for killing people" from the WISC-R).

Administration and Scoring Pointers

1. Read the scoring guide completely before scoring a questionable response.

Psychometric Properties

Average reliability = .87

"g" loading = .80

Loading on verbal comprehension factor = .79

Loading on perceptual organization factor = .22

Loading on third factor = .18

Loading on fourth factor = .16

Subtest specificity = .24 (adequate)

Behaviors to Note

1. Word retrieval (finding) problems

2. Preponderance of 1-point responses

3. Misarticulation

Cognitive Hypotheses to Investigate

1. Knowledge base

2. Verbal expression

3. Long-term memory (information processing)

4. Knowledge acquisition components (Sternberg)

5. Verbal comprehension (factor analysis)

6. General intelligence (factor analysis)

7. Verbal meaning (Thurstone)

8. Crystallized ability (Cattell)

9. Executive system (Borkowski)

10. Vocabulary knowledge

Biographical and Behavioral Hypotheses to Investigate

1. Parental cognitive stimulation

2. Quality of schooling

3. Achievement motivation

4. Interest in reading

5. English language proficiency

Object Assembly

This test is also an analog of a test from the World War I effort (Reynolds & Kaufman, 1990). Object Assembly, like Block Design, has a strong spatial component and a minor fine motor component. The stimuli used are relatively common, so knowledge base is rarely a factor.

Object Assembly is a rather unique test in the annals of intellectual assessment because it has only five items (plus a sample item that is completed by the examiner). Based on the relationship between reliability and test length, one may think that the test is wholly unreliable. The reliability problem, however, has been conquered by awarding partial credit and bonus points for speedy performance for each item. Because of the small number of items it is, nevertheless, important to note how a child obtained his or her raw score. A careless error on one of the items may have a dramatic effect on the overall score. As was the case with Block

Design, a child may be punished for having careful work habits, as speed is integral to obtaining a high score.

Administration and Scoring Pointers

1. Practice the rules for assigning partial credit to imperfect responses.

Psychometric Properties

Average reliability = .69

"g" loading = .61

Loading on verbal comprehension factor = .26

Loading on perceptual organization factor = .69

Loading on third factor = .11

Loading on fourth factor = .14

Subtest specificity = .26 (inadequate)

Behaviors to Note

1. Overconcern with the stopwatch
2. Inability to verbally "label" an item, resulting in a failure

Cognitive Hypotheses to Investigate

1. Perceptual organization (factor analysis)
2. Spatial ability
3. Holistic (simultaneous) processing (Luria, Das)
4. Fine motor coordination
5. Visual-motor coordination
6. Executive system (Borkowski)
7. Puzzle-solving skill

Biographical and Behavioral Hypotheses to Investigate

1. Visual acuity and discrimination
2. Anxiety related to the stopwatch
3. Achievement motivation
4. Attention span/impulsivity

Comprehension

The Comprehension test requires the child to respond orally to questions posed by the examiner. This verbal test places a premium on the child's verbal expression skills. Also, Comprehension more than any other WISC-III subtest is known as having the potential to elicit rich clinical cues about a child's personality (Zimmerman & Woo-Sam, 1985). This test is clinically rich in that it not only assesses knowledge but also conformity to societal conventions. An adolescent with a conduct disorder may respond in a socially deviant manner.

Every child begins with Item 1 on this test regardless of age, which creates the opportunity for older children to respond to very easy items.

Administration and Scoring Pointers

1. Remember to cue items requiring a second response when necessary.
2. Read the scoring guide completely before scoring a questionable response.

Psychometric Properties

Average reliability = .77

"g" loading = .68

Loading on verbal comprehension factor = .65

Loading on perceptual organization factor = .19

Loading on third factor = .17

Loading on fourth factor = .19

Subtest specificity = .30 (adequate)

Behaviors to Note

1. Word retrieval (finding) problems
2. Responses that are deviant from societal norms

Cognitive Hypotheses to Investigate

1. Knowledge base
2. Verbal expression

3. Long-term memory

4. Verbal comprehension (factor analysis)

5. Knowledge acquisition components (Sternberg)

6. Verbal meaning (Thurstone)

7. Executive system (Borkowski)

8. Crystallized ability (Cattell)

Biographical and Behavioral Hypotheses to Investigate

1. Quality of schooling

2. English language proficiency

3. Acculturation

4. Parental cognitive stimulation

5. Achievement motivation

6. Interest in reading

7. Fatigue (the child has taken several tests at this point and Comprehension is among the least interesting)

8. Values and moral development

Symbol Search

This new test measures mental processing speed and visual search skills akin to Coding. Symbol Search also has two levels, like Coding (under 8, and 8 and over), and its oral instructions are rather lengthy. This test is reminiscent of the speed of processing test of the Differential Ability Scales (see Chapter 11).

The clinical value of this test is not well known nor is its distinctiveness from the Coding subtest. Symbol Search does covary with Coding, yet it has a significant secondary loading on the perceptual organization factor, unlike Coding (see below and section on factor analysis). This finding reveals that the Symbol Search test shares more with the Performance scale than Coding, making it a more suitable substitute for another Performance scale subtest than the Wechsler original—Coding. While such a substitution is warranted by the data, the advice in

the manual is contrary, in that Symbol Search is only allowed to be substituted for the Coding test.

Administration and Scoring Pointers

1. Be sure to have two pencils without erasers.

2. Use only the standardized instructions given.

Psychometric Properties

Average reliability = .76

"g" loading = .56

Loading on verbal comprehension factor = .20

Loading on perceptual organization factor = .35

Loading on third factor = .19

Loading on fourth factor = .56

Subtest specificity = .34 (adequate)

Behaviors to Note

1. Rechecking the target symbols indicating that they are not memorized

2. Squinting or other evidence of difficulty seeing

Cognitive Hypotheses to Investigate:

1. Fluid ability (Cattell)

2. Clerical speed and accuracy

3. Sequencing or successive processing (Luria, Das)

4. Coping with novelty (Sternberg)

5. Pencil and paper skill

6. Short-term memory (information processing theory)

7. Following instructions

8. Level I processing (Jensen)

9. Visual-motor coordination

10. Processing speed

Digit Span

This test requires the child to orally reproduce a string of numbers that are dictated by the examiner. Digit Span has a long history as part of intellectual assessment (Reynolds & Kaufman, 1990). Digit Span requires the child to attend at least briefly, and the child will benefit from rehearsal of the numbers in short-term memory. Some children rehearse more overtly than others—one can hear them or see their lips move. Other children show no evidence of rehearsal. This test also requires adequate auditory perception and discrimination skills.

For the first time the cumulative frequency of raw scores for the Digits Forward and Digits Backward items is included in the manual (Table B.6, Wechsler, 1991). Clinicians have always noted that some children are much more adept at repeating forward digits than at backward digits, although no data have been available to allow clinicians to check their informal impressions. The data presented in the manual do suggest that the forward digits are in fact considerably easier than the backward digits. The average longest string of forward digits for the entire sample was 5.81, whereas the mean of only 4.01 was obtained for the backward digits.

The factor loadings for Digit Span lead one to conclude that it is the most unique subtest on the WISC-III in that it loads poorly on all factors and only slightly better on factor three than on factor one. It is almost as if Digit Span is dependent on a rather unique skill (short-term memory) that is simply not measured well by other WISC-III subtests. This lack of covariation with the remainder of the WISC-III will make this test more likely to deviate from other tests as a strength or weakness. Consequently, examiners will have to become comfortable interpreting this test, and/or add similar tests to corroborate Digit Span findings.

Administration and Scoring Pointers

1. Practice the 1-second administration interval between stimuli in order to develop a "rhythm."

Psychometric Properties

Average reliability = .85

"g" loading = .47

Loading on verbal comprehension factor = .26

Loading on perceptual organization factor = .19

Loading on third factor = .34

Loading on fourth factor = .18

Subtest specificity = .63 (ample)

Behaviors to Note

1. Absence of evidence of rehearsal
2. Comments about their memory skills
3. Responds before examiner gives complete stimulus, suggesting impulsivity

Cognitive Hypotheses to Investigate

1. Fluid ability (Cattell)
2. Architectural system (Borkowski)
3. Knowledge of numbers
4. Sequencing or successive processing (Luria, Das)
5. Short-term memory span (information processing theory)
6. Level I processing (Jensen)

Biographical and Behavioral Hypotheses to Investigate

1. Auditory acuity and discrimination
2. English language proficiency
3. Attention span/impulsivity
4. Anxiety
5. Fatigue or boredom

Mazes

Mazes, another component of the old Army examinations (Reynolds & Kaufman, 1990), assesses the ability of a child to complete a series of mazes with pencil and paper. This task is not unlike the mazes that many children complete for their own enjoyment. It requires adequate spatial ability and fine motor skill to guide the pencil through each maze.

This test can also be difficult to score, especially if a child changes his or her mind frequently or is sloppy. Mazes also lacks difficulty (ceiling) for older children, resulting in lower reliability coefficients for older age groups. In fact, the test-retest coefficients (corrected for variability) for Mazes for the 10–11 and 14–15 age groups were .56 and .57 respectively. These factors have contributed to its lack of popularity with practicing clinicians.

Administration and Scoring Pointers

1. Practice scoring a variety of responses.

Psychometric Properties

Average reliability = .70

"g" loading = .30

Loading on verbal comprehension factor = .06

Loading on perceptual organization factor = .36

Loading on third factor = .11

Loading on fourth factor = .12

Subtest specificity = .57 (ample)

Behaviors to Note

1. Numerous changes of course, indicative of impulsivity

2. Squinting or other evidence of vision problems

Cognitive Hypotheses to Investigate

1. Short-term memory (information processing)

2. Spatial ability (Thurstone)

3. Holistic (simultaneous) processing (Luria, Das)

4. Fine motor coordination

5. Visual-motor coordination

6. Pencil and paper skill

7. Executive system (Borkowski)

Biographical and Behavioral Hypotheses to Investigate

1. Visual acuity and discrimination

2. Anxiety related to the stopwatch

3. Attention span/impulsivity

4. Achievement motivation

5. Fatigue or boredom

6. Experience with mazes

THE VERBAL AND PERFORMANCE SCALES

Hypotheses for V/P Differences

Theories abound regarding the abilities and skills assessed by the Verbal and Performance (V/P) scales, some of which were discussed earlier in the section on factor analysis. This section explores a variety of explanations for score differences between the scales as a prelude to competent WISC-III interpretation (to be discussed in Chapter 7).

What are the factors that contribute to V/P discrepancies, and how do these factors affect diagnosis, prognosis, treatment plans, and the like? Kaufman (1979b) suggested several possible hypotheses for interpreting WISC V/P discrepancies. These and some additional hypotheses are discussed next. Accompanying a discussion of each hypothesis, some "suggestive evidence" will be offered. Such evidence refers to behaviors, background information, other test scores, and information that *may be consistent* with a child's performance on these scales.

Verbal versus Nonverbal Content (V > P or P > V)

It is quite possible that a child may simply be more adept at responding to verbal stimuli than nonverbal stimuli (or stimuli that elicit less verbal response). This hypothesis should always be considered when entertaining reasons for Verbal/Performance discrepancies on the WISC-III because this distinction does enjoy a history of factor analytic support (Kaufman, 1979b). Vernon (1984) labels verbal and nonverbal abilities as "major group factors" because they have emerged in countless factor analytic investigations.

The distinction between the ability to apply cognitive operations to verbal as opposed to more nonverbal content is an ideal one for application to the WISC-III. This hypothesis is supported not only by factor analytic findings but by the fact that it was the basis upon which the Wechsler tradition is premised. Wechsler's development of a clinical test of intelligence mirrors the experience of World War I psychologists, who found that many non–English-speaking immigrants to this country obtained inappropriately low scores on the primarily verbal Army Alpha. As a result of this experience, the requirement to access intelligence through the use of nonverbal procedures was met by the military through the creation of the Army Beta. Hence, the measurement of intelligence has a long tradition of conceptualization based upon the nature of the content to be processed cognitively.

Even when there is a substantial Verbal/Performance discrepancy, some subtests may still not align themselves with either the Verbal or Performance scales. In fact, this misalignment is probable given that the Arithmetic, Symbol Search, Coding, and Digit Span subtests have their primary loadings on the third and fourth factors and Picture Arrangement does not load well on any WISC-III factor. The examiner, then, should not expect unanimity of performance within the Verbal and Performance scales given these findings. The clinician will more commonly find a trend for most of the Verbal

and Performance subtest scores to fall together. In other words, *the Verbal/Performance distinction may still be the most parsimonious explanation for a child's scores, even when some of the subtests do not support this distinction.*

I have seen a number of children display a P > V pattern that seemed to center on the child's preference for dealing with nonverbal stimuli (again, the term "nonverbal" is a misnomer, but a convenient term to denote subtests with visual stimuli). The children who come to mind when thinking of this pattern have been reticent during the testing. They seem to be genuinely enthusiastic about the Performance tests (as indicated by moving closer to the table and working intently) and dread the Verbal scale tests (as suggested by frowning, pushing away from the table, and so on). Less frequently, I have observed children who obtain a V > P pattern who take delight in the Verbal tests and appear confident in their verbal skills. On Performance tests, by contrast, their confidence withers and they seem unsure as to how to solve the problems. Frequently, these children will express interest in highly verbal activities, such as reading. Test behaviors such as these may be helpful in corroborating verbal or nonverbal content differences.

SUGGESTIVE EVIDENCE

1. Poor (or strong) academic achievement scores
2. Poor (or good) articulation
3. Delayed (or precocious) language development
4. Lack of interest (or interest) in mechanical skills or hobbies
5. Interest (or lack of interest) in reading
6. Good (or poor) conversational skills
7. Strong (or poor) school grades

Linguistic Differences (P > V)

Related to the notion of a verbal/nonverbal content distinction is the hypothesis that a V/P discrepancy is the result of linguistic differences (limited English proficiency in most cases). Numerous research studies have noted a P > V profile for groups of children for whom English is not their primary language (Shellenberger & Lachterman, 1976; Gerken, 1978; Fourquean, 1987). This hypothesis is reasonable for a P > V profile whenever information documenting linguistic differences in home and/or the school setting is available.

A linguistic difference hypothesis should enter the clinician's mind when testing any non–English-speaking child, including Spanish-speaking, Asian-American, and Native American children. There may also be forms of English that differ somewhat from the terminology used on the WISC-III. Most clinicians have tested children with whom they have considerable difficulty communicating and, more importantly, difficulty interpreting responses to Verbal scale items.

A linguistic difference hypothesis may also be confounded by cultural differences. A child may conceivably be self-conscious about his or her lack of English proficiency and make a limited attempt to use English. An examiner could assess this possibility before the evaluation by observing the child in school or other social settings or by asking the child's teacher or parent to describe the child's English language proficiency.

SUGGESTIVE EVIDENCE

1. Non-English first language
2. Primary language of the home is not English
3. Immigrant from non-English culture
4. Child was reared with a "nonstandard" form of English (e.g., Cajun)
5. Poor reading skills

Speech or Language Impairment (P > V)

The presence of a speech or language impairment may also depress Verbal scores in relationship to Performance scores. This hypothesis, like the linguistic difference hypothesis, is again typically suggested based upon thorough knowledge of background information regarding the child being assessed. Clearly, a child who has a verbal expression problem will have difficulty on the Verbal scale more than on the Performance scale.

SUGGESTIVE EVIDENCE

1. Delayed language development
2. History of speech/language services
3. Poor reading skills
4. Poor Vocabulary test scores (WISC-III and other Vocabulary tests such as PPVT-R)

Hearing Impairment (P > V)

Research findings support a clear Performance > Verbal profile for children with significant hearing impairments. Sullivan and Burley (1990) state that typical practice involves using only the WISC Performance scale in the assessment of the cognitive skills of hearing-impaired children (see Chapter 14).

A clinician may also encounter children with mild or undetected hearing loss that produce a P > V pattern. Behaviors that may suggest hearing loss include unclear, loud, or delayed speech; requests to repeat items or instructions; or difficulty understanding instructions. Children who have been prescribed hearing aids should wear them for the evaluation. When a child's speech is not easily interpretable or the child uses sign language, a specialist should conduct the intellectual evaluation.

SUGGESTIVE EVIDENCE

1. History of hearing impairment
2. Does not hear well during evaluation
3. Wears hearing aids
4. Uses sign language

Novelty (V > P)

Sternberg (1987) contends that some children, especially some minority group children, have trouble coping with novelty. This hypothesis may explain why some samples of African-American children show a V > P profile on the WISC-R (Reynolds, 1981). The Performance scale poses a number of unfamiliar item types to children, in contrast to the familiar words used on the Verbal scale. Children who are not used to having novel stimuli presented to them lack coping skills for dealing with novelty.

Clinicians can "test the limits" in order to assess the effects of novelty on WISC-III Performance scores. An examiner could ask the child, once testing is completed, if certain items were more recognizable than others.

SUGGESTIVE EVIDENCE

1. Uses unsystematic (trial and error) approach to Performance scale items
2. Seems uncomfortable in test setting (e.g., reluctant to speak or make eye contact)
3. Low scores on other nonentrenched tests such as Ravens Progressive matrices

Achievement Motivation (V > P or P > V)

Since the Verbal scale of the WISC-III is more highly correlated with school achievement than the Performance scale, a child may have a V > P profile that is due to a high level of achievement motivation and associated academic achievement. A relatively high Verbal score could not only be the *cause* of a high level of academic achievement, but it could also be the *product* of high levels of academic achievement, especially on tests highly related to in-school achievement, such as Information and Arithmetic.

A child who is the product of a striving family may exhibit this profile. Behaviors that may be exhibited by the child include tenacity, great concern about whether or not he or she gave correct responses, and curiosity about correct responses for items solved incorrectly.

A contrasting lack of achievement motivation could be associated with a P > V profile. While this is theoretically possible, it may be more clinically rare. The unmotivated child or adoles-

cent may also not put forth good effort during administration of the Performance scale, resulting in a lack of bonus points. This scenario could produce an overall underestimate of the child's skills. This hypothesis could be tested by readministering some tests or a new intelligence test, and giving rewards (e.g., toys, money, praise, etc.) for competent performance (see Chapter 4 Research Report). If a child's scores increase dramatically (beyond what would be expected based on the standard error of measurement for the subtest or composite score) on retesting, then an achievement motivation weakness may be suspected as contributing to low scores or a P>V split.

This hypothesis is more likely to be sensible for older children. It assumes that the child has already had ample opportunity to demonstrate tenacity, hard work, or apathy in school.

SUGGESTIVE EVIDENCE

1. Parents who do (or do not) emphasize education and achievement
2. Academic achievement scores higher (or lower) than Performance score
3. Good (or poor) effort in school
4. Child expresses like (or dislike) for school
5. Lack (or excess) of behavior problems in school
6. Low (or high) level of aspiration as indicated by career goals or other data

Hemispheric Specialization (V > P or P > V)

Researchers have hypothesized for some time that the Verbal scale of the WISC-III measures primarily left brain processing, and the Performance scale right brain processing (Kaufman, 1979b), based upon the groundbreaking research of Sperry (1968) (see Chapter 2). The hypothesis that left hemisphere processing is more related to Verbal scale performance is due to the theorizing that the left brain is specialized for language and the right hemisphere is primarily nonverbal (Gazzaniga, 1975) (see Chapter 14). The right hemisphere has been associated with Performance scale abilities because tests such as Block Design were included by Sperry and colleagues as exemplary measures of the spatial-holistic processing abilities of the right hemisphere. Unfortunately, while this left hemisphere versus right hemisphere dichotomy seems logical and intuitively appealing, it is apparently not consistently documented in children (Kamphaus & Reynolds, 1987). A number of research investigations have shown no clear-cut relationship between Verbal and Performance IQs and left and right hemisphere functioning for children (Kaufman, 1979b; Morris & Bigler, 1985; Shapiro & Dotan, 1985) (see also Chapter 14). Part of the problem is that the attribution of a child's problems to one hemisphere is an oversimplification of a dynamic and complex system. There are cases, however, where this model may be at least partially helpful.

One of the more salient cases in my memory is of a child who displayed a P > V profile shortly after recovering from a drug-induced coma. The child was given the wrong medication by his pharmacy. He lost almost all speech but did recover much of it. Later, he still showed a P > V profile that was statistically significant, although his speech had apparently returned to normal.

SUGGESTIVE EVIDENCE

1. History of head trauma
2. History of seizures
3. Delayed early developmental milestones
4. History of medical condition associated with neurological insult (e.g., tuberous sclerosis)

Spatial Ability (P > V or V > P)

Due to the preponderance of visual stimuli on the Performance scale, performance deficits relative to the Verbal scale may sometimes be explained by poor spatial problem-solving abilities. Related to this the clinician may, in fact, find evidence of visual problems that could certainly

interfere with Performance scale results. Alternately, well-developed spatial skills may explain a P > V profile.

A colleague told me of a child with mild cerebral palsy who had a V > P difference of 50 points! Even on visual perception measures that did not require motor skill he had extreme difficulty. According to physician reports, his eyesight was normal. He just had extraordinary difficulty interpreting most spatial stimuli. As one would expect, his major school problem was in mathematics.

Visual acuity could also be the explanation for a V > P profile. Children should always be assessed for vision problems prior to an evaluation. Clinicians should also check to ensure that a child with corrective lenses is wearing them during the evaluation.

SUGGESTIVE EVIDENCE

1. History of vision problems (V>P)
2. Difficulty (or success) in academic areas requiring spatial skills (e.g., geometry, fine motor skills)
3. Congenital or traumatic neurological insult to visual/spatial processing areas of the brain (V > P)
4. Poor scores on visual-motor tests such as Bender or Beery

Motor Problem (V > P)

A child with a motor deficit, particularly a fine motor deficit, may have extraordinary difficulty with Performance scale subtests resulting in a Verbal > Performance profile. I once had a case where I was asked to assess a hydrocephalic child. This child, even at age 12, was still suffering cerebral damage due to marginally controlled hydrocephaly. Occasionally her cerebral shunt would clog, resulting in an exacerbation of her physical condition. Among the sequelae of her hydrocephaly was a significant gross and fine motor coordination problem. This individual showed a very clear pattern of V > P intelligence scores on the WISC-III. This hypothesis may also apply to other handicapping conditions with associated motor problems. Such conditions may include cerebral palsy and muscular dystrophy.

SUGGESTIVE EVIDENCE

1. Sloppy construction of Performance items
2. Frustration during construction
3. History of motor disability (cerebral palsy, muscular dystrophy, etc.)
4. Poor scores on visual-motor tests such as Bender or Beery

Deliberate Response Style (V > P)

A child may also obtain a V > P profile because of a very deliberate response style. A child may achieve nearly perfect scores but receive few bonus points on Performance scale subtests. Sometimes, a child may have solved a Block Design item correctly but will then spend considerable time "tidying up" the design. Some children will not leave any blocks out of perfect alignment. These compulsive behaviors can preclude a child from earning bonus points for quick performance.

Kaufman (1979c) demonstrated the clear effects of speed on WISC-R performance and concluded that speed of response becomes increasingly important for obtaining high Performance scale scores with increasing age. In parallel fashion, a deliberate response style hypothesis should become more viable for older children and adolescents.

SUGGESTIVE EVIDENCE

1. Compulsive neatness when constructing designs
2. Child earns few, if any, bonus points

Time Pressure (V > P)

Since the only timed items are on the Performance scale, a V > P pattern may occur because of an inability to handle the pressure associated with being timed by a stopwatch. Some children become visibly upset, with hands shaking and face flushed, on tests such as Block Design and Object Assembly.

Underlying anxiety may set the stage for responding to time pressures. The following observations taken from a WISC-III evaluation of a 13-year-old exemplify this pattern. "Significant weight loss lately. Many, many self-deprecating statements throughout exam despite continuous successes. Extreme somatic tenseness: cracking vertebrae, clenching jaw, trembling hands, sitting rigidly in his seat, breathing heavily. Careless mistakes on portions of timed tests. *Too much pressure for him.*" This adolescent obtained a Verbal score of 137 and Performance score of 121!

SUGGESTIVE EVIDENCE

1. Signs of anxiety during timed tests (e.g., sweating, increased respiration, etc.)
2. Rushes through timed tests

Academic Problems (P > V)

The general trend for children with learning disabilities is to have a P > V profile (Kavale & Forness, 1984). The differences in a number of investigations, however, are small. In the Kavale and Forness (1984) metaanalytic investigation of 94 studies of learning disabled children, the average Verbal standard score was 94 and the Performance standard score average was 98. This difference of a few standard score points, although small, is persistent.

A trend toward a P > V profile for learning-disabled children is intuitive since the Verbal scale is more highly correlated with school achievement. Children are referred for learning disability services because they are performing poorly in the classroom (Kaufman, 1979b). More recent investigations have also corroborated the findings of a "mild" P > V profile (Fourquean, 1987; Rethazi & Wilson, 1988). This profile, however, is of virtually *no value in making the differential diagnosis of a developmental learning disability* (e.g., Dyslexia) since other academic problems such as poor schooling, poor cognitive stimulation at home or behavior problems in school could produce this profile. The learning disability diagnostic process depends heavily on non-intelligence test data. In fact, some have argued that intelligence tests not be used for making such a diagnosis (see Chapter 15).

1. Delayed acquisition of basic academic skills, particularly in reading

2. History of diagnosis of reading disability in immediate family members

3. Teacher and parent suspicions of a learning disability

Long-Term Memory/Word Retrieval (V > P or P > V)

A V/P discrepancy could be highly influenced by long-term memory processes if one subscribes to an information processing perspective (see Chapter 2). The efficiency with which a child solves Verbal scale items is determined to a large extent by his or her ability to store and retrieve information from long-term memory. A child who does not use good strategies to store verbal information or lacks retrieval cues may display a P > V profile. The Performance scale does not require a child to retrieve substantial amounts of information from memory.

Children sometimes struggle through a variety of Verbal tests making comments like, "I know that." One hypothesis that this type of statement suggests is that the child did not do a good job of storing class material and, therefore, was unable to efficiently retrieve the information (P > V profile). A child may also have word retrieval problems that are due to neuropsychological insults (see Chapter 15).

1. Good (or poor) school performance

2. Exhibits obvious memory strategies during the evaluation (e.g., repeats numbers on Digit Span)

3. Spontaneously expresses knowledge of memory strategies (e.g., "I repeat names to myself so I can remember them better")

4. Good (or poor) performance on delayed recall tests such as those on the Woodcock-Johnson or Differential Ability Scales

WISC-III STRENGTHS AND WEAKNESSES

Clinicians must be familiar with the strengths and weaknesses of the WISC-III in order to decide when to use it (principles of test selection and use will be discussed in Chapter 17). This premise of test selection assumes that there is no such thing as a perfect intelligence test that should be used with all children under all circumstances. In fact, this point of view is a consistent bias underlying this textbook. Just as there are numerous word processing programs available for writing a textbook such as this one, there are also an increasing number of intelligence tests and procedures, all of which have some virtues and problems. It is hoped that by having a clear understanding of the strengths and weaknesses of each test discussed in this book, examiners can make informed choices that meet their assessment needs and serve their clients best.

WISC-III Strengths

Glasser and Zimmerman (1967) note that one advantage of the WISC is the Verbal/Performance division of subtests. This enhances the assessment of blind, deaf, orthopedically handicapped, culturally deprived, and bilingual children. This allows the examiner to administer nonpenalizing portions of the WISC to a variety of children. This could even include administration of the Performance scale to learning-disabled children, many of whom have language-related learning disabilities (Stanovich, 1986).

The WISC-R also possesses an extraordinary research base that can be used to guide assessment practice (Reynolds & Kaufman, 1990). The collection of well over a thousand research studies in the scholarly literature allows clinicians to predict how children will perform and alerts the examiner to inconsistencies between a child's scores and previous research, thus allowing the examiner to engage in more sophisticated interpretation of scores. Much of this research applies to the WISC-III. The WISC-III also possesses a comprehensive manual that includes considerable evidence of reliability and validity.

The factorial validity of the WISC-III appears good. The third and fourth factors are clear-cut but small and, consequently, they do not play a large role in interpretation (see Chapter 7 for sample cases).

The WISC-III can effectively diagnose mental retardation and giftedness. Such findings establish the WISC-III as a competent intelligence test in the tradition of Binet's early work and that of the Army mental testers.

The WISC-III measures verbal expression to a greater extent than several other intelligence tests. The WISC-III allows the examiner the opportunity, in a sense, to hear the child think aloud when trying to verbally reason through a word definition, verbal concept, or practical problem-solving situation. Allowing the child or adolescent greater opportunity to "reveal" him- or herself provides valuable clinical insight into the nature of a child's problems or assets.

The WISC-III possesses many admirable psychometric properties. It is a good measure of "g," it has ample concurrent validity, and it has excellent reliability estimates for the composite scores. The new norming sample is consistent with current high standards.

WISC-III Weaknesses

A major weakness of the WISC-III is its lack of theoretical clarity. This limitation is shared by a variety of intelligence tests that were developed prior to the 1980s when no premium was placed on the use of theory in the test development process (see Chapter 1). Glasser and Zimmerman (1967) eloquently describe this limitation:

In many ways, the WISC is essentially a revamped Binet, composed of various tasks (most of which are also found on the Binet) which are assumed to be components of intelligence. The WISC is thus based solely on the pragmatic inferences about the nature of intelligence first advanced by Binet. The rationale for interpreting subtest scores remains obscure. (p. 7)

Another weakness of the WISC-III is its low interest level for early elementary-grade children. Most of the tasks are merely downward extensions of Wechsler's original adult scale, and some of the subtests, such as Comprehension, are too lengthy.

The verbal instructions given by the WISC-III examiner are too long, and they require too much verbal comprehension on the part of the child (Kaufman, 1977). This makes the test, including Performance tests, more difficult to administer to limited English-proficient and hearing-impaired children than some other measures. The WISC-III also places more emphasis on speed in comparison to the WISC-R. Kaufman (1992) observes:

The WISC-III allots three bonus points for solving one Block Design item in one to five seconds, and does the same for a Picture Arrangement item. I have only one label for a person who responds to a problem in five or fewer seconds: foolish. (p. 157)

Conclusions

The WISC has a long clinical and research history that supports interpretation by clinicians. The WISC-III is yet another milestone in the development of the Wechsler series that promises to receive widespread acceptance. Its longevity is testimony to the accuracy of Wechsler's original ideas about the practical needs of clinicians involved in intellectual assessment. Other assets of the WISC-III are its long clinical and research history. This legacy has led to the development of strong interpretive systems (Kaufman, 1979b) that further enhance the utility of the scale. The WISC-III possesses numerous strengths that enhance the Wechsler tradition, including a clarification of the WISC-R factor structure that promises to enhance interpretation.

The WISC-III's history is also its greatest liability. Much has been learned about children's cognitive development since the conceptualization of the Wechsler scales, and yet few of these findings have been incorporated into revisions. New tests that capitalize on current research findings will be the greatest challenge to the WISC-III.

CHAPTER SUMMARY

1. The Wechsler/Bellevue offered many features that were not available in previous editions of the Binet scales, including separate norms for children and adults, the provision of subtest standard scores, a separate Performance scale to allow for the assessment of linguistic and cultural minorities, and a Standard Score (Deviation IQ) that solved many of the psychometric problems associated with Ratio IQ scales. The Wechsler series of tests are among the few popular measures of intelligence that continue to use the term "IQ." Most modern tests have dropped the terminology.

2. Wechsler did not consider the Verbal and Performance scales to represent separate abilities, but, rather, he considered them as two additional "languages" through which the underlying general intelligence may express itself.

3. The WISC-III comprises 10 mandatory and 3 supplementary subtests, all of which span the age range of 6 through 16 years. The 5 mandatory subtests on the Verbal scale are Information, Similarities, Arithmetic, Vocabulary, and Comprehension. The supplementary subtest on the Verbal scale is Digit Span. Traditionally, Digit Span is administered with the remainder of the Verbal subtests.

4. The Performance scale of the WISC-III comprises 5 subtests including Picture Completion, Picture Arrangement, Block Design, Object Assembly, and Coding. The supplementary subtests on the Performance scale are Mazes and Symbol Search.

5. The WISC has been criticized for being outdated.

6. Wechsler subtest scaled (standard) scores have a mean of 10 and standard deviation of 3, whereas the IQs have a mean of 100 and standard deviation of 15.

7. The WISC-III norming sample was stratified so as to match 1990 U.S. Census statistics.

8. The reliability of the WISC-III is exemplary.

9. The average standard error of measurement for the Full Scale IQ across all age groups for the WISC-III is 3.20.

10. Gain scores for the Verbal scale are small (2–4 points), whereas on the Performance scale the average gain upon short-term retesting is in the 8–11 point range.

11. WISC-R predictive validity coefficients are in the range of .50 to .60 for most investigations.

12. The WISC-III produces a large first or general intelligence "g" factor.

13. Kaufman's (1975) seminal investigation showed the WISC-R to have a very comparable factor structure to its predecessor, the 1949 WISC, including three factors that were labeled "verbal comprehension," "perceptual organization," and "freedom from distractibility."

14. There was considerable controversy over

the naming of the WISC-R freedom from distractibility factor. Alternate names that were proposed for this factor included symbolic ability, sequential processing, and short term memory.

15. WISC-III factor analytic findings are the clinician's most potent weapons for interpreting WISC-III results.

16. Some of the examiner instructions on the WISC-III are wordy and inappropriate for early elementary-grade children.

17. The WISC-III Verbal tests of Similarities, Vocabulary, and Comprehension seem to be particularly difficult for new examiners to score correctly.

18. The WISC-III possesses an extraordinary research base that can be used to guide assessment practice.

19. The WISC-III possesses many admirable psychometric properties. It is a good measure of "g"; it has ample criterion-related validity, a modern norming sample, and excellent reliability estimates for the composite scores.

20. A major weakness of the WISC-III is its lack of theoretical clarity, which, in turn, hinders interpretation.

21. There are many hypotheses for WISC-III V/P differences.

An Integrative Method of Interpretation

CHAPTER QUESTIONS:

What are some of the problems with intelligence test interpretation?

How do modern clinicians interpret test results?

This chapter presents a scientific approach to intelligence test (and other test) interpretation based on the scientific method of offering hypotheses and testing them against data. Furthermore, this interpretive system emphasizes the integration of intelligence test results with all other information about the child. There are many reasons for offering such an interpretive system, which are discussed in the following paragraphs.

The status quo of psychological test interpretation must change (Matarazzo, 1990; McDermott, Fantuzzo, & Glutting, 1990). Recent writers have called into question some longstanding practices in intelligence test interpretation that portend change in interpretive practice.

Matarazzo (1990) identifies some problems in the assessment process, including a lack of knowledge of the psychometric properties of the tests psychologists use and a lack of congruence between test results and other information about the client. McDermott, Fantuzzo, and Glutting (1990) assail the age-old practice of investigating strengths and weaknesses in a child's subtest profile by revealing measurement flaws underlying the practice.

The crux of these criticisms is that clinicians' interpretations of intelligence tests are now held to a higher standard. Put in psychometric terms, *our interpretations of intelligence test results must routinely have demonstrated validity.* While this point now seems axiomatic, this has frequently not been the case. Matarazzo (1990) explains how assessment practice is now held to a higher standard.

These congressional and judicial decisions had a clear message for psychology: Given the human costs involved, in the event a mistake was made, society now wanted firmer evidence of the validity of opinions offered by psychologists in job hiring and in the schools. Society had spoken out 25 years ago that turning down a job applicant or placing a minority child or a poor child in a special education class for slow learners entailed human costs that were too high to be based solely on the professional belief of the consulting psychologist (or technician surrogate) that the tests, which formed a core part of his or her assessment decision, had been adequately validated. (p. 1001)

As this quotation suggests, clinicians not only have to do a better job of offering valid conclusions, but they also have to consider the *consequences* of their conclusions. This point is necessary because a reliable and valid measure of intelligence may still be used for doing harm (Jensen, 1980; Matarazzo, 1990; Thorndike, 1990). Now clinicians (as many have in the past) must consider the *effects* of making the diagnosis of giftedness or mental retardation (Anastasi, 1988) (ethics and standards will be discussed in Chapter 17).

The increased demands for validity and for adherence to high standards of ethical practice are forcing clinicians to reconsider their interpretive practices. The following interpretive system is designed to meet the need for drawing the most valid conclusions possible, which also foster the development of children.

AN INTEGRATIVE METHOD OF INTERPRETATION

I chose the term "integrative" for this interpretive approach with a specific idea in mind. The term "integrate" has been defined as "to make into a whole by bringing all parts together; unify" (*American Heritage Dictionary:* New College Edition). For years now I have seen my students struggle to integrate test results—to make all the pieces of data for a child fit together to lead to sensible and practical interpretations and recommendations. One of the most disconcerting problems that I have seen is that my

students all too often ignore their own observations and intuitions, preferring instead to derive "the answer" to a child's profile from a textbook such as this one. Here is a concrete example. Given a Digit Span weakness a clinician might conclude that the child has an auditory short-term memory deficit. This conclusion is what many textbooks would suggest as a plausible one. In fact, the clinician may make this conclusion based on the writings of others without considering the fact that the child was more inattentive during this test than during any others. What I have observed all too often is that clinicians will favor the textbook interpretation in this case and ignore, or fail to integrate, the relevant observations that provide a defensible interpretation of the subtest score. (Matarazzo [1990] offers similar observations for practicing clinical psychologists.)

I have also observed that my students are even more likely to fail to integrate findings with other data if the interpretive textbook they are using requires numerous calculations and manipulation of statistical and interpretive tables as part of the interpretive process. Hence, the integrative approach described herein attempts to unify all test- and nontest-based data for a child in order to draw conclusions and to deemphasize statistical calculations that dissuade examiners from integrating assessment results.

The integrative approach described next is basically a codification of what has always been considered sound clinical assessment practice. There are several hallmarks of sophisticated assessment practice, including an emphasis on the collection of multiple data sources, searching for hypotheses that can be corroborated by more than one source of data, and supporting conclusions with theory and research.

Principle 1: Collect and Integrate Data from Numerous Sources

Intelligence test interpretation is fraught with problems when these tests are interpreted in isolation. The integrative approach emphasizes collecting data from a variety of sources so that intelligence test results can be checked against other sources of information. Consider, for example, the case of an adolescent who obtains a relative weakness (a lower subtest score than on any other subtest) on the Arithmetic subtest when there is a lack of information regarding the student's mathematics in school. The clinician may conclude, based on WISC-III performance, that the child shows arithmetic difficulties. A clinician could look foolish if he or she cited a mathematics problem in the report, which could easily happen, if the examiner lacked information from the child's teacher regarding school performance. It may be that the child excels in math in school. Matarazzo (1990) gives a similar example from a neuropsychological evaluation of the failure to integrate test results with background information.

> There is little that is more humbling to a practitioner who uses the highest one or two Wechsler subtest scores as the only index of a patient's "premorbid" level of intellectual functioning and who therefore interprets concurrently obtained lower subtest scores as indexes of clear "impairment" and who is then shown by the opposing attorney elementary and high school transcripts that contain several global IQ scores, each of which were at the same low IQ levels as are suggested by the currently obtained lowest Wechsler subtest scaled scores. (p. 1003)

The point is, *all intelligence test results should be integrated with other information about the child to portray a more valid picture of a child's intelligence.* This integration can only be accomplished if multiple data sources are available.

This principle should not be interpreted as meaning that each child should be administered multiple intelligence measures. There are numerous test and nontest data sources available for corroboration, such as background information, observations during testing, and parent and teacher reports.

Principle 2: Corroborate Conclusions with Multiple Data Sources

This is a corollary of Principle 1 in that it is assumed that multiple data sources are available for the child being evaluated. This principle emphasizes the importance of ensuring that each conclusion drawn by a psychologist about a child's intelligence be corroborated by at least one piece of data external to the WISC-III. *I suggest, however, that each conclusion drawn in a psychological report be supported by at least two additional data sources.*

A clinician, for example, may see a Full Scale score of 84 (below average) for a child and conclude that she possesses below average intelligence. Even this seemingly obvious conclusion should be corroborated by two external sources of information. If the majority of the child's achievement scores are in this range and her teacher says that she seems to be progressing more slowly than the majority of the children in her class, then the conclusion of below-average intelligence has been corroborated by two sources of information external to the WISC-III. On the other hand, if this child had been previously diagnosed as having attention deficit hyperactivity disorder and she missed her morning dosage of medication prior to the testing, one would worry about the veracity of the WISC-III scores. If she were also extremely active during the testing session one would question the obtained scores even more.

The criterion of two pieces of corroborating information sounds stringent, although this is not the case in actual practice. Substantial evidence for corroborating hypotheses frequently may be obtained from caretakers, other clinicians, and teachers.

Principle 3: Support Conclusions with Research

The "clinical impressions" of examiners are no longer adequate for supporting interpretations

Characteristic WISC-R profile types

A study by McDermott et al. (1989) applied multistage cluster analysis to the WISC-R standardization sample in order to identify core profile types. The authors cite a number of flaws with existing research on profile analysis. They question the utility of the various profiles for exceptional populations that have been identified in numerous research investigations. They cite numerous methodological flaws in this previous line of inquiry, the most serious of which is best explained in their own words.

Perhaps the most important consideration in profile research is the choice and evaluation of relevant hypotheses. In our review of research from the past fifteen years, we found few instances where claims for discovery of a unique WISC-R profile were assessed against a viable null hypothesis—namely, that such a profile was commonplace in the general population of children and thus unremarkable. Instead, claims for profile uniqueness tend to be grounded in surmises that the average profile for a group of similarly diagnosed youngsters is inherently characteristic for the diagnostic category and uncharacteristic of alternative categories, or that evidence for differences in average profiles between diagnostic categories is tantamount to prove that such profiles are unlikely to emerge in the overall normal population. Frankly, without a normative typology of core profiles commonly existing among children, we simply cannot know whether subtest profiles elsewhere discovered are uncommon, distinctive, or clinical meaningful. (McDermott et al., 1989, p. 293)

All 2,200 children and adolescents that were included in the WISC-R national norming program were used for this analysis. Multistage cluster analyses were used to sort profiles according to similar level and shape. The resulting profiles were then replicated. The final solution consisted of seven profile types. The seven profile types, their percentage of occurrence in the norming sample, and their mean Full Scale IQ are shown below.

Name	% in Sample	Mean FS IQ
High	13.9	121
Above average	18.4	109
Slightly above average	15.1	105
Average	22.6	98
Slightly below average	8.3	91
Below average	17.7	84
Low	4.0	70

Adapted from tables 1 and 2 of McDermott et al. (1989).

The authors then tallied and described the demographic and other characteristics associated with each profile type. For example, they noted that the high profile tends to have more V > P differences than P > V differences. They also found that of the high cluster groups 60% were boys, and the majority were preadolescents. One-third of the families were of the professional occupational status and two-thirds of the families were of at least "white-collar" occupational status. More than half of the fathers and half of the mothers had some postsecondary education. More of the children in this group came from two- and three-children families than from families having five or more children. By contrast, the low profile type included families led by semi- or unskilled workers. The number of fathers having no more than elementary school education is more than double what would be expected of the population at large, and the number of fathers completing high school is considerably less than what would be expected. Approximately 40% of the children in this profile came from families having five or more children.

These findings for the high and low groups are highly consistent with the research regarding SES, educational attainment, and family size that was presented in Chapter 3. McDermott et al. (1989) provide specific methods for using these core profile types to test the null hypothesis. A procedure is given for comparing the child's obtained profile to the core profile types.

One of the most interesting findings of this investigation from a theoretical standpoint is the association of the core profile types with Full Scale IQ. This supports the robust finding of a large general intelligence factor for the WISC-R.

---

of a child's intelligence test scores (Matarazzo, 1990). Consider again the example above in which the child with persistent school problems obtained a WISC-III Full Scale score of 84. Given the data showing the positive relationship between intelligence and achievement scores, the results seem consistent with the research literature and lend support to the interpretation of below-average intelligence. If necessary, the clinician could give testimony citing studies supporting the correlational relationship between intelligence and achievement test scores to support the conclusion of below-average intelligence (Matarazzo, 1990).

As is stated clearly in the *Code of Fair Testing Practices in Education* and in the *Test Standards* (see Chapter 17), all conclusions that are made based on intelligence tests must have empirical support. As such, clinicians will be asked to apply the knowledge gained in earlier chapters and in previous coursework to the process of intelligence test interpretation. In this way, test users will acquire the habit of keeping abreast of recent research on intelligence testing so as to keep their assessment practice current. One must keep current because there may be a kernel of truth in the saying, "Today's accepted practice is tomorrow's malpractice."

This is not to say that clinicians have to routinely give formal written citations supporting their conclusions. While providing citations may be desirable because they reflect rigor, this is too burdensome. Clinicians should simply retrieve whatever theory or research knowledge

they have regarding a conclusion that they draw about a child's intelligence. Even without formal citations, this recommendation at least fosters the practice of clinicians checking their results against their knowledge base of intelligence research and theory.

Knowledge of theory is important above and beyond research findings because theory allows the clinician to do a better job of conceptualizing a child's scores. Having a clear conceptualization of the child's cognitive status then allows the clinician to better explain the child's results to parents, teachers, colleagues, and other consumers of the test findings. Parents will often want to know the etiology of the child's scores. They will ask, "Is it my fault for not sending her to the best preschool?" or "Did he inherit this problem—my brother had the same problems when he was in school." Clinicians will find themselves unprepared to give plausible answers to such questions without adequate theoretical and research knowledge.

Principle 4: Interpretation Should Be Individualized

As Anastasi (1988) observes, the emphasis on individualized interpretation espoused by Kaufman (1979b) is a major contribution to the sophisticated use of intelligence tests. The "intelligent tester" has to search for theories and research findings to explain the child's scores, in contrast to making the child's scores fit the theory of the test or some other valued theory.

Another assumption of the approach is that no currently available theory of intelligence fits all children all of the time, and the examiner must find the match between theory and the child. This interpretive model requires considerable skill and flexibility on the part of the examiner.

As absurd as it may sound, I try to accomplish this goal of flexible interpretation by using the names of individuals who are associated with particular theories to help me conceptualize the child's performance. Even while testing a child, I will say to myself things such as, "Sternberg would love to see this child; she cannot allocate her time resources. This is dramatically lowering her Performance IQ." Examiners can refer to Chapter 2 and similar sources to gauge the fit between theory and a child's scores.

Principle 5: Emphasize Reliable and Valid Conclusions

The hierarchical aspects of Kaufman's (1979b) approach to WISC-R interpretation have been emphasized previously (Kamphaus & Reynolds, 1987). This text also emphasizes drawing conclusions based on the most reliable and valid scores yielded by the WISC-III.

Given what is known about the relationship between test length and reliability, one can easily guess how this principle will be applied in this text. A conceptualization of the hierarchy is as follows.

SOURCE OF CONCLUSION	DEFINITION	RELI-ABILITY	VALIDITY
Composite scores	Wechsler IQs	Good	Good
Shared subtest scores	Two or more subtests combined to draw a conclusion	Good	Fair to poor
Single subtest scores	A single subtest score	Fair	Poor

The composite score level should receive priority during interpretation for a variety of reasons. The superior reliability of the composite scores is intuitive; they constitute a larger sample of behavior. The shared subtest hypotheses are a somewhat smaller sample of behavior, and the single subtests are smaller samples yet. In addition, interpreting single subtest scores is most treacherous when one takes into account the issue of subtest specificity (see Chapter 5). The reliability evidence, then, divides intuitively into three levels of interpretation.

In terms of validity, the wealth of factor analytic research on the Wechsler scales lends support to the Verbal and Performance scales. No such validation exists for the many hypotheses that may be generated for alternative combinations of subtests and single subtests. In most cases the concern is not that many of the shared or single subtest hypotheses have been disproved, but rather that most have not been tested. The combinations that have been tested, however, have not fared well (see ensuing sections of this chapter).

Principle 6: Deemphasize Subtest Profile Analysis

This principle is a corollary of Principle 5. For the purposes of this discussion a subtest profile consists of a pattern of subtest strengths (high subtest scores) and weaknesses (low subtest scores) that are considered distinctive for a particular child or group of children and thereby warrants interpretation. The centerpiece of profile analysis is *ipsative interpretation*—the process of discovering intraindividual strengths and weaknesses in cognitive areas. In ipsative interpretation the child is used as his or her own standard or norm. In contrast, in normative-based interpretation a child's score is compared to that of a reference group of his or her peers. An example of a hypothesis from a normative approach would be, "James has above-average intelligence as measured by the WISC-III." An ipsative interpretation would be something like, "James's mathematics skills are better than his reading skills."

Shared Hypotheses

One of the most popular methods of ipsative interpretation involves interpreting clusters of subtests that are relatively high or low in relation to the other subtests. When a conclusion is based on two or more subtests that are deviant from the remainder of the profile, this has been referred to as "shared abilities" or "shared hypotheses" (Kaufman, 1979b). The crucial problem with interpreting shared hypotheses is their lack of validity evidence (Lyman, 1965). Unfortunately, the validity of many combinations of subtests as shared hypotheses is not known because it simply has not been studied. One of the few shared hypotheses that has been studied is the regrouping of WISC-R subtests proposed by Bannatyne (1974). His recategorizations are shown below.

SPATIAL	CONCEP-TUALIZATION	SEQUENCING	ACQUIRED KNOWL-EDGE
Block Design	Vocabulary	Digit Span	Information
Object Assembly	Similarities	Coding	Arithmetic
Picture Completion	Comprehension	Arithmetic Picture Arrangement	Vocabulary

Matheson, Mueller, and Short (1984) studied the validity of Bannatyne's recategorization of the WISC-R using a multiple group factor analysis procedure with three age ranges of the WISC-R and data from the WISC-R standard-

ization sample. They found that the acquired knowledge, conceptualization, sequencing, and spatial categories of the WISC-R had high reliabilities but problems with validity. They found, for example, that while the acquired knowledge category had sufficiently high reliabilities, it was not independent of the other three categories, particularly conceptualization (Matheson, Mueller, & Short, 1984). This finding is sensible given that the conceptualization and acquired knowledge categories have one subtest in common (Vocabulary) and that previous factor analytic studies of the WISC-R revealed three, not four, factors. The subtests from the conceptualization and acquired knowledge categories form the large first factor labeled verbal comprehension. As a result, Matheson, Mueller, and Short (1984) advise that the acquired knowledge category not be interpreted as a unique entity. Said another way, these results suggest that the acquired knowledge and conceptualization categories are best interpreted as one measure of verbal intelligence, which is more consistent with the factor analytic research on the WISC-R.

In a similar investigation, Naglieri, Kamphaus, and Kaufman (1983) tried to test the accuracy of Kaufman's (1979b) recategorizations of the WISC-R into successive and simultaneous tests based on Luria's theory (see Chapter 2). They met with mixed results. While there was some support for Kaufman's recategorization, it was not robust. Mazes, for example, was hypothesized to be a strong sequential test, yet it had its highest loadings on the simultaneous factor. Again, a recategorization of the WISC-R subtests failed to gain validity support as strong as that which has been found for the three-factor structure of the WISC-R.

In one sense the Matheson, Mueller, and Short (1984) and Naglieri, Kamphaus, and Kaufman (1983) investigations support the hierarchical aspects of the integrative method of interpretation proposed in this chapter, whereby interpretation of the composite scores, in this case the Verbal and Performance Scales, receives primacy over interpretation of recategorizations such as Bannatyne's. Fortunately, the validity of Bannatyne's and Kaufman's recategorizations has at least been tested. The vast majority of other proposed recategorizations that will be discussed in upcoming sections *have not been tested to determine the extent of their validity.* (See also McDermott, Fantuzzo, and Glutting [1990] and Anastasi [1985] for a discussion of measurement issues in profile analysis.) *Most importantly, clinicians need to be aware of the fact that profile analysis depends exclusively on the clinical acumen of the examiner, not on a sound research base.*

All of this negative information on profile analysis is given as a backdrop in order to make the new user of intelligence tests appropriately cautious in evaluating Wechsler profiles. A child's profile simply cannot be matched to some of the theoretical profiles mentioned in the literature, and a conclusion cannot be drawn without the consideration of other pieces of evidence. Similarly, *a diagnosis should never be made solely on the basis of a subtest profile.*

Subtest Interpretation

There is, however, some suggestive evidence that a single subtest score or set of subtest scores should be interpreted. Although most current research suggests that the overall composite score possesses better evidence of validity (especially predictive validity) than subtests (McDermott, Fantuzzo, & Glutting, 1990), there is some research evidence to support interpretation of subtests. One example of such support for subtest interpretation is a series of investigations by Siegel (1990, 1988) that show that basic word reading tests are more highly correlated with reading performance than composite scores from intelligence measures. This finding suggests that a single subtest, for example, the Reading/Decoding subtest of the K-ABC (to be discussed in a later chapter), could be interpreted with some research support.

It is conceivable that WISC-III or other intelligence test subtests or subtest combinations would also be shown to have *better* validity than an overall composite score. This has not been the case to date, but not much research attention has been paid to the validation of subtests or subtest combinations. It is too early, however, to conclude that subtest or subtest combinations should be routinely ignored, especially if there is research evidence or overwhelming clinical evidence to support interpretation. It is for this reason that this principle used the term "deemphasize" rather than "eliminate" subtest or profile interpretation. Some subtest interpretation in particular could be supported by future research.

Principle 7: Minimize Calculations

An effort was made to keep calculations to a minimum in this interpretive system in order to avoid taking quantitative interpretation to its illogical extreme and to prevent new examiners from getting bogged down in calculations. I have seen many of my students focus so much on the calculations involved in test interpretation that they overlook their own experiences with the child and other important pieces of qualitative information. In addition, computers are now readily available to make whatever calculations that may be needed easily accessible (see Chapter 12).

In keeping with this philosophy of minimal calculation, only average values are used in the interpretive process proposed in this text. Statistical accuracy should not take preeminence over knowledge of how to apply relevant theory and research. Besides, clinicians cannot search through all of the tables and calculations in this book and get a "right" answer. In addition, Kaufman (1979b) points out that average values are usually more appropriate and trustworthy because they are based on the largest samples available for a test.

Principle 8: Interpretation Is an Iterative Process

Test interpretation is something like detective work, where the clinician follows clues and develops leads until eventually a clear picture of a crime emerges. Intelligence test interpretation works in similar ways. A clinician, for example, may find a low Digit Span score that was unexpected. This finding is difficult to interpret in isolation without corroborating evidence. This finding, then, results in another "iteration" in that additional tests will be administered to determine whether or not this is an anomalous or irrelevant finding. The next test given may provide additional "leads" allowing the clinician to follow up with additional data collection in order to narrow down the possibilities for this finding.

Another potential scenario requiring the use of an iterative approach is for there to be two or more pieces of consistent evidence *and* two or more pieces of inconsistent evidence for a hypothesis. This is a rather unusual situation that warrants discussion. Say, for example, a child has depressed scores on the Arithmetic, Digit Span, and Coding subtests of the WISC-III (the old distractibility factor of the WISC-R). The corroborating evidence includes the fact that the child's mother is concerned about hyperactivity and distractibility, and she wants to know if her child has an attention deficit disorder. She reports that her child is highly active and difficult to manage at home. The disconfirming evidence is that the child was exceedingly cooperative and attentive throughout the evaluation and seemed to be paying attention to every item presented. The child was simply a delight to test! In addition, the teacher reports that the child is active and talkative in school although there are no distractibility problems noted when the child is completing worksheets or reading silently. One approach to this dilemma is to simply make a decision somehow (by flipping a coin or whatever). Another approach is to defer interpretation and continue the iterative process of collecting more data in order to make a conclusion that the examiner feels comfortable placing his or her reputation on. As a general rule, *I advise examiners not to draw conclusions because of time or other pressures* in a nonemergency case. An analogous situation would be for a pediatrician to examine a child with stomach problems, administer an office examination, collect a history, and conclude that the child has an ulcer without seeing X-rays or other test results. Similarly, the psychologist should feel equally free to "order" (to use medical parlance) additional diagnostic tests before a definitive diagnosis or intervention is offered. Given the locus of the child's problems to the home environment, family assessment or other methods may be in order.

This iterative process is especially useful when surprising findings occur. A clear understanding that this type of detective work is often necessary has the additional advantage of precluding clinicians from making premature and potentially erroneous conclusions. The necessity of viewing intelligence test interpretation as an iterative process will be highlighted in upcoming sections on "aposteriori" methods of interpretation.

Principle 9: Emphasize Apriori Interpretation

The interpretive method advocated in this book involves offering apriori hypotheses prior to the calculation of the child's scores. This is a powerful method for encouraging the integration of test results with other information. The word *apriori* is defined as "proceeding from a known or assumed cause to a necessarily related effect; deductive . . . based on a hypothesis or theory rather than on experiment or experience" (*American Heritage Dictionary*, 1981). This definition is in contrast to the term *aposteriori*, which is defined as "denoting reasoning from facts or particulars to general principles, or from effects to causes; inductive; empirical" (*American Heritage Dictionary*, 1981). In this case aposteriori is meant specifically to refer to the latter parts of the above definition, which emphasize inferring causes from effects. The aposteriori approach has a long tradition of use in clinical assessment.

Apriori hypotheses are based on previous information about the child, including reports from teachers, clinicians, and parents, previous school grades, medical and developmental histories, and observations during the test session. The clinician, for example, may observe that a child entered the test session begrudgingly because she had to leave her favorite playmate to attend the test session. She had a noticeable scowl on her face during administration of the Picture Completion subtest and she offered minimal effort with no elaboration of her answers. After the Information subtest the examiner was able to more firmly establish rapport and the child's effort improved substantially thereafter. The examiner may then hypothesize based on these observations that the child will score lower on the Picture Completion subtest than on others because of her poor motivation. If, in fact, this finding obtains, then the examiner can feel confident that the apriori hypothesis is confirmed. This method virtually guarantees integration of intelligence test results with other findings since the hypotheses are already based on other findings.

The apriori approach also forces consideration of research and theory because the clinician is operating on the basis of research and theory when the hypothesis is drawn (see Table 7.1). Another example will clarify the element of applying previous research. A child is referred for psychological evaluation because of a failure to make academic gains in the first grade. He does not yet know his letters and numbers, and he is being retained in grade one while receiving remedial assistance. Based on the known correlation between intelligence and academic achievement (see Chapter 3) the examiner would hypothesize below-average intelligence test scores. If the child obtains a WISC-III Full Scale of 89 or below, the hypothesis would be

TABLE 7.1   Sample research findings and supporting evidence for apriori hypotheses

Research Finding	Evidence
Intelligence tests correlate moderately with measures of academic achievement.	Grades, retentions, achievement test scores, reading or mathematics instructional group placement, special education placement.
Developmental delays (or disabilities) are associated with lower-than-average intelligence test scores.	Delayed language, motor, or cognitive milestones; disorders such as Down's Syndrome, Fragile X, Tuberous Sclerosis.
Brain injuries are associated with lower-than-average intelligence test scores.	Low Apgar scores, high sustained fevers, intractable seizures, traumatic head injuries (e.g., automobile accidents).
Prenatal teratogens are associated with lower intelligence test scores.	Maternal alcohol or drug use, maternal illnesses (e.g., rubella), traumatic injuries during pregnancy (e.g., a mother suffers an abdominal injury in a fall).
Parental educational attainment is associated with child intelligence test scores	Number of years of schooling completed by birth parents, parental occupation (e.g., professor, etc.).
Previous intelligence test scores are highly correlated with future intelligence test scores.	Scores from individually and group-administered intelligence tests.

Citations for these findings are provided in Chapter 3 and other chapters throughout this book.

confirmed and, additionally, the examiner's conclusion would be based on research findings.

Yet another example demonstrates the link between apriori hypotheses and theory. A child is referred subsequent to a brain injury with complaints of short-term memory deficits and declining school performance. The child's grades have deteriorated from primarily As to mainly Cs. The psychologist conducting the evaluation may hypothesize that Digit Span would be a weakness on the WISC-III because of the reported short-term memory deficits. In addition, the psychologist may also hypothesize that the child will show a lower WISC-III Full Scale than would be predicted (in the average as opposed to the above-average range) based on the child's previous academic record. Borkowski theorizes (see Chapter 2) that the architectural system must be intact for the executive system to work adequately. This theory may lead the psychologist to predict an overall deficit (in comparison to previous estimates) in intelligence test scores due to damage to the architectural system, which in turn damages the executive system. If one of the child's lowest scores is on Digit Span and his Full Scale falls somewhere in the average range or below, then the clinician's hypotheses would be confirmed.

This approach to interpretation is analogous to one of the differences between exploratory and confirmatory factor analysis, where in the latter procedure, theories about the factor structure are offered apriori (see Chapter 5). Traditional "exploratory" methods of interpretation give the clinician a data set (i.e., Wechsler scores) and ask the clinician to make sense of them, which is similar to what a researcher does by labeling exploratory factors post hoc. I have found this exploratory method of interpretation to be difficult for new students because it is bereft of theory and it does not emphasize the integration of intelligence test results with other findings. New trainees, in particular, feel very insecure about "naming factors" or drawing conclusions post hoc, causing them to sometimes revert to "cookbook" methods of in-

terpretation that are far from insightful or helpful. *Apriori hypotheses should receive priority in the interpretive process because these hypotheses are already based on substantial information, suggesting that they are likely to be highly meaningful in the context of the child's referral problem(s).*

APPLYING AN INTEGRATIVE METHOD TO THE WECHSLER SCALES

Apriori Method of Interpretation

This section presents a systematic approach for interpreting Wechsler and other intelligence test results. The interpretive steps are given in summary fashion in Box 7.1.

Interpretive Step 1: Offer Apriori Hypotheses

The first step in intelligence test interpretation is to draw hypotheses based on previous information (see Principle 8 above). These hypotheses should be written on a sheet of paper (or on a computer file) for later reference. Recording hypotheses in writing is an important step because the writing process often forces clinicians to think through their hypotheses more carefully than when offering armchair opinions.

Ideas for apriori hypotheses based on research findings may be gleaned from Table 7.1. There are generally four categories of apriori hypotheses based on their sources. The four major sources of information are developmental history, educational progress, family characteristics, and observations from test sessions (see Table 7.1).

Listed below are some examples of hypotheses that emanate from data acquired prior to the calculation of Wechsler scores. The hypotheses that are based on research and theory take

Box 7.1

Sequence of steps for the integrative interpretation method

1. Collect background information.
2. Offer apriori hypotheses.
   A. Full Scale (global) composite
   B. Other composites (e.g., V and P)
   C. Profiles (i.e., two or more subtests)
   D. Single subtest
3. Test apriori hypotheses against obtained scores.
   A. Full Scale (global) composite against apriori descriptive category
   B. Other composites hypotheses against composite score significant and rare differences
   C. Profile hypotheses against subtest strengths and weaknesses
   D. Single subtest hypotheses against subtest strengths and weaknesses
4. Draw conclusions.
If not all results are explained by apriori hypotheses then:
5. Offer aposteriori hypotheses.
   A. Full Scale (global) composite
   B. Other composites (e.g., V and P)
   C. Profiles (i.e., two or more subtests)
   D. Single subtests
6. Collect data (information) to test aposteriori hypotheses.
7. Test aposteriori hypotheses against other data.
   A. Full Scale (global) composite against aposteriori descriptive category
   B. Other composites against aposteriori significant and rare differences
   C. Profiles against aposteriori subtest strengths and weaknesses
   D. Single subtest against subtest strengths and weaknesses
8. Accept hypotheses corroborated by two pieces of evidence.
9. Offer accepted hypotheses as conclusions.

---

their premise from findings such as those listed in Table 7.1. This table culls findings from elsewhere in this book in summary form to help the clinician form apriori hypotheses to be tested.

Background Information

Elizabeth is starting school and has a *prior diagnosis of Down's syndrome*, a genetic abnormality that is frequently associated with mental retardation.
Hypothesis: Significantly below-average Wechsler scores
Reference: Chapters 2, 14

Background Information

Greg's mother reports that his *language developmental milestones were delayed.* He did not use single words until 2 years of age.
Hypothesis: Average to below-average Wechsler scores
Reference: Chapter 14

Background Information

Chloe's mother complains of a *decline in school performance* subsequent to a *head injury* that occurred when her daughter was struck by a car while riding a bicycle.

Hypothesis: Lower intelligence test scores than premorbid levels (i.e., her Wechsler scores may be lower than estimates of her intelligence prior to the accident).
Reference: Chapters 2, 15

Background Information

Beda was referred for evaluation for a second opinion. Some of the previous evaluation data (i.e., *achievement test scores at the 99th percentile*) suggested that she would be a good candidate for the gifted program; other data were inconsistent.
Hypothesis: Significantly above-average Wechsler scores
Reference: Chapter 3

Background Information

Rowanda has a history of a *mild hearing deficit* and *chronic otitis media* (ear infections). She is also *receiving speech therapy* for articulation difficulties.
Hypothesis: Relative strength on the Performance scale and weakness on the Verbal scale
Reference: Chapters 3, 6, 14

Background Information

Caroline has made *poor progress in school.* She is currently in the third grade and was *retained in both the first and second grades.* She has lived in foster care since she was 3 years of age. She was taken from her parents because of evidence of paternal child sexual abuse and parental neglect.
Hypothesis: Average to below-average intelligence test scores
Reference: Chapter 3

Background Information

Chauncey is 6½ years old and virtually all of his *developmental milestones are delayed.* His mother was addicted to *alcohol during pregnancy.* He was born premature and he has a previous diagnosis of *fetal alcohol syndrome.*

Hypothesis: Below-average to significantly below-average intelligence test scores
Reference: Chapter 3

Background Information

A teacher notes that Ricky's *retention of facts is poor.* Information does not seem to "stick with him."
Hypothesis: Two hypotheses may be drawn here. One is that his Wechsler scores may be below average and the other is that his scores on tests requiring long- or short-term memory may be poor.
Reference: Chapters 3 and 6

Background Information

Pilar's academic performance is uneven in the first grade this year. One of her problems is very *poor motor skills.* She is *clumsy,* has an *odd gait,* and her *written work is messy and disorganized.* She does *express herself well in class* and *she conversed readily and competently with the examiner.*
Hypothesis: Relative weakness on Performance scale and higher Verbal scale
Reference: Chapter 6

Background Information

Antonio was *highly distractible* when observed in the classroom. Similarly, he was *highly distracted during the Digit Span, Picture Arrangement, Block Design, Coding, and Symbol Search subtests.*
Hypothesis: Relative weaknesses on the Digit Span, Picture Arrangement, Block Design, Coding, and Symbol Search subtests
Reference: Chapters 4 and 15

Background Information

Ashley *gave up easily on the Coding subtest.* She did not seem willing to work quickly on this test.
Hypothesis: Relative weaknesses on the Coding and Symbol Search subtests
Reference: Chapter 6

Background Information

Kristin is 16 years old. She has a history of *poor school performance* and *truancy*. She is on probation for automobile theft, and she has run away from home for weeks at a time. *Hypothesis:* Below-average WISC-III scores *Reference:* Chapters 3 and 16

It is noteworthy that the vast majority of the hypotheses drawn above pertain to the Full Scale, Verbal, and Performance scores and few are ipsative (single subtests or profiles) in nature. This is the case because the composite scores have the most research associated with them (McDermott, Fantuzzo, & Glutting, 1990) (see Principles 5 and 6 above). Subtest apriori hypotheses, on the other hand, are often based on observations during testing and background information rather than research findings.

Interpretive Step 2:
Test Global Composite
Score Apriori Hypothesis

These hypotheses are then tested against WISC-III data. If an examiner predicts above-average intelligence and the child's scores are in the average range, then this apriori hypothesis is discarded. Similarly, if an examiner predicts that Picture Arrangement will be a relative weakness for a child, then this subtest should deviate significantly from the child's average subtest score. If this score does not deviate significantly, then the hypothesis is discarded.

Typical Full Scale score (standard score) apriori hypotheses are offered on five levels of performance. These include:

1. 130 and above: significantly above average (see Chapter 8)

2. 110–129: above average

3. 90–109: average

4. 71–89: below average

5. 70 and below: significantly below average

If the child's obtained Full Scale is within the hypothesized category or within 3 standard score points (about 1 SEM) of the hypothesized category, then the apriori hypothesis can be accepted. If, for example, a significantly below-average Full Scale is hypothesized because of a previous diagnosis of mild mental retardation and the child obtains a 69, the apriori hypothesis is confirmed. Additionally, if the child obtains a 73 the hypothesis is also confirmed.

Step 3: Test Other Composite Score Apriori Hypotheses

The next level of hypotheses to test are those associated with Verbal and Performance scale differences. The interpretive value of the Full Scale score may be gauged in two ways. The first procedure is to test the statistical significance (or reliability — Silverstein, 1981) of the difference between Verbal and Performance standard scores. In this way the examiner can determine if the difference between Verbal and Performance scores is likely accurate and not a statistical artifact (i.e., due to chance). The average values across ages are a Verbal/Performance difference of 12 standard score points at the .05 level and 15 points at the .01 level (Wechsler, 1991). In other words, a difference of 12 points between the Verbal and Performance scales is likely a reliable one that is not due to chance factors. Said another way, there is only a 5% probability (.05) that the difference is due to chance and there is a 95% probability that it is an accurate difference. An apriori hypothesis of a V/P difference would be confirmed if a statistically significant difference is obtained.

Because of the difference between statistical significance and clinical significance, Kaufman (1979b) advised that examiners also consider the relative rarity of discrepancy scores in the national population. Values for determining the proportion of the WISC-III standardization sample that obtained a given discrepancy score or larger are given in the WISC-III manual. As a general guide, I suggest that *a discrepancy of 25 points that occurs in 5% or less of the standardization sample is rare* (see table B.2, Wechsler, 1991) and renders the overall composite standard score, in this case the Full Scale standard score, relatively useless as an overall estimate of intelligence. When a difference this unusual and this large occurs in an individual's intelligence test performance at the composite score level, the child's intelligence is simply too multifaceted to be summarized with a single number. (See later section on illusory V/P differences for an exception.)

Differences between Index scores may also be hypothesized and tested. Tables B.1 and B.2 of the WISC-III manual (Wechsler, 1991) also allow examiners to test for reliable and rare differences between many pairwise comparisons of Index scores. An examiner may hypothesize, for example, that the Processing Speed Index will be lower than the Perceptual Organization Index because a child is said to be extremely slow to complete written work in the classroom. A reading of table B.1 reveals that a 15-point difference between these two Index scores is reliable (i.e., statistically significant at the .05 level), and table B.2 shows that a difference between these scores of 31 points or more occurs in less than 5% of the population.

Step 4: Test Shared Subtest Apriori Hypotheses

The next step is to test apriori shared subtest hypotheses. Experienced examiners will be able to merely glance at the subtest scores for an individual child and discover significant fluctuations in the profile. The new examiner, however, requires specific guidelines for determining when a fluctuation in a child's profile may be of significance. Kaufman (1979b) produced tables for determining the statistical significance of profile fluctuations for the WISC-R. This principle is the same as was used in determining significant or reliable differences between Verbal and Performance scores. The difference in this case is determining whether or not there are reliable peaks or valleys, or strengths or weak-

nesses, in a child's profile of Wechsler subtest scores.

The common procedure for determining significant strengths and weaknesses in Wechsler subtest profiles is to consult table B.3 of the WISC-III manual (Wechsler, 1991). The WISC-III manual offers a bewildering number of possibilities for determining subtest strengths and weaknesses—eight, to be exact, depending on the number of subtests administered and whether or not one uses the mean of all subtests for comparison or the mean of the Verbal and Performance scales separately (the issue of which subtest mean is preferable will be discussed later). The values needed for this section are given on page 264 of the WISC-III manual.

The advised procedure for determining significant fluctuations in a profile is as follows:

1. Compute the mean scaled score of all 12 subtests (or 10 or 13 subtests as appropriate) combined and round this value to the nearest whole number.

2. Compute the difference between each subtest scaled score and the mean scaled score.

3. Compare each difference score to the corresponding subtest difference score value for the .05 level (the second column in the table) presented in table B.3 (p. 264) of the WISC-III manual. Round the values in table B.3 to make these comparisons. If a difference between a subtest score and the mean *meets or exceeds the rounded tabled value*, then it is marked as a strength (S). Mark a weakness (W) if the subtest scaled score is lower than the mean but at least as large as the tabled value.

The WISC-III profile for Connie in Figure 7.1 will serve as an example of how subtest strengths and weaknesses are determined. This child obtained a mean scaled score for 12 tests of 11. The subtest scores are compared to the mean, revealing the strengths and weaknesses shown in Figure 7.1.

In order to confirm shared subtest hypotheses

FIGURE 7.1

Sample case—Connie

Composite Scores

Full Scale Standard Score	108
Verbal Standard Score	117
Performance Standard Score	96

Subtest Scores

VERBAL SCALE	SCORE	MEAN	DIFFERENCE	SIGNIFICANCE VALUE (TABLE B.3)	S or W
Information	13	11	2	3	—
Similarities	13	11	2	4	—
Arithmetic	13	11	2	4	—
Vocabulary	12	11	1	3	—
Comprehension	13	11	2	4	—
Digit Span	13	11	2	4	—
PERFORMANCE SCALE					
Picture Completion	14	11	3	4	—
Picture Arrangement	10	11	−1	4	—
Block Design	10	11	−1	3	—
Object Assembly	10	11	−1	5	—
Coding	4	11	−7	4	W
Symbol Search	9	11	−2	4	—

Overall Mean = 11
(11.36)

in the sample profile, *all, or virtually all, of the scores for the subtests that are a part of the hypothesis should be at or below the subtest mean of 11.* If, for example, an apriori hypothesis of slow processing speed were offered, the Coding and Symbol Search subtest scores should be at or below the subtest mean of 11. In Connie's case such a hypothesis would be supported by the Coding and Symbol Search scores of 4 and 9 respectively.

Step 5: Test Single Subtest Apriori Hypotheses

Finally, single subtest apriori hypotheses should be tested against the obtained scores. These hypotheses are confirmed if the subtest score upon which the hypothesis is based is determined to be a statistically significant (or nearly significant) strength or weakness.

Step 6: Draw Apriori Conclusions

The final step in the interpretive process is to consider the hypotheses that have been corroborated and determine which ones, if any, should be reported orally or in writing. The important rule at this stage is to *try to subsume less reliable and valid hypotheses under more reliable and valid ones.* By doing so, examiners are erring in the direction of drawing conclusions based on greater evidence of reliability and validity (see Principle 5).

If a child had a lone weakness on the Information test, one may be tempted to interpret this as a single subtest weakness and say something about fund of general information in an oral or written report. This same child, however, could also have a P > V discrepancy. In most cases it will be more sensible to subsume the Information weakness under the Verbal standard score and conclude that the child simply has a relative weakness in verbal skills. This conclusion is more psychometrically robust than the single subtest conclusion.

Similarly, if a child obtains an Information relative strength, this too could be subsumed under high composite scores. If this same child has a high Full Scale score, it would be best to attribute the Information strength to overall strong cognitive skills.

This emphasis on composite scores over shared and single test hypotheses is an interpretive bias that shows respect for psychometric properties. Shared or single subtest hypotheses may still be viable, but they should be corroborated to the point that they are *clearly superior* to composite score hypotheses.

It is also possible to draw conclusions at all three levels of interpretation for the same case. A composite score and single subtest conclusion can coexist, as will be seen in some of the sample cases. In fact, in some situations it will be eminently reasonable to draw conclusions at all three levels of interpretation.

A second overriding rule for drawing conclusions is to favor apriori hypotheses that are based on background information. Most importantly, they are "ecologically" valid in that they are directly related to the referral questions. In addition, apriori hypotheses can be highly valid because they are frequently based on considerable historical data. If, for example, a child has a history of language delays, is receiving speech/language services, and his teacher observes language weaknesses, then a relative weakness on the Verbal scale is predictable and important to interpret.

Aposteriori Method of Interpretation

Aposteriori hypotheses may also be offered at the composite, shared subtest, and single subtest levels. These hypotheses should be considered *only when apriori hypotheses do not explain the observed scores*. If apriori hypotheses account for all of the obtained scores, then there is no need to entertain aposteriori hypotheses and the clinician may proceed directly to report writing. If, for example, there are large unanticipated V/P differences or subtest strengths and weaknesses, then proceed to the next step.

Step 1: Composite Score Hypotheses

This step involves listing on paper all hypotheses based on composite scores. The first composite score hypothesis is based on the overall composite score, in this case the Full Scale standard score of the WISC-III.

Step 2: Shared Subtest Hypotheses

Shared subtest hypotheses for Wechsler subtests are given in Table 7.2. This table is given to assist clinicians in the process of generating hypotheses as to why a child's score may be particularly high or low. Table 7.2 includes cognitive factors, background variables, test behaviors, and emotional traits and states that may affect performance. This list is also provided for the purpose of generating hypotheses during interpretation.

For a number of reasons these lists should not be treated like a "cookbook." Lists of this nature can be a "double-edged sword." They do help new clinicians think through a profile, yet trainees can easily become too dependent on them. These lists emanate from theory and experience more so than research. They are based primarily on the work of Kaufman (1979b), Zimmerman and Woo-Sam (1985), the larger body of WISC-R literature, and on my own experiences and those of my colleagues and students with the WISC-R. Another important realization is that each item in these lists is relative. For example, quality of schooling probably influences performance on every WISC-R subtest, but it is not listed for all. By inference, then, these lists are suggestive and certainly not all-inclusive.

TABLE 7.2   Shared and single subtest hypotheses for WISC-III strengths and weaknesses

Hypotheses	Inf	Sim	Arith	Voc	Comp	DS	PC	PA	BD	OA	Cod	Maz	Sym
Knowledge Base	✓	✓	✓	✓		✓	✓		✓				
Sequencing			✓			✓					✓		
Short-term Memory			✓			✓					✓		✓
Long-term Memory	✓	✓	✓	✓	✓		✓			✓			
Achievement Motivation	✓		✓								✓		
Level II Processing		✓	✓						✓				
Verbal Comprehension	✓	✓		✓	✓								
Verbal Expression	✓	✓		✓	✓								
Knowledge Acquisition Components	✓	✓	✓										
Auditory Acuity and Discrimination			✓			✓							
Categorical Thinking		✓											
Mathematics Knowledge		✓											
Social Studies Knowledge	✓												
English Vocabulary				✓									
Common-sense Reasoning				✓									
Short-term Memory Span						✓							
Perceptual Organization							✓		✓	✓		✓	
Visual Acuity and Discrimination							✓	✓	✓	✓	✓	✓	✓
Holistic Processing							✓		✓	✓		✓	
Spatial Ability							✓		✓	✓		✓	
Fine-motor Coordination							✓	✓	✓	✓	✓		✓
Coping with Novelty		✓				✓	✓		✓		✓		✓
Visual-Motor Coordination									✓	✓	✓	✓	✓
Distinguishing Essential from Nonessential Details							✓						
Inferring Cause-and-Effect Relationships								✓					
Right Hemisphere Processing									✓				
Clerical Speed and Accuracy											✓		✓
Pencil and Paper Skill											✓	✓	✓

(continued)

TABLE 7.2   *(continued)*

Hypotheses	Inf	Sim	Arith	Voc	Comp	DS	PC	PA	BD	OA	Cod	Maz	Sym
Following Instructions											✓		
Quality of Schooling	✓	✓	✓	✓	✓								
English Language Proficiency	✓	✓	✓	✓	✓	✓							
Acculturation (to American Culture)	✓	✓	✓	✓	✓								
Parental Cognitive Stimulation	✓	✓	✓	✓	✓								
Interest in Reading	✓	✓		✓	✓								
Anxiety Related to Stopwatch							✓	✓	✓	✓	✓	✓	✓
Willingness to Guess							✓						
Attention Span/Impulsivity			✓				✓	✓	✓	✓	✓	✓	✓
Experience with Comic Strips								✓					
Experience with Social Interaction								✓					
Fatigue/Boredom					✓	✓					✓	✓	✓
Values and Moral Development					✓								
Distractibility						✓							
Experience with Mazes												✓	
Processing Speed											✓		✓

The significant fluctuations in a profile give some guidelines as to where to search for profiles that may be of importance for understanding a child's cognitive skills. The profile in Figure 7.1 has only one significant fluctuation—a weakness on the Coding subtest. The next step is to *enter Table 7.2 and write down all shared subtest hypotheses* for Coding.

For a hypothesis to be listed as potentially viable, it has to include, of course, Coding and all, or nearly all, of the subtests that are lower than the subtest mean of 11. If one enters Table 7.2 the following hypotheses may be listed as plausible for shared subtest weaknesses that in-

clude Coding. The first hypothesis that includes the Coding subtest is sequencing. Across the page there are two other subtests that are hypothesized as placing a premium on this skill—Arithmetic and Digit Span. In order to list sequencing as a hypothesis worth investigating further, *all, or virtually all, of the scores for the subtests that are a part of this hypothesis should be at or below the subtest mean of 11.* Arithmetic does not lend support because of its score of 13. Digit Span mitigates further against listing this hypothesis because of its score of 13. Given this state of affairs, the sequencing hypothesis is discarded as a possible weakness and the search continues.

The next step is to reenter Table 7.2 and check the next hypothesis that includes the Coding subtest—short-term memory. This hypothesis will also not work because it includes the same subtests as the prior hypothesis—Arithmetic and Digit Span. This process continues until all shared subtest hypotheses are exhausted.

Step 3: Single Subtest Hypotheses

The level of single subtest interpretation was saved for last because it is the most treacherous, as it lacks reliability and validity support even more than the shared subtest level. This step involves taking the subtests that emerge as strengths or weaknesses and entering Table 7.2 in order to generate hypotheses for the Coding subtest in isolation. Entering Table 7.2 with Coding in mind, one can write the following list of hypotheses: weaknesses in clerical speed and accuracy, following instructions, and fatigue or boredom. A hypothesis not offered in Table 7.2 is dysgraphia (a written expression learning disability that could be secondary to a brain insult). This is but one of many potential hypotheses that is not offered in Table 7.2 because it is low-incidence, lacks research support, or is speculative. It is, however, an example of a hypothesis that may be offered based on the examiner's knowledge of the case.

Examiners also need to refer back to information on subtest specificity when offering a single subtest hypothesis. It would be helpful to record the subtest specificity on the sheet used for making case notes and listing hypotheses. The subtest specificity for Digit Span may bolster the clinician's confidence in the hypothesis, and for Object Assembly the clinician may decide apriori to not even entertain single subtest hypotheses.

Step 4: Corroborating or Rejecting Aposteriori Hypotheses

Now the clinician must determine which hypotheses have the most support by "testing" each hypothesis listed against background information, observations during testing, interview information, school or clinic records, reports of parents and teachers, other test scores, and WISC-R and WISC-III research findings.

Each hypothesis should be taken in turn, and the corroborating or conflicting evidence is recorded. *Two pieces of evidence* are generally adequate to corroborate or reject a hypothesis. In some cases one strong piece of evidence may corroborate a hypothesis. If, for example, the Arithmetic subtest of the WISC-III emerged as a lone weakness and it was subsequently learned that a previous teacher suspected a mathematics disability, then the previous suspicion of a mathematics learning disability may be a strong piece of evidence that explains the Arithmetic weakness. A more cloudy case would be the situation where Arithmetic is the lone weakness in a profile and there is no evidence of a mathematics problem.

The disconfirming evidence for a hypothesis can also be compelling. Low scores on Object Assembly and Block Design could be used to form a shared subtest hypothesis having to do with part–whole relationships. This is a difficult hypothesis to corroborate as is, but if the child had strengths on Pattern Analysis (a Block Design look-alike on the Stanford-Binet), the Bender (a design drawing task), and no problems with part–whole relationships are noted by parents or teachers, then the disconfirming evidence forces the clinician to attribute the findings to chance variation or some other factor. This hypothesis is then discarded as important.

Most aposteriori hypotheses will not be corroborated without collecting additional information (see Principle 9 above). If the clinician has done a careful job of offering apriori hypotheses, corroborating evidence will have been exhausted on these. Sometimes this additional data collection will be minor, requiring simply calling a child's teacher to find out about mathematics performance in order to corroborate an Arithmetic subtest weakness, for example.

Step 5: Draw Aposteriori Conclusions

If, however, apriori hypotheses are confirmed by WISC-III results, then these become important conclusions that should be favored over other conclusions that are discovered by aposteriori methods. *Specifically, if an apriori conclusion subsumes an aposteriori conclusion derived from aposteriori interpretive steps, then the apriori conclusion should receive priority in the interpretive process.*

There are also numerous situations in which apriori hypotheses are not confirmed by the data. In fact, these can be some of the most interesting cases. Such cases also tend to be those where intelligence tests are most insightful because the results are so incongruent with background information or the predictions of others. For this reason, aposteriori approaches to interpretation remain a necessity.

SAMPLE CASES

Connie

The basics of interpretation are now demonstrated with a sample case. Connie is a 16-year-old female who was evaluated subsequent to receiving hospital treatment for drug dependency. Her scores and significant profile fluctuations are shown in Figure 7.1. Connie's significant profile fluctuations were determined using the aforementioned procedures.

Apriori Hypotheses

Connie's teacher noted some strengths and weaknesses in school. Connie has a history of mathematics difficulties and writing problems and stronger skills in verbal/language arts areas. She was also noted to be highly verbal during the test session. Similarly, Connie smiled more during verbal tasks and displayed more motivation during verbal activities. The examiner noted "excellent verbal skills — expressed herself well." She also talked aloud when solving Performance scale tasks.

These behaviors and background information suggest relatively stronger verbal skills and a V > P difference for Connie. The size of this V > P difference can subsequently be tested to determine its statistical significance. A statistically significant V > P difference would support the hypothesis of a relative strength in verbal skills.

There are also no indications that Connie suffers from significant intellectual deficits or strengths. She has no record of special education or gifted referral or placement, for example. Social/emotional factors loom largest in conceptualizing her case. Hence, a second reasonable apriori hypothesis for Connie is that she possesses at least average intellectual skills. A third plausible apriori hypothesis would be a relative weakness on the Arithmetic subtest given her history of mathematics difficulties.

Test Apriori Hypotheses

Connie's intelligence is in the average to above-average range, which supports the apriori hypothesis of average intelligence.

In Connie's case there is a 21-point discrepancy between her Verbal standard score of 117 and Performance standard score of 96, supporting the V > P hypothesis. A difference this large is statistically significant (P < .05) and therefore warrants further investigation. Statistical significance, however, does not tell the whole story regarding differences between Verbal and Performance scales. This is the case because significant differences between Verbal and Performance standard scores is common in the national population. For example, although an 11-point discrepancy between Verbal and Performance standard scores is statistically significant at the .05 level, a difference this large or larger was obtained for approximately 40% of the standardization sample (table B.2, Wechsler, 1991). Consequently, a statistically significant difference can indicate whether or not a discrepancy is likely to be reliable; it may or may not be indicative of any abnormality that is unusual or that could be attributed to a particular disorder or handicapping condition.

A difference of 21 points is relatively rare (occurring in 11% of the population—see table 3.2, Wechsler, 1991); it begins to call into question the utility of the Full Scale standard score as a good summary score of Connie's intelligence.

Connie's apriori hypothesis of relative weakness on the Arithmetic subtest was not confirmed (see Figure 7.1) since this was not a significant weakness.

Aposteriori Hypotheses

Aposteriori hypotheses at the Composite score level are unnecessary since all of her scores were explained by the apriori method. Shared subtest hypotheses were obtained for Connie from Table 7.2. Coding is used as the "routing" test to enter the table since it is the lone significant profile fluctuation. If there were more than one strength or weakness, then each would be used to enter the table and derive possible shared hypotheses. Since all of the tests except Coding and Symbol Search hover at or above the mean of 11, shared hypotheses are not going to be easily derived from Figure 7.1. The search to find other tests on the same side of the mean as Coding that measure similar skills yielded only Symbol Search. Consequently, shared subtest hypotheses will be sought that link only these two tests. Hypotheses derived from Table 7.2 include clerical speed and accuracy, pencil and paper skill, and processing speed. Since Mazes was not administered it does not rule out pencil and paper skills.

A search for single subtest hypotheses for the Coding subtest in Table 7.2 yielded only "following instructions." These shared and single subtest hypotheses are recorded for the next stage of interpretation.

Drawing Conclusions

One can easily corroborate the apriori composite score hypothesis of average to above-average intelligence. First, Connie's achievement test scores were average to above average, and, secondly, the examiner noted that she was highly motivated to do well on the tests. For example, she frequently asked whether or not she solved items correctly. She also appeared somewhat confident of her skills. Both terms, "average" and "above average" are necessary because of the size of her V/P difference. It is appropriate in this case to deemphasize the value of the Full Scale score.

Connie's V > P profile hypothesis of a relative strength in verbal skills and weakness in nonverbal skills is also easily corroborated. It is noteworthy that her highest score on the Performance scale was on the only subtest on that scale that *elicits a verbal response* (i.e., Picture Completion).

It is also possible to support the aposteriori shared subtest hypothesis of a deficit in pencil and paper (writing) skill. According to her teacher she has particular difficulty expressing herself in writing. She also had a difficult time on the spelling test that was administered as part of the test battery. She erased frequently, which resulted in a messy written product. Connie's weakness in written expression was also shown in the following written responses to the sentence completion blank.

"I want to be like myself off of drugs"

"I hate to hear people say that I ain't tall"

"My greatest fault is to be avoiding"

No data were found to support the single subtest weakness of following instructions. This hypothesis is most appropriately subsumed under the shared subtest hypotheses.

In summary, in Connie's case there are only two reasonable hypotheses at the composite score level (average to above-average intelligence and verbal > nonverbal skills), and one at the shared subtest level (pencil and paper, or writing, skill). The remaining task is to take the pencil and paper skill hypothesis and try to attribute it to the more reliable and valid relative weakness in nonverbal areas. The goal here is to say that Connie's pencil and paper skill weakness is merely a reflection of her overall relative weakness in nonverbal areas.

In this case such a statement is not logical. While ideally one would like to err in the direction of "higher" levels of interpretation, the evidence for the shared subtest weakness in pencil and paper skill is compelling. Among the evidence that supports interpreting this weakness for Connie is:

1. Coding is one of two tests on the WISC-III requiring the child to use a pencil. The Symbol Search subtest score is Connie's next to lowest.

2. Coding is not slightly lower than the other tests but considerably lower. The next highest scaled score is 6 points higher. This is more than a 1½ standard deviation difference.

3. Writing problems were obvious on other tests administered as part of the evaluation.

4. A written expression weakness is well documented by teacher report.

5. Coding and Symbol Search possess ample subtest specificity (see Chapter 6).

In light of the aforementioned considerations, the following *conclusions* will be listed in Connie's report (see Chapter 8).

1. Connie's measured intelligence is in the average to above-average range.

2. Connie's verbal skills are stronger than her nonverbal skills. Her verbal skills are above average and her nonverbal skills are average.

3. Connie's written expression weakness was also reflected on the WISC-III, where she performed most poorly (well below average) on a test requiring her to copy nonsense symbols with a pencil as rapidly as possible and another test requiring her to work quickly with pencil and paper. While this conclusion is consistent with a written expression weakness, more testing would be recommended to document a bonafide learning disability.

Janna

Janna was referred by her teacher for being extremely loud in class, making facial contortions that caused others to be distracted during class activities, and throwing tantrums including stomping around the room and slamming doors.

Apriori Hypotheses

Janna's performance went from A's to D's during the past fourth-grade school year, primarily in the area of mathematics. She reportedly has a high activity level, including being constantly talkative, sitting on the edge of her seat, and constantly interacting with others. She is also aggressive toward other children and is frequently inattentive.

Janna's mother is a banker and her father is a store manager. Janna has a dramatic fear reaction to fire because when younger she was severely burned by a trash fire.

On a recent administration of an achievement test, Janna obtained the following national percentile ranks:

Reading Composite	97
Mathematics Composite	63
Writing	87
Spelling	58

Janna appeared for the test session as a friendly child who sat on the edge of her seat and engaged in animated conversation with the examiner. By the beginning of the Information subtest Janna was already bored with the testing. She was squirming in her chair and sighing. She became more serious, however, when Picture Arrangement was reached. She began to quiet down and work more diligently. Her behavior on the later subtests reflected this new-found diligence.

Janna was also observed in her classroom. On the day that Janna was observed, the children were engaged in an activity involving cutting and pasting incomplete sentences on construc-

Janna's WISC-III scores

Composite Scores

Full Scale Standard Score	118
Verbal Standard Score	118
Performance Standard Score	112

Subtest Scores

VERBAL SCALE	SCORE	MEAN	DIFFERENCE	SIGNIFICANCE VALUE	S OR W
Information	12	12	0	3	—
Similarities	14	12	2	4	—
Arithmetic	10	12	−2	4	—
Vocabulary	14	12	2	3	—
Comprehension	15	12	3	4	—
Digit Span	10	12	−2	3	—
Performance Scale					
Picture Completion	14	12	2	4	—
Coding	10	12	−2	4	—
Picture Arrangement	11	12	−1	4	—
Block Design	14	12	2	3	—
Object Assembly	10	12	−2	5	—
Symbol Search	12	12	−0	4	—

Overall Mean = 12
(12.2)

tion paper. Janna was observed to be talking with her neighbor occasionally. She was the only child who was standing most of the time while cutting the paper. She dawdled more than others before going to lunch. She also responded more slowly to teacher requests to be seated and prepare for lunch. She smiled frequently during the class session at other children and once at the student teacher in the classroom.

Available information for Janna suggests the following apriori hypotheses.

1. Average to above-average intelligence test composite scores. This hypothesis is suggested by average to above-average achievement test scores and the lack of any teratogens that may be associated with low intelligence.

2. Janna may have a weakness on the Information test because of less-than-optimal test behavior during the administration of that test.

No shared subtest hypotheses or V/P or Index score hypotheses are offered for Janna.

Test Apriori Hypotheses

Janna exhibits above-average to well-above-average intelligence as hypothesized. She also does not have a significant difference between her Verbal and Performance scores.

The hypothesis of an Information weakness was not supported by the data. In fact, Information was at the mean of her scores. The lack of subtest strengths and weaknesses produced no shared or single subtest hypotheses.

Aposteriori Hypotheses

Janna's test results do not suggest any aposteriori hypotheses.

Drawing Conclusions

Janna's profile is best interpreted at the composite score level. The overall conclusion to be reached is that on the majority of cognitive tasks she performs in the average to above-average range. Her subtest scores are clustered between 10 and 15, with no substantial strengths or weaknesses. Similarly, the 6-point difference between Verbal and Performance scores is not noteworthy.

Janna's case is interesting in that it shows how independent intelligence test scores can be from social/emotional factors. There were some hints of Janna's behavioral difficulties in the test session, but they were not overwhelming. Intelligence is not the focus of her evaluation, and the intelligence test scores may receive little emphasis when the assessment results are reported. Other types of assessment, such as behavioral assessment, are more relevant to understanding Janna's school difficulties.

Jerry

Jerry is a third-grader who was referred by his teacher for academic problems in all areas.

Apriori Hypotheses

When Jerry was 6 years old, he was in a serious automobile accident that resulted in head injuries. He returned to school approximately six months later and entered a class for the physically handicapped. He still suffers from hemiparesis on his right side. He drags his right foot when he walks and he has little strength in his right arm. Even before the accident, Jerry had significant school problems. According to his mother, he would become very frustrated and angry when he could not complete assignments on time. When tested *before* the accident he obtained a

Full Scale IQ of 68; approximately two months after the accident he obtained a Full Scale IQ of 54. On both tests Jerry showed a P > V pattern. According to his teacher, his strengths are social interaction and completing assignments. His weaknesses are visual memory and following instructions.

Jerry was administered the BASIS by his teacher, on which he obtained the lowest possible standard score of 65 on the Mathematics, Reading, and Spelling tests.

Observations during testing were that Jerry talks and walks slowly. He was slow to respond to many of the questions presented to him. At one point during the evaluation he asked what the word "arithmetic" meant. On the Picture Completion test he used pointing responses in lieu of verbal responses.

The aforementioned information suggests that following apriori hypotheses.

1. Significantly below-average intelligence test scores (less than 70) are suggested by his language delay, history of head trauma, and his previous WISC-R scores.
2. Jerry will likely have a P > V profile based on his previous WISC-R results, his history of language delays, and his observed difficulty expressing himself.
3. Jerry may have a shared subtest weakness in visual memory that would depress his Coding and Symbol Search scores.

No single subtest hypotheses are offered for Jerry.

Test Apriori Hypotheses

Jerry's intelligence test scores are significantly below average, which confirms the first hypothesis. The second hypothesis was not confirmed but was "hinted" at by his test results. Jerry's present P > V profile has occurred in previous evaluations but is statistically insignificant (unreliable).

Jerry's WISC-III scores

Composite Scores

Full Scale Standard Score	69
Verbal Standard Score	66
Performance Standard Score	75

Subtest Scores

VERBAL SCALE	SCORE	MEAN	DIFFERENCE	SIGNIFICANCE VALUE (TABLE B.3)	S OR W
Information	3	5	−2	3	—
Similarities	5	5	0	4	—
Arithmetic	4	5	−1	4	—
Vocabulary	4	5	−1	3	—
Comprehension	4	5	−1	4	—
Digit Span	3	5	−2	4	—
Performance Scale					
Picture Completion	8	5	−3	4	—
Coding	1	5	−4	4	W
Picture Arrangement	7	5	−2	4	—
Block Design	6	5	1	3	—
Object Assembly	8	5	−3	5	—
Symbol Search	1	5	−4	4	W

Overall Mean = 5
(4.5)

The hypothesized visual memory (Processing Speed index) weakness is supported by the emergence of Symbol Search and Coding as weaknesses. *When a member of the WISC-III third and fourth factors* (i.e., Arithmetic, Digit Span, Coding, Symbol Search) *emerges as a strength or weakness, the WISC-III index scores should be calculated in order to determine if these scores are a better interpretation of the results than the V/P distinction* (see later section on index scores). Jerry's index scores are as follows:

Verbal Comprehension (VC)	68
Perceptual Organization (PO)	85
Freedom from Distractibility (FFD)	64
Processing Speed (PS)	50

These scores shed a very different light on Jerry's profile. First, they support the apriori hypothesis of a relative weakness in verbal skills and relative strength in nonverbal skills, which is consistent with considerable background information. The VC, PS, and FFD scores are both significantly lower than the PO score at the .05 level (see table B.1 of the WISC-III manual).

In complementary fashion, these scores also support the apriori hypothesis of a relative weakness in visual memory. In this case the processing speed index score is not being interpreted as a measure of speed but rather as a measure of visual memory because of teacher information and observations during testing that suggested memory problems on these tests. This is not an unusual practice since WISC-III subtests are complex and many abilities are assessed by each one.

Aposteriori Hypotheses

Jerry's test results do not suggest any aposteriori hypotheses since all strengths and weaknesses were accounted for by apriori hypotheses.

Drawing Conclusions

The bulk of evidence identifies Jerry's intelligence as significantly below average. This consistent evidence makes it reasonable to emphasize the composite score conclusion in a report.

In Jerry's case, however, the WISC-III index scores give the clearest picture of his intellectual strengths and weaknesses. The index scores are also strikingly consistent with previous information. Because of the clarity with which the index scores describe Jerry's cognitive skills, these should be highlighted in written reports along with the Full Scale.

Many implications could be drawn from Jerry's WISC-III results. The relative strength in perceptual organization, for example, may be a valuable strength to emphasize in vocational planning.

Advanced WISC-III Interpretive Issues

Factor Analysis and WISC-III Interpretation Revisited

Now that case studies have been discussed, the importance of factor analysis for competent WISC-III interpretation should again be recognized. In many of the cases, which were a relatively random sample of children with a variety of presenting problems, the factor structure of the WISC-III was supported. For most children the Verbal and Performance scales were relatively unitary. When they were not, the results

mimicked closely the four-factor structure of the WISC-III. Specifically, when subtests deviated from the child's average, they tended to be those that correlated least with the Full Scale score, such as Coding, Symbol Search, and Digit Span. These and other factor analytic findings are probably *the clinician's most potent weapons* for making sense of WISC-III results.

Illusory V/P Differences and Subtest Scatter

One way of evaluating whether or not a Verbal/Performance discrepancy is illusory is to investigate *scatter* (the difference between the highest and lowest subtest scaled scores) within the Verbal and Performance scales. The normal range of scaled scores (the difference between the lowest subtest scaled score and the highest scaled score within the Verbal and Performance scales) is approximately 6 points for six Verbal tests and six Performance tests (table B.5, Wechsler, 1991). If the intrascale scatter is somewhat unusual, then it becomes difficult to interpret the Verbal and Performance scales as unitary dimensions. With considerable scatter the Verbal and Performance scales are best considered as assessing a variety of cognitive skills. When within-scale scatter is fairly large, reasonable conclusions may not lie in the Verbal/Performance scales or at the composite score level but at the shared or single subtest levels of interpretation.

Jerry's case provides a good example of the meaningfulness of intrascale scatter. Jerry's level of scatter with the Verbal and Performance scales is 2 (scaled scores of 3 to 5) and 7 (scaled scores of 1 to 8) respectively. The Verbal scale scatter is not unusual in that a difference of 2 points or larger between the lowest and highest subscale score occurred in 99.5% of the WISC-III norm sample (table B.5, Wechsler, 1991). A difference of 7 points or more for the Performance scale occurred in 46% of the norming sample (table B.5, Wechsler, 1991). The 7-point scatter on the Performance scale is not unusual by any standard, but it does hint that there is more diversity of skills on this scale than on the Verbal scale. A difference of 11 points on the Performance scale would indicate significant scatter, as a difference this large or larger occurred in 5% or less of the norming sample (table B.5, Wechsler, 1991).

Drawing Multiple Conclusions

Clinicians often seem reluctant to draw more than one conclusion for a child. The sense one gets is that they are searching for "the problem." Experienced intelligence test users recognize that a child may be suffering from numerous problems, including poor spatial skills, distractibility, a limited memory span, family dysfunction, and the like, and multiple weaknesses may not even be related to each other. The need to draw multiple conclusions is reflected in the previous cases, where it was recognized that children's behavior is multidimensional, multifaceted, and multidetermined. The psychologist who recognizes this complexity will provide more sophisticated evaluation results. Although parents and others may sometimes yearn for simple answers from psychologists, they will also recognize when they are receiving simplistic answers and lose respect for the psychologist's work.

Tell the Truth

On a similar note, psychologists do not gain by pretending to know answers when they do not. Admitting to unclear findings is not symptomatic of incompetence, but, rather, such acknowledgments typically signify that the examiner is thoughtful, careful, and concerned.

Clinicians can also make *tentative* conclusions in a report if further data are required to test a theory or hypothesis. If an uncorroborated Information subtest weakness is found, for example, an examiner should not feel compelled either to overinterpret the finding or to ignore it. The examiner in this case could write:

> *A clear explanation for Al's lower score on the Information subtest is not yet apparent. A second Information-like measure should be obtained to see if this is a reliable finding. One source of additional information could be scores on file such as Al's scores on the science, history, and social science sections of the achievement test used by his school.*

Inferring Cause-and-Effect Relationships

A particularly disconcerting problem of assessment reports is the tendency to offer cause-and-effect relationships between intelligence test profiles and a child's school or other problems. Concluding that a child cannot write because of poor visual-motor skills seems sensible, but it is nevertheless a *supposition*.

The examiner who offers such conclusions is inferring etiology, a tricky proposition at best. A similar temptation occurs in medical diagnosis. When a pediatrician diagnoses a problem, parents often ask questions such as, "How did he get this?" If a child were diagnosed with leukemia, a physician would be unlikely to say that the child acquired the condition from the chemical waste dump down the street. While this may be true, it would be difficult to prove given the multiple etiologies of leukemia. Similarly, the argument that a child's visual-motor weakness as identified on Block Design and other Wechsler tests is the "cause" of a reading problem is highly inferential. It is entirely possible that these two problems exist but are not related.

Other examples of inferring cause-and-effect relationships are:

> "Jason's mathematics problem is due to his problem with psychomotor speed."
> "Michelle's inattentiveness is caused by her school failure, which is adversely affected by her poor verbal intelligence."

"Aaron's writing problem is the result of his spatial processing problem."

Of course, the psychologist's (and the physician's) job in many cases *is* to infer cause-and-effect relationships. The point of this section is to ensure that psychologists clearly recognize when they are making such a conclusion so that they think critically about these inferences before making them. Examiners should also label an interference as such when they are offering it to the consumer of the results.

Supplementary WISC-III Procedures for Profile Analysis

Kaufman (1979b) popularized a method of WISC-R hypothesis generation involving determining subtest strengths and weaknesses *separately* for the Verbal and Performance scales. This procedure requires the examiner to compute separate mean scaled scores for the Verbal and Performance scales, then compare each subtest to its respective means. In order to use this procedure the following means must be computed.

1. Compute the mean scaled score of the Verbal scale subtests administered and round it to the nearest whole number.
2. Compute the mean of the Performance scale subtests administered and round it to the nearest whole number.

The examiner then computes significant strengths and weaknesses (table B.3, Wechsler, 1991) and then uses shared ability tables (Kaufman, 1979b) to develop hypotheses. Kaufman (1979b) then advises examiners to compute a grand subtest mean (as was done in the cases previously discussed), determine strengths and weaknesses, and search for additional shared hypotheses. The integrative approach described earlier did not determine significant fluctuations within scale, simply identifying subtest strengths and weaknesses based on all of the subtests administered.

The first step of the Kaufman (1979b) method is not featured in this text for the following reasons.

- Kaufman (1979b) does not provide a compelling rationale for determining fluctuations separately within scale.
- Since the rationale for profile analysis is to violate the apriori organization of the scales and the factor analytic findings, it seems incongruous to determine strengths and weaknesses separately for each scale.
- Newer tests determine strengths and weaknesses for all subtests combined (the K-ABC and Binet-4).
- The method used in this text deemphasizes profile analysis, which is consistent with recent research.
- The one-step method used in this text is easier for new students to learn.

The within-scale approach may be useful for testing the homogeneity of a child's performance on that scale. *This approach is most likely to be useful when there is a significant V/P discrepancy* (a V/P discrepancy of 11 points or more).

The WISC-III manual includes all of the data necessary to determine strengths and weaknesses separately for the Verbal and Performance scales in table B.3 (Wechsler, 1991). Examiners may want to initially use both methods for determining strengths and weaknesses—particularly if they are using computer scoring, which makes computation easy.

When to Retest

In some cases a psychologist may feel that the current intelligence test results are invalidated by other factors. In these instances there are basically two choices. The psychologist can make a "guesstimate" of the child's intelligence or retest the child. An example of using background information to help gauge if a child's scores were valid may help explicate the issue of retesting.

> *A 15-year-old female was hospitalized in a psychiatric unit of a general hospital for severe depression with psychotic features. She was suffering from visual hallucinations and an inability to "slow down" her thought processes. She had also slit her wrists in a suicide attempt just prior to admission. The patient was the product of a supportive family background. Her father was an engineer and her mother a school teacher. She had nearly a straight A average in her high school advanced placement program.*

On the WISC-R the subject above obtained a Full Scale of 115, which corresponds to the 84th percentile rank. While this score is above average, there is considerable evidence that her score could have been adversely affected by her mental illness. In this case the client should be tested again once her depressive and psychotic symptoms are under better control. Unfortunately, inaccurate intelligence test scores can remain in children's files or cumulative folders for some time and potentially result in misperceptions of their skills.

CONCLUSIONS

The integrative method of interpretation offered in this chapter is empirically based and emphasizes interpretation of intelligence test scores in the larger context of the child's life. One of the hallmarks of this approach is an emphasis on the corroboration of intelligence test results with other data. The case studies in this chapter emphasized the use of intelligence tests as one component of the diagnostic decision-making process, where sometimes the intelligence test results are primary and in other cases they are not as relevant. Clinicians must remember that *intelligence tests do not make decisions about children's lives—professionals*

do (Kaufman, 1990). In this more limited context, intelligence tests are much less likely to be overused or overinterpreted and more likely to be of value for helping to understand children.

CHAPTER SUMMARY

1. In the early days of psychological assessment, a premium was placed on interpretation of subtests and composite scores and subtest profiles. The Wechsler scales were instrumental in fostering this emphasis because of the provision of subtest scores.

2. Characteristics of an integrative method of intelligence test interpretation include the following:
   Principle 1: Collect and integrate data from numerous sources
   Principle 2: Corroborate conclusions with multiple data sources
   Principle 3: Support conclusions with research
   Principle 4: Interpretation should be individualized
   Principle 5: Emphasize reliable and valid conclusions
   Principle 6: Deemphasize subtest profile analysis
   Principle 7: Minimize calculations
   Principle 8: Interpretation is an iterative process
   Principle 9: Emphasize apriori interpretation

3. An interpretive hierarchy that is consistent with an integrative method is as follows.

SOURCE OF CONCLUSION	DEFINITION	RELIABILITY	VALIDITY
Composite scores	WISC-III IQs	Good	Good

SOURCE OF CONCLUSION	DEFINITION	RELIABILITY	VALIDITY
Shared subtest scores	Two or more subtests combined to draw a conclusion	Good	Fair to Poor
Single subtest scores	A single subtest score	Fair	Poor

4. The process of discovering intraindividual strengths and weaknesses in cognitive areas is a process commonly referred to as "ipsative interpretation." Ipsative interpretation refers to the situation in which the child serves as his or her own norm.

5. Profile analysis is the process of drawing conclusions based on differences between scores on the same test, combinations of subtests, and single subtests, as opposed to the composite score level of interpretation.

6. Shared subtest hypotheses possess some evidence of reliability but suffer from a lack of validity data.

7. Matheson, Mueller, and Short (1984) found that the acquired knowledge, conceptualization, sequencing, and spatial categories of Bannatyne had high reliabilities but problems with validity.

8. Profile analysis depends heavily on the clinical acumen of the examiner more than on research findings.

9. The typical procedure for determining significant strengths and weaknesses in Wechsler subtest profiles is to consult a table of values for determining the significance of a difference between a subtest score and the child's average subtest score.

10. Two pieces of evidence are generally adequate to corroborate or reject a hypothesis.

11. Always try to subsume less reliable and valid hypotheses under more reliable and valid ones. By doing so, the examiner errs in the direction of drawing hypotheses based on greater evidence of reliability and validity.

12. Always attempt to offer research and theory to support confirming or rejecting evidence.

13. One way of evaluating potentially illusory V/P differences is to investigate scatter within the Verbal and Performance scales.

14. Clinicians should feel free to draw more than one conclusion for a child.

15. It is generally risky to draw cause-and-effect relationships between WISC-III profiles and a child's school or other problems.

16. Kaufman (1979b) popularized a method of WISC-R hypothesis generation involving determining strengths and weaknesses separately for the Verbal and Performance scales.

17. Examiners should consider retesting if there is reason to believe that current intelligence test results were invalidated by other factors.

Report Writing and Oral Reporting

CHAPTER QUESTIONS

What is the best way to tell parents of their child's test results?

What are the common mistakes made in report writing?

Presenting test results in writing has been an often loathed aspect of the psychology profession. Fears of litigation, insecurities about interpretive skill, and nightmares of embarrassing spelling or grammatical errors have all contributed to making the writing process onerous for clinicians who use intelligence tests. Because of concerns such as these a chapter on report writing is crucial for every assessment text. As examiners know full well, their written products may "live in infamy."

Effective psychological report writing is taking on increased importance for practicing psychologists. Psychological reports are frequently made available to parents, judges, lawyers, and other nonpsychologists, creating the opportunity for improper interpretation of the results by untrained individuals. Often parents and others cling to the notion that the IQ is an entirely genetically based and fixed entity that is not associated with measurement error. Other misconceptions about intellectual assessment and the nature of intelligence make it imperative that psychologists communicate clearly, both orally and in writing.

An example of a situation in which a child's intelligence test scores should not be considered as fixed in stone could occur for a child who is diagnosed as having an attention deficit hyperactivity disorder (ADHD) and the child was tested prior to being placed on medication. This child could have been uncooperative in the test session, and the intelligence test scores could change markedly as a result of medical intervention. If the child's test scores have been adversely affected by his or her activity level and follow-up testing was not recommended, then the child's test scores collected under adverse

Interacting with parents

In a recent handbook contribution Tuma and Elbert (1990) gave some advice for understanding and dealing with parents in the assessment process. Children are often referred by their parents. If a parent defines a problem or set of problem behaviors, then the psychologist must deal directly with these problems in the assessment process. Parents are most concerned about child problems that increase the child's demands on them (Tuma & Elbert, 1990). However, parents may be less responsive to a child's problems at school and prefer to attribute these problems to the teacher or school situation. Parents of a delinquent child may have other issues requiring consideration in the assessment process. These parents may be unwilling or reluctant to obtain an evaluation and complain that they have been compelled by some authority to seek help with their child or adolescent.

Guilt is another issue that may arise with parents. Sometimes parents are racked with guilt about their child's behavior problems, assuming perhaps too much responsibility for their etiology. Another group of parents that may be difficult to deal with in the assessment situation is the parent(s) who is reluctant to become involved for fear that his or her own problems, learning disabilities, or psychopathology may be discovered. These parents may delay seeking help for their child until late adolescence or early adulthood (Tuma & Elbert, 1990), when they are seeking help primarily in order to get the child to leave the "nest."

Tuma and Elbert (1990) go on to identify four important phases of the parent feedback conference. The four components are: (1) *initial conference analysis*, in which the parents are asked for their own observations, impressions, and/or concerns about the child's behavior during an evaluation or any other concerns about the assessment process; (2) *problem discussion*, in which the psychologist presents the various assessment findings and discusses the implications of the assessment results; (3) is akin to a *consultation process*, in which recommendations and intervention planning are considered and recommendations may include those related to family, the child, the clinical facility, or the child's school; and (4) *summary*, in which the examiner reiterates the nature of the referral, significant assessment findings, and the recommendations and interventions to be carried out.

Tuma and Elbert (1990) further recommend that if a psychologist also has to present findings at the child's school where a large meeting will be called, it is incumbent upon the examiner to meet with the parents prior to the larger school conference. This allows parents and the psychologist to discuss aspects of the evaluation that would be inappropriate in a larger meeting because some topics may be invasions of the child's (or parents') privacy and confidentiality.

circumstances may be taken too seriously by the child's parents.

In addition, psychological reports remain particularly useful to other clinicians who evaluate a child who has previously been seen by a psychologist. A previous psychological report could be extremely valuable in a case of brain injury, if a child was given an intelligence test prior to the injury. The previous psychological report could be crucial as a measure of premorbid status. Estimates of premorbid status are extremely valuable because they allow the psychologist to determine the extent of cognitive impairment that may be due to brain insult (see

Chapter 15 for a detailed discussion of assessing brain-injured children).

As Glasser and Zimmerman (1967) correctly recognize, "the clarity of the original presentation will determine the use made of the examination at a later date." In the case of the ADHD and brain-injured children such as the ones just cited, the written psychological report becomes an extremely important piece of information for treatment planning and diagnosis because of its role in clarifying the nature of the obtained scores.

Despite its importance, the topic of report writing is a neglected one in the research literature (Ownby & Wallbrown, 1986). While a number of treatises are available on this topic (Teglasi, 1983; Tallent, 1988), little research has been done on the effects of report writing on important outcomes such as the likelihood that a recommendation will be followed (Ownby & Wallbrown, 1986).

Of the research on psychological report writing collected to date, Ownby and Wallbrown (1986) draw several discouraging conclusions. They conclude that psychological reports:

1. Are considered useful to some extent by consumers such as psychiatrists and social workers

2. Are frequently criticized by these professional groups on both content and stylistic grounds

3. May (or may not) make substantial contributions to patient management.

In addition to works concerning psychiatrists and social workers, a number of studies have assessed teachers' satisfaction with psychological reports, and here the news is not good (Ownby & Wallbrown, 1986). Researchers have found that teachers are frequently dissatisfied with these reports (Ownby & Wallbrown, 1986).

One can get a sense of why teachers and other professionals are dissatisfied with psychological reports by reading the following excerpt that was taken verbatim from a psychological report that was given to me several years ago by a colleague. All of the conclusions drawn by the evaluator in this case *are based on one test requiring the child to simply reproduce nine designs with pencil and paper.* In other words, this report was written by either an incredibly gifted or inept clinician!

The Bender-Visual Motor Gestalt test suggests delinquency and an acting out potential. He is anxious, confused, insecure and has a low self-esteem. He may have difficulties in interpersonal relationships and tends to isolate himself when problems arise. . . . (He) also seems to have a lot of anxiety and tension over phallic sexuality and may be in somewhat of a homosexual panic.

This examiner was apparently using a cookbook approach to interpretation to prepare this report. A report such as this is of no help to anyone, especially not the child being evaluated.

One of the difficulties with report writing is that different audiences require different reports. For example, a psychometric summary (a psychometric summary is a portion of the report that presents only test scores and is usually given as an appendix at the end of a report) given out of context is likely to be of little use to parents, but of great potential use to colleagues and perhaps teachers. An important decision that each psychologist must make prior to report writing is to determine the primary audience for the report. For example, a psychometric summary may be of minimal use to parents who have contracted with the psychologist in private practice for an evaluation. In this case it is more sensible to present test results in context in order to communicate effectively to parents. A psychometric summary is more in order in a clinic situation where it is imperative that a psychologist communicate effectively with knowledgeable colleagues.

PITFALLS OF REPORT WRITING

Norman Tallent (1988) produced a landmark textbook (now in its third edition) on report writing in which he summarized the literature on the strengths and weaknesses of reports as identified by psychologist colleagues in mental health care, most notably social workers and psychiatrists. Some of the highlights of Tallent's (1988) review will be outlined next.

Vocabulary Problems

As the reader may surmise from reading the report vignette given previously, the problem of using vague or imprecise language in report writing persists. The colloquial term used to describe such language is "psychobabble." Siskind (1967), for example, studied the level of agreement between psychologists and psychiatrists in defining words such as the following:

Abstract	Bizarre	Defense	Hostility
Affective	Bright Normal	Dependent	Immaturity
Aggression	Compulsive	Depressive	Impulsive
Anxiety	Control	Constriction	Emotional

The results of the study showed very little correspondence between the definitions proffered by the two groups of professionals.

Harvey (1989) explains how this problem of vague or imprecise language applies to school psychologists, who probably do the greatest amount of assessment work with children and adolescents. Harvey also points out that, because of the passing of the "Buckley Amendment" and the increasingly common practice of giving reports to parents, the educational level of the typical consumer of psychological reports is lower than in the past. While many writers of psychological reports use language consistent with their graduate-level training, such language may be at a reading level far beyond the capability of the target audience, particularly if the audience is parents or even adolescents. Harvey (1989) notes that even respected magazines are written at a high school level. The *Atlantic Monthly* is written at a 12th-grade level, and *Time* and *Newsweek* at 11th-grade levels (Harvey, 1989).

Tallent (1988) refers to one aspect of this problem with language as "exhibitionism," which seems to be a frequent criticism of reports, particularly on the part of other psychologists. One commentator stated, "They are written in stilted psychological terms to boost the ego of the psychologist."

Other pertinent observations (Tallent, 1988) on the use of language by psychologists in reports include:

"Semantics have a tendency to creep in, and the phenomenon of 'verbal diarrhea' occurs too often."

"They are too often written in a horrible psychologese — so that clients 'manifest overt aggressive hostility in an impulsive manner' — when, in fact — they punch you on the nose."

"They are not frequently enough written in lay language. I believe it requires clear thinking to write without use of technical terms."

And my personal favorite is:

"Scores have little meaning even to the psychologist who understands their rationale, unless he knows how they fit together in terms of cause and effect regarding behavior. To cover up his ignorance he resorts to the reporting of percentages, ratios, etc., and overwhelms his reader with such technical language that little information is conveyed."

Actually, I have one more favorite.

"They are not clear enough to be wrong."

Of course, psychologists cannot be singled out as the only profession with a preference for its own idiosyncratic terminology, as anyone who reads a physician's report or legal contract will admit.

Eisegesis

Eisegesis is the problem of "faulty interpretation based on personal ideas, bias, and what not" (Tallent, 1988). It is most readily seen in reports where the psychologist is clearly using the same theories or drawing the same conclusions in every report. A psychologist may conclude that all children's problems are due to poor ego functioning, neuropsychological problems, or family system failure. Psychologists who aspire exclusively to behavioral principles, for example, will attribute all child problems to faulty reinforcement histories. The savvy consumer of this psychologist's reports will eventually become wary of the skill of the psychologist, as the relevance of this theory to some cases is questionable. One can imagine the skepticism that may be engendered by a psychologist who concludes that a child whose school performance has just deteriorated subsequent to a traumatic head injury merely needs more "positive reinforcement" to bring his grades up to pretrauma levels.

The problem of eisegesis may also occur if a psychologist draws conclusions that are clearly in conflict with the data collected for a child. I have seen an extraordinarily large number of students who never seemed capable of assessing intelligence accurately because they always found some mitigating circumstance. Either the child was not sitting still, the room was too hot, or the child just did not seem motivated to take the test. If a child obtained a low standard score (which is typical because children are usually referred because of problems), it was considered invalid and the conclusion drawn that the child's "true ability" was undoubtedly considerably higher. Teachers who receive this interpretation consistently from the same psychologist may eventually pay more attention to the data presented in the reports and ignore the psychologist's conclusions.

Report Length

Psychologists, more so than other groups, complain about the excessive length of reports (Tallent, 1988). However, length may not be the real issue. Perhaps long reports are used to disguise incompetence, fulfill needs for accountability, or impress others. The possibility that length is a cover for other ills is offered in the following quotation (Tallent, 1988).

> *A certain business executive likes to relate the anecdote about the occasion when he assigned a new employee to prepare a report for him. In due time a voluminous piece of writing was returned. Dis-*

mayed, the executive pointed out that the required information could be presented on one, certainly not more than two, pages. "But sir," pleaded the young man, "I don't know that much about the matter you assigned me to." (p. 72)

It may also be worth considering that the Ten Commandments are expressed in 297 words, the Declaration of Independence in 300 words, and the Gettysburg Address in 266 words (Tallent, 1988).

A Number Emphasis

Psychologists are also infamous for having sections of their report entitled something like "Test Results." In this part of the report the reader usually gets the sense that the child is of secondary importance and the numbers are of greatest importance (Tallent, 1988). The psychologist needs to keep clearly in mind that the child is the loadstar of the evaluation, and the numbers obtained from intelligence tests and the like are only worthy of emphasis if they contribute to the understanding of the child being evaluated. All too frequently the numbers take precedence in assessment results sections. One way to think of the scores is as a means to an end, the end being better understanding of the child. The same numbers for two children can mean two quite different things. Just as a high temperature reading can be symptomatic of a host of disorders from influenza to appendicitis, so, too, a low intelligence test score can reveal a host of possible conditions.

One horrendous error made often in reporting test scores is when a psychologist reports a child's IQ and then says that it's invalid. Then why report it (Tallent, 1988)? If a test score is invalid, how does it serve the child to have this score as part of a permanent record? Is it to record for all time the lack of logic on the part of the psychologist? This purpose seems to be the only one served by reporting scores in which the clinician has little, if any, faith. Reporting invalid scores is akin to a physician making a diagnostic decision based on a fasting blood test where the patient violated the fasting requirements. In all likelihood the flawed results would not be reported; rather, the patient would be required to retake the test. *Clinicians do not have to report scores for a test if they think that the results are invalid.*

Failure to Address Referral Questions

Tallent (1988) points out that psychologists too often fail to demand clear referral questions and, as a result, their reports appear vague and unfocused. This very obvious point is all too frequently overlooked. Psychologists should insist that referral sources present their questions clearly, and, if not, the psychologist should meet with the referring person to obtain further detail on the type of information that is expected from the evaluation (Tallent, 1988). Many agencies use referral forms to assist in this process of declaring assessment goals. A form similar to those used by hospitals is shown in Figure 8.1 and one suitable for use by school systems is given in Figure 8.2.

THE CONSUMER'S VIEW

A few studies have evaluated psychological reports from the viewpoint of the consumer (Mussman, 1964; Rucker, 1967; Brandt & Giebink, 1968). One rather clever study evaluated teacher preferences for and comprehension of varying report formats (Weiner, 1985). This study required a group of elementary school teachers to read and rate their comprehension of and preferences for three different reports for the same child.

The three reports used were a "short form," a "psychoeducational report," and "question-and-answer." The short form report was one page, single spaced. It used some jargon, such as

acronyms, to shorten length; conclusions were drawn without reference to a data source; and recommendations were given without elaboration. The psychoeducational report format was 3½ single-spaced pages. It used headings such as "Reason for Referral," "Learning Style," "Mathematics," "Conclusions," and "Recommendations." Observations were stated in behavioral terms with examples used freely. Recommendations were given and elaborated, and acronyms and other jargon were only used when they were defined in text. The question-and-answer report was similar to the psychoeducational report in many ways, but it did not use headings per se. This report listed referral questions and then answered each question in turn. This report was 4½ pages long.

Now the time has come to crown the winner! Was it the short form, the psychoeducational, or the question-and-answer format? Amazingly enough, in this study *length* was preferred. First, teachers comprehended the two longer reports better. Second, of the two longer reports, the teachers preferred the question-and-answer report over the psychoeducational report. The short form was clearly preferred least.

These are interesting results in that they hint that length may be overrated as a problem in report writing, and that teachers may prefer a question-and-answer report format. This latter finding is interesting to me because I have never seen anyone use this format in my entire career as a psychologist!

Do parents have different preferences from teachers? In a follow-up study with parents, using the same methodology, Weiner and Kohler (1986) found that teachers and parents have similar preferences. In this second study the same three report formats were used. As was the case with teachers, parents comprehended the two longer reports significantly better than the short form report. An interesting additional finding was that parents with a college education comprehended reports better than parents with a high school diploma. Parents also tended to prefer the question-and-answer format to the other

Patient Name_____

Medical Record Number_____

Attending Physician_____

Type of Consultation_____

Signed_____Title_____Date_____

Results of Consultation:_____

Date of Consultation_____

Signature of Consultant_____Title_____Date_____

FIGURE 8.1

Sample referral form

two formats, although the difference in preference scores between the psychoeducational and question-and-answer reports failed to reach statistical significance.

Taken together, these two studies suggest that the two most frequent consumers of child and adolescent psychological reports, parents and teachers, consider the clarity of reports to be more important than their absolute length. They also show a preference for reports that have referral questions as their focus.

SUGGESTED PRACTICES

Report Only Pertinent Information

One of the most difficult decisions to make when writing a report involves gauging the relevance of information included (Teglasi, 1983). Examiners happen onto a great deal of information during the course of an evaluation, some of

School District_____Referring School_____
Student's Name _____Date of Referral_____
Address_____Phone_____Birthdate_____
Grade_____Grade Repeated_____Attendance (days absent)_____
Is the student now receiving speech therapy? ___yes   ___no

Communications Problems	Never	Sometimes	Often
Expressive Language (Problems in grammar, limited vocabulary)	—	—	—
Receptive Language (Comprehension, not following directions)	—	—	—
Speech (Poor enunciation, lisps, stutters, omits sounds, infantile speech)	—	—	—

Physical Problems	Never	Sometimes	Often
Gross Motor Coordination (Awkward, clumsy, poor balance)	—	—	—
Fine Motor Coordination (Eye-hand, manual dexterity)	—	—	—
Visual (Cannot see blackboard, squints, rubs eyes, holds book too close)	—	—	—
Hearing (Unable to discriminate sounds, asks to have instructions repeated, turns ear to speaker, often has earaches)	—	—	—
Health (Example: epilepsy, respiratory problems, etc.)_____	—	—	—

Medication: __ yes   __ no   Type:_____

Classroom Behavior	Never	Sometimes	Often
Overly energetic, talks out, out of seat	—	—	—
Very quiet, uncommunicative	—	—	—
Acting out (Aggressive, hostile, rebellious, destructive, cries easily)	—	—	—
Inattentive (Short attention span, poor on-task behavior)	—	—	—
Doesn't appear to notice what is happening in the immediate environment	—	—	—
Poor Peer Relationships (Few friends, rejected, ignored, abused by peers)	—	—	—

Academic Problems	Never	Sometimes	Often
Reading (word attack, comprehension)	—	—	—
Writing (Illegible, reverses letters, doesn't write)	—	—	—
Spelling (Cannot spell phonetically, omits or adds letters)	—	—	—
Mathematics (computation, concepts, application)	—	—	—
Social Science, Sciences (Doesn't handle concepts, doesn't understand relationships, poor understanding of cause and effect)	—	—	—

Other Problems_____
What methods/materials have you tried to solve the problems?_____
_____

_____   _____
Signature and Position of referring person   Chairperson/School Position

FIGURE 8.2

Sample student referral form

which is tangential. Say, for example, a child is referred for an evaluation of a suspected learning disability. During the course of an interview with the child's mother, she recounts at length her disappointment with her husband. She tells the examiner that her husband is dating other women, and she believes that he is not spending adequate time with their son.

In writing the report on this case, the clinician has to determine whether or not this information is pertinent to the learning disability evaluation. This example is used because it is rather obvious that the husband's infidelity is not directly linked with learning disabilities, and the mother's report about her husband may or may not be able to be corroborated. In most cases, however, the decision is not so obvious. If, for example, the above case were a referral for behavioral problems at home, the parents' marital satisfaction might be of relevance to the referral problem. Clinicians must think critically about the information that they include in reports and consider its relevance to the case. If information is not relevant to the referral problem and if it is very personal information, the psychologist should consider carefully the decision to invade the family's privacy and include the information in the report.

Define Abbreviations and Acronyms

Acronyms are part of the idiosyncratic language of psychological assessment. They can greatly facilitate communication among psychologists but hinder communication with nonpsychologists. Psychologists, just like other professionals, need to use nontechnical language to communicate with parents, teachers, and other colleagues in the mental health field. A pediatrician would not ask a mother if her child had an emesis; rather, the physician would inquire whether or not the child vomited.

When writing a report, psychologists should try to *avoid using acronyms*, at least undefined

ones. To simply use the acronym "WISC-III" is inappropriate. On the other hand, the use of the complete name, the "Wechsler Intelligence Scale for Children-Third Edition," repeatedly throughout a report seems clumsy and laborious. *Acronyms and short forms can be used effectively if they are defined.* However, short names (abbreviations) of tests should be used for reports geared toward parents and teachers, and acronyms should be used in reports for mental health care colleagues that are familiar with test scores. Examples of how one could define abbreviations or acronyms for later reference in a report are shown below.

- Wechsler Intelligence Scale for Children-Third Edition (Wechsler Scale)
- Wechsler Intelligence Scale for Children-Third Edition (WISC-III)

At later points in the report, the psychologist can then refer to the WISC-III or Wechsler Scale.

Emphasize Words Rather than Numbers

Particularly in the test results section of a report, clinicians must resist the "wizardry of numbers" (Zimmerman & Woo Sam, 1967). Words communicate more effectively than numbers because they communicate more directly. The typical question is not what the child obtained on the WISC-III but, rather, determining how the child's intelligence compares to others. As an example, instead of saying, "Demetrius obtained a Full Scale standard score of 106," say something like "Demetrius' intelligence is in the average range."

Reduce Difficult Words

This issue is by now an obvious one. The difficult part for report writers is following through on this advice. Consider the following two paragraphs that differ greatly. The first vignette uses a level of vocabulary that is too high for most consumers of reports. The second example is a rewrite of the first paragraph that uses a lower vocabulary level:

> *There is also evidence from the cognitive test data to suggest that Pam is very obdurate in response to anxiety. She may also tend to be concrete and not notice some of the subtleties of interpersonal discourse. Given these idiosyncrasies, she may find it difficult to generate effective social problem-solving strategies and strategies for coping with life's stressors.*

The next paragraph tries to communicate more clearly by using, among other things, simpler language.

> *Pam responds to stress by withdrawing from others (e.g., in her room or leaving a group of friends while on a social outing), which seems to be the only method she uses for dealing with stress. She also has trouble understanding and responding to messages given by others in social situations (e.g., body language or verbal hints). Because of these behavior patterns, Pam has trouble keeping friends.*

Related to the use of difficult words is the issue of using the correct person. Occasionally, instead of using the child's name, he or she is referred to as "the child" or "the subject." This usage sounds too mechanistic and impersonal for a psychological report. In most cases the use of the child's name is better. In a sentence such as the following: "The child scowled at the examiner," a better alternative would be: "Sandy scowled at the examiner."

Describe the Tests Used

In many cases it is safe to assume that parents or other readers of the report have little knowledge of the tests being used. This is why I suggest that report writers describe the nature of the assessment devices. Prior to the ready availability of personal computers, this task would have been onerous. Now it is relatively easy, since a description of each test can be stored, retrieved, and inserted as necessary. The following paragraph could be used to describe the WISC-III to parents.

> *(Child's Name)* was evaluated with the Wechsler Intelligence Scale for Children-III (WISC-III). This test is a popular scale made up of 13 subtests that assess various aspects of intelligence although 12 tests are typically used. The tests are divided into two types: Verbal and Performance. Verbal tests have items such as defining vocabulary words, answering common-sense questions, and answering factual questions on topics such as science. The Performance tests have items such as constructing puzzles and abstract designs and identifying missing parts of a picture. The WISC-III produces three scores: Verbal, Performance, and Full Scale, where the Full Scale is based on the sum of the scores on all of the tests.

An introductory paragraph for a test such as the WISC-III is probably not as crucial because of the WISC-R's longstanding popularity. Even so, the WISC-III means nothing to most parents the examiner will encounter. An introductory paragraph describing the intelligence test being used is even more appropriate for newer tests such as the K-ABC, Binet-4, and Woodcock-Johnson Cognitive, since these tests are not as widely used as the WISC-III.

The naive reader of a report will also be assisted by a description of the subtest that is being discussed. This fact is particularly true for tests that are not adequately described by their names. Take, for example, the Coding subtest of the WISC-III. The name "Coding" could conjure up a variety of images in a report reader's mind. Instead of concluding that a child had a weakness in Coding, the report writer could state that the child had a weakness on a test that required using a pencil to copy as many geometric symbols (which are to follow a code given at the top of the page) as possible in a

2-minute period. For verbal tests, examples of items may be given to communicate the nature of a task. One example may be to say that a child "showed a wide range of knowledge that was demonstrated on the Information subtest (sample item: Who was Pablo Picasso?) of the WISC-III." When sample items are used, however, they should be analogous items and not actual test items. This suggestion is in keeping with the ethical guidelines of the American Psychological Association that charge psychologists with maintaining the security of test items (see Chapter 17).

Edit the Report at Least Once

I have found that a number of my students do not take a critical eye toward editing their own work. Editing is necessary to ensure the most accurate communication in the least amount of space. Tallent (1988) provides the following excellent example of how an editor thinks:

> There is the tale of the young man who went into the fish business. He rented a store, erected a sign, FRESH FISH SOLD HERE, and acquired merchandise. As he was standing back admiring his market and his sign, a friend happened along. Following congratulations, the friend gazed at the sign and read aloud, "FRESH FISH SOLD HERE. Of course it's here. You wouldn't sell it elsewhere, would you?" Impressed with such astuteness, the young man painted over the obviously superfluous word. The next helpful comment had to do with the word sold. "You aren't giving it away?" Again impressed, he eliminated the useless word. Seemingly that was it, but the critic then focused on the word fresh. "You wouldn't sell stale fish, would you?" Once more our hero bowed to the strength of logic. But finally he was relieved that he had a logic-tight sign for his business; FISH. His ever alert friend, however, audibly sniffing the air for effect, made a final observation: "You don't need a sign." (p. 88)

Psychologists do not need to engage in such severe editing, but they should at least make an attempt to think critically about their word usage in order to reduce report, sentence, and paragraph length. The problem with editing is that for some people it can become a "neurosis" in itself, as was the case in the smelly fish story above. Despite this down side, judicious editing can go a long way toward clarifying meaning in a report.

An examiner could conclude, for example, that, "Roy performed in a manner on the WISC-III that is indicative of intelligence in the average range when compared to his peers." An editor might suggest the following alternative for this statement: "Roy's WISC-III score is in the average range."

Sometimes new examiners are not used to critiquing their own writing. One readily available option is to have a colleague read reports. Confidentiality, however, should be kept in mind if an editor is used.

Use Headings and Lists Freely

Headings and lists can serve to enhance the clarity of communication (Harvey, 1989). If, for example, an examiner draws a number of conclusions about a child, these can sometimes lose their impact if they are embedded in paragraphs. Here is an example.

"Shirley has a specific learning disability in mathematics reasoning. In addition to this, she is having difficulty interacting with her peers. She appears to have a social skills deficit. Shirley exhibits strong reading skills and a great deal of interest in reading for pleasure."

These conclusions could have an increased impact if headings and lists were used as shown below.

Conclusions

1. Shirley has a specific learning disability in mathematics reasoning.
2. Shirley has social skills problems that are adversely affecting relationships with her peers.

3. Shirley's strength is in reading, which she nourishes with a great deal of leisure reading.

As one would predict, the use of headings and lists to excess has a down side. A report that uses too many lists, for example, becomes stilted, and it may not communicate all of the texture and subtleties of the child's performance. Report writers should consider using additional headings if a section of their report stretches for nearly a page (single spaced) without a heading. Examiners should consider lists if they want to add impact to statements that they want to ensure the reader remembers.

Use Examples of Behavior to Clarify Meaning

Since there is some disagreement as to the meanings of particular words, report writers should clarify meaning in order to ensure accuracy. Words that may conjure up a variety of interpretations include *anxiety, cooperation, dependent, hyperactive,* and *low self-esteem.* One way to foster clarity is to use examples of the child's behavior. Here, for example, are two ways to say that Emilio was anxious.

1. "Emilio exhibited considerable anxiety during the testing."
2. "Emilio appeared anxious during the testing. He frequently asked whether or not he had solved an item correctly, he would occasionally look at the ticking stopwatch during an item and then hurry, and his face became flushed when it was obvious to him that he did not know the answer to a question."

An additional benefit of using examples of behavior is that it forces the psychologist to consider the extent of supporting evidence for a conclusion about a child's behavior. If a psychologist writes that a child is anxious but cannot think of behaviors to buttress this observa-

tion, then the conclusion should not be drawn, as it is unsupportable.

Direct quotations are also very helpful in clarifying meaning. If a clinician concludes that an adolescent is "suicidal," a quotation from the child may help clarify this statement considerably. The child may have said, "I thought about taking some pills once" or "I feel like I want to run out in front of a car tonight and if that doesn't work, I will steal my father's gun and kill myself." These are obviously varying degrees of suicidal intent that are most clearly differentiated by knowing what the child or adolescent actually said.

Reduce Report Length

Tallent (1988) gives the following instances as indices of undue length. A report is too long when:

- The psychologist is concerned that it took too long to write it.
- The psychologist has difficulty organizing all of the details for presentation.
- Some of the content is not clear or useful.
- The detail is much greater than can be put to good use.
- Speculations are presented without a good rationale for them.
- The writing is unnecessarily repetitious.
- The organization is not "tight."
- The reader is irritated by the length or reads only a few sections such as the summary or recommendations sections.

The issue of length is primarily a concern of other psychologists, and it is intertwined with other issues, such as clarity. Hence, the psychologist in training should not assume that shorter is better. Quality may be a more important issue than quantity. Concern about length should never interfere with the need to portray a child's performance accurately.

Check Scores

An all too frequent and grievous error is to report scores that are incorrect. Psychological expertise and clerical skill may not be highly correlated variables. One major breakthrough that is helping with this problem is computerized scoring. In fact, if the facilities are available, *each test protocol that is scored by hand should be checked against computer scoring.* If this is not possible, the test scores should at least be checked prior to finalizing a report. Having to recant scores because an error was caught by someone else is very embarrassing.

One way of checking scores is to be alert to inconsistencies. If a child who was referred for possible mental retardation obtains a score in the average range, then the score should be checked to see if a scoring error is the source of the incongruity. Other situations that may make an examiner suspicious would include a child suspected of a learning disability in math whose Arithmetic score is the child's highest score on the WISC-III, a child with a 50-point discrepancy between Verbal and Performance IQs, or the case where the examiner thought that the child was doing rather well on a test and yet it turned out to be the lowest score in the profile. The clinician needs to be ever vigilant in order to avoid scoring errors. If a score doesn't seem sensible, then the examiner should always check for a scoring error in order to rule out this possibility.

Check Spelling

Another problem with reports that detracts from the credibility of the examiner is the presence of spelling errors. Most examiners today have access to a microcomputer and word processing—and checking—programs, which makes spelling errors almost inexcusable. Careless errors in a written report reduce the likelihood of readers crediting an examiner with sage wisdom.

Many psychologists now have more sophisticated tools at their disposal, such as an electronic thesaurus and grammar/usage checker. These tools can also be beneficial in that they can help to further "polish" the final report.

Avoid Stating Etiologies Routinely

An often confused aspect of interpretation is the difference between inferring *etiologies versus consistencies.* It is clear from research findings, for example, that low SES is associated with lower intelligence test scores (as it is with health problems and other difficulties). It is quite a different matter to conclude that low SES *causes* low scores for a particular child. It is more sensible to conclude that if a child from a low-SES background obtains a high score this finding is *inconsistent* with research on the relationship between SES and intelligence test scores. Similarly, if this same child obtains a slightly below-average Full Scale score, one may conclude that this score is *consistent* with research findings, which suggests the Full Scale score is a predictable finding. In this case, however, the clinician should not conclude that the child's low-SES circumstances *caused* the lower-than-average scores. It could be that a brain injury caused the lower scores independent of SES.

Inferring etiologies is speculative. The clinician may offer *theories,* but they should be presented as such, not as *facts.* The difference between inferring etiologies and simply stating findings and consistencies is exemplified by medical diagnostic practice. Many people have been affected by cancer. They have had a relative who suffered from cancer or had cancer themselves. One of the first questions leveled at the attending physician in such circumstances by the patient and family members is the question of etiology. Was it my diet, sunbathing, smoking, genetic inheritance, or other factors that are associated with various cancers? What about the case of the individual with lung cancer who has never smoked? When sharing such dreadful news of cancer with patients, physicians will hedge on the issue of etiology or present a theory, just as psychologists often do when sharing intelligence test results. It is most accurate in routine evaluations to simply cite consistencies that support current intelligence test results.

Often psychologists are asked to infer etiologies in court testimony or other forums. These occasions require careful study, exhaustive data collection, and presentation of results with appropriate caveats. Often consumers of intelligence test data want simple answers regarding etiologies, but these are indeed rare in everyday practice. Often children experience multiple insults (as will be shown in many of the case studies herein), making the determination of a single insult as *the* etiological agent a veritable impossibility. These comments are not intended to convey the idea that the assessment of cognitive development or skills lacks utility; to the contrary, knowledge of cognitive status can be revealing. *These cautions are given to discourage the routine determination of etiology in oral or written psychological reports when substantial evidence is lacking.*

ADAPTING REPORTS TO AUDIENCE AND SETTING

It is probably a truism that no report format is optimal. Different audiences have different characteristics, such as literacy levels, but, more importantly, different audiences have different questions.

In a school setting, where most of the psychological assessment of children is conducted, the most frequent referral is for a learning problem. As such, the intelligence test results are of great concern and are usually the featured aspect of the report. Teachers are also seeking information to assist them with curriculum decisions.

In a psychiatric hospital setting the most frequent referrals are likely to be for problems such as depression, conduct disorder, and alcohol or drug abuse. In this setting, intelligence test results are frequently of little concern to the treatment team. Of greater concern are issues such as suicide potential and coping strategies. These questions are very different than those of the school setting, requiring a focus on topics other than intelligence.

Parents are yet another audience with different questions. When conducting an evaluation for parents in a private practice setting, the emphasis is on what the parents can do to effect a change in their child's behavior. The three reports given next reflect the variety of report writing styles that may be used in different settings.

Private Practice—Parents

The following report was written for the adolescent being evaluated and for the parents (who paid for the evaluation). Both the parents and client were looking for explanations and assistance in dealing with the client's difficulties in high school.

Psychological evaluation for Harry (confidential)

NAME: Harry   GRADE: 12
DATE OF BIRTH: 3/28/70   SCHOOL: Valley Preparatory School
AGE: 16 years, 2 months

Assessment Procedures   Date
Wechsler Intelligence Scale for Children-Revised (Wechsler)   May 22, 1987
Diagnostic Interview   May 22, 1987

Mental Status Exam	May 22, 1987
Sentence Completion Test	May 22, 1987
Kaufman Test of Educational Achievement—Comprehensive Form (K-TEA)	May 22, 1987
Family History	By mail
Minnesota Multiphasic Personality Inventory (MMPI)	May 22, 1987

Referral Information

Harry's father initiated the evaluation process. He was referred by a local tutoring service. Harry is having some difficulty with his coursework at the residential high school he attends. Harry also expressed an interest in determining whether or not he has a learning disability and in deciding whether or not to attend college.

Background Information

Harry grew up in a large eastern city with his parents and his older sister. His father and mother both have some college education. His father is a manager, and his mother is a nurse.

Harry's parents describe his developmental history as normal. He was also described as having school problems at an early age. During his elementary years, he had difficulty with reading, writing, and arithmetic and had a generally slow rate of learning. His parents provided for tutoring beginning in the fourth grade. Harry also had ear surgery when he was 9 years old to correct a mild hearing loss. His parents were told by his teachers that he had a reading comprehension problem. His mother also reported being told that Harry had a below-average IQ and that he would probably never be able to succeed in college. He was never retained.

Harry had many friends in grammar school, but he has had some problems with social relationships in high school. Harry describes himself as being rebellious during his teenage years. He obtained primarily average grades. He stated that he did not like himself until his junior year when he read a self-help book. When he was 10, he was seriously injured in a train wreck. He has a large scar on his cheek that he said is the result of being thrown into a seat during the accident. Harry reported that he was unconscious for about a week. Harry was in a rehabilitation program at University Hospital for about a month, where he received speech and physical therapy. Harry said that he had to learn how to write and speak all over again. He said that his school grades were about the same before and after the accident. He did miss a great deal of school because of the accident.

At school Harry lives in a dormitory. He had particular problems this past year with a political science class, for which he received tutoring. He has also received poor grades in the sciences, mathematics, and history. He has received better grades in art, physical education, and music. His cumulative grade point average is now a 2.0 (where 2.0 = C). He has scored poorly on college entrance exams. He reports that "studying does not help."

Harry is involved in student activities, including a French club and band. He likes dancing, conversation, "hanging out with friends," and parties. Harry expressed some concern about not having a girlfriend.

Behavioral Observations and Interview Data

Harry appeared very open and honest in the interview situation. He maintained excellent eye contact and did not hesitate before responding to questions. Harry said that he enjoyed being interviewed.

Harry's behavior during testing was similarly exemplary. He tried very hard on all of the tests. He was so reluctant to give up when faced with test items too difficult for him that the testing session lasted longer than one would anticipate for an individual his age. At one point during the testing he said, "I'm slow." He was cooperative and hard working throughout the session.

Test Results and Conclusions

Harry was evaluated with the Wechsler Intelligence Scale for Children-Third Edition (WISC-III). This popular scale is made up of several subtests (usually 12 tests are used) that assess various aspects of intelligence. The tests are divided into two types: Verbal and Performance. Verbal tests have items such as defining vocabulary words, answering common-sense questions, and answering factual questions on topics such as science. The Performance tests have items such as constructing puzzles and abstract designs and identifying missing parts of a picture. The Weschler produces three scores: Verbal, Performance, and Full Scale; the last is based on the sum of the scores on all of the tests.

(continued)

Psychological evaluation for Harry (confidential) *(continued)*

Harry's performance on the Weschler indicates that overall he is currently functioning in the well below-average range of intelligence. There is a 90% probability that his performance meets or exceeds that of approximately 3–12% of his agemates. While this is a low estimate of intelligence in comparison to the general population, it is of particular concern when one considers the fact that his prep school competitors typically have higher test scores than the population at large.

This overall intelligence score is, however, something of a misrepresentation of his skills in that on some subtests he scored in the average range, while on others his performance was well below average. He performed in the average range on tests of vocabulary (knowledge of word meanings) and short-term memory for strings of numbers. By contrast, he performed very poorly on a test requiring him to construct puzzles and one requiring him to solve practical, everyday problems (e.g., what to do if someone steals your wallet). A complete summary of Harry's Wechsler performance is attached. Generally, he performed better on tests that were familiar to him or on tests requiring only rote learning. Harry had greater difficulty on more novel or unfamiliar tasks.

Harry was administered the K-TEA in order to obtain more diagnostic information regarding his school problems. His K-TEA profile is somewhat consistent with his measured intelligence in that his scores in mathematics applications, calculation, and reading comprehension are below what one would expect for his age. On the other hand, his performance in spelling and word decoding was considerably better. In these two areas he performed in the average range. Again, Harry is capable of performing in the average range for his age when the task is amenable to rote or overlearning. On cognitive tasks that require more conceptual skills or an ability to deal with novel problems, he has great difficulty.

A K-TEA error analysis was conducted for the three weak academic areas. The error analysis for the two mathematics tests shows that Harry makes similar errors whether the problem is applied or calculation. He had particular problems with fractions on both mathematics subtests. He also had problems with advanced number concepts and with algebraic equations. On the reading comprehension test, Harry showed problems with both literal and inferential comprehension. This difficulty is probably one of Harry's major stumbling blocks in college preparatory–level work, since in many classes test performance is a direct reflection of the student's ability to read and comprehend textbooks.

Harry's personality functioning seems to be well within normal limits at the present time. His responses to interview questions, the MMPI, and to the sentence completion test showed stable personality functioning. Harry does seem to be sensitive to interpersonal feedback and desirous of close interpersonal relationships. His family is a very important source of support for him.

Recommendations

1.   Harry requires an approach to tutoring that minimizes his weaknesses and maximizes his strengths. He learns best in a situation where he can apply his language skills to familiar problems. He also seems to thrive on warm personal attention. These factors should be considered in designing any intervention program. For example, in preparing for college entrance examinations, he should work with a tutor who is not only competent but also personable in order to help maintain his motivation. He should also receive instruction on tasks very similar to those included on the examination. If the task on the examination is to read a paragraph about a topic and answer multiple-choice questions, then he should practice taking this type of test. This procedure will make the taking of the exam a more familiar problem-solving situation for him and will avoid problems with transfer of training. Language skills may also be used to help him understand areas such as mathematics. He could, for example, memorize verbal rules for solving mathematics problems involving fractions. Harry's interpersonal strengths also argue for the use of study groups. He may learn more by discussing a topic with his peers than by solitary study.

2.   For certain areas where Harry may receive tutoring, some further diagnostic testing may be necessary. Writing is a curricular area in which further assessment is required. His tutors in a particular content area should be able to conduct any further academic testing that is necessary.

3.   Harry should take only the minimum number of classes required to stay enrolled. To date he has been able to overcome some significant cognitive weaknesses with relatively few signs of undue stress. However, Harry should

not overly commit himself. Given his academic weaknesses, he is going to have to take extra time to complete his degree.

4. Harry should consult with the adult learning disabilities clinic at the university where he intends to enroll. He may be able to access appropriate services from the university to help him complete his degree.

5. If it appears that Harry is going to have difficulty completing requirements for his high school degree, he should seek counseling from the high school counseling service.

Summary

Harry is a 16-year-old male who has a history of academic problems. His language ability, ability to solve familiar problems, and rote learning ability are in the average to low average range. By contrast, his ability to solve unfamiliar problems and his higher cognitive skills are in the well below-average range. Recommendations for Harry include that he take a reduced course load and receive tutoring that capitalizes on his rote learning, interpersonal, and language strengths and does not depend on transfer of training, and that he consult with the learning disabilities clinic at the university he attends.

Wechsler Intelligence Scale for Children-Third Edition

SCORE SUMMARY

Full Scale Score	76
Performance	74
Verbal	81

VERBAL TESTS

Information	5
Similarities	9
Arithmetic	6
Vocabulary	10
Comprehension	5
Digit Span	8

PERFORMANCE TESTS

Picture Completion	6
Coding	10
Picture Arrangement	5
Block Design	5
Object Assembly	5
Symbol Search	9

Clinic/Hospital—Colleagues

The following report follows the guidelines of Tallent (1988) for a "case-focused report," or at least I hope that Dr. Tallent would agree that it follows his guidelines! In this case the audience consists of the treatment team at the hospital, which includes the attending psychiatrist, nurses, aides, teachers, and social workers.

Psychological evaluation for Natalie (confidential)

Natalie is a 13-year-old female who was admitted to the hospital yesterday for treatment and evaluation of suicidal threats and oppositional behavior at home. This evaluation was designed to assess for suicidal risk and to pinpoint her coping strategies and personality structure in order to assist the treatment team in designing interventions for her.

Natalie was evaluated with the Wechsler Intelligence Scale for Children-III (WISC-III), the Comprehensive form of the Kaufman Test of Educational Achievement (K-TEA), Kinetic Family Drawing, Sentence Completion Test, Reynolds Adolescent Depression Scale (RADS), and Suicidal Ideation Questionnaire. Information was also gathered from Natalie's chart and from a diagnostic interview.

Psychological evaluation for Natalie (confidential) *(continued)*

Natalie's assessment results portray her as a shy and anxious adolescent who is responding poorly to the stresses associated with early adolescence. Most problematic for her is her self-effacing nature. Because of this characteristic, she would rather meet the needs of others to the exclusion of her own. She is likely, for example, to be extremely compliant at home until she becomes so frustrated with not being able to spend as much time with friends as she would like that she eventually explodes with a verbal tirade and breaks rules such as curfews. Similarly, she has a very low tolerance for interpersonal conflict. She ruminates unduly about any conflict between herself and her parents or peers, all of which contributes to cognitions associated with depression such as thoughts of worthlessness and hopelessness.

Natalie's personality structure has proved inadequate for dealing with the emotionally charged early adolescent years, resulting in her experiencing significant depression. While she was formerly a good student, her academic achievement has declined dramatically over the last year to primarily failing grades. This decline cannot be explained by intellectual reasons, since the current estimate of her intellectual skills is in the average range (WISC-III Full Scale of 103, Performance scale of 101, and Verbal scale of 106). She has also reported having severe crying spells two to three times a week, irritability, mood swings, feelings of sadness, poor appetite, difficulty sleeping, and a tendency to withdraw by spending increasingly more time in her room. Recently her depression has exacerbated to a point that she has thought of suicide. She was unable, however, to produce a "plan" for how she would attempt suicide, and she currently denies such ideation.

Natalie expresses an interest in receiving treatment. Her treatment should focus on helping her develop skills for dealing with others, especially in emotionally charged situations. Depending on what is discovered in the psychotherapeutic process, she may benefit from approaches such as cognitive behavior therapy aimed at controlling ruminations and other maladaptive cognitions (Aaron Beck's approach should be considered) that reinforce feelings of depression. She is also a good candidate for assertiveness training and social skills training aimed at developing interpersonal coping skills. In the latter area, strategies from the skillstreaming series used on the unit would likely be of benefit.

A diagnosis of major depression, single episode, moderate (296.22) seems most appropriate given all of the information collected to date.

School—Educators/Parents

This report is pitched more directly to teachers who are making a special education classification decision and are interested in curricular planning. In this case, parents will likely review the report.

Psychological evaluation for Shawn (Confidential)

NAME:	Shawn	GRADE: 9th
DATE OF BIRTH:	9/3/69	SCHOOL: Washington High School
AGE:	15 yrs, 6 months	CLASS: Educable Mentally Retarded with one-third of his time in regular education classes

Assessment Procedures	Date
Wechsler Intelligence Scale for Children-Third Edition (Wechsler)	5/14/89
Vineland Adaptive Behavior Scales-Survey Form (Vineland)	5/14/89

Basic Achievement Skills Individual Screener (BASIS)	5/14/89
Clinical Interview	5/14/89
Teacher Interview	5/14/85
Record Review	5/14/89
Classroom Observation	5/13/89

Referral Information

Shawn was referred by the Director of Psychological Services for a 3-year reevaluation to determine whether or not his educational placement was still appropriate.

Background Information

Shawn's mother describes his early development as uneventful. She did note, however, that many of his early milestones were delayed. He did not speak in sentences until about age 5. She describes him as a compliant child who has not presented any significant behavior problems.

Similarly, his special education teacher describes him as hard working and polite. She also reports that he is well liked by the other students and is a leader in the class. She does wonder if he sometimes does not work up to his ability.

According to Shawn's school, he seems to be the product of a normal developmental history. His last evaluation 3 years ago yielded a WISC-R Verbal of 82, a Performance of 91, and a Full Scale of 85. Six years ago he obtained a Stanford-Binet IQ of 79, and 9 years ago he obtained a WISC-R IQ of 74. Shawn has recently had a vocational evaluation.

Behavioral Observations and Interview Data

Shawn was somewhat skeptical of the testing situation at the outset. His special education teacher indicated that he had a previous bad experience with a mental health professional. Hence, she tried to reassure Shawn. While somewhat reserved for the first 5 to 10 minutes of the testing, Shawn eventually warmed up. Once he was assured that this experience was not going to be negative, he cooperated fully in the evaluation process. In fact, Shawn was delightful to work with. He was cooperative and consistently gave his best efforts.

One did get the sense from working with Shawn that he was conscious of his history of poor academic achievement. When faced with an academic task that was difficult for him, he trembled slightly when responding.

Test Results and Conclusions

On the WISC-III Shawn obtained a Full Scale score in the below-average range, with a 90% probability that his score falls between the standard scores of 73 and 83. He obtained a Verbal score in the well below-average range and a Performance score in the low average range. There is a 90% probability that Shawn's Verbal and Performance scores fall within the standard score ranges of 66 to 78 and 80 to 96 respectively. The percentile rank confidence bands, indicating the percentage of agemates Shawn's performance met or exceeded for the Full Scale, Verbal, and Performance scores were 4 to 13, 1 to 7, and 9 to 39, respectively.

Shawn's performance on the WISC-III is indicative of an individual who suffers from a lack of acquired knowledge. His lowest scores on the WISC-III were on the Information, Arithmetic, and Vocabulary subtests. All three of these subtests are heavily dependent on both schooling and out-of-school intellectual stimulation. In addition to the subtests requiring acquired information, he also performed very poorly on one subtest of high-level nonverbal reasoning skills. This result is consistent with his overall Full Scale standard score, which is in the below-average range. In direct contrast, Shawn's performance on many of the WISC-III tasks that require "practical reasoning skills" was in the average range. For example, on a puzzle-solving task his performance was even slightly above average for his age.

Hence, Shawn's performance on the WISC-III does indicate that he is currently functioning in the below-average range of intelligence. On the other hand, he shows good potential in practical problem-solving situations. This relative strength makes one optimistic about his vocational possibilities. His academic deficits in acquired information/academic achievement, however, also need to be addressed in order to enhance the probability of his eventual vocational success.

(continued)

Psychological evaluation for Shawn (Confidential) *(continued)*

Shawn achieved the following age-based percentile ranks on the BASIS: mathematics 1, reading 1, and spelling 1. Shawn's performance in mathematics indicated that he had only successfully acquired basic addition and subtraction skills involving one- and two-digit numerals. On items requiring addition and subtraction of three- and four-digit numbers, multiplication, or division, his performance waned. His mathematics performance indicates that he possesses only rudimentary skills, which are not adequate for functioning independently as an adult. Shawn's performance in reading, although only at the 1st percentile, was closer to a literate level. He showed adequate comprehension at about the third- or fourth-grade levels but considerable problems with decoding several words. He was unable to decode the following words: *creatures, suggested, dwarfed, despair, successful, gasped,* and *bugs.* His comprehension could seemingly improve if he were better able to decode words in context. Finally, Shawn's spelling performance was also at a rudimentary level. He was able to spell words such as *wall, left, child, apple, near,* and *butter.* In contrast, he was unable to spell the following words: *woke, rubber, corner,* and *month.*

In summary, his BASIS performance indicates that he possesses a very basic level of academic skills. Most importantly, his academic skills are not up to par with his intelligence test scores on the Full Scale, Verbal, or Performance scales of the WISC-III. Based on these results, he may need more intensive intervention accompanied by higher academic standards for his performance.

On the Survey Form of the Vineland, Shawn obtained standard scores of 95, 105, and 111 on the Socialization, Communication, and Daily Living Skills Domains respectively. Shawn seems to possess many adaptive skills that are important for independent functioning as an adult. Generally, his adaptive behavior as measured by the Vineland indicates that his adaptive functioning is well within the average range. This finding precludes Shawn from obtaining a dual deficit in intelligence and adaptive behavior indicative of the mildly mentally retarded child. In other words, Shawn's level of adaptive functioning indicates that he clearly is not functioning in the mild level of mental retardation outside the school environment.

Summary

Shawn seems to be a congenial adolescent who is functioning in the well below-average range intellectually and possesses an average level of adaptive behavior skills. He shows particular strengths in practical problem-solving and adaptive life skills. These skills are most critical for vocational success. However, his vocational success could be hindered drastically by his lack of academic achievement. Therefore, his vocational plans should be addressed as soon as possible by giving him appropriate training for a career. Also, his academic program should be intensified to bring his academic skills up to par with his intellectual skills. Once he has accomplished this goal, Shawn shows potential for responsible and independent functioning as an adult.

Recommendations

1.   Shawn's vocational plans should be considered as an entry on his individual educational plan. He should begin working with vocational rehabilitation personnel in order to plan career training. His individual education plan should be adjusted to be congruent with his career objectives.

2.   Shawn's academic expectations should be raised. He shows more intellectual and adaptive behavior potential than he is applying to the academic situation. He may respond, because of his very pleasant personality, to tutoring by peers. This practice would have the added benefit of allowing him to interact with positive peer models.

3.   An attempt should be made to get Shawn involved in extracurricular school activities. Indications from Shawn and the peer group that he interacts with are that he may be tempted to drop out of school prior to high school graduation. Involvement in extracurricular activities would perhaps provide the immersion necessary to keep him in school through graduation.

4.   Shawn should be referred to the dropout prevention program for evaluation.

OTHER REPORT WRITING ISSUES

This section discusses a number of issues that are commonly considered in report writing, in addition to the consideration of gearing a report for a particular audience. These are issues that psychologists and other report writers have been grappling with for some time. Hence, this book must also consider these issues.

Confidence Bands

It is customary practice always to report confidence bands to represent the amount of error associated with intelligence test scores (Kamphaus & Reynolds, 1987). These have been included when reporting intelligence test results in a variety of ways. Some examples of how report writers have included confidence bands are shown below.

"Janie obtained a WISC-III Full Scale standard score of 109 ± 3."

"Janie obtained a WISC-III Full Scale standard score of l09 ± 3.19."

"Janie obtained a WISC-III Full Scale standard score of 109 (106–112)."

"There is a 68% probability that Janie's three Full Scale standard scores lie within the range of scores of 106–112."

Report writers also use differing levels of confidence. While the above examples use 1 SEM (68%), many report writers adhere to Kaufman's (1979b) advice and use a 90% confidence band. Of course, the decision is up to the examiner, who must consider factors such as the nature of his or her audience. In order to promote this flexibility, most test manuals offer 68%, 85%, 90%, 95%, and 99% confidence bands. One of the examples above uses decimals; most manuals use only whole numbers for simplicity of calculation. Computer software makes the use of decimals much more practical.

This text will use 90% confidence bands because of Kaufman's (1979b) precedent, but also because this book emphasizes using percentile ranks in report writing. Higher levels of confidence (95% and 99%) produce such large percentile rank bands that the scores look grossly inexact. This is an artifact of the nature of the percentile rank scale and its unequal intervals between scores (see Chapter 5).

Score Classification Schemes

Some of the score classification systems used today are old and in need of revision in light of changes in terminology. The Wechsler/Binet classification systems can be traced to the early part of this century. They are very similar to descriptive schemes proposed by writers such as Pintner (1923) and Levine and Marks (1928). Pintner's (1923, p. 77) early classification scheme is shown below.

CLASSIFICATION	INTELLIGENCE QUOTIENTS
Feebleminded	0–69
Borderline	70–79
Backward	80–89
Normal	90–109
Bright	110–119
Very Bright	120–129
Very Superior	130 and above

The classification system of Levine and Marks (1928, p. 131) is as follows:

LEVEL	RANGE IN IQ
Idiots	0–24
Imbeciles	25–49
Morons	50–74
Borderline	75–84
Dull	85–94
Average	95–104
Bright	105–114

Very Bright	115–124
Superior	125–149
Very Superior	150–174
Precocious	175 and over

The typical procedure used by modern psychologists is to place the Full Scale standard score into the Wechsler classification system given in the WISC-R manual (Wechsler, 1974). This classification system is given below. This system is very similar to that of Levine and Marks (1928).

CLASSIFICATION	FULL SCALE STANDARD SCORE
Very Superior	130 and above
Superior	120–129
Above Average (bright)	110–119
Average	90–109
Below Average (dull)	80–89
Borderline	70–79
Mentally Deficient	69 and below

Using the classification system of Wechsler, if a child obtains a score of 105, he or she is classified as average, 84 as below average, 126 as superior, and so on. What is to be said, however, if a child obtains a score of 109? It does not seem fair, given what we know about the standard error of measurement, to assign this child to the "average" classification. In order to address this problem I have devised a rule for my own students. Given that the standard error of measurement for the Full Scale standard score of the WISC-III rounds to about 3 standard score points at most age ranges, I recommend that *if a child's composite score is within 3 standard score points of the next classification, both bordering classifications should be given.* For example, a Full Scale standard score of 93 would be classified as average, whereas a score of 92 would be given two classifications, below average to average.

Although the Wechsler classification system for intelligence test scores is by far the most popular, it may not be the most appropriate (Reynolds & Kaufman, 1990). The Wechsler classification system does use a great deal of antiquated terminology. This includes terminology such as "bright" and "dull" to describe the performance of children. By the way, these two classifications are not parallel. Should it not be "bright" and "dim"?

Besides its age, there are other problems with the use of the Wechsler classification system that may lead to inappropriate use. For example, scores of 69 or below are classified as "mentally deficient," an older term for mental retardation. The reader of a psychological report that describes the child's performance as in the mentally deficient range may interpret the report as indicating, in fact, that the child is mentally retarded. Intelligence tests were designed for use as the sole criterion for the diagnosis of mental retardation. This practice, however, is no longer appropriate since most modern diagnostic systems, such as the Diagnostic and Statistical Manual of Mental Disorders, Third Edition-Raised *(DSM III-R)* and Public Law 94-142, require dual deficits in intelligence *and* adaptive behavior in order to make the diagnosis of mental retardation. Further, describing a child's score as being in the borderline range may be potentially confusing because of the existence of diagnoses such as Borderline Personality Disorder from DSM III-R. Examiners need to be careful when using Wechsler's classification system because it may lead to some confusion on the part of the reader of the psychological report, especially parents and teachers.

The WISC-III offers an update of the WISC-R classification system that addresses some of these criticisms. The new classification system is listed below. It still retains some terminology from the early days of testing including the categories of "Superior" and "Borderline." Whether or not this new system will become popular is not known.

CLASSIFICATION	FULL SCALE STANDARD SCORE
Very Superior	130 and above
Superior	120–129
High Average	110–119
Average	90–109
Low Average	80–89
Borderline	70–79
Intellectually Deficient	69 and below

An alternative classification system proposed by Lyman (1965, p. 177) is shown below. This system may be adequate for some purposes, but it is still too evaluative as opposed to descriptive. The use of terms such as "weak" or "excellent" should be avoided.

PERCENTILE RANKS	DESCRIPTIVE TERMS
95 or above	Very high; Superior
85–95	High; Excellent
75–85	Above average; Good
25–75	About average; Satisfactory or fair
15–25	Below average; Fair or slightly weak
5–15	Low; Weak
5 or below	Very low; Very weak

Another alternative system of classification was proposed by Kaufman and Kaufman (1983). This system is more in keeping with modern practice in that it uses parallel terminology above and below the mean, and it describes a level of performance without promoting diagnostic confusion. Their system is as follows:

Upper extreme	130 and above
Well above average	120–129
Above average	110–119
Average	90–109
Below average	80–89
Well below average	70–79
Lower extreme	69 and below

Yet another nonevaluative classification system is offered by the new Differential Ability Scales (DAS, Elliot, 1990) (see Chapter 12).

Recently, Fish (1990) offered an intelligence classification scheme that is also descriptive and yet is not easily confused with diagnostic categories. Fish's scheme includes the following score ranges and classifications (where $M = 100$ and $SD = 15$).

Significantly below average	69 and below
Moderately below average	70–79
Below average	80–89
Average	90–109
Above average	110–119
Moderately above average	120–129
Significantly above average	130 and above

I will use the Kaufman and Kaufman (1983) and Fish (1990) systems throughout most of this book because these seem less evaluative.

Undoubtedly, psychologists will find that other systems are more appropriate for particular settings. The point being made by offering so many different classification schemes is that the decision to use a particular system should be made by the psychologist writing the report. The psychologist should choose a system based upon the setting in which the report is being written, the purpose(s) of the evaluation, the audience for the report, and other factors. Clinicians should not use a system just because it is written in a test manual, particularly if the system is likely to promote confusion or even inappropriate practice.

Reporting Scores

Another debate in report writing is the issue of whether or not, or how, to report scores. Some professors argue that IQs should never be given in a report because they are prone to misinterpretation, particularly overinterpretation, by parents and others. Yet other professors and supervisors do not see including scores in the report as an issue at all. I am sympathetic to the point of view that parents do tend to take scores too seriously. Much to my chagrin, I have even seen IQ scores used by parents to play "one upmanship" at cocktail parties. On the other hand, test scores can enhance the clarity of communication. If I were told that my child was below average I would not be satisfied. I would want to know exactly how far below average.

One option is that clinicians find a middle ground by reporting scores but also clearly stating the error associated with them. The score that many prefer is the percentile rank, as this score seems to be the most easily understood by parents (Lyman, 1965). In addition, Lyman (1965) suggested using percentile rank confidence bands. This practice is consistent with my bias of gearing reports to the least sophisticated audience. If a psychologist can communicate effectively with an unsophisticated audience, then he or she will have no difficulty with other audiences. In addition, percentile ranks are less apt to produce inaccurate reactions that are more typically associated with IQ scores (Kellerman & Burry, 1981). A sample sentence from a report using these guidelines may read something like this:

> "Laura's intelligence test scores fell in the average range. Her performance exceeded that of anywhere from 25 to 50 percent of the children her age."

This practice is in contrast to the more traditional practice of giving the obtained score with a confidence band. This approach would read something like:

> "Laura obtained a WISC-III Full Scale IQ of 95 ± 5."

An excellent example of using percentile rank confidence bands to communicate with parents is available for the Peabody Individual Achievement Test-Revised (PIAT-R) (Markwardt, 1991) report to parents. The following quotation is taken directly from the PIAT-R report to parents.

> *Results on each part of the test . . . are reported as percentile ranks. This type of score tells what percentage of other students at the same grade or age level scored below your child's score. In other words, a percentile rank of 50 indicates achievement above that of 50 percent of students at the same level. . . .*
>
> *A common way to interpret percentile ranks is shown in the chart below. For example, a percentile rank of 50 could be interpreted as indicating average performance.*

PERCENTILE RANKS OF	ARE CONSIDERED
1 to 5	low
6 to 24	below average
25 to 75	average
76 to 94	above average
95 to 99	high

> *Because no test score can be perfectly accurate and any student might score higher or lower if tested again on another day, it is said that the "true" score can only be estimated. To account for the possible variation in test results, a range of scores has been calculated for your child. (This range is written in parentheses following the test score obtained by your child.) In interpreting the test results, you should think of your child's score as falling somewhere in that range. (p. 2)*

A Proposed Format for New Students

That which follows is intended as a rudimentary beginning for report writing. Consequently, there are several characteristics of the proposed report format that need to be made explicit. First, the report is intended for an unsophisticated audience. Secondly, the format is highly structured in order to satisfy the need of many new students for specific guidance. Each section of the report will now be discussed in turn.

Identifying Information

Most report formats provide some identifying information on the top of the first page of the report. This section can include information such as name of the child, age, grade, birthdate, and perhaps the name of the school or agency where the child is currently attending or being served. Also, most reports caution that the nature of the report content is confidential. A sample of the identifying information section of a report for Connie (from Chapter 7) is shown in Box 8.1.

Assessment Procedures

I prefer to use the term "assessment procedures" to describe the tests administered because in everyday practice not all of the assessment devices used in an evaluation are tests per se. Evaluation procedures can and frequently do include interviews, reviews of records, and classroom or other observations. A sample of this type of section is also shown in Box 8.1.

Referral Questions

The referral section is too often overlooked (Tallent, 1988). It is crucial because the referral questions dictate the design of the evaluation. In addition, the lack of clear referral questions may lead to consumer or referral source dissatisfaction with the report. As Tallent (1988) suggests, psychologists may have to contact the referral source in order to clarify the nature of the question(s). Again, a sample is given for Connie in Box 8.1.

Background Information

This section should include all of the pertinent information that may affect interpretation of a

child's scores. The key word here is *pertinent*. The clinician should report only information that is relevant to the current evaluation, not information that is superfluous or an undue invasion of privacy (Teglasi, 1983). Material should only be included if it has some potential impact on the interpretation of the child's scores in order to answer the referral question(s).

While parental occupation and marital status are generally private subjects, these may be important pieces of information, given what is currently known about the effects of SES and parental strife (divorce) on a child's cognitive functioning (see Chapter 3). A sample of how background information may be written in a report is provided in Box 8.1.

The report writer should also be clear about the sources of information. If the father views his son as lazy, then this statement should be attributed to the father. Statements that could be used for making such attributions include the following:

"According to . . ."
"His father/mother said . . ."
"His mother's/father's opinion is . . ."
"His teacher's view of the situation is . . ."
"___ reports that . . ."
"___ acknowledges that . . ."

If care is not taken to make clear the sources of information, questions may arise when feedback is given to involved parties.

Sensitive background information should be corroborated or excluded from the report if it is inflammatory and cannot be corroborated. For example, a 5-year-old may say something like "Mother shoots people," and later the psychologist discovers that the child's mother is a police officer.

Previous assessment results should also be included in this section (Teglasi, 1983). Also, previous experiences with psychological or educational interventions should be noted here.

If several evaluations are already available, the report writer can simply refer the reader to an-

BOX 8.1

Sample Psychological Report for Connie (confidential)

Name: Connie P.   Gender: female
Birthdate: 7/31/73   Grade 11
Age: 16 years, 2 months   Evaluated by: Ashley S. Kamphaus, B.A., psychology practicum student
Date of Report: 10/6/89

Assessment Procedures

Wechsler Intelligence Scale for Children-Third Edition (WISC-III)

Referral Questions

This evaluation was requested by Connie's treatment team coordinator at the psychiatric hospital while she was being treated as an inpatient. Specifically, the treatment team wanted to rule out mental retardation as a possible contributory factor to her depression.

Background Information

Connie has had a tumultuous family background. She has never known her biological father. For the first three years of her life she was reared by foster parents. Since that time she has lived with her biological mother. Her mother has married and divorced three times. Consequently, Connie has moved and changed schools frequently, resulting in her missing a considerable amount of school. Her mother currently works as an administrative secretary.

Connie has always been cited by her teachers as being an underachiever. Although she has never failed a grade, she reportedly tends to do just the minimum to get by. Her grades have ranged from B's to D's.

According to her mother, Connie's current problems with alcohol abuse can be traced to the eighth grade. During this year she moved to a less-than-desirable neighborhood. She began to associate with a group of older children who were heavy users of alcohol and drugs. For some reason, Connie has avoided significant drug use in spite of peer influence. She has been drinking beer and/or hard liquor at least five days a week since the eighth grade.

Observations and Interview Results

Connie seemed highly motivated to achieve a high score on the WISC-III. She frequently asked, "How'd I do?" Connie complained bitterly when she was unable to solve an item correctly. She also tried to hurry in order to obtain bonus points. No urging was required on the part of the examiner.

Connie seemed quite capable of expressing herself. She appeared to thrive on conversation and spoke freely and often throughout the assessment process.

Assessment Results and Interpretation

Connie was evaluated with the Wechsler Intelligence Scale for Children-Third Edition (WISC-III). This popular scale is made up of several subtests (usually 12 tests are used) that assess various aspects of intelligence. The tests are divided into two types: Verbal and Performance. Verbal tests have items such as defining vocabulary words, answering common-sense questions, and answering factual questions on topics such as science. The Performance tests have items such as constructing puzzles and abstract designs and identifying missing parts of a picture. The WISC-III produces three scores, Verbal, Performance, and Full Scale; the last is based on the sum of the scores on all of the tests.

Connie's overall estimate of intelligence, the Full Scale, places her in the average to above-average range. Taking measurement error into account, this score indicates that her performance meets or exceeds anywhere from 61% to 82% of the children her age. An estimate of her intelligence in the above-average range is consistent with a number of pieces of information about Connie. Her teachers have always argued that she does not use her

BOX 8.1 *(continued)*

ability in school, and she displayed an interest in getting items correct, suggesting that she has some confidence in her cognitive skills.

This description of her intelligence test performance, however, is not complete because she obtained a Verbal score in the above-average to well above-average range and a considerably lower Performance score—in the average range. Again, taking measurement error into account, Connie's Verbal score indicates that she exceeds anywhere from 81% to 95% of the adolescents her age, whereas on the Performance scale she exceeds 23% to 58% of her peers. Her relatively stronger verbal skills were even reflected on one of the Performance scale subtests. On the only Performance subtest requiring a verbal response, she obtained her highest subtest score on the scale. As mentioned earlier, her relative verbal strength was also evident during the evaluation, in which she showed excellent conversational skills and ability to express herself verbally.

These test results all rule out a problem with mental retardation. Even her relative weakness in Performance scale skills is still in the average range compared to other 16-year-olds.

Summary

Connie is a 16-year-old female who was evaluated while receiving inpatient treatment for alcohol abuse. She has a history of alcohol abuse and academic underachievement dating back to the eighth grade. The purpose of this evaluation was to rule out mental retardation. Connie exhibited a high level of cooperation and motivation during the administration of the WISC-III. Her Full Scale and Verbal standard scores were in the above-average range and her Performance standard score was in the average range. Her relative strength on Verbal subtests was pervasive in that it appeared to even help her on one of the Performance tests. This strength is also consistent with her conversational skills. These findings effectively rule out a diagnosis of mental retardation.

Recommendations

1. Connie's verbal strength should be tapped to assist her with difficult school subjects. She could be advised by teachers to use verbal encoding and rehearsal strategies even for subjects that are more nonverbal, such as mathematics. She could, for example, be required to verbally rehearse the steps involved in solving algebraic equations.

2. Connie's enjoyment of conversation suggests that this high-frequency activity may serve as a good reinforcing stimulus for her. If she completes a satisfactory amount of schoolwork, for example, she might be allowed to converse with someone.

Ashley S. Kamphaus, B.A.
Psychology Practicum Student

Psychometric Summary for Connie

Wechsler Intelligence Scale for Children-Revised

COMPOSITE SCORES

Full Scale Standard Score	108
Verbal Standard Score	117
Performance Standard Score	96

SUBTEST SCORES

Verbal Scale

Information	13

(continued)

BOX 8.1 *(continued)*

SUBTEST SCORES *(continued)*

Similarities	13
Arithmetic	13
Vocabulary	12
Comprehension	13
Digit Span	13

PERFORMANCE SCALE

Picture Completion	14
Coding	4
Picture Arrangement	10
Block Design	10
Object Assembly	10
Symbol Search	9

BOX 8.2

Interpretation and Report Writing Worksheet

This form is an interpretation and report writing worksheet that is intended to assist examiners in the process of organizing their thoughts prior to dictating or writing a report. The form follows the interpretive logic used in Chapter 7. It may be photocopied as necessary with permission of the publisher. Additional space may be added to the form in order to allow for the inclusion of nonintelligence test data, which in many cases is going to be most important for answering referral questions.

NAME:_____GRADE:_____

BIRTHDATE:_____SCHOOL:_____

AGE:_____DATE OF EVALUATION:_____

Referral Questions:

1._____

2._____

3._____

4._____

5._____

6._____

Background Information:

1._____

2._____

BOX 8.2 *(continued)*

3._____
4._____
5._____
6._____
7._____
8._____
9._____
10._____
11._____
12._____
13._____
14._____
15._____

Assessment Procedures:

1._____
2._____
3._____
4._____
5._____
6._____
7._____
8._____
9._____
10._____
11._____
12._____

Observations During Evalution:

1._____
2._____
3._____
4._____
5._____
6._____
7._____
8._____
9._____
10._____
11._____
12._____

(continued)

BOX 8.2 *(continued)*

Apriori Hypotheses

Composite Score Hypotheses:

Strengths	*Evidence*
1._____	_____
2._____	_____
3._____	_____

Weaknesses

1._____

2._____

3._____

Shared Subtest Hypotheses:

Strengths

1._____

2._____

3._____

4._____

5._____

6._____

7._____

Weaknesses

8._____

9._____

10._____

11._____

12._____

13._____

14._____

Single Subtest Hypotheses:

Strengths

1._____

2._____

3._____

Weaknesses

4._____

5._____

6._____

BOX 8.2 *(continued)*

Composite Scores

_____Standard Score	—		_____Standard Score	—
_____Standard Score	—		_____Standard Score	—
_____Standard Score	—		_____Standard Score	—
_____Standard Score	—		_____Standard Score	—

Subtest Scores

_____Scale		*Mean*	*Difference*	*Significance Value*	*S or W*
1._____	—	—	—	—	—
2._____	—	—	—	—	—
3._____	—	—	—	—	—
4._____	—	—	—	—	—
5._____	—	—	—	—	—
6._____	—	—	—	—	—

_____Scale					
1._____	—	—	—	—	—
2._____	—	—	—	—	—
3._____	—	—	—	—	—
4._____	—	—	—	—	—
5._____	—	—	—	—	—
6._____	—	—	—	—	—

Overall Mean =

_____Scale	—	—	—	—	—
1._____	—	—	—	—	—
2._____	—	—	—	—	—
3._____	—	—	—	—	—

Aposteriori Hypotheses:

Composite Score Hypotheses:

	Confirming Evidence	*Rejecting Evidence*

Strengths

1._____	1._____	1._____
	2._____	2._____
2._____	1._____	1._____
	2._____	2._____
3._____	1._____	1._____
	2._____	2._____

(continued)

BOX 8.2 *(continued)*

Weaknesses

1._____   1._____   1._____
   2._____   2._____

2._____   1._____   1._____
   2._____   2._____

3._____   1._____   1._____
   2._____   2._____

Shared Subtest Hypotheses:

Strengths

1._____   1._____   1._____
   2._____   2._____

2._____   1._____   1._____
   2._____   2._____

3._____   1._____   1._____
   2._____   2._____

4._____   1._____   1._____
   2._____   2._____

5._____   1._____   1._____
   2._____   2._____

6._____   1._____   1._____
   2._____   2._____

7._____   1._____   1._____
   2._____   2._____

Weaknesses

8._____   1._____   1._____
   2._____   2._____

9._____   1._____   1._____
   2._____   2._____

10._____   1._____   1._____
   2._____   2._____

11._____   1._____   1._____
   2._____   2._____

12._____   1._____   1._____
   2._____   2._____

13._____   1._____   1._____
   2._____   2._____

14._____   1._____   1._____
   2._____   2._____

BOX 8.2 *(continued)*

Single Subtest Hypotheses:

Strengths

1._____   1._____   1._____
                      2._____   2._____

2._____   1._____   1._____
                      2._____   2._____

3._____   1._____   1._____
                      2._____   2._____

Weaknesses

4._____   1._____   1._____
                      2._____   2._____

5._____   1._____   1._____
                      2._____   2._____

6._____   1._____   1._____
                      2._____   2._____

Other Assessment Data:

1._____
2._____
3._____
4._____
5._____
6._____
7._____
8._____
9._____
10._____
11._____
12._____

Drawing Conclusions:

1._____
2._____
3._____
4._____
5._____
6._____
7._____
8._____
9._____
10._____

(continued)

BOX 8.2 (continued)

11._____

12._____

Answers to Referral Questions:

1._____

2._____

3._____

4._____

5._____

6._____

7._____

8._____

9._____

10._____

11._____

12._____

other source (Zimmerman & Woo Sam, 1976). This practice can substantially reduce bulk.

Observations and Interview Results

In this section the behaviors that the child exhibits during the assessment are recorded. The behaviors that may be significant were cited in Chapters 3 and 5. When writing this section, the number of observations made, the setting where the observations were made (e.g., school, clinic, etc.), and the person who made the observations should be included (Teglasi, 1983). Observations for Connie are shown in Box 8.1.

This section is also the place to enter interview results that may assist in the process of corroborating or rejecting hypotheses.

Assessment Results and Interpretation

This section is where the intelligence test results for the child are reported. For the beginning report writer who is trying to communicate with parents, the following sequence for reporting intelligence test results is suggested.

First paragraph

1. Introduction to the WISC-III

2. Global composite score (e.g., Full Scale or overall composite from other tests) classification, conclusions, and supporting evidence

3. Global composite score percentile rank confidence bands

Second paragraph

4. Area composite score (e.g., Verbal, Performance, or other composite scores based on

two or more subtests) classification, conclusions, and supporting evidence

5. Area composite score percentile rank confidence bands

THIRD PARAGRAPH

6. Shared subtest conclusions and supporting evidence

FOURTH PARAGRAPH

7. Single subtest conclusions and supporting evidence

This outline, of necessity, may promote stilted writing at first. It is intended to ensure that students apply the same interpretive logic to their report writing that they applied to interpretation. At this point in the report the intelligence test results should also be integrated with other findings, as "the I.Q. score . . . does not exist in a vacuum" (Kellerman & Burry, 1981).

Less stilted usage of this and similar report formats will be demonstrated in subsequent chapters. A sample of this section of a report is given in Box 8.1.

Summary

The final section of the report is intended to give an overview of the major findings (see Box 8.1). This review helps ensure that the reader understands the major points made in the report. A rule of thumb for writing summaries is to use one sentence to summarize each section of the report. In addition, a sentence should be devoted to each major finding presented in the test results section and to each recommendation. In some cases, one sentence can be used to summarize multiple findings and recommendations, as was done for the sample report given in Box 8.1.

One of the common pitfalls in preparing summaries is including new information in the summary section. If an examiner introduces a new finding in the summary, then the reader is lost. The reader has no idea as to the source or rationale behind the conclusion. Students should read their draft summaries carefully and check every conclusion made in the summary against the body of the report.

Signatures

Reports typically require signatures in order to attest to their authenticity. It is important for clinicians to use titles that represent them accurately. Some states, for example, do not have specialty licensure, and as such the use of a title such as "licensed pediatric psychologist" is not appropriate. In this case, a more generic term such as "licensed psychologist" should be utilized.

Students should also be careful to represent themselves accurately. A title such as "practicum student," "intern," "trainee," or something similar should be used. Psychological custom also determines the inclusion of the highest degree obtained by the clinician.

Writing Recommendations

The recommendations section of a report is often the most difficult for new students to write. It is difficult primarily because it requires students to draw on information from several graduate training, practicum, and internship experiences. Regardless of the source of knowledge for writing recommendations, some principles can be followed. Recommendations should be specific and clear (Teglasi, 1983). Writing a recommendation for extra drill and practice, for example, may be difficult to carry out if the curriculum content area and other aspects of the recommendation are not made explicit. Some recommendations may also not be easy to communicate succinctly in writing. In almost all cases the examiner should relay recommendations in person to teachers, parents, and colleagues (Teglasi, 1983) in order to ensure that they are followed.

Another way of offering suggestions in a way that they will be carried out is to offer a "sliding scale" (Zimmerman & Woo Sam, 1967). If, for example, special class placement is warranted but not practical, then perhaps tutoring should be recommended in lieu of school intervention services.

Psychometric Summary

Some clinicians include a listing of all of the child's obtained scores with the report. While this summary will be of limited value to the less knowledgeable reader, it may be of great value to another examiner who reviews the report. This summary is best placed on a separate sheet of paper, which makes it convenient for the examiner to be selective about who receives the summary. A report writing self-test is provided in Figure 8.3.

COMMUNICATING RESULTS ORALLY

Parent Conferences

Imparting intelligence test results to parents requires considerable savvy, as the individual differences between families are multitudinous. Ricks (1959) summarizes the heart of the dilemma.

> The audience of parents to which our test-based information is to be transmitted includes an enormous range and variety of minds and emotions. Some are ready and able to absorb what we have to say. Reaching others may be as hopeless as reaching TV watchers with an AM radio broadcast. Still others may hear what we say, but clothe the message with their own special needs, ideas, and predilections. (p. 4)

Regardless of the potential pitfalls, parents must be informed of the results of a psychological evaluation of their child (the legal, ethical, and regulatory mandates for this practice are given in Chapter 17).

Hints for communicating intelligence test results to parents include:

1. Avoid excessive hedging or deceit. The problem with excessive hedging or failure to report the "bad news" is that parents may sense this deceit and respond to the psychologist with great mistrust. Honesty on the part of the clinician is also easily sensed by parents, which ultimately enhances the clinician's credibility.

2. Use percentile ranks heavily when describing levels of performance.

3. Instead of lecturing, allow parents opportunities to participate by asking about things such as their opinion of the results and how they fit with their knowledge of their child.

4. Anticipate questions prior to the interview and prepare responses. How would a psychologist answer the question, "Will my son's intelligence get better?" (One way of preparing would be to reread Chapter 3 of this book.)

5. Schedule adequate time for the interview. Parent conferences often become more involved than one has planned. A session, for example, could turn into therapeutic counseling for the mother, who had just separated from the child's father. Allow 2 hours for such a session with parents. If it does not take this long, then the clinician can take a long lunch or, even less likely, see another child earlier than planned.

6. Practice communicating with parents from a variety of backgrounds. Some parents can be addressed as colleagues, while others may have only a limited education. Sometimes translators may be needed.

7. Never make an overly explicit prediction (Lyman, 1965). A phrase to be avoided would be something like, "She will never go to college" or "She will always have trouble with school."

In order to help report writers think critically about their work, the following checklist is offered. This "test" can be completed periodically to help ensure that reports are carefully prepared.

Item	True	False
	(circle one)	
1. Was the report edited?	T	F
2. Are there unnecessary invasions of privacy?	T	F
3. Is the referral question(s) explicitly stated?	T	F
4. Is the referral question answered?	T	F
5. Does the report emphasize numbers over words?	T	F
6. Can a person with a high school education understand the wording used?	T	F
7. Is the report so long that the major findings are lost?	T	F
8. Are the conclusions drawn without undue hedging?	T	F
9. Do the conclusions fit the data?	T	F
10. Are invalid results presented?	T	F
11. Are percentile ranks included for the benefit of parents and client?	T	F
12. Was a spellchecker used?	T	F
13. Are supporting data integrated with conclusions?	T	F
14. Are the recommendations clear and specific?	T	F
15. Are headings and lists included to enhance impact?	T	F
16. Are acronyms defined?	T	F
17. Are acronyms overused?	T	F
18. Is new information included in the summary?	T	F
19. Were scores double-checked?	T	F
20. Are examples of behavior used to clarify meaning?	T	F
21. Are test instruments described adequately?	T	F
22. Is a conference scheduled to accompany the written report?	T	F

23. Was written parental consent obtained prior to releasing the report to

    interested agencies or parties?   T   F

24. Is a feedback session scheduled with the child or adolescent?   T   F

25. Are the type and paper of professional quality (e.g., no dot matrix print or

    onion skin paper)?   T   F

FIGURE 8.3

Report writing self-test

These types of statements can be very offensive to parents, not to mention very inaccurate.

8. Use good basic counseling skills. Every parent likes to talk about the trials, successes, and tribulations of raising a child. Give parents at least some opportunity to do this, as it allows you to show interest in the child by your listening to the parent's story.

9. Do not engage in counseling that is beyond your level of expertise (Lyman, 1965). Parents are often very eager to obtain advice from a professional. It is inappropriate (and unethical by most standards) for a psychologist to provide services for which he or she is not trained. If, for example, a parent requests marital counseling and you have no training in this area, you should inform the parent of this fact and offer a referral. In fact, the psychologist will be helped by having referral sources readily available for such eventualities.

10. Be aware that some parents are not ready to accept some test results. Some parents will impugn your skills because psychologically they cannot accept the fact that their child has a severe handicap. They may leave the session angry, and you may feel inept. The idea that every parent conference will end on a happy note is unrealistic. Examine your skills critically in response to parent feedback, but realize that some parents simply will not accept the results because of their own personal issues. You will likely encounter this problem, particularly if a parent had a subtle handicap. If a parent was labeled "slow" and ridiculed by peers, then this parent may become defensive and angry at the suggestion that his or her child may have a handicap. The session with such a parent will likely end on a tense note. In many of these cases, however, the parent will accept the news only after a number of evaluations of the child reveal the same results. Thus, the parent may be able to interact more positively with the clinician on their next encounter.

Teacher Conferences

Many of the principles used in parent conferences will apply to teachers also. Two "nuances," however, deserve special listing.

1. Never starve a teacher! Some teachers get few breaks in a day. Most do get a brief lunch, at which they prefer to unwind with colleagues and prepare for the remainder of the day. A clinician is unlikely to command a teacher's undivided attention during this lunch break. If a teacher has an additional free period, it may be a good time for a conference. After school is frequently the best time to get a teacher's undivided attention for a meeting. Teachers are generally very busy people, so the pace of the meeting will be quicker than for parents.

2. Teachers are interested in schooling issues. The diagnosis of conduct disorder is of less con-

cern to teachers than getting specific recommendations for helping the child in the classroom (Teglasi, 1983). If an examiner is not trained and/or has little experience in teacher consultation, then the assistance of someone like a qualified school psychologist should be enlisted to assist with the teacher conference.

The most important thing to remember about teacher conferences is that they should take place (Zimmerman & Woo Sam, 1967; Teglasi, 1983). Such a conference is desirable because teachers are usually involved somehow in the treatment of children and adolescents. An accurate portrayal of the child's intelligence can assist teachers in designing interventions to assist a child in school.

Child Feedback

The child feedback session may be the most challenging for many clinicians, but it is a skill that must be acquired nonetheless. The practice of giving a child feedback about an evaluation is now commonplace.

The major decision that a clinician needs to make before giving feedback to a child is to determine the type of information that is appropriate for a child's developmental level. Clearly, the kind of feedback given to parents is inappropriate for a 5- or 6-year-old, who may have extraordinary difficulty understanding the concept of a percentile rank. A child this age, however, may be able to understand the consequences of the evaluation. In this situation the child may be able to understand something like, "Remember those tests I gave you? Well, your scores were low on a couple of them. Because of this I suggested to your parents that you be tutored after school. So now you will be going to visit a teacher after school who will help you with schoolwork."

The older the child, the more similar the feedback session becomes to the one for parents. Another dramatic difference, however, is that negative feedback to a child or adolescent can have the opposite of the intended effect. That is, in most cases the goal is to improve variables such as academic achievement. A child who is told that he or she has low intelligence test scores may decide to stop trying in school. In some cases the examiner's honesty could harm the child. A few options are available in cases where an examiner is concerned about such negative consequences. One option is to have someone who knows the child well and has a positive relationship with him or her help the psychologist communicate the results in a non-threatening manner to the child. A good person to fill this role is a teacher. A second possibility is to have the child's primary therapist or counselor eventually share the results with the child in a counseling session. The counselor or therapist would then be able to help the child cope with the results in a supportive setting.

CONCLUSIONS

Report writing and oral reporting are central, not ancillary, considerations in the intellectual assessment process. The most insightful and elegant of evaluations is lost if not translated to usable information in written reports and treatment team meetings. Unfortunately, these central assessment skills are easily overlooked in the training of clinicians, who are left to acquire these skills through trial and error. Clinicians should seek out expert supervision in this area if it is not readily offered. In addition, most clinicians should enlist the aid of a competent (and preferably brutal) editor to review their written work. Writing is not easy. Writing skills, however, can be acquired with diligence and patience. George Orwell described the writing process well when stating why he writes. Orwell said that writing a book "is a horrible, exhausting struggle, like a long bout of some painful illness." Unfortunately, writing good assessment reports can be just as laborious.

CHAPTER SUMMARY

1. Psychological reports are essentially in the public domain, as they are frequently made available to parents, judges, lawyers, and other nonpsychologists, creating the opportunity for improper interpretation of the results by untrained individuals.

2. Psychological reports can be useful to other clinicians who evaluate a child who has previously been seen by a psychologist.

3. Ownby and Wallbrown (1986) conclude that psychological reports: (1) are considered useful to some extent by consumers such as psychiatrists and social workers, (2) are frequently criticized by these professional groups on both content and stylistic grounds, and (3) may (or may not) make substantial contributions to patient management.

4. Different audiences require different types of written reports.

5. Some of the common problems with report writing include:

Vocabulary problems

Eisegesis

Report length

A number emphasis

Failure to address referral questions

6. Some research has shown that teachers prefer a question-and-answer report format.

7. Parents also tend to prefer a question-and-answer format to other formats, although the difference in preference scores between the psychoeducational and question-and-answer reports in one study failed to reach statistical significance.

8. Suggested report writing practices include:

Report only pertinent information.

Define abbreviations and acronyms.

Emphasize words rather than numbers.

Reduce difficult words.

Describe the tests used.

Edit the report at least once.

Use headings and lists freely.

Use examples of behavior to clarify meaning.

Reduce report length.

Check scores.

Use a spelling checker.

9. Some of the score classification systems used today are old and in need of revision in light of changes in terminology. The Wechsler/ Binet classification systems can be traced to the early part of this century.

10. If a child's composite score is within 3 standard score points of the next classification, both bordering classifications should be given.

11. A continuing debate regarding report writing is the issue of whether or not, or how, to report scores.

12. Percentile ranks are less apt to produce inaccurate reactions that are more typically associated with IQ scores.

13. A proposed report format for new students includes the following sections.

Identifying Information

Assessment Procedures

Referral Questions

Background Information

Observations and Interview Results

Assessment Results and Interpretation

Summary

Signatures

Recommendations

Psychometric Summary

14. Hints for communicating intelligence test results to parents include:

- Avoid excessive hedging or deceit.
- Use percentile ranks heavily when describing levels of performance.
- Allow parents opportunities to participate.
- Anticipate questions prior to the interview and prepare responses.
- Schedule adequate time for the interview.
- Practice communicating with parents from a variety of backgrounds.
- Never make an overly explicit prediction.
- Use good basic counseling skills.

- Do not engage in counseling that is beyond your level of expertise.
- Be aware that some parents are not ready to accept some test results.

15. The most important thing to remember about teacher conferences is that they should take place.

16. The major decision that a clinician needs to make before giving feedback to a child is to determine the type of information that is appropriate for the child's developmental level.

CHAPTER 9

Kaufman Assessment Battery for Children (K-ABC)

CHAPTER QUESTIONS

Who created the K-ABC and how is it different from other popular tests?

With what groups of children is the K-ABC likely to be most useful?

The Kaufman Assessment Battery for Children (K-ABC) (Kaufman & Kaufman, 1983a) has been the subject of scores of research investigations (at least several hundred). It is particularly surprising that a test this new would be so extensively used in research investigations. A book published in 1987 by Kamphaus and Reynolds containing a rich collection of research indicates that the pace of K-ABC research shows no sign of slowing.

The K-ABC is also becoming a frequently used test in everyday assessment practice. In a nationwide survey of school psychologists conducted in 1987 by Obringer (1988), respondents were asked to rank the following instruments in order of their usage: Wechsler's scales, the K-

ABC, and both the old and new Stanford-Binets. The Wechsler scales earned a mean rank of 2.69, followed closely by the K-ABC with a mean of 2.55; then came the old Binet (1.98) and the Stanford-Binet Fourth Edition (1.26). A more recent survey of school psychologists has confirmed these findings (Bracken, 1989). This survey revealed that 41% of the practitioners used the McCarthy Scales of Children's Abilities with preschoolers (see Chapter 12), 28% used the Binet-4, and 25% used the K-ABC. For ages 5 to 11 years the WISC-R was endorsed by 82%, the K-ABC by 57%, and the Binet-4 by 39% of the practitioners. These results argue that child clinicians should have at least some familiarity with the K-ABC. Whether its relative popularity stems from the novelty of the instrument (it differs from other scales in theory, organization of subtests, and other ways), its ease of use, or other factors is not clear. It does, however, appear to be around for the long haul.

From the outset the K-ABC has been the subject of great controversy, as attested to by the

Research Report

Use of the K-ABC with children diagnosed as attention deficit disordered

A recent study by Carter and colleagues (1990) appears to be the only study of the use of the K-ABC in relationship to the WISC-R for evaluating the intelligence of attention deficit disordered children with hyperactivity. This study used 38 consecutive clinic referrals. Girls were, however, subsequently eliminated from the sample because there were a disproportionate number of females in the clinic control sample and the girls tended to be younger than the boys. Consequently, two male-only groups were formed. One group was composed of 23 children who were diagnosed as attention deficit hyperactivity disorder (ADHD) and who had a mean age of 9.1 years. The other group consisted of 15 clinic control subjects with a mean age of 9 years. The average grade level for the ADHD group was 3.70 and for the clinic control group was 3.33. Children were eliminated from either group if they had any evidence of neurological impairment or seizures, chronic mental illness, major psychiatric disorder, significantly subnormal intelligence, or other evidence of developmental disabilities.

Children were diagnosed as ADHD based upon a variety of criteria. One of the criteria included a score of 15 or more on the Parent 10-item Conners Abbreviated Symptom Questionnaire. The same criteria were used for the Teacher's Conners. Additional criteria included a T-score above 60 on the hyperactivity scale of the Personality Inventory for Children and a score in the "significant" range or higher on the attention scale of the Burke's Behavioral Rating Scale that was completed by the children's fathers. When there was more than one rater on a particular measure, the ratings were averaged. All of the subjects were dependents of military personnel who were seen at an outpatient pediatric clinic of an Air Force Medical Center. The two groups did not differ significantly on socioeconomic status or ethnicity. The vast majority of the children in the sample were of an Anglo-culture origin. The scores on the various ratings scales for the ADHD group and the clinic control group differed substantially. For example, the mean Parent Conner's rating for the ADHD group was 19.26, versus 11.87 for the control group. On the PIC Hyperactivity Scale, the mean for the ADHD group was 72.13, versus 52.40 for the clinic controls. Fifteen of the 23 ADHD children were subsequently prescribed stimulant medication. In order to control for the possible confounding effects of medication on K-ABC and WISC-R performance, a 48-hour abstinence period from medication was required prior to the cognitive testing. The children were tested by a psychometrist or clinical psychologist and examiners were blind to group membership for the study.

The K-ABC composite scores and the WISC-R composite scores were used for all analyses. In addition, a WISC-R freedom from distractibility factor score was computed for the purposes of analysis. A multivariate analysis of variance was used to determine whether the two groups differed on various composite scores of the WISC-R and the K-ABC. There were statistically significant differences between the ADHD and clinical groups on only two composite scores—the sequential scale of the K-ABC and the freedom from distractibility factor of the WISC-R. The Sequential standard scores for the ADHD group produced a mean of 91.44; the mean for the clinic control group was 100.87. Similarly, the mean freedom from distractibility score for the ADHD group was 87.65, versus 100.00 for the clinic control group. Although not statistically significant, the groups did differ in overall intelligence score. The mean MPC for the control group was 104.87, versus 105.33 for the WISC-R. In contrast, the mean MPC for the ADHD group was 99.83, versus 107.44 for the WISC-R. The correlation between the MPC and Full Scale score was also very high at .77. In order to more clearly determine the contribution of the individual subtests to the group differences, subtest group comparisons for the K-ABC Sequential scale were conducted. All of the Sequential scale subtests were lower for the ADHD than for the control group, but only the Word Order test was statistically significant, with a mean of 8.39 versus a mean of 10.53 for this same subtest for the control group.

The authors interpret these findings as suggesting that the Sequential scale of the K-ABC is adversely affected by attentional problems. This, in turn, results in a correspondingly lower MPC than Full Scale score. While the freedom from distractibility subtests of Arithmetic, Coding, and Digit Span were also adversely affected, their effect on total score is diluted by the fact that only two of these subtests influence the Full Scale score. It is also interesting that the MPC and the subtest scores on the Sequential scale subtests are still within the average range for this particular sample.

(continued)

Research Report

Use of the K-ABC with children diagnosed as attention deficit disordered *(continued)*

A major interpretive problem for these results is produced by the low correlation of .38 between the Sequential scale of the K-ABC and the freedom from distractibility factor of the WISC-R for the sample of ADHD children. This suggests that these scales are depressed for different reasons. It could be that the distractibility factor of the WISC-R is assessing something different for the ADHD sample from the Sequential scale of the K-ABC. Is one scale adversely affected by distractibility and the other by sequential processing problems? The answer is currently unknown, and examiners will have to interpret results for individual children based upon their clinical acumen. Given the small sample size and some of the controversy regarding the appropriate methods for diagnosing ADHD, these results require replication.

---

strongly pro and con articles written for a special issue of the *Journal of Special Education* devoted to the K-ABC (Miller & Reynolds, 1984) (see Box 9.1). Many of the controversies, especially those regarding the validity of the K-ABC theory, will likely endure unresolved for some time. In the meantime, however, a wealth of research can lead clinicians in interpreting the K-ABC because so much is known about how it correlates with other measures.

Despite its apparent nuances, the K-ABC should be viewed as a logical outgrowth of the history of intelligence testing. The K-ABC authors have extensive experience with other measures, notably the WISC-R. Alan Kaufman had a major impact on the assessment of children's intelligence in his role as a researcher at The Psychological Corporation. Kaufman was project director for development of the WISC-R and the McCarthy scales, tasks to which he was well suited because of his studies at Columbia under the tutelage of the famed psychometrician Robert L. Thorndike.

The Kaufmans' first book, *Clinical Evaluation of Young Children with the McCarthy Scales* (1977), provided a training ground for their work on the K-ABC by immersing them in the work of Dorothea McCarthy, a well-respected child clinician. Alan Kaufman is probably best known for his text *Intelligent Testing with the WISC-R* (1979b). This text laid the groundwork for modern intelligence test interpretation, much of which is incorporated into early chapters of this book. As Anastasi (1988) observes: "The basic approach described by Kaufman undoubtedly represents a major contribution to the clinical use of intelligence tests. Nevertheless, it should be recognized that its implementation requires a sophisticated clinician who is well informed in several fields of psychology" (p. 484).

One can readily see that the Kaufmans entered the arena of intelligence test development with well-deserved laurels. This fact may explain in part why the K-ABC has enjoyed some acceptance.

THEORETICAL FRAMEWORK

The K-ABC intelligence scales are based on a theoretical framework that differs greatly from the approach of Wechsler, who emphasized the assessment of "g" (see Chapter 2). The Kaufmans put much more emphasis on their sub-scales, Sequential and Simultaneous information processing, which are roughly equivalent to the Verbal and Performance scales. Wechsler used the Verbal and Performance scales as means to an end, that end being the assessment of general intelligence. The Kaufmans, however, elevate the Sequential and Simultaneous scales so that they rather than the overall score—the Mental Processing Composite (MPC)—are the focus of interpretation.

The theoretical underpinnings of the Se-

Box 9.1

Now I'm really confused

Reviews of tests by experts are important sources of information when making intelligence test purchase and use decisions. The clinician should, however, read more than one review as experts often disagree, as shown in the examples below that were taken from a 1984 special issue of the *Journal of Special Education* devoted entirely to reviews of the K-ABC. Often intelligence test users will have to read several reviews and even try out a new test before deciding on its utility. While at first these reviews of the K-ABC appear confusing, they are enlightening in at least several respects. They highlight the controversial nature of the K-ABC when it was first published and they show that the K-ABC appeared at the time to be different from its predecessors.

Dean (1984)

The K-ABC represents a theoretically consistent battery of tests that offers insights into children's cognitive processing beyond presently available measures of intelligence.

Sternberg (1984)

The creators of the Kaufman Assessment Battery for Children have attempted to put together a unique, innovative test that will solve the problems created by existing tests. Unfortunately, the test generates more problems than it solves. It is based upon an inadequate conception of intelligence, and as a result, it is not a good measure of intelligence. The data of others cited to support the conception do not in fact support it, and the data collected specifically to evaluate the K-ABC also do not support it. The external validations, if anything, contraindicate the validity of the theory, and the internal validations are inadequate. I cannot think of any circumstance under which I would advocate use of this test over its major competitors, such as the WISC-R or the Stanford-Binet. I am sorry to have to conclude with such a negative evaluation, because ideally, innovation should be rewarded. In the present case, the innovation did not succeed, and the value of the test appears to be a media phenomenon rather than a new measure of intelligence.

Majovsky (1984)

The K-ABC appears to have adequate construct validity as supported by its theoretical basis from the research of cognitive psychology, clinical neuropsychology, cerebral lateralization studies, and other psychological supporting evidence. Secondly, the K-ABC can be most useful in research studies on normal neuropsychological development in young children, as well as impaired brain-behavior functions in diverse childhood populations. Thirdly, the K-ABC is seen to be useful in neuropsychological investigations offering the experienced clinician to see how the information processing style of a child is utilized and on what kinds of tasks. The K-ABC can give a wider degree of information that is not readily obtained by other intelligence measures or test batteries. Fourthly, the K-ABC can be used to supplement a child's clinical neuropsychological evaluation of the level at which the child is processing specific kinds of information, what cognitive strategies are employed, and the efficiencies of the child's information processing styles. The K-ABC in the hands of an experienced clinician offers qualitative observation plus well-standardized and well-defined reliability and validity for making generalizations when and where appropriate.

Goetz and Hall (1984)

To conclude, attempts to revise intelligence testing in light of work in information processing are to be applauded; information-processing theory and research hold great promise for improving educational practice associated with intellectual assessment. In our view, however, development of the K-ABC has left this promise largely unfulfilled.

Telzrow (1984)

. . . this colorful and appealing instrument appears to be well-suited to the unique requirements of preschool assessment.

Salvia and Hritko (1984)

We take the position that there should be empirical validation before ability training is introduced in the schools. In the absence of such empirical validation, the educational uses that the Kaufmans advocate for the K-ABC are currently

(continued)

Box 9.1 *(continued)*

unacceptable. Ysseldyke and Salvia (1974) argued that implementation of unvalidated educational programs on the basis of theoretical derivation, speculation, and good intentions (rather than data) constituted experimentation. Experimentation should be governed by the procedures for research with human subjects, including obtaining informed consent and systematically collecting data. Those requirements seem appropriately employed with the K-ABC.

Anastasi (1984)

The use of multiple scores and profile analysis are a commendable feature of the K-ABC, a feature that enhances the diagnostic value of the battery and facilitates the planning of individualized educational programs. But such multiple assessment can be implemented without introducing a distinction that encourages misuse. In the hands of a highly qualified professional, the K-ABC is a promising instrument for dealing with important practical testing needs. It should be presented to the testing community with adequate safeguards against popular misinterpretation.

Jensen (1984)

The diminished black-white difference on the K-ABC seems to be largely the result of psychometric and statistical artifacts: lower g loadings of the mental processing scales and greater heterogeneity of the standardization sample, which causes mean group differences to be smaller when they are expressed in standard score units. The general factor measured by the K-ABC is essentially the same g as that of the Stanford-Binet and Wechsler scales. But the K-ABC yields a more diluted and less valid measure of g than do the other tests. The K-ABC factors of successive and simultaneous mental processing, independent of the g factor, constitute only a small fraction of the total variance in K-ABC scores, and the predictive validity of these small factors per se is probably nil.

Kaufman (1984)

If the widespread use of the K-ABC shows that the WISC-R/Binet monopoly can be challenged, and if that realization spurs the development of numerous new well-normed and well-conceived intelligence tests from a plethora of practical, clinical, and theoretical perspectives, then I will be the first to applaud. That, to me, would be the K-ABC's finest legacy.

---

quential and Simultaneous scales are really an updated version of a variety of theories (Kamphaus, 1990). They were gleaned from a convergence of research and theory in diverse areas including clinical and experimental neuropsychology and cognitive psychology. The Sequential and Simultaneous theory was distilled primarily from two lines: the information processing approach of Luria (e.g., Luria, 1966) and the cerebral specialization work done by Sperry (1968, 1974), Bogen (1969), Kinsbourne (1975), and Wada, Clarke, and Hamm (1975).

Simultaneous Processing

Simultaneous processing refers to the mental ability of the child to integrate input all at once to solve a problem correctly. Simultaneous processing frequently involves spatial, analogic, or organizational abilities (Kaufman & Kaufman,

1983b; Kamphaus & Reynolds, 1987). Often there is a visual aspect to the problem and visual imagery may be involved in solving it. The Triangles subtest on the K-ABC (an analogue of Wechsler's Block Design task) is a prototypical measure of simultaneous processing. To solve these items correctly one must mentally integrate the components of the design to "see" the whole. Such a task seems to match up nicely with Luria's qualifying statement of synthesis of separate elements (each triangle) into spatial schemes (the larger pattern of triangles, which may form squares, rectangles, or larger triangles). Whether the tasks are spatial or analogic in nature, the unifying characteristic of simultaneous processing is the mental synthesis of the stimuli to solve the problem, independent of the sensory modality of the input or the output. Simultaneous processing is also required on the Photo Series subtest of the K-ABC. This finding is sometimes a surprise to the new user because of the similarities between this test and Wechsler's Picture Arrangement. The Photo Series test, however, is a marker task of the Simultaneous scale, as it is tied with Triangles for having the best factor loading on the simultaneous factor (Kaufman & Kamphaus, 1984). Hence, even though the Photo Series subtest appears to have a sequential component (and the Kaufmans theorized that it was a sequential task but were surprised themselves [Kamphaus & Reynolds, 1987]), the process that most children elect to use places it on the Simultaneous scale. Evidently the more crucial aspect of solving Photo Series items correctly involves developing a sense of the whole series of pictures and how they connect to one another.

Sequential Processing

Sequential processing, on the other hand, emphasizes the arrangement of stimuli in sequential or serial order for successful problem solving. In every instance each stimulus is linearly or temporally related to the previous one (Kaufman & Kaufman, 1983b) creating a form of serial interdependence within the stimulus. The K-ABC includes sequential processing subtests that tap a variety of modalities. The Hand Movements subtest involves visual input and a motor response; the Number Recall subtest involves auditory input with an auditory response. Word Order involves auditory input and a visual response. Therefore, the mode of presentation or mode of response is not what determines the scale placement of a task, but rather the *mental processing demands* are important (Kaufman & Kaufman, 1983b).

Process versus Content

Unfortunately, this distinction between type of mental process as opposed to type of content or stimulus makes the K-ABC theory more difficult to grasp than the verbal/nonverbal content distinction of the WISC. The logic of the Wechsler scales as to why subtests belong on either the Verbal or Performance scale is easy to understand. In the case of the Wechsler scales, if it "looks like a duck, and walks like a duck, it is probably a duck." Alternately, the K-ABC subtests were placed on the Sequential and Simultaneous scales empirically regardless of the authors' intuitions or hopes. Consequently, the K-ABC intelligence scales require a higher level of inference than the Wechsler scales, making them more difficult for the student to understand. In the case of the K-ABC theory, if it "looks like a duck, and walks like a duck, it may in fact be a groundhog!"

Achievement versus Intelligence

While the empirical nature of the intelligence scales of the K-ABC may be novel, an equally controversial move was to take the equivalent of the WISC-III Verbal scale and say that these types of tests are no longer intelligence tests—they are now achievement tests (Kamphaus & Reynolds, 1987), which is what the Kaufmans did by taking analogues of Wechsler tests such as Information (Faces and Places), Vocabulary (Riddles and Expressive Vocabulary), and Arithmetic (Arithmetic) and putting them on their own scale as achievement tests. The K-ABC authors (Kaufman & Kaufman, 1983b) give the following rationale for this move.

> *Unlike the theoretically based mental processing scales, the K-ABC Achievement Scale was derived from only rational and logical considerations. . . . We see these diverse tasks as united by the demands they place on children to extract and assimilate information from their cultural and school environment. Regardless of more traditional approaches to the definition and measurement of intelligence, the K-ABC is predicated on the distinction between problem solving and knowledge of facts. The former set of skills is interpreted as intelligence; the latter is defined as achievement. This definition presents a break from other intelligence tests, where a person's acquired factual information and applied skills frequently influence greatly the obtained IQ. (p. 2)*

The label "achievement" may, however, not be the best for this scale (Kamphaus & Reynolds, 1987) because of its similarity to the

WISC-III Verbal scale. In some cases this scale may function as two—verbal intelligence and reading (Kamphaus & Reynolds, 1987). This division of the Achievement scale is especially appealing in light of the factor analytic data on the K-ABC, which suggests that the K-ABC possesses three factors that are very similar to those of the WISC-R and WISC-III.

ORGANIZATION
OF THE K-ABC

The intelligence scales of the K-ABC consist of subtests that are combined to form scales of Sequential Processing, Simultaneous Processing, and the Mental Processing Composite, a summary score reflective of the Sequential and Simultaneous scales. On the separate Achievement scale, subtests are combined to form a global Achievement score.

The K-ABC differs greatly from the WISC-III in its developmental focus. Instead of giving all subtests to all children, the K-ABC has subtests that are designed only for specific age groups. As a result, children at different ages not only are administered different subtests but also different numbers of subtests, with young children receiving far fewer subtests than older children.

The K-ABC also includes a special short form of the Mental Processing Composite, known as the Nonverbal scale (composed of tasks that can be administered in pantomime and that are responded to motorically) to assess the intelligence of children with speech or language handicaps, of hearing-impaired children, and of those who do not speak English. It is particularly useful as part of the assessment of children suspected of aphasias or other expressive or receptive language disorders. However, the Nonverbal scale is useful as an estimate of general intellectual level only and cannot be subdivided into Sequential or Simultaneous Processing scales.

Supplementary Scales

Kamphaus and Reynolds (1987) proposed new supplementary scales for Verbal Intelligence, Reading Composite, and a Global Intelligence Composite. These supplementary scales are intended for specialized uses (see Table 9.1).

All of the K-ABC global scales (Sequential Processing, Simultaneous Processing, Mental Processing Composite, Achievement, and Nonverbal) yield standard scores, with a mean of 100 and standard deviation of 15, to provide a commonly understood metric and to permit comparisons of mental processing with achievement for children suspected of learning disabilities. Furthermore, use of this metric allows for easy comparison of the K-ABC global scales to other major tests of intelligence and to popular individually administered tests of academic achievement. The Mental Processing subtests yield standard scores with a mean of 10 and standard deviation of 3, modeled after the familiar Wechsler scaled score. Achievement subtests, on the other hand, yield standard scores with a mean of 100 and a standard deviation of 15, which permits direct comparisons of the Mental Processing global scales with individual achievement areas. The K-ABC achievement tests are

TABLE 9.1   Kamphaus and Reynolds supplementary scales

	Verbal	Reading
Expressive Vocabulary	x	
Faces & Places	x	
Arithmetic	x	
Riddles	x	
Reading/Decoding		x
Reading/Understanding		x
Global Intelligence = Seq + Sim + Verbal		

*Norms for these scales can be found in Kamphaus and Reynolds (1987).

also longer than similar tests on the WISC-III, which allows them to support a more familiar metric.

PSYCHOMETRIC PROPERTIES OF THE K-ABC

Standardization

The K-ABC was standardized on a sample of 2,000 children, using primarily 1980 U.S. Census figures. The sample was stratified by age, gender, geographic region, race/ethnic group, parental educational attainment (used as a measure of SES), community size, and educational placement (regular class placement versus placement in a variety of programs for exceptional children). In the past, exceptional children have been excluded from the standardization samples for individually administered tests (Kaufman & Kaufman, 1983b). The K-ABC authors attempted to include representative proportions of learning-disabled, mentally retarded, gifted and talented, and other special populations in the standardization sample according to data provided by the National Center for Education Statistics and the U.S. Office of Civil Rights. Overall, the match of the sample to Census statistics is quite good, although high-SES minorities (specifically African-Americans and Hispanics) were statistically significantly oversampled (Bracken, 1985). The effect of this sampling, however, was probably rather small (Kamphaus & Reynolds, 1987).

Reliability

Split-half reliability coefficients for the K-ABC global scales range from 0.86 to 0.93 (mean = 0.90) for preschool children and from 0.89 to 0.97 (mean = 0.93) for children age 5 to 12½. All of the K-ABC subtests show internal con-

sistencies that are comparable to those of other measures except one — Gestalt Closure. This test had mean internal consistency coefficients of .72 for preschoolers and .71 for school-age children. These results suggest that this test has a relatively heterogeneous item pool.

I have seen this heterogeneity reflected in my own clinical assessment practice, where I will frequently see children perform inconsistently on this test. A child may solve easy items incorrectly and later, more difficult, items correctly. The Gestalt Closure subtest is also a good example of the difference between internal consistency coefficients and test-retest coefficients. The stability or test-retest coefficients are considerably higher for this test (.74 for preschoolers, .84 for early elementary grades, and .86 for later elementary grades) than the internal consistency estimates. These data suggest that although this test has a heterogeneous item pool, the overall scores obtained by a child are relatively stable over time.

A test-retest reliability study was conducted with 246 children retested after a 2- to 4-week interval (mean interval = 17 days). The results of this study showed good estimates of stability that improved with increasing age. For the Mental Processing Composite, coefficients of .83, .88, and .93 were obtained for each age group (for preschoolers, for early elementary grades, and for later elementary grades). Achievement scale composite reliabilities for these same age ranges were .95, .95, and .97 respectively. (Further details of the test-retest study can be found on pp. 81–84 of the *K-ABC Interpretive Manual* [Kaufman & Kaufman, 1983b]).

The test-retest reliability coefficients for the global scales — and to a lesser extent the internal consistency (split-half) coefficients — show a clear developmental trend, with coefficients for the preschool ages being smaller than those for the school-age range. This trend is consistent with the known variability over time that characterizes preschool children's standardized test performance in general (Kamphaus & Reynolds, 1987).

Box 9.2

Interview with Alan S. Kaufman, Research Professor, University of Alabama

You are well known because of your work with the McCarthy scales, the WISC-R, and of course, your own K-ABC. Do you have any new assessment instruments in the works?

Nadeen and I have continued to develop tests ever since the publication of the K-ABC in 1983. The Kaufman Test of Educational Achievement (K-TEA), published in 1985, has become increasingly popular; so has a more recent test, the 1990 Kaufman Brief Intelligence Test (K-BIT). The K-BIT, for ages 4 to 90, is composed of measures of vocabulary and matrices, and provides a quick, reliable assessment of verbal and nonverbal IQ for professionals who have a legitimate reason to bypass more comprehensive testing. The K-BIT was developed to provide an alternative to the kinds of brief instruments, like the Slosson Intelligence Test, that are usually found wanting when their norms and other psychometric properties are evaluated. The K-BIT is also intended as an alternative choice for psychologists who routinely administer short forms of well-normed comprehensive intelligence tests. The norms and psychometric properties of short forms are invariably obtained from administration of the complete batteries; data from administration of just the abbreviated form are rare.

We also contributed the cognitive and language portions of the 1990 screening battery known as the *AGS Early Screening Profiles*, a comprehensive instrument that also includes assessment of adaptive functioning and motor coordination. Most of our current test development efforts, however, have been for adolescents and adults. Three new tests have been standardized, and all should be available in late 1992 or early 1993. The most comprehensive is the Kaufman Adolescent and Adult Intelligence Test (KAIT), for ages 11–90 years, that offers Fluid and Crystallized IQs and follows the Horn-Cattell fluid-crystalized theory. Tasks composing both major IQ scales were selected to emphasize the measurement of high-level planning processes and formal operational thought. Additionally, the KAIT offers assessment of immediate and delayed recall.

The other two tests are brief: the Kaufman Adaptive and Functional Skills Test (K-FAST) spans the 15–90 year age range and assesses a person's ability to apply cognitive skills in the areas of reading and arithmetic to everyday life situations; the Kaufman Screener for Neuropsychologists and Physicians (K-SNAP), for ages 11–90 years, includes tasks at three levels of mental functioning, and is intended to help clinicians determine whether a patient requires comprehensive neuropsychological assessment. The four subtests that compose the K-SNAP can be interpreted from several frameworks, such as Luria's: Block 1, Arousal (Mental Status); Block 2, Successive and Simultaneous Processing (Number Recall, Gestalt Closure); and Block 3, Planning (Four-Letter Words).

When assessing children, psychologists have a number of excellent options in their testing libraries. For adults, however, the situation is different. The WAIS-R (and before it, the Wechsler-Bellevue and WAIS) has had a stranglehold in this area for a half-century, and we believe that examiners need alternatives. If we've learned one thing from the K-ABC, it is that the Wechsler-Binet monopoly can be challenged, and that test users are eager to have alternatives to the existing tests—even if many prefer to stick to the more established tests for routine assessments. Also, competition from new tests helps keep the older test publishers on their toes; they realize that if relative newcomers such as the K-ABC and Woodcock-Johnson have manuals filled with validity studies, then they will have to exert similar efforts to stay number one. Nowhere is this infusion of new blood required more than in the field of intellectual evaluation of adults.

Why did you decide to devote your efforts to the area of adult intellectual assessment?

The seed of our interest in adult assessment began with conversations Nadeen and I had with David Wechsler back in 1975 when he graciously visited with our school psychology students at the University of Georgia. I had worked closely with Dr. Wechsler from 1971 to 1974 while employed by The Psychological Corporation when we were engaged in the revision and restandardization of the WISC. He remains the most important mentor of my career, and is the most talented clinician I have ever met. (He claimed that he could diagnose a person based on just a few items—such as the response to the population of the United States—without looking at the IQs or scaled scores. I

Box 9.2 *(continued)*

believe him.) The evening of his visit, Nadeen and I took out Dr. Wechsler and his lovely wife Ruth for dinner; throughout the meal he directed the conversation to focus primarily on one topic: "How do you measure an adult's intelligence?" He was clearly dissatisfied with the use of the WAIS for the elderly, remarking that he could no longer respond quickly to some of his own Performance items, and that he was contemplating developing a test for the elderly that would have had the wonderful acronym WISE (even the revision would have been appropriately named the WISE-R!). The meal was not a relaxing one. We had wanted to talk about casual topics after a grueling day, but he was insistent on getting our opinions—in between mouthfuls—about adult intelligence, especially of elderly individuals. Simply put, when David Wechsler talked about intelligence, people listened. And when he asked questions about it, Alan and Nadeen (despite the panicky feeling of sounding stupid) responded.

We tucked away that evening's conversation and the insights that arose from the four-way interaction somewhere in our long-term store of information, and proceeded to focus on children's intelligence for nearly a decade. After all, we were still 30-something and old age seemed far away. But after the K-ABC was published in 1983 and we spent the next year or so amid public and professional controversy, we were close to 40 and began taking stock of where we wanted to head professionally. That long-ago conversation with the Wechslers surfaced in each of us, perhaps simultaneously, and we began to wonder whether an alternative to the WAIS-R might enhance the assessment of adult intelligence across the life span. David Wechsler, too, sought to supplement the WAIS with the WISE for elderly adults as a means of enhancing life-span mental assessment.

Interestingly, the more we worked on the development of the KAIT, the more fascinated we became with the topic of intelligence and aging. Much of the library research that I immersed myself in on developmental psychology and neuropsychology, while writing my 1990 text *Assessing Adolescent and Adult Intelligence*, was illuminating and provocative. So were the results of the series of studies that I conducted with my colleagues, Jim McLean and Cecil Reynolds, on the relationship of aging to the WAIS-R IQs across the 20–74-year range. Finally, one event triggered Nadeen and my continued interest in life-span development from a personal perspective: In 1987, the birth of sweet Nicole made us permanently and irrevocably grandparents.

How will the KAIT differ from other scales such as the WAIS-R and K-ABC?

The KAIT has its foundation in three theoretical models: (1) the Cattell-Horn distinction between fluid and crystallized intelligence, (2) Piaget's notion of formal operational thought, and (3) the Luria-Golden conceptualization of the planning functions that are associated with the prefrontal lobes. The latter two theories were instrumental in our selection of subtests for the battery. We tried to ensure that virtually every task measured the high-level, decision-making, executive, problem-solving capacities that are associated with both formal operational thought and planning ability. But it is the Cattell-Horn theory that forms the foundation of the KAIT, providing the two-pronged scale structure tentatively labeled Fluid and Crystallized.

Both scales measure aspects of the hypothesis-generation skills that define formal operations and planning; however, as befits scales derived from the Cattell-Horn model, the Fluid scale focuses on novel problem-solving situations while the Crystallized scale is dependent on knowledge obtained through acculturation and formal education. All research on the relationship between intelligence and aging converges on the Cattell-Horn distinction between fluid and crystallized intelligence. When education and other cohort variables are controlled to the degree possible, the same findings emerge from cross-sectional, longitudinal, and cross-sequential investigations: Crystallized skills maintain throughout the life span before declining gradually in old age, while fluid skills peak in the late teens or early 20s before plunging rapidly and dramatically throughout the adult life span. The sequential-simultaneous model was fine for the K-ABC, geared for preschool and elementary school children, but we felt that the Cattell-Horn approach had no peer as a model to guide the assessment of adolescent and adult intelligence. We did not want to be locked into a children's model for our adult test, or to the specific tasks that comprise the K-ABC. Instead, we developed a new set of tasks with only a slight K-ABC overlap, preferring to focus in on research in adult developmental psychology, and explored the fit of the sequential-simultaneous model

(continued)

Box 9.2 *(continued)*

along with several other approaches. We found that the fluid-crystallized dichotomy fit our tasks psychometrically and conceptually better than did the cerebral specialization or Luria-Das constructs.

The WAIS-R Performance versus Verbal distinction is often interpreted from the fluid-crystallized model, but it falls a little short. Research suggests that Picture Arrangement has a healthy dose of crystallized ability, while age-related changes on Similarities and Digit Span often resemble the life-span decrements that characterize Performance subtests. Also, Coding, according to Horn, is a measure of general speed, not fluid intelligence. The KAIT, in contrast to the WAIS-R, has strong construct validity support for a fluid-crystallized interpretation of its scales. Additionally, the KAIT Crystallized Scale includes pictorial stimuli as well as verbal stimuli, while the Fluid scale assesses novel problem solving with a variety of stimuli (including verbal). Whereas speed of information processing is an essential aspect of fluid ability on the KAIT, visual-motor speed and coordination—so much a part of a person's success on Wechsler's Performance Scale—is greatly deemphasized.

There's no question that we've departed substantially from the K-ABC model in constructing the KAIT, although there are some similarities as well. In the *K-ABC Interpretive Manual*, we discuss how the Mental Processing Composite (Sequential + Simultaneous) resembles fluid ability, whereas the Achievement scale is a crystallized analogue; hence, the K-ABC is easily interpretable from the Horn-Cattell model. Also, from Luria's theory, sequential and simultaneous processing are associated with Block 2, the second functional unit, while planning ability is within the domain of Luria's Block 3. Consequently, our definition of intelligence for children stresses Luria's Block 2, or coding, processes; in contrast, our definition of adolescent and adult intelligence is entrenched in the planning processes that define Luria's third functional unit. This distinction in definitions is consistent with a body of research from both the Piaget and Luria-Golden perspectives that identifies the emergence of formal operational thought, and the maturity of the prefrontal lobes needed for that type of abstract thought, at about 11–12 years of age. That is precisely where the K-ABC leaves off and the KAIT begins.

Another difference between our tests for children versus adults is whether so-called measures of achievement should be classified as intelligence. For the K-ABC, we say no; for the KAIT, we say yes. Here the reason is pragmatic rather than theoretical, and relates to the reasons for assessing individuals at different ages. Children within the K-ABC age range are commonly referred for a school-related problem, whether examiners are trying to assess possible mental retardation, learning disabilities, or emotional disturbance in school-age children, or "high-risk" behavior in preschoolers. The children are commonly from minority groups, often where their primary language is not English, and from disadvantaged backgrounds. The amelioration of school achievement difficulties is usually one of the prime reasons for the evaluation. Consequently, we kept the Achievement scale out of the K-ABC intelligence score to avoid unfairly penalizing children from culturally different or disadvantaged backgrounds. At the preschool and elementary school ages, one of the main developmental tasks is to continue to improve one's achievement.

During adolescence and adulthood, people are usually referred for different reasons, having to do with neuropsychological, clinical, and vocational issues. Educational concerns are less pertinent, and the separation of new problem-solving ability from old learning seems artificial at best for individuals who are beyond the elementary school grades. Nonetheless, when the KAIT is administered to an illiterate, to a person known to have dyslexia, or to other individuals for whom the Crystallized scale will surely provide a poor estimate of intelligence, examiners are encouraged to interpret *only* the Fluid Scale.

The KAIT model differs from the Horn (*not* Cattell-Horn) model that underlies the cognitive portion of the Woodcock-Johnson Psycho-Educational Battery-Revised. The revised WJ relies on Horn's most recent refinement of his theoretical approach, which identifies many fairly pure dimensions of intelligence. Woodcock and Johnson measure seven of these cognitive factors, each with only a few subtests. We adhere to the older Horn-Cattell approach that placed primary emphasis on the fluid-crystallized distinction, and defined these constructs fairly broadly. We have found that specific, "pure" factors are fine for laboratory research, but they fall short when used to measure the complexities of intelligence, particularly the mental functioning of adolescents and adults. That observation stems directly from David Wechsler's philosophy.

Box 9.2 *(continued)*

The KAIT fluid-crystallized dichotomy also resembles one aspect of the model that forms the theoretical foundation of the fourth edition of the Stanford-Binet. However, the new Binet has a third category called Memory, whereas the KAIT integrates its memory tasks into the two main scales. Also, the Binet does not provide good factor analytic support for the Horn-Cattell dichotomy, and its oldest age group is only 18–23 years.

We are eagerly awaiting KAIT's entrance onto the assessment scene. If the reactions of professionals to the K-ABC serve as any type of yardstick, then there just might be some excitement and controversy in store.

Validity

The eagerness to conduct research on the K-ABC may have been spurred by the Kaufmans themselves. The *K-ABC Interpretive Manual* (Kaufman & Kaufman, 1983b) includes the results of 43 validity studies, an impressive amount of prepublication research that at the time was all too uncommon in test manuals. Studies were conducted on aspects of construct, concurrent, and predictive validity. In addition, several of the studies were conducted with samples of exceptional children, including samples classified as hearing impaired, physically impaired, gifted, mentally retarded, and learning disabled.

Developmental Changes

The K-ABC yields satisfactory growth curves for most age groups (Kamphaus & Reynolds, 1987). It has, however, some problems with a lack of easy items for preschoolers (inadequate floor) and difficult items for older children (inadequate ceiling)(Kamphaus & Reynolds, 1987). At the preschool level the K-ABC generally lacks difficulty for 2½- and 3-year-olds with below-average intelligence. Since children are usually referred at this age for developmental problems, a child will likely obtain at least one raw score of zero. A child who obtains more than one raw score of 0 has not been measured because the examiner does not know how far below 0 this child's skill or ability lies. When this situation occurs, it makes interpretation of the child's scores difficult and results in the examiner having to engage in a high level of in-

ference. The examiner would do better to avoid such problems by choosing a test with more floor. The problem with this age group is that there are not many alternatives to the K-ABC with evidence of adequate floor (see Chapter 13).

The parallel problem is the lack of ceiling for older age groups, which occurs for children beginning at about 10 years of age. The major problem here is on the Simultaneous scale, on which a child may obtain a perfect score on tests such as Photo Series and Matrix Analogies. If this eventuality occurs, then, again, the child has not been measured. The K-ABC is perhaps not the test of choice for gifted children 10 years old or older.

In summary, age differentiation validity is an issue of greater relevance to the K-ABC than to the WISC-III. The K-ABC introduces new tests at a variety of ages and spans the preschool and school age ranges, and both of these factors make the scale more prone to zero and perfect raw scores than the WISC-III. Clinicians have to keep knowledge about age differentiation validity clearly in mind in order to use this test effectively.

Item Bias/Content Validity

The K-ABC is also unusual in that the Kaufmans apparently went to great lengths to remove biased items. As such, the K-ABC has an extremely well-scrutinized set of items. Many items were removed at various stages of the test development process due to concern over gender, regional, or racial/ethnic group bias. A more thorough discussion of this issue and examples of biased items can be found in Kamphaus and Reynolds (1987).

Correlations with Other Tests

Despite the fact that the K-ABC differs in numerous ways from tests such as the WISC, overwhelming evidence shows that these measures correlate very highly (Kamphaus & Reynolds, 1987). In a study of 182 children enrolled in regular classrooms, the Mental Processing Composite (MPC) correlated 0.70 with WISC-R Full-Scale IQ (FSIQ) (Kaufman & Kaufman, 1983b). Hence, the K-ABC Mental Processing scales and the WISC-R share a 49% overlap in variance. They correlate similarly to the relationship between older versions of the Wechsler and Binet scales. The correlations between the K-ABC and WISC-R for numerous nonhandicapped and exceptional populations shown in the *Interpretive Manual* range from .57 to .74. The K-ABC overlaps with the WISC-R a good deal, and yet it also shows some independence. Also of interest in the sample of 182 children is the standard score difference between the MPC and FSIQ. The K-ABC, based on 1980 U.S. Census data, was shown to be about 3 points "tougher" (mean MPC = 113.6) than the WISC-R (mean FSIQ = 116.7) based on this sample of children from regular classes (Kaufman & Kaufman, 1983b).

These findings suggest that *just because the K-ABC and WISC-R correlate relatively highly with one another does not mean that they will yield the same score.* Cases discussed later in this chapter will demonstrate this phenomenon. The K-ABC and WISC-R are organized very differently with different item types on their intelligence scales, resulting in the K-ABC yielding very different scores than the WISC-R for some populations.

Predictive Validity

Predictive validity evidence for the K-ABC is generally comparable to that of the WISC-R

(Kaufman & Kaufman, 1983b). Murray and Bracken (1984), for example, evaluated the predictive validity of the K-ABC over an 11-month interval for a group of 29 children. They found the MPC to predict PIAT Total Test scores at a .79 level over this time period. The Achievement scale composite from the K-ABC was an even better predictor, with a validity coefficient of .88. In a 6-month predictive validity study by Childers and colleagues (1985) the MPC was found to correlate .65 with the Total score on the California Achievement Test (CAT). The relationship of the K-ABC Achievement scale to the CAT was .77. These studies, along with those in the *K-ABC Interpretive Manual* (Kaufman & Kaufman, 1983b), suggest good predictive validity evidence for the MPC and exemplary predictive validity evidence for the K-ABC Achievement scale.

Factor Analysis

The K-ABC initially sparked a flurry of factor analytic investigations. These studies are helpful for understanding the K-ABC better, and, because of similar results, they have the potential to enhance interpretation of the WISC-III and Binet 4. The factor structures of these three measures are looking more similar with each new factor analytic investigation.

A first point to consider is the "g," or unrotated first factor, loadings of the K-ABC in comparison to the WISC-R. Initially researchers thought that the K-ABC, particularly the Sequential scale, was a more diluted measure of "g"—that the Mental Processing subtests measured more simple memory and spatial skills than high-level intellectual abilities (Jensen, 1984; Sternberg, 1984). Subsequently these researchers have been proven wrong, as the similarity between the "g" factors of the K-ABC and the WISC-R have proved strikingly similar (Kamphaus & Reynolds, 1987). Also of interest is the finding that the Sequential and Simultaneous scales measure "g" to the same extent (Kamphaus & Reynolds, 1987). This is a somewhat surprising finding given that for most children the Simultaneous scale has two more tests than the Sequential scale and is slightly more reliable. In addition, the Sequential scale subtests also have a distinct short-term memory component.

The first well-known factor analytic evidence offered in support of the Sequential and Simultaneous scales was by Kaufman and Kamphaus (1984). These authors identified three factors for the K-ABC and labeled them as sequential, simultaneous, and achievement.

Some problems with the sequential/simultaneous model, however, were apparent even in this early investigation. Hand Movements had a split loading, particularly at the school-age level. Even though Hand Movements was consistently the third-best measure of the sequential factor, it had a consistent and significant secondary loading on the simultaneous factor. In addition, Photo Series, long thought to be a sequential task, loaded consistently higher on the simultaneous factor. As a result, after norming, this test was switched from the Sequential to the Simultaneous scale (Kaufman & Kaufman, 1983b). There was, however, some support for the K-ABC theoretical model that emerged from the "nonloadings" in this investigation for Hand Movements and Spatial Memory. The Hand Movements subtest had an insignificant loading on the simultaneous factor for preschoolers. Similarly, Spatial Memory never had an important loading on the sequential factor. These two sets of loadings support the processing (versus content) distinction of the Kaufmans. Hand Movements has an obvious visual component, and yet it never loads higher on the more visual simultaneous factor than it does on the sequential factor. Spatial Memory, with its obvious short-term memory component (it has a five second exposure of the stimuli before their placement must be recalled), never joins the sequential factor. These two findings suggest that there may be problems applying hierarchical (memory versus reasoning) and content (verbal versus nonverbal), content models to the K-ABC.

Kamphaus and Kaufman (1986) conducted an exploratory factor analysis for boys and girls. This investigation yielded similar results to the Kaufman and Kamphaus (1984) study, finding virtually no differences in factor structure attributable to gender. There was a tendency for Hand Movements to have a higher simultaneous loading for girls at the school-age level than for boys. Again, however, Hand Movements and Spatial Memory remained aligned with their respective scales, providing some support for the Kaufmans' processing distinction.

In a series of studies, Keith and his colleagues (Keith, 1985; Keith & Dunbar, 1984; Keith et al. 1985) have called the K-ABC processing model into question by applying Wechsler-like content labels to the K-ABC scales. Keith (1985) has used labels such as "nonverbal/reasoning" (Simultaneous), "achievement/verbal reasoning" (Achievement), and "verbal memory" (Sequential) for the K-ABC factors, making the scales similar to the tradition of psychological assessment. In a study of a sample of 585 referred children (Keith et al., 1985) three factors emerged in an exploratory factor analysis. Virtually all of the factor analyses were similar to those found in previous studies, but their interpretation differed greatly. Hand Movements, for example, loaded highest on the verbal memory factor, and Faces & Places, Riddles, and Arithmetic had substantial secondary loadings on the nonverbal/reasoning factor. The issue of what to call the K-ABC factors remains debated but unresolved (see, for example, Kamphaus, 1990).

Kaufman and McLean (1987) conducted a factor analytic investigation for a sample of learning disabled children and obtained a factor structure that was similar to the model proposed by Keith. Findings of this nature suggest that the interpretive model applied to the K-ABC may depend on sample (child) characteristics. In this way, K-ABC interpretation is entirely consistent with Kaufman's (1979b) intelligent testing model.

One confirmatory factor analytic investigation has provided strong support for the two-factor sequential and simultaneous processing model (Willson et al., 1985) but less enthusiastic support of a distinct Achievement scale. The subtests of the Achievement scale do show their largest loadings on a separate factor, as Kaufman and Kaufman (1983b) proposed, yet each shows large secondary loadings on the two mental processing factors. This supports Anastasi's (1984) contention that the K-ABC MPC/Achievement distinction is more theoretical than practical as there is a substantial correlation between the MPC and Achievement scales.

ADMINISTRATION AND SCORING

Administration and scoring procedures for the K-ABC are available in the *K-ABC Administration and Scoring Manual* (Kaufman & Kaufman, 1983a). One important aspect of K-ABC administration that deserves special mention, however, is the notion of *teaching items.* The first three items of each mental Processing subtest (the sample and the first two items appropriate for a child's age group) are designated as teaching items. On these items the examiner is required to teach the task if the child fails on the first attempt at solving the item. The phrase "teaching the task" means that the examiner is allowed the flexibility to use alternate wording, gestures, physical guidance, or even a language other than English to communicate the task demands to the child. The examiner is not allowed to teach the child a specific strategy for solving the problem, however. This built-in flexibility was designed to be particularly helpful to preschoolers, minority-group children, and exceptional children, who sometimes perform poorly on a task from a traditional IQ test not because of a lack of ability but because of an inability to understand the instructions given. Kaufman and Kaufman (1983b) discuss the concept of teaching items in greater detail and note

that this built-in flexibility has not adversely affected the reliability of the K-ABC. Sample items are now common fare, as they were subsequently embraced by both the Binet-4 and WISC-III.

The K-ABC basal and ceiling rules, referred to as *starting and stopping points* in the *K-ABC Administration and Scoring Manual* (Kaufman & Kaufman, 1983b), also differ from those of many existing intelligence tests. The first rule for administering the K-ABC subtests is straightforward: Examiners are instructed to start and stop testing at the items designated as starting and stopping points for the child's age group. The set of items between the starting and stopping points are, therefore, designed based on standardization data to represent a full range of difficulty for the child's age group. This first basal and ceiling rule is very straightforward, but it is also rigid. Hence, several supplemental rules are given to allow examiners to find items of appropriate difficulty for children at the ends of the distribution of ability (Kaufman & Kaufman, 1983a). The K-ABC also incorporates a very simple discontinue rule (discontinue testing after 1 unit of incorrect items) that is the same for all K-ABC subtests.

The K-ABC Subtests

In contrast to the WISC-III, the K-ABC subtests are a rather unique collection. The WISC-III subtests, for example, were taken primarily from the early Army group tests. The K-ABC subtests are taken from a wider range of sources including the WISC-III (Number Recall and Triangles), experimental cognitive science (Face Recognition), neuropsychology (Hand Movements), and early psychometricians such as Raven (Matrix Analogies), among other sources. In addition, some of the K-ABC subtests are novel, such as Magic Window and Faces & Places.

The K-ABC subtests, however, do have a common lineage in the K-ABC theoretical model, the division of the Sequential, Simultaneous, and Achievement scales. The K-ABC subtests had to show a great deal of consistency with the test's theoretical model in order to be retained. This philosophy is illustrated by the large number of tests that were discarded in the developmental process (Kaufman & Kaufman, 1983b). This section is organized in the same manner as for the WISC-III; a test overview, administration and scoring pointers, noteworthy observations, and psychometric properties.

Psychometric properties are taken from the *K-ABC Interpretive Manual* (Kaufman & Kaufman, 1983b). Some factor analytic results are from Jensen (1984).

Magic Window (Ages 2½–4)

Magic Window requires the child to identify a picture that the examiner exposes by moving it past a narrow slit or "window" (making the picture only partially visible at any one point in time). This subtest appears to be one of the few subtests that can justifiably be described as novel, as it has no clear counterpart in the history of intellectual assessment. This test is designed as the first measure of simultaneous processing and the first test to be administered to preschoolers. It appears to be appropriately placed as the first subtest for preschoolers, as viewing through the window to try to discover the object behind it is a genuinely intriguing task for young children.

It is also an interesting task from the standpoint that while the stimulus is visual, the response is clearly verbal, demonstrating again the relative independence of test content from the mental process used to solve the item. This task was found to be one of the best measures of simultaneous processing for preschoolers (Kaufman & Kaufman, 1983b).

ADMINISTRATION AND SCORING POINTERS

1. Practice the 5-second exposure interval used on this subtest. While the marks on the back of the window are a helpful guide, it does take some experience to get used to this exposure interval.

BEHAVIORS TO NOTE

1. Squinting or other indication that the child is having extraordinary difficulty seeing the items
2. A lack of curiosity about the task
3. Poor articulation
4. Curiosity as to the correct answer
5. An ability to describe the correct answer yet not name it accurately (for example, it has tires and doors)

PSYCHOMETRIC PROPERTIES

Average reliability = .72
"g" loading = N/A
Loading on sequential factor = .24
Loading on simultaneous factor = .53
Loading on achievement factor = .23
Subtest specificity = .40 (ample)

Face Recognition (ages 2½–4)

This test requires a child to select from a group photograph the one or two faces that were shown briefly in a preceding photograph. This task is also a good early task on the K-ABC, as children seem to have a natural curiosity about photographs. This test has its roots in neuropsychological assessment, in which it has been used for the diagnosis of cerebral dominance (Benton, 1980). The Kaufmans (Kaufman & Kaufman, 1983b) chose this task not only because it was a good measure of simultaneous information processing but also because it was a measure that produced few group differences for children from disparate cultures (Kagan & Klein, 1973).

The Face Recognition subtest was excluded from the school age level of the K-ABC because it switched factor loadings for older children. For older children it became more of a measure of sequential processing, suggesting a developmental change in the way that children process these types of photographs. Perhaps young children process faces more as a whole and older children try to break them down into component parts and describe them verbally.

ADMINISTRATION AND SCORING POINTERS

1. Practice the 5-second exposure to develop a rhythm.

BEHAVIORS TO NOTE

1. Squinting or some indication that the child is having difficulty seeing the photographs

PSYCHOMETRIC PROPERTIES

Average reliability = .77

"g" loading = N/A

Loading on sequential factor = .24

Loading on simultaneous factor = .44

Loading on achievement factor = .33

Subtest specificity = .48 (ample)

Hand Movements (2½–12½ years)

For this test the child has to imitate a series of hand movements in the same sequence as the examiner performed them. This test is taken directly from the work of Luria (1966), who used a similar test to asses motor function as part of his neuropsychological evaluation. This test also gives the examiner a clinical sense of the child's fine motor skill (Kaufman & Kaufman, 1983b) and eye-hand coordination.

ADMINISTRATION AND SCORING POINTERS

1. This test unfortunately requires fine motor skill also on the part of the examiner. Be sure to practice using your right hand to administer the items.

2. Be especially vigilant during the most difficult items, as they may become rather difficult to score.

PSYCHOMETRIC PROPERTIES

Average reliability—preschool = .78

Average reliability—school age = .76

"g" loading = .54

Loading on sequential factor = .46

Loading on simultaneous factor = .31

Loading on achievement factor = .18

Subtest specificity—preschool = .49 (ample)

Subtest specificity—school age = .41 (ample)

BEHAVIORS TO NOTE

1. Inability of the child to form the three different hand movements adequately

2. Demonstrating all of the correct movements but failing the items primarily because of difficulty in sequencing

3. Vocalization or subvocalization being used as a strategy to solve the items correctly

Gestalt Closure (2½–12½)

The child is required to name an object or scene pictured in a partially completed "inkblot" drawing. Not unlike some Rorschach items, this test requires a child to visually "complete" drawings. On the face of it, this test is another classic measure of simultaneous/holistic right brain types of processing. This is borne out by factor analytic findings (Kaufman & Kaufman, 1983b; Kamphaus & Kaufman, 1984).

This test has a long history, dating back to the early 1930s (Street, 1931), and yet the Kaufmans were the first to include it in a major test of intelligence.

ADMINISTRATION AND SCORING POINTERS

1. Study the scoring criteria for each item carefully before administering the test.

2. It is important to remember that a nonverbal response can be considered correct (in lieu of a verbal response) on this subtest.

PSYCHOMETRIC PROPERTIES

Average reliability—preschool = .72

Average reliability—school age = .71

"g" loading = .47

Loading on sequential factor = .10

Loading on simultaneous factor = .49

Loading on achievement factor = .28

Subtest specificity—preschool = .39 (ample)

Subtest specificity—school age = .38 (ample)

BEHAVIORS TO NOTE

1. Squinting or other indications that the child is having difficulty seeing the items

2. Seeming realization of the identity of the item but having difficulty naming it

3. Describing parts of the item but inability to label the whole

4. An unwillingness to guess

5. Bizarre responses (e.g., "A frog with blood on it")

Number Recall (2½–12½)

This task is a familiar adaptation of Digits Forward from the WISC-III. Of course, this type of task has been part of intelligence testing since the days of Binet (Binet, 1905). This test is, however, different from Wechsler's in at least a few respects. Most importantly, it includes only Digits Forward.

ADMINISTRATION AND SCORING POINTERS

1. Remember that the examiner's voice may not be dropped at the end of each item.

PSYCHOMETRIC PROPERTIES

Average reliability—preschool = .88

Average reliability—school age = .81

"g" loading = .55

Loading on sequential factor = .66

Loading on simultaneous factor = .16

Loading on achievement factor = .24

Subtest specificity—preschool = .51 (ample)

Subtest specificity—school age = .34 (ample)

BEHAVIORS TO NOTE

1. Recalls all of the digits correctly but errs because of an incorrect sequence

2. Unwillingness to respond or guess when uncertain

3. Self-deprecating statements about memory ability

Triangles (4–12½)

The Triangles subtest is also an adaptation of Wechsler's Block Design task—which is an adaptation of Kohs's (1927) Block Design test. Like Gestalt Closure, this test, too, seems to be a clear measure of simultaneous processing. This supposition is also born out by factor analytical results (Kaufman & Kaufman, 1983b; Kamphaus & Kaufman, 1984; Kamphaus & Reynolds, 1987). Wechsler's Block Design task has also been used in split-brain research investigations as a marker task of right brain processing (Reitan, 1974) (see Chapter 2).

Although the Triangles test is obviously related to Wechsler's Block Design test, the absolute correlations between these two tests is not all that high, generally in the .50s (Kaufman & McLean, 1987). It appears that these two tests, while tending to correlate with one another, should not be viewed by clinicians as interchangeable.

ADMINISTRATION AND SCORING POINTERS

1. Remember that there are no time bonus points for these items.

2. Remember that the child is not allowed to stand the triangles on end.

3. Remember that there is no penalty for rotations.

Average reliability—preschool = .89

Average reliability—school age = .84

"g" loading = .65

Loading on sequential factor = .21

Loading on simultaneous factor = .63

Loading on achievement factor = .27

Subtest specificity—preschool = .51 (ample)

Subtest specificity—school age = .37 (ample)

BEHAVIORS TO NOTE

1. Squinting or other indications that the child is having difficulty seeing the stimulus pictures

2. Dependence on one hand or difficulty using hands to construct the designs

3. Numerous 90° rotations

Word Order (4–12½)

Word Order is the third and last Sequential Processing subtest on the K-ABC. It ranks behind Number Recall as the premier measure of sequential processing. This task requires a child to touch a series of pictures in the same sequence as they were named by the examiner. On more difficult items a color interference task is used. The Kaufmans (Kaufman & Kaufman, 1983b) see this task as an auditory-vocal test of the McCarthy (1972) Verbal Memory ilk. This task is also similar to tests such as Memory for Sentences on the Stanford Binet-4. The Kaufmans borrowed some aspects of this test, including the interference task component, from a clinical neuropsychological test used by Luria (1966).

The color interference task of Word Order may also provide some valuable clinical information. Denckla (1979) observed that disabled readers perform more poorly than capable readers on rapid naming tests that include the naming of colors, letters, and objects.

ADMINISTRATION AND SCORING POINTERS

1. Remember that examiners are not allowed to drop their voice at the end of each sequence.

2. The color interference task can be especially awkward, and the examiner requires some practice in order to administer it properly.

Average reliability—preschool = .84

Average reliability—school age = .82

"g" loading = .64

Loading on sequential factor = .68

Loading on simultaneous factor = .22

Loading on achievement factor = .29

Subtest specificity—preschool = .33 (ample)

Subtest specificity—school age = .28 (ample)

BEHAVIORS TO NOTE

1. The child recalls the stimuli correctly but misses items because of recalling them in incorrect sequence.

2. The child makes self-deprecating statements about memory ability.

3. The child responds with considerable anxiety at the introduction of the color interference task and fails all items thereafter.

Matrix Analogies (5–12½)

The Matrix Analogies test requires the child to select a picture or abstract design that completes a visual analogy. In many ways the Matrix Analogies test resembles Raven's Progressive Matrices (1956, 1960). As such, Matrix Analogies is one of the better measures of simultaneous processing skills. In fact, Raven's Progressive Matrices was used by Das, Kirby, and Jarman (1979) as part of their simultaneous/successive test battery.

One of the interesting aspects of this task is that it may also have a sequential component at older age groups. A separate factor analysis conducted for boys and girls in the K-ABC standardization sample found that when the sample was divided by gender, Matrix Analogies began to take on more substantial loadings on the Sequential Scale for 11- and 12-year-olds, especially for girls. This result suggests that children may apply different, perhaps more sequential/analytic, skills to solving the matrices at older ages. This occurrence may be inferred through observation of the child during testing.

ADMINISTRATION AND SCORING POINTERS

1. Be sure to lay out the "chips" in the same sequence as shown on the easel.

PSYCHOMETRIC PROPERTIES

Average reliability = .85
"g" loading = .62
Loading on sequential factor = .30
Loading on simultaneous factor = .50
Loading on achievement factor = .26
Subtest specificity = .44 (ample)

BEHAVIORS TO NOTE:

1. Use of verbal strategies to solve the items

Spatial Memory (5–12½)

Spatial Memory requires the child to recall the placement of pictures on a page that was exposed for a 5-second interval. Although memory tasks such as this one have not previously appeared on popular tests of intelligence, they have suddenly appeared on the K-ABC and on the Stanford Binet-4. This test serves to round out memory assessment on the K-ABC in that it provides for a nonverbal stimulus and response, like Hand Movements. This subtest, however, is somewhat unique from the other K-ABC memory tasks in that it shows a substantial loading on the simultaneous processing factor. This test, along with Face Recognition at the preschool level, make it difficult to apply a memory versus reasoning

dichotomy to the Sequential/Simultaneous Processing scales. This relatively large number of memory tests, however, provides the basis for a strong measure of children's memory.

ADMINISTRATION AND SCORING POINTERS

1. Like Hand Movements, this task can become extremely difficult to score at more advanced difficulty levels.

PSYCHOMETRIC PROPERTIES

Average reliability = .80
"g" loading = .56
Loading on sequential factor = .26
Loading on simultaneous factor = .58
Loading on achievement factor = .15
Subtest specificity = .39 (ample)

BEHAVIORS TO NOTE

1. Strategies such as a child configuring his or her fingers while watching the stimulus page and then applying this configuration on the response page

2. Focusing more attention on the content of the stimuli (e.g., naming the stimuli or asking questions about them) than on the location of the stimuli on the page per se

3. Difficulty in rapid naming of the colors

Photo Series (6–12½)

Photo Series requires the child to place photographs of an event in chronological order. This test, on the face of it, looks similar to Wechsler's Picture Arrangement subtest. However, several investigations of these two batteries show modest to poor intercorrelations between these two subtests (Kaufman & Kaufman, 1983c; Kaufman & McLean, 1987). The Photo Series test also appears to have a distinctly sequential component. However, factor analyses of the K-ABC have shown that this subtest, along with Triangles, is a marker task of simultaneous processing ability (Kamphaus & Reynolds, 1987). One hypothesis is that in the case of Photo Series the sequential response is anticlimactic to the holistic processing of the stimuli that is required prior to producing a response. In other words, a child has to first visually interpret and verbally label the series (e.g., as a car backing up) before he or she can put the pieces in their correct sequence in the examiner's hand.

ADMINISTRATION AND SCORING POINTERS

1. Examiners must hold the cards in their hands so that they are visible to the child at all times.
2. This test has a number of administration and scoring procedures that share nothing in common with Wechsler's Picture Arrangement task.

PSYCHOMETRIC PROPERTIES

Average reliability = .82
"g" loading = .67
Loading on sequential factor = .25
Loading on simultaneous factor = .64
Loading on achievement factor = .26
Subtest specificity = .33 (ample)

BEHAVIORS TO NOTE

1. Impulsive responding, where the child does not survey the stimulus cards adequately prior to producing a response
2. Trial-and-error responding, where the child obviously does not have a Gestalt for how the picture should be placed together and tries to compare each card to every other card

Expressive Vocabulary (2½–4)

Expressive Vocabulary requires the child to name objects that are pictured in photographs. This test is the first one encountered by pre-

schoolers on the Achievement scale. The Expressive Vocabulary test is intended to follow in the tradition of Wechsler and Binet Vocabulary tests (Kaufman & Kaufman, 1983b). The Kaufmans propose that the assessment of verbal intelligence is essential as part of an intellectual evaluation, but they prefer that the "verbal intelligence" subtests on the K-ABC be included on the Achievement scale and not labeled intelligence as such (Kaufman & Kaufman, 1983c; Kaufman & Reynolds, 1987).

ADMINISTRATION AND SCORING POINTERS

1. Poorly articulated responses that are otherwise correct can be accepted as correct responses.

PSYCHOMETRIC PROPERTIES

Average reliability = .85
"g" loading = N/A
Loading on sequential factor = .25
Loading on simultaneous factor = .61
Loading on achievement factor = .77
Subtest specificity = .27 (ample)

BEHAVIORS TO NOTE

1. Poor articulation
2. Responses in languages other than English
3. Word retrieval problems

Faces & Places (2½–12½)

Faces & Places involves having a child name a well-known person, fictional character, or place pictured in a photograph or illustration. This test is designed as an analogue of Wechsler's Information subtest. It is sensitive, just as is the Information subtest, to factors such as linguistic and cultural background. This test is also sensitive to academic stimulation in school.

This test, however, presents general information items in a novel format. This format has led to considerable criticism of some of the items, the main complaint being that some of them are out of date (most notably Mohammed Ali) (Kamphaus & Reynolds, 1987). Although the content of the individual items is controversial, the test still correlates rather highly with Wechsler's Information subtest (Kamphaus & Reynolds, 1987).

ADMINISTRATION AND SCORING POINTERS

1. Correct last names can be accepted as correct responses even if the first name is not given.

PSYCHOMETRIC PROPERTIES

Average reliability—preschool = .77
Average reliability—school age = .84
"g" loading = .69
Loading on sequential factor = .21
Loading on simultaneous factor = .39
Loading on achievement factor = .67
Subtest specificity − 2.5-4 = .27 (ample)
Subtest specificity—school age = .24 (ample)

BEHAVIORS TO NOTE

1. Responses given in languages other than English
2. A pattern of correct responses for the preschool cartoonlike items and incorrect responses for school-age items that assess more academic/school-related knowledge

Arithmetic (3–12½)

The Arithmetic subtest of the K-ABC requires a child to answer questions that assess knowledge of math concepts or the manipulation of numbers. This Arithmetic subtest resembles more the Arithmetic subtest of Wechsler's genre as opposed to pencil and paper subtests found on clinical measures of mathematics achievement. As such, this test should be considered as a measure of verbal intelligence or a screening measure of mathematics as opposed to a mathematics subtest per se (Kamphaus & Reynolds, 1987). While designed as an analogue of Wechsler's Arithmetic test, this test is somewhat unique because it is considerably longer and assesses a wider range of mathematics skills and content than Wechsler's. This test does show substantial correlations with more traditional mathematics achievement tests (Kamphaus & Reynolds, 1987).

ADMINISTRATION AND SCORING POINTERS

1. Remember that the child is not allowed to use pencil and paper for this subtest.

PSYCHOMETRIC PROPERTIES

Average reliability—preschool = .87
Average reliability—school age = .87
"g" loading = .82
Loading on sequential factor = .46
Loading on simultaneous factor = .48
Loading on achievement factor = .49
Subtest specificity—preschool = .28 (ample)
Subtest specificity—school age = .20 (adequate)

BEHAVIORS TO NOTE

1. Failures on items that are part of a particular content domain (e.g., all subtraction items or multiplication or division items are failed)
2. Self-deprecating statements regarding academic or mathematics achievement

Riddles (3–12½)

Riddles requires a child to name an object or concept that is described by a list of three of its characteristics. From a psychometric standpoint it appears to be a close analogue of vocabulary tests that have always been a part of intelligence tests (Kamphaus & Reynolds, 1987). While this subtest does not require the eloquent multiword expression of the Vocabulary test of the WISC-III, it does seem to require a high level of vocabulary knowledge. This test mimics vocabulary tests from other batteries in other ways, including the fact that it is one of the premier measures of general intelligence ("g") on the K-ABC.

ADMINISTRATION AND SCORING POINTERS

1. This test uses only a 1-0 scoring system with no bonus points.

PSYCHOMETRIC PROPERTIES

Average reliability—preschool = .83
Average reliability—school age = .86
"g" loading = .78
Loading on sequential factor = .34
Loading on simultaneous factor = .42
Loading on achievement factor = .62
Subtest specificity—3–8 = .23 (adequate)
Subtest specificity—9–12½ = .19 (inadequate)

BEHAVIORS TO NOTE

1. Word retrieval problems
2. Self deprecating statements regarding academic achievement

Reading/Decoding (5–12½)

This test requires a child to read words out of context. This is a simple word recognition task similar to those found on screening measures of academic achievement such as the Wide Range Achievement Test-Revised. This test is intended as a measure of basic reading skill.

This test may not serve as a substitute for other clinical tests of reading achievement, in spite of its high correlations with these measures. This prohibition is primarily because of questionable content validity. There are, for example, a number of items with silent consonants. These items may lack "social validity" or utility

since they may not be frequently used by children or appear regularly in their reading materials.

ADMINISTRATION AND SCORING POINTERS

1. Pronunciation is crucial, and the child's response cannot be scored as correct unless pronounced correctly.

PSYCHOMETRIC PROPERTIES

Average reliability = .92
"g" loading = .79
Loading on sequential factor = .39
Loading on simultaneous factor = .26
Loading on achievement factor = .68
Subtest specificity = .21 (adequate)

BEHAVIORS TO NOTE

1. Frustration on the part of the child with his/her reading ability
2. Self-deprecating statements regarding reading ability
3. Reversals
4. Problems with particular item types (e.g., silent consonants)

Reading/Understanding (7–12½)

This task requires a child to act out commands that are given in words or sentences. While intended as a measure of reading comprehension, it is an extraordinarily novel way of assessing reading comprehension. In contrast to many academic achievement measures, this task requires a child to follow commands. While this approach makes the task somewhat controversial, it correlates in the expected fashion with other measures of basic reading skills and reading comprehension (Kamphaus & Reynolds, 1987).

This test also has the potential to yield some insights into the child's personality. A child's refusal to do the task or demonstration of no reluctance whatsoever may be used to corroborate findings from personality measures.

This test should be interpreted cautiously if a child seems reticent, and perhaps more so at the older ages (10 and above) since the reliability tends to dip somewhat.

ADMINISTRATION AND SCORING POINTERS

1. Older children may require considerable encouragement to act out commands.

PSYCHOMETRIC PROPERTIES

Average reliability = .91

"g" loading = .71

Loading on sequential factor = .37

Loading on simultaneous factor = .28

Loading on achievement factor = .76

Subtest Specificity = .11 (adequate)

BEHAVIORS TO NOTE

1. Refusal to act out commands
2. Self deprecating statements regarding reading skills

INTERPRETATION

The K-ABC is amenable to the same interpretive framework that was espoused for the WISC-III.

The following steps should be taken to begin the K-ABC interpretive process.

1. Offer apriori hypotheses.
2. Assign a verbal classification to the MPC (e.g., average).
3. Band the MPC with error (the 90% level of confidence is recommended).

4. Assign verbal classifications to the Sequential and Simultaneous scales.
5. Band the Sequential and Simultaneous scales with error.
6. Test the difference between the Sequential and Simultaneous scales for statistical significance (a reliable difference at the .05 level) using table 10 of the *K-ABC Administration and Scoring Manual* (Kaufman & Kaufman, 1983b).
7. Test the difference between the Sequential and Simultaneous scales for clinical rarity (where a difference that occurred in 5% of the population or less is considered rare) using table 5.12 (p. 193) of the *K-ABC Interpretive manual*) (Kaufman & Kaufman, 1983b).
8. Test apriori hypotheses.
9. Develop aposteriori hypotheses at the composite, shared subtest, and single subtest level.
10. Test aposteriori hypotheses.
11. Draw conclusions.

Apriori Hypotheses

In order to offer apriori hypotheses, one must know the cognitive and behavioral factors that affect K-ABC composite and subtest scores. The characteristics of subtests have already been discussed. Now the Sequential and Simultaneous scales will be considered.

Hypotheses for Sequential/ Simultaneous (Seq/Sim) Differences

While the K-ABC is built around a fairly explicit theoretical stance, Kaufman's own intelligent testing philosophy (Kamphaus & Reynolds, 1987) would encourage examiners to entertain other possible reasons for Seq/Sim differences. Various explanations for such differences are offered next.

SEQUENTIAL VERSUS SIMULTANEOUS PROCESS-ING (SEQ > SIM OR SIM > SEQ) The relative-ly clear factor structure of the K-ABC Mental Processing scales makes a difference in Se-quential and Simultaneous Processing a neces-sity to investigate (Kaufman & Kamphaus, 1989). The major question regarding the K-ABC is in regard to the range of application of the Seq/Sim model. Just how many and what types of children have Seq/Sim discrepancies? The answer to the latter question is only recent-ly becoming apparent. Learning-disabled or mentally retarded children do not show clear patterns (Kamphaus & Reynolds, 1987). Hence, the meaning of a Seq/Sim discrepancy is going to be difficult to establish in many cases, thereby testing the clinical acumen of the examiner to the same extent as V/P differences did.

LINGUISTIC DIFFERENCES (SIM > SEQ) Two of the three Sequential scale subtests have English language content (Number Recall, Word Order). In contrast, the one test with obvious English language content on the Simultaneous scale (Gestalt Closure) makes up only one-fifth of that composite (versus two-thirds for the Se-quential scale) for school-age children. Con-sequently, where English language proficiency is in question a Sim > Seq pattern is likely. A Navajo sample cited in the *Interpretive Manual* demonstrated this problem (Kaufman & Kauf-man, 1983b). The sample spoke the Navajo lan-guage both at home and at school. They ob-tained a mean Sequential score of 88 and a mean Simultaneous score of 100. This pattern of Sim > Seq for a linguistically different group was also found by Valencia (1985) in an in-vestigation of 42 Mexican-American preschool-ers. Here the mean Sequential score of 100 was again lower than the Simultaneous score of 106.5. Another interesting finding from this in-vestigation was the WISC-R Verbal score of only 96 compared to a Performance score of 109, suggesting that the WISC-III Verbal scale

is even more sensitive to linguistic difference than the Sequential scale of the K-ABC.

Whether or not a Sim > Seq pattern can be attributed to a linguistic difference can be checked by the Achievement scale. For that same Navajo group the K-ABC analogue of Wechsler's Vocabulary, Riddles, was the group's lowest Achievement score, with a score of 75 (where mean = 100 and SD = 15).

These findings regarding linguistic differ-ences on the K-ABC are also enlightening from a test design standpoint. The Kaufmans clearly wanted to limit the influence of cultural and linguistic factors on the K-ABC intelligence (Mental Processing) scales. As is clear from these data, the effects of language may be deem-phasized on the K-ABC Mental Processing scales, but its influence may still be powerful, especially on the Sequential scale.

MOTOR PROBLEM (SIM < SEQ) Motor problems may adversely affect a child's performance on the Simultaneous scale of the K-ABC. While the K-ABC Simultaneous scale requires only mini-mal fine motor skill, it does require enough dex-terity that children with substantial motor in-volvement may produce lower scores on this scale due to a motor problem as opposed to a simultaneous processing weakness.

A potentially difficult aspect of evaluating the potential effects of a motor deficit is teasing out the effects of visual problems or simultaneous processing problems. This "unmasking" or clar-ification process can be aided by administering additional tests. One case I observed involved a child with cerebral palsy who obtained a whop-ping 55 standard score point discrepancy in favor of sequential processing. In order to de-termine if the simultaneous weakness was only the result of motor problems, the clinicians in-volved administered the Motor Free Visual Per-ception Test (MVPT) to assess visual perception skills relatively independently of motor skill. The MVPT score was very similar to the Simul-taneous score, suggesting that the child's visual perception problems were more important than the motor problem in determining the low Simultaneous score. This finding was also sensible in light of the K-ABC profile, which showed that even tests such as Gestalt Closure, which has a visual perceptual component but no motor involvement, was also depressed.

For some children with motor problems *both* the Simultaneous and Sequential scales may be well below the mean of 100. This possibility is exemplified by a study of hemiplegic children (Lewandowski & DiRienzo, 1985). In this study a group of children with cerebral palsy (and documented congenital neurodevelopmental delays localized primarily to one of the cerebral hemispheres) were compared to a group of control children without neurodevelopmental problems. These children with obvious hemiplegia on one side achieved mean K-ABC Sequential and Simultaneous scores that were significantly below that of the control group, which achieved means near 100. The mean Sequential scores of the two brain-injured groups with associated motor problems were 95 and 95, whereas their Simultaneous scores were 84 and 95. These data hint that the Simultaneous scale may be more sensitive to motor problems, but they also suggest that the Sequential scale, with tests such as Hand Movements, may show some depression due to severe motor problems.

AUDITORY SHORT-TERM MEMORY PROBLEM (SIM > SEQ) This profile seems to be all too frequent and tests the interpretive savvy of clinicians (Kamphaus & Reynolds, 1987). It occurs relatively frequently because it is consistent with the factor structure of the K-ABC. The Hand Movements test "switches allegiance" because of its equivocal factor loadings for school age children (Kamphaus & Reynolds, 1987). This test's loading on the Sequential factor is consistently *but not considerably* higher than its loading on the Simultaneous factor.

The often observed consequence of this factor structure is that the Number Recall and Word Order tests will yield similar scores that are both discrepant from the rest of the profile. The difficult call in this instance is to determine if these two tests are reflecting sequential processing or auditory short-term memory. Several suggestions for testing these hypotheses are:

1. If a child's responses on these two tests indicate good recall but poor sequencing, then a sequencing hypothesis is supported. For example, a child who responds to the stimulus "8-2-5-1" with "2-5-1-8" may have greater problems with sequencing in recall than memory span per se.

2. If Spatial Memory and Hand Movements scores are more in line (not necessarily strong or weak to the same degree) with Number Recall and Word Order than with the Simultaneous scale subtests, then hypotheses related to a memory problem are more plausible.

3. Teacher reports can also help test an auditory short-term memory versus sequencing hypothesis. A child's teacher may produce evidence of sequencing problems from worksheets or other student products. The child's teacher should also be asked whether or not examples of significant memory failure can be cited.

VERBAL VERSUS NONVERBAL INTELLIGENCE (ACH > SEQ > SIM) Factor analyses of all K-ABC subtests have consistently produced three factors similar to the Sequential, Simultaneous, and Achievement scales. Factor labels, however, are dictated to a large extent by the theoretical orientation of the test author or researcher conducting the investigation (Kamphaus, 1990). Kamphaus and Reynolds (1987) have taken this work one step further by developing new scores for the K-ABC that facilitate the application of a verbal/nonverbal intelligence dichotomy. Use of the Wechsler model, however, is not only a change in labels but a change from a process to a content distinction.

Kamphaus and Reynolds (1987) divide the Achievement scale into two components: verbal intelligence, which includes all of the Achievement scale subtests exclusive of the two reading tests, and a reading composite, which consists of the two reading subtests. Even without the use of these supplementary procedures (see Kamphaus & Reynolds, 1987) the verbal/nonverbal distinction may be of some value.

Two of the Sequential tests (Number Recall and Word Order) use verbal stimuli, and so do the Achievement scale subtests. A child with an oral expression deficit, speech problem, language processing problem, or similar difficulty that may adversely impact performance on verbal subtests may produce a profile of Ach < Seq < Sim. Similarly, a child with strong verbal skills may produce the reverse.

Examples

Examples of apriori hypotheses for the K-ABC are given next. The reader will note that many of these overlap with WISC-III hypotheses because the K-ABC possesses a similar research base.

Source of hypothesis	Hypothesis
Jesse is a first-grader who is referred for a suspected reading disability. His teacher reports that he is slow to acquire phonics skills and has difficulty sequencing.	Sim > Seq
Jack is referred for language delays by his social worker. His native language is Navajo, although he speaks primarily English at school. His mother is concerned because he spoke much later than her other children and his Navajo and English articulation are poor.	MPC > Ach
Peter was diagnosed with fetal alcohol syndrome shortly after birth. His mother used alcohol daily during pregnancy and she smoked one to two packs of cigarettes per day. His developmental milestones were delayed and he was retained in kindergarten for next year. His family is poor. His mother and father cannot read.	below avg Seq, Sim, MPC, and Achievement scores
Monja is in the gifted class at her school. She was referred by her teacher for behavior problems in class and inattention.	Ach > Sim > Seq
Cheng was born with cerebral palsy.	Ach & Seq > Sim
Gina has missed 60 days of school this past year due to frequent relocations of her family.	MPC > Ach. Arithmetic may be particularly low.

Shared Subtest Hypotheses

The *K-ABC Interpretive Manual* (Kaufman & Kaufman, 1983b) uses the same procedure for determining strengths and weaknesses as was outlined previously in Chapter 7. Rounded values for determining subtest strengths and weaknesses are again advised.

This interpretive step is analogous to the WISC-III in the process of forming aposteriori shared subtest hypotheses. Numerous possible hypotheses are given on pages 197–201 of the *K-ABC Interpretive Manual* (Kaufman & Kaufman, 1983b). The same process for generating hypotheses should be used here as was used for the WISC-III.

Single Subtest Hypotheses

The K-ABC Mental Processing subtests are rather brief, like those of the WISC-III, and produce similar reliabilities. This fact suggests that a similar amount of caution be used when interpreting K-ABC subtests. The same process for generating single subtest hypotheses should also be used.

When recording single subtest hypotheses from the *K-ABC Interpretive Manual* (Kaufman & Kaufman, 1983b), the amount of subtest specificity associated with the test should also be noted. Specificity values and ratings were given earlier in this chapter, and more information can be found in tables 5.9, 5.10, and 5.11 of the *K-ABC Interpretive Manual* (Kaufman & Kaufman, 1983b).

SAMPLE CASE—WALTER

Referral Information

Walter is a 3-year-old male who was referred for hyperactivity and attention problems. His pediatrician wanted to know if he suffered from attention deficit hyperactivity disorder.

Behavioral Observations

Walter was brought to the clinic by his birth father. It was clear in the waiting room that his father had trouble controlling him. Walter immediately opened the candy jar on the receptionist's desk upon entering the waiting area. He unwrapped and ate a piece of candy despite his father's protests. He talked almost constantly to whomever would listen. He tried to strike up a conversation with every adult in the waiting room. He removed most of the toys from the toy box, and he refused to replace any of them.

After entering the testing room, Walter grabbed several games and a whistle from a shelf. He asked to play with these rather than "your games." He protested taking the test at least once during every subtest. At the end of

Number Recall, for example, he said, "I told you I don't want to do this anymore." During Gestalt Closure he feigned illness by slouching in his chair and complaining of a stomach ache. After the examiner asked him about his not feeling well, he perked up and said, "Gotcha! You thought I was sick, didn't you." After Gestalt Closure, Walter ran from the room, saying that he had to use the restroom. He played with water in the restroom for several minutes before agreeing to come out.

Walter required continuous monitoring and reminders to stay in his seat and pay attention. He missed some Number Recall items because the examiner could not maintain his attention. On some Gestalt Closure items he gave the impression that he preferred to not put forth an effort. When Walter was asked where his mother was, he responded, "Doin' drugs."

Background Information

Walter's maternal grandmother currently has custody of him. Custody was removed from his birth mother because of numerous accusations of child abuse and neglect. His mother has a longstanding history of chemical dependency.

Walter's grandmother's account of his early development was sketchy. She was able, however, to provide vivid descriptions of his current behavior problems. She reports that Walter is highly active, strong-willed, manipulative, disobedient, accident-prone, and disorganized. He has had conduct problems, including setting another child's hair ablaze.

Apriori Hypotheses

Walter's history of attentional problems, his less-than-optimal behavior during testing, and the possibility of prenatal insult due to maternal drug addiction suggest an apriori hypothesis of below-average MPC and Achievement scores. His lack of attention and dislike for two of the

K-ABC Scores

	STANDARD SCORE	MEAN	DIFF.	DIFF.	SIGNIFICANT S OR W
SEQUENTIAL SCALE					
Hand Movements	10	11	−1	3	
Number Recall	14	11	3	3	S
SIMULTANEOUS SCALE					
Magic Window	11	11	0	4	
Face Recognition	10	11	−1	3	
Gestalt Closure	10	11	−1	4	
ACHIEVEMENT SCALE					
Expressive Vocabulary	128	117	11	13	
Faces & Places	130	117	13	15	
Arithmetic	90	117	−27	12	W
Riddles	122	117	5	13	

GLOBAL SCALES	STANDARD SCORES
Sequential Processing	112
Simultaneous Processing	104
Mental Processing Composite	109
Achievement	121

Sequential subtests suggest a Sim > Seq pattern. His test behavior also suggests a weakness on the Number Recall subtest. No additional Achievement scale hypotheses are in order since he has not yet attended school.

Testing Apriori Hypotheses

This is a fascinating case in that all of the apriori hypotheses are rejected because they are such a poor fit to the data. All scores are above average, and Number Recall emerged as a strength. Aposteriori methods of interpretation of necessity must come into play.

Aposteriori Hypotheses

1. Above-average intelligence based on MPC
2. Above-average academic achievement
3. Strength in auditory recall of digits (Number Recall); Weakness in Mathematics (Arithmetic).

Drawing Conclusions

With a child this age one has few pieces of data to use for corroboration. In such a case the aposteriori hypotheses of above-average intelligence and achievement should be presented cautiously and additional testing recommended. Even these scores could be a fairly drastic underestimate of Walter's cognitive development given his misbehavior during testing. In this case the scores serve an important function as baselines for further evaluations.

The Number Recall test could be interpreted as a unique strength, but such an interpretation would be highly speculative for the following reasons: (1) there is no corroborating evidence for this strength; (2) more cautious interpretation of Walter's profile is advised because of his age and the potential confounding of his behavior problems; and (3) the Number Recall strength is consistent with his overall above-average performance, making it easy to subsume this under the global scale hypothesis.

Any interpretation of the Arithmetic weakness would be similarly highly speculative. This weakness, however, is more plausible because it flies in the face of the above-average trend in the profile. The child's history of neglect provides some corroborating evidence for this hypothesis. On the other hand, why did the neglect not affect his other measures of knowledge acquisition? This hypothesis also requires further corroboration.

The main conclusions based on the K-ABC are above-average intelligence and academic achievement. A hypothesis of an Arithmetic weakness could either not be offered or offered as a hypothesis that requires further evaluation. Walter's volatile living situation and behavior beg for ongoing monitoring of treatment and periodic reevaluation of numerous domains including intelligence. In Walter's case, intelligence and achievement may be bright spots. In this situation the psychologist will likely focus attention on other domains and let intelligence fade into the background for the time being.

Assessing Exceptional Children with the K-ABC

Given that for most children the K-ABC correlates substantially with the WISC-R, it is likely that the K-ABC and WISC-III will covary to a great extent when used for evaluating exceptional children. Some groups of children, however, show substantial differences. For these groups the selection of one test over another can be crucial in the diagnostic process. Moreover, the clinician has to be especially alert when dealing with individual cases where research does not apply or is lacking. This section summarizes research on the utility of the K-ABC for assessing exceptional children, with special emphasis on its assets and liabilities as identified by Kamphaus and Reynolds (1987).

Mental Retardation

There is a tendency for mentally retarded children to have higher K-ABC than WISC-R scores (Naglieri, 1985). K-ABC data for samples of previously identified (usually with the WISC-R) mentally retarded children (Kamphaus & Reynolds, 1987) (see Chapter 13) show mean Mental Processing Composite scores ranging from the mid 60s to about 70. Naglieri (1985a) administered the K-ABC to 37 children who were diagnosed previously as mildly mentally retarded. When these children were reevaluated, the K-ABC and WISC-R were administered in counterbalanced fashion. The resulting WISC-R Full Scale mean was 58 and the K-ABC mean was 65. The correlation of the K-ABC and WISC-R for this sample was very high (.83), suggesting that the rank order of the children on these two tests was highly similar, but the K-ABC distribution of scores was tilted more toward the normative mean of 100.

The K-ABC has some practical limitations that examiners must consider in using the test to diagnose mental retardation. First is the issue of subtest floor. Kamphaus and Reynolds (1987) observed that the K-ABC lacks easy items for some developmentally delayed children. In other words, a 5-year-old mentally retarded child may obtain too many raw scores of zero. This risk of a lack of floor, however, is less likely to occur for an 8-, 9-, or 10-year-old mildly retarded child. For moderately to severely mentally retarded children, however, there is a substantial risk of a lack of floor for most ages, as the K-ABC has new subtests introduced at virtually every age group from 2½ through 7. Second, the K-ABC composite score norms usually do not extend below a standard score of 55, which makes the K-ABC less useful for the diagnosis of moderate or severe levels of mental retardation. Tests such as the Stanford-Binet Fourth Edition and the DAS may be better suited for the purpose since their composite score norms often extend down below 55 (see Chapters 10 and 11).

The availability of sample and teaching items and the intuitive nature of the K-ABC task demands are advantages for the assessment of delayed children. A potential benefit of the use of teaching items is that they allow the examiner to see how a child responds to instruction. This opportunity can be a primitive assessment of a child's zone of proximal development (ZPD) (Vygotsky, 1962; see Kamphaus & Reynolds, 1987), where the ZPD is the difference in performance on a task with and without instruction.

Learning-Disabled Children

Mean K-ABC global scale and subtest scores for a number of samples of learning disabled children suggest that children with learning problems tend to score in the below-average to average ranges, exhibit a "mild" Simultaneous greater than Sequential profile (6 to 8 standard score points), and have their lowest scores on the Achievement and Sequential scales (Kamphaus & Reynolds, 1987) (see Chapter 14). There is also a consistent trend for the average MPC to be greater than the average Achievement scale score. This is consistent with the operational definition of learning disabilities, where a discrepancy between "ability" and achievement must be identified.

Fourqurean (1987) identified a substantial pattern of underachievement for a sample of limited English proficient Latino learning-disabled children. These results support the hypothesis that the K-ABC Achievement scale is adversely affected not only by learning problems but also by cultural and/or linguistic differences. In addition, the MPC in this study appeared to be less influenced or confounded by linguistic or cultural differences. This study highlights the theoretical differences between the K-ABC and the WISC-R. The mean WISC-R Verbal IQ of 68.1 for these children, for example, was almost identical to their mean Achievement scale score on the K-ABC of 67.7. As a result, the MPC for this sample was considerably higher (82.9) than the Full Scale IQ (76.7). The K-ABC may prove valuable in cases where a clinician is trying to differentiate among intellectual, cultural, and linguistic influences on learning.

Intellectually Gifted Children

No typical global scale profile emerges for samples of gifted children (Kamphaus & Reynolds, 1987) (see Chapter 13). Gestalt Closure is one of the worst subtests for gifted children. Relative strengths on Triangles and Matrix Analogies may suggest that the higher the "g" loading of the subtest, the more likely the gifted samples will score higher (Kamphaus & Reynolds, 1987). The K-ABC MPC is consistently lower than Stanford-Binet and Wechsler scores for these children. Naglieri and Anderson (1985), for example, obtained a K-ABC mean of 126.3 and WISC-R mean of 134.3. McCallum, Karnes, and Edwards (1984) obtained a mean Stanford-Binet L-M IQ (1972 edition) that was about 16.19 points higher than the mean K-ABC MPC. One explanation for the difference between the 1972 Stanford-Binet and the K-ABC for gifted children is that the 1972 Stanford-Binet may give higher bound estimates of intelligence for academically capable children. This is suggested by a study by Zins and Barnett (1984) that showed an extremely high correlation (.86) between the 1972 Stanford-Binet and the K-ABC Achievement scale. In addition, a study in the Stanford-Binet Fourth Edition *Technical Manual* (1986) indicates that the 1972 Stanford-Binet produces much higher scores (mean IQ = 135.3) than the 1986 Fourth Edition (mean IQ = 121.8). It may be that the 1972 Stanford-Binet shared extensive overlap with measures of academic achievement.

EDUCATIONAL REMEDIATION RESEARCH

The K-ABC is unique in that one of the test development goals was to produce a test that is helpful in the educational remediation process (Kaufman & Kaufman, 1983c). This is an ambitious goal that is similar to saying that a cure exists for low intelligence (i.e., mental retardation). Hence, the mere statement of intent to be useful for educational remediation was controversial and led to immediate attack (Salvia & Hitcko, 1984).

The Kaufmans went much further than their predecessors by including an entire chapter on educational translation of K-ABC scores in the *Technical Manual* (Kaufman & Kaufman, 1983b). They reviewed some models of special education intervention, identified problems, and proposed solutions. They offered a "strength" model of remediation (Reynolds, 1981) that borrows heavily from neuropsychological models of remediation. The Kaufmans' model proposed that one should not try to remediate weaknesses (e.g., prescribe exercises that would improve a child's simultaneous weakness), but rather a child's cognitive strengths should be utilized to improve academic skills. This model is a familiar one in medical rehabilitation. A stroke victim, for example, may never regain the strength of his dominant hand that he used to dress himself. In cases such as this an occupational therapist will teach the patient dressing skills that capitalize on the patient's strengths. The therapist may show the patient clever ways to fasten fasteners partially before the garment is worn. Similarly, the Kaufmans propose that a child with reading problems and a sequential deficit not be taught sequencing skills (this would be nonsensical since sequencing is the predictor variable not the criterion variable), but rather be taught how to use simultaneous skills to compensate for sequential weaknesses in the reading process.

Recently the whole idea of using intelligence tests with the goal of a *direct* link to intervention has been questioned (Kamphaus, 1990). As Kamphaus (1990) observes: "I think that intelligence tests will never have *direct*, and I emphasize the word *direct*, effects on treatment planning. . . . Take, for example, measures of height, such as feet and inches. Do these measures have 'treatment validity' for measuring height?" (p. 366).

Kamphaus (1990) proposes that intelligence tests will be more likely to have *indirect* effects on treatment. Medical tests such as the MRI scan do not possess strong evidence of treatment validity, but they do allow for more sophisticated research on a disorder that may indirectly lead to treatment. This discussion calls into question the inclusion of a "remediation" chapter in the K-ABC manual. It also renders criticism of the K-ABC intervention model less important.

Some pilot data presented in the K-ABC *Interpretive Manual* (Kaufman & Kaufman, 1983b) suggest that the K-ABC may be useful for designing educational interventions. In direct contrast, a study by Ayres, Cooley, and Severson (1988) suggests that the K-ABC will not be useful for treatment planning. Both of those pieces of research have methodological weaknesses. The Kaufman and Kaufman (1983b) studies were based on small samples and they were not well controlled. The Ayres, Cooley, and Severson (1988) investigation used criterion measures of sequential and simultaneous processing that had no strong evidence of validity. The question of whether or not the K-ABC remedial model is effective is still not answered. There are simply no large-scale, well-controlled studies available on this topic. Unfortunately, it does not appear likely that research on this issue will become available in the near future. This model of intervention, however, is perhaps not so important as far as the K-ABC goes; rather, this approach to pedagogy for exceptional children deserves more research and consideration.

K-ABC SHORT FORMS

Kaufman and Applegate (1988) developed short forms of the K-ABC that may be useful when only general estimates of mental processing and achievement that can be administered in relatively brief amounts of time are needed. Examples of uses of short forms include preschool screening for identification of at-risk or potentially gifted children, research, and certain clinical or educational circumstances. Although the administration of a short form can never replace the multiple scores and clinical evaluations obtained from administration of a complete battery, short forms of the K-ABC demonstrate excellent psychometric properties and offer useful estimates of functioning.

Extensive analysis of the reliability and validity of various combinations of subtests led to the selection of the following short forms for age 4 through 12½ years. (Short forms were not developed for younger children because the K-ABC is already relatively brief for these ages.)

Mental Processing Dyad: Triangles, Word Order

Mental Processing Triad: Triangles, Word Order, Matrix Analogies

Mental Processing Tetrad: Hand Movements, Triangles, Word Order, Matrix Analogies

Mean reliability coefficients for the short forms are excellent and range from .88 to .93. Although the corrected validity coefficient between the Mental Processing dyad and the complete K-ABC is a marginal .80, the remaining short forms demonstrate excellent validity, with corrected coefficients of .86 for the Mental Processing triad, .88 for the Mental Processing tetrad, and .93 for an Achievement dyad. Kaufman and Applegate (1990) recommend using either the Mental Processing triad or tetrad along with an Achievement dyad whenever a short form of the K-ABC is needed. Tables for computing *Estimated* Mental Processing Composites and Achievement standard scores (X = 100, SD = 15) based on the sum of subtest scaled or standard scores are provided in Kaufman and Applegate (1988). The word *estimated* should be used whenever scores from short forms are reported.

NONVERBAL SCALE

The Nonverbal scale is intended for use with children for whom administration of the regular K-ABC (and virtually all other well-normed, standardized measures of intelligence) would be inappropriate: those who are hearing impaired, have speech or language disorders or other communication handicaps, or have limited English proficiency. The Nonverbal scale yields a global estimate of intelligence (see Chapters 11 and 13). Most well-normed intelligence tests that are applicable to communications-handicapped children are narrow and give a quite limited view of these children's intelligence (e.g., the Columbia Mental Maturity Scale)(Glaub & Kamphaus, 1991). Although the K-ABC Nonverbal scale has limitations in this regard, of those tests of mental ability with adequate technical/psychometric characteristics the K-ABC Nonverbal scale provides the broadest sampling of abilities and their development. The lack of adequately normed scales with any breadth of assessment has been a hindrance not only to clinical assessment of children with communication disorders but also to research in the area (Reynolds & Clark, 1983). The Nonverbal scale of the K-ABC is one of the best-normed, psychometrically most sophisticated nonverbal scales presently available.

K-ABC STRENGTHS AND WEAKNESSES

Strengths

1. The theory underlying the K-ABC is explicit, making it easier to understand why the test is organized as it is. The theory also yields a predictable factor structure that is the beneficiary of some research support.

2. The K-ABC is lawfully related to other intelligence measures. It does differ from other measures when language is an important variable for a child.

3. The K-ABC is relatively fun and easy to administer and score. The new "K-ABC Lite" (a more portable and lighter version) is also a boon to the mobile clinician.

4. The psychometric properties of the K-ABC, including norming, reliability, and validity, are strong.

5. From a neuropsychological standpoint the K-ABC is helpful in that it assesses more memory functions.

Weaknesses

1. While the MPC may be easily interpreted, the meaning of the Sequential and Simultaneous scores is not as clear, making the test more of an interpretive challenge for clinicians.

2. The K-ABC suffers from floor and ceiling effects at a number of ages. This problem is compounded by changing subtests at various ages.

3. The K-ABC Achievement scale is enigmatic. It is a Wechsler-like verbal intelligence scale in some regards, but it also resembles clinical measures of achievement that are used for diagnosing learning disabilities. The Achievement scale, then, seems to require some experience if one is to interpret it properly.

4. The Kaufmans' remedial model should be used cautiously until some research is available to support it.

Conclusions

The K-ABC is a unique contribution to the intellectual assessment scene. This bold stroke by the Kaufmans has resulted in polarized viewpoints on the instrument—either you like it or you do not. The K-ABC has made some important contributions to children's intellectual assessment. The most important one is that it has served as a catalyst for research on children's intellectual assessment. The K-ABC has also been adopted by clinicians, suggesting that it has proven clinical value for some children in some settings. This is a well-known test because of all of its related research, which will likely foster its use for the foreseeable future.

Chapter Summary

1. Surveys have found that the K-ABC is heavily used by practitioners.

2. The K-ABC has been the subject of great controversy, as attested to by the strongly pro and con articles written for a special issue of the *Journal of Special Education* devoted to the K-ABC.

3. Simultaneous processing is the mental ability of the child to integrate input all at once to solve a problem correctly.

4. Sequential processing, on the other hand, emphasizes the arrangement of stimuli in sequential or serial order for successful problem solving. In every instance, each stimulus is linearly or temporally related to the previous one.

5. A controversial move was to take the equivalent of the WISC-III Verbal scale and say that these types of tests are no longer intelligence tests—they are now achievement tests.

6. Kamphaus and Reynolds (1987) proposed new supplementary scales for verbal intelligence, reading composite, and a global intelligence composite.

7. The K-ABC global scales (Sequential Processing, Simultaneous Processing, Mental Processing Composite, Achievement, and Nonverbal) yield standard scores, with a mean of 100 and standard deviation of 15.

8. The K-ABC was standardized on a sample of 2000 children, using primarily 1980 U.S. Census figures.

9. Split-half reliability coefficients for the K-ABC global scales range from 0.86 to 0.93

(mean = 0.90) for preschool children, and from 0.89 to 0.97 (mean = 0.93) for children age 5 to 12½.

10. The K-ABC yields satisfactory growth curves (age differentiation validity) for most age groups.

11. The K-ABC has an extremely well-scrutinized set of items, which benefited from item bias studies.

12. In a study of 182 children enrolled in regular classrooms, the Mental Processing Composite (MPC) correlated 0.70 with WISC-R Full-Scale IQ (FSIQ).

13. Predictive validity evidence for the K-ABC is comparable to that of the WISC-R.

14. The first well-known factor analytic evidence offered in support of the Sequential and Simultaneous scales was by Kaufman and Kamphaus (1984). These authors identified three factors for the K-ABC and labeled them as sequential, simultaneous, and achievement.

15. In a series of studies, Keith and his colleagues have called the K-ABC processing model into question by applying Wechsler-like content labels to the K-ABC scales.

16. The Nonverbal scale of the K-ABC is one of the best-normed, psychometrically most sophisticated nonverbal scales presently available.

17. The following steps should be taken to begin the K-ABC interpretive process.

    1. Assign a verbal classification to the MPC (e.g., average).

    2. Band the MPC with error (the 90% level of confidence is recommended).

    3. Assign verbal classifications to the Sequential and Simultaneous scales.

    4. Band the Sequential and Simultaneous scales with error.

    5. Test the difference between the Sequential and Simultaneous scales for

statistical significance (a reliable difference at the .05 level) using table 10 of the *K-ABC Administration and Scoring Manual* (Kaufman & Kaufman, 1983b).

    6. Test the difference between the Sequential and Simultaneous scales for clinical rarity (where a difference that occurred in 5% of the population or less is considered rare) using table 5.12 (p. 193) of the *K-ABC Interpretive Manual* (Kaufman & Kaufman, 1983b).

    7. Develop hypotheses for reliable (not necessarily rare) differences between Sequential and Simultaneous scores.

18. Hypotheses for Sequential/Simultaneous (Seq/Sim) differences include:

Sequential versus Simultaneous Processing (Seq > Sim or Sim > Seq)

Linguistic differences (Sim > Seq)

Motor problem (Sim < Seq)

Auditory short-term memory problem (Sim > Seq)

Verbal versus nonverbal intelligence (Ach > Seq > Sim)

19. Children with learning problems tend to score in the below-average to average ranges, exhibit a mild Simultaneous greater than Sequential profile (6 to 8 standard score points), and have their lowest scores on the Achievement and Sequential scales.

20. A typical global scale profile does not emerge for samples of gifted children.

21. The question of whether or not the K-ABC remedial model is effective is still not answered.

22. Kaufman and Applegate (1980) developed short forms of the K-ABC.

23. The K-ABC is a well-known test because of all of its related research, which will likely encourage its use for the foreseeable future.

Stanford-Binet Fourth Edition

CHAPTER QUESTIONS

How does this Binet differ from its predecessors?

How does factor analytic research for the Binet-4 affect interpretation of its composite scores?

The latest (fourth) edition of the Stanford-Binet in some ways follows in the tradition of Alfred Binet's original work and Terman's American revision of his scale (see Chapter 1). Some of the items found on the Binet-4 have long histories and can be traced directly to Binet's original work. On the other hand, this newest version of the Binet departs from its predecessors to such an extent, especially in terms of its structure and theory, that it should be considered a new test, as opposed to what is typically considered a mere revision of an earlier scale. The Binet-4, however, does remain a significant achievement in intelligence test technology, and, as such, it warrants serious consideration by individuals who use these measures.

THEORETICAL BASIS

The Binet-4 differs from its forebears by proposing a theoretical model that was used to guide test development endeavors, and which is described in detail in the Binet-4 *Technical Manual* (Thorndike, Hagen, & Sattler, 1986). This theoretical model had not been used in any previous editions of the Binet scales. In this hierarchical model, "g," or general intelligence, remains the premier cognitive ability at the top of the hierarchy (Thorndike, Hagen, & Sattler, 1986). The Binet-4 authors observed: "Still, the general ability factor, g, refuses to die. Like a phoenix, it keeps rising from its ashes and will no doubt continue to be an enduring part of our psychometric theory and psychometric practice" (Thorndike, Hagen, & Sattler, 1986, p. 6).

Regarding whether to assess "g" with a single test or a variety of tests, the authors (Thorndike, Hagen, & Sattler, 1986) decided to side with the wisdom of Wechsler, as shown in the following quotation.

265

RESEARCH REPORT

The Binet factor structure arbitrated

Robert M. Thorndike (the son of Robert L. Thorndike) has made a valiant attempt to tie together all of the factor analytic research on the Binet-Fourth Edition. This is a monumental task given the considerable disagreement in the research literature. Thorndike (1990) begins by making critical comments about existing factor analytic studies of the Binet-4. He cites problems with the exploratory analyses of Thorndike, Hagen, and Sattler (1986), Reynolds, Kamphaus, and Rosenthal (1988), and Sattler (1988). He then proposes an exploratory factor analytic procedure as the "right" answer.

He used a principal axis factor analytic method where squared multiple correlations were used in the diagonal of the correlation matrix as initial commonality estimates. His first analysis was conducted on 17 correlation matrices corresponding to the age groups of the Binet-4. Two- and three-factor solutions were rotated using the Oblimin (Oblique, see Chapter 5) rotation procedure. For ages 2–6, the first factor yielded relatively large eigenvalues, ranging from a low of 3.46 for age 2 to a high of 4.72 for age 5. Similarly, the eigenvalues for the second factor were substantial at most ages, ranging from .80 at age 5 to 1.18 at age 2. By comparison, however, the eigenvalues for the third factor were considerably lower, ranging from .55 at age 3 to .81 at age 2. Thorndike (1990) concluded that a three-factor solution was the best fit for the 2-year olds but a two-factor solution representing primarily verbal and nonverbal subtests was the most sensible for ages 3 through 6. Hence, he concluded that at ages 2 through 6, a two-factor solution representing primarily verbal and nonverbal skills was most supportable for the Binet-4. Subtests with high loadings on the verbal factor included Vocabulary (loadings from .83 to .89), Comprehension (loadings from .62 to .98), Absurdities (loadings from .34 to .75), and Memory for Sentences (loadings from .56 to .71). The subtests that marked the nonverbal factor included Pattern Analysis (loadings of .63 to .82), Copying (loadings of .61 to .76), Quantitative (loadings from .39 to .73), and Bead Memory (loadings from .59 to .78). These results gained some additional support because they are consistent with the analysis favored by Sattler (1988).

Thorndike used the same procedures to evaluate the factor structure for the middle age group, ages 7 through 11 years. In this age group, the first factor produced eigenvalues ranging from 4.97 for 7-year-olds to 6.62 for 11-year-olds. The second factor yielded eigenvalues ranging from .83 for 11-year-olds to 1.24 for 7-year-olds. The third factor produced eigenvalues ranging from .71 for 11-year-olds to 1.02 for 9-year-olds. The fourth factor was considerably and inconsistently smaller, with eigenvalues ranging from .66 for 8-year-olds to .78 for 7-year-olds. Thorndike interpreted these results as supporting a three-factor solution. This solution was also supported by evaluation of Scree plot results.

Thorndike identified the first factor as verbal ability because it included strong loadings for subtests such as Vocabulary (loadings of .43 to .94), Comprehension (loadings of .41 to .87), and Memory for Sentences (loadings of .45 to .73). The Absurdities subtest takes a minor role in the verbal factor at this age, producing loadings ranging from .14 to .45. The second factor is interpreted as a nonverbal factor that is marked by subtests including Pattern Analysis (loadings of .58 to .88), Copying (loadings of .52 to .59), Matrices (loadings of .15 to .75), Bead Memory (loadings of .36 to .63), and Absurdities (loadings of .43 to .88). At this age range the Absurdities subtest switches factors from its place on the verbal factor at the preschool ages. Thorndike attributes this switch to the use of visual stimuli on this primarily verbal subtest. It is also noteworthy, however, that, as with the analyses of younger children, there is a melding of Quantitative and Short-Term Memory tests (Bead Memory) with the abstract/visual factor.

The new factor to emerge at this age is labeled as memory by Thorndike. This factor is marked primarily by Memory for Digits, with loadings ranging from .52 to .83. Memory for Objects contributes somewhat to this factor, with loadings ranging from .15 to .58. Similarly, Memory for Sentences contributes some variance to this factor, with loadings ranging from .21 to .58. Memory for Sentences, however, continues to have considerably higher loadings at this age range on the verbal factor.

The final age range to be investigated was ages 12 through 23 years (the last age group is 18–23). Again, three factors were obtained using the Kaiser criterion and Scree plots. Eigenvalues for the first factor ranged from 6.79

RESEARCH REPORT (*continued*)

for 15-year-olds to 7.91 for ages 18 to 23. Eigenvalues for the second factor ranged from .92 for 14-year-olds to 1.36 for 12-year-olds. Eigenvalues for the third factor ranged from .83 for 16-year-olds to 1.15 for 12-year-olds. All of the eigenvalues for the fourth factor were below 1, with a range of .63 for 17-year-olds to .86 for 12-year-olds.

The first factor was marked by loadings for verbal subtests and was identified as a verbal factor. It had uniformly high loadings by Vocabulary (loadings of .61 to .88), Comprehension (loadings of .34 to .78), and Memory for Sentences (loadings of .32 to .94) subtests. Again, the loadings for the Absurdities subtest were equivocal, ranging from .30 to .71 for ages 12 through 14 years. The abstract/visual factor for ages 12–23 was marked by high loadings on the part of Pattern Analysis (loadings of .25 to .89), Matrices (loadings of .25 to .68), Paper Folding and Cutting (loadings of .68 to .82), Number Series (loadings of .31 to .84), Equation Building (loadings of .07 to .85), and, to a lesser extent, Bead Memory (loadings of .06 to .48). The memory factor again was marked by the Memory for Digits subtest, with factor loadings ranging from .17 to .78. This factor was supported to a lesser extent by Memory for Sentences, with loadings of .14 to .69, and Memory for Objects, with loadings of .12 to .68. The Bead Memory subtest contributed very little to the memory factor, with a median factor loading of .28.

Most apparent from these factor analytic results is that they agree with those of researchers such as Sattler (1988) and Reynolds, Kamphaus, and Rosenthal (1988) in that a quantitative factor could not be identified. As Thorndike (1990) states, "Attempts to clarify this situation by finding a factor common to the three quantitative tests were not successful" (p. 427).

Thorndike concludes that these factors are also identified by Sattler (1988). He also notes, however, that the strong correlation of about .40 to .70 between the factors suggests a strong "g" component.

Thorndike then turns his attention to reviews of the confirmatory factor analyses. He concludes: "Although the evidence from these confirmatory analyses may be gratifying to those who have an interest in four factors, the support is rather weak" (p. 433). He also criticizes the method used by some confirmatory factor analytic researchers who are using these models in an "exploratory" fashion.

There are numerous practical implications of these research findings. One can follow the road taken by Sattler (1988) and reinvent the Binet-4 by using factor scores for interpretive purposes. Another approach is to use the existing Binet-4 with the lessons from these factor analytic findings clearly in mind. These lessons suggest that a Verbal Reasoning area score is most homogeneous and distinct from other area scores when it is made up of the Vocabulary and Comprehension subtests. Similarly, the Short-Term Memory area score is most robust when it includes Memory for Digits. The Abstract/Visual area score is most robust when using Pattern Analysis, Copying, Paper Folding and Cutting, and Matrices. The Abstract/Visual score comes closest to the original conceptualization of the Binet developers. The Quantitative area score of the Binet-4 is a wash. This is sounding all too familiar, isn't it? The Binet-4 area scores resemble the Verbal and Performance standard scores from the WISC-III when supplemented by a Digit Span subtest!

It is our strong belief that the best measure of **g**— *and consequently broad effective prediction—will stem from a diverse set of cognitive tasks that call for relational thinking in a diversity of contexts. We have tried to provide this both in* CogAT *and in the Fourth Edition of the Stanford-Binet. (p. 6)*

The second level of the Binet hierarchy (see Figure 10.1) is based on the work of Cattell and his fluid and crystallized dimensions of in-

telligence (see Chapter 2). The crystallized abilities, those abilities that are most influenced by schooling, familial, and other environmental factors, are measured by subtests from the Verbal Reasoning and Quantitative Reasoning areas. The fluid analytic abilities at the second level of the hierarchy consist of primarily abstract/visual reasoning tasks. The authors of the Binet-4 added a third theoretical construct, short-term memory, to this second-most important level of interpretation (see Figure 10.1). Short-term memory is a theoretical construct that is more associated with human information processing theories than the theories of Cattell (Glutting & Kaplan, 1990). Nevertheless, it is added to Cattell's work to create a triumvirate, so to speak, at the second level of the Binet-4 theoretical hierarchy. This hierarchical framework of intelligence is highly consistent with the British approach to intelligence.

The third level in the Binet theoretical hierarchy consists of finer discriminations of the fluid and crystallized abilities. The crystallized abilities are subdivided into Verbal Reasoning and Quantitative Reasoning areas. The Abstract/Visual Reasoning area or group of subtests represents the assessment of fluid analytic abilities. This third level of interpretation, Verbal Reasoning, Quantitative Reasoning, and Abstract/Visual Reasoning, was designed to receive less emphasis in interpretation than the two higher levels (Thorndike, Hagen, & Sattler, 1986). Finally, the Binet-4 consists of 15 subtests, 4 subtests each for Verbal Reasoning, Abstract/Visual Reasoning, and Short-Term Memory, and 3 subtests for Quantitative Reasoning.

Some of the areas assessed by the Binet-4, such as Verbal Reasoning and Abstract/Visual Reasoning, are also reminiscent of Vernon's (1950) well-known hierarchical model of intelligence (see Chapter 2 and Glutting & Kaplan, 1990). In many ways, then, the Binet interpretive hierarchy is based upon a confluence of theories from a variety of individuals who wrote extensively on theories of intelligence in this century. As such, the Binet-4 theory should in no way be considered as new or novel or, for that matter, modern. The emphasis on an overall composite score dates back to Spearman's work in the 1920s; the second level of interpretation is based upon the fluid/crystallized dichotomy, which dates back to the 1940s; and the third level of interpretation, which is reminiscent of Vernon's theory, dates back to the

1940s and 1950s. Hence, the Binet-4, although published in 1986, is not an intelligence test that capitalizes on what has been known as the "cognitive revolution" of the 1960s, 1970s and 1980s.

PSYCHOMETRIC PROPERTIES

Standardization

The Stanford Binet Fourth Edition was normed on 5,013 children between the ages of 2 and 23 years. Cases were drawn from 47 states in the United States, including Alaska and Hawaii, so as to be representative of the 1980 U. S. Census. A stratified random sampling procedure was employed, with stratification variables that included geographic region, community size, gender, ethnicity, and socioeconomic status. Parental occupation and education were used as the measures of SES (Thorndike, Hagen, & Sattler, 1986).

One of the early controversies that occurred shortly after the release of the Binet-4 was the apparent mismatch between Census Bureau statistics and the Binet-4 standardization sample. The Binet-4 *Technical Manual* (Thorndike, Hagen, & Sattler, 1986) showed clearly that the sample was biased toward the inclusion of children from higher socioeconomic status families than would be indicated by the appropriate census statistics. This oversampling of high-SES groups and undersampling of low-SES children could have contributed dramatically to the development of norms of inappropriate difficulty level. In order to counteract this sampling problem the authors weighted the norming cases to create a proper SES distribution. In other words, since high-SES children were overrepresented, the scores of children from high-SES families counted as less than one case in the development of norms. On the other hand, the scores of children from low-SES families were counted as greater than one—thus weighting them more heavily in the development of norms for the individual subtests. This weighting procedure, then, served to change the composition of the sample to match very closely 1980 Census figures. Weighting samples this way is not typical of clinical tests of intelligence such as the WISC-R (Wechsler, 1974) and the K-ABC (Kaufman & Kaufman, 1983). Consequently, questions arise as to the appropriateness and accuracy of the weighting procedure.

All indications are, however, that the weighting procedure was rather effective in producing norm-referenced scores that are consistent and predictable in relationship to other tests of intelligence (Glutting & Kaplan, 1990). Several studies of nonhandicapped children have shown the Binet-4 norm-referenced scores to be slightly lower (2–3 standard score points) than those of older tests normed in previous eras. (See Table 10.1, the Binet-4 *Technical Manual*, and Sattler, 1988).

Reliability

Internal Consistency

Reliability, as measured by indices of internal consistency for the Binet-4 composite score, is extraordinarily high over the 2- to 23-year age span of the Binet-4. Internal consistency reliabilities for the composite score range from .95 to .99. The reliabilities for the four area scores of the Binet-4 are also extremely high, ranging from .80 to .97. The reliabilities of the Binet-4 subtests are also strong. These high reliabilities are likely due to their length, resulting in a larger sample of behavior. Consider, for example, the Pattern Analysis subtest of the Binet-4, which has 41 items in comparison to the similar Block Design subtest on the Wechsler scales, which contains only 12 items. In virtually all cases, the Binet-4 subtests are considerably longer than subtests typically found on intelligence batteries such as the Wechsler series or the K-ABC.

Test-Retest

Test/retest reliabilities for the Binet-4 are somewhat lower than the internal consistency coefficients. The test-retest reliability of the quantitative subtest is especially noteworthy in that a study of 55 elementary school–age children (Thorndike, Hagen, & Sattler, 1986) yielded a reliability coefficient of only .28. In the same investigation, reliability coefficients for the four area scores ranged from a .51 for the Quantitative Reasoning scale to a .87 for the Verbal Reasoning scale. The composite score reliability coefficient for this investigation was .90. Since stability coefficients are of practical importance, these test-retest coefficients should be kept clearly in mind. This advice is particularly true for problematic tests such as those on the quantitative scale. Further test-retest studies on the Binet-4 could yield higher test-retest coefficients. Unfortunately, the single study included in the *Technical Manual* (Thorndike, Hagen, & Sattler, 1986) is all that is currently available.

Validity

The Binet-4 has amassed considerable validity evidence to date, particularly evidence of concurrent and factorial validity. Some of the earliest studies of concurrent validity are reported in the *Technical Manual* and Table 10.2. These studies show a strong correlational relationship between the Binet-4 and its predecessors, suggesting that the Binet-4 is very much like other well-respected intelligence measures. Studies reported in the *Technical Manual* (Thorndike, Hagen, & Sattler, 1986) and elsewhere have produced coefficients for nonhandicapped samples ranging from .72 to .91. The focus of these studies, however, is on the composite score of the Binet-4. The area scores of the test are less well-known entities, particularly the Short-Term Memory and Quantitative scales, since these are not offered on tests such as the WISC-III.

TABLE 10.1   Mean differences between the Binet-4 and other test composites

Authors/Date	Sample	N	Means
Carvajal, Gerber, Hewes, & Weaver (1987)	NH	32	WAIS-R = 103.5 Binet-4 = 100.9
Carvajal & Weyand (1986)	NH	23	WISC-R = 115.0 Binet-4 = 113.3
Clayton, Hartwig, & Sapp (1987)	NH	30	Binet-LM = 113.1 Binet-4 = 114.4
Rothlisberg (1987)	NH	32	WISC-R = 112.3 Binet-4 = 105.5
Rothlisberg & McIntosh (1991)	referred	40	K-ABC = 86.6 Binet-4 = 86.5
Thorndike, Hagen, & Sattler (1986)	NH	139	Binet-LM = 108.1 Binet-4 = 105.8
Thorndike, Hagen, & Sattler (1986)	NH	205	WISC-R = 105.2 Binet-4 = 102.4
Thorndike, Hagen, & Sattler (1986)	NH	75	WPPSI = 110.3 Binet-4 = 105.3
Thorndike, Hagen, & Sattler (1986)	NH	47	WAIS-R = 102.2 Binet-4 = 98.7
Thorndike, Hagen, & Sattler (1986)	NH	175	K-ABC = 107.4 Binet-4 = 112.7
Thorndike, Hagen, & Sattler (1986)	gifted	82	Binet-LM = 135.3 Binet-4 = 121.8
Thorndike, Hagen, & Sattler (1986)	gifted	19	WISC-R = 117.7 Binet-4 = 116.3
Thorndike, Hagen, & Sattler (1986)	LD	14	Binet-LM = 76.9 Binet-4 = 79.9
Thorndike, Hagen, & Sattler (1986)	LD	90	WISC-R = 87.8 Binet-4 = 84.8
Thorndike, Hagen, & Sattler (1986)	LD	30	K-ABC = 94.2 Binet-4 = 92.5
Bell, Phelps, & Scott (1988)	LD	35	WISC-R = 95.6 Binet 4 = 92.3
Thorndike, Hagen, & Sattler (1986)	MR	22	Binet-LM = 49.5 Binet-4 = 50.9
Thorndike, Hagen, & Sattler (1986)	MR	61	WISC-R = 67.0 Binet-4 = 66.2
Thorndike, Hagen, & Sattler (1986)	MR	21	WAIS-R = 73.1 Binet-4 = 63.8

TABLE 10.2 Concurrent validity studies of the Binet-4 composite and other test composites

Authors/Date	Sample	N	r with Binet-4
Carvajal, Gerber, Hewes, & Weaver (1987)	NH	32	WAIS-R = .91
Carvajal & Weyand (1986)	NH	23	WISC-R = .78
Clayton, Hartwig, & Sapp (1987)	NH	30	Binet-LM = .72
Rothlisberg (1987)	NH	32	WISC-R = .77
Rothlisberg & McIntosh (1991)	referred	40	K-ABC = .85
Thorndike, Hagen, & Sattler (1986)	NH	139	Binet-LM = .81
Thorndike, Hagen, & Sattler (1986)	NH	205	WISC-R = .83
Thorndike, Hagen, & Sattler (1986)	NH	75	WPPSI = .80
Thorndike, Hagen, & Sattler (1986)	NH	47	WAIS-R = .91
Thorndike, Hagen, & Sattler (1986)	NH	175	K-ABC = .89
Thorndike, Hagen, & Sattler (1986)	gifted	82	Binet-LM = .27
Thorndike, Hagen, & Sattler (1986)	gifted	19	WISC-R = .69
Thorndike, Hagen, & Sattler (1986)	LD	14	Binet-LM = .79
Thorndike, Hagen, & Sattler (1986)	LD	90	WISC-R = .87
Thorndike, Hagen, & Sattler (1986)	LD	30	K-ABC = .74
Bell, Phelps, & Scott (1988)	LD	35	WISC-R = .92
Thorndike, Hagen, & Sattler (1986)	MR	22	Binet-LM = .91
Thorndike, Hagen, & Sattler (1986)	MR	61	WISC-R = .66
Thorndike, Hagen, & Sattler (1986)	MR	21	WAIS-R = .79

Exceptional Children

The relationship of the Binet-4 to other tests for samples of handicapped children is less clear, however. The findings of the Thorndike, Hagen, and Sattler (1986) study of gifted children are particularly striking. This study involved 82 children who were administered both the Binet-4 and the Binet-LM. The resulting means differed greatly, with the Binet-4 mean being 13 points lower than the Binet-LM mean. This finding did not occur in the other Thorndike, Hagen, and Sattler (1986) study of gifted children that used the WISC-R. In this study the Binet-4 mean was only 1 point lower than the WISC-R. A first hypothesis to consider for the difference between the two Binet scales is simple regression toward the mean. One may then ask, however, why was no regression apparent in the WISC-R study? It could also be that the old and new Binet measure very different things that belie their high correlation. The item content of the scales is different, with the old Binet being more verbally loaded and the Binet-4 giving more weight to spatial, memory, and quantitative skills in addition to verbal skills. This hypothesis of content differences is supported by some of the concurrent validity studies. In the Thorndike, Hagen, and Sattler (1986) study of 82 gifted children, the correlation between the Binet-4 Verbal Reasoning scale and Binet-LM composite (.40) was higher than that between the two test composites (.27). This result also occurred for the study of 19 children in which the correlation between the Binet-4 and WISC-R verbal scores was .71 and the correlation between the two composites was lower at .62. These results suggest that the older Binet may be more influenced by verbal skills than the new one and when the two tests differ, the verbal ability of the sample (or child for that matter) may be the culprit.

The Binet-4 produces results very similar to the WISC-R for mentally retarded and learning-disability samples, with the Binet-4 consistently yielding slightly lower scores (see Chapter 14). A reasonable question, however, is why doesn't the Binet-4 exhibit regression effects for mentally retarded samples? Regression effects would certainly be expected given the low WISC-R scores for these groups. The studies for mentally retarded children are consistent with those for the WISC-R in a number of respects. As is the case with the WISC-R (Kaufman, 1979b), the mentally retarded samples had a relative strength in the Abstract/Visual area (Thorndike, Hagen, & Sattler, 1986). For mentally retarded children, however, the Binet-4 is not likely simply another form of the WISC-R, given the modest correlations between the two (see the Binet-4's *Technical Manual*). Seeing the range of scores for the samples on both measures would also be more helpful. It could be that because the Binet-4 norms extend to 35, as opposed to the WISC-R's lowest possible score of 45, the Binet could "allow" more low scores thus mitigating against regression effects. Only one investigation, however (Thorndike, Hagen, & Sattler, 1986), gives evidence of a larger standard deviation on the part of the Binet-4. For the moment the Binet-4 must be assumed to yield similar mean scores to the WISC-R for groups of mentally retarded children regardless of the reason for it.

Factor Analysis

For clinicians one of the most confusing aspects of the Binet-4 is the disagreement over the amount of factor analytic support for the various scales. It is important that composite scores show some evidence of factor analytic support in order to allow psychologists to use them for interpretive purposes. For the Binet-4, most of the subtests ideally would have high loadings on a large first factor (or general intelligence factor.) Such a finding would lend support to the use of the test composite for interpretive purposes. Similarly, there are four other featured composites on the Binet-4: Verbal Reasoning, Abstract/Visual Reasoning, Quantitative Reasoning, and Short-Term Memory. Since these are the four featured area scores, supportive factor analytic studies should show four factors that intuitively correspond to these groupings of subtests.

Factor analytic studies have created some confusion because various researchers, using similar procedures, have produced different conclusions. Keith et al. (1988) used confirmatory factor analytic procedures to conclude that there was general support for the four area scores, while Kline (1989) used these same procedures to conclude that Sattler's (1988) two- and three-factor models were a better fit to the data. Hence, confusion seems to reign supreme! Actually, upon closer inspection one can find considerable agreement among these studies. The agreement across studies will be captured next in an effort to develop an interpretive system for the Binet-4.

"g" Loadings

General intelligence ("g") loadings are typically defined as the loading of each test on an unrotated first factor. Analyses of the Binet-4 suggest that tests such as Vocabulary, Quantitative, Number Series, Comprehension, and Matrices are likely to produce scores that are consistent with one another (i.e., they have high "g" loadings)(Reynolds, Kamphaus, & Rosenthal, 1988; Sattler, 1988; Thorndike, Hagen, & Sattler, 1986). On the other hand, Memory for Digits, Memory for Objects, and Copying are likely to produce discrepant scores from the remainder of the test battery (i.e., they have low "g" loadings) (Reynolds, Kamphaus, & Rosenthal, 1988; Sattler, 1988; Thorndike, Hagen, & Sattler, 1986).

The Area Score Controversy

While all factor analytic researchers have concluded that the Binet-4 test composite is a good measure of "g" (Glutting & Kaplan, 1990), there is not unanimity on the factorial validity of the four area scores: Verbal Reasoning, Abstract/Visual Reasoning, Quantitative Reasoning, and Short-Term Memory. Several researchers have used confirmatory factor analytic methods to support the validity of the area scores (Keith et al., 1988; Ownby & Carmin, 1988; Thorndike, Hagen, & Sattler, 1986), and yet, several studies using both comfirmatory and exploratory methods have concluded that some of the four Area Scores lack factor analytic support (Kline, 1989; Reynolds, Kamphaus, & Rosenthal, 1988; Sattler, 1988). These contrasting findings provide a dilemma for the clinician who needs to know how much faith can be placed in the area scores. Fortunately, despite the obvious differences, consistency can be found across many of these studies when one looks closely at the results of these articles and chapters.

First, there is agreement that the Verbal Reasoning and Abstract/Visual Reasoning areas show strong evidence of factorial support (Keith et al., 1988; Kline, 1989; Ownby & Carmin, 1988; Reynolds, Kamphaus, & Rosenthal, 1988; Sattler, 1988; Thorndike, Hagen, & Sattler, 1986). This is hardly surprising given the well known verbal/nonverbal factors that have been well documented since World War I.

There is also considerable agreement that the Quantitative scale lacks clear evidence of a corresponding factor (Kline, 1989; Reynolds, Kamphaus, & Rosenthal, 1988; Sattler, 1988). This is true even when one inspects the results of "supportive" studies. The analysis of Thorndike, Hagen, and Sattler (1986) that generally supports the area scores shows some problems with the Quantitative Reasoning scale. In this analysis the Quantitative and Number Series subtests have paltry loadings of .21 and .26 respectively on the Quantitative factor. The Quantitative Reasoning area score is also suspect because it is most appropriate for older children. The typical procedure used by many clinicians is to only administer one or two subtests from this domain. If a clinician uses the general-purpose six-subtest battery, then only one subtest (Quantitative) from this area is used. Finally, it could be argued that the Quantitative area, although certainly measuring aspects of intelligence, is so similar to mathematics tests that it is difficult to establish its content validity as an intelligence measure (Kaufman & Kaufman, 1983).

The Short-Term Memory area score is a mixed bag. Some researchers have found support for it (Keith et al., 1988; Ownby & Carmin, 1988; Thorndike, Hagen, & Sattler, 1986), others have not (Reynolds, Kamphaus, & Rosenthal, 1988), and some have found support for it for elementary and secondary age groups but not for preschoolers (Kline, 1989; Sattler, 1988). The two subtests that seem to contribute to the disagreement regarding this area score are Memory for Sentences and Bead Memory.

Memory for Sentences loads as highly, and in some cases higher, on the verbal reasoning factor as on the Memory factor. Sattler (1988), for example, found Memory for Sentences to have an average loading of .57 on the memory factor and .58 on the verbal factor. Keith et al. (1988), although generally supportive of the Binet-4 structure, found that in their "relaxed" confirmatory model, Memory for Sentences loaded .43 on the memory factor and .40 on the verbal factor.

The scenario for Bead Memory is strikingly similar. Sattler (1988) found the average loading for this test on the memory factor to be .36, and on the abstract/visual factor its loading was higher at .51. Again, in the Keith et al. (1988) relaxed model, Bead Memory loaded higher on the abstract/visual (.49) than on the memory factor (.27). These results all bring into question the routine interpretation of the Quantitative Reasoning and Short-Term Memory area scores as homogeneous scales. These results do suggest that the Verbal and Abstract/Visual area scores are the most robust and that other subtest scores from other areas may be subsumed under these two factors.

Developmental Differences in Factor Structure

Sattler (1988) and Kline (1988) call attention to possible developmental factors in the interpretation of the Binet-4 by concluding that two factors (Sattler calls them verbal comprehension and nonverbal reasoning/visualization) constitute the most parsimonious solution for children ages 2 through 6, and three factors for ages 8 and above (where a memory scale is added). This structure is also supported by the confirmatory factor structure of Kline (1989). The finding of developmental differences in factor structure is also consistent with the factor analytic findings for the K-ABC (Kaufman & Kaufman, 1983). These findings also cast further doubt on the robustness of the Quantitative and Short-Term Memory area scores.

Binet 4 and Wechsler Research

Perhaps one way of reconciling this overwhelming amount of data is to compare these findings to those for other tests. This can be done rather easily. The literature is replete with the findings of two and three factors for multisubtest intelligence measures. Of course, the Wechsler scales are notable for this finding.

The WISC-R third factor has been assigned various labels such as freedom from distractibility, sequencing, and yes, short-term memory (see Chapter 5). The WISC-III also produces a memory factor. The search for a short-term memory factor has, however, proved elusive. It has not emerged for the K-ABC, where one of the short-term memory tests, Spatial Memory, continues to load on the simultaneous factor (Kamphaus & Reynolds, 1987). Similarly, Elliott (1990) has not offered a short-term memory scale for the new *Differential Ability Scale (DAS)* because of a lack of factor analytic support for such a factor. In this larger context it would have been surprising for the Binet-4 to produce a clear-cut short-term memory factor that would consistently support the corresponding area score.

Certainly the Binet-4 is not a Wechsler clone. It has many new subtests that measure a great variety of skills. It could well be that although the Quantitative score lacks support, it could be extremely useful for identifying the mathematically gifted, or perhaps for other uses. The labeling of the two major factors of the Binet-4 is open to question and debate. It is clear, however, that one emphasizes verbal content and the other less verbal, more visual, content.

Implications for Interpretation

With these findings in mind, the following applications of the Binet-4 factor analytic results are offered.

1. The Binet-4 test composite can be interpreted in much the same way as other tests that have been shown to be good measures of general intelligence, such as the WISC-III. One must also consider, however, the numerous criticisms of the general intelligence school of thought (see Chapter 2).

2. The Quantitative and Short-Term Memory Area Scores have little factor analytic support and would have to be heavily supported by other data in order to be emphasized in the interpretive process.

3. The Short-Term Memory Area Score may have more validity at ages 7 and above, but its validity is still less impressive than that for the two major factors.

4. Tests such as Memory for Digits, Memory for Objects, and Copying have poor "g" loadings. Therefore, they are more likely to deviate from the remainder of the profile and cause interpretive difficulties.

Conclusions about Binet Factors

Glutting and Kaplan's (1990) conclusion after reviewing factor analytic studies of the Binet-4 is:

In sum, the first conclusion that can be drawn for SB4 is that its factor structure is far from clear. Secondly, it is quite evident that attempts to uncover interpretable SB4 factors will, at the very least, be difficult. Finally, the possibility exists that the nature of SB4's data may ultimately preclude the

discovery of substantially meaningful dimensions for this test. (p. 293)

I am more optimistic. I think that at least the first two Binet factors are similar to the verbal/nonverbal dimensions of other tests.

ADMINISTRATION AND SCORING

Administration and scoring of the Binet-4 depart dramatically from the 1972 Stanford-Binet Form LM. The 1972 version and all previous editions of the Binet-4 had a number of brief subtests or small clusters of items that were different for every age level. The current edition conforms more closely to modern intelligence tests such as the Wechsler, K-ABC, and Woodcock-Johnson. The Binet-4 consists of 15 subtests, only a portion of which are administered to each age group. This design is laudable in that it shows some developmental sensitivity on the part of the Binet designers.

While Binet-4 subtests and items were devised in accordance with its theoretical model, an attempt was also made to include as many item types as possible from previous editions of the Binet scales (Anastasi, 1988). To some extent, however, this decision has complicated the administration of some of the individual subtests. On some subtests two different item types from earlier versions of the Binet were, in a sense, collapsed in order to form one subtest with different item types used at different age levels. This situation creates problems from an administration standpoint because the examiner may have to become familiar with two distinct sets of procedures for an individual subtest. One example is the Copying subtest, on which items for preschoolers require the examiner to become facile with the administration of items using single color blocks. The item type then switches at older ages, requiring the child to use pencil and paper skills. Perhaps more important than the issue of adding an additional "wrinkle" to the administration of this particular subtest, this switch in item type may make the interpretation of the scores on the Copying subtest more difficult. Another example of this situation is the Pattern Analysis subtest, on which early items use a three-piece form board. The next set of items requires a child to match a model made of single-color cubes, and more difficult items involve constructing intricate designs. Internal consistency coefficients for the Binet subtests, which are typically very impressive, do not preclude an individual child responding very differently to two item types. No evidence is reported to suggest that the different item types used in some Binet-4 subtests measure comparable or the same skills.

The Binet-4 items are more attractive than its predecessors', and the manipulatives and the stimuli involved are more easily stored and used by the examiner than in previous editions. For example, Form LM's version of Bead Memory required the examiner and child to string wooden beads on a shoestring. This apparatus was difficult for young children to handle, and many of them spilled considerable numbers of small beads. The newer version is somewhat more manageable, requiring the child to place beads on a stalk (stick). The stimuli used on the Bead Memory subtest, however, still have been criticized because at least two of the pieces are able to be pushed through a "choke-tube," a device that indicates whether or not an object is small enough to easily be swallowed and induce choking in a young child (Glutting & Kaplan, 1990). Concern has also been expressed that a couple of items on the Binet-4 may not be readily interpreted by children with color blindness. Glutting and Kaplan (1990) identify item 1 of the Vocabulary test, which depicts a red car on a brown background, as potentially extremely difficult for the color-blind child to interpret. Similarly, the form-board items of the early portion of the Pattern Analysis subtest depicts red pieces against a green background, making this item difficult to interpret for children with red/green color blindness.

One aspect of Binet-4 administration that is potentially troublesome is the question of which subtests to administer. This has not been an issue with the tests discussed thus far. The Binet-4 differs in that the use of short forms is discussed in its various manuals, including short forms for mental retardation and gifted diagnosis. A six-subtest, general-purpose, abbreviated battery includes Vocabulary, Bead Memory, Quantitative, Memory for Sentences, Pattern Analysis, and Comprehension. The various reliability and validity data reported in the *Technical Manual* (Thorndike, Hagen, & Sattler, 1986), however, are based on research studies in which each child was administered the number of subtests deemed appropriate by his or her scores on the Vocabulary routing test—usually about eight subtests. Reynolds (1987) cautions against the use of short forms because of their lack of theoretical and research support. Until clearer research support exists for the Binet-4 short forms, they should likely be used as secondary or back-up procedures as opposed to batteries of first choice. Use of the battery in the same manner as the standardization edition would give the user more confidence in the obtained scores.

Adaptive Testing

The Binet-4 uses an adaptive testing design. This design was one of the unique features of previous editions of the Binet. Adaptive procedures are included primarily to make testing time most efficient and brief (Thorndike, Hagen, & Sattler, 1986). The basic procedure described in the Binet-4 is to administer the Vocabulary subtest first to all children. This Vocabulary subtest then serves as a "routing" subtest to appropriate entry points on subsequent subtests that are administered to the child. The Vocabulary test is an excellent candidate for a routing test because traditionally it has been an excellent measure of "g" (Kamphaus & Reynolds, 1987), and on the Binet-4 it is an extremely high correlate of all the other subtests in the battery (Reynolds, Kamphaus, & Rosenthal, 1988). If a test is a high correlate of various other tests in the battery, then it will do a good job of routing the examiner to items of appropriate difficulty level on subsequent subtests.

Consistent with theories of adaptive testing, the Vocabulary test serves as an initial estimate of the child's ability. Based upon this initial estimate of ability, the examiner can be routed to the various levels of the Binet (which are grouped by letters of the alphabet) that are most likely to be of appropriate difficulty for the child. This procedure should facilitate starting at appropriate points on individual subtests so as to quickly identify basal and ceiling levels in order to reduce testing time. This approach is in contrast to others such as those used on the Wechsler and the K-ABC, on which starting points for children are designated by the child's chronological age. The Binet-4 routing procedure may be a very efficient procedure for a child whose mental age is very different from his or her chronological age. If a child is precocious, beginning at a point appropriate for his or her chronological age is not a wise use of testing time. The Binet-4 adaptive testing strategy using the Vocabulary subtest is intended to counteract this problem by basing starting points for individual subtests on ability rather than on chronological age.

The efficiency of this adaptive testing strategy, however, is dependent on the correlation of the Vocabulary subtest with the other subtests of the Binet-4. Consequently, the Vocabulary subtest is going to be a better routing test for some tests than for others. It is likely to be an excellent routing test for the Comprehension subtest, with which it shares a high intercorrelation (Thorndike, Hagen, & Sattler, 1986). On the other hand, the Vocabulary subtest is likely to be an inefficient and perhaps inaccurate routing test for a test such as Bead Memory, which has a considerably lower correlation with Vocabulary.

This is the reason why, in everyday practice, the wisdom of an adaptive testing strategy is not overwhelmingly evident. The Binet-4 is likely ushering in a new era in children's intellectual assessment where eventually many tests will be administered and scored via computers and routing procedures can then be made more efficient.

Comprehension of Instructions

Glutting and Kaplan (1990) reviewed the comprehension level of Binet-4 directions for preschoolers by evaluating the number of basic concepts that are used in the instructions to children. They used the same procedure as Kaufman (1978), who found that several preschool tests require children to understand basic concepts that may be too difficult for the typical preschooler. Kaufman (1978) found, for example, that the McCarthy Scales of Children's Abilities (McCarthy, 1972) included 7 basic concepts in the instructions and the Wechsler Preschool and Primary Scale of Intelligence (WPPSI) (Wechsler, 1967) used 14 basic concepts in its instructions. By comparison, the Glutting and Kaplan (1990) analysis of the Binet-4 revealed that 8 basic concepts were included in the instructions for this measure. This review suggests that the comprehension level of Binet-4 instructions is about the same as that of other popular preschool measures of intelligence.

Similarity to the K-ABC

The Binet-4 administration and scoring procedures are in many ways more consistent with those of the K-ABC than they are with the WISC-III. Dichotomous scoring was used on the Vocabulary subtest of the Binet-4, as opposed to the three-point system used on the Wechsler scales. In fact, all of the Binet-4 subtests use a dichotomous scoring system. Also, like the K-ABC, the Binet-4 makes extensive use of sample items. This practice creates the opportunity for a child to make mistakes on initial items without having his or her score affected. Similarly, it allows the examiner greater opportunity to explain the nature of the various tasks to the child before continuing with the test.

Derived Scores

One of the complications of the Binet-4 for examiners is the use of a standard score metric that is not comparable with other modern tests of intelligence and, for that matter, with tests of academic achievement. While all the tests discussed so far use standard score metrics with a mean of 100 and standard deviation of 15, the Binet-4 defies this trend. The Binet-4 in a sense goes "back to the future" and resurrects an older metric in which the mean of the standard score distribution is set at 100 and the standard deviation is set at 16. This metric is used for the Binet-4 test composite score and for the four area scores. While this problem is not insurmountable, it can be an annoyance. For example, the standard score to percentile rank conversion table for all tests that use normalized standard scores with the mean of 100 and standard deviation of 15 is universal. One can use the percentile rank tables for the WISC-III, K-ABC, or the Woodcock-Johnson, for example. However, because of the standard deviation of 16, the percentile rank distribution for the Binet-4 is different from that of other measures. A conversion table is presented in the Binet-4 *Expanded Guide for Scoring and Interpretation* (Delaney & Hopkins, 1987) and the *Technical Manual* (Thorndike, Hagen, & Sattler, 1986).

Perhaps the most confusing of the different metrics used by the Binet-4 is that used for the subtest scores. These are normalized standard scores with a mean of 50 and a standard deviation of 8. This metric seems to be wholly idiosyncratic and is not used by any other popular tests. It is reminiscent of the t-score method used heavily in personality assessment, where

the mean is 50 and the standard deviation 10. However, this subtest score metric on the Binet-4 differs enough from the t-score metric to make for little transfer of training. As a result, examiners have to think very differently when interpreting Binet-4 composite, area, and subtest standard scores since these scores have different percentile rank conversions than those of other popular tests.

A scoring procedure that is unique to the Binet-4 is the use of common Area Score norm tables regardless of the tests used to assess the child. For example, the manual includes only one norm table for converting the sum of the Short-Term Memory subtest score to an area composite score, and yet anywhere from one to four of the Short-Term Memory subtests may be used to enter the table and derive a composite. A clinician may use Bead Memory and Memory for Sentences, or Memory for Digits and Memory for Objects to enter the norm table and obtain a composite score. Without separate tables for the specific tests used, one basically assumes that all subtests intercorrelate equally—an untenable assumption. This problem also argues against the use of highly abbreviated batteries.

BINET-4 SUBTESTS

The Binet-4 subtests are described next in that same manner that was used for the WISC-III and K-ABC. Reliabilities, "g" loadings, and specificities are from Thorndike, Hagen, and Sattler (1986), and factor loadings are from table 19 of Thorndike (1990).

Verbal Reasoning Area

Vocabulary

For the first 15 items in the Vocabulary subtest, the child has to point to a picture named by the examiner. Items 16 through 46 require the child to define words given by the examiner. While the word definition portion of this test appears similar to that of the Wechsler scales, scoring of the individual items has been simplified. Instead of the more complex 2-1-0 scoring system used by the Wechsler scales, only dichotomous scoring is used on this particular subtest (1 or 0), thus simplifying scoring.

Performance on this test may be affected by language stimulation at home, school, and among peers. Scores may also be impacted by linguistic and schooling differences and language-based handicapping conditions such as oral expression learning disabilities. Information about the child's language development and environmental stimulation may be helpful in corroborating hypotheses.

ADMINISTRATION AND SCORING POINTERS

1. Study the scoring criteria carefully in order to be able to query responses appropriately.

2. Be sensitive to cultural/linguistic differences and local dialects.

3. Record actual responses if possible to assist with report writing.

4. Check the pronunciations of unclear words with the child's parent.

BEHAVIORS TO NOTE

1. Poor or misarticulation

2. Description of the word or examples of use of the word in lieu of a definition

3. Word retrieval problems (Follow up with a word retrieval test if necessary.)

4. Reticence to speak, point, or use gestures ("Test the limits" by readministering items if the child becomes more expressive on later items than on earlier items.)

PSYCHOMETRIC PROPERTIES

Average reliability = .87

"g" loading = .76

Loading on verbal factor = .86

Loading on memory factor = .06

Loading on quantitative factor = -.00

Loading on abstract/visual factor = .03

Subtest specificity = .25 (adequate)

Comprehension

For the first six items, a child is required to identify body parts on a card with a picture of a child. For items 7 through 42, the child has to respond to Wechsler-like questions about everyday problem situations ranging from survival behavior to civic duties.

Performance on this test may be particularly affected by oral expression skills and language stimulation at school and at home. Acclimation to American culture is also an important determining factor. This test should not be used in situations where cultural factors may be preeminent. Information about the child's language development, environmental stimulation, and culture may be helpful in corroborating hypotheses.

ADMINISTRATION AND SCORING POINTERS

1. Study the scoring criteria carefully in order to be able to query responses and score them appropriately.

2. Be sensitive to cultural/linguistic differences and local dialects.

3. Record actual responses if possible to assist with scoring and report writing.

4. Check the pronunciations of unclear words with the child's parent.

BEHAVIORS TO NOTE

1. Poor or misarticulation

2. Use of words or phrases from another language in responses

3. Word retrieval problems (Follow up with a word retrieval test if necessary.)

Average reliability = .89

"g" loading = .71

Loading on verbal factor = .70

Loading on memory factor = .07

Loading on quantitative factor = -.00

Loading on abstract/visual factor = .11

Subtest specificity = .47 (adequate)

Absurdities

The child has to point to inaccurate pictures that show a situation that is contrary to common sense or that is false for items 1 through 4. For items 5 through 32 the child has to describe the absurdity that is depicted.

Absurdities items are especially prone to idiosyncratic or creative interpretations. Performance on this test may be affected by a child's tendency toward conformity or nonconformity to societal expectations. Interpretation of this test can be difficult because of the confounding of visual and verbal skills and its lack of research or substantial clinical history. Reynolds, Kamphaus, and Rosenthal (1988) found this test to load on its own factor, which further suggests that it possesses some unique properties.

ADMINISTRATION AND SCORING POINTERS

1. Study the scoring criteria carefully in order to be able to query responses and score them appropriately.
2. Be sensitive to cultural differences that may influence interpretation of the stimuli.
3. Record actual responses if possible to assist with scoring and report writing.

BEHAVIORS TO NOTE

1. Reluctance to respond to the stimuli that may be due to an inability to respond when uncertain
2. Creative responses to stimuli that are not

included in the scoring criteria and are yet somewhat plausible (Such responses may violate the validity of this test for a particular child.)

PSYCHOMETRIC PROPERTIES

Average reliability = .87

"g" loading = .67

Loading on verbal factor = .40

Loading on memory factor = .03

Loading on quantitative factor = -.14

Loading on abstract/visual factor = .45

Subtest specificity = .57 (ample)

Verbal Relations

Given four words by the examiner, the child has to state how three words out of the four-word set are similar. This test assesses aspects of concept development—specifically, the ability to relate concepts to one another. Certainly a strong fund of verbal information is necessary to solve these items correctly. Subtleties of meaning are central to obtaining correct items, making linguistic and cultural differences a potential confound. Research on concept development may be helpful in interpreting scores on this test (see, for example, Bruner, Olver, & Greenfield, 1966). Information on SES and quality of schooling may be helpful in corroborating hypotheses.

ADMINISTRATION AND SCORING POINTERS

1. Study the scoring criteria carefully in order to be able to query responses appropriately.
2. Be sensitive to cultural/linguistic differences.
3. Record actual responses if possible to assist with report writing.

BEHAVIORS TO NOTE

1. Questions about the meanings of words used in the stimuli

Average reliability = .91

"g" loading = .66

Loading on verbal factor = .74

Loading on memory factor = −.07

Loading on quantitative factor = .18

Loading on abstract/visual factor = −.01

Subtest specificity = .54 (ample)

Quantitative Reasoning Area

Quantitative

In the Quantitative subtest, children are required to solve applied mathematics problems and show knowledge of mathematics concepts. This test uses visual as well as oral stimuli, making it perhaps more similar to the Arithmetic subtest of the K-ABC than to the Arithmetic test of the WISC-III. In addition, the child is allowed to use scratch paper and pencil on this test.

Quantitative scores are likely affected by the child's mathematics knowledge, which in turn may be determined by interest, quality of schooling, and other factors. Scores on this test can be compared to scores from other mathematics measures to test hypotheses. Scores for young children on this test may be difficult to interpret since a different item type is used for items 1 to 3 and 6 to 8. These early items place a premium on spatial perception and reasoning skills. While the items used in this test assess a variety of mathematics skills, the authors do not suggest that the test is a comprehensive measure of mathematics ability.

ADMINISTRATION AND SCORING POINTERS

1. Be sure to give the child scratch paper beginning with item 19.

BEHAVIORS TO NOTE

1. Self-deprecating statements about mathematics skills

2. Limited or no use of the scratch paper on difficult items (This may indicate poor achievement motivation or lack of confidence.)

3. Impulsive responding

4. Sweating, tearfulness, shaking, or other signs of anxiety

5. Statements suggesting low self-esteem (e.g., "I can't do this, I'm not as smart as my friends")

Average reliability = .88

"g" loading = .78

Loading on verbal factor = .25

Loading on memory factor = .20

Loading on quantitative factor = .37

Loading on abstract/visual factor = .21

Subtest specificity = .48 (adequate)

Number Series

The child has to review a series of four or more numbers presented by the examiner, identify the principle underlying the series of numbers, and then generate the next two numbers in the series consistent with the principle.

This test is also affected by academic achievement in mathematics. Scores on this test may also be affected by related factors such as achievement motivation and academic self-concept. Scores on this test can be compared to scores from other mathematics measures to test hypotheses.

ADMINISTRATION AND SCORING POINTERS:

1. Record responses as an aid to understanding the nature of a child's reasoning errors.

BEHAVIORS TO NOTE

1. Self-deprecating statements about mathematics skills

2. Indicators of poor achievement motivation or lack of confidence (e.g., an expressed dislike for schoolwork)

3. Impulsive responding

Average reliability = .90

"g" loading = .79

Loading on verbal factor = .05

Loading on memory factor = .26

Loading on quantitative factor = .42

Loading on abstract/visual factor = .33

Subtest specificity = .45 (adequate)

Equation Building

The child has to take numerals and mathematical signs and resequence them in order to produce a correct solution (equation). This test is clearly a measure of advanced mathematics skill. It may be wholly inappropriate as a measure of intelligence for a 12-year-old who has not yet taken related coursework such as algebra. This test may be more useful for assessing the mathematically precocious child who is a candidate for some type of advanced coursework.

1. Brush up on your algebra! The manual states that not all of the correct solutions may be given.

1. Responses to failure
2. Level of interest in the task

Average reliability = .91

"g" loading = .65

Loading on verbal factor = .13

Loading on memory factor = .11

Loading on quantitative factor = .71

Loading on abstract/visual factor = .01

Subtest specificity = .49 (ample)

Abstract/Visual Reasoning Area

Pattern Analysis

The first six items require the child to place puzzle pieces into a form board. Items 7 through 42 require the child to reproduce patterns with blocks. This test is a clone of Wechsler's Block Design, which was a clone of Kohs's (1923) Block Design from earlier in this century (see Chapter 6). The test, however, can be somewhat confounded for younger children because of the use of the form board. The task effectively changes from puzzle solving to abstract design reproduction.

This test can be dramatically affected by speed of performance. A large number of time failures (three or more items) would call into question the obtained score for this test. This test may also serve as a marker of right hemisphere skills, as is the case of Block Design.

1. Practice timing items

1. Attempts to align the sides of the blocks in addition to the tops
2. Frequent time failures
3. Impulsive responses where the child does not survey the stimulus before constructing the design

Average reliability = .92

"g" loading = .67

Loading on verbal factor = .00

Loading on memory factor = .00

Loading on quantitative factor = .08

Loading on abstract/visual factor = .74

Subtest specificity = .22 (adequate)

Copying

For the first 12 items the child is required to produce models with single-color blocks. For items 13 through 28 the child has to use pencil and paper to draw a variety of geometric and similar designs to match a model. This test follows in the tradition of visual-motor skill assessment popularized by Lauretta Bender (1938). These item types (i.e., drawing geometric designs) have, however, been included on previous editions of the Binet. As with all visual-motor tests, the Copying test items are most appropriate for younger children. The skills required for this type of test evidently develop early and peak by about the middle of the elementary school years. Performance on this test can be affected by visual activity, motor problems, or neuro-developmental problems.

ADMINISTRATION AND SCORING POINTERS

1. The Copying test has two item types: blocks are used for early items and pencil and the record form for older ages.
2. Scoring of the design items may take some practice.

BEHAVIORS TO NOTE

1. Poor pencil grip
2. Frequent erasures
3. Failure to scan the stimuli adequately before responding (impulsive responding)

PSYCHOMETRIC PROPERTIES

Average reliability = .87

"g" loading = .60

Loading on verbal factor = .09

Loading on memory factor = .13

Loading on quantitative factor = −.08

Loading on abstract/visual factor = .54

Subtest specificity = .69 (ample)

Matrices

The child is presented figural matrices in which one portion of the matrix is missing. The child has to identify the missing element from multiple-choice alternatives.

The Matrices test uses a format similar to that used by the Ravens Progressive Matrices and the Matrix Analogies of the K-ABC. Tests of this nature are known for strong correlations with composite scores or "g" loadings. This test requires strong spatial skills.

ADMINISTRATION AND SCORING POINTERS

1. Although this test is difficult for younger children, it may be appropriate for some younger precocious children.

BEHAVIORS TO NOTE

1. Good success on early items compared with no success on the later pencil and paper items

PSYCHOMETRIC PROPERTIES

Average reliability = .90

"g" loading = .75

Loading on verbal factor = .12

Loading on memory factor = .16

Loading on quantitative factor = .27

Loading on abstract/visual factor = .39

Subtest specificity = .57 (ample)

Paper Folding and Cutting

The child has to choose the correct picture from a multiple-choice format that shows how a piece of paper might look if it were folded as shown in a drawing. This test has a long history with the Binet and is relatively unique. It assesses spatial skills with little confound from motor skills.

1. Administration of this test can be inefficient if the examiner has not practiced folding and cutting the paper. Examiners should practice this if they have not used the test in some time.

BEHAVIORS TO NOTE

1. Excessive help (teaching) required in order for the child to grasp the nature of the task

PSYCHOMETRIC PROPERTIES

Average reliability = .94
"g" loading = .69
Loading on verbal factor = .09
Loading on memory factor = .09
Loading on quantitative factor = .35
Loading on abstract/visual factor = .55
Subtest specificity = .60 (ample)

Short-Term Memory Area

Bead Memory

For the first 10 items, the child has to recall which of one or two beads was exposed briefly by an examiner. For items 11 through 42 the child has to place beads on a stick in the same sequence as shown by the examiner in a picture.

Bead Memory can be a challenge to interpret because of its tendency to not correlate with the remainder of the Short-Term Memory area subtests. The substantial loading by Bead Memory on the abstract/visual factor suggests that frequently this test will produce a score more similar to the A/V than the STM subtests. Evidently the spatial aspects of this task loom large as a factor affecting performance.

ADMINISTRATION AND SCORING POINTERS

1. Do not present the box of beads before being ready to begin the test because access to the beads may be difficult for many children to resist.

BEHAVIORS TO NOTE

1. Inability to resist "playing" with the beads
2. Motor coordination problems (e.g., child has difficulty placing beads on the stalk)

PSYCHOMETRIC PROPERTIES

Average reliability = .87
"g" loading = .69
Loading on verbal factor = .04
Loading on memory factor = .31
Loading on quantitative factor = .05
Loading on abstract/visual factor = .44
Subtest specificity = .59 (ample)

Memory for Sentences

The child has to repeat a sentence exactly as it was stated by the examiner. This test seems to possess "ecological" validity in that it assesses an important and practical cognitive skill—the ability of a child to recall a series of words. This is similar to the task of following directions given by teachers or parents. This is a classic example of a fluid ability task that can be adversely affected by medical or neurodevelopmental problems. This test may be a poor test of memory for a child whose first language is not English.

ADMINISTRATION AND SCORING POINTERS

1. Practice may be required in order to read the items at an even rate.

BEHAVIORS TO NOTE

1. Heavy use of colloquial language, which results in low scores.

PSYCHOMETRIC PROPERTIES

Average reliability = .89
"g" loading = .67

Loading on verbal factor = .44

Loading on memory factor = .52

Loading on quantitative factor = −.06

Loading on abstract/visual factor = −.07

Subtest specificity = .53 (ample)

Memory for Digits

The child has to repeat digits exactly as they were stated by the examiner and, for some items, in reverse order. This is a clone of Wechsler's Digit Span test, a "classic" short-term memory test that traces its roots to the earliest days of intellectual assessment.

Administration and scoring pointers

1. The 1-second presentation rate may require practice in order to administer the items in consistent fashion.

Behaviors to note

1. Little evidence of rehearsal
2. Impulsivity, as shown by the child responding before the examiner completes the stimuli

Psychometric properties

Average reliability = .83

"g" loading = .58

Loading on verbal factor = .01

Loading on memory factor = .70

Loading on quantitative factor = .13

Loading on abstract/visual factor = −.02

Subtest specificity = .49 (adequate)

Memory for Objects

The examiner presents a group of objects on a page and the child has to identify the objects in the correct order from a larger array. In some ways this test resembles Spatial Memory of the K-ABC. This test may require adequate verbal skills to encode the stimuli properly.

Administration and scoring pointers

1. Practice may be required to flip the stimulus pages quickly.

Behaviors to note

1. Inattention
2. Absence of rehearsal strategies

Psychometric properties

Average reliability = .73

"g" loading = .51

Loading on verbal factor = .00

Loading on memory factor = .50

Loading on quantitative factor = .00

Loading on abstract/visual factor = .18

Subtest specificity = .50 (adequate)

Interpretation

The Binet-4 is amenable to the same interpretive approach described in previous chapters; however, because of its relative "youth" it is a less well-known entity. An example of this is the Absurdities subtest, which, although present on previous editions, is not well researched and is factorially unclear (Sattler, 1988). Considerably more research will help the Binet-4 user discern the meaning of its subtest, area, and composite scores.

The Binet-4 authors are also in general agreement with the interpretive approach of this test (Thorndike, Hagen, & Sattler, 1986). They clearly emphasize the importance of the composite score and relegate the area and subtest scores to a lesser status. Factor analytic findings generally support this approach, with one exception: the equal treatment of the Area Scores. The Verbal Reasoning and Abstract/Visual area scores are factorially more viable than the Quantitative and Short-Term Memory scores. Given the lack of validity evidence for these latter two scales, they are more similar to shared hypotheses than composite score hypotheses. The three levels of Binet-4 interpretation may then be conceptualized as follows.

COMPOSITE SCORE HYPOTHESES

Composite

Verbal Reasoning area

Abstract/Visual area

SHARED SUBTEST HYPOTHESES

Combinations of two or more subtests

Short-Term Memory area

Quantitative area

SINGLE SUBTEST HYPOTHESES

Individual subtest scores

An alternative approach to placing two Area Scores at the composite score level and two Area Scores at the shared subtest level is the factor score interpretation approach provided in Sattler (1988). For various reasons (see Chapter 6), the factor score approach is eschewed in this text. The factor score method of interpreting the Binet-4 is particularly unattractive given the availability of numerous factor analytic studies upon which a factor score method could be based and the increasingly obvious limitations of exploratory factor analytic techniques such as those used by Sattler (Keith & Reynolds, 1990).

Apriori Hypotheses

The development of apriori hypotheses for the Binet-4 is hindered somewhat because of limited research findings. Clinicians will have to depend primarily on their experience. Listed below are some potential apriori hypotheses that may be offered for the Binet-4.

SOURCE OF HYPOTHESIS	HYPOTHESIS
Ali is referred for mathematics problems.	Quantitative area score lower than other Area Scores.
Rosa suffered head trauma in an automobile accident. She now has numerous motor problems and a previous report notes "spatial" deficits.	Abstract/Visual area score lower than other area scores. Bead Memory lowest of the STM subtests.
Shalica is highly inattentive and overactive in school. According to her teacher, she never finishes her assigned work. She has never received medical treatment for hyperactivity.	STM area score lower than other area scores. Composite below average.
Nigel is referred for a developmental evaluation at age 2½. He has a history of language and motor delays. He did not walk until age 20 months and he did not speak until 24 months of age.	Composite score below average.

Composite Score Hypotheses

Tables for determining significant composite score differences and the rarity of differences can be found in Hopkins and Delaney (1988), Spruill (1988), and Rosenthal and Kamphaus (1988). The average differences between the A/V and V/R area scores for the norming sample are shown in Table 10.3.

Hypotheses for the Test Composite, Verbal Reasoning, and Abstract/Visual area scores can be generated based on information in previous chapters, particularly the WISC-III chapter. By now scores of this variety are familiar, as are the factors that may influence them. Various composite score hypotheses will be offered and interpreted in the case studies to follow.

TABLE 10.3   Clinical rarity of differences between Abstract/Visual and Verbal Reasoning area scores for two age groups

A/V vs V/R DIFFERENCE	Percentage of Norm Sample Obtaining a Difference This Size or Larger	
	AGES 2–10	AGES 11–23
10 points	48	39
15 points	29	20
20 points	16	8
25 points	8	3
30 points	3	1
35 points	1	1

Table values were computed based on data provided by Rosenthal and Kamphaus (1989).

Shared Subtest Hypotheses

Table 10.4 offers a number of shared subtest hypotheses for Binet-4 subtests that are adapted from Delaney and Hopkins (1987) and from factor analytic results. As always, these hypotheses should be considered cautiously because of their lack of validity evidence. Additionally, something unique to the Binet-4 is the listing of the Quantitative and Short-Term Memory area scores as shared, *not* composite, score hypotheses.

Subtest strengths and weaknesses can be determined using the rule of thumb offered by Delaney and Hopkins (1987). They suggest using ±7 points as indicative of a significant subtest deviation from the overall subtest mean.

The Binet-4 subtests are relatively lengthy. This subtest length—and its associated reliability—is unusual. It also may produce some quite high ratios of subtest specificity to error variance for several subtests (e.g., .59 for Bead Memory), suggesting that some of the Binet-4 subtests are amenable to interpretation as assessing a relatively unique cognitive skill or set of skills. The validity of such interpretations, however, is still dependent on the clinician's judgment rather than on an available body of validity research. Single subtest hypotheses are also given in Table 10.4.

REPORT WRITING

The Binet-4 poses several interesting challenges for report writing. It is one of the few tests where the subtests administered to a child should be clearly listed. Since the array of subtests that can be administered is large, the reader of a Binet report will likely question which "version" of the Binet was used. I recommend that each report list the *Binet-4 subtests administered* and any that were spoiled or eliminated for whatever reason. Report writers should explain why subtests were eliminated in order to ensure that they were not eliminated capriciously.

The Binet report also needs an introductory paragraph. Here is one example of such an introduction.

The Stanford-Binet Intelligence Scale-Fourth Edition (Binet 4) is a major test of intelligence that yields a composite that is comparable to the overall score of other major intelligence tests and similar to the traditional IQ score. The Binet-4 subtests are divided into four subscales—Verbal Reasoning, Abstract/Visual Reasoning, Quantitative Reasoning, and Short-Term Memory. Typically a minimum of two subtests from each area are administered, although the specific subtests used and scores interpreted may vary depending on the case.

For the Binet-4 it may also be necessary to describe the nature of a particular subtest when writing about it. Some of the Binet items, such as those on the Number Series test, are infrequently used and/or new to this edition of the Binet. This situation creates the possibility that even other psychologists may be unfamiliar with the task.

TABLE 10.4   Shared subtest hypotheses for the Stanford-Binet-Fourth Edition

	Verbal Reasoning Area				Abstract/Visual Reasoning Area				Quantitative Reasoning Area				Short-Term Memory Area			
	VOC	Com	Abs	VR	PA	Cpy	Mat	PF&C	Qun	NS	Eq	Bld	BM	MfS	MfD	MfO
Vocabulary knowledge	✓	✓		✓										✓		
Verbal expression	✓	✓	✓	✓												
Verbal concept formation	✓			✓												
Verbal comprehension		✓												✓		
Part-to-whole synthesis					✓	✓										
Visual analysis					✓	✓	✓	✓					✓			✓
Mathematics knowledge									✓	✓		✓				
Fluid ability					✓		✓	✓					✓	✓	✓	✓
Crystallized ability	✓	✓	✓	✓					✓							
Memory strategies													✓	✓	✓	✓
Short-term auditory memory														✓	✓	
Short-term visual memory													✓			✓
Visual-motor coordination					✓	✓										
Knowledge of social conventions		✓	✓													
Attention													✓	✓	✓	✓
Response to novelty							✓	✓								
Manual dexterity					✓	✓							✓			
Time pressure					✓											

CASE STUDY

The Binet-4 case study of Jerri (see Box 10.1) differs from those of earlier chapters. This case is presented as a final report with apriori hypotheses offered. This format assumes that the new clinician has progressed to the point that he or she can apply an integrative approach to a larger set of data that includes information in addition to intelligence test data.

Jerri is referred for school difficulties. There is concern about her poor academic performance. She is currently being served in a special

Box 10.1

Psychological Evaluation using Binet-4

Name: Jerri   Age: 12 years, 3 months
Grade: Fifth   School: East End Middle School
Sex: Female

Assessment Procedures

Parent, teacher, and child interviews

Parent rating scales

Parenting Stress Index (PSI)

Parent Achenbach Child Behavior Checklist (Parent Achenbach)

Teacher rating scale

Teacher Achenbach Child Behavior Checklist (Teacher Achenbach)

Child rating scales

Piers-Harris Children's Self-Concept Scale (Piers-Harris)

Revised Children's Manifest Anxiety Scale (RCMAS)

Reynolds Adolescent Depression Scale (RADS)

Stanford-Binet Intelligence Scale-Fourth Edition (Binet-4)

Bender Gestalt

Kaufman-Test of Educational Achievement/Comprehensive Form (K-TEA)

Draw-A-Person (DAP)

Thematic Apperception Test (TAT)

Reason for Referral

Jerri was referred for evaluation by her mother and teachers for poor performance in many academic areas.

Background Information

Background information was provided by Jerri's mother. Her mother reports that throughout her pregnancy she smoked cigarettes and experienced significant depression and crying spells. Jerri's birth was uneventful except for the use of forceps during the delivery. Developmental milestones were reported as achieved within normal limits.

Significant head injuries occurred on two occasions. At age 20 months, Jerri fell from her bed, resulting in a concussion. While at her preschool at age 2, she again experienced a head injury, but her mother was not aware of specific details of the accident. Jerri was toilet trained at 24 months, yet she continued to wet the bed periodically until age 7. Her mother attributes this problem to frequent kidney infections.

Jerri currently lives with her mother, stepfather, and two brothers, one 14 years of age and one 5 years of age. Her mother and biological father have been divorced for several years. Jerri's mother says that Jerri is emotionally close to her stepfather. She also gets along well with her brothers.

Jerri's mother reports a number of emotional problems in the past. In the first grade Jerri was sexually fondled by an adult male.

Jerri attends regular classes for a portion of the school day with the remainder of the day spent in a resource classroom for behavior-disordered children. In the resource room she is receiving remedial instruction in reading and math. She also receives some voluntary afterschool tutoring. She was retained in the third grade.

(continued)

Box 10.1 (*continued*)

Test Observations

Jerri was extremely cooperative during testing. She was compliant and attentive. She did, however, display a poor academic self-concept. She called herself "stupid" and "dumb" on numerous occasions.

Assessment Results

The Binet-4 intelligence scale comprises 15 subtests, of which usually 6 to 9 are administered to a given child or young adult. These tests are divided into four areas including Verbal Reasoning, Abstract/Visual Reasoning, Quantitative Reasoning, and Short-Term Memory. The Verbal Reasoning area contains tests such as defining words and answering common-sense questions. Abstract/Visual Reasoning tests include items such as constructing puzzles, assembling abstract designs with blocks, and drawing figures. The Quantitative Reasoning area includes test items that assess applied mathematical problem solving and advanced mathematical skills such as algebra. Finally, Short-Term Memory items require children to recall digits, sentences, and arrangements of multicolored and multishaped beads. The subtests in each area are combined to produce an area score (e.g., Abstract/Visual). These area scores in turn are combined to derive a Test Composite score. Jerri obtained a Test Composite in the well below-average range. Her Test Composite score corresponds to a percentile rank of 7, indicating that she performed better than approximately 7% of other 12-year-olds taking the test and worse than approximately 93%. Jerri's performance on this measure is highly consistent with her mother's report of Jerri being "low" in all skill areas.

These results are also highly consistent with those from the K-TEA. Individual academic area and composite standard scores for Jerri ranged from 70 to 85, which corresponds to percentile ranks ranging from 2 to 16 (see psychometric summary). No significant pattern of strengths and/or weaknesses were evident between subtest areas; rather, all skill areas assessed were below average. Again, this result is supported by maternal reports and school records of Jerri's past and present academic achievement.

Social/Emotional Area

According to results of the Parenting Stress Index, area of stress revealed between Jerri and her mother appear to be related to her mother's frustration with what she perceives as her daughter's excessive activity level and lack of fulfillment of her mother's expectations for her. On the Parent Achenbach, the only clinically significant area was immature/hyperactive. Interview information obtained from Jerri's mother confirms these findings, with her reporting that she sees Jerri as extremely distractible and overactive.

Jerri's teacher ratings revealed no significant scale elevations. Her teacher says that Jerri cannot concentrate long enough to complete her schoolwork and that she is constantly asking for assistance for even the simplest assignments. Socially, she reports that Jerri has few friends.

Rating scales and an interview were used to determine Jerri's personal perception of her social and emotional functioning. Jerri's Piers-Harris scores in all areas assessed were extremely low, with the exception of the area of Happiness and Satisfaction. This profile tends to be associated with an adolescent who feels incompetent but denies it when directly questioned about it. A significant amount of inconsistency in Jerri's responses was noted on the RCMAS, which is usually associated with adolescents having a distorted or inaccurate view of themselves and their current level of emotional stability. Finally, RADS results indicate that Jerri does not see herself as depressed at this time.

On the DAP and TAT, Jerri tended to give responses that were considered developmentally immature. Interview information from Jerri supports these findings. She relates that she is anxious and that she gets upset easily "like her mother." She is concerned about not having any close friends, and she feels that the other children in school "talk about her behind her back." Surprisingly, she reports that she is generally a happy person. Regarding her poor performance in school subjects, she says that she is "real slow" and that it takes her a long time to learn things. She, like her mother and teacher, feels that she has a very hard time concentrating and that it is easy for her to be distracted.

(continued)

Box 10.1 *(continued)*

Conclusions and Recommendations

Jerri is a 12-year old female who was referred for evaluation for determination of significant factors related to her academic problems. Intellectual and achievement testing indicate that she functions as a "slow learner" with below-average skills evident in all achievement areas assessed. Evaluation of social-emotional areas indicates that Jerri is an extremely distractible child. She has a poor self-image and may be experiencing significant feelings of anxiety and apprehension at this time.

Recommendations based on assessment results include:

1. Jerri's behavior meets the diagnostic criteria for attention deficit disorder, undifferentiated as specified by the *Diagnostic and Statistical Manual of Mental Disorders* (3rd ed., Rev.). This diagnostic category is somewhat vague, but it seems appropriate for Jerri because of her high level of distractibility without hyperactivity. This diagnosis suggests that Jerri will need some type of intervention to control her distractibility at school.

2. A number of risk factors appear to be present in areas related to Jerri's emotional functioning. It is recommended that individual counseling and group counseling be sought to lessen the risk of Jerri's development of future emotional problems.

3. Jerri has been identified as a slow learner in academic areas. A formal tutorial program is recommended to enhance her development of academic skills. In conjunction with tutoring, curriculum-based assessment is advised to help pinpoint specific areas of academic weakness.

Psychometric Summary

Stanford-Binet Intelligence Scale - Fourth Edition

AREA/SUBTEST	STANDARD AGE SCORE
Verbal Reasoning	73
Vocabulary	36
Comprehension	39
Abstract/Visual Reasoning	86
Pattern Analysis	43
Copying	43
Quantitative	84
Quantitative	42
Short-Term Memory	74
Bead Memory	36
Memory for Sentences	42
Composite	76 (7th percentile)

Kaufman - Test of Educational Achievement

SUBTESTS	STANDARD SCORES	PERCENTILE RANK	GRADE EQUIVALENT
Mathematics Applications	80	9	3.9
Reading Decoding	79	8	3.6
Spelling	70	2	2.6

Box 10.1 *(continued)*

Subtests	Standard Scores	Percentile Rank	Grade Equivalent
Reading Comprehension	85	16	4.5
Mathematics Computation	77	6	4.1
Composites			
Reading	81	10	4.0
Mathematics	78	7	4.0

Bender Gestalt Test

Errors = 5

Age Equivalent = 7-6 – 7-11

Percentile = less than 5th

Achenbach Child Behavior Checklist

	Mother
Internalizing Scale	57
Anxious/Obsessive	57
Somatic Complaints	67
Schizoid	67
Depressed/Withdrawn	55
Immature/Hyperactive	74*
Externalizing Scale	59
Delinquent	66
Aggressive	55
Cruel	65

	Teacher
Internalizing Scale	61
Anxious	59
Social Withdrawal	63
Depressed	64
Immature	62
Self-Destructive	62
Inattentive	68
Externalizing Scale	69
Unpopular	67
Delinquent	63
Aggressive	69

Box 10.1 *(continued)*

Piers-Harris Children's Self-Concept Scale

CLUSTERS	RAW SCORES	PERCENTILE	STANINE	T-SCORE
Behavior	10	25	4	43
Intellectual and School Status	5	6	2	34
Physical Appearance and Attributes	4	11	2	37
Anxiety	8	37	4	47
Popularity	3	5	2	34
Happiness and Satisfaction	9	72	6	56
Total Score	18	1	1	27

CHILD SUBSCALE SCORES   PARENT SUBSCALE SCORES

Adaptability	26	Dependent	21
Acceptability	19*	Attentive	14
Demonstrative	21	Restraint	16
Mother	12	Competent	30
Distractibility	32*	Isolation	13
Reinforcement	10	Health	10

Sum of Child Domain Score = 120
Sum of Parent Domain Score = 121
Total Stress Index = 241

Revised Children's Manifest Anxiety Scale (RCMAS)

CLUSTERS	PERCENTILE	T-SCORE OR SCALED SCORE
Total Anxiety	38	47
Lie	90	13

Reynolds Adolescent Depression Scale (RADS)

Raw Score = 53

Total Percentile = 28

Only one critical item noted (# 30)

---

education program on a resource basis with an emphasis on basic academic skill development. She was retained once for academic failure and she has received after-school tutoring. She also has a history of head injury and questionable prenatal care or environment. All of these fac-

tors are associated with lower-than average-intelligence test scores. A reasonable apriori hypothesis is that her Binet scores will be below average. Jerri also estimated her intelligence to be below average, as was indicated by her numerous self-deprecating statements during testing.

BINET-4 STRENGTHS AND WEAKNESSES

Strengths

1. The age and standard score ranges of the Binet-4 are strengths that make it useful in a wide variety of applications. The large age range allows for some continuity of assessment to track development. The larger-than-usual standard score range makes the test more useful for children at the tails of the normal distribution (i.e., the mentally retarded and gifted).

2. The flexibility of administration is a "mixed blessing" in that it is helpful for devising a test that is customized for use with a client. This flexibility, however, does create the opportunity for unjustified uses.

3. Some Binet-4 subtests, such as Number Series, are unprecedented in individual intellectual assessment. Novel tests such as this create the opportunity for specialized clinical and research uses.

4. The Binet-4 concurrent validity and reliability research is solid and impressive.

5. The dichotomous scoring system of the Binet-4 facilitates the scoring of verbal response item types.

Weaknesses

1. Factor analytic support for the Test Composite score is good, but support for the Area Scores is unusually poor.

2. The current Binet does not have as much ceiling and floor as its predecessor. It is not unusual for adolescents to obtain perfect scores on tests such as Pattern Analysis. Nor is it unusual for a 2-year-old to obtain raw scores of zero on one or more tests.

3. The Copying test drawing items are relatively difficult to score in comparison to other visual-motor tests.

CONCLUSIONS

The Binet-4 represents a significant step forward in the development of Binet's original technology. The new scale is so comprehensive and different from its predecessors that it cannot draw upon its earlier research base; hence, it may take several years of research to understand the nature of its contributions and limitations.

CHAPTER SUMMARY

1. The Binet-4 departs from its predecessors to such an extent, especially in terms of its structure and theory, that it should be considered a new test, as opposed to what is typically considered a mere revision of an earlier scale.

2. In the Binet-4 hierarchical model, "g," or general intelligence, is the premier cognitive ability at the top of the hierarchy.

3. The second level of the Binet hierarchy is based on the work of Cattell and his fluid and crystallized dimensions of intelligence.

4. The third level in the Binet theoretical hierarchy consists of finer discriminations of the fluid and crystallized abilities. This level includes the area scores and subtests.

5. The weighting procedure used to correct for norming sampling problems was effective in producing norm-referenced scores that are consistent and predictable in relationship to other tests of intelligence.

6. The Binet-4 produces results very similar to the WISC-R for mentally retarded and learning disability samples, with the Binet-4 consistently yielding slightly lower scores.

7. Internal consistency reliability for the Binet-4 Composite score is extraordinarily high over the 2- to 23-year age span of the test.

8. Concurrent validity studies show a strong correlational relationship between the Binet-4 and its predecessors, suggesting that the Binet-4 is very much like other well-respected intelligence measures.

9. Factor analytic studies of the Binet-4 have created some confusion because various researchers, using similar procedures, have produced different conclusions.

10. Vocabulary, Quantitative, Number Series, Comprehension, and Matrices have high "g" loadings. Memory for Digits, Memory for Objects, and Copying have poor "g" loadings.

11. The verbal reasoning and abstract/visual reasoning factors show strong evidence of factorial support.

12. The Quantitative scale lacks clear evidence of a corresponding factor.

13. The Short-Term Memory area score receives support in some factor analytic studies yet not in others.

14. The Binet-4 consists of 15 subtests, only a portion of which are administered to each age group.

15. Until more clear research support exists for the Binet-4 short forms, they should likely be used as secondary or back-up procedures as opposed to batteries of first choice.

16. The Binet-4 uses an adaptive testing design. The Vocabulary subtest then serves as a "routing" subtest to appropriate entry points on subsequent subtests that are administered to the child.

17. The comprehension level of Binet-4 instructions is about the same as that of other popular preschool measures of intelligence.

18. The Binet-4 uses a standard score metric that is not comparable with other modern tests of intelligence and, for that matter, with tests of academic achievement.

19. In a report, clinicians should list the Binet 4 subtests administered and any that were spoiled or eliminated for whatever reason.

CHAPTER 11

Woodcock-Johnson and Differential Ability Scales

CHAPTER QUESTIONS

What theory drove the development of the Woodcock-Johnson?

What are some special features of the DAS that make it attractive to users?

Two relatively new multisubtest comprehensive test batteries are the Differential Ability Scales (DAS) (Elliott, 1990a) and the Woodcock-Johnson Psycho-Educational Battery-Revised (W-J) (Woodcock & Johnson, 1989) Tests of Cognitive Ability (the preschool forms of these tests are discussed in Chapter 13). While there is considerable research available on these measures, all of it is publisher-sponsored. In a sense, then, the debate has really not yet begun on these tests since few independent reasearchers or critics have made their voices heard. These tests have also not been widely available for clinical purposes. Thus, the extent of their use is not known and the clinical diagnostic value of the

instruments, independent of their psychometric quality, is unknown. Perhaps in a second edition of this volume these measures will be provided more space—time will tell. *The fact that each test does not have its own chapter is not an indication that it is not recommended for use*; rather, it is an indication that the test is new.

W-J TESTS OF COGNITIVE ABILITY

The W-J was published in 1989 as a revision to the 1977 edition. While this chapter focuses on the cognitive battery, the W-J actually is one of the most comprehensive test batteries available for the clinical assessment of children and adolescents. The W-J Tests of Achievement have enjoyed considerable popularity since their original release, much more than the cognitive battery. The system also includes the W-J Scales of Independent Behavior (SIB), an adaptive behavior scale.

The current W-J Cognitive, however, differs significantly from its predecessor in many ways. Most obvious is its closer tie to John Horn's work with Cattell's fluid/crystallized model of intelligence (see Chapter 2). Woodcock and Horn align the subtests of the W-J with eight of the cognitive abilities isolated by Horn, as shown in Table 11.1.

The W-J is extensive, as revealed by the breadth of its theoretical model. The scale also includes two sets of subtests: standard and supplemental.

Some of the W-J abilities are already familiar to readers because they have been used in other tests and/or they are described in earlier chapters. The greater dependency of the W-J revision on an explicitly stated theoretical orientation is a major improvement over the original

TABLE 11.1   Cognitive factors and subtests of the Woodcock-Johnson

Cognitive Factor		Subtests
Long-Term Retrieval	Stand. Supp.	1. Memory for Names 8. Visual-Auditory Learning 15. Delayed Recall—Memory for Names 16. Delayed Recall—Visual Auditory Learning
Short-Term Memory	Stand. Supp.	2. Memory for Sentences 19. Memory for Words 17. Numbers Reversed
Processing Speed	Stand. Supp.	3. Visual Matching 10. Cross Out
Auditory Processing	Stand. Supp.	4. Incomplete Words 11. Sound Blending 18. Sound Patterns
Visual Processing	Stand. Supp.	5. Visual Closure 12. Picture Recognition 19. Spatial Relations
Comprehension Knowledge	Stand. Supp.	6. Picture Vocabulary 13. Oral Vocabulary 20. Listening Comprehension 21. Verbal Analogies
Fluid Reasoning	Stand. Supp.	7. Analysis-Synthesis 14. Concept Formation 19. Spatial Reasoning 21. Verbal Analogies
Quantitative Ability	Supp.	24. Calculation* 25. Applied Problems*

*These two tests are from the W-J Tests of Achievement.
Stand. = Standard Battery
Supp. = Supplemental

W-J. The closer tie between the W-J subtests and theory should enhance the ability of the new W-J user to learn to interpret the test. The theoretical orientation should allow the user to interpret the scales with greater confidence and accuracy. Some data are presented in the manual to support the theoretical organization of the subtests, but independent factor analytic and other investigations are needed.

Standardization

The W-J was normed on 6,359 cases using a stratified sampling procedure to match U.S. Census Bureau statistics. The sample for ages 2 to 5 consisted of 705 cases, while the sample for grades kindergarten through 12th included 3,245 cases. Stratification variables included gender, geographic region, community size, and race (white, black, Native American, Asian Pacific, other, and Hispanic origin). The W-J used a different approach from the other tests discussed thus far to control for family SES. Communities were selected for the standardization program based on SES. Community SES was gauged by adult educational attainment, type of occupation, occupational status, and household income. Educational attainment and occupation were used as direct measures of SES for the adult norming sample. Over all, there is a relatively close match between Census statistics and the characteristics of the norming sample.

The W-J Cognitive was normed concurrently with the W-J Tests of Achievement. Because of the conorming of the W-J Tests of Cognitive Ability and Achievement, the W-J fosters ability/achievement comparisons. Ability/achievement discrepancies, which may be particularly useful for learning disability diagnosis, can be computed based on the frequency of occurrence of these discrepancies in the standardization sample. The manual and software program provide for the systematic evaluation of such discrepancies (see Chapter 14 for a discussion of the issue of ability/achievement discrepancies and learning disability diagnosis).

This conorming is particularly necessary in the case of the W-J since the Quantitative cluster is made up of two subtests from the Tests of Achievement.

Reliability

Internal consistency estimates for the standard battery subtests are quite high. The median coefficients are above .80 for five of the seven subtests. It is noteworthy that the Visual Closure subtest yields coefficients in the .60s for ages 6 through 39. This test is similar to the Gestalt Closure subtest of the K-ABC, which has some of the lowest internal consistency coefficients for that battery. At other ages the Visual Closure subtest has some coefficients in the .80s, but the primary use of the test will occur in the age range with the worst coefficients. The Visual Closure subtest may produce some difficult scores to interpret, as is the case with the K-ABC. The other test with lower coefficients is Visual Matching. Reliability estimates in the .70s for this test, however, are comparable to those for the WISC-R Coding subtest. (These coefficients are test-retest coefficients since internal consistency coefficients are inappropriate for timed tests.)

The Broad Cognitive Ability (BCA) composite score for the seven standard battery subtests yields a median internal consistency coefficient of .94. The Broad Cognitive Ability Early Development scale is also highly reliable for preschoolers, with a coefficient of .96 at ages 2 and 4. Internal consistency reliabilities for the clusters (composites) that are derived when supplemental scales are used are also high. They range from a median coefficient of .80 for Fluid Reasoning to .96 for Short-Term Memory. While composites on the WISC-R and other tests produce consistent reliability estimates in the .90s, some of the W-J cluster scores do not produce estimates this high. The Auditory Processing, Visual Processing, Comprehension-Knowledge, and Fluid Reasoning clusters all have coefficients that average in the .80s. With this finding in mind, these clusters may represent something of an intermediate score that is more reliable than the typical intelligence test subtest and yet somewhat less reliable than the typical intelligence test composite score. At the time of this writing, stability coefficients were not available. Depending on the nature of validity evidence, these scores should be interpreted in like fashion—that is, receive more emphasis than a subtest score but less emphasis than a composite score. Only research and clinical experience will tell for sure.

Validity

Some attention was paid to the establishment of content validity for the W-J, but no evidence is presented. According to the *Examiner's Manual* (Woodcock & Mather, 1989), "Items included in the various tests were selected using item validity studies as well as expert opinion" (p. 7). Some results of the experts' judgments or description of the methods and results of the studies would have been desirable.

Several prepublication concurrent validity studies were also completed. The concurrent validity coefficients show some overlap with existing measures, but the magnitude of the correlations is somewhat less than one would expect for a multisubtest measure of intelligence. For a study of 64 three-year-olds, the W-J BCA Early Development score correlated .69 with the K-ABC MPC, .62 with the McCarthy GCI, and .69 with the Binet-4 Composite. For a sample of 9-year-olds the BCA Standard Battery composite correlated .57 with K-ABC MPC, .68 with Binet-4 Composite, and .68 with the WISC-R Full Scale. These relationships are lower and less impressive than some would have hoped. Correlations with the WAIS-R also stayed below .70 in a study involving 51 seventeen-year-olds. The W-J BCA Standard Battery correlated .65 with the Binet-4 and .64 with the WAIS-R Full Scale. All of these coefficients are lower than one would expect based on correlations among previously published lower measures,

where coefficients have been above rather than below .70. This finding stands in some contrast to data for the tests discussed thus far, where more often than not correlations among the measures are above .70.

The factor analytic validity of the W-J was evaluated recently by Woodcock (1990), Reschly (1990), and Ysseldyke (1990). Woodcock (1990) presents the results of several factor analytic studies. He found support for eight factors underlying the W-J, which gives this measure considerably more breadth than other measures. He also argued that other tests are underfactored and that other tests do not possess enough breadth and depth of measurement of intelligence.

The tendency to emphasize breadth in the intellectual assessment process is emphasized in the following remarks from Woodcock (1990).

Horn (1988) conceptualizes intellectual functioning as a "Milky Way" of human abilities. Just as we do not know how many stars make up the Milky Way, we also do not know precisely how many unique intellectual abilities exist. In the Milky Way, we infer constellations. In the "Milky Way of intellectual abilities," we infer common-factor concepts of constellations that help us describe and understand human intellectual functioning. (p. 233)

Woodcock (1990) first presents a confirmatory factor analysis of 16 subtests with eight factors identified. The fit indices are all strong (above .95) and the root mean square residual was only .02. Details regarding the specifications of the model (e.g., whether some or all tests were allowed to have coloadings, although some were apparently allowed to coload) were not given. The factor loadings themselves are also supportive of the W-J model, although there are some hints of problems. Picture Recognition does not appear to be a marker of the Visual Processing cluster as its loading was .38 on this scale and .24 on the Long Term retrieval cluster. This finding is also consistent with the lower reliability coefficients for this cluster.

An exploratory factor analysis using oblique rotation replicated these findings in that there was considerable resemblance to the W-J model, but there were also some inconsistencies. Picture Recognition again was a poor measure of the Visual Processing cluster, with a small loading (less than .20 although the actual coefficient is not given) on this cluster and a loading of .25 on the Long Term Retrieval cluster. In effect, the Visual Processing cluster looks like a one-subtest cluster where Visual Closure devours the lion's share of the variance. Some questions are also raised by this analysis for the Quantitative Ability cluster, as the Applied Problems test had loadings of .44 on Quantitative, .20 on Fluid Reasoning, and .27 on Comprehension-Knowledge. Remember the Binet-4? The W-J may be having similar problems identifying a homogeneous quantitative scale.

Reschly (1990) and Ysseldyke (1990) are impressed by the W-J factor analytic data. Reschly (1990) observes, "The psychometrically sound, relatively clean measures of the eight factors are a major accomplishment" (p. 265). Ysseldyke (1990) similarly points out that "it appears that the WJ-R adequately represents many of the major components of human ability as suggested by the extant factor analytic research in intelligence" (p. 274). Independent factor analyses of the W-J are not available and are sorely needed.

Administration

The W-J is designed for ages 2 to 90+ and is administered in an easel format. The cognitive battery consists of 21 subtests, only 7 of which are considered as part of the standard battery (see Table 11.1). Many of the W-J subtests are familiar ones. Visual Matching, for example, is highly similar to the Coding subtest of the WISC-R. On the other hand, Memory for Names uses a novel and clever format (i.e., teaching the child the names of space creatures) that is interesting, time efficient, and clinically rich in that it allows the examiner to actually observe the child "learning." The administration of several tests is also aided by the use of an audiotape. For the Incomplete Words test the word fragments are presented by a female voice on the tape. This procedure not only fosters the use of uniform administration procedures, but it also hastens the pace of administration.

As strange as it may sound, the easel format of the W-J makes it so easy to administer that the W-J does not resemble other tests of intelligence. It resembles academic achievement measures to a greater degree. For example, manipulatives (or toy-like materials) are not available for the assessment of preschoolers. Similarly, while most intelligence tests have a visual-motor measure (e.g., Block Design, Triangles, Pattern Analysis), the W-J does not. While the W-J is extremely easy to administer, its lack of similarity to other well-known tests may deter transfer of training from other measures. On a practical level, the test may also not be as inviting as others (e.g., McCarthy) for preschoolers who require manipulatives to maintain their attention (see Chapter 12). The W-J does have an Early Development scale for preschoolers consisting of the Memory for Names, Incomplete Words, Visual Closure, and Picture Vocabulary subtests.

Scoring

The scoring options for the W-J are limitless, so much so that they may be bewildering, especially to clinicians who primarily use standard scores for interpretation. The composite or IQ-like score is called Broad Cognitive Ability, thus avoiding the inappropriate connotations of the IQ score. The overall composite for preschoolers is called Early Development. Latent trait scores ("W" scores) are offered as intermediate scores for later score calculations. The composites and individual subtest scores have a mean of 100 and standard deviation of 15, and percentile ranks are offered. Cluster scores are available for the eight cognitive factors shown in Table 11.1. Other scores offered include t-scores, normal curve equivalents (NCEs), and stanines. Grade-based scores where grade is used as the norm or reference group are offered in addition to the traditional age-based scores.

One of the more novel scores offered by the W-J, which has previously been used more in achievement testing, is the Relative Mastery Index (RMI). The RMI is similar to a ratio with the second part of the ratio set at a value of 90. Sample RMIs look like the following: 40/90, 55/90, 95/90. The 90 is based on the performance of the norm sample (either age or grade reference groups). The denominator means that children in the norm sample can perform the intellectual task with 90% accuracy. The first number of the ratio represents the child's performance in relationship to the 90% level of accuracy (mastery). If a child obtained an RMI of 45/90, it would mean that the child's proficiency on the subtest is at a 45% level whereas the typical child of his or her age (or grade) mastered the material at a 90% level. The RMI is similar to the rationale behind the Snellen Chart used for visual screening. Some of us have vision of 20/20, some 20/60, and so on. In the case of the Snellen Chart, however, the first number is fixed and the second one varies. The rarity of the use of the RMI score in intellectual assessment makes it difficult to gauge its value in everyday cognitive assessment practice. No other major test of intelligence offers such a score. The notion of "mastery" is more common and appropriate for achievement testing.

The W-J also offers extended age and grade equivalent scales that may facilitate the evaluation of children at the tails of the normal distribution. Instead of having a lowest possible age equivalent of 2-0 (2 years, 0 months), the W-J offers an age equivalent of 2-0[1], where the superscript one represents the first percentile rank. An age equivalent of 2-0[48] means that the child obtained a score at the 48th percentile rank for 2-year-olds.

The easel format of administration and scoring is assisted by a user-friendly and fast software program. The foregoing paragraphs make scoring of the W-J sound formidable and, in fact, it is. This fact undoubtedly makes the software of the W-J very popular.

Interpretation

Descriptive terms for levels of W-J performance are modern in that they describe levels of performance as opposed to offering a diagnosis. The W-J descriptive labels corresponding to standard scores are given below.

STANDARD SCORE	LABEL
131 and above	Very superior
121–130	Superior
111–120	High average
90–110	Average
80–89	Low average
70–79	Low
69 and below	Very low

One caveat to consider when interpreting W-J scores is the relatively small number of items per subtest. The W-J covers an extraordinarily large age range with a small number of items. If a child is not attending on a few of the items of a subtest, the derived scores could change rather dramatically. On Memory for Sentences, for example, a raw score of 49 corresponds to an age equivalent of 16.3, but a raw score of 50 corresponds to an AE of 20. Incomplete Words is another brief subtest. For this test a raw score of 24 corresponds to an AE of 7-0 and a raw score of 26 corresponds to an AE of 8-5. These conversions hint that some of the W-J subtests may have too few items to assess such a large age range. This situation results in some unexpected relationships between raw scores and derived scores where small increases in raw scores may produce larger-than-expected differences in derived scores, creating more opportunity for test behavior such as inattention to influence scores.

In lieu of providing extensive tables of difference score values for profile interpretation, the W-J advises using confidence bands to compare cluster and subtest scores. The rules for comparing scores via this method are given on page 82 of the *Examiner's Manual* (Woodcock & Mather, 1989).

Apriori hypotheses for the W-J are somewhat difficult to make. The offering of such hypotheses is hindered by the lack of clinical history of the W-J and lack of concurrent validity and other studies. The individual W-J user will have to depend on accumulated clinical experience to generate hypotheses until more research becomes available.

Sample Case

The case reported in Box 11.1 demonstrates the use of the W-J Cognitive in a test battery for Kathy, an adolescent who is being evaluated upon admission to an inpatient treatment unit of a general hospital. The report is written in a style that may be more appropriate for hospital practice where a brief stay is anticipated. Intelligence is not the major referral question and therefore is not highlighted in the report.

Kathy demonstrates few risk factors for low intelligence test scores. Her development and medical histories are unremarkable. She has not been in special education nor has she been retained. On the other hand, there are no suggestions of high intelligence test scores either. She has not been identified as precocious and she is not in the college preparatory curriculum at her school. Kathy's test behavior suggested at least average intelligence test scores. Her effort in the test session was good despite her depression. All of these factors argue for an apriori hypothesis of average intelligence.

In addition, Kathy worked extremely hard on the Visual Matching test. This test is a Wechsler Coding subtest analogue where a premium is placed on speed of performance. Kathy responded well to the demands of the tasks and seemed to push herself hard to respond. This test also seemed to elicit Kathy's tendency to be extremely compliant and to try to meet the de-

mands of others. Her behavior on this test leads to the hypothesis that this would be one of her higher subtest scores.

Conclusions

The W-J is clearly the product of a thorough test development process. The result is a test with substantial psychometric support. The W-J has not attracted the research attention that the K-ABC has, for example. This edition of the W-J deserves serious research attention and a clinical trial.

DIFFERENTIAL ABILITY SCALES

The Differential Ability Scales (DAS) (Elliott, 1990a) is a new entrant onto the individual clinical assessment scene. The DAS is a comprehensive battery of cognitive and achievement tests that are designed for children and adolescents between the ages of 2 1/2 and 17 years. The DAS is not, however, a new measure. Rather, it is a revision and U.S. adaptation of the British Ability Scales (BAS) (Elliott, Murray, & Pearson, 1979). There were, however, several changes made in the DAS from its predecessor in addition to the collection of the U.S. normative sample, such as the addition of several new subtests and the creation of a standard "core" battery. The DAS Cognitive Battery has a preschool level and a school-age level. For school-age children there are reading, mathematics, and spelling achievement tests that are described primarily as "screeners." All of these measures were normed on the same sample to make the comparison of cognitive and achievement domains more appropriate.

Theory and Features

The DAS differs in some ways from other recently developed tests by not basing the construction of the scale on a particular theory.

Box 11.1

Psychological evaluation/consultation using the W-J

Name: Kathy
Age: 16 years, 8 months
Grade: 11
School: Comprehensive High School

Class: Regular
Occupation: Part-time employment at a fast-food restaurant approximately 25 hours per week

Assessment Procedures

Diagnostic interview

K-TEA Comprehensive Form

Achenbach Youth Self-Report

Woodcock-Johnson Test of Cognitive Ability

Sentence Completion Test

Rorschach

Thematic Completion Test

Referral Information

Kathy was referred by her attending physician for a psychological evaluation subsequent to admission to the hospital. Her admitting diagnosis was major depression, single episode, moderate. The referral question was whether or not psychological evaluation would confirm this diagnosis.

Background Information

Kathy has been experiencing symptoms of depression for the past 6 months. These symptoms have included withdrawal, feelings of hopelessness, depressed affect, crying spells, periodic suicidal ideation (without a specific plan), difficulty falling asleep, and declining school grades. Kathy sought help from her high school English teacher and was subsequently referred to the hospital.

Kathy lives with her birth father, mother, and three younger siblings. Her father works as a custodian and her mother as a seamstress. She has never been retained nor has she received special education. She enjoys math and art class. Kathy works 25–30 hours a week and seems to enjoy this activity. She reports that she has many friends. She says that she is experiencing difficulty in her relationship with her mother. She feels that her mother is not giving her appropriate attention or care. As an example, she cited that occasionally she has come home after drinking some alcohol with friends and that although there was a notable change in her behavior, she received no comment from her mother.

Observations During Testing

Kathy displayed depressed mood throughout the test session. She was, however, compliant and exceedingly polite. Her effort during the testing sessions was commendable and suggestive of good achievement motivation. She exhibited some confidence in her mathematics and spelling skills. She showed good concentration and attention.

Test Results and Conclusions

All of Kathy's cognitive test scores were within the average range. Her percentile ranks on the Woodcock-Johnson Cognitive ranged from a low of 30 to a high of 86 with no significant strengths or weaknesses being evident. She obtained her highest percentile rank of 86 on the Visual Matching subtest. She worked extremely hard on this test, showing good manual speed, dexterity, and motivation to comply with the demand for speed. On the K-TEA her percentile ranks were also average, ranging from a low of 47 to a high of 66.

Kathy gave numerous indications of dysthymic tendencies in her personality test results. She seems plagued by anxiety, low self-concept, emotional dependency, ruminations, and perhaps compulsive tendencies. For example,

(continued)

Box 11.1 *(continued)*

she admitted to some excessive hand washing and concern with cleanliness. There is also some indication that she is willing to suppress her own feelings and desires in favor of those of others. She may also engage in passive-aggressive behaviors in order to meet her emotional needs. There are also indications in the personality test results that she may be a "well-compensated" depressive. In other words, she may have been hiding feelings of depression considerably longer than the past 4-6 months.

Recommendations

The current findings suggest that Kathy may require long-term (more than a few weeks) psychotherapeutic intervention and that she may be passively resistant to it. She may require fairly aggressive approaches to psychotherapy. There are also suggestions of family difficulties, indicating a need for family assessment with the potential requirement for family therapy. Regardless of therapeutic modality, there are suggestions that while Kathy may appear to be rather forthcoming, it may not be easy for her to change her behavior patterns.

Diagnosis

Major depression, single episode, moderate.

Comments

In this case, both of the apriori hypotheses, one based on background information and the other based on test behavior, were confirmed. The single subtest conclusion for the Visual Matching subtest is interesting because it shows how personality variables—namely, compliance and need to please others—may occasionally affect intelligence test scores.

Instead the scale seems to be built on a number of test development goals and assumptions about cognition. Elliott (1990b) describes his approach to the development of the DAS as "eclectic," at various times citing the work of Cattell, Horn, Das, Jensen, Thurstone, Vernon, and Spearman. Which aspects of these theories he ascribes to is not clear. Elliott (1990b) appeals to Thurstone's notion of primary mental abilities. He agrees with Thurstone's idea that the emphasis on intellectual assessment should be on the assessment and interpretation of distinct abilities as opposed to the assessment process focusing exclusively on an overall composite score. For this reason the DAS subtests were constructed to enhance their subtest specificity (that is, their reliable unique variance), which in turn should make the subtests more interpretable as measures of unique abilities. Elliott presents evidence of higher subtest specificities than for the WISC-R and the K-ABC. Keith (1990) points

out that subtest specificities can be affected by the method of computation and shows how using an alternate method might result in lower subtest specificity estimates for the DAS. Even if one accepts the data showing that the DAS offers higher subtest specificities, there is no evidence that this is a "clinical" advantage. Presumably, higher specificities would lead to clearer profiles (Elliott, 1990b). Empirical evidence of meaningful DAS profiles for types or subtypes of clinical populations, however, are not available. In addition, there is not strong evidence that the abilities measured by the DAS subtests are important for clinical diagnostic use. One important piece of evidence to support subtest interpretation would be enhanced predicted validity, over and above the values for a composite score (McDermott, Fantuzzo, & Glutting, 1990). Such data are not available, relegating the higher DAS subtest specificities to the class of an "interesting" finding the value of which is not known.

Elliott (1990b) also ascribes to the theoretical stance of Spearman and others of the British school. He suggests that:

1. *All ability measures are intercorrelated and, thus, are likely to yield a general factor, "g."*

2. *Ability measures, if developed to be homogeneous, are likely to form subgroupings at a lower level of generality than "g," as well as showing a proportion of reliable specific variance. The structure of abilities is, therefore, likely to be hierarchical, with "g" at the apex, followed by group factors and with subtests at the lowest level.*

3. *The hierarchical structure will differentiate and develop with age. (p. 378)*

We are seeing considerable agreement here between the DAS approach to test development and the Binet-4 in that both offer apriori hierarchical models. The most obvious difference between the Binet-4 and DAS is the emphasis on subtest specificity on the part of the DAS. Elliott (1990b) clearly places more emphasis on subtest interpretation than the Binet-4 authors, offering "diagnostic" subtests that are interpreted individually because they are not part of any cluster (composite) scores.

Elliott (1990b) defines the "g" measured by the DAS thusly: "Psychometric "g" is the general ability of an individual to perform mental processing that involves conceptualization and the transformation of information" (p. 380). This definition is strikingly similar to Jensen's definition of Level II processing (reasoning ability; see Chapter 2), especially the emphasis on the transformation of information. Such a definition also clearly makes Elliott's work consistent with that of Spearman, Vernon, Jensen, and others of the "British school" (see Chapter 2).

It appears that Elliott reaches far and wide, adopting theoretical notions from hierarchical models (lumpers) and those espousing the value of assessing specific abilities (splitters; see Chapter 2). This eclecticism reveals Elliott's (1990b) grasp of the issues and provides support for the inclusion of the GCA, cluster, and diagnostic subtest scores. The value of this eclecticism, however, is not clear. There is no evidence, pro or con, regarding the utility of this approach for interpretation.

Standardization

The DAS was normed on a representative national sample of 3,475 children tested between 1987 and 1989. The normative sample includes 200 cases per 1-year age group between the ages of 5 and 17 years. At the younger age groups the sample includes 350 cases between 2 1/2 and 4–11 per year. Exceptional children were also included in this standardization to make it as representative as possible of the population of children. Socioeconomic status was gauged using the average education level of the parent or parents living with the child. Sex, race/ethnicity, geographic region, community size, and enrollment (for ages 2-5 through 5-11) in an educational program were also controlled.

One of the difficulties in the assessment of mentally retarded individuals is the problem of differentiating levels of mental retardation. The DAS attempts to address this dilemma by developing extended GCA norms. These extended norms, which go down to a standard score of 25, are obtained by scoring each subtest on norms for a younger age and then converting the sum of subtest scores to an appropriate standard score for the child's actual age.

Out-of-level norms allow the examiner to use subtests that are designed for a particular age group at a lower level in order to provide the child with an easier set of items. These out-of-level norms can be interpreted in the same way as other norms because they were based on the complete standardization sample.

Reliability

Composite score reliabilities for the GCA are generally quite good, ranging from .89 to .95

depending on the age range studied. Internal consistency reliability estimates for the cluster scores (a second tier of composites similar to Binet-4 Area Scores) range from .83 for Nonverbal Reasoning at age 5 to .94 for Spatial at several ages (although Elliot cautions that the values for Spatial Ability are slightly inflated). The mean internal consistency estimates for the clusters at the school-age level are .88 for Verbal Ability, .90 for Nonverbal Reasoning Ability, and .92 for Spatial Ability. These coefficients are high for composites that each comprise only two subtests. They are slightly lower than the internal consistency estimates for composites made up of more subtests, such as those on the Binet-4.

Internal consistency reliabilities of the subtests are also relatively strong, with a few exceptions. The mean reliability coefficient for Recall of Objects, for example, is only .71 and for Recognition of Pictures only .73.

Test-retest coefficients for the composite scores are slightly lower, primarily at the preschool ages. At the preschool level the test-retest reliability of the GCA is still a respectable .90. However, the reliability of the Verbal and Nonverbal Ability composites are .84 and .79 respectively. Some of the individual subtest reliabilities are also low at these young ages. For example, Picture Similarities obtained a test-retest coefficient at the preschool level of only .56, and Recognition of Pictures obtained a reliability coefficient of only .58. The average test-retest coefficient for the subtests is .78.

Subtest specificities for the school-age level of the DAS are given in the *Handbook* (Elliott, 1990a). Recall of Digits and Speed of Information Processing have particularly favorable ratios of subtest specificity to error variance. Speed of Information Processing, for example, has a mean specificity of .82 and error variance of only .09.

The DAS is unusual in that item bias was systematically assessed during the test development process. No other test besides the K-ABC has conducted this procedure. There is no detailed information, however, on the types of items that were eliminated based upon bias analyses.

Validity

Several correlational studies show good evidence of concurrent validity for the DAS. Studies with school-age children have yielded strong GCA correlations with the WISC-R Full Scale (.84 for 8- to 10-year-olds and .91 for 14- and 15-year-olds), Binet-4 Composite (.88 for 9- and 10-year-olds and .85 for a sample of gifted children), and K-ABC MPC (.75) for 5- to 7-year-olds. The DAS did produce lower mean scores than the criterion test in each of these investigations. The GCA was 6 points lower than the WISC-R Full Scale score in one study and 8 points lower in another. The DAS was only 3 points lower than the Binet-4 Composite in one study but 6 points lower in the study for gifted children. The GCA was 9 points lower than the K-ABC MPC. It is difficult to explain these differences based on the norming samples since some of these measures have older norms and some do not. Score differences of about 5 points with the WISC-R and about 2 points with the K-ABC would be expected because of the time intervals between norming, but the actual differences exceed these expectations. This trend for the DAS to yield lower scores requires further study. It would be particularly helpful to have studies conducted with referral populations, since these are the children for whom the test was designed.

The correlations of the DAS ability measures and achievement tests with academic achievement tests mimic closely the results found for the K-ABC. Namely, the achievement tests are consistently more highly correlated with other achievement measures than are the ability measures. A correlational study of the DAS with the BASIS (Basic Achievement Skills Individual Screener) clearly demonstrates this finding (Elliott, 1990b). Correlations of the GCA with the three achievement subtests of the BASIS ranged from .46 (Spelling for 11-year-olds) to .66 (Reading for 7-year-olds). In direct contrast, the DAS achievement test correlations ranged from .64 (DAS Word Reading and BASIS Reading) to .88 (DAS Spelling and BASIS Spelling).

The .64 coefficient was the only one in the .60s; all others were .75 and above. This trend was repeated in a study of the DAS and K-TEA (Kaufman Test of Educational Achievement) with 7- to 11-year-old gifted education referrals. In this study the GCA correlated .56 with the K-TEA composite, and the DAS Basic Number Skills, Spelling, and Word Reading skills correlated .71, .78, and .81 respectively with the K-TEA composite. The DAS Achievement scale advantage even obtained when school grades were used as the criterion of achievement. In a study of approximately 626 cases (some of the *N*s for individual comparisons were smaller) the correlation between Mathematics grades and GCA was .40, and between Mathematics grades and Basic Number Skills .43. The pattern is more striking for Spelling and Word Reading, where the correlations with their achievement grades in these areas and GCA were .25 and .38, and correlations of grades with the achievement tests were .60 and .48 respectively. These results argue convincingly that *the GCA should not be used for predicting school achievement if the DAS achievement test scores are available.* Actually, this conclusion applies to all intelligence tests.

Factor analyses of the DAS were conducted using confirmatory and exploratory factor analytic techniques. At the school-age level the first factor (a confirmatory factor that could also be interpreted as a "g" factor) was marked by core subtests including Word Definitions, Similarities, Matrices, Sequential and Quantitative Reasoning, and Pattern Construction. At ages 2 1/2 to 3 1/2 the Verbal Comprehension and Naming Vocabulary subtests are the premier measures of "g." At ages 4 and 5 the Verbal Comprehension and Early Number Concepts are premier measures (Elliott, 1990a). These results hint that there may be a developmental component to "g" since there is a tendency for the "g" factor to be marked by verbal tests at younger ages and spatial/nonverbal tests at older ages. This developmental trend may require the clincian to ascribe different interpretations to the GCA depending on the child's age. Subtests with low "g" loadings included Speed of In-

formation Processing, Recognition of Pictures, Recall of Digits, and Recall of Objects. These results corroborate the subtest specificity and intercorrelation findings for Recall of Digits and Speed of Information Processing showing that these subtests measure discrete skills that overlap little with other tests in the battery. Elliott (1990a) interprets these results as supporting the idea that "g" is a "mental complexity factor." The paltry factor loadings for the Speed of Information Processing test also suggest that this test may correlate very little with other intelligence tests. Hence, this test may be an interesting supplement to other test batteries as an additional clinical or research tool. The relationship of the Speed of Information Processing test to the remainder of the DAS is also intriguing in that it is theoretically lawful given the history of poor relationships between criterion measures of achievement and speed of information processing measures (see Chapter 2).

Elliott (1990a) also incorporates findings regarding general intelligence factor loadings into the computation of the GCA score. At ages 2 1/2 through 3 1/2 the GCA only includes four subtests, and at ages 3 1/2 and above, six subtests are included. In contrast to the WISC-III for example, where subtests with small first factor loadings such as Coding were included in the computation of the Full Scale, the DAS only includes tests in the computation of the GCA if they have substantial first-factor loadings. The day-to-day advantage of this approach is yet to be seen, but it is a theoretically defensible practice that is loyal to the data.

Questions about the DAS Factors

The factors analytic study of the DAS included in the *Handbook* (Elliott, 1990a) is as thorough as in any intelligence test manual. As of this writing, however, the results of these early studies have not been corroborated by independent researchers with independent samples. Confidence in the robustness of the DAS factors is essential to proper interpretation of the composite scores in particular. Without evidence of cross-validation, clinicians could feel more confident in interpreting the DAS clusters if they resembled well-known group factors identified on other clinical measures with similar subtests. In addition, if the DAS factors resemble "familiar" scales, then clinicians can more readily transfer their training to the DAS. How do the DAS factors compare?

Elliott (1990a) concluded that at ages 2 1/2 through 3 1/2 a single general factor was the most appropriate explanation for the intercorrelation matrix. Elliott (1990a) and colleagues tried to fit two- and three-factor models to the data with less success. The DAS scores remain loyal to these data by offering only the GCA at these ages, without lower-level "cluster" scores.

At ages 3-6 through 5-11 a two-factor model was proposed as the best fit to the data. These two factors were labeled as verbal and nonverbal. Confirmatory factor analyses that included the memory subtests in a third factor did not produce an increase in fit. It was concluded that not only were the memory subtests relatively independent of the verbal and nonverbal factors, but, in addition, they were relatively independent of one another. Elliott (1990a) cites some information processing research to support his view that a conceptualization of memory as a unitary dimension is not defensible. This finding of a lack of a clear memory factor is also consistent with the research for the Binet-4, where the memory factor has been disputed (see Chapter 10) and for the K-ABC, where Spatial Memory never joins the other Short-Term Memory subtests (see Chapter 9). So far the DAS factors resemble closely those of other tests, which should enhance transfer of training and competent interpretation.

At the school-age level of the DAS, three factors were deemed most appropriate (Elliott, 1990a). These factors were identified as representing verbal, nonverbal reasoning, and spatial abilities. The verbal factor seems intuitive and familiar in that it is marked by loadings for the Word Definitions and Similarities subtests. The nonverbal reasoning and spatial factors, however, differ somewhat from tradition.

The confirmatory factor analyses suggested that Matrices and Sequential and Quantitative Reasoning be combined to form the nonverbal reasoning factor and Pattern Construction and Recall of Designs to form the spatial cluster. These findings are more difficult to juxtapose on previous research.

The exploratory factor analytic findings reported in Elliott (1990a) do not show a clear differentiation between Pattern Construction (spatial) and the Nonverbal Reasoning subtests. The exploratory procedure used a Promax rotation. The three-factor solution shows a lack of clarity for the Pattern Construction test. The loadings of Pattern Construction, Matrices, and Sequential and Quantitative Reasoning on the second factor were .40, .62, and .67 respectively. The Pattern Construction subtest loaded .42 on the third factor. These equivocal loadings for Pattern Construction (i.e., its shared variance with the other nonverbal reasoning subtests) make the case that the distinction between the nonverbal reasoning and spatial cluster scores may not be consistently apparent in clinical assessment practice with the DAS. The Recall of Designs subtest may be the one that is "driving" the distinction between these two clusters. The loading for the Recall of Designs subtest on factor three of the exploratory analysis was .83 (versus .42 for Pattern Recognition), making Recall of Designs the clear marker of this factor.

Finally, for assessment purposes it is important to keep in mind that the zero-order correlations between the nonverbal reasoning and spatial clusters show considerable overlapping variance. The correlation between nonverbal reasoning and spatial ranges from a low of .55 at ages 5 and 8 to a .71 at age 13; for the full range, the value is .61. The zero-order correlations also suggest that the overlap in these two scales is due primarily to the correlation between Pattern Construction and the Nonverbal Reasoning subtests. Pattern Construction has correlations with the Nonverbal Reasoning cluster ranging from .43 at age 5 (this is the only coefficient in the .40s) to .70 at age 13; the overall value is .60. These substantial relationships hint that Pattern Construction could align itself with either the Spatial or Nonverbal cluster for many children tested.

The Nonverbal Reasoning/Spatial distinction clearly requires more study. One study of value may be a joint factor analysis of the DAS with other intelligence measures or with its own achievement tests. These scales may split further. A lack of distinction between the spatial and nonverbal reasoning factors may also be more difficult to interpret because of Elliott's (1990a) atheoretical approach to test development. Elliott (1990a) is bucking the trend of recent intelligence test developers by not offering apriori hypotheses regarding the organization of the cluster scores. This fact can make interpretation of obtained factors less clear and result in the use of confirmatory factor analysis in an exploratory fashion (Thorndike, 1990), which makes this statistical technique less powerful. In the interim, DAS users should be wary of the separation of the nonverbal reasoning and spatial dimensions. They may not be highly interpretable as unique dimensions.

Administration and Scoring

The DAS manual is clever in that it has its own built-in stand. Whether or not the apparatus is durable remains to be seen. The DAS norm tables use a small typeface and are "busy." This is a particular problem with the achievement tests, where it seems that this typeface could lead to the incorrect calculation of scores.

There are two sets of subtests on the cognitive scales of the DAS. One set is a group of "core" subtests that are used to derive the GCA composite score and cluster scores. In addition to these there are a number of "diagnostic" subtests that are intended to measure relatively independent abilities (see Table 11.2). The core battery is made up of four to six subtests. These

subtests were selected because they were "the best measure of reasoning and conceptual abilities" (Elliott, 1990b) that were available in the test battery. They include a balance of verbal and nonverbal content and are administered in a prescribed sequence. The General Conceptual Ability (GCA) score is a summative score for the cognitive domains that is similar to what is typically called a full scale IQ or other cognitive score for other intelligence tests.

Subtest norms use a rather nonstandard metric in intellectual assessment, using t-scores with a mean of 50 and a standard deviation of 10. This metric is commonly used in personality assessment but may provide a challenge for the intelligence examiner who is used to a metric with a mean of 100 and a standard deviation of 15 or subtest scores with a mean of 10 and standard deviation of 3. The GCA score uses the more familiar metric with mean 100 and standard deviation of 15. The various diagnostic and core subtests for the DAS are shown in Table 11.2.

Like the Stanford-Binet, the administration of the DAS is somewhat flexible, allowing for out-of-level testing and selection of diagnostic subtests. This practice of using diagnostic subtests is especially appealing since administration of the core subtests is relatively brief, anywhere from 25 to 65 minutes in comparison to the typical 1-hour administration of a test such as the WISC-R. This flexibility allows the examiner the opportunity to supplement the core DAS with additional diagnostic subtests.

The DAS also takes great care to ensure that each child is administered a set of items that is most appropriate for his or her ability level. This task can be difficult to carry out with the DAS as it is with other tests (e.g., Binet-4) that use forms of adaptive testing (see Chapter 16). The DAS tries to mimic adaptive testing practices by having varied starting points for age groups and using "decision points." Children begin at a point that is designated for their age group. They respond to items until a decision point is reached. At this decision point the examiner uses

TABLE 11.2 Differential Ability Scale subtests

Ages	Cluster Subtests	Diagnostic Subtests
2-6 to 3-5	Block Building Picture Similarities Naming Vocabulary Verbal Comprehension	Recall of Digits Recognition of Pictures
3-6 to 5-11	*Nonverbal:* Copying Pattern Construction Picture Similarities *Verbal:* Naming Vocabulary Verbal Comprehension Early Number Concepts	Block Building Matching Letter- like Forms Recall of Digits Recall of Objects Recognition of Pictures
6 to 17	*Nonverbal Reasoning:* Matrices Sequential and Qualitiative Reasoning *Spatial:* Pattern Construction Recall of Designs *Verbal:* Similarities Word Definitions	Recall of Digits Recall of Objects Speed of Information Processing

the child's performance as a basis for deciding to stop testing, administer more difficult items, or return to easier items. In addition to designated stopping points, there are also "alternative" stopping points that should be used when a child is failing numerous items in succession. Some DAS subtests do not use these procedures but revert to using the traditional basal and ceiling approach. This variety of procedures is unusually burdensome to the new user.

The implementation of these various approaches to item administration also requires a record form that is very busy by comparison to tests such as the WISC-III. A raw score to ability score conversion for the subtests contributes further to the complexity of the record form. Once the DAS has been mastered, however, the wealth of information offered on the record form will likely be valued. It is also unusual to have separate record forms for the preschool and

school-age ranges. Examiners must, therefore, keep track of supplies of two record forms as opposed to one for tests such as the Binet 4. (As a professor I have enough difficulty getting the University to order one record form correctly for my classes, let alone two for the same test!) The DAS also employs many manipulatives that may require some practice to use handily.

There are three achievement tests on the DAS. These measures include arithmetic computation, spelling, and word recognition (decoding). These subtests use the convenient standard score metric where mean = 100 and SD = 15. Grade-based percentile ranks, NCEs, and grade equivalents are in addition to the usual age-based scores available. The estimated administration times for these subtests are anywhere from 15 to 25 minutes. Like the K-ABC, the DAS makes provisions for out-of-level testing. This is especially helpful for preschoolers of either very high or very low ability levels and for low-scoring children age 6 and older. Examiners may select particular subsets of items in order to get the best match between the items and the child's ability level. In addition, examiners may select a set of subtests normally given at younger or older ages.

The DAS also includes a nonverbal scale to allow for even greater flexibility in the assessment of children with limited verbal abilities, linguistic differences, hearing impairments, or other factors that the examiner feels may confound the administration of a verbal test. The nonverbal scale, however, is relatively brief, producing a slightly lower reliability coefficient than when using the core subtests.

Interpretation

The DAS manual provides interpretive information and a framework for interpretation for the composite scores and subtests. This is an admirable characteristic of the DAS manual that is all too uncommon in intelligence test manuals. Interpretive information, by comparison, is given little attention in the W-J Cognitive manual.

The DAS offers yet another classification system for intelligence test scores (see Chapter 8). This system is similar to newer systems in that it offers categories that are more descriptive than diagnostic. The classification system is as follows.

GCA and cluster scores	Category
130 and above	Very high
120–129	High
110–119	Above average
90–109	Average
80–89	Below average
70–79	Low
69 and below	Very low

The DAS manual then proposes an interpretive system including appropriate tables of statistical values. For example, values are given on the record form for determining the statistical significance of a difference between cluster scores. The values given in conjunction with the cluster scores indicate that a 9-point difference is required to have a statistically significant difference between any of the three cluster scores and the GCA. Similarly, a 16-point difference is required for a statistically significant difference between two cluster scores. Why is the value of 16 points larger than values for composite score comparisons for the WISC-III or K-ABC, for example? The DAS values are larger because they are dependent on the reliability of the obtained scores (see previous section on reliability). Since the DAS clusters are made up of only two subtests, they are slightly less reliable than Verbal or Simultaneous scores, which comprise five tests (at most ages). The DAS difference values are also adjusted for multiple comparison.

Values for determining significant strengths and weaknesses within a cluster are also given on the DAS record form. A difference of 12 points or more between the two verbal tests would be significant. Finally, values are given for comparing a child's subtest score to the mean of all core subtest scores in order to determine significant strengths and weaknesses. Although there is potential for confusion by including all of these interpretive values on the record form, some would likely argue that for the frequent DAS user the advantages of speed and convenience would outweigh the disadvantages.

Supplementary interpretive methods and associated values are offered for evaluating the child's diagnostic subtest performance. Tables of shared subtest hypotheses are also offered on pages 101 and 102 of the handbook (Elliott, 1990a). This allows the examiner to apply numerous theories to the interpretation of the DAS. For example, Elliott (1990a) shows how the K-ABC simultaneous/sequential distinction can be applied to the DAS.

The DAS also offers tables and procedures for interpreting ability/achievement discrepancies for the purposes of learning disability diagnosis. The DAS manual and handbook offer values for determining the statistical significance and frequency of a difference between the DAS ability and achievement tests. Similarly, the manual and handbook provide tables of the frequency significance and of differences in the population between a child's *expected* achievement level and his or her actual achievement. This *regression* approach is not offered by many tests but is of potential value as it is a popular method for the determination of ability/achievement discrepancies (see Chapter 14).

The DAS manual also includes some validity study research for samples of exceptional children. The mean scores for a sample of gifted children were rather low (mean GCA = 118.1). This finding may be due to regression effects since all of the children were previously identified with other tests based on high intelligence test scores (see Chapter 5). The mean GCA was 59.4 for a sample of 25 students who were previously identified as mildly retarded. A sample of 110 children who were identified by their school as learning disabled obtained a mean GCA of 89.6 with a consistent composite score pattern. There was, however, a consistent discrepancy in that DAS Achievement test scores were consistently lower than the ability scores especially in Spelling (mean = 78.2) and Word Reading (mean = 76.5). This finding suggests that the GCA/Achievement test discrepancy may be consistent with much of current practice in the assessment of learning problems.

Testimony to the thoroughness of the DAS manual is the fact that a cluster analytic study was included. This type of study is unusual in intelligence test manuals but is perhaps a harbinger of the future. The researchers selected 136 children from the DAS standardization sample who had GCA scores > 85, Word Reading scores < 85, and Word Reading scores at least 15 points below the score predicted by their GCA. These children were considered reading-disabled, and their scores were submitted to a cluster analysis. The analysis produced four clusters. Three of the clusters were marked by a

relative strength in spatial ability and one by a relative strength in verbal ability. All mean GCAs were in the middle to high 90s. Although the sample was selected on the basis of reading scores, spelling scores were also low. Spelling scores for the four clusters ranged from 77.1 to 82.1. Basic Numbers Skills scores were not as depressed, but they were consistently lower than the GCAs, with means in the high 80s to low 90s. The ranks of the achievement tests in this study are the same as those for the school-selected sample cited previously. The ability/achievement profile is striking in this study, and the cluster scores are consistent with one another.

Interpretive notes to keep in mind for the DAS might include the following.

1. Be aware of the lesser reliabilities of clusters and composites at the preschool level.

2. Definitive profiles for exceptional children are not present (and they may never be or never should be; see Chapter 14).

3. The Spatial score may be difficult to interpret given the hefty relationship between Pattern Construction and the Nonverbal Reasoning ability score.

4. The Speed of Information Processing test may be difficult to support with other test results because many tests do not include similar measures. This test may relate to scores on other tests such as the new WISC-III because of its enhanced speed component.

5. The Pattern Construction subtest may be a good analogue of Wechsler's Block Design since two studies produced correlations of .80 and .86 between these two measures (Elliott, 1990a).

Sample Case

The report in Box 11.2 is a report of a psychological evaluation in which the DAS was used as part of a comprehensive test battery. This case is

Box 11.2

Psychological report using DAS

Name: Dahlia   Birthdate: 11/16/77
Age: 12 years, 10 months   School: County Middle
Gender: Female   Grade: 7

Assessment Procedures

Differential Ability Scale (DAS)

Wechsler Intelligence Scale for Children-Revised (WISC-R)

Woodcock-Johnson Tests of Achievement-Revised (WJ-R)

Kaufman Test of Educational Achievement-Comprehensive Form (K-TEA)

Bender-Gestalt Test of Visual-Motor Development (Bender)

Achenbach Youth Self-Report (YSR)

Social Skills Rating System-Student Form (SSRS)

Sentence Completion Survey

Reynolds Adolescent Depression Scale (RADS)

Kinetic Family Drawing (KFD)

Achenbach Child Behavior Checklist (ACBCL)

Social Skills Rating System-Parent Form (SSRS)

Parenting Stress Index (PSI)

Behavior Assessment System for Children-Developmental History Questionnaire (BASC)

Achenbach Child Behavior Checklist-Teacher Report Form (ACBCL)

Reason for Referral

Dahlia was evaluated at her parents' request because of concerns about her achievement motivation, failure to complete assignments, poor organizational skills, inattention, and deterioration in grades. Parents and teachers alike feel that Dahlia is an underachiever. The parents in particular want to rule out the presence of a learning disability.

Background Information

Dahlia lives with her birth mother and father. Both her mother and father are faculty members at a local junior college. The parents could not describe any particular strife at home, with the exception of some arguments over homework.

Dahlia's mother reports a normal pregnancy and delivery. At age 3, Dahlia contracted chicken pox, which is the only childhood illness that was reported.

According to her mother, Dahlia's developmental milestones were delayed. However, once she acquired these skills, she did not differ noticeably from her peers. Her mother also reported that she was given a readiness test before entering kindergarten, on which she did very poorly. The school decided to admit Dahlia, contingent upon her performance.

Dahlia's academic performance has been inconsistent, which has been of considerable concern to her parents. They stated that after approximately 3 weeks of this school year, her attitude seemed to change for the worse and she seemed "stressed." Of all her academic subjects, Dahlia's mother is most concerned with mathematics. After an

(continued)

Box 11.2 *(continued)*

initial parent/teacher conference at the beginning of the school year, Dahlia's teachers decided to help her work on her organizational skills and completion of assignments. They incorporated a plan of initialing her assignment list to verify that Dahlia had copied her assignments.

Dahlia's most recent vision and hearing exams were given in the fall of this year. The results were negative.

Behavioral Observations

Dahlia was pleasant and well mannered during the testing session. She was reticent at first, but rapport was quickly established. A notable observation was her attempt to control her inattention and impulsivity. On one test she said aloud, "Think," which seemed to be aimed at ensuring a nonimpulsive response. On some tests she seemed disinterested (e.g., she sat far away from the test table), and on some she responded impulsively by not surveying problems before responding.

Assessment Results

Cognitive

Dahlia's performance on the intelligence measures was variable, making it difficult to summarize her performance with a single score. Her WISC-R revealed a Verbal greater than Performance profile with a difference of 19 points. Her Verbal score was a relative strength, with a score in the above-average range and her Performance in the average range.

The Differential Abilities Scales (DAS) includes subtests that assess verbal, nonverbal Reasoning, and spatial skills. Dahlia's summary score on this measure, the General Cognitive Ability composite score (GCA), was also less relevant (as were WISC-R composites) because of variability in her subtest scores. Her WISC-R and DAS scores taken together suggest that Dahlia has problems with subtests that require sustained effort and concentration. These tests happen to be on nonverbal reasoning scales of the DAS and WISC-R. These tests usually involve manual activities and good visual/spatial skills in which the child has to copy a pattern or solve figural analogies. Her performance is somewhat better, by contrast, when she solves verbal items. These items involve abilities such as defining words or giving oral descriptions of how to solve practical problems.

Academic Achievement

Dahlia's academic achievement was evaluated with the WJ-R and the KTEA. Both of these measures contain subtests similar to school-related tasks, such as reading comprehension, mathematics calculation, and spelling.

Dahlia's scores on both achievement measures are commensurate with her intellectual skills in that all of her scores hover in the average to above-average ranges. There was also no suggestive evidence of a specific learning disability or a particular academic weakness.

Visual-Motor Skills

Dahlia's visual-motor skills were evaluated by using the Bender and the Recall of Designs subtest of the DAS. These tests are similar and consist of copying several designs that are presented to the examinee.

Dahlia's performance was below average on the Bender. This low score may be due to the fact that she drew each design quickly without referring back to the stimulus. Her performance on the Recall of Designs subtest of the DAS meets or exceeds 82% of the children her age. Again, she was quick to reproduce these designs, which is consistent with previous observations of impulsive tendencies. Dahlia's scores on the Recall of Designs test may be higher because there is also a memory component for this test. Impulsive tendencies may have worked to her benefit somewhat as she responded quickly, which may have allowed her adequate access to the memory traces.

Box 11.2 *(continued)*

Social-Emotional Status

Self-Report Information

Dahlia completed the Reynolds Adolescent Depression Scale (RADS), Social Skills Rating System (SSRS), Achenbach Youth Self-Report (YSR), Kinetic Family Drawing (KFD), and the Sentence Completion Survey. There were no apparent problems indicated on these measures.

According to the SSRS, Dahlia views herself as cooperative, assertive, empathic, and as having self-control. Dahlia's responses on the YSR also support these views of herself; however, these self-reports are in direct contrast to the way her parents view her behavior. The KFD, RADS, and the Sentence Completion Survey did not indicate that there are any emotional or family problems of significance.

Parent Information

Dahlia's mother completed the Parenting Stress Index (PSI), Social Skills Rating System (SSRS), and the Achenbach Child Behavior Checklist (ACBCL). The scores obtained on the ACBCL indicated that she views Dahlia's behavior as being in the normal range. She did, however, endorse items such as inattention and disorganization that were noted in the original referral.

Teacher Information

All of Dahlia's teachers completed the Achenbach Child Behavior Checklist-Teacher's Report Form. There were no problems indicated in the areas of adaptive functioning or classroom behavior.

Summary and Conclusions

Dahlia is a 12-year-old female who was evaluated at her parents' request to determine if she has a learning or motivational problem that may explain a perceived problem with academic underachievement. Dahlia is functioning in the average to above average ranges of intelligence, with a relative weakness in attention that becomes apparent on tests that require concentrated and sustained effort and planful problem solving. This estimate is commensurate with her estimates of achievement. There is no evidence currently of a specific learning disability. Although Dahlia views herself as socially and emotionally well-adjusted, her parents are concerned about her tendencies to appear stressed and make self-deprecating statements.

All assessment results indicate that Dahlia seems unable rather than unwilling to perform up to her ability in school. This was most apparent on tasks requiring sustained attention. She has difficulty attending and poor organizational skills that she is aware of and tries to control occasionally through self-talk. No evidence of motor hyperactivity is present.

Diagnosis

Dahlia's longstanding symptoms of inattention and impulsivity without motor hyperactivity are consistent with the now out-of-date diagnosis of Attention Deficit Disorder without Hyperactivity. The closest terminology from *DSM III-R* is Attention Deficit Undifferentiated. Given the rarity of this diagnosis, it is best considered as provisional until it is clarified during the course of therapeutic intervention.

Recommendations

1. Consultation should be sought by the district's school psychologist in order to enhance Dahlia's motivation and self-control at school.

2. Psychotherapy aimed at improving self-control and organizational skills as well as assistance in understanding and coping with her problems should be initiated.

3. Dahlia's parents should receive some professional consultation in order to help them manage Dahlia's behavior.

4. Dahlia should be reevaluated a few months after the initiation of treatment to assess her progress.

(continued)

Box 11.2 *(continued)*

Psychometric Summary Wechsler Intelligence Scale for Children-Revised (WISC-R)

COMPOSITE SCORES	STANDARD SCORES	PR
Full Scale	111	77
Verbal Scale	119	90
Performance Scale	100	50

SUBTESTS	SCALED SCORES
Verbal	
Information	14
Similarities	11
Arithmetic	14
Vocabulary	9
Comprehension	18
Digit Span	6
Performance	
Picture Completion	11
Picture Arrangement	15
Block Design	8
Object Assembly	6
Coding	10
Mazes	13

Differential Ability Scales (DAS)

SUBTESTS	T-SCORE	PR
Recall of Designs	59	82
Word Definitions	50	50
Pattern Construction	50	69
Matrices	37	10
Similarities	56	73
Sequential & Quantitative Reasoning	51	54

Box 11.2 *(continued)*

COMPOSITE SCORES	STANDARD SCORES	PR
Verbal	104	61
Nonverbal Reasoning	89	23
Spatial	111	77
General Cognitive Ability	102	55

Kaufman Test of Educational Achievement (K-TEA)

COMPOSITE SCORES	STANDARD SCORES	PR
Reading	105	63
Mathematics	120	91
Battery	112	79
Subtests		
Mathematics Applications	130	98
Reading Decoding	110	75
Spelling	102	55
Reading Comprehension	100	50
Mathematics Computation	107	68

Woodcock-Johnson Psychoeducational Battery (WJ-R)

COMPOSITE SCORES	STANDARD SCORES	PR
Broad Reading	111	77
Broad Math	111	77
Broad Written Language	100	50
Skills	108	70
Subtests		
Letter-Word Identification	118	88
Passage Comprehension	100	50
Calculation	103	59
Applied Problems	115	84
Dictation	90	25
Writing Samples	125	95

(continued)

Box 11.2 *(continued)*

Bender-Gestalt Test of Visual-Motor Development (Bender)

Score = 2   Age equivalent 9:0 to 9:11

Reynolds Adolescent Depression Scale (RADS)

SCALE	RAW SCORE	PR
Depression	36	4

Social Skills Rating System-Student Form

SCALE	STANDARD SCORE	PR
Social Skills	108	70

Achenbach Youth Self-Report (YSR)

	T-SCORE
Depressed	55
Unpopular	55
Somatic Complaints	55
Self-Destructive	55
Thought Disturbances	55
Delinquent	55
Aggressive	55
Sum	**33**
Activities	48
Social	55
Total Competence	**52**

Parenting Stress Index (PSI)

	PR
Child Domain Score	**78**
Adaptability	17
Acceptability	12
Demandingness	19
Mood	3
Distractibility/Hyperactivity	20
Reinforces Parent	7

Box 11.2 *(continued)*

Parent Domain Score	**90**
Depression	12
Attachment	11
Restriction of Roles	5
Sense of Competence	25
Social Isolation	10
Relation with spouse	10
Parent Health	10
Total Stress Score	5

Social Skills Rating System-Parent Form

	STANDARD SCORES	PR
Social Skills	120	91
Problem Behaviors	92	30

Achenbach Child Behavior Checklist-Parent Form (ACBCL)

	T-SCORE
Somatic Complaint	63
Schizoid	56
Uncommunicative	61
Immature	55
Obsessive-Compulsive	56
Hostility-Withdrawal	62
Delinquent	61
Aggressive	60
Hyperactive	65
Sum	**61**
Activities	55
Social	38
School	43
Total	45

(continued)

Box 11.2 *(continued)*

Child Behavior Checklist-Teacher Report Form

T-SCORES

	Teacher:	1	2	3	4
Adaptive Functioning					
School Performance	60	41	51	51	51
Working Hard	37	37	37	47	47
Behaving Appropriately	54	51	51	51	54
Learning	34	53	40	40	**
Happy	**	32	32	**	**
Behavior Problems					
Social Withdrawal	61	59	65	61	59
Anxious	55	55	58	55	55
Unpopular	55	63	55	55	55
Obsessive-Compulsive	60	55	63	60	56
Immature	62	55	62	62	62
Self-Destructive	55	59	55	55	55
Hyperactive	62	60	64	60	60
Aggressive	55	55	55	55	55

**Indicates too many responses omitted to arrive at a score.

interesting in that the DAS and WISC-R scores do not correspond closely with one another.

Apriori hypotheses Dahlia's background and test behavior may be described as erratic. She has not failed a grade, been retained, or placed in special education, and yet her academic performance has been inconsistent. Her test behavior was similarly inconsistent, suggesting that she may achieve high scores on some tests and low scores on others. Given her lack of risk factors an apriori hypothesis of average intelligence test scores seems warranted. Given the lack of evidence of specific cognitive strengths or weaknesses no additional apriori hypotheses can be made.

Dahlia's WISC-R shows a verbal strength and the DAS does not. The WISC-R and DAS scores were also somewhat erratic. On the DAS, for example, there is a relative nonverbal reason-

ing weakness, but it occurs as a result of one test (Matrices) and the other nonverbal test, Sequential and Quantitative Reasoning, is average. Hence, several of Dahlia's composite scores are heterogeneous. Even scores that typically correlate highly, namely Block Design and Pattern Construction, are inconsistent. What's wrong here? I suspect that the answer lies in Dahlia's behavior. She is inattentive and disorganized, and her motivation wavers. The report does not make a great deal of her intelligence test profile because it seems secondary to social/emotional/behavioral issues *and* tainted by them.

Summary

The DAS is yet another promising intelligence test instrument. There is every indication that the developers of the DAS erred in the direction of quality at every turn. The manual is extraordinarily thorough, the psychometric properties are strong, and the test materials are of high quality. This test also deserves more research and clinical trials. The extended range of scores to a standard score of 25 makes this an especially appealing test to those who are trying to differentiate among levels of mental retardation. Other unique features include the Nonverbal scale and provisions for out-of-level testing. Early indications are that there is great potential here. The learning curve for administration and scoring may be quite steep, but for some if not many clinicians the effort may be well worth it.

CONCLUSIONS

The W-J and DAS make unique contributions to the field of intellectual assessment. It was not that long ago that the Wechsler and Binet series completely dominated intellectual assessment practice. With these new entries, examiners have even more options for meeting children's specialized needs. It will take some time to gather data and experience with these new measures. If they hold up to their initial promise they will demonstrate further the necessity of being familiar with numerous intelligence tests.

CHAPTER SUMMARY

1. The W-J Cognitive is designed for ages 2 to 90+ and is administered in an easel format. The test battery consists of 21 subtests, only 7 of which are considered as part of the standard battery.

2. The W-J was normed on 6,359 cases using a stratified sampling procedure to match U.S. Census Bureau statistics.

3. The W-J concurrent validity coefficients show some overlap with existing measures, but the magnitude of the correlations is somewhat less than one would expect for a multisubtest measure of intelligence.

4. Reschly (1990) and Ysseldyke (1990) are impressed by the W-J factor analytic data.

5. One caveat to consider when interpreting W-J scores is the relatively small number of items per subtest, which may compromise the reliability and validity of scores for an inattentive child.

6. The DAS is a comprehensive battery of cognitive and achievement tests that are designed for children and adolescents between the ages of 2 1/2 and 17 years.

7. The DAS borrows from numerous theorists and research findings.

8. There are two sets of subtests on the cognitive scales of the DAS. One set is a group of "core" subtests that are used to derive the GCA composite score. In addition to these there are a number of "diagnostic" subtests that are intended to measure relatively independent abilities.

9. There are three achievement tests on the DAS. These include arithmetic computation, spelling, and word recognition (decoding).

10. The DAS also includes a Nonverbal scale to allow for even greater flexibility in the assessment of children.

11. The DAS was normed on a representative national sample of 3,475 children tested between 1987 and 1989.

12. Several correlational studies show good evidence of concurrent validity for the DAS.

13. The DAS GCA should not be used for predicting school achievement if the DAS achievement test scores are available.

14. The learning curve for DAS administration and scoring may be steep.

Other Measures of Intelligence

CHAPTER QUESTIONS

What are some common problems with "nonverbal measures"?

How will the computer affect intelligence test development?

The variety of intelligence tests currently available is befuddling. Along with newer comprehensive individually administered tests, there are brief measures, nonverbal tests, group tests, and adaptations for various linguistic groups. Since this book clearly emphasizes comprehensive individually administered measures, these will be the focus of the chapter.

This discussion may give the impression of being a "grab bag" of lesser measures of intelligence. This is not the case. There are many good measures of intelligence available that are not featured in previous chapters for a variety of reasons. One reason is that some tests are so new that little research and experience are available for them. Tests of this variety include the

Differential Ability Scales (Elliott, 1990a) and the Woodcock-Johnson Psycho-Educational Battery-Revised (Woodcock & Johnson, 1989) Tests of Cognitive Ability, which were considered in the previous chapter.

Other tests are included here because they may be viewed as ancillary measures, or screeners, and not comprehensive test batteries. The Peabody Picture Vocabulary Test-Revised (PPVT-R) is a good example of such a measure. Others are also discussed. The tests described in this chapter do vary in quality and popularity, and these characteristics will be described. Again, *the fact that a test does not have its own chapter is not an indication that it is not recommended for use.*

NONVERBAL INTELLIGENCE TESTS

There is a long history, especially in the United States, of the use of nonverbal intelligence tests.

The need for nonverbal measures of the intelligence construct has been present since the early days of World War I (see Chapter 1). In fact, Wechsler (1939) clearly recognized this need for a nonverbal measure by including the Performance scale as part of his original test battery. Over the past 70 years the assessment of nonverbal intelligence has continued to evolve. Now there are numerous instruments designed specifically to be nonverbal measures of intelligence.

Prior to the discussion of individual tests, some conceptual issues regarding nonverbal intelligence testing require consideration. An important first question is, what is nonverbal intelligence? Some suggest (Naglieri & Prewett, 1990) that "nonverbal intelligence tests are those that are designed to measure a theoretical construct called nonverbal intelligence" (p. 348). Others have argued that there is no such construct as nonverbal intelligence (Glaub & Kamphaus, 1991). They have proposed that the use of the word "nonverbal" simply describes a methodology for accessing the same general intelligence that has always been of interest to psychologists since the early part of the century. This distinction may seem to be minor, but it is an important one that all psychologists should consider when they use these tests. At this point it is probably more reasonable to consider nonverbal intelligence tests as simply a clever and unusual means for assessing the same general intelligence. Currently there are no detailed and compelling theories of a separate nonverbal intelligence, and most theorists who discuss the term do so similarly to Wechsler (1974), who describes nonverbal measures as simply being different means for uncovering the underlying general intelligence.

The development of nonverbal scales of intelligence seems to have come full circle since the time of Wechsler. Wechsler included the more nonverbal Performance scale as a integral part of his intellectual assessment battery. Subsequent to this development, some authors prepared nonverbal intelligence tests that were designed exclusively as nonverbal measures. These include tests such as the Hiskey-Nebraska Tests of Learning Aptitude and the Leiter International Performance Scale. Now intelligence test developers are reverting back to the practice of Wechsler. Many test batteries offer nonverbal intelligence tests or scales as supplemental scales or specialized short forms. Tests of this variety are multipurpose test batteries such as the K-ABC and the Differential Ability Scales. This chapter will also discuss nonverbal measures that are part of other comprehensive measures.

A final important point to consider before discussion of specific tests is the need for nonverbal intelligence tests. More comprehensive measures such as the WISC were not deemed ideal for use with a variety of populations in which language/hearing variables loom as confounds. The WISC-III oral instructions to examinees, for example, are exceedingly wordy for tests such as Coding. Popular nonverbal (or perhaps a better term is "less verbal") tests such as the Hiskey-Nebraska and the Leiter include nonverbal instructions and use pantomime as part of the administration process. This method allows these measures to be used with hearing-impaired children with a greater degree of confidence.

Nonverbal intelligence measures later become popular for use with children who do not speak English (the most popular language used by test developers). While English is the dominant language in the United States, for example, the United States continues to be a multilingual society. Just as the Army Beta was used to assess the intelligence of waves of immigrants after World War I, so too modern nonverbal tests of intelligence are attractive to psychologists who work in areas of the United States with large non–English-speaking populations.

Nonverbal measures can also be helpful for assessing children with significant speech impairments. A child or adolescent who has lost speech due to a head injury may be a good candidate for the use of nonverbal measures of intelligence. These three audiences—non-English-speaking, hearing-impaired, and speech-impaired children—provide a healthy demand for the use of nonverbal measures.

There is also a cadre of nonverbal intelligence assessment screeners. Some of the more well-known names here are the Raven Progressive Matrices, Test of Nonverbal Intelligence-2 and the Columbia Mental Maturity Scale. Some instruments will be discussed here. Detailed information on these brief measures can be found in Naglieri and Prewett (1990).

Hiskey-Nebraska Tests of Learning Aptitude (HNTLA or Hiskey)

The Hiskey was designed specifically to assess the cognitive skills of deaf children and adolescents (Hiskey, 1966). The Hiskey-Nebraska age range extends from 2½ years through 17½ years. This measure suggests the use of pantomimed instructions for hearing-impaired individuals. There are five subtests that are administered to ages 3 to 10 and four subtests that are specific to ages 11 to 17. There are three subtests on the Hiskey that extend across all age ranges. Administration of the Hiskey takes approximately 45–50 minutes for an experienced examiner.

Item Selection

The procedures used for the selection of items were specified prior to test development and explicitly stated. Item selection criteria included:

1. Tasks should be similar to those that young children encounter in school.

2. The item had to be adaptable for use in a nonverbal test.

3. The item had to accommodate presentation of directions through simple pantomime.

4. The item had to be one that in previous research had been shown to yield high cor-

relations with acceptable criteria of intelligence.

5. The item had to be capable of being constructed and presented in such a way that made the scoring objective and easily done.

6. The item had to be appealing and attractive to children.

7. The item should be capable of being scored without the score being based on time.

8. The difficulty of the item should appear to be within the age range of the standardization group.

9. The item had to be likely to show high discriminative capacity.

The seventh point about time is an interesting one. This criterion makes the Hiskey more of a power test than the WISC-III. It is in contrast to tests such as Object Assembly, where the only means of obtaining a high score is through quick performance. Hiskey clearly differentiated his test development philosophy from Wechsler on this point. The Hiskey does, however, use "tried and true" items. No attempts were made to develop novel item types. The use of novel items would not have been consistent with item specification #4. One weakness of the Hiskey may be a lack of creativity in item development.

The Hiskey is designed to be a broad-based measure of intellectual skills. For this reason the test consists of a number of subtests as opposed to using only one or two item formats to assess a child's intelligence. In this way the Hiskey is analogous to the WISC-III, as numerous types of "languages" may be used by the child or adolescent to express his or her intelligence.

The subtests of the Hiskey are:

1. Bead Patterns (ages 3–10)

2. Memory for Color (ages 3–10)

3. Picture Identification (ages 3–10)

4. Picture Association (ages 3–10)

5. Paper Folding (ages 3–10)

6. Visual Attention Span (all ages)

7. Block Patterns (all ages)

8. Completion of Drawings (all ages)

9. Memory for Digits (ages 11 and above)

10. Puzzle Blocks (ages 11 and above)

11. Picture Analogy (ages 11 and above)

12. Spatial Reasoning (ages 11 and above)

Standardization

The Hiskey was standardized on 1,079 deaf children and 1,074 hearing children between the ages of 2½ years and 17½ years. Specific information on the standardization sample is lacking. An attempt was made to stratify the hearing sample based on the 1960 U.S. Census data using parental occupation as a measure of SES. Beyond that, there is little evidence that systematic efforts were made to match Census Bureau or other statistics for gender, type or severity of hearing impairment, geographic region, or ethnic group or race. The normative sample of the Hiskey is lacking by modern standards.

The scaling of the Hiskey is consistent with the early Binet tradition. Early versions of the Binet emphasized the interpretation of mental ages (or learning ages for hearing-impaired children) for interpretive purposes. Hiskey (1966) argued that mental ages were more readily understood and interpreted than standard scores or percentile ranks. This statement was perhaps true back in the 1960s, as the Binet at that time also emphasized mental ages in computing scores.

Mental ages are derived for each of the Hiskey subtests and a median mental age is computed as an overall rating of intelligence. This median age rating can then be converted to a deviation IQ (DIQ), which uses the traditional Binet metric of a mean of 100 and standard deviation of 16. The computation of scores is slightly different when the deaf norms are used. For the deaf norms the median learning age can be converted to a learning quotient (LQ) using the old Ratio IQ approach, the forerunner of modern standard scores (see Chapter 5). The formula for computing an LQ is LQ = LA/CA × 100. As is apparent, the Hiskey scaling technology is also far behind current standards.

Reliability

Split-half reliability coefficients are reported in the Hiskey manual with the use of the Spearman-Brown correction formula (Hiskey, 1966). Split-half internal consistency coefficients are generally high. The lowest one reported for the composite score is .90. Test-retest data for the Hiskey is not reported in the manual nor is information on standard errors of measurement or individual subtest reliability. One study that evaluated the use of the Hiskey for 41 hearing-impaired children and adolescents produced a test-retest coefficient for the composite score of .79 after a 1-year interval (Watson, 1983).

Validity

The manual produces strong evidence of concurrent validity for the Hiskey for hearing children. The 1966 manual reports a correlation of .82 with the 1949 WISC and .86 for younger children and .78 for older children with Form LM, the 1960 edition of the Stanford-Binet. Further information on validity is not provided in the manual. A recent study by Phelps and Branyan (1988) with 31 hearing-impaired children ages 6 through 10 years yielded LQ correlations of .66 with the WISC-R Performance score, .57 with the K-ABC Nonverbal scale, and .67 with the Leiter. An investigation by Watson and Goldgar (1985) with 71 hearing-impaired children ages 5 through 18 yielded a correlation of .85 between the LQ and the WISC-R Full Scale. The Hiskey yielded a greater number of extreme scores (scores < 70 and > 119), which caused Watson and Goldgar to advise cautious use of the Hiskey.

Kennedy and Hiltonsmith (1988) correlated the Hiskey with the K-ABC Nonverbal scale and the Pictorial Test of Intelligence. The Hiskey correlation with the K-ABC was .72 and with the PTI .80. The Hiskey yielded 10 scores above a standard score of 116. The K-ABC yielded the lowest scores, but the authors stated that this result is to be expected because of the out-of-date (and therefore softer) Hiskey and PTI norms. An independent factor analytic investigation by Bolton (1978) found that the factor structures of the Hiskey differed for hearing and deaf children for the 3–10-year-old age group. Specifically, the Memory for Colors and Block Pattern subtest loaded on different factors for the hearing and deaf children. Unfortunately, the Hiskey does not seem to be the recipient of much recent research interest.

Summary

The Hiskey-Nebraska Test of Learning Aptitude is a multisubtest comprehensive intellectual assessment battery designed specifically for hearing-impaired children and adolescents between the ages of 2½ and 17½ years. The Hiskey is primarily an adaptation of earlier editions of the Stanford-Binet. In fact, some of the items can be traced directly to the Binet scales. The Hiskey was the first of its genre in that it was specifically defined for the deaf population, making it particularly attractive for use with this group of children. In many ways, however, the Hiskey is also wedded to earlier intelligence tests, and to earlier Stanford-Binet assessment technology in particular. The standardization and scaling procedures used by the Hiskey would not be acceptable today. The manual may have been adequately prepared for the 1960s, but it is in dire need of revision in order to meet modern standards of assessment practice. For all practical purposes, in light of current developments in nonverbal intellectual assessment the Hiskey is psychometrically inadequate and cannot be recommended for use. This is not to say that the test battery does not have potential. A clever redevelopment of the earlier instrument may provide yet another desirable alternative for the assessment of hearing-impaired children, a group that has traditionally challenged the assessment skills of clinicians.

Leiter International Performance Scale (Leiter)

The Leiter (Leiter, 1948) is one of the most venerable of nonverbal intelligence tests. This measure was most recently revised in 1979. While the Leiter retains many characteristics of the older Binet scales such as using mental ages as an integral aspect of the scoring process, its administration and item types are relatively novel.

The Leiter is designed to be administered with as few verbal instructions as possible. It can be administered effectively in pantomine. Essentially, most of the items are matching. This test is relatively heavy and cumbersome since most of the items involve the use of square wooden blocks that have pictures of a shape, design, color, or figure on them. Each test item on the Leiter consists of a set of four to eight blocks and a paper strip corresponding to the number of stimuli in the item. Each stimulus on the paper strip is related in some way, either spatially or analogically, to one of the blocks. The paper strip is situated on a wooden frame containing eight notches where each stimulus is aligned with a particular notch. The child or adolescent then places the block corresponding to the stimulus in the appropriate notch on the wooden frame. The test is designed for ages 2 through 18.

In addition to requiring little if any verbalization, the Leiter is designed to require little fine motor skill, unlike more complex puzzle solving, block building, or block design types of tests. Similar item types are solved on the Leiter by simply picking up and placing individual blocks in the wooden frame.

Standardization

Standardization is one of the most glaring deficiencies in the Leiter in that the standardization sample is not described in the test manual. One can say with certainty, however, that its standardization sample is outdated and that it predates 1948. The age of the sample makes the norm reference scores on the Leiter highly suspect and likely to produce higher scores than a more modern test. The Leiter is scored in much the same way as were earlier versions of the Binet. A child's total raw score is converted to a mental age that is then entered into a table in the Leiter manual for conversion to a Ratio IQ score. Leiter (1979), however, argued that the scale tended to score too low and created a revised scoring procedure whereby 5 points are added to the IQ score and the mental age is adjusted to account for this problem.

Reliability

As with other psychometric properties, reliability data are conspicuously lacking from the manual. A test-retest study by Weiner (1971) found the reliability coefficient of .64 with a retest interval of 6 months and .63 after a 2-year test-retest interval with the same sample of preschool handicapped children.

Validity

The correlations between the Leiter and intelligence scales such as the Stanford-Binet intelligence scale Form LM are consistently high. In a review of the literature, Ratcliffe and Ratcliffe (1979) found a median correlation of .77 for 13 concurrent validity investigations. The greater controversy regarding the concurrent validity of the Leiter with tests such as the WISC-R and the Stanford-Binet is the direction of mean score differences. Naglieri and Prewett (1990) found striking inconsistencies here in the research literature, with a number of studies reporting that the Leiter produced significantly lower scores than other intelligence measures and yet other studies drawing the opposite conclusion. The Leiter has not been the beneficiary of a lengthy research effort. Resolution of this difference may not be forthcoming.

Summary

While the Leiter has been used by many professionals in the assessment of mentally retarded individuals and hearing-impaired children, its psychometric properties are so lacking in comparison to more modern instruments that the Leiter is of more historical than clinical value.

WISC Performance Scale

The WISC-R Performance Scale has traditionally been one of the most popular tests for use in the assessment of hearing-impaired children (Levine, 1974). This fact is congruent with the original design of the Wechsler series. It appears that Wechsler was well aware of the fact that an intelligence test had to provide flexible adminstration options especially in assessing individuals in a multicultural society. According to Sullivan and Burley (1990), "the WISC-R performance scale is an excellent test for use with school-aged hearing impaired children" (p. 784).

It is typically recommended that six or seven subtests of the Performance scale be administered when assessing a hearing-impaired child. Hearing-impaired children seem to have particular difficulty with the Picture Arrangement and Coding subtests. This fact is not suprising given the lengthy oral instructions on these tests, particularly those on Coding, which require considerable comprehension. The problem of verbal comprehension may also interfere with valid administration of the WISC-III Symbol Search test. It has been recommended that if these tests seem inappropriate, the Performance score may be prorated so that the Performance scale is effectively serving as a four-subtest nonverbal short form of the WISC (Sullivan & Burley, 1990).

Standardization

Typically the regular WISC norms are used for computing the Performance IQ when the Performance scale is used as a nonverbal test of intelligence. Alternatively, a nonrepresentative but large sample of norms collected for hearing-impaired children is available for the WISC-R and has been used (Anderson & Sisco, 1977).

The utility of these hearing-impaired norms, however, has been questioned (see Chapter 14 on testing children with hearing impairments) and their practical utility not clarified (Sullivan & Burley, 1990).

Reliability and Validity

Separate validity evidence for the use of the WISC-R for hearing-impaired children has typically been supportive. The mean WISC-R Performance score for hearing-impaired children, however, is somewhat lower than for the standardization sample (standard score = 95). This mean is also slightly lower than, for example, the average K-ABC Nonverbal scale for hearing impaired children (median = 98). The more substantial level of verbal comprehension that is required on the part of the child on tests such as Coding may account for this small difference (Sullivan & Burley, 1990).

The only study available for the WISC-III produced higher PIQ scores (Wechsler, 1991). This relatively small sample of 30 children with severe and profound hearing impairments achieved a Verbal score of 81.1, Performance score of 105.8, and Full Scale of 92.2. The Coding and Symbol Search subtests yielded lower scores than many of the Performance subtests, resulting in a Perceptual Organization Index of 106.0 and Processing Speed Index of 101.4. It remains to be seen whether or not these data will be replicated.

Summary

The WISC-III Performance Scale is likely to continue to be a popular nonverbal test of intelligence. One caution is that the Performance subtests seem to require substantially more verbalization on the part of the examiner and verbal comprehension on the part of the child than some nonverbal measures (e.g., K-ABC).

K-ABC Nonverbal Scale

Analogous to the inclusion of the Performance scale in the Wechsler series, the Kaufmans (Kaufman & Kaufman, 1983b) included a Nonverbal scale as part of the K-ABC development process. The K-ABC Nonverbal Scale is a subset of K-ABC Mental Processing subtests that spans the ages of 4 to 12 1/2 years. It is considered a "special short form of the mental processing composite, one that correlates quite well with this total score" (Kaufman & Kaufman, 1983b, p. 35). The test is designed for use with "deaf, hearing-impaired, speech- or language-disordered, autistic, and non–English-speaking children" (Kaufman & Kaufman, 1983b, p. 35).

The subtests comprising the K-ABC Nonverbal Scale include Face Recognition (age 4 only), Hand Movements, Triangles, Matrix Analogies, Spatial Memory, and Photo Series (ages 6 and up only).

Given that the K-ABC instructions require little oral expression on the part of the examiner and verbal comprehension on the part of the child, this test can be adminstered readily using pantomime and gestures. Several studies (Porter & Kirby, 1986; Ulissi, Brice, & Gibbons, 1985) have shown no specific problems with the administration of the Nonverbal scale to hearing-impaired children.

Standardization

The K-ABC Nonverbal Scale norms are derived from the same national standardization sample that was selected to meet 1980 U.S. Census data (see Chapter 9). The featured score for the K-ABC Nonverbal scale is a composite with the mean of 100 and standard deviation of 15. Other derived scores for the Nonverbal scale such as percentile ranks are also included as part of the regular K-ABC manuals and software.

Reliability

Internal consistency coefficients for the K-ABC Nonverbal Scale are strong, ranging from a .87 coefficient for 4-year-olds to a .94 for a number of the older age groups. The average coefficient for school-age children is .93. One study of the test-retest reliability of the Nonverbal scale reported a coefficient of .87 (Kaufman & Kaufman, 1983c).

Validity

There is substantial evidence from the K-ABC *Interpretive Manual* (Kaufman & Kaufman, 1983c) that the Nonverbal scale correlates highly with the Mental Processing composite of the K-ABC. This finding holds true even when the coefficients are corrected for spurious overlap. Correlations between the Nonverbal short form and the Mental Processing composite range from .88 at age 4 to .94 at several of the older age groups. Studies by Ulissi, Brice, and Gibbons (1985), Ham (1985), and Porter and Kirby (1986) all yielded significant correlations (typically in the .60s and above) between the K-ABC and other nonverbal intelligence measures. These three investigations also yielded mean K-ABC Nonverbal composites for hearing-impaired children ranging from 97 to 101, suggesting that the normal distribution of intelligence for hearing-impaired children is strikingly similar to that of the population at large when using the K-ABC Nonverbal Scale. Although the samples for these studies were relatively small, the trend is clear. Hearing-impaired children have relatively normal intelligence test scores as assessed by the K-ABC Nonverbal scale.

The Porter and Kirby (1986) study also tested the utility of pantomimed versus sign language administrations of the K-ABC Nonverbal Scale. The means for the pantomimed and sign language administration groups were 98.8 and 96.8 respectively. For this relatively small sample this difference was not statistically significant. These results argue for administering the K-ABC Nonverbal Scale as it was originally intended, in pantomime.

Summary

The K-ABC Nonverbal Scale carries on the tradition of using portions of a larger intelligence test battery as a nonverbal intelligence measure. The K-ABC Nonverbal Scale holds promise as a nonverbal intelligence measure for a variety of populations (Kamphaus & Reynolds, 1987).

Differential Ability Scales Nonverbal Scale

The DAS takes a similar route to the K-ABC by including a Nonverbal scale as part of a larger test battery. The rationale for use of the DAS Nonverbal Scale is given in the following quote:

> *If the examiner judges that subtests involving verbal presentation or response may not be reliable and valid measures of a particular child's ability, a briefer battery may be administered in order to obtain a special nonverbal composite score in place of the GCA score. . . . [S]by preschoolers, those reluctant to talk to an unfamiliar adult, children with delayed language or speech problems, elective mutes, children from culturally different backgrounds, children whose primary language is not English, and children with middle ear infections or suspected hearing loss frequently are referred for assessment. Directions for the subtest of the special nonverbal scale may be conveyed through gestures, and the child's responses require only pointing, drawing, or manipulation of objects. (Elliott, Guiton, & Daniel, 1990, p. 17)*

The DAS subtests that can be used to compute a Nonverbal composite at each age include the following:

Ages 2.6 through 4.11 – Block Building, Picture Similarities

Ages 3.6 through 7.11 – Pattern Construction, Copying, Picture Similarities (i.e., the Nonverbal cluster)

Ages 5.0 through 17.11 – Pattern Construction, Recall of Designs, Matrices, Sequential and Quantitative Reasoning

Standardization

The norms for the Special Nonverbal Composite (SNV) are derived from the regular DAS norming program. The Nonverbal Composite yields a standard score with a mean of 100 and standard deviation of 15. (See the earlier parts of this chapter for a detailed description of the DAS normative sample and the various scores available for the DAS.)

Reliability and Validity

Special Nonverbal Composite score reliabilities are generally high. The mean Nonverbal Composite reliability coefficient for ages 3.6 through 5.11 is .89; for ages 6 through 17 the mean is .94. The reliability of the two-subtest composite for ages 2.6 through 4.11 is somewhat lower, averaging .81. The SNV is a high correlate of the GCA. Correlations between the SNV and GCA scores at their lowest are .85 for ages 2.6 through 3.5 and .88 for ages 3.6 through 5.11, suggesting good concurrent validity for the SNV score (Elliott, 1990a). Separate validity evidence for the Special Nonverbal Composite particularly for hearing-impaired or non–English-speaking children is currently lacking.

Summary

As a nonverbal scale of intelligence, the special Nonverbal scale of the DAS is relatively brief at some ages, yet it remains as a multisubtest battery with a variety of items types that can be used for assessing intelligence while limiting the confounding effects of verbal and hearing issues. Early reliability studies of this specialized composite are favorable. Given the recency of the publication of the DAS, it is not suprising that validity evidence is lacking. Considering the norming and reliability properties of the DAS Nonverbal Scale, this scale requires further study and consideration for at least trial clinical use. At this point the DAS Nonverbal Scale shows promise as another useful alternative in the area of nonverbal intellectual assessment.

Columbia Mental Maturity Scale

The Columbia Mental Maturity Scale (Burgmeister, Blum, & Lorge, 1972) is designed to assess the "general reasoning ability" of children from 3½ to 9 years 11 months of age. The test is designed for children who may have communication or motor problems, including those with problems such as mental retardation, hearing loss, speech impairment, or cerebral palsy. The test does not require the child to read or speak English. The Columbia consists of 92 items, each presented on cards with three to five drawings per card. These items are divided among eight levels where the child is primarily administered items at a level appropriate for his or her chronological age. However, additional levels of items may be administered depending upon the child's score on the first level administered. The stimulus cards used show drawings and the child is asked which drawing does not belong in the set. The objects used on the cards are intended to be familiar to American children.

The feature score of the Columbia is an age deviation score (ADS). The ADS is a standard score with mean of 100 and standard deviation of 16. ADS scores can be converted to percentile ranks and stanines. The Columbia also offers a Maturity Index (MI). This is in effect an age equivalent developmental norm.

Standardization

The Columbia standardization sample is now somewhat dated since it was collected in the late 1960s and early 1970s and based on 1960's U.S. Census data. At the time the standardization sample was first-rate, consisting of 2,600 children including 200 children in each age group of the Columbia. The sample was stratified based on geographic region, race, sex, and parental occupation.

Reliability

Considering that this is a single-subtest measure, reliability estimates for the Columbia are quite good. Split-half reliability coefficients are high for most age groups, ranging from .85 to .91. They are more consistently in the mid .80s range between the ages of 6 and 9 years. Test-retest reliability coefficients are slightly lower, ranging from .84 at age 5 and 6 to .86 at age 4.

Validity

The Columbia depends primarily on correlations with other tests as evidence of its validity. An extensive study in the manual showing correlations between the Columbia and the 1964 edition of the Stanford Achievement Test showed moderate correlations between the two batteries. Most of these correlations were in the .40s, .50s, and .60s. A study comparing the Columbia and the Stanford-Binet Intelligence Scale Form LM for a sample of 52 preschool and first-grade pupils yielded a coefficient of .84.

Summary

The Columbia is a rather unique single-subtest measure of "reasoning ability" for children of ages 3½ to 9 years of age. At the time of its publication in 1972 it exceeded standards of psychometric quality for clinical instruments. Now, however, the Columbia is thoroughly in need of revision. It would be especially desirable to have a revised standardization sample.

Raven's Progressive Matrices

As the name implies, the Raven's is composed of a set of figural matrices that can be used as a measure of general intelligence. Again, given the minimal language involvement and requirement of this item type, this test is particularly suited to assessing the intelligence of individuals with hearing impairments and language disabilities and children whose native language is not English.

The two most popular matrices are the Standard and the Coloured. The Coloured Progressive Matrices includes 30 items and the Standard Progressive Matrices contain 60 items. Each item consists of 2×2 or 3×3 figural matrices presented in a multiple-choice format where the child has to identify the missing element.

The Standard and Coloured matrices raw scores can be converted to percentile ranks.

These percentile conversions are available for ages 6½ to 16½. Percentile ranks can also be converted to other derived scores such as standard scores. This conversion, however, is not very effective at the tails of the distribution. The conversion of percentile ranks to standard scores will not yield a very wide range of standard score below 70 and above 130.

Standardization

Both the Standard and Coloured Progressive Matrices were recently renormed in the United States (Raven, 1986). This renorming, however, was somewhat unusual in that the 1986 publication does not describe a set of national norms for the Raven but rather a collection of norm tables from 10 local norming investigations conducted in various areas of the United States. There was an attempt to provide combined norms for the United States for the Standard and Coloured matrices. However, descriptions of how these norms were derived, including descriptions of socioeconomic status, geographic, race, age, gender, and other representations of the samples, are not included in the manual. The undetailed description given by Raven (1986) leads one to believe that these were more or less "convenience" samples. Certainly, more detail is needed on the description of these samples to help clinicians understand the value of using these norm tables.

Reliability

Reliability data are not presented in the 1986 Raven manual. Given the number of the items, one would be surprised to see poor reliability coefficients. However, some data should certainly be provided.

Validity

Validity evidence for the Raven's extends primarily from correlational studies with other tests. A correlational study with the California Achievement Test yielded a coefficient of .76

with the Standard Progressive Matrices. A correlation of .69 was found with the Standard matrices and WISC-R Full Scale score and .61 between the Coloured matrices and WISC-R Full Scale score for a sample of Mexican-American students.

Summary

On the face of it, the Raven's seems to be a reasonable though older member of the intelligence screening market. The disappointing aspect of the Raven's Standard and Coloured matrices is that, despite their long history, they have not been the beneficiary of continuing sophisticated psychometric development. The 1986 "Compendium of Local Norms" is an example of this problem. These norms may be well collected and adequate for users of the Raven's. However, there is not enough information provided to determine whether or not this is the case. Given the paucity of technical information, the Raven's should likely be considered as a research instrument, an area in which it has enjoyed a great deal of historical popularity. This status should change, however, once the psychometric properties and/or information on the Raven's become more compelling.

Matrix Analogies Test

Yet another variation on the Raven's theme is this modern version of a figural matrices test by Naglieri (1985). There are two forms of the Matrix Analogies Test, a group administered short form (MAT-SF) consisting of 34 multiple-choice items and an expanded form (MAT-EF) consisting of 64 multiple-choice items that is individually administered. The age range of the Matrix Analogies Test Short and Expanded forms is from 5 through 18.

The uses for this measure are the same as those for figural matrices tests mentioned earlier. Raw scores on the expanded form of the Matrix Analogies Test can be converted to standard scores with mean of 100 and standard deviation of 15. These scores in turn can be converted to age equivalents and percentile ranks. Raw scores on the short form can be converted to percentiles, stanines, and age equivalents.

Standardization

The expanded form was standardized using a sample of 5,718 children in the United States in the early 1980s. The sample was stratified according to U.S. Census statistics by race, sex, age, geographic region, community size, and socioeconomic status. The match between the sample and Census statistics is adequate.

Reliability

Internal consistency reliability of the expanded form is generally high, ranging from .88 to .95. As is the case of several of the measures discussed previously, test-retest coefficients are considerably lower. Test-retest reliability of the total test score over a 1-month interval is only .77.

Validity

The validity of the expanded form has been assessed primarily via correlations of other tests such as the WISC-R. Correlations with the WISC-R for a sample of 82 nonhandicapped children were .41, for Native American children .43, and for hearing-impaired children .68. The expanded form correlation with the Wide Range Achievement Test Reading subtest was .45. Several studies have found the expanded form to produce consistently lower scores than the WISC-R Performance Scale score. The trend across studies is for the expanded form to score about 10 points lower than the Performance score of the WISC-R (Naglieri & Prewett, 1990). Another study of 3,022 students in the fourth through twelfth grades yielded moderate correlations for the MAT-SF. The MAT-SF correlations with reading scores ranged from .47 at grade 6 to .66 at grade 12.

Summary

The Matrix Analogies Test, particularly the expanded form, follows in the tradition of the use of figural matrices as a means of assessing the intelligence of children with communication problems or motor problems and children for whom English is not their first language. The Matrix Analogies Test, however, is considerably more modern than many of its predecessors. Its norming sample is more recent, larger, and more psychometrically sophisticated. As a single-subtest screener of intelligence for a particular purpose or for conducting research on the mental processing of figural matrices by children, the Matrix Analogies Test expanded form would be a viable candidate.

Test of Nonverbal Intelligence-2 (TONI)

The TONI was first published in 1982 and revised in 1990 by Brown, Sherbenou, and Johnson (1990). The TONI is intended as a nonverbal measure of intelligence for children and adults. It has an age range of 5 years, 0 months to 85 years, 11 months. The TONI attempts to assess "problem solving."

It does so by using variance of figural matrices. It also uses a multiple-choice format where the child or adult has to select the response that best completes the problem. Typically, the examiner does not use language but rather administers the test in pantomime and the child responds simply by pointing. In order to assist pantomimed or language-free administration, there are several training items at the beginning of the test. The TONI takes approximately 15 minutes to administer. It includes two parallel forms, A and B.

The two featured derived scores are a TONI quotient, which is a standard score with mean of 100 and standard deviation of 15, and percentile ranks.

Standardization

The TONI was standardized on a large national sample (over 2,500 cases) reflecting the age range of 5 to 85. The sample was stratified based on sex, race, ethnicity, parental educational-occupational attainment for school-age children and current educational-occupational attainment for the adult sample, and geographic region. The majority of the standardization sample received both forms A and B in counterbalanced but successive order.

Reliability

Evidence for reliability of the TONI is adequate. Internal consistency coefficients are generally in the .80s and .90s. Test-retest coefficients are slightly lower, generally in the .80s.

Validity

Evidence for validity of the TONI comes primarily from correlations with other multiscale intelligence test batteries.

Summary

The TONI-2 has a number of attributes to recommend its use, including a fairly recent standardization sample, ease of administration, and an extordinarily wide age range. The TONI-2 manual leaves some things to be desired in terms of detail. The TONI-2 also has not been studied extensively as far as its concurrent validity. This test, however, is reminiscent of the Matrix Analogies Test in that it is a recent, well-developed entry in the area of single-subtest measures of nonverbal intelligence.

INTELLIGENCE SCREENERS

Beginning around World War I, researchers investigated other measures of intelligence in addition to the Binet scales. Several alternatives

RESEARCH REPORT

Questioning the relationship of the draw-a-person technique to school achievement

A recent study by Prewett, Bardos, and Naglieri (1989) investigated the relationship between the Matrix Analogies Test-Short Form (MAT-SF), Draw-A-Person: A Quantitative Scoring System (DAP), and the Kaufman Test of Educational Achievement Comprehensive Form (K-TEA). The purpose of the study was to evaluate the utility of the MAT-SF and the DAP as screening instruments for the diagnosis of mental retardation. The study involved 46 nonhandicapped and 39 developmentally handicapped children from fourth- and fifth-grade classrooms from a suburban school district. The developmentally handicapped (DH) children were previously diagnosed based on obtaining a standard score of 80 or lower on an individually administered intelligence test. This group also had concurrent deficits in adaptive behavior.

The MAT-SF and the DAP were group-administered by two school psychologists on the same school day. The MAT-SF was administered first and the DAP was administered immediately afterward. The K-TEA was individually administered to all subjects within 3 weeks by the same examiner.

Significant differences between each of the tests within group were evaluated with repeated measures analyses of variance. Tukey's procedure was used for post hoc analyses. Zero-order correlation coefficients were computed between Reading and Mathematics Composite scores of the K-TEA and the various scores of the screening measures. The correlations for only the normal sample were corrected for restriction of range.

The mean scores for the nonhandicapped and developmentally handicapped groups differed significantly. On most of the measures the nonhandicapped group scored in the average range and the developmentally handicapped group scored in the 70s and 80s. Interestingly, the range of scores for the DAP for the developmentally handicapped group was considerably higher than for the other two measures. The DAP means for the two groups were 80.3 and 83.6. In addition, the other screener, the MAT-SF, produced a higher score of 75.8 for the DH group than either the Reading Composite (mean = 70.3) or the Mathematics Composite (mean = 72.2) of the K-TEA. Generally, it appears that the screening measures gave more generous estimates of cognitive skills than the K-TEA. Most importantly, however, the DAP scores were consistently higher than the initial intelligence test scores—all of which had to be less than 80 to qualify children for services.

The most striking findings of this study were the poor correlations between the two screening measures and the two composites of the K-TEA Comprehensive Form. For the nonhandicapped sample the correlation for the DAP total score with the Reading Composite score of the K-TEA was only .17, and the correlation between the DAP total and Mathematics Composite of the K-TEA was .00. The MAT-SF correlations were also not impressive, with a .63 with Reading Composite and .37 correlation with Mathematics Composite. The correlations among the various measures for the clinical sample were worse. The correlation of the Reading Composite with DAP total was .11. The correlation of the Mathematics Composite with DAP total was only .47. The correlations of the Reading and Math Composites with the MAT-SF were .35 and .57 respectively for the DH sample.

The mean score differences and the poor-to-moderate correlational relationships between the screeners and the criterion measure of academic achievement suggest that the screeners may classify children differently than the original intelligence measure and possess less evidence of criterion-related validity. Prewett, Bardos, and Naglieri (1989) used a generous test of the effectiveness of the screeners. Instead of using a standard score of 80 or below as was used for the original diagnostic purposes, they used a standard score of 85 or below as a criterion for evaluating the effectiveness of the screening measure. Using this criterion, 32 of the 39 in the DH group would have been screened accurately by the MAT-SF. The results were considerably worse for the DAP, where only 22 of the 39 developmentally handicapped students would have been accurately screened. These results do not bode well for the use of draw-a-person techniques, even as screeners of intellectual development (Kamphaus & Pleiss, 1991).

---

were offered, including drawing techniques. Florence Goodenough (1926) popularized the use of draw-a-person techniques as brief measures of "mental development." This type of measure has enjoyed continued popularity as a screening measure. In the 1960s the Peabody Picture Vocabulary Test became extremely popular as a screening measure of intelligence. Today figural matrices item types are gaining popularity as screening measures of intelligence or mental development. Tests such as the Raven's and the Matrix Analogies Test may serve this screening function (Naglieri & Prewett, 1990).

The authors of most of these instruments recommend them as screeners when the use of a more broad-based, multisubtest measure of intelligence is either unwarranted, unnecessary, or unavailable. There is some question about the ability of these short forms to estimate intelligence test scores of comprehensive measures (Kamphaus & Pleiss, 1991). Such criticisms are likely to continue, especially since modern multisubtest intelligence test batteries are now producing their own short forms. These include nonverbal short forms and other varieties that are intended for use as screeners much in the same way as the tests discussed in this section are designed for screening purposes. The short forms from the multisubtest batteries tend to have more credibility because these short forms assess a broader range of cognitive skills by usually including more than one item type.

Goodenough's Draw a Man Test (1926)

Florence Goodenough experimented with a variety of figure drawings and decided that a "man" was the ideal stimulus because of greater uniformity in clothing that may allow for standardized scoring procedures. In the fall of 1920 Goodenough collected 4,000 drawings from children in the kindergarten through fourth grades of the public schools in Perth Amboy, New Jersey. The drawings were made under standardized conditions. From these a group of 100 was selected for preliminary study (20 from each grade). She and her coworkers reviewed these drawings to determine how drawings in the upper grades appeared to differ from those in the lower grades. After several revisions a scoring scale of 51 points was finalized. This test became the standard against which other drawing techniques were judged.

Goodenough-Harris Draw a Person (DAP) Test (1963)

This revision of the original scale attempted to extend the Goodenough scale to include adolescent years and to develop an "alternative form" to the man scale by deriving an analogous point scale for the figure of a woman. The second objective was successful, but the first was not. A drawing of the self was included as a potential third form, a possible avenue for studying the emerging self-concept, and a possibly more valid projective device for the study of affect and interest than impersonal figures.

Administration

The test covers ages 3-0 to 15-11, but it functions best with ages 3 to 10. The DAP can be administered either individually or in groups. Preschool children and children being studied clinically should have the DAP individually administered and the drawing followed by an "informal interrogation" to clarify the child's intent. A #2 pencil with eraser and 8.5'' × 11'' unlined paper should be provided. Examiners are admonished not to make criticisms or give suggestions. In fact, some children are self-conscious and should not be openly watched while they are drawing. There is no time limit for the DAP.

Scoring

The point scale for the man has 73 items and the one for the woman has 71 items. Points are awarded for various body parts drawn by the child. Each item is scored pass (1) or fail (0). The child's raw score is used to obtain a standard score where M = 100 and SD = 15. A quality scale permits a much more rapid evaluation of drawings than the point scale, but results are not as precise. The quality scale has 12 drawings representing various levels of maturity, where 1.0 = least mature and 12.0 = most mature. These values can then be converted to standard scores and percentile ranks.

Standardization

The man and woman point scales were standardized on more representative samples than were available to Goodenough in 1920s. A total of 2,975 boys and girls in the United States were selected as representative of the 1960 Census figures. Four geographical areas were used, and 75 children were included at each age level from 5 to 15 years.

Reliability

Split-half reliability of the DAP is reported at .89 and test-retest at .68. Interscorer reliability is estimated at .90.

Validity

Correlations with the Stanford-Binet ranged from .45 to .92 and with the Full Scale WPPSI from .72 to .80 for 5-year-olds (Kamphaus & Pleiss, 1991).

The moderate correlations with intelligence measures make the DAP an *acceptable* (not extraordinary) screening instrument for use as a nonverbal measure of cognitive ability, particularly with children 3 to 15 years of age.

Koppitz Human Figure Drawing (HFD) (1968)

Elizabeth Koppitz (1968) developed a human figure drawing test for use with children ages 5 through 12. This measure is intended for use in building rapport, as a stimulus for interviewing the child, and as a *gross* estimate of maturity or developmental level.

Standardization

The HFD was normed on 1,856 public school pupils representing 86 entire classes in 10 elementary schools. Of the sample, 33% were from 2 schools in residential sections of a midwestern city, 54% attended 5 schools in three small industrial towns in a midwestern and an eastern state, and the remaining 13% were from 3 schools in small villages or rural areas of these same states. Systematic efforts at stratification were not apparent.

Reliability and Validity

These values are very similar to those for the Goodenough-Harris. An interrater reliability coefficient of .97 was obtained. A correlation of .68 with the WISC Full Scale was reported.

Administration and Scoring

Administration procedures are identical to those for the Goodenough-Harris. Koppitz generated 30 items that can be converted into *broad categories of intellectual functioning* rather than specific IQ scores. These broad categories of mental ability are considered sufficient for differentiating between children who are mentally retarded and those who have average or above-average intellectual ability. Koppitz's most unique contribution is the "emotional indicators." Emotional indicators (1) had to have clinical validity, (2) they must be unusual and occur infrequently on HFDs of normal children, and (3) they must not be related to age and maturation. Emotional indicators may reveal information about issues ranging from attitudes toward life to concern about school achievement.

Draw-A-Person: A Quantitative Scoring System

The Draw-a-Person: A Quantitative Scoring System (DAP) (Naglieri, 1988a) is a revision and update of the classic draw-a-person technique. The DAP uses human figure drawings as an "estimate of ability." The three drawings used for the DAP are of a woman, a man, and self. There are 64 scoring items for each of the three drawings. Critical scoring criteria include the number of body parts included, the elaboration of the drawings, and the drawing of body parts and their various connections in appropriate proportions and locations. The scoring was devised to try to avoid rating fashions and dress.

The DAP is featured for use with populations of children where language and verbal skills may be an issue. There was also an attempt to produce scoring criteria so as not to penalize children with fine motor coordination problems. Furthermore, Naglieri sees this test as useful because it produces smaller between-group differences for ethnic groups such as samples of Greek and American (Naglieri & Bardos, 1987) and Canadian and American children (Bardos, Softas, & Petrogiannis, 1989). The question of whether drawing techniques measure the same constructs for different ethnic groups is still debatable (Oakland & Dowling, 1983).

The DAP includes an examiner record form and a student response form. The scoring system is included in the DAP manual and on a two-page scoring chart. The DAP also includes a helpful training procedure that clinicians can use to learn the scoring system. Administration time for the DAP is approximately 5 minutes for producing each of the three stimuli, and the author states that once the scoring of the 64 items is mastered, a clinician can score a typical DAP in less than 5 minutes.

The range of raw scores on the DAP is from 0 to 64 for each drawing and 0–192 for the total test. The drawings of the three stimuli are combined to form a DAP total test score, which is a standard score scale with a mean of 100 and standard deviation of 15. This score can then be converted to percentile ranks or age equivalents. A standard score may also be computed for the individual drawings. The manual offers confidence intervals for the total test and tables for determining significant standard score differences for each of the drawings separately.

Norming

The DAP norming sample consisted of 2,622 children between the ages of 5 and 17 years. It was a stratified sample based on 1980 U.S. Census Bureau statistics and used the stratification variables of age, gender, race, geographic region, ethnic group, socioeconomic status, and community size.

Reliability

Reliability coefficients for the DAP are generally quite high considering the brevity of this measure. The median total test internal consistency coefficient for the standardization sample is .86. The internal consistency coefficients for the drawings of the man, woman, and self scored separately were .70, with a range of .56 to .78. A test-retest reliability study involving 112 children in the first through seventh grades produced coefficients ranging from .60 to .89 with a mean of .74 for the total test. Also, interscorer reliability is good, ranging from .93 to .95 (Gottling, 1985).

Validity

The validity of the Draw-a-Person is discussed on pages 17 to 20 of the manual. Evidence of age differentation validity is supportive. Much of the concurrent validity evidence is based on strong correlational relationships between the DAP and other drawing techniques such as the Goodenough-Harris system (Naglieri & Prewett, 1990). These coefficients are generally very high, in the range of the .70s to the .90s.

More crucial, however, if the DAP is to be considered for use as an "estimate of ability," is the relationship between the screener and comprehensive measures of children's intelligence. Here the correlations are relatively mediocre, although consistent with previous research on drawing techniques (see other portions of this chapter). A study by Wisniewski and Naglieri (1989) found a correlation of only .51 between the DAP Total Test and WISC-R Full Scale for a sample of 51 children who ranged in age from 6 to 16 years. These findings of mediocre validity coefficients led a recent reviewer to conclude that: "The DAP is an improvement over other draw-a-figure measures. It was constructed to provide a clear, objective scoring system for scoring drawings; it yields high reliabilities. As with other draw-a-figure measures, however, construct validity is arguable . . ." (Neisworth & Butler, 1990, pp. 194–195). Data regarding the relationship of the DAP to an academic achievement measure show low correlation between the DAP and reading and mathematics scores for a sample of 1,328 nonhandicapped children. The correlation of the DAP total with mathematics was .21 and with reading .24.

Concluding Comments Regarding Drawing Techniques

There has always been a need for techniques to serve as screeners of intelligence. Drawing techniques have fulfilled this need for 70 or so years. Times are changing though, and now most of the multisubtest batteries discussed in this book have short forms (screeners) for a variety of purposes. These abbreviated batteries also have stellar psychometric properties, including strong correlations with total composite scores. New tests such as the *Kaufman Brief Intelligence Test (K-BIT)* (Kaufman & Kaufman, 1990) are being marketed solely as screeners. All of this suggests that clinicians have many options for screeners of intelligence, most of which have stronger psychometric properties than drawing techniques. Drawing techniques are so fitting for the young child that they will undoubtably enjoy continued use, but an important technological breakthrough is necessary to bring them back to preeminence. There are simply too many better options available.

Peabody Picture Vocabulary Test-Revised (PPVT-R)

The PPVT-R (Dunn & Dunn, 1981) is the successor to the original PPVT (Dunn, 1959). The PPVT-R is perhaps one of the briefest measures of intelligence ever developed. It is a rather unique test in that it has an identity problem. In its first edition published in 1959 it was offered to clinicians as a quick screening measure of general intellectual ability. This claim, however, was attacked by a number of reviewers because of the brevity of the measure. In its most recent edition the claim of being a measure of general intelligence was withdrawn. The PPVT-R is now a measure of "hearing vocabulary." One suspects, however, that many clinicians continue to use the PPVT as a brief screening measure of overall intellectual ability or cognitive development.

The concept behind the PPVT is a simple one. The test consists of two equivalent forms, L and M, with 175 items per form. Each item consists of a "plate" or page with four line drawings. The examiner dictates a word and the child or adult is to point to the picture that best describes the meaning of the word given by the examiner. The examiner then uses basal and ceiling rules to determine, based upon the child's performance, the appropriate range of the 175 items to be administered to the child. The PPVT-R spans an age range of 2½ through 40.

The combination of simple administration and scoring (a composite is offered with a mean of 100 and standard deviation of 15) and a broad age range serves to make the PPVT-R an attractive screening measure. It also has specialized uses in the area of speech and language assessment. For example, a child with intact hearing but impaired oral communication skills could be assessed with the PPVT-R since the items require only a pointing response.

Norming

The PPVT-R was developed through two norming programs, one for children and adolescents and one for adults. The child and adolescent program spanned the ages of 2½ through 18 and data were collected in May through December of 1979. The sample of 4,200 children was stratified in order to meet 1970 Census Bureau statistics using the stratification variables of age, gender, geographic region, occupation of parent (major wage earner for the adult sample), race, and community size. The norming program was quite sophisticated and yielded a very close match to 1970 Census Bureau statistics.

Reliability

Internal consistency estimates for the PPVT-R range from .67 to .88 for Form L and from .74 to .86 for Form M. These are lower coefficients than what we are typically used to as users of intelligence tests. Test-retest coefficients were similar to the internal consistency coefficients. The test-retest coefficients are also alternate forms coefficients between Forms L and M. The median alternate forms (test-retest) coefficient is .84, which is slightly higher than the average internal consistency coefficients.

Validity

The validity of the PPVT-R rests on concurrent validity, at least in terms of its ability to serve as a screening measure of intelligence. Intelligence tests seem to correlate with each other in the .70s and sometimes in the .80s. A comprehensive review by Bracken, Prasse, and McCallum (1984) shows that the PPVT-R yields correlation coefficients with popular intelligence tests in a similar range, although in some individual studies the correlations have been poor. However, since correlations do not assess agreement of scores per se (as opposed to agreement of rankings), Bracken, Prasse, and McCallum (1984) examined the mean score differences between the PPVT-R and other intelligence measures. They noted that the PPVT-R tended to yield scores consistently slightly lower than popular measures such as the WISC-R and the Stanford-Binet. On the other hand, agreement between the PPVT-R and the McCarthy GCI scores is more consistent. Bracken, Prasse, and McCallum (1984) concluded that the PPVT-R, because of its occasionally low to moderate relationship with other measures of intelligence, is "not a measure of general cognitive ability" (p. 59).

Summary

The PPVT-R has a long tradition as a screening measure of intelligence. Its simple format, administration, and scoring have proved attractive to psychologists and others who have used it as a screener. I have colleagues, for example, who use the PPVT-R and a drawing technique as an initial screener for children whom they are charged with evaluating. They then use this information to select a comprehensive test battery for use in the full-blown evaluation. This practice seems acceptable in that the PPVT-R in this case (and the draw-a-person for that matter) is being used truly as a screener. In effect, it is only for the "in-house" use of the psychologist conducting the evaluation. One of the problems with the PPVT-R in the past is that its brevity has made it prone to misuse and overuse by clinicians. Occasionally the PPVT-R has been used as a substitute for a more comprehensive measure of intelligence.

EMERGING INTELLECTUAL ASSESSMENT TECHNOLOGIES

WISC Screeners

Short forms have typically been frowned upon by clinicians engaged in assessment practice. Yet, on the other hand, a number of articles have been written on the use of short forms with intelligence tests (Silverstein, 1982; Reynolds & Kaufman, 1990).

Short forms can be useful in a variety of settings. While a short form is not useful when conducting a comprehensive intellectual evaluation, it can serve a useful screening purpose. Situations where a screening measure of intelligence would be used include the following:

1. For the purposes of some evaluations a comprehensive measure of intelligence is not needed. Many referrals to psychologists do not have questions about intelligence. A child who is referred for treatment of depression and not for a psychological evaluation may be such a case. A psychologist may just want some general information about the child's cognitive skills before treatment begins.

2. Mass screening. When large numbers of children are screened, an intelligence test short form may serve as an initial screener for cognitive problems.

3. Supporting evidence. An examiner may have given a child an intelligence test and not felt too confident of the results. A short form may serve as a quick check of the validity of a previous test administration.

The commonality of all of these circumstances is that the short form measure is serving as *supporting evidence* and not as the primary source of evidence in an evaluation.

The most popular WISC-R short form was composed of the Vocabulary, Arithmetic, Picture Arrangement, and Block Design subtests (Kaufman, 1976). This short form had strong validity evidence. The average correlation between Arithmetic-Vocabulary and the Verbal score was .92, and the correlation of Picture Arrangement–Block Design and the Performance score was .89 (Kaufman, 1976b). Clinicians could administer these four tests and obtain an estimate of the Full Scale standard score.

A two-subtest short form composed of Vocabulary and Block Design has been proposed by Silverstein (1983a). This short form, however, had a considerably larger standard error of estimate (about 9 points) than the four subtest short form of Kaufman (about 5 points)

(1976). Other WISC-R short form research has been conducted by Silverstein (1974, 1983b).

Recently, Kaufman and Kaufman (1990) published the *Kaufman Brief Intelligence Test (K-BIT)*, which is essentially a two-subtest short form of the Wechsler scales that includes one verbal and one nonverbal subtest. The K-BIT shows strong correlations with the WISC-R and WAIS-R (Kaufman & Kaufman, 1990). Undoubtedly, short forms of the WISC-III will be forthcoming.

Learning-Potential Assessment

One of the promising intelligence assessment movements of the 1970s and 1980s is the learning-potential movement. Names and research traditions associated with this movement include Feuerstein, Budoff (1987), and Brown and French (1979). There is a common theoretical thread to these methods in that most of them draw heavily on the theories of the Russian developmentalist L. S. Vygotsky.

Vygotsky (1978) viewed cognitive development as a social process whereby the child's interaction with competent adult models resulted in cognitive growth. He viewed learning and development as interactive processes. Maturation provided the platform for learning, new learning in turn promoted further maturation, and so the process continued in synergistic fashion.

Vygotsky offered the notion of the zone of proximal development (ZPD) to explain this process of cognitive growth. The ZPD is the difference between the child's current level of development (as determined by the child's history of learning and its influence on the maturation process) and the level of development that can be achieved when a child is assisted by a competent model such as a parent, teacher, or accomplished peer. In Vygotsky's (1978) own words the ZPD is: "the distance between actual developmental level as determined by independent problem solving and the level of potential development as determined through problem solving under adult guidance or in collaboration with more capable peers" (p. 86).

The aforementioned researchers have attempted to use assessment of the ZPD as an intellectual assessment system. The work of Feuerstein, Rand, and Hoffman (1979) in this area is most well known. Feuerstein developed the Learning Potential Assessment Device (LPAD) as a method of gauging the malleability (modifiability) of a child's intelligence by assessing the child's ZPD. This paradigm is frequently referred to as a "test-teach-test" paradigm. The first test is the assessment of the initial developmental level, the teaching portion of the assessment allows the child to benefit from the "coaching" and guidance of a competent model, and the final portion of the assessment measures the developmental level reached as a result of "teaching." The distance (gain) between first and second tests then serves as an estimate of the child's modifiability. A "gainer" would be a child with a large difference between initial scores and second tests.

There are several attractive theoretical aspects to the notion of the ZPD and the theoretical work of Feuerstein, Budoff, and Brown. Traditional intelligence measures are criticized by those ascribing to dynamic assessment paradigms as "static" measures that do not provide insight into the "processes" by which a child solves problems. In addition, traditional intelligence measures do not provide insights that may be useful for treatment.

Overview of Techniques.

Feuerstein, Rand, and Hoffman (1979) state that the purpose of the LPAD is to "identify and locate specific cognitive deficiencies and then evaluate, by intrachild comparisons, responses to instruction in general cognitive principles" (p. 297). The LPAD consists of a variety of tests, some of which are familiar to intelligence test users and some of which are not. Theoretically the size of the LPAD test battery is infinite given the number of possible cognitive functions and

skills that could be assessed (Glutting & McDermott, 1990). The child is first assessed with tests that might include the Representational Stencil Design Test, Numerical Progressions Test, Raven's Progressive Matrices-LPAD Variations Test, and Organization of Dots Test, The Test of Verbal Abstraction, and Plateaux Test. "Mediated learning experiences" are offered by the examiner during the administration of these tests. If a child has some difficulty with an item the examiner provides increasingly explicit prompts until the child is able to solve the item. Examiners record the *amount* and *type* of assistance required to solve the item. After the LPAD is administered along with appropriate mediated learning experiences a posttest is administered to assess the transference of the mediated learning experiences.

Budoff's (1975) system uses traditional nonverbal intelligence tests to pretest intelligence so as to avoid language-based measures that may be influenced by cultural differences (Glutting & McDermott, 1990). The pretest consists of the Kohs Block Designs Test and Raven's Progressive Matrices. The Kohs is the forerunner of the Block Design subtest used by Wechsler. In Budoff's system no prompts, teaching, or coaching are offered during the pretest.

Items that are similar to those of the pretest measures are used during the teaching phase. During this part of the assessment the examiner assists the child in using maximally effective problem-solving strategies including avoidance of impulsive responding, defining the problem, and comparing responses carefully to the models. The final part of the assessment is the posttest where the Raven's and Kohs are readministered. The gain score between the first and second tests then serves as the measure of the ZPD.

Arguments for Dynamic Assessment

Feuerstein, Rand, and Hoffman (1979) argue that traditional IQ tests underestimate the extent to which children are modifiable, especially children diagnosed as mildly retarded and children who are outside the "dominant" culture. Such a rationale has encouraged the perception that the LPAD holds promise as a multiculturally sensitive intelligence assessment technique since little emphasis is placed on labeling.

Bransford and colleagues (1987) make several arguments in favor of dynamic assessment techniques, including the idea that in dynamic assessment the locus of failure is not the child but the instructional techniques that have failed to produce cognitive maturation. Bransford et al. (1987) also note that some of Budoff's research shows that (1) children who perform competently following dynamic assessment do better in other learning and social situations; (2) students with high learning potential status have higher achievement scores and have a better self-concept when they are mainstreamed, as opposed to segregated in self-contained special education classes; and (3) dynamic assessment profiles are frequently inconsistent with children's traditional assessment classification.

Braden (1984) finds some promise in the LPAD in that (1) the instrument yields concrete educational objectives that may be useful to teachers for educational intervention planning, (2) psychological reports based on the LPAD tend to be "noncategorical and growth oriented," and (3) the LPAD results are frequently very descriptive of the student being evaluated. Glutting and McDermott (1990) praise the fact that there is great flexibility in the tests that can be used to assess a child. Examiners can choose LPAD instruments based on the child's personal competencies and learning characteristics.

Arguments against Dynamic Assessment

Glutting and McDermott (1990) cite a central problem with the LPAD research. The pliability of the LPAD methodology and haphazard

adherence to a test-teach-test model make documentation of the effectiveness of the LPAD virtually impossible. Braden (1984) concludes that the LPAD requires extensive training and that the amount of social interaction required on the part of the examiner may be difficult to provide for multihandicapped children, new immigrants, or children from a cultural group that is different from the examiner's.

Glutting and McDermott (1990) provide numerous methodological criticisms of the LPAD and Budoff methods. Regarding the LPAD, they conclude that because of its methodological problems "it is impossible to determine empirically whether test performance subsequent to the experimental inducement of mediated learning is due to the treatment or to a host of problems, not the least of which is IQ" (p. 300). Regarding Budoff's approach, Glutting and McDermott (1990) conclude that "Budoff's system identifies gainers twice as often as do diagnostic decision rules that control statistical artifacts better (20.3% vs. 9.0%, respectively)" (p. 304). Furthermore, gainer diagnoses are incorrect over 50% of the time, suggesting that "the initial optimism raised by diagnoses of gainer status is destined to change to disappointment when children fail to manifest prophesied potential." Glutting and McDermott (1990) also question a central premise of dynamic assessment approaches that dynamic assessment methods are best suited to helping high-risk children. They point out:

Over 83% of those studies demonstrated that higher-functioning subjects profited more from LP assessments than lower-functioning subjects. Such results are contrary to expectations from the LP hypothesis. In comparison to higher-IQ subjects, subjects with lower IQs appeared relatively worse off on the LP posttest than they were initially on the traditional LP pretest. (p. 309)

The PASS Model

The Planning-Attention-Simultaneous-Successive (PASS) model developed by Naglieri and

Das (1990) will sound familiar to readers since its theoretical basis traces the same roots as the K-ABC. The PASS approach, however, does differ substantially from the K-ABC even though both ascribe to Luria's theories of cognitive function.

While there is some resemblance of the simultaneous and successive components, the PASS model is intended to be a more comprehensive system for measuring "cognitive function" (a term preferred to intelligence by Naglieri and Das). The PASS tests measure all three of Luria's functional units. The first functional unit, the brain stem and subcortical areas, is concerned with functions of attention and arousal. The second functional unit "is located in the posterior regions of the neocortex including the visual (occipital), auditory (temporal) and general sensory (parietal) regions of the hemispheres" (Naglieri & Das, 1990, p. 308). The second functional unit is concerned with the simultaneous or successive coding of information. The third functional unit "comprises the frontal lobes, in particular, the prefrontal region (anterior to the precentral gyrus), which are responsible for programming, regulation, and verification of cognitive activity" (p. 310). The subtests used to assess these four functions are listed below.

Planning Tests	*Simultaneous Tests*
Visual Search	Figure Memory
Planned Connections	Matrices
Planned Codes	Simultaneous Verbal
Attention Tests	*Successive Tests*
Expressive Attention	Sentence Repetition
Number Finding	Sentence Questions
Receptive Attention	Word Recall

These tests form the basis for a test instrument that is referred to as the Das-Naglieri Cognitive Assessment System (CAS). Naglieri and Das (1990) cite numerous studies that have evaluated the factorial, concurrent, and dis-criminant validity of the CAS and produced generally supportive results. Several factor analytic investigations have produced evidence in support of factors that correspond to the planning and attention scales (Naglieri & Das, 1990). Despite these findings, early reviewers (Lambert, 1990; Telzrow, 1990) of the CAS maintain that more validity data are required before the CAS can become part of assessment practice.

Measures of Reaction Time

Reaction time measures fell into disfavor early on in the history of intelligence test development (Vernon, 1990) (see Chapter 1). Since the 1960s, however, there has been a resurgence of interest in such measures (Vernon, 1990). The typical reaction time paradigm involves an apparatus of some sort, in some cases not unlike the bar press mechanism in Skinner boxes, where the examinee must respond as quickly as possible to some stimuli (usually a choice task) that is administered by an examiner or computer. The score derived from such measures is usually the latency of the examinee's response. In some cases numerous trials are used and average latencies are computed in order to serve as the person's "score." Much of the validity research on reaction time tasks assesses concurrent validity with tests such as the WISC-R serving as the criterion. One would predict that the correlations of reaction time with WISC-R scores would be minimal, as was the case with Galton's early research. More recent methodologies produce moderate correlations with the WISC-R (Vernon, 1990). Modern-day concurrent validity coefficients are better than the predictive and concurrent validity coefficients of Galton's day for two reasons. Jensen (1987) has made efforts to increase the complexity of reaction time tasks. For example, he has systematically increased the number of decisions that an examinee must make before responding. In addition, reaction time tasks have been added to produce a composite score that is more highly correlated with traditional intelligence test scores than the individual reaction time tasks that enter into the composite. Vernon (1990) reviewed four studies of the concurrent validity of reaction time measures with WISC-R IQs and found substantial multiple correlations between multiple reaction time measures and IQ scores (values for mean reaction times across all studies ranged from .434 to .737). In addition, Vernon (1990) points to data showing that reaction time measures produce similar heritability coefficients to those of traditional IQ tests.

The Computer and Intelligence Testing

Computers have taken on more and more assessment tasks since the advent of their widespread availability in the 1970s. The increasing use of computers in assessment-related activities eventually led to attempts by psychological organizations such as the American Psychological Association (APA, 1985, 1986) to create guidelines for computer usage by those engaged in psychological assessment.

Shortly after microcomputers became widely available, psychologists created their own test-related software programs before many were commercially available (Roid & Gorsuch, 1984; Roid, 1986). In many ways the development of testing software programs has mimicked the history of test development, where in the early days of both industries many publishers were "mom and pop" operations where a psychologist created a program to meet a personal need and then began to share it.

Psychologists in schools have made heavy use of computers in the assessment process because of the ready availability of computers in this setting. Increasingly professionals in other settings such as clinics and hospitals are making greater use of computers. Testimony to the increasing popularity of computers for assessment purposes is the growth of the publisher of the MMPI-2, National Computer Systems, which offers a computerized testing program for psychologists with a great variety of tests available.

Types of Computer Programs

McCullough (1990) provides categorizations of different types of computer use in psychology. These include:

> *Computer-Adapted Testing (CAT). CAT starts with a database or large collection of facts, skills, and concepts from an array of subject areas placed into memory banks or secondary storage devices of a computer. For any given area, the computer selects and tests a subset of skills, facts, and concepts, and the individual's basal and ceiling levels are then determined for each area. The adapted or "tailored" part of the test program comes from the branching capabilities used to determine which questions should be asked of which persons. (p. 724)*

> *Computer-Administered Interviews. Computerized interviews or questionnaires help to identify problem behavior areas and etiological factors. They are found most often in university counseling centers, child guidance centers, and outpatient mental health centers. (p. 726)*

> *Computerized Scoring and Analysis (CS). Test scoring involves identifying responses as correct or incorrect, computing raw scores for each subtest of a battery, and then converting the raw scores to standard scores using norm tables prepared by the publisher/researcher. (p. 728)*

> *Computerized Interpretation (CI). Test-scoring and interpretation programs include publisher-authorized, privately produced, and public domain versions, and vary in quality and ease of use. The best interpretation programs are designed on the basis of empirically validated decision rules and are intended for the use of trained professionals experienced with the test instrument and its supportive research. (p. 730)*

CS and CI will be the focus of this section, with limited discussion of CAT.

Computerized Scoring

Computerized scoring (CS) is by far the most popular computer use for psychologists who work with children (Jacob & Brantley, 1987). These types of programs are popular because they handle clerical tasks more accurately and expeditiously than the clinician. Features of these types of programs usually include:

1. *Error trapping of data input.* These programs usually require the psychologist to compute raw scores for an intelligence test and enter these. More programs, however, now require raw score input. CS programs will "trap" for impossible data such as impossible raw scores or item scores. For example, the highest possible raw score on the Binet-4 Pattern Analysis subtest is 45. A good program would error trap an entry of 46 and not allow it to be entered. The program may make an audible noise or display a message on screen indicating the nature of an error. Good programs also trap for other problems such as the entry of an inappropriate or impossible age (e.g., a 13th month) or a subtest score that is inappropriate for a child's age (e.g., K-ABC Face Recognition for a 6-year-old). These features greatly enhance the accuracy of the clinician's work with intelligence tests. They can help one avoid the embarrassment—and perhaps liability—of making unintentional errors.

2. *Computation of chronological age.* Virtually all software programs take the child's birthdate and test date as entered and compute the child's chronological age in years, months, and days. For some reason, computation of a child's age is fraught with problems, and CS programs almost guarantee accuracy.

3. *Inclusion of biographical information.* Many programs include open fields (empty spaces where an examiner is cued to enter information such as parental educational attainment) or checklists (parental educational attainment may be indicated by marking the number of years of school completed given a list of options) for providing background information. Popular types of information for such programs include child gender, race/ethnicity, primary language, parental education or occupation, number of grades retained, school grades, and scores from other tests.

4. *Computation of scores.* A major advantage of these programs is that they compute various derived scores virtually without error. Most psychologists have caught themselves making scoring errors. Newer tests are most problematic because of the increasing number of available scoring options and norm tables. Whereas older tests offered only one or two scores (usually IQs and mental ages) for interpretation, newer tests offer local norms (e.g., the sociocultural norms of the K-ABC), out-of-level norms (e.g., DAS), and a plethora of other options. These various derived scores can be both time consuming and confusing. CS programs ease this clerical burden and prevent clinicians from using norm tables incorrectly.

5. *Increased scoring options.* Some computer programs offer scoring options that are not available in the test manual. Some scores are not provided in the manual for a test, and they can be burdensome to compute with a calculator or look up in a research article or other secondary source. Factor scores are good examples of scores that may have value for interpretation but are not readily available because of the difficulty of their computation. Another difficult hand-scoring option is asymmetrical confidence bands (see Chapter 5). Asymmetrical confidence bands require the computation of true scores, which is not conveniently done with a hand calculator. These various supplementary scores are easily delivered via computer, thus increasing the scope of heretofore data for interpretation.

6. *Intraindividual interpretation.* Most CS programs also compute subtest strengths and weaknesses (e.g., in a similar manner to the way subtest strengths and weaknesses are determined by the worksheets accompanying this text), significant and rare composite score differences (e.g., Verbal and Performance differences), pairwise comparisons of subtests, and other score comparisons. These computations can be very time-

consuming and are much more conveniently and accurately done by CS programs.

7. *Printed summaries.* The majority of these programs also provide a printout and/or screen display summarizing the obtained scores and score comparisons. There are vast differences in the quality of program output. Some printouts are easily read and understood, but others are more difficult. Some printouts are busy with a number of derived scores reported side by side. Other programs group scores by section, making the output more interpretable.

8. *Hypotheses.* Rather than offering conclusions, some programs offer hypotheses based on the obtained data and ask the user to confirm or reject them. These hypotheses are often based on tables of shared or unique abilities from well-known texts such as Kaufman (1979b). Some programs offer research summaries and citations for consideration by the user in interpreting the results.

9. *Data storage.* Some programs allow for the storage of multiple cases—25, 100, or more. This allows the clinician to more easily access previous intelligence test results for a child. It also provides a space-efficient back-up for "hard copy" files. Most professionals have had the experience of not being able to find a client's file when needed. A computer file is a viable back-up in these circumstances. Storage capabilities also enhance the ability of the clinician to conduct local research studies because of the ready availability of archival test data. A few programs include data summary features that allow users to prepare reports. An examiner, for example, can calculate mean scores or tally the number of children tested in a given period of time.

10. *Word processing features.* A few newer programs offer traditional word processing features such as insert, delete, typeover, and text moving. These features can be used to modify program output before printing or storing reports. Many programs also include import/export features that enable an examiner to export data in ASCII

or other format to a word processing or other program for further work.

11. *Files of recommendations.* Another useful feature of software programs is the ability to browse through banks of recommendations and include the desired ones in printed output. Such electronic files of recommendations enhance the examiner's ability to include recommendations that are consistently well written.

12. *Password protection.* This feature can help protect against unnecessary access or use of the program. When the user is required to enter a password in order to be allowed to use a program, the intelligence test data is protected from unauthorized access.

Evidence of the popularity of CS programs is that it is now axiomatic that new intelligence tests be published with CS software. The following is just a short list of the intelligence tests with CS programs available.

Wechsler Preschool and Primary Scale of Intelligence-Revised (WPPSI-R)

Wechsler Intelligence Scale for Children-Revised (WISC-R)

Kaufman Assessment Battery for Children (K-ABC)

Woodcock-Johnson Psychoeducational Test Battery-Revised

Wechsler Adult Intelligence Scale-Revised (WAIS-R)

Computerized Interpretation

A controversial type of available software is computerized interpretation (CI) software (Jacob & Brantley, 1987). Psychologists are often wary of CI programs because they differ substantially from CS programs, although sometimes the two types of programs are hard to differentiate. Often CI programs do everything that a CS program does. These types of programs differ in that CI software provides interpretation of the results, something that up to now was the sole province of the clinician. Some common features of CI programs are described next.

1. *Hypothesis generation.* Some intelligence test CI programs use decision rules similar to or the same as those given earlier in this text. For example, a program may use the rule that a Sequential/Simultaneous difference of 12 points is statistically significant and therefore warrants the study of hypotheses for the difference. The program will then access hypotheses that are consistent with the direction of the difference (i.e., either Seq > Sim or Sim > Seq). Hypotheses are frequently also offered for subtest strengths and weaknesses. The software may then use various algorithms for drawing conclusions about a child's performance. For example, a child with a P > V difference whose native language is Spanish (as indicated by the examiner when the biographical data were entered) may have the composite score difference attributed to being non-English dominant. This conclusion would then be offered as the reason for the V < P difference in the printed report.

2. *Expert decisions.* Expert systems technology has not seen widespread use in intelligence test CI programs. A CI expert system is derived by recording the wisdom of experts, sometimes for a period of years, and then applying the expert clinicians' accumulated experience to the interpretation of the test results. This technology has been popularized by personality tests such as the MMPI and the Louisville Behavior Checklist (McCullough, 1990), where expert clinicians' experience with the instrument has been applied to interpreting the test. An analogous situation in intelligence testing would be to present Dr. Collin Elliott with hundreds of DAS protocols and have him interpret them. These solutions could then be coded into a software program. The desirability of this approach is that it makes the knowledge of Dr. Elliott available to *every* DAS user. It is only a matter of time before expert systems become available for intelligence tests.

3. *Actuarial analysis.* This method involves matching a child's profile of scores to the most similar set of score profiles that have been found for a test. The CI program can then access the database pertaining to that profile and report information on the child's profile match such as interventions, diagnoses, course, and prognosis. Again, this technology has been widely applied in personality assessment but not in intellectual assessment. The availability of the work of McDermott and Glutting (see the discussion of cluster analysis in Chapter 7) will likely enhance the likelihood that actuarial analysis will be applied to intelligence tests.

4. *Printed reports.* After the various interpretations of the data are made by a CI program a report is produced. This is one of the most controversial aspects of CI programs because there is great concern by psychologists that these computer-generated reports, many of which look very much like the typical psychological report, will be used by consumers in lieu of an individualized report written by a psychologist. Some of these reports can look very official and authoritative, and they can even allow the clinician to enter his or her name and leave space to sign the report.

Concerns about CI

The advantages of CS and CI programs such as improved clerical accuracy, time savings, and the potential for more sophisticated interpretation have already been discussed. The potential disadvantages of CI, however, require further consideration by professionals. McCullough (1990) cites the following potential disadvantages of CI programs.

1. *Unauthorized use.* In some ways computer technology enhances the availability of psychological services. It also creates greater accessibility for unauthorized users such as technicians, administrators and others who are not familiar with the research on intelligence and its assessment. This creates

opportunities for the unsophisticated or un-professional use of CI without due considera-tion being given to its caveats.

2. *Documentation of decision rules.* Many pro-grams do not include detailed information about the decision rules used by the program. For example, a program could use the .05 or .01 level to determine significant strengths or weaknesses. A program could offer a hypoth-esis of "brain damage" for V/P differences of 12, 15, 20, or 30 points. Clinicians clearly need to know the bases upon which a CI program makes hypotheses or decisions.

3. *Insufficient validation.* The many conclusions drawn by CI programs may have no validity evidence. Some interpretations may be very difficult to validate. At the very least, CI pro-grams should at least make it clear which interpretations are based on theory, intuition, or research.

4. *Selecting experts.* Some may question the qual-ification of an "expert" whose clinical wisdom is used to produce a CI expert system. The selection of experts is likely to always be con-troversial. Even experts, however, should supply the rationale for their decisions.

Standards aimed at encouraging the proper use of CS and CI programs have been offered by some professional organizations. Guidelines are offered by the Committee on Professional Stan-dards (COPS) and the Committee on Psycho-logical Tests and Assessment (CPTA) of the American Psychological Association.

Future Trends in CS and CI

In many ways computerized scoring and in-terpretation of intelligence tests is still in its infancy. There have been several impediments to its development, not the least of which is the limitations of personal computers. As small computers become more powerful they will pro-vide the platform necessary for the development of advanced scoring programs and expert sys-tems.

The advent of more powerful computers will also allow the introduction of the next wave of testing technology, computerized adaptive test-ing (CAT). Online administration of intel-ligence tests, or even portions of intelligence tests, should be just around the corner. The advantages of computerized adaptive testing are many. Clinicians have always struggled to give a child the most appropriate set of test items. They know that items that are either too diffi-cult or too easy do not provide good measure-ment and increase disinterest or frustration on the part of the child. Test developers have attacked this problem by applying basal and ceil-ing rules and routing tests. These methods, however, have proved cumbersome. Clinicians would likely welcome some aspects of CAT, particularly its ability to customize the test for each child by selecting a group of items that is best suited to the child's ability. This approach holds the potential to minimize testing time and improve accuracy of measurement. There is some research emerging to show that computer-ized test administration is acceptable to clients (Lennon, 1985).

CAT will likely first occur for group-ad-ministered tests of intelligence, although they are not called intelligence tests. They are usually called "ability" tests. Group-administered tests would be ideal for computerized administration because of their lack of manipulatives and objec-tive multiple-choice item format (Lennon, 1985). The time savings to clinicians would be substantial, allowing them to place greater em-phasis on test interpretation and treatment planning.

Features to Consider

There are several characteristics of a computer program that should be considered by clinicians before making a choice. Some of the questions that a clinician may want to ask when evaluating a program include:

1. Is the interface user friendly? Many older programs developed their own interface that

was not consistent with that of popular programs such as popular word processing programs. The more the program resembles other programs that the psychologist uses frequently the more likely it is that the psychologist will be comfortable using it.

2. Is the program fast? Many intelligence tests are easy to score, thus obviating the need for software. A slow program is unlikely to be used frequently.

3. Does the program provide helpful interpretive information? Since most intelligence tests are easy to score, a software program should provide information above and beyond that which can be easily accessed by hand-scoring methods. Well-documented interpretive information, profile matching, treatment recommendation banks, and other less convenient types of information would make the program more advantageous.

4. Can the program be run from a hard disk drive? Many professionals use programs loaded on their hard drives and make little use of floppy diskettes. Such users would find it inconvenient to use a test scoring program that cannot be copied from floppy to hard drive.

5. Does the program come with strong manual and troubleshooting support? There are few things more frustrating than a software program that is difficult to install or run. A clearly written and comprehensive guide to the use of the program is of substantial benefit, as are telephone support and consultation from the software publisher.

6. Is the program compatible with a large array of printers? The array of printers available to computer users continues to expand. It can be extremely frustrating for users to purchase a program and then find that it is either difficult or impossible to configure it for their printer. Some users also have a computer in their home that may be attached to a different printer than their one at work.

7. Are the program files transportable? The ability to transfer files (e.g., computer-gener-

ated reports or test results) to another software program such as a word processor or spreadsheet can be a useful feature.

Conclusions

This chapter has taken the reader on a whirlwind tour of new, nonverbal, and brief intelligence tests. It is clear that the pace of research and development of intelligence measures has not slowed and has probably quickened.

While there are numerous signs of research and development regarding intelligence test measures, there is no clear evidence to date of a breakthrough. The new measures discussed here have not made headlines because they have not been shown to be *better* or substantially different from current approaches. Until a new method produces better predictive validity coefficients or some other convincing evidence, the WISC-III and similar tests will likely reign supreme.

Chapter Summary

1. Nonverbal intelligence tests are best considered as simply a clever and unusual means for assessing the same general intelligence, not a different "nonverbal intelligence" construct.

2. The Hiskey was designed specifically to assess the cognitive skills of deaf children and adolescents.

3. The standardization and scaling procedures used by the Hiskey would not be acceptable today. The manual may have been adequately prepared for the 1960s, but it is in dire need of revision in order to meet modern standards of assessment practice.

4. The psychometric properties of the Leiter International Performance Scale are so lack-

ing in comparison to more modern instruments that the Leiter is of more historical than clinical value.

5. The K-ABC Nonverbal Scale holds promise as a nonverbal intelligence measure for a variety of populations.

6. Given the strong norming and reliability properties of the DAS Nonverbal Scale, this instrument warrants further study and consideration for at least trial clinical use.

7. The WISC-III Performance Scale is likely to continue to be a popular nonverbal test of intelligence.

8. In 1920 Goodenough collected 4,000 drawings from children in the kindergarten through fourth grades of the public schools in Perth Amboy, New Jersey to standardize the scoring scale of her Draw a Man test.

9. Elizabeth Koppitz developed a human figure drawing test for use with children ages 5 through 12.

10. A study by Wisniewski and Naglieri (1989) found a correlation of only .51 between the DAP Total Test (Draw-a-Person: A Quantitative Scoring System) (Naglieri, 1988) and WISC-R Full Scale for a sample of 51 children who ranged in age from 6 to 16 years.

11. Clinicians now have many options for screeners of intelligence, most of which have stronger psychometric properties than drawing techniques.

12. The simple format, administration, and scoring of the PPVT-R have proved attractive to psychologists and others who have used the test as a screening measure.

13. Vygotsky viewed cognitive development as a social process whereby the child's interaction with competent adult models resulted in cognitive growth.

14. The zone of proximal development (ZPD) is the difference between the child's current level of development (as determined by the child's history of learning and its influence on the maturation process) and the level of development that can be achieved when a child is assisted by a competent model such as a parent, teacher, or accomplished peer.

15. Feuerstein, Rand, and Hoffman (1979) state that the purpose of the Learning Potential Assessment Device (LPAD) is to "identify and locate specific cognitive deficiencies and then evaluate, by intrachild comparisons, responses to instruction in general cognitive principles" (p. 297).

16. During the administration of the LPAD, examiners record the amount and type of assistance required to solve the item.

17. Budoff's system uses traditional nonverbal intelligence tests to pretest intelligence so as to avoid language-based measures that may be influenced by cultural differences (Glutting & McDermott, 1990). The pretest consists of the Kohs Block Designs Test and Raven's Progressive Matrices.

18. Bransford et al. (1987) delineate some advantages of dynamic assessment by noting that some of Budoff's research shows that (1) children who perform competently following dynamic assessment do better in other learning and social situations; (2) students with high learning potential status have higher achievement scores and have a better self-concept when they are mainstreamed, as opposed to segregated in self-contained special education classes; and (3) dynamic assessment profiles are frequently inconsistent with children's traditional assessment classification.

19. Glutting and McDermott (1990) cite a central problem with the LPAD research. The pliability of the LPAD methodology and haphazard adherence to a test-teach-test model make documentation of the effectiveness of the LPAD virtually impossible.

20. The Planning-Attention-Simultaneous-Successive (PASS) model serves as the basis for the Das-Naglieri Cognitive Assessment System.

21. Since the 1960s there has been a resurgence of interest in reaction time measures (Vernon, 1990).

22. Computerized scoring is by far the most popular use of intelligence testing software for clinicians who work with children.

23. Some common features of computerized scoring programs include error trapping of data input, computation of chronological age, inclusion of biographical information, computation of scores, increased scoring options, intraindividual interpretation, printed summaries, generation of hypotheses, data storage, word processing features, files of recommendations, and password protection.

24. Computerized interpretation software provides interpretation of the results, something that up to now was the domain of the clinician.

25. Some common features of CI programs include hypothesis generation, expert decisions, actuarial analysis, and printed reports.

26. McCullough (1990) cites some potential disadvantages of CI programs including unauthorized use, poor documentation of decision rules, insufficient validation of interpretive rules, and controversy regarding the selection of experts.

CHAPTER 13

Infant and Preschool Intellectual Assessment

CHAPTER QUESTIONS

What are the special reliability and validity issues associated with the assessment of young children?

What are some strengths and weaknesses of the Bayley scales?

Infant and preschool measures, which are usually associated with the age range of 1 year to 6 years, differ from other intelligence tests in scope. Infant measures in particular are usually multidimensional. Infant tests frequently assess cognitive and motor domains simultaneously. The McCarthy Scales of Children's Abilities (McCarthy, 1972), for example, are designed for ages 2½ through 8 and include a motor domain. Motor domains are even more common for infant measures. Some measures also assess behavioral, temperamental, and emotional status. The *Battelle Developmental Inventory* (Newborg,

et al., 1984) is a broad-based diagnostic measure that assesses personal-social, adaptive, motor, communication, and cognitive skills.

Many tests for young children focus on screening. Screening refers to the identification of "at-risk" children, who are then referred for a more thorough evaluation. Usually cut-off scores for at-risk status are rather generous in order to err in the direction of more false positives (children identified by the screener as at risk who are subsequently found to not be at risk) than false negatives (children who were not identified as at risk by the screener who may in fact have developmental problems). Cut scores for screening measures are also more inclusive because of the need for screeners to reduce false negatives. Screeners are brief by definition and more prone to measurement error. They are designed for use by professionals or trained paraprofessionals and are multidimensional. These measures are designed for the screening of large numbers of young children in a variety of settings ranging from neonatal clinics to pre-kindergarten schools. These devices have brief intellectual/cognitive tests, and in some cases they are not emphasized any more than any other part of the battery. The *Developmental Indicators for Assessment of Learning-Revised (DIAL-R)* and the *Denver Developmental Screening Tests* are examples of multidimensional screening measures.

This chapter focuses on comprehensive measures. It discusses intelligence test batteries that emphasize the assessment of cognitive functions and that are typically used for making diagnostic, as opposed to screening, decisions.

ISSUES IN PRESCHOOL ASSESSMENT

U.S. Public Law 99-457

Just as PL 94-142 provided impetus for increased assessment of children and adolescents by the public schools, PL 99-457 is a major extension of these services for preschool children and infants. The major provisions of the law are twofold. It mandates the extension of services under PL 94-142 downward to the 3- to 5-year-old age group. Handicapped preschoolers are entitled to a free and appropriate public education beginning in the 90–91 school year. The second component is the creation of a new federal Handicapped Infants and Toddlers Program for children from birth to 2 years of age. Children are eligible for the birth to 2 program if they are experiencing developmental delays, have a physical or mental condition that places them at risk for later delays (e.g., Down's syndrome), or are at risk for physical or emotional delays. These provisions are potentially far-reaching and should create renewed interest in the assessment and diagnosis of very young children, and there should be an associated increase in the number of available instruments for the cognitive assessment of this age group.

The psychometric quality of infant and pre-school intelligence measures is improving substantially as a result of renewed interest in the assessment of this age group. Bracken (1987) provides a review of the psychometric qualities of a number of preschool instruments that were available at that time and notes some shortcomings. He reviewed subtest and composite score reliabilities, ceiling and floor effects, and validity evidence. The quality of some of the instruments was high, particularly for some of the newer tests. Since this article, however, the standards continue to be raised as tests such as the DAS and others enter the arena.

Sources of Items

There is a notable lack of differentiation between the item pools of infant measures. Most of the widely used tests of infant intelligence can trace their roots to a single item pool, that of Arnold Gesell, the famous developmentalist.

This item similarity among preschool instruments was formally evaluated by Lewis and Sullivan (1985), who compared the items of 11 different tests spanning 50 years of test development. The tests that they reviewed are listed below.

Gesell Developmental Schedules (1939)

Uzgiris-Hunt (1976)

Denver Developmental Screening Test (1976)

Iowa Tests for Young Children (1936)

Merrill-Palmer (1926)

Kuhlman-Binet (1922)

Minnesota Pre-School Scale (1932)

Kuhlman Tests of Mental Development (1939)

Cattell Infant Intelligence Scale (1940)

Bayley Scales of Infant Development (1969)

Griffiths Mental Development Scale (1945–70)

Lewis and Sullivan (1985) noted remarkable similarity among the items in these tests, and most of the items could be traced to the pioneering work of Gesell. This situation is reminiscent of the rush to copy Binet early in this century. At that time there were numerous adaptations of the original Binet scales, all of them bearing striking similarities to the original. If imitation is indeed a sincere form of flattery, then Gesell's work on measuring mental development has been much appreciated as a measurement of infant intelligence.

Intelligence versus Developmental Status

It is interesting that, although he provided the basis for so many test development activities, *Gesell did not believe that intelligence could be assessed.* He was more interested in measuring the general maturation of the child (Goodman, 1990). Gesell conducted his important research as a contemporary of Terman, Goddard, Binet, and other early workers. In those heady days intelligence testing had become known as the major practical contribution of psychology. Many scientists of the day believed that Binet's test measured only or primarily biologically determined intelligence (see Chapter 1). Others, such as Gesell, believed that while intelligence was a construct worth studying, direct measures of this biological entity were not yet available and likely not to be discovered for some time. This idea is similar to the widely held view today that intelligence tests measure psychometric intelligence (Hebb's Intelligence B, 1949; Eysenck's psychometric intelligence, 1988), not biological intelligence.

The view that infant tests measure a multi-determined general developmental status has been carried forward by Nancy Bayley, the author of the respected *Bayley Scales of Infant Development* (1969). Bayley (1969) does not use the word "intelligence" in the title of her test or in her manual. She prefers to refer to her test as a measure of "developmental status." She states further that there are not "factors" of intelligence for preschoolers but rather clusters of abilities that differentiate at school age. As

Bayley states, ". . . any classification of abilities into parallel arrays purporting to designate different factors that develop concurrently is artificial and serves no useful purpose" (1969, p. 3). This point of view appears to be supported by subsequent factor analyses of preschool measures such as the Binet-4, where numerous researchers identified only one factor for 2- and 3-year-olds. The Bayley was also not devised to make inferences about past history or etiology. It was intended only as a measure of the current status of a child's cognitive development. The Bayley and the Gesell, by the way, do not offer "IQ" scores.

Gesell, Bayley, and Binet were all cautious about the interpretation of their scales as measures of intelligence. Does this caution have anything to do with their experiences with young children? Perhaps, but these viewpoints are currently important as *they emphasize the fairly low level of inference that is appropriate for all intelligence measures.* According to these great researchers, modern-day psychologists should regard preschool intelligence assessment as the evaluation of developmental status in the cognitive domain.

Assessing Developmental Status at All Ages

Sandra Scarr (1981) provides a theoretical framework for the viewpoint of these early workers, and she advances the idea that assessment of older children follow the lead of the early childhood tests by emphasizing the assessment of multiple domains. Analogous to the term "developmental status," Scarr proposes that clinicians measure "intellectual competence" (as opposed to intelligence). Scarr concludes that school personnel in particular measure three domains: cognitive (similar to current intelligence tests), motivation, and adjustment. She summarizes her argument for broadening intellectual assessment by saying:

Whenever one measures a child's cognitive functioning, one is also measuring cooperation, attention, persistence, ability to sit still, and social responsiveness to an assessment situation. This is certainly not an original thought; David Wechsler, for one, said this for nearly 50 years. Binet, before him, was aware that testing sampled far more than cognitive development. (p. 1161)

In many ways Scarr is describing the history of the practice of early childhood assessment, where there is a longer tradition of not placing one domain at a higher premium than others. Why did this orientation not take a foothold in the assessment of school-age children? The reasons are likely multitudinous and speculative. It is clear, however, that the intelligence test has historically been the lodestar of the school-age child's evaluation, in comparison to preschoolers.

Stability

One of the unusual aspects of preschool intellectual assessment is that psychologists cannot depend on these measures to show strong evidence of stability of past and future intelligence test scores (see Chapter 3). Stability research with preschoolers also differs in that there are significant differences in stability for normally developing and developmentally delayed infants and preschoolers.

The typical stability coefficients for intelligence tests hover in the .70s range and higher when tests are first administered at ages 6–7 or above and a second test is given about a year later (see Chapter 3). For normally developing children evaluated between birth and 2½ years of age the correlation with scores obtained at ages 3 to 8 range from .01 to .59 (Goodman, 1990). These coefficients are particularly unimpressive given that the correlation between parental intelligence or SES and child's scores on the Bayley approximate these values with coefficients as high as .50 for normally developing children. The trend, however, does differ for children showing developmental delays.

Developmentally delayed young children's intelligence test scores are considerably more stable. Whereas stability coefficients between early (below 2 years of age) and later tests (taken at age 4–5 or above) for normal children reach .50 at their zenith, stability coefficients for handicapped children are in the .70 to .90s range for children tested at 1 year of age and older. There is a substantial likelihood that a child diagnosed as developmentally delayed during the first 2 years of life will retain such a diagnosis (Goodman, 1990) (see Chapter 3).

Inadequate Theory

Some of the same problems that have plagued all intellectual assessments of course apply also to the assessment of infants and preschoolers. The pernicious problem of a lack of theory to guide test and item selection also affects this area of assessment. Since most of the items currently in use can be traced to Gesell's pioneering work in the 1920s, the item content of many of these measures is not specified by a theory unique to each test author. Early developers of infant tests were driven by the same empiricism as Binet, who sought high correlations with school achievement. Infant and preschool test developers used the same approach but gave attention to a different type of validity. These test developers were seeking strong evidence of age differentiation validity. Goodman (1990) eloquently states the problem:

From today's distance, one wonders why the one fundamental criterion for item selection was goodness of fit with evolving age. Apparently no effort was made to predefine the nature of intelligence and then to select items that most adequately fit the construct(s), regardless of how smoothly they paralleled age changes. Theories of mental growth were generated by, rather than generating, item development. (p. 187)

Infant and preschool assessment has not been the beneficiary of recent test development efforts. The most popular infant scale, the Bayley, was published in 1969. Some tests that are designed for wide age ranges may make some theoretical contributions to preschool assessment. The K-ABC, Woodcock-Johnson, and DAS have tried to develop theory-based items down to age 2 years. Perhaps would-be developers of new tests in this area will be able to create an even stronger link between theory, research, and assessment.

Preschool and Infant Assessment as a Specialty

Infant and preschool intellectual assessment is often full of pitfalls for the clinician. The test instruments offer choices ranging from the psychometrically inadequate to the antique. The usual thinking regarding predictive validity and stability does not apply to these measures, and the challenges presented by this age group, ranging from adorable manipulation to soiled pants, require a skilled clinician.

Given that intellectual assessment of preschoolers requires a different set of knowledge and skills than for older children, there seems to be a need for specialized training in this area. It is akin to the assessment of hearing-impaired children, children from cultures vastly different from that of the examiner, and other children who require new sets of knowledge and skills. While formal guidelines for the training of individuals to assess young children are lacking, it seems wise for clinicians to seek specialized coursework and supervised practice before conducting evaluations of young children (see Box 13.1).

The trend toward specialized training is increasingly being recognized. In the newly published *System for Planning Early Childhood Services (SPECS)* (Bagnato & Neisworth, 1989), a new professional title is used: Developmental School Psychologist. I have not heard this term previously, but I think that its use reflects the recognition on the part of the authors that the infant age range in particular requires special-

ized training in order to carry out intellectual evaluations. Specialized training for child clinicians who assess infants and preschoolers might include strong coursework in normal and handicapped child development, preschool assessment coursework, and supervised experience in an early childhood setting.

TESTING INFANTS

The assessment of children under 24 months of age typically involves some modifications in the standard assessment procedure. While tests administered to older children are to be administered in prescribed order, this is not the case for younger children. Standardized procedures for infants are more of a "guide" than a rigid set of rules. Examiners should feel free to violate the prescribed test's sequence in order to maintain the infant's interest in the tasks. Scoring is even more flexible. On the Bayley, for example, an item may be scored correct if the child demonstrates the criterion behavior outside the test session (e.g., in the waiting room).

It is also conventional wisdom that mothers or other caretakers are not to be present for intellectual evaluations. Not only are parents "allowed" to be present for the testing of preschoolers; they may also administer some items if the infant is more likely to respond to the parent (Bayley, 1969). This also requires that the examiner develop a good rapport with the parent as well as with the baby. In fact, rapport with the parent is probably more important. In this setting the word "doctor" may not be wise to use when introducing oneself to the child's parent since it may remind the child of some painful medical procedure. Rapport with the parent will be facilitated by making eye contact, smiling, and approaching her in a direct and friendly manner. The reason for the assessment and/or neutral topics such as the weather and parking difficulties may provide good material for an opening conversation. It is also important to

BOX 13.1

Preschool escapades

Preschoolers are so cute that they may seem to be an appealing audience to many people. Hence, I think that a few cautions are in order. When I worked as a school psychologist, I was charged with reevaluating high-risk kindergarteners annually as part of an experimental intervention program. I gave the McCarthy scales to about 40 children each winter, and I was always ill with an upper respiratory infection until spring break! I tried washing my hands psychopathologically, taking vitamins, sitting farther away from the kids—everything short of wearing a mask—but it was of no avail. I was miserably sick for three months every year.

In addition to the colds, I was orthopedically impaired for these same three months. This difficulty was due to my having to sit every day in a preschooler's chair, or on the floor, in order to conduct the evaluations. At 6 foot 3 inches tall and inflexible, I had great difficulty adjusting to talking through my knees.

There was no escaping the little cuties. At the time I had a preschooler at home, and a vengeful one at that. I'll never forget the day that she became angry at her older sister and used her sister's shoe for her bowel movement in lieu of the commode. I vividly remember her proudly walking out of the bathroom with her sister's shoe full of you know what.

Yes, young children can be delightful, in the hands of the right clinician, which apparently was not me!

explain the testing procedures thoroughly to the parent and to continue to explain what one is doing as the assessment progresses (Kamphaus, Dresden, & Kaufman, in press).

The child should not be approached abruptly (Bayley, 1969). The examiner may place a toy or other object near the child, then speak with the child's caregiver for a brief time or arrange the test setting. The examiner may then gradually approach the child while interacting with the parent. Approaching the child with the parent will help allay the baby's fears.

The examiner should be aware of the context surrounding the individual testing session. This awareness is particularly important when testing infants because the examiner has the opportunity to provide the parent with some information about his or her child. For example, the examiner may use the session to model appropriate interaction with an infant for a parent whose parenting skills need strengthening or may highlight the child's capabilities in order to reassure an overly anxious parent (Kamphaus, Dresden, & Kaufman, in press).

Scheduling is a crucial consideration with infants. Young infants may have only an hour or two of alert time each day, and it is imperative that examiners attempt to schedule testing for this time (Bayley, 1969). Unfortunately, predicting these alert times is often difficult and thus makes the testing of infants very tricky indeed. A testing session should never be scheduled during a regular nap or feeding time (Kamphaus, Dresden, & Kaufman, in press). Breaks may also be taken for feeding, nursing, or changing diapers as needed.

Recommendations regarding the environment differ for infants and preschoolers compared to older children. The floor should be carpeted or otherwise be made comfortable, and there should be homelike places for the young infant—a blanket on the floor or an infant seat, for example. If infant seats are not available the parent can be asked to bring the infant to the testing session in his or her car seat and the car seat can be used instead (Kamphaus, Dresden, & Kaufman, in press). Some preschoolers may respond better to an examiner sitting across the table from as opposed to beside the child (Bayley, 1969). This arrangement may work better for the reticent child who may feel uncomfortable if the examiner comes too close.

Because infants have such brief periods when they are happy and alert, the examiner must pace the session carefully and be extremely flexible. The pace of the session must be rapid in order to catch as much optimal behavior as possible, *and* very calm and gentle in order not to overstimulate the baby. As Bayley (1969) aptly states, "Hurry yourself but do not hurry the child" (p. 27). Too many repetitions of an item or too many items in too little time can cause the baby to be overwhelmed and fall apart. Flexibility is also necessary—the examiner may have to follow a toddler around the room administering whatever item seems most likely to attract the child's attention. Generally, young children respond better when the session begins with manipulatives such as blocks or other test toys (Bayley, 1969). Oral questions or items involving following instructions should be administered after working with a few manipulatives. Finally, as the child tires and needs a break from sitting, gross and fine motor activities may be optimal.

The key to flexible, swift, yet relaxed administration of a test is a thorough knowledge of the test and total familiarity with the materials. This knowledge enables the examiner to move rapidly from one item to another while focusing on the child and maximizes the likelihood that the child will perform up to the level of his or her true capability (Kamphaus, Dresden, & Kaufman, in press). Test familiarity will also allow the examiner to collect valuable nontest data for domains such as parent–child interaction, parenting skill, and child temperament.

INFANT TESTS

Bayley Scales

The most popular of infant developmental status intelligence measures is the *Bayley Scales of Infant Development* (Bayley, 1969). This scale extends from 2 to 30 months of age and includes a Motor Scale, Mental Scale, and Infant Behavior Record. Nancy Bayley's test is somewhat unique in that it is the result of a long career of research on the mental development of children, primarily with the Berkeley Growth Study. Based on this research, Bayley concluded that infants' mental development was highly unstable, and that no general factor of intelligence existed (Goodman, 1990).

The Bayley scales differed from other infant tests of its day because of its technical superiority. For example, it broke with tradition by offering standard scores instead of the Ratio IQ that was typical of its predecessors. The two Bayley composite scores of interest are the Mental Development Index (MDI) and the Psychomotor Development Index (PDI). The MDI and PDI are normalized standard scores using the familiar Stanford-Binet metric with a mean of 100 and standard deviation of 16. Their values range from 50 to 150, and Naglieri (1981) provides extrapolated indexes down to a standard score of 28 for some age groups. These are not, however, IQs or meant to serve as measures of intelligence per se, but rather as measures of developmental status. According to Bayley (1969), the three scales serve as "a tripartite basis for the evaluation of a child's developmental status in the first two and one half years of life" (p. 3). The Bayley manual, however, does not elaborate on this point to articulate the nature of "developmental status" and explain its implications for interpretation (Damarin, 1978).

The Bayley was also designed to be psychometrically superior to its predecessors, many of which had norms dating back to the middle of this century. At the time of its collection the norming study of the Bayley was clearly superior to that of its competitors.

Virtually all infant and preschool tests are difficult to administer given the behavioral characteristics of this age group, especially the difficulties in gaining and sustaining their attention. Consequently, test developers make heavy use of manipulatives, resulting in test kits that resemble toy boxes and weigh nearly as much. All parents know how difficult it is to find the toy you want in a toy box! Finding—and using—the test materials of the Bayley and other scales is similarly difficult. The Bayley requires extraordinary familiarity with its materials in order to administer it properly.

Standardization

The Bayley was standardized in the 1960s for children 2 through 30 months of age. The sample was divided into 14 age groups of 100 children each and evenly divided by gender. The goal of 1,400 cases was not met, resulting in a slightly smaller sample of 1,262 children. The smallest sample for any age group was 83 cases at age 2 months. Children had to be tested within 1 week of their designated age categorization.

The sample was stratified so as to be representative of the U.S. population at the time, based on gender, age, ethnicity (white and non-white), geographic region, community size (urban or rural residence), and SES (parental occupation and education). Another interesting variable collected during the norming was the percentage of children by birth order. First-borns made up 27% to 44% of the sample for any age group. Ninth-born children made up only 0% to 2% of any age group. While these norms were state of the art for the time, their appropriateness for use in the 1990s is questionable (see Chapter 5).

Reliability

Split-half coefficients for the scales are high, in the .80s and .90s. The coefficients for the MDI range from a low of .81 at age 8 months to .93 at age 3 months. Internal consistency coefficients for the PDI are slightly lower. Test-retest coefficients are reported as indexes of agreement rather than coefficients, making their interpretation difficult.

Validity

There is clear evidence to support Bayley's (1969) point that the abilities assessed by the MDI change *qualitatively* over time. As one piece of evidence, Damarin (1978) points out that at 4, 5, and 6 months the average proportion of true score variance of the MDI that can be explained by the PDI is high at .66. This proportion changes at 12 months to .08, and at 21 to 30 months to .13. Clearly the question as to the degree to which the MDI and PDI can be interpreted as unique constructs varies substantially by age. Correlations between the MDI and PDI given in the manual range from .18 at 30 months to .75 at 5 months. There is somewhat of a trend for the correlations between the two scales to attenuate with age, suggesting that these two constructs begin to differentiate with increasing age.

These is also one study of the relationship between the Stanford Binet-LM and the Bayley reported in the manual. At age 24 months the correlation between the two measures was .53, at 27 months .64, and at 30 months it was .47. These are moderate relationships that show some independence of the two measures.

Summary

The Bayley is generally considered an important psychometric achievement in the development of infant tests. It does, however, require a new set of interpretive skills because of the undifferentiated nature of the cognitive skills of young children.

Administration of the Bayley demands considerable study on the part of the new examiner. The materials, however, are toy-like, making them appealing to young children. Bayley's extensive experience with young children is evident in the selection of stimulus materials.

The major strength of the Bayley, its strong psychometric properties, is now becoming a liability. The norm sample is too old to be used with a great degree of confidence for making norm-referenced comparisons. On the other hand, the psychometric properties of the Bayley remain strong compared to its contemporaries such as the Cattell and Gesell that are more out of date. The Bayley is also said to be currently undergoing a major revision.

Measures of Infant Information Processing

Tests of infant mental processing skills have received considerable attention lately as a potential breakthrough in the assessment of infant intelligence. Although many of them are experimental, these "tests" have received attention because of claims of stronger predictive validity coefficients, even for nonhandicapped children. They measure attention, retrieval, encoding, and other processing skills, using a variety of paradigms.

One of the well-known information processing characteristics of infants is *habituation*. Most of these paradigms present face-like stimuli to infants. As the child becomes familiar with the visual stimulus, his or her interest in it and attention to it begins to wane. This decrement in attention to a familiar stimulus signifies habituation. In other words, more capable children direct less attention to the familiar stimulus.

Another habitation measure is to measure recovery of attention when a novel stimulus (e.g., face-like pattern) is introduced. This paradigm, commonly referred to as *novelty preference* or *dishabituation*, measures the attention that a child gives to a newly introduced stimulus. Children with impaired intelligence do not recognize or respond to the novel stimulus as quickly in such procedures.

A novelty preference task was used by Fagan (1984b), who tested 36 suburban nonhandicapped children on a novelty preference task at age 7 months. Each infant was shown pairs of pictures (black and white) of women and babies until the child fixated on one of the faces for 20 seconds. The child was then shown this face again, paired with a novel face, for two five-second test intervals to determine the child's preference for novelty. The children were then evaluated again at 3 years on a recognition memory task and the PPVT-R. The children were given these same tests again at 5 years of age.

The reliability of the novelty preference measures was quite low at .32. The predictive valid-

ity of the novelty preference task at 7 months for PPVT-R scores at age 5 was higher at .42. Another finding was that recognition memory scores at age 3 were more highly correlated with PPVT-R scores at age 5 (r = .66) than novelty preference at age 7 months. These are all modest stability and validity coefficients that do not differ significantly from the data for more traditional measures.

The finding of significant predictive validity coefficients for the novelty preference task is robust (Fagan, 1984b). A novelty preference task has also been found effective for differentiating low birth weight and high-risk monkeys (Gunderson, Grant-Webster, & Fagan, 1987; Gunderson, Grant-Webster, & Sackett, 1989) from normal monkeys. This line of research has resulted in the *Fagan Test of Infant Intelligence* (Joseph F. Fagan, Department of Psychology, Case Western Reserve University, Cleveland, OH, 44106). Fagan (1984b) also draws theoretical implications from his work, suggesting that visual preference and visual recognition tasks measure developmentally continuous intellectual skills that may shed light on the nature of g.

Goodman (1990) is critical of Fagan's work on a variety of levels. She notes that there are reliability problems with these types of tasks because of the difficulties involved in measuring infants' attention. Typical reliability coefficients are in the .40s. Predictive validity coefficients for normal children are higher than those of tests such as the Bayley, but coefficients for handicapped samples are similar to those for traditional tests (Goodman, 1990). After a thorough review of the data on measures of infant information processing, including Fagan's work, Goodman (1990) concludes: "Until we have more predictors and criteria, it will remain unclear just what the visual recognition tasks are measuring and how much reliance can be placed on them" (p. 199).

Ross (1989) assesses the practical utility of Fagan's and similar approaches and draws two conclusions: (1) information processing approaches are less satisfactory from a clinical standpoint, and (2) their predictive validity advantage is insignificant for clinical cases. The narrow set of skills assessed by information processing measures results in less of an information yield than that obtained from traditional measures that sample a larger variety of infant behavior.

The predictive superiority of information processing measures is insignificant for handicapped infants when ranges of scores are utilized. Ranges may include broad categories such as > 85 (normal), 70–85 (at risk), and < 70 (handicapped). These ranges correspond to typical diagnostic practice, where children are classified or diagnosed based on the range in which their scores lie. Ross (1989) found a correct classification rate of 87% using the Bayley with a sample of 94 preterm infants. Siegel (1979) obtained an 84% correct classification rate when using the Bayley. Fagan, Singer, and Montie (1986) found a classification rate of 86% with preterm infants when a novelty preference task was used.

The novelty preference task, however, does show more consistent superiority when used to predict the performance of nonhandicapped children (Ross, 1989). The information processing approaches of Fagan and similar methodologies are promising. They do, however (please excuse the lame attempt at humor), seem to be in their "infancy." More large-scale investigations and greater attention to issues of norming, reliability, and validity are necessary before wide acceptance is warranted.

Battelle Developmental Inventory

The Battelle Developmental Inventory (BDI) was developed as part of a large-scale federal research program concerned with planning and evaluating intervention programs for at-risk infants, toddlers, and preschoolers. The BDI was published in 1984 and the manual and norms were updated in 1988. The BDI was designed for children from birth to 8 years of age, and it includes five major domains. These domains include Cognitive, Personal-Social, Adaptive, Motor, and Communication. Each domain comprises numerous subdomains. Consequently, the BDI is extremely comprehensive, capable of producing a profile of 30 scores. These scores include:

1. Adult Interaction
2. Expression of Feeling-Affect
3. Self-concept
4. Peer Interactions
5. Coping
6. Social Role
7. Personal-Social Total
8. Attention
9. Eating
10. Dressing
11. Personal Responsibility
12. Toileting
13. Adaptive Total
14. Muscle Control
15. Body Coordination
16. Locomotion
17. Gross Motor
18. Fine Muscle
19. Perceptual Motor
20. Fine Motor
21. Motor Total
22. Receptive
23. Expressive
24. Communication Total
25. Perceptual Discrimination
26. Memory
27. Reasoning and Academic Skills
28. Conceptual Development
29. Cognitive Total
30. Total Battery

The BDI is in many ways similar to the Bayley scales because of its multidimensional emphasis and because it includes a cognitive domain, which is the focus of this review.

Administration and Scoring

The BDI because of its comprehensive nature is somewhat more lengthy to administer than many preschool and infant test batteries. A study by Bailey et al. (1987) evaluated several practical aspects of BDI administration and scoring. They included a study of 76 teachers who had administered the BDI to 247 handicapped preschoolers as part of a statewide study evaluating the use of the BDI. One of the findings of this implementation study was that the BDI required on the average 2½ sessions to administer. Average administration time was 93.4 minutes and the mean amount of scoring time was 34.4 minutes. Hence, the BDI on average will require 2 hours of examiner time.

The BDI offers a variety of scores, including percentile ranks, age equivalents, and developmental quotients (DQ) (standard scores with a mean of 100 and SD of 15). One of the problems identified with BDI scoring is the difficulty in obtaining extreme DQ values for domains. In the Cognitive domain, for example, the lowest value available for the DQ is 65. The manual, however, provides a procedure for calculating (extrapolating) DQs below this level. This procedure, however, is somewhat cumbersome and has resulted in what appear to be spurious values (Bailey et al., 1987). McLinden (1989) clarified the nature of the problem of calculating extreme BDI scores. Apparently it is possible to obtain negative developmental quotients. In the implementation study by Bailey et al., 28% of the children obtained a negative developmental quotient. In addition, McLinden (1989) has criticized the wide age ranges used in developing the norms. It was noted, for example, that a toddler tested at 23 months of age with a total raw score of 243 would receive a DQ of 99. If this same child was tested *1 month later* at 24

months of age and again obtained a raw score of 243, the developmental quotient would be 65.

The BDI also requires a considerable number of manipulatives in the administration process. Many of the manipulatives have to be produced by the examiner. The examiner, for example, must cut out puzzles and pictures for administration purposes—materials that may show considerable wear and tear (Paget, 1989).

Standardization

Standardization of the BDI was conducted from December 1982 to March 1983. A stratified national sample was collected consisting of 800 children, approximately 50 boys and 50 girls at each 1-year age level. The sample was constructed to reflect 1980 Census Bureau statistics. The sample, however, was not specifically stratified for socioeconomic status, leading to some question about the accuracy of the sampling program (McLinden, 1989).

Reliability

Reliability coefficients for the BDI are extremely high. A study of 183 children involved in a test-retest reliability study produced coefficients ranging from .71 to .99, with a .99 also being yielded for the BDI total score. Interrater reliability coefficients for the BDI are similarly high. Several authors have cited the small standard errors of measurement of the BDI as a potential strength of the instrument (Oehler-Stinnett, 1989; Paget, 1989). McLinden (1989), however, challenges the values for the standard errors of measurement included in the BDI manual. McLinden suggests that the test authors used the incorrect formula to calculate the SEMs. It appears that the authors of the BDI used the formula for the standard error of the mean as opposed to the formula for SEM. Correctly computed SEMs for the BDI are reported in an article by McLinden (1989) and they are considerably more realistic and larger than the "SEMs" reported in the manual.

Validity

An early concurrent validity study by Guidubaldi and Perry (1984) shows substantial correlations between BDI Cognitive DQ scores and other cognitive measures in a sample of first-grade children. In this investigation the BDI Cognitive DQ correlated .38 with the PPVT-R and .31 with the Stanford-Binet Third Edition Vocabulary subtest. A similar investigation by Mott (1987) was conducted on 20 children diagnosed as having significant speech-language disorders. For this small sample the BDI Cognitive DQ correlated .32 with the PPVT-R.

A classification study by McLean et al. (1987) involved 30 handicapped and 35 nonhandicapped children between the ages of 7 months and 72 months of age. The handicapped sample included primarily children diagnosed as developmentally delayed or multihandicapped. A small number of children were diagnosed as hearing-impaired or behaviorally disordered. This study compared the diagnostic agreement between the BDI screening test (a short form of the BDI) and the Denver Developmental Screening Test-Revised. These authors found that the Denver and the BDI disagreed substantially in identifying children for follow-up evaluation. Specifically, "out of a group of 35 children with no prior indication of exceptionality, the BDI identified 22 as needing further testing while the Denver Developmental Screening Test-Revised identified all as normal" (McLean et al., 1987, p. 19). An interesting investigation by Sexton et al. (1988) compared the BDI to the Bayley scales for a sample of 70 handicapped children who were less than 30 months old. The correlation between the BDI Cognitive and Bayley Mental Score was quite high at .93. This high coefficient led Sexton et al. (1988) to conclude that "the correlation coefficients . . . indicate that the scales within both measures tend to place the 70 children in roughly the same order. The results strongly support the concurrent validity of the newly developed BDI" (p. 22).

One of the frequently cited strengths of the BDI is its content validity (Paget, 1989). The final BDI item pool was selected from an initial pool of 4,000 items that were derived from other tests and evaluated carefully in two preliminary studies.

The factor structure of the BDI in an early investigation suggests some correspondence between the five domains of this measure and its factor structure for children from birth to 5 years of age. At ages 6 through 8 more than five factors were yielded, suggesting that factorial support is strongest for younger age groups (Newman & Guidubaldi, 1981).

Conclusions

Although a relatively new entrant into the field of preschool assessment, the BDI has been noted as having several strengths. Among these assets are its careful selection of item content, comprehensive sampling of preschool and infant behavior, extended age range, administration flexibility, and concurrent validity with the Bayley scales. Negative aspects of the BDI include questionable scaling, lack of SES stratification for the norming sample, mediocre concurrent validity with well-known cognitive measures such as the WISC-R and Stanford-Binet (Oehler-Stinnett, 1989), and lengthy administration time.

It is perhaps reasonable and predictable for the BDI not to show a close correspondence with multisubtests measures of intelligence at the preschool level. The domains assessed by the BDI are frequently not assessed by intelligence measures (e.g., adaptive behavior), which could adversely affect the correlation between BDI Total Score and traditional intelligence measures. In addition, the Cognitive domain of the BDI is somewhat brief in comparison to other preschool measures, which again could adversely affect its correlational relationship with well-known competitors. The BDI differs in concept to such a substantial extent from many multisubtest measures of intelligence that one has to evaluate its utility in a much larger context. The decision regarding selection of the BDI has more to do with the nature of the assessment purpose that the clinician has in mind. Clinicians have to decide how the BDI or its competitors in a particular age range fit into the larger context of the assessment of an infant or preschooler.

PRESCHOOL TESTS

McCarthy Scales of Children's Abilities

The McCarthy scales (McCarthy, 1972) have been the recipient of considerable research attention (Kaufman, 1982; Valencia, 1990). There is even a well-written textbook on the use of the McCarthy (Kaufman & Kaufman, 1977). The McCarthy warrants consideration by all clinicians who evaluate children because of its long research tradition and other strengths. These strengths include a design that considers the developmental needs and interests of preschoolers, use of cognitive developmental research and theory in test design, and utility for diagnostic decision making (Kaufman & Kaufman, 1977).

The McCarthy consists of 18 subtests designed for use with children between the ages of 2½ and 8½. This brief age range may be a hindrance to the popularity of the McCarthy since it does limit opportunities for continuity of follow-up assessment. The subtests of the McCarthy are combined to produce six composite scores. The Verbal, Perceptual-Performance, and Quantitative scales assess important content or knowledge, whereas the Memory and Motor scales are designed to assess how well a child processes information (Valencia, 1990). The subtests of the McCarthy and their scale membership are shown in Table 13.1 in their order of administration. The sixth scale of the McCarthy is an overall composite score called a General Cognitive Index (GCI) (mean = 100, SD = 16). The GCI is made up of 15 subtests from all

TABLE 13.1   Subtests of the McCarthy scales of children's abilities

Subtest	Scale(s)
Block Building	Perc-Perf, GCI
Puzzle Solving	Perc-Perf, GCI
Pictorial Memory	Ver, Mem, GCI
Word Knowledge	Ver, GCI
Number Questions	Quant, GCI
Tapping Sequence	Perc-Perf, Mem, GCI
Verbal Memory	Ver, Mem, GCI
Right-Left Orientation*	Perc-Perf, GCI
Leg Coordination	Motor
Arm Coordination	Motor
Imitative Action	Motor
Draw-A-Design	Perc-Perf, Motor, GCI
Draw-A-Child	Perc-Perf, Motor, GCI
Numerical Memory	Quant, Mem, GCI
Verbal Fluency	Ver, GCI
Counting and Sorting	Quant, GCI
Opposite Analogies	Ver, GCI
Conceptual Grouping	Perc-Perf, GCI

*This test is only administered at age 5 and above.

of the scales (three of the Motor tests are omitted from the GCI and two are retained).

The McCarthy is designed so that all of the tests are to be administered to all children (with the exception of Right-Left Orientation, which is only administered at ages 5 and above). This may sound lengthy to a novice, but the McCarthy subtests are designed to be relatively short so as to hold the child's interest. The brevity of the subtests precludes subtest interpretation. The subtests also vary in terms of motor activity (i.e., gross motor tasks are included that allow the child to get out of his or her seat), which is clearly congruent with the activity level of young children. The McCarthy is one of the few tests that has these built-in "breathers" for young children. This design can be seen in Table 13.1.

The Motor subtests are administered halfway through the evaluation; thus, the child is provided with a reprieve from sitting.

Standardization

The standardization sample consisted of 1,032 boys and girls divided equally among 10 age groups ranging from 2½ to 8½ years. The sample was selected based on 1970 U.S. Census statistics. Stratification variables included gender, age, father's occupation, ethnicity, geographic region, and urban/rural residence. The standardization sample used sophisticated procedures for its day (Nagle, 1979); however, it cannot be considered to be representative of the national population of young children today.

Reliability

The McCarthy scales show good evidence of reliability for the six composite scores (Kaufman, 1982). Valencia (1990) reviewed five studies of the internal consistency reliability of the McCarthy and eight studies of stability. Internal consistency estimates were generally high across the investigation, with most of them being in the .80s and .90s, which is commendable given the lower reliabilities that are associated with preschool assessment. The Motor scale was an exception to this trend in that coefficients for this scale were typically lower, in the .60s and .70s. Test-retest studies produced lower reliabilities overall. Of the eight studies reported by Valencia (1990), only one produced a GCI test-retest reliability of .90—the remainder were primarily in the .80s. The Motor scale again had lower reliabilities, with coefficients ranging from .33 to .77. These results suggest that McCarthy scores, while highly stable for many children, will be unstable for a few children. This is likely to be a particular problem for some of the composites other than the GCI. It is also predictable from previous research on preschoolers that stability will be an even greater problem with children toward the bottom of the McCarthy age range.

Validity

Factor analytic studies of the McCarthy have produced inconsistent results (Valencia, 1990). Some studies have produced a large first, or "g," factor (Kaufman & Hollenbeck, 1973; Keith & Bolen, 1980), whereas others have not (Kaufman & DiCuio, 1975; Teeter, 1984). There has been consistent evidence, however, of factors that correspond to the Verbal, Motor, and Perceptual-Performance scales (Kaufman, 1982; Valencia, 1990). The Quantitative and Memory scales, in contrast, do not show consistent factorial support (Kaufman, 1982; Valencia, 1990). This sounds vaguely familiar, does it not? These results are strikingly consistent with the Binet-4 findings indicating a lack of factor analytic support for its Quantitative and Short-Term Memory scores and with the DAS data that showed no indication of a separate memory scale. In light of these findings for other tests, the McCarthy results seem predictable and reasonable.

Valencia (1990) concluded that there is strong evidence for the concurrent validity of the McCarthy. He reviewed the available correlational studies comparing the McCarthy with the Binet, WPPSI, and other scales and found a mean correlation of .74, a substantial correlation. The greater controversy regarding the McCarthy deals with the issue of mean differences between McCarthy GCI and overall composite scores of other measures, notably the WISC-R Full Scale score. (See the discussion of the difference between correlation and agreement in Chapter 5.) Many studies have addressed this issue, and the conclusion across investigations is that the GCI underestimates intelligence test scores from the Wechsler scales and the Binet-LM (which is now superseded by the Binet-4) by about 4 standard score points. This finding has led some clinicians to view the McCarthy skeptically. Unfortunately, this difference between the McCarthy and the WISC-R and the Binet-LM cannot be explained by differences in dates of norming sample as one might predict, since all were normed in the early

1970s. An interesting finding is that the McCarthy and K-ABC agree more closely (Valencia, 1990).

Evidence for the predictive validity of the McCarthy is strong, with coefficients from most studies being in the .60s and .70s. This type of validity evidence is of particular relevance for a preschool instrument designed to identify children at risk for educational problems. The McCarthy has also piqued interest in predictive validity issues because of its well-known screening short form, the *McCarthy Screening Test* (MST) (The Psychological Corporation, 1978).

Smith and Lyon (1987) compared the McCarthy and the K-ABC performance of groups of repeating and nonrepeating preschoolers. One group had been recommended for kindergarten (N = 27) and a second group of children had been recommended for retention in the preschool program (N = 13). Both the McCarthy and K-ABC scores discriminated between the two groups. The mean GCI for the repeaters was 67.0, whereas for the nonrepeaters the mean GCI was 86.5. In parallel fashion the MPC for the repeaters was 76.2, as opposed to 91.4 for the nonrepeaters. It is noteworthy in this study that the McCarthy scores are lower for both the repeater and nonrepeater groups. This finding is consistent with other research showing that the McCarthy tends to produce lower scores than other tests (Valencia, 1988).

McCarthy Screeners

The MST consists of six subtests: Right-Left Orientation, Draw-A-Design, Numerical Memory (Parts 1 and 2), Verbal Memory (Part 1), Leg Coordination, and Conceptual Grouping. In lieu of a GCI or other total score, the MST offers two decision points: "at-risk" at one of three cutoffs of the 10th, 20th, or 30th percentile rank and "failure" of one, two, or three subtests.

Some controversy regarding the construction of the MST has resulted in the development of alternative screening forms of the MST (Taylor,

Slocumb, & O'Neill, 1979). The most serious challenge to the MST is the Kaufman short form (Kaufman, 1977, hereafter referred to as the KSF). This short form for screening purposes also includes six McCarthy subtests: Puzzle Solving, Word Knowledge, Numerical Memory, Verbal Fluency, Counting and Sorting, and Conceptual Grouping. The KSF has impressive psychometric properties, with correlations with complete GCI being in the low .90s in the majority of investigations (Valencia, 1990). Perhaps because of these impressive psychometric properties, the KSF has spawned a number of studies comparing the MST and the KSF. (See Valencia, 1990, for an excellent review of the McCarthy research, including screener investigations.) The available research has been somewhat more supportive of the KSF. Based on his extensive and insightful review, Valencia (1990) concludes: "Taken together, the available research on the three McCarthy short forms clearly points to the Kaufman SF as the instrument of choice, and thus I endorse it as a useful screening tool. Both psychometric and "hands-on" studies speak to its effectiveness as a screening tool" (p. 233).

Summary

The McCarthy is a unique instrument that is especially suited to assessing the emerging cognitive abilities of preschool and young school-age children. Research abounds on the use of the McCarthy and its various screeners as predictors of later academic problems. The McCarthy is well constructed and alluring to young children. It is game-like, which can demand some motor skill on the part of the examiner.

The McCarthy could benefit from greater floor. While the materials are childlike, there are not enough easy items for 2½ year olds. Evidence of this problem is the fact that for 11 of the 17 subtests the raw score standard deviation at age 2½ is *larger* than the mean raw score.

Although the McCarthy norms may need updating, the extensive supportive research base of the McCarthy suggests that every clinician who assesses the intelligence of young children should become familiar with this scale. The well-known psychometrician Cronbach (1989) rates the McCarthy highly, saying, "The McCarthy scales, despite out-of-date norms, appear to be the instrument of choice at early ages" (p. 775).

The Binet-4

The release of the Binet-4 was generally not greeted with enthusiasm by those who assess preschoolers. In comparison to previous editions, the Binet-4 lacked manipulatives (toys, dogs, cats, scissors, etc.) and clinicians thought that it would be less likely to hold preschoolers' interest. Anastasi (1989) notes this poor early acceptance among clinicians, saying, "At this stage, its principal limitation centers on communication with test users, especially in clinical settings" (p. 772). Cronbach (1989) echoed some of the concerns of clinicians when he observed, "My impression is that the SB4 is less game-like than some other individual tests and will be less attractive to children" (p. 773).

I also question the arrangement of Binet-4 subtests for preschoolers. Pattern Analysis, for example, uses three different item types and the child shifts abruptly from one to the other as the test becomes more difficult (see Chapter 10). This procedure complicates the examiner's duty to administer a variety of item types correctly.

Practical problems and concerns aside, the Binet-4 is being used with preschoolers, and it has a number of positive attributes to recommend its use. The continuity of measurement with the Binet-4 is one admirable characteristic. Its wide age range and extended standard score scale (to a low of 35) make it a useful tool for assessing developmentally delayed young children and following them through their school years. The psychometric properties of the Binet-4 are also excellent (see Chapter 10).

Reliability

Internal consistency coefficients for the Binet-4 for preschoolers are excellent (see Chapter 10 for a discussion of reliability and norming properties). Furthermore, test-retest coefficients reported in the Binet-4 *Technical Manual* (Thorndike, Hagen, & Sattler, 1986) are also impressive. The test-retest reliability of the composite scores ranges from a low of .71 for Quantitative Reasoning to a high of .91 for the Composite. These findings are sensible given the robust factor analytic support for the Composite score and validity problems of the Quantitative area score. Most of the Binet-4 subtests have test-retest coefficients in the .70s for preschoolers except for Bead Memory, which had a coefficient of .56 (Thorndike, Hagen, & Sattler, 1986). One can imagine how preschoolers' eagerness to play with the beads may have adversely affected their performance on this test.

Validity

Given that Binet-4 debuted in 1986, it is surprising to find so little research available on the use of the test with preschoolers. One concurrent validity study available in the *Technical Manual* (Thorndike, Hagen, & Sattler, 1986) used the old WPPSI with 5-year-olds. The correlation between the two composite scores was high at .80.

Factor analytic data for preschoolers shows that the four area score model is a poor fit for this age group (see Chapter 10). Thorndike (1990), Kline (1988), and Sattler (1988) use a variety of methods but come to the same conclusions. The composite score is the most important to interpret for preschoolers because of a strong "g" factor. The Verbal and Abstract/Visual area scores are the only two with any substantial support. This leads one to consider altering the administration of the Binet-4 for this age group. Is it wise to administer only the Verbal and Abstract/Visual domains and reserve the other domains for supplementary information? This is an important topic that I hope someone will address.

Summary

The advantages of the Binet-4 for preschool assessment include a large age range that supports continuity of measurement, an extended standard score scale, factor analytic validity evidence to support the composite score, relative brevity, and strong concurrent validity. Disadvantages include area scores that lack validity, less game-like materials, and a limited research base. More than anything else, the Binet-4 is in need of more research with this population. Currently the Binet-4 is too enigmatic considering its publication date.

K-ABC

The K-ABC enjoys considerable popularity for use with preschoolers (Kamphaus & Kaufman, 1991). The Kaufmans had young children clearly in mind when developing the K-ABC, and they included several characteristics that make the test useful for this age group.

The K-ABC differs greatly in its appearance from many widely used tests. It was designed to attract the interest of preschoolers by using colorful and true-to-life materials, not unlike the McCarthy scales. Tests such as Magic Window, Face Recognition, Expressive Vocabulary, and Arithmetic use either full-color artwork or photographs. As Telzrow (1984) notes: "Unlike other measures of preschool intelligence . . . the K-ABC utilizes marvelous color photographs in place of static (and too often unfamiliar) line drawings" (p. 312). On the other hand, although the K-ABC is attractive to young children, it could benefit from more manipulatives, which tend to pique the interest of children at the youngest age levels. Some clinicians bemoan the fact, for example, that the Triangles subtest is not administered until age 4. Additionally, Telzrow (1984) remarks: "The easel format facilitates the direction of attention where it should

be—on the child—instead of on myriad boxes, manuals, and test materials. And the child's attention is easy to maintain, given the attractiveness of the materials and their appeal to the children" (pp. 311–312).

The K-ABC authors also took great care to ensure that young children are able to understand the test instructions. This feat was accomplished by removing potentially difficult verbal concepts from the examiner instructions. Such concepts as "middle" and "after," which Boehm (1969, 1971) found to be difficult for young disadvantaged children, appear commonly in the directions spoken by the examiner when administering various standardized preschool instruments (Kaufman, 1978). Many examiners have asked why, for example, the Photo Series instructions do not use the words "sequence" or "order." These words were not used because it was believed that they would be difficult for some 6-year-olds to understand. In the K-ABC, however, there is an additional fall-back position if a young child does not understand even these simplified directions: Sample and Teaching Items (see Chapter 9).

Telzrow (1984) described several potential uses of the K-ABC with preschoolers. She proposed that the Nonverbal scale is a needed addition for preschoolers. She noted the deficiencies in other nonverbal measures (see Chapter 11) and suggested that the Nonverbal scale should be given a trial by those charged with the evaluation of hearing-impaired and severely speech-impaired preschoolers. Telzrow cautioned that some severely language-disordered children may be misidentified, possibly as mentally retarded, by many existing measures of intelligence that depend heavily on the assessment of verbal skills and knowledge.

Telzrow (1984) also argued that the K-ABC offers two advantages in the identification of preschool gifted children. One of these advantages is the availability of an achievement scale that is normed down to age 2½. She noted that academic achievement has been proposed as an important measure of early academic potential and that the K-ABC is unusual in that it possesses one of the few achievement scales appropriate for this age group.

Reliability

The test-retest coefficients for the K-ABC are generally in the middle .80s for the Mental Processing Composite scales for preschool children. The test-retest coefficients are generally higher (in the middle .90s) for the Achievement scale. This is an interesting finding in that the K-ABC Achievement scale is similar to traditional measures of verbal intelligence (Kamphaus & Reynolds, 1987). Furthermore, the K-ABC Achievement scale is the test's best predictor of future achievement. Since prediction of future achievement is one of the central purposes of preschool intelligence testing, it is fortuitous for practitioners that the best predictor on the K-ABC clearly possesses the best reliability.

Lyon and Smith (1986) assessed the long-term stability of the K-ABC with at-risk preschoolers. The K-ABC was administered at a 9-month interval to 53 children between the ages of 49 and 73 months who had been referred for early intervention. The stability coefficients ranged from .84 for the MPC to .73 for the Sequential scale. The coefficient was .76 for the Simultaneous scale and .82 for the Achievement scale. While these results support the overall accuracy of the K-ABC, an equally useful finding for practitioners was the level of gain over this time period. The Simultaneous scale was the big gainer (87.9 on test 1 to 97.2 on test 2), which is consistent with the test-retest data presented in the K-ABC *Interpretive Manual* (Kaufman & Kaufman, 1983b). The Sequential and Achievement scales each improved by about 3 points. The MPC improved by about 8 points over the 9-month time period.

In fact, the Achievement scale of the K-ABC yields comparable or higher stability coefficients at the preschool level than do the composite scores of tests such as the Stanford-Binet Fourth Edition, WPPSI-R, and McCarthy scales (see Bracken, 1987, for a review of the stability of preschool tests).

Validity

The K-ABC Achievement scale, like the Verbal scale of the WISC-R, is the best predictor of subsequent school achievement (Kamphaus & Reynolds, 1987). This finding is an important reminder to psychologists that measures of achievement, basic concepts, readiness skills, and related measures are likely to be better predictors of future school achievement than intelligence measures. I recommend that the Achievement scale be routinely administered when assessing preschoolers. This is consistent with the recommendations of Kaufman and Kaufman (1983b) that the Achievement scale always be administered in conjunction with the Mental Processing scales of the K-ABC.

Other research with at-risk preschoolers compares the K-ABC to other popular tests. Lyon and Smith (1986) compared the K-ABC, Stanford-Binet Form LM, and McCarthy scales for a group of 72 children referred for early intervention. The children ranged in age from 49 to 73 months. The correlations between the K-ABC and the other tests were moderate: .59 with the GCI and .45 with the Binet IQ. The correlation between the K-ABC Achievement scale and the GCI was also .59. The correlation between the Achievement scale and the Binet IQ, however, was considerably higher (.71). In this study the K-ABC MPC (M = 85.9) and McCarthy GCI were highly consistent (M = 86.3). The Binet mean IQ of 82.4 was somewhat lower.

Factor analytic studies of the K-ABC for preschoolers are consistent with the three-factor structure identified for older ages (see Chapter 9) but less robust. The distinctiveness of the achievement factor is particularly lacking, with the Achievement subtests having numerous significant coloadings on sequential and simultaneous factors. These results suggest that the

Achievement scale in particular may not be interpreted as a distinct entity with confidence (Kamphaus & Reynolds, 1987).

Summary

The K-ABC has some floor problems. As a result, K-ABC users have to be wary of obtaining too many zero raw scores when assessing handicapped children. The K-ABC has plenty of difficulty to challenge precocious preschoolers, especially beginning at age 4½, where tests such as Reading/Decoding can be administered via the out-of-level norms procedure.

The K-ABC has a number of characteristics to recommend its use with preschoolers. At present the K-ABC is among the most frequently used tests in handicapped children's early education programs (HCEEP) (Lehr, Ysseldyke, & Thurlow, 1987) and in programs for preschool children with learning disabilities (Esterly & Griffin, 1987).

Wechsler Preschool and Primary Scale of Intelligence-Revised

The WPPSI-R (1989) is a revision of Wechsler's WPPSI (1967). There were several test development goals for this revision, including updating the norms, improving the appeal of the content to young children, and expanding the original age range of the WPPSI so that it now applies to children aged 3 years, 0 months through 7 years, 3 months of age (Gyurke, 1990).

The WPPSI-R follows loyally in the original Wechsler-Bellevue tradition by emphasizing intelligence as a global capacity but having Verbal and Performance scales as two methods for assessing this global entity. The subtests of the WPPSI-R consist primarily of adaptations of Wechsler-Bellevue subtests. The subtests of the WPPSI-R are shown in Table 13.2.

The content of the WPPSI-R subtests has changed substantially in an effort to be more attractive to children. This change reminds me of the controversy over the colorization of old movies that were filmed in half-tones. The

WPPSI-R, in effect, is a "colorized" version of the Wechsler scales that is more appropriate for young children.

A new feature of the WPPSI-R is in line with modern tests of intelligence such as the K-ABC and the DAS. Examiners are allowed to give extra help on early items of subtests in order to ensure that the young child understands what is expected of him or her. This practice is vitally important for testing preschoolers, especially reticent ones. The only subtest that does not allow for this type of assistance is the Arithmetic test.

Computation of WPPSI-R scores is familiar to Wechsler users. Subtest scores are provided with a mean of 10 and standard deviation of 3. These in turn are converted to Verbal, Performance, and Full Scale IQs with a mean of 100 and a standard deviation of 15. In addition, the WPPSI manual is considerably more comprehensive than previous editions of the Wechsler scales. Interpretive tables are provided that allow the examiner to determine the statistical significance and clinical rarity of Verbal and Performance score differences, determine strengths and weaknesses on WPPSI-R subtests, and make pairwise comparisons among subtests. These interpretive data are likely to be extremely helpful to the new WPPSI-R user.

Norming

The WPPSI-R norming sample was obtained via a stratified sampling procedure based on 1986 U.S. Census Bureau estimates. The sample included 1,700 children. The stratification variables included gender, race, (white, black, Hispanic, other), geographic region, parental occupation, and parental education. The 1,700 cases were divided among nine age groups that each included 200 children. The 7-year-old age group was the lone exception in that it included only 100 children. There is generally good correspondence between the sample statistics and the Census statistics.

Reliability

The WPPSI-R appears to be highly reliable. The average Verbal, Performance, and Full

TABLE 13.2   WPPSI-R subtests

Verbal Tests

- *Information*: The information subtest of the WPPSI-R is a simplified version of the traditional Wechsler Information test in that it requires the child initially to point to a picture to answer a question and later give oral responses to questions from the examiner.
- *Comprehension:* The child is required to give oral responses to questions about commonplace actions, or consequences of events.
- *Arithmetic:* The child must demonstrate elementary counting, number concept, and computation skills on pictorial item types and word problems.
- *Vocabulary:* The child has to orally identify pictures of objects. On more difficult items the child has to provide verbal definitions of words.
- *Similarities:* There are three item types on this test. The first requires the child to choose a group of objects that is most similar to another group of objects that share a common feature. The second part requires the child to orally complete a sentence that reflects an analogy. The last portion of the test is similar to the traditional Wechsler item type that requires the child to orally identify commonality among verbal concepts.
- *Sentences:* The child has to repeat sentences from memory exactly as dictated by the examiner.

Performance Tests
- *Object Assembly:* The child has to assemble colorful puzzles.
- *Geometric Design:* The first part of the task requires the child to look at a design and find a similar one to match it. The second part of the task requires the child to draw a geometric figure based on a model.
- *Block Design:* The child uses flat, two-colored chips to construct patterns based on a model. This is a timed task.
- *Mazes:* The child uses pencil and paper to trace mazes. This is a timed task.
- *Picture Completion:* The child has to identify a missing element of pictures of common events or objects.
- *Animal Pegs:* Much as with the Coding test for other versions of the Wechsler scales, the child has to match particular color pegs to a series of pictured animals. This is also a speeded test.

Scale internal consistency coefficients across age groups are .95, .92, and .96 respectively. The internal consistency estimates are slightly lower at age 7, where it is recommended that the WPPSI-R is most appropriate for below-average children and the WISC-R for use with other children.

The reliability coefficients for the individual subtests vary substantially, from an average internal consistency coefficient of .86 for the

Similarities subtest to an average of .63 for the Object Assembly subtest. Typically, stability estimates are somewhat lower than internal consistency estimates. A test-retest investigation of 175 children from the standardization sample yielded coefficients in the high .80s and low .90s. The test-retest coefficient for the Full Scale was .91.

Validity

While the WPPSI-R manual goes much further than the older WPPSI or other Wechsler scale manuals in providing validity evidence, it still comes up short in relationship to newer measures such as the DAS, K-ABC, and Binet-4. For example, no predictive validity data are included in the WPPSI-R manual.

Exploratory factor analytic investigations reported in the manual show generally good congruence with the well-known verbal and nonverbal dimensions from the research literature. The data, however, may not be as clear-cut as they first appear. The Arithmetic subtest, for example (See table 64 in the WPPSI-R manual) has a substantial loading of .57 on the verbal factor and .44 on the performance factor. Similarly, Picture Completion loads .39 on the verbal factor and .53 on the performance factor. The Animal Peg subtest does not have a particularly strong loading on either factor, with a .25 on the verbal and a .41 on the performance. The factor structure of the WPPSI-R will likely be better understood when additional analyses are conducted by independent researchers. For example, the notion of the WISC-R third factor was not explored thoroughly in the analysis conducted in the WPPSI-R manual. Similarly, confirmatory factor analyses would be helpful in clarifying the nature of the WPPSI-R structure.

There are a number of concurrent validity studies showing correlations between the WPPSI-R and other well-known measures of intelligence. The correlation between WPPSI and WPPSI-R Full Scale IQs was reported at .87, and the correlation between WPPSI-R and

WISC-R IQs for a sample of 50 children was reported at .85. The correlations between the WPPSI-R and other preschool cognitive measures is somewhat lower than the .80s, which is to be expected. The correlation of the composites from the WPPSI-R with the Stanford-Binet is .74, with the McCarthy .81, and with the K-ABC .55. The low correlation of .49 with the K-ABC is curious and inconsistent with the study correlating the K-ABC and the old WPPSI (Kaufman & Kaufman, 1983b). Otherwise, these concurrent validity coefficients provide strong evidence for the construct validity of the WPPSI-R. To date there is no research available on the use of the WPPSI-R with developmentally delayed preschoolers.

Summary

The WPPSI-R is a major update and improvement of its predecessor, the 1967 WPPSI. Strengths of the WPPSI-R include more attractive materials than its predecessor. The use of materials that are more intrinsically interesting to young children should improve child interest and motivation. The flexible administration allowing examiners to teach the tasks should also improve the utility of the test with young children. Other practical features of the WPPSI-R are the extended age range and a more comprehensive and well-written manual.

The psychometric quality of the WPPSI-R is unimpeachable, including the updated standardization sample. The reliability and validity evidence was carefully gathered, and it buttresses the quality of the instrument (Bracken & Delugach, 1990).

The WPPSI-R, however, is burdened by its heritage. Its primary weaknesses are due to the fact that it is inextricably linked to the work of Wechsler in adult intellectual assessment. Potential weaknesses include the fact that it clings to the individual subtest format that Wechsler popularized in the 1930s. The use of subtests that are in and of themselves reliable and interpretable is most appropriate for the more patient and cooperative adult client. For extremely young children, however, the use of brief sets of items, as was popularized by the original Binet and intelligence tests such as the Bayley and McCarthy scales, is more suitable to the attention spans of young children. In addition, the WPPSI-R still suffers from a limited age range. A broader age range extending down to 2½ years of age is offered by numerous other tests, including the Binet-4, K-ABC, McCarthy scales, and Differential Ability Scales. In addition, the WPPSI-R competitors also have upper age limits beyond that of the WPPSI-R.

Another holdover from the Wechsler tradition that makes the test more cumbersome for use with preschoolers is the use of 10 subtests as the standard battery. The WPPSI-R has always been known for its high reliability; however, this reliability has always come at a price, and the price is having to push a young child through a minimum of 10 subtests. Block Design itself could theoretically take 25 minutes to administer (Slate & Saddler, 1990). Other preschool measures such as the Binet-4 (abbreviated battery), Woodcock-Johnson Revised, McCarthy scales, K-ABC, and DAS are much more realistic in their demands on the attention of preschool children. With these caveats and strengths in mind, the WPPSI-R should be considered a contribution to preschool assessment that warrants consideration for use by clinicians who work with young children. Perhaps one of the major differences between the WPPSI and the WPPSI-R is that in 1967 there was little competition, but in 1990 there are numerous excellent instruments that may be used with this age group.

Case Study

The case study in Box 13.2 is of a young child who was evaluated with the WPPSI-R and the Binet-4. One interesting aspect of this case is that the examiner hypothesized that this highly active child enjoyed taking the Binet-4 more than the WPPSI-R.

Differential Ability Scales

The DAS is a new and largely untested measure of preschool cognitive development (see Chapter 11). Elliott (1990a) too eschews the term "intelligence." The DAS has a battery of tests designed specifically for preschoolers beginning at age 2½. The core and diagnostic (supplementary) subtests for the DAS are shown in Table 13.3. The Block Building, Verbal Comprehension, Picture Similarities, and Naming Vocabulary tests contribute the GCA (General Conceptual Ability) score at ages 2½ through 3½. Block Building is not used in the GCA at the remaining preschool ages, and Early Number Concepts, Copying, and Pattern Construction subtests are added to the aforementioned core subtests to create a battery of six subtests for 3½- through 6-year-olds. The four diagnostic subtests shown in Table 13.3 are also available for various young age groups. The preschool battery gets equal emphasis with the school-age battery of the DAS and it has its own record form.

The item types on the DAS are well known, most of them being variants of Binet-type tasks. Tests such as Block Building, Verbal Comprehension, Naming Vocabulary, and Copying are reminiscent of similar items on previous editions of the Binet. The use of toy-like objects for the Verbal Comprehension test is most similar to the earlier Binet editions. Given that these are tried and true item types for these age groups, one would predict that they should work well with young children. One unknown aspect of the DAS is its interests level for young children. New clinicians should make an effort to consult DAS users to assess this variable, as it is crucial for the successful use of the DAS with this age group.

The DAS also offers some administration flexibility at this age range. Most of the subtests allow for out-of-level testing so that an examiner could give a test that is ordinarily too difficult for an age group to a precocious child and, conversely, give a subtest that is normally too easy for an age group to a developmentally delayed child.

Box 13.2

Case study of preschooler using the Binet-4 and the WPPSI-R

Reason for Referral

Matt is a 4-year-old preschooler who was referred for evaluation at his parents' request due to attentional problems at preschool. He is considered hyperactive at home and demanding of adult attention.

Medical History

Information provided by the parents suggested that Matt's condition at birth was good. He was delivered by Caesarean section with a birth weight of 6 lbs., 5 oz. No difficulties were noted in his early developmental history. His medical history is significant for asthma, which seems to be improving, and scarlet fever at age 3. Frequent rashes around Matt's mouth are treated with hydrocortisone cream. Parental report indicates that Matt passed vision and hearing screenings administered at school within the last year.

Background Information

Matt lives with both parents and one sister, age 11. Matt's sister has been previously diagnosed as having an attention deficit disorder, and Matt's father reported having experienced similar difficulty in school: "daydreaming" and an inability to complete tasks. A psychoeducational evaluation was desired as part of a comprehensive assessment.

Parents report that their most difficult problems with Matt involve discipline. Although very loving, Matt can be stubborn, and he "talks back." When he doesn't get his way, he becomes angry, whines, and cries. Matt reportedly loves preschool, but last year he had difficulty listening, following directions, and making wise use of his time. He often screamed or made other loud noises, disrupted the activities of other children, and demanded attention.

Behavioral Observations

Matt was nicely dressed in casual clothes and appeared comfortable. He was brought to the testing session by his father and mother. Throughout the evaluation Matt was responsive and candid in his responses. He demonstrated fair to low task persistence yet seemed to try hard on some tasks presented. Rapport was established and maintained throughout the testing session. At times Matt cooperated fully with the examiner, but for the most part he was uncooperative, and he was very difficult to keep in his seat. Matt was able to be redirected.

Assessment Results

Matt was evaluated with the Stanford-Binet Intelligence Scale: Fourth Edition. Matt obtained a Test Composite score of 90 ± 6. The chances are 95 out of 100 that Matt's scores meet or exceed 16% to 40% of the children his age. This estimate of his current cognitive functioning classifies him in the average to low-average range. On the Wechsler Preschool and Primary Scale of Intelligence-Revised (WPPSI-R) his Full Scale score was slightly lower. He obtained a score of 80 ± 6, which means that the chances are 95 out of 100 that Matt's scores meet or exceed 4% to 18% of the children his age. This estimate classifies him in the low-average range. This lower score may be due in part to fatigue, inattention, and overactivity, which were more evident during administration of the WPPSI-R than during the Stanford-Binet.

Matt demonstrated a weakness in his ability to mentally compute arithmetic problems and to complete visual-motor tasks. His weakness in perceptual-motor skills was mainly due to his lack of attention and concentration on tasks that demanded tedious and accurate work. Matt demonstrated strengths in his verbal ability to comprehend words and verbal concept formation.

The Developmental Test of Visual Motor Integration (VMI), a measure of the degree to which visual perception and motor behavior are integrated, yielded a Standard Scaled score of 80. This score is consistent with Matt's ability scores and his weakness in visual-motor coordination.

The Bracken Basic Concepts Scale provides a measure of readiness skills in the areas of basic concept

Box 13.2 *(continued)*

knowledge. The results indicate that Matt's Total Test standard score of 97 classifies him as meeting or exceeding 42% of the children his age on basic readiness skills.

Matt's mother completed the Parenting Stress Index. The total stress score and the parent domain score were within normal limits. The overall child domain score was high. This suggests that this family would be viewed as experiencing a normal amount of stress and that characteristics of the child that may need to be the focus of intervention include demandingness (compliance), child mood (crying, fussing), and distractibility/hyperactivity. These results are consistent with referral concerns.

Both parents and Matt's preschool teacher completed the Achenbach. Parents' ratings reflected social competence within normal limits, including Matt's participation and performance in activities, social relationships, and school performance. Teacher reports of adaptive functioning suggest that Matt is working much less than his classmates and he is behaving somewhat less appropriately. He was, however, considered to be happy and learning at an average rate. No difficulties were noted by the teacher in Matt's attainment of readiness skills.

The teacher and the mother's ratings on the behavior problem scales suggest that Matt's characteristics are more externalizing (undercontrolled) than internalizing. Both parents' responses reflect similar concerns, with primary elevations on the Hyperactive scale and on the scale labeled Delinquent. Only Matt's mother's ratings exceeded the upper limit of the normal range in these two areas (T > 70). His mother indicated that she handles most of the child management in the home. Items endorsed on the Delinquent scale reflect Matt's disobedience at school and destructiveness of things.

On the Structured Interview for Diagnostic Assessment of Children (SIDAC), Matt's behavior was rated as being characteristic of Attention Deficit Disorder with Hyperactivity *(DSM III)* and Attention Deficit Hyperactivity Disorder *(DSM III-R)*.

On the Family Kinetic Drawing his visual-motor coordination was shown to be consistent with the other measures of perceptual-motor integration. Although he seems to have a weakness in this area, caution should be taken in interpreting these results because of his young age.

During the child interview the examiner noted many inconsistencies in Matt's description of his environment. Matt was constantly changing facts, especially when talking about his behavior at the preschool.

Diagnosis

Matt's behavior is characteristic of children diagnosed as having Attention Deficit Hyperactivity Disorder (314.01 *DSM-III-R)*.

Summary

Matt is a 4-year-old boy who will soon be entering kindergarten. He is very active and inattentive at times. Current assessment data suggest that Matt's cognitive functioning is in the average to low-average range but this should be considered merely an "estimate" because of his youth and inattentiveness. Matt's basic concept scores are commensurate with his cognitive ability.

Recommendations

Matt should be further evaluated in his preschool setting and appropriate consultation to his teachers provided. A home visit should also be made and parent training and consultation initiated.

Psychometric Summary

Parenting Stress Index

SUBTEST	PERCENTILE*
Child Domain	90
Adaptability	55

(continued)

Box 13.2 *(continued)*

Subtest	Percentile*
Acceptability	60
Demandingness	95
Mood	95
Distractibility/Hyperactivity	95
Reinforces Parent	55
Parent Domain	39
Total Stress Index	69

*Normal is 15th–80th percentile.

Achenbach Child Behavior Checklist-Parent Report

	T-SCORES	
	Mother	Father
Schizoid-Anxious	59	63
Depressed	55	61
Uncommunicative	55	55
Obsessive Compulsive	55	55
Somatic Complaints	55	55
Withdrawal	57	55
Hyperactive	73	67
Aggressive	63	55
Delinquent	72	65
Internalizing	54	57
Externalizing	67	59
Sum	63	59

Achenbach Child Behavior Checklist-Teacher Report

	T-SCORE
Anxious	55
Social Withdrawal	57
Unpopular	64
Self-Destructive	65
Obsessive-Compulsive	59
Inattentive	66
Nervous-Overactive	70
Aggressive	63
Internalizing	55
Externalizing	66
Sum	65

Box 13.2 *(continued)*

VMI

PERCENTILE	SCALED SCORE
9	80

Binet-4

SUBTESTS	STANDARD AGE SCORE
Vocabulary	54
Comprehension	50
Absurdities	49
Verbal Reasoning	102
Pattern Analysis	41
Copying	49
Abstract/Visual Reasoning	87
Quantitative	39
Quantitative Reasoning	78
Bead Memory	54
Memory for Sentences	45
Short-Term Memory	99
Test Composite	90

WPPSI-R

SUBTESTS	SCALED SCORE	IQ
Object Assembly	6	
Geometric Design	5	
Block Design	6	
Mazes	7	
Picture Completion	7	
Animal Pegs	9	
Performance tests	31	76
Information	8	
Comprehension	7	
Arithmetic	7	
Vocabulary	7	
Similarities	11	
Sentences	11	
Verbal tests	40	87
Full Scale score		80

(continued)

Box 13.2 (*continued*)

Bracken Basic Concepts Scale

SUBTESTS	STANDARD SCORE	PERCENTILE
School Readiness Composite	12	75
Direction/Position	9	37
Social/Emotional	9	37
Size	11	63
Texture/Material	9	37
Quantity	9	37
Time/Sequence	8	25
Total Test Score	97	42

Norming and Reliability

The psychometric properties of the DAS are commendable, including its standardization program (see Chapter 11). Some of the subtests do not have an extraordinary amount of floor. If, for example, a child obtains a raw score of only 1 on Block Building, the corresponding t-score is 37, which is slightly less than 1½ standard deviations below the mean. The GCA, on the other hand, appears to have plenty of evidence of floor.

Both internal consistency and test-retest reliabilities for the GCA are strong, rarely dipping below .90. A rather unusual feature of the manual is to report reliability estimates separately for ability levels for the purposes of out-of-level testing. This practice shows clearly the amount of confidence an examiner can place in a test that is administered out of level. Pattern Construction, a test that is relatively difficult for young children, has a slightly positively skewed distribution for 3-year-olds. Because of this fact the test is less reliable for low-achieving 3-year-olds (t-score < 40) because it does not have enough easy items to measure these children well (.47). It is for this reason that Pattern Construction is not part of the regular battery for this age. For high-ability 3-year-olds (t-score > 60), however, the reliability of the test is considerably better (.93). The opposite is true where

there are ceiling effects (negatively skewed). These reliability data for out-of-level testing are reported on page 183 of the DAS *Introductory and Technical Handbook* (Elliott, 1990a).

The DAS manual (p. 191) also reports subtest specificity values for the preschool subtests. Some of the subtests with the most specificity and correspondingly low error variances include Pattern Construction, Copying, and Recall of Digits. The ratio of specificity to error variance is lowest for Naming Vocabulary, which has a mean specificity of .34 and error variance of .22.

Validity

Intercorrelations of the subtests and composites at the preschool age level (p. 199 of the handbook, Elliott, 1990a) suggest that the memory tests, particularly Recall of Objects Immediate and Delayed, are least likely to covary with the GCA. In addition, Matching Letter-Like Forms and Block Building have relatively low correlations with the GCA. Block Building does have a higher correlation with GCA at ages 2½ to 3½. The core subtests clearly have the higher correlations with the GCA, which is their reason for inclusion in the GCA (see Chapter 11).

The "g" factor at ages 2½ through 3½ is marked by Verbal Comprehension and Naming Vocabulary, with loadings of .80 and .74 respectively. The remaining four subtests have load-

TABLE 13.3 Differential ability scale preschool subtests

Ages	Core Subtests	Diagnostic Subtests
2–6 to 3–5	Block Building Picture Similarities Naming Vocabulary Verbal Comprehension	Recall of Digits Recognition of Pictures
3–6 to 5–11	Copying (NV) Pattern Construction (NV) Picture Similarities (NV) Naming Vocabulary (V) Verbal Comprehension (V) Early Number Concepts	Block Building Matching Letter-like Forms Recall of Digits Recall of Objects Recognition of Pictures

ings only in the .50s (Elliott, 1990a). Subtests with high first-factor loadings (using a one-factor confirmatory model) at ages 4 and 5 include Verbal Comprehension, Naming Vocabulary, and Early Number Concepts. Subtests with low loadings on this factor included Recall of Digits and Recall of Objects. These results, therefore, parallel the intercorrelation matrices cited earlier and show which subtests are not likely to align themselves with the GCA.

Based on factor analytic evidence, Elliott (1990a) concluded that at ages 2½ through 3½ a single general factor was the most appropriate explanation for the intercorrelation matrix. At ages 4 through 5-11 a two-factor model was proposed as the best fit to the data. These two factors were labeled as verbal and nonverbal.

Concurrent validity studies reported in the handbook (Elliott, 1990a) show strong and lawful correlations between the DAS and other popular preschool tests. In a variety of studies of preschoolers the GCA of the DAS correlated .89 and .81 in two studies with the WPPSI-R Full Scale, .77 with the Binet-4 Composite, .76 and .82 with the McCarthy GCI, and .68 with the K-ABC MPC. There was also a consistent trend for the GCA to be 1 to 4 standard score points lower than these other measures. It is a small difference, but it occurred in every study. The GCA was considerably lower than the McCar-

thy GCI, being about 8 points lower in two separate studies. One plausible explanation for this substantial difference is the age of the McCarthy norms, although this is somewhat surprising given the concern about the McCarthy scoring lower than other tests (Valencia, 1990).

Summary

The DAS possesses a number of characteristics of good measures of preschool intelligence, including provisions for teaching, familiar and attractive item types, factor analytic support, good reliability and concurrent validity, good norming, out-of-level testing, and strong manuals. Some questions remain about the ability of the DAS to hold the interest of young children and about ease of administration. The DAS now needs to be "road tested" with clinicians who assess preschoolers.

CONCLUSIONS

The state of the art in infant and preschool intelligence testing is changing rapidly. While there are few current competitors for the Bayley, there are likely some under development. New procedures based on cognitive science research may change the face of infant testing. For clients as young as 2½, examiners have their choice of a wide range of high-quality instruments. Many of these are new, and the truly valuable instruments may not be known until there are more clinical trials.

CHAPTER SUMMARY

1. Infant measures of intelligence are usually multidimensional.

2. PL 99-457 is a major extension of the provision of educational services for preschool children and infants.

3. Lewis and Sullivan (1985) noted remarkable similarity among the items in infant tests, and most of the items could be traced to the pioneering work of Arnold Gesell.

4. Gesell, while providing the basis for so many test development activities, did not believe that intelligence could be assessed.

5. For normal children evaluated between birth and 2½ years of age the correlation with scores obtained at ages 3 to 8 range from .01 to .59.

6. Stability coefficients between early and later tests for normal children reach .50 at their best, but stability coefficients for handicapped children are in the .70s to .90s range.

7. Specialized training for child clinicians who assess infants and preschoolers might include strong coursework in normal and handicapped child development and preschool assessment, and supervised experience in an early childhood setting.

8. The assessment of children under 24 months of age typically involves some modifications in the standard assessment procedure.

9. The most popular and respected of infant intelligence measures is the Bayley Scales of Infant Development.

10. The major strength of the Bayley, its strong psychometric properties, is now becoming a liability.

11. Tests of infant information processing skills have received considerable attention lately as a potential breakthrough in the assessment of infant intelligence.

12. The McCarthy scales have been the recipient of considerable research attention.

13. There has been some controversy regarding the construction of the McCarthy Screening Test, which has resulted in the development of alternative screening forms of the MST (Taylor, Slocumb, & O'Neill, 1979).

14. Although the McCarthy norms may need updating, the extensive supportive research base of the McCarthy suggests that every clinician who assesses the intelligence of young children should become familiar with this scale.

15. Cronbach concluded that the Binet-4 was likely to be as interesting to preschoolers as its predecessor or other measures.

16. The K-ABC enjoys considerable popularity for use with preschoolers, and it possesses a strong research base.

17. The WPPSI-R (1989) is a revision of Wechsler's 1967 WPPSI.

18. The psychometric quality of the WPPSI-R is unimpeachable.

19. The Differential Ability Scales (DAS) is a new and largely untested measure of preschool intelligence.

20. The DAS possesses a number of characteristics of good measures of preschool intelligence, including provisions for teaching, familiar and attractive item types, factor analytic support, good reliability and concurrent validity, good norming, out-of-level testing, and strong manuals.

Assessing Exceptional Children: Mental Retardation, Giftedness, Hearing and Visual Impairments

CHAPTER QUESTIONS

What are the different levels of mental retardation?

Why is the use of intelligence tests as the sole criterion of giftedness criticized?

How should intelligence tests be used when diagnosing important and prevalent childhood disorders? The range of presenting problems of children is enormous, requiring the intelligence test user to be aware of a variety of issues presented by exceptional children. Some children may be "untestable," and others may require specialized measures. Clinicians require specialized knowledge to use intelligence measures effectively with such groups. The next three chapters address issues related to the use of intelligence measures with exceptional children and various cultural and linguistic groups. Such specialized knowledge is as crucial for fostering sophisticated interpretation as it is for avoiding simplistic or damaging uses. These chapters also challenge some long-held beliefs of psychologists about the utility of profile analysis and other issues.

The issues discussed in the next three chapters should not be considered as supplemental or optional but, rather, as central to the knowledge base of the intelligence test user. These chapters are placed here because some of the concepts are difficult and an in-depth understanding of more basic issues is required prior to considering these specialized uses. If a clinician encounters children with special needs or characteristics (and all will), a lack of familiarity with these issues will mitigate against a high-quality evaluation. The use of intelligence tests with children with mental retardation, giftedness, or hearing and vision problems will be discussed in this first chapter.

MENTAL RETARDATION

Since intelligence tests were designed originally to diagnose mental retardation (see Chapter 1), it is eminently appropriate that this group be discussed first. Mental retardation has been recognized by societies for some time—at least since the Roman Empire. It has been said that Roman parents often threw their mentally retarded children into the Tiber River in order not to have to care for them and that the Spartans killed or abandoned mentally retarded individuals. It was not until the Middle Ages that some societies began to care for these individuals' needs (Weiss & Weisz, 1986). Given such potential dire consequences, one cannot help but wonder about the accuracy of the diagnoses that were made in those days!

Most modern diagnostic systems are based on the criteria set by the American Association on Mental Deficiency (AAMD) (Grossman, 1983). The AAMD has for some time considered mental retardation as a condition that can only be diagnosed if *dual deficits* in intelligence and adaptive behavior exist during the developmental period (usually considered to be about age 18). All of the major diagnostic systems have adopted this view that an intelligence deficit is only half of the mental retardation diagnosis. Most diagnostic systems also mimic the *DSM-III-R* by defining significantly below-average intelligence as a standard score (M = 100, SD = 15 or 16) of about 70 or below. The *DSM-III-R* also stipulates that the standard error of measurement may be taken into account and that scores of 65 to 75 may be considered as either qualifying or disqualifying a child for the diagnosis of mental retardation when other variables, such as adaptive behavior and age of onset, are taken into account.

These criteria for the diagnosis of mental retardation can be easily applied to the following examples.

Case	Intelligence Composite	Adaptive Behavior	Onset Age	Mental Retardation
1	55	62	27	No
2	60	81	2	No
3	84	63	7	No
4	58	59	2	Yes

The sample cases above, while oversimplifications of the diagnostic principles involved in mental retardation diagnosis, do give some indication of the general parameters that are considered in making the diagnosis. Case 1 is probably the trickiest because the sole reason that the diagnosis cannot be made is because the age of onset is outside what is typically considered the developmental period.

Adaptive Behavior Scales

Adaptive behavior scales assess the degree to which an individual meets the standards of personal independence and social responsibility expected for a child's age or cultural group (Grossman, 1983). This construct is more nebulous than intelligence since the standards of behavior and achievement are determined by an individual's society. For example, adult expectations to vote may be relevant to some societies and not others. Cooking skills may be deemed necessary for some cultural groups and not for others. As it turns out, however, there are some standards of adaptive behavior that are relatively universal, such as toilet training, control of aggression, and respect for authority figures. These skills are the ones typically assessed by adaptive behavior scales.

One of the oldest and premier measures of adaptive behavior is the *Vineland Adaptive Behavior Scale* (Sparrow, Balla, & Cicchetti, 1984). This is a revision of the *Vineland Social Maturity Scale* that was developed by Edgar Doll in the 1930s. Doll essentially founded the field of adaptive behavior assessment by noting that although all of his patients at the Vineland (NJ) State Training School suffered from intellectual problems, there were vast differences in their day-to-day life and coping skills. If, for example, two children have intelligence test composite scores of 60 and one is toilet-trained and the other is frequently incontinent, these children would place considerably different demands on an adult's time. The toilet trained child is more mobile and can be involved in many more activities than the incontinent child, who requires considerably more attention and care (see Box 14.1).

The list of domains assessed by the Vineland gives a sense of the type of skills that are considered to be within the realm of adaptive behavior.

Communication Domain: Receptive, Expressive, Written

Daily Living Skills Domain: Personal, Domestic, Community

Socialization Domain: Interpersonal Relationships, Play and Leisure Time, Coping Skills

Motor Skills Domain (for young children primarily): Gross, Fine

Some of the more popular adaptive behavior scales currently available include:

Vineland Adaptive Behavior Scales: Survey, Classroom, and Expanded Forms (Sparrow, Balla, & Cicchetti, 1984)

Adaptive Behavior Inventory for Children (ABIC) (Mercer & Lewis, 1978)

AAMD Adaptive Behavior Scale, School Edition (Nihira et al., 1981)

*Scales of Independent Behavio*r (Bruininks et al., 1984)

Adaptive behavior assessment was invigorated in the 1980s because of the need for fairer assessment practices. Assessing adaptive behavior served to round out the diagnostic picture for a child by providing information on out-of-school behavior and day-to-day life skills. The recent special education emphasis on successful transition to adulthood should continue to provide impetus for research and development in adaptive behavior assessment (DeStefano & Thompson, 1990).

Levels of Mental Retardation

A standard score of less than 70 has long been accepted as a criterion of mental retardation (Flynn, 1985). To date there are very few who have questioned the ability of the WISC-R or other intelligence tests to provide a meaningful criterion of mental retardation. This acceptance exists in spite of research such as that by Flynn (1985), who in an interesting investigation shows how sampling problems and changes in norms over time have served to effectively change the numbers of individuals (the percentage of the population) that are identified by the standard score = 70 criterion. He found the criterion of mental retardation to vary as much as a full standard deviation on the particular Wechsler scale selected. Among other results, Flynn (1985) concludes that in order to have a coherent and consistent cut score for mental retardation, The Psychological Corporation would have to renorm the WISC-III every 7 years. Despite such contrary findings, a WISC-III standard score of less than 70 will likely be used as a cut-off for some time.

Different levels of mental retardation are recognized by most diagnostic systems. Some descriptions of the various levels of mental retardation are given below. These descriptions are adapted from Weiss and Weisz (1986).

1. *Mild Mental Retardation* (standard score range 50–55 to approximately 70): This group constitutes approximately 80% of the cases of mental retardation. In most cases these individuals look relatively normal and often are not identified until they begin school and experience considerable difficulty. They can develop social and basic life skills and achieve up to about a sixth-grade level in some academic areas. Mildly retarded individuals usually become self-supporting, but the jobs that they do are viewed by most as tiresome.

2. *Moderate Mental Retardation* (standard score range 40–45 to 50–55): About 12% of the mental retardation cases fall into this range. These children often have obvious physical abnormalities and appear awkward or clumsy. They frequently show language delays in the preschool years and do not obey social conventions. These individuals may be able to

Box 14.1

The difference between intelligence and adaptive behavior

I learned to appreciate the difference between intelligence and adaptive behavior early in my career. My third job after completing college (yes, I had trouble finding a job I liked with a bachelor's degree in psychology) was a temporary position as Rehabilitation Workshop Supervisor in a modern version of a state mental hospital. I helped patients build birdhouses and stools, and I served as the favorite target for the conduct-disordered adolescents who felt the need to throw paint at someone—but that is another story. I vividly recall an experience with a young man, about age 30, who was in the hospital for alcoholism treatment. I remember this man so well because he was well groomed, mannered, and pleasant. We had many enjoyable conversations about his family and his work, and I looked forward to his visits to the workshop. I also remember being stunned when one of the staff members from the alcoholism treatment unit told me that the young man was mildly mentally retarded. I remember feeling a sense of empathy and also wishing that all of the clients would be as polite and enjoyable to work with as this man.

---

work in a sheltered workshop setting but rarely live independently.

3. *Severe Mental Retardation* (standard score range 20–25 to 35–40): This group constitutes approximately 7% of the mental retardation cases. During early childhood they show significant speech and motor delays. Their schooling focuses on the development of personal hygiene and basic communication skills. As adults these individuals can only perform simple occupational tasks under close supervision.

4. *Profound Mental Retardation* (standard score less than 20–25): Individuals in this 1% of mentally retarded individuals suffer from physical abnormalities and neurological problems that often preclude them from walking and speaking. They require constant supervision and life-long custodial care (p. 349).

It is in the differentiation of levels of mental retardation that psychologists have come face to face with the limitations of intelligence tests. The academic nature of many of the items does not provide easy enough items for children with severe impairments. Infant and some preschool tests do have enough easy items because intelligence is defined differently, more globally,

for these ages. Motor scales, for example, are common and contribute to developmental indices (see Chapter 12). Some individuals have advised using infant scales such as the Bayley with children who are beyond the test's age range and yet have mental ages that are within the age range (Sullivan & Burley, 1990). Differentiating levels of retardation remains a murky area where clinicians are seeking guidance (see the later section on range of scores).

Profile Research

Much of the research on the use of intelligence tests with children has focused on identifying characteristic composite scores or subtest profiles. Kaufman (1979b) identified a WISC-R profile in which mildly mentally retarded children obtained relative strengths on spatial tests such as Block Design, Picture Completion, and Object Assembly and relative weaknesses on school-related tests such as Arithmetic, Vocabulary, and Information. While this profile suggests that there may be a characteristic P > V profile, this does not appear to be the case. As Kaufman (1979b) emphasizes, the WISC-R profile is merely a trend in the data.

Mean WISC-R scores for numerous samples of mentally retarded children are shown in Table 14.1. Inspection of this table shows clearly that a mild P > V pattern and the aforementioned subtest profile are trends that are potentially and theoretically significant but *useless for making differential diagnoses*. In the majority of studies the P > V profile is only in the 8 to 10 point range (Naglieri, 1979; Gutkin, 1979; Kaufman & Van Hagen, 1977). A *V/P difference of this magnitude is not reliable enough for individual assessment purposes* and, therefore, not a valuable group trend that can be used as a diagnostic sign.

Why does this mild subtest and P > V pattern occur? It certainly makes sense that mentally retarded children would have a deficit in school-related skills such as those assessed by the Arithmetic and Vocabulary subtests since the diagnosis of mental retardation is usually made by schools, and children who are referred for suspected mental retardation are likely referred because of substantial school failure (Kaufman, 1979b). It is also conceivable that the cumulative deficit phenomenon (see Chapter 2) comes into play and adversely affects school achievement. This would be particularly true for mathematics tests since later skill development is dependent on prerequisite skill acquisition. The relative strength on nonverbal tasks with a strong spatial component may be explained similarly. This profile could be affected by the nature of mild mental retardation. Most mild mental retardation (about 75% of cases) is described as familial (Weiss & Weisz, 1986), where problems such as poverty and illiteracy are associated with the syndrome. Perhaps Block Design, Object Assembly, and Picture Completion are less affected by adverse cultural conditions. Yet another possibility is that some mentally retarded children exhibit subtle neurological differences from the population at large that could be due to prenatal or postnatal factors.

Composite score profiles for other tests reinforce the WISC-R findings, which leads one to believe these profiles may be scientifically meaningful. Profiles for a few other tests are also shown in Table 14.1.

Reynolds and Kaufman (1990) have also summarized the extent of WISC-R subtest scatter (intercomposite or intersubtest differences) that has been found for populations of mentally retarded children. They found that subtest scatter in the typical investigation was in the 6 to 7 point range (when the lowest subtest score is subtracted from the highest subtest score). This finding is well within the range of +7 or –2 points that was found to be within the average range for the WISC-R standardization sample (Kaufman, 1979b).

Which Score Do I Use?

An important issue regarding the use of intelligence tests for the purposes of mental retardation diagnosis is the decision about which composite score to use in making a diagnosis when there is a composite score difference (e.g., V/P) and one of these scores is outside the mental retardation range. For example, a child could obtain a WISC-R Verbal score of 78 and a Performance score of 65. Here the Full Scale score of 70 is not too problematic. If the child's adaptive behavior score is 70 or less, the diagnosis of mental retardation becomes more likely, as dual deficits in intelligence and adaptive behavior are clearly documented.

What if, however, a more difficult case with a large V/P discrepancy is considered? A good example of this scenario would be a child who obtains a Performance score of 88, Verbal score of 60, Full Scale score of 72, and adaptive behavior composite score of 71. This is a more difficult case to decide based on scores alone, forcing logic to come into play. This case is also a good example of why *rigid cut-off scores should not be used when making diagnoses based on intelligence test results* (Kaufman, 1990). One may make quite different diagnostic decisions with this same set of scores, depending on other information about the child. This child may be

TABLE 14.1   Mean intelligence test scores for samples of children diagnosed as mentally retarded

Author(s)/Date	N	Composite Score	Sample Mean
WISC-R (WISC-III)			
STUDIES			
Wechsler (1991)	43	Verbal	59.2
		Performance	59.2
		Full Scale	55.8
Naglieri (1985a)	101	Verbal	70.8
		Performance	83.5
		Full Scale	75.1
Thorndike, Hagen, & Sattler (1986)	61	Verbal	66.2
		Performance	71.9
		Full Scale	67.0
Catron & Catron (1977)		Verbal	61.62
		Performance	63.93
		Full Scale	59.66
Avery, Slate, & Choven (1989)	26	Verbal	65.6
		Performance	67.6
		Full Scale	63.3
K-ABC STUDIES			
Naglieri (1985a)	33	Sequential	77.9
		Simultaneous	81.9
		MPC	77.8
Naglieri (1985b)	37	Sequential	67.2
		Simultaneous	67.7
		MPC	69.7
Nelson, Obrzut, & Cummings (1984)	30	Sequential	72.4
		Simultaneous	72.8
		MPC	69.7
BINET-4 STUDIES			
Thorndike, Hagen, & Sattler (1986)	61	Verbal	69.4
		Abstract/Visual	71.6
		Quantitative	73.9
		Short-Term Memory	67.5
		Composite	66.2
Thorndike, Hagen, & Sattler (1986)	22	Verbal	56.2
		Abstract/Visual	55.5
		Quantitative	57.9
		Short-Term Memory	51.8
		Composite	50.9
DAS STUDIES			
Elliott (1990a)	25	Verbal	63.8
		Nonverbal	63.4
		Spatial	65.8
		GCA	59.4

diagnosed as mentally retarded given information that he or she:

1. Is 9 years old and has failed several subjects every school year despite the fact that his or her parents have hired tutors and he or she seems to be putting forth great effort in school.
2. Was born in the United States and speaks English as his or her native language.
3. Has a developmental history indicating that he or she achieved major language and motor milestones considerably later than normal.

A child with the scores cited above may just as well not be diagnosed as mentally retarded if he or she:

1. Is 7 years old, has lived in the United States for only 1 year, and Spanish was his or her first language acquired.
2. Has only failed language arts subjects.
3. Was reared in a high-SES family environment where his needs were met by others and the acquisition of adaptive life skills was not emphasized or deemed necessary (e.g., the household employed both a maid and a cook), resulting in a very low score on the Daily Living Skills domain of the Vineland, with other domain scores being considerably higher.

Since background information, other test scores, developmental history, and other factors are so important in making diagnostic decisions with intelligence tests, perhaps the most reasonable approach is to consider developmental history, other test scores, and related information as *central to the diagnostic process.* In cases where there are composite score differences with some scores within the mental retardation range and others outside this range, *the examiner should explain why the diagnostic decision was made,* whatever that decision may be. This practice at least allows for peer review and collaboration. If the reason is defensible to other professionals who know the child's circumstances, then the clinician can feel more comfortable with the decision made. Writing the rationale for the diagnosis has an additional benefit in that it may help the clinician clarify his or her thought processes regarding the diagnosis.

Unfortunately, the use of intelligence tests in isolation has been reinforced by statutory guidelines such as those offered by state departments of education and U.S. federal agencies such as the Social Security Administration. A cut-off score of 70 has been identified by various agencies to decide everything from special education class placement to eligibility for monetary benefits. One can imagine the ire of physicians if the use of medical diagnostic tests were similarly regulated. What if some governmental body decided that a person had to have a cholesterol level of 200 (LDL) to be eligible to receive medicine to reduce serum cholesterol? The patients with levels of 195 would likely be very angry at being denied treatment, and those patients with levels of 205 who wanted to treat themselves with diet modifications would be similarly angry. This scenario sounds ludicrous, but it is not far removed from current mental retardation diagnostic practice that occurs with school-age children under the aegis of various education regulatory bodies. If intelligence tests are going to be used in a larger context for decision making, then clinicians have to use discretion as opposed to rigid cut scores or diagnostic formulae. To do otherwise is to promote the simplistic and inappropriate use of intelligence tests, which serves no one, certainly not children!

Intelligence and Adaptive Behavior Revisited

The relationship between adaptive behavior scales and intelligence scales should also be kept in mind for appropriate use of intelligence tests in diagnosing mental retardation (Kamphaus, 1987). My review of the literature in 1987 drew the conclusion that the correlation between the

WISC-R and the K-ABC and adaptive behavior scales such as the *Vineland Adaptive Behavior Scales* where parents serve as the informants is moderate to low in most studies (i.e., correlations in the .20 to .60 range). This finding has several practical implications for the use of an intelligence test along with an adaptive behavior scale in the diagnosis of mental retardation. These implications include:

1. Psychologists should not expect intelligence and parent-reported adaptive behavior scores to show much agreement, especially when the child is outside the mental retardation range.

2. The limited correlation of these measures with intelligence tests suggests that adaptive behavior scales are adding information to the diagnostic process that is different from that of intelligence tests (Kamphaus, 1987).

3. The correlation between intelligence tests and adaptive behavior scores as rated by teachers may be somewhat higher (Kamphaus, 1987). Teacher-rated adaptive behavior, therefore, may not be considered as a substitute for parent-reported adaptive behavior and vice versa.

All of these findings also support the notion that adaptive behavior is likely to become more central to the diagnosis of mental retardation and to treatment plan design (DeStefano & Thompson, 1990).

Regression Effects

Yet another issue to consider in the diagnosis of mental retardation is the likelihood of regression effects (see Chapter 5). Since intelligence tests are not perfectly reliable, one can expect the composite score means for samples of mentally retarded children to move toward the normative mean. A good example of this is a study by Spitz (1983) where the original mean for the mentally retarded group was 55 (54.96) at age 13 and 58

(58.33) at age 15. Changes such as this can make diagnosis very difficult, especially if a child moves from a score of 68 to 74. Is this child still appropriately diagnosed as mentally retarded? At least a few of the possibilities to consider include:

1. The child's first evaluation was conducted under less than ideal circumstances, and the first test results were inordinately low.

2. The second score is higher primarily due to regression effects. This hypothesis is especially plausible when the difference between the first and second scores is rather small— less than 10 points or so.

3. Practice effects could play a role in the second score being higher. This could also be the case when the difference between tests is very small—about 6 points or less—and there is greater gain on nonverbal/spatial/simultaneous tests that are more prone to practice effects.

4. The second score could reflect gains in cognitive development. This explanation is more likely when the first evaluation was conducted when the child was very young—in the preschool years. The child's intellectual skills could have simply unfolded during the early school years when cognitive development is fairly rapid. Another possibility is that the child has been the beneficiary of an effective intervention program. An intervention program may have succeeded in placing an impoverished child back onto a favorable "creode" (see Chapter 2).

These and other possibilities should be considered when evaluating a child's gain on retest. However, equally important are the child's scores on other measures or other constructs. If a child's overall composite is 74 on retest and his or her achievement and adaptive behavior test scores are both 69 and below, then it is more difficult to argue that there has been a substantial and important cognitive change for the better, and regression and practice effects are more likely. On the other hand, if a child with this same composite on retest has achievement test and adaptive behavior scores that have also moved above 70, then retaining the diagnosis of mental retardation becomes questionable.

Another phenomenon that could mitigate against regression effects is the cumulative deficit (see Chapters 2 and 3). If a child scores lower on retesting and is the product of an impoverished environment, then the effects of the impoverishment may accumulate over development (Haywood [1986] refers to this as the "MA deficit") and result in a child achieving increasingly lower scores.

The Range of Scores Issue

A common complaint about intelligence tests is their inability to differentiate between the various levels of mental retardation. Few intelligence tests offer standard scores that go low enough to differentiate between moderate, severe, and profound levels of retardation. Many popular scales only produce standard scores as low as 45 or 50 (see the sections and chapters for other tests to determine their range of standard scores). The DAS is a notable exception here (see Chapter 11).

It is first important to consider the psychometric limitations inherent in this situation. One limitation is the availability of data for calculating norms for these groups. If, for example, a test has collected only 200 cases at age 7 for norming purposes, then there are only going to be about 4 cases, or data points, below a standard score of 70 (the 2nd percentile). Consequently, the calculation of norms below the 2nd percentile may be based more on the computer algorithms used for calculating the norms than actual data for handicapped children.

Even if this psychometric limitation is conquered with statistical or sampling procedures, the practice may still may be questionable. At very low levels of functioning, the type of scholastic intelligence assessed by most intelligence tests is less relevant. Adaptive behavior issues such as ambulation, speech, toileting, and eating skills are more important at these low levels of functioning. Reschly (1982) recognizes this difference between mild and other levels of mental retardation by pointing out that mild retardation is not characterized by physical abnormalities, it is usually only apparent in school settings, and it may not be permanent. It may well be that not only does the nature of mental retardation differ across levels, but also that the relative importance of adaptive behavior and intelligence tests changes across the levels of mental retardation. Intelligence tests may be important for differentiating between mild and moderate levels of mental retardation. Adaptive behavior scales such as the Vineland, however, do produce standard scores as low as 20. Adaptive behavior scales are also more likely to produce much more important information for intervention design than intelligence scales. It is also theoretically defensible to *use adaptive behavior scales as measures of intelligence* with the severely handicapped because the content domain at low levels of adaptive behavior scales is strikingly similar to that of infant intelligence tests such as the Bayley. Motor skills are part of intelligence scales for preschoolers; why can't they be part of a developmental assessment for the older child or adolescent who has a significant cognitive impairment? My opinion is that *adaptive behavior scales are the tests of choice for differentiating between moderate, severe, and profound levels of mental retardation or developmental disability.*

Unfortunately, many regulatory agencies, such as state departments of education, still insist that every child diagnosed as mentally retarded have an intelligence test score. This requirement results in psychologists engaging in questionable practices such as using preschool tests to obtain a mental age for mentally retarded adolescents and using the old Ratio IQ formula MA/CA × 100 = IQ) to produce an IQ score. *An intelligence test should never be used out-*

side its age range to produce a norm-referenced score to be used in making diagnostic decisions. If an intelligence test is used this way it is likely no better, and it may be worse, than an educated guess by a skilled professional. The sample case in this chapter shows how a credible evaluation of a severely handicapped child may be completed without using an intelligence test.

Other Diagnostic Issues

Despite some problems (Flynn, 1985; Spitz, 1988, 1983, 1986), intelligence tests will likely continue to play an important role in the diagnosis of mental retardation. The potential for misuse of intelligence tests in making the mental retardation diagnosis, however, looms large, especially when intelligence test scores are interpreted in isolation without giving due consideration to adaptive behavior evaluations and background information. A good example is the case of Daniel Hoffman, who was diagnosed by a school board psychologist as mentally retarded (Payne & Patton, 1981). He spent *12* years in a class for the mentally retarded before it was discovered that the initial diagnosis was incorrect. He, in fact, was above average intellectually, but he had a severe speech defect. He had even accepted the fact that he was mentally retarded!

The reasons for making the diagnosis of mental retardation, since it does depend so heavily on the use of intelligence test results, *should be explained in writing.* Simply reporting scores that are 70 or below and concluding that a child is mentally retarded is not adequate for modern assessment practice. Above all, intelligence test results should not be used rigidly in making mental retardation diagnoses. The use of strict cut-off scores places too much emphasis on those very scores and causes evaluators to lose sight of the child's full spectrum of strengths and weaknesses. Gone are the days when the diagnosis of mental retardation is based solely on one measure — intelligence tests. The practice of

using intelligence tests in isolation is analogous to using only a sphygmomanometer (blood pressure cuff) in isolation to diagnose diabetes. There are a host of reasons why a person's blood pressure may be high, only one of which is diabetes!

Case Study

The case study of Kent (Box 14.2) is interesting in that it is clearly a difficult case. This child provided the ultimate challenge for the examiner in that he was young, medically involved, severely developmentally delayed, and could not communicate with anyone other than his mother. Kent lacked school experience, making it even less likely that he would respond to a stranger. Suggestions for evaluating challenging children like Kent are given in Box 14.3.

The case is also interesting in that it makes the diagnosis of mental retardation without appealing to questionable assessment practices. It would have been tempting to use an intelligence test outside its age range or simply make an educated guess as to the child's IQ (e.g., "somewhere below 20"). *Instead, the examiner focused more on determining the child's needs,* making appropriate programming recommendations, and developing appropriate answers to the referral questions, rather than expending great effort to produce "the IQ." This report also follows the guideline that a good report presents and answers referral questions in a straightforward manner (see Chapter 8).

GIFTED CHILDREN

Definition

The most widely accepted definition of gifted and talented children is from the 1978 Gifted and Talented Children's Education Act. The following excerpt gives the central aspects of this definition.

Box 14.2

Psychological report involving mental retardation

NAME:	Kent	CHRONOLOGICAL AGE:	4 years, 7 months
SEX:	Male	ORDINAL POSITION	(birth order): 2nd
GRADE:	Preschool—not attending a formal program	SIBLINGS:	1 older brother

Referral Question(s)

Kent was referred for assessment to determine an appropriate educational placement for the next school year. Questions to be addressed were:

At what developmental level is Kent currently functioning?

Will Kent require special class placement?

If so, what type of placement is appropriate for Kent's needs?

Background Information

Health and Physical Development

The pregnancy with Kent was complicated by hemorrhaging in the first 6 weeks, followed by a high fever that resolved without treatment. His mother reported experiencing mild PET (toxemia) near term. Kent was born at term via an elective Caesarian section; birth weight 5 pounds, 12 ounces.

According to his mother, a milk allergy was diagnosed at 2 days of age. Kent continued to experience vomiting and diarrhea from 10 days to 6 weeks of age. In addition, a ventricular septal defect was diagnosed at 10 days of age, which later closed spontaneously. At 2 months of age, Kent's pediatrician queried deafness and blindness. In addition, Kent was again experiencing vomiting and diarrhea. Kent's mother reported that he exhibited "strange shaking of the feet, arms, and grimacing of the face" around 2 1/2 months of age. An EEG was performed at 5 months of age and Kent was diagnosed as having hypsarrhythmia (infantile spasms). At the present time, additional diagnostic problems, as specified by the pediatric neurologist, include probable Cerebral Dysgenesis, Mental Retardation, Cerebral Palsy: mild Spastic Diplegia, Microcephaly, Seizure Disorder, Congenital Renal Problems, and Recurrent Otitis Media.

According to his mother, Kent held up his head at 3–4 months, sat at 10 months, pulled to a stand and crawled at 12 months, and walked at 23 months of age. However, due to subsequent heel cord lengthening operations, Kent again walked independently at 3 years of age. His mother reports that Kent has an expressive language vocabulary of 15–20 words.

Kent wears corrective lenses for astigmatism. His hearing was assessed at Children's Hospital, and he was diagnosed as having "functional hearing for communication purposes." At the present time, Kent undergoes physical and occupational therapy and is on a waiting list for kindergarten.

Family Background

Kent is the youngest of two children, the first also being a boy. The family is intact, and relationships appear to be healthy. His mother was observed to verbally reprimand Kent when he played inappropriately. This discipline technique was appropriate for the situation. Both parents appeared to interact and cope with their handicapped child at a high degree of proficiency. The social worker at the Child Development Center expressed concern that Kent's parents are overly involved with his handicap such that their requests for services are at times unreasonable. Although his parents inquired intensely about school district services, their questions were appropriate and indicative of considerable thought and insight.

(continued)

Box 14.2 *(continued)*

Previous Test Results

Kent underwent psychological assessments at Children's Hospital at ages 2 and 2½. Test results from the Bayley Scales of Infant Development were as follows:

AGE	MENTAL AGE	MOTOR SCALE
2	13 months (below 50)	16 months (below 50)
2½	15 months (below 50)	16 months (below 50)

Current Psychoeducational Assessment

Formal psychological assessment was attempted, but reliable and valid results were unobtainable due to the extensive nature of Kent's communication disorder. Kent appeared to be at the exploratory level of functioning and was unable to point to any object upon command or sit at an activity for a sustained period of time.

Observations

Due to Kent's not being presently engaged in a preschool program, observations were made at the evaluation center and at Kent's home. Each observation was approximately 1 hour in duration.

Mobility

Kent walked independently, although he exhibited awkward gait and tended to lean forward with his arms stretched forward while walking. Kent walked independently up and down stairs. His mother reported that Kent is unable to run, jump, hop, or catch a ball.

Speech and Language

Kent did not attempt any vocalizations at home. However, he frequently gestured and whined for a coloring book at home. These behaviors appeared to be an attempt to communicate with others. Kent did not voice any discernable words during either observation.

Awareness of Environment and Exploratory Behavior

Kent demonstrated awareness (visual and auditory) of his environment. He was interested in watching and attempting to engage in activities being conducted within his immediate visual field. He responded to loud noises by visually orienting to the sound source. Kent wore glasses during both observations. He also actively explored his surrounding environment. When at the center, Kent took objects from their container and replaced them upon command from his mother. He actively sought new toys. When at home, Kent attempted to color in a coloring book. He held the crayon incorrectly within his fist. When reprimanded for not completing his task, Kent left the room and searched for a photograph album. His mother reported that Kent is unable to cut with scissors.

Interaction with Others

Kent attempted to solicit the examiner's attention on a variety of occasions. He readily approached the examiner upon initial meeting and appeared pleased (i.e., smiled) when placed on the examiner's lap.

Following Instructions and Attending to Tasks

When requested by his mother to color on the page instead of the table, Kent readily complied. Kent did not follow instructions provided by the examiner.

Box 14.2 *(continued)*

Peabody Picture Vocabulary Test-Revised

This receptive vocabulary test was administered, but Kent was unable to produce a satisfactory pointing response. He appeared to point at the pictures at random.

Brigance Inventory of Early Development

Self Help Skills: His mother answered these questions. The ratings assigned by his mother are as follows:

Feeding and Eating—approximately a 2-year developmental level

Undressing and Dressing—approximately a 2-year developmental level

Fastening and Unfastening—approximately a 2-year developmental level

Toileting—approximately a 2-year developmental level (verbalizes toilet needs consistently)

Bathing—approximately a 2-year developmental level (washes face with assistance)

Grooming—approximately a 3-year developmental level (brushes teeth with assistance)

Household Chores—approximately a 2-year developmental level (imitates housework but does not avoid hazards)

General Knowledge and Comprehension: Kent did not perform these tasks due to his inability to provide a reliable pointing response and his inability to remain at this task.

Vineland Adaptive Behavior Scales (Expanded Form)

This instrument was administered to Kent's mother to obtain additional information for program development.

DOMAIN	STANDARD SCORE	ADAPTIVE LEVEL	AGE EQUIVALENT
Communication	53 ± 4	Low	1-5
Daily Living Skills	58 ± 4	Low	1-6
Socialization	59 ± 4	Low	1-6
Motor Skills	46 ± 8	Low	1-7
Adaptive Behavior Composite	50 ± 3		

(Mean = 100, SD = 15)

On the basis of these test results, when compared to his same-age peers, Kent is presently functioning 3–4 standard deviations below the mean, which is indicative of a Severe/Profound Mentally Handicapped child. (Please refer to the protocol for an analysis of Kent's behavioral strengths and weaknesses.)

Summary of Assessment Results

Due to the nature and severity of Kent's handicapping condition, a formal standardized assessment was not possible. However, based on interviews with his parents and observations at school and at home, it appears that Kent's overall developmental level is within the 1 to 2 year range. In most respects, Kent is presently at the exploratory stage of development.

Response to Referral Questions

At what developmental level is Kent currently functioning? On the basis of the present assessment, Kent appears to be functioning at the 1 to 2 year developmental level.

(continued)

Box 14.2 *(continued)*

Will Kent require special class placement? If so, what type of placement is appropriate for his needs? Based on the current evaluation, Kent will require special class placement. Kent meets the entrance criteria for the Special Learning Resource classroom: performance of 4 or more standard deviations below the mean on a test of intelligence and an adaptive behavior profile that is below the moderately mentally handicapped range.

Recommendations

1. Referral for consideration for entrance into Special Education
2. An individualized program be developed by the appropriate teacher and school psychologist. Kent's parents should participate in program development.

For the purposes of this part, the term "gifted and talented children" means children and, whenever applicable, youth, who are identified at the preschool, elementary, and secondary level as possessing demonstrated or potential abilities that give evidence of high performance capability in such areas as intellectual ability, creative ability, specific academic ability, leadership ability, ability in the performing and visual arts and who by reason thereof, require services or activities not ordinarily provided by the school. (Sec. 902)

An important and often confused aspect of this definition is the emphasis on two types of gifts—intellectual giftedness and creative, musical, artistic, and other nonintellectual talents (Maker & Schiever, 1989). This section focuses more on the former, not because intellectual giftedness is viewed as more important or reified in any manner, but because this volume focuses on intelligence assessment. In addition, the reality of the gifted population that clinicians will be charged with evaluating is that most are referred for high intellectual skill. Hence, when this text uses the term "gifted," it applies primarily to children suspected of having high intelligence test scores.

Some researchers suggest broadening the process of gifted and talented education in order to be more inclusive (Maker & Schiever, 1989). This trend has resulted in less emphasis on the use of intelligence test scores in the gifted identification process. For example, some school districts collect a great variety of data, some of which is nontest-based data, in order to identify gifted children. A checklist used by the Los Angeles Unified School District (shown in Perrine, 1989) asks teachers to rate behaviors such as:

Demonstrates ability to absorb information rapidly

Tries to discover the how and why of things

Sustains interest span in selected topics

Is creative and productive in small groups

Exhibits verbal fluency in native language

Assumes adult responsibility at home and in the community

Has ability to relate well with peers and adults

While this broadening of the gifted identification process is continuing, there is ample evidence that intelligence tests will remain as part of the diagnostic process at some level for some students. Consequently, intelligence test use with this population should be studied.

There is also some concern that intelligence tests do not measure all aspects of intelligence. Haensly and Torrance (1990) cite Osborn's (1963) distinction between "critical intelligence," that which is assessed by most intelligence tests, and "creative intelligence," which has not been addressed by popular tests.

Box 14.3

Procedures for assessing the severely and profoundly developmentally handicapped

Listed below are some unusual aspects that should be considered when assessing the intelligence of substantially handicapped children and adolescents. Children such as Kent (see sample case in Box 14.2) require special skills to evaluate with intelligence tests or other measures. Some ideas for assessing significantly impaired children are given below.

1.   Sometimes severely handicapped individuals are disrupted by new individuals in their environment. For this reason, examiners should always observe the child first before introducing themselves. Frequently repetitive, stereotypic, or self-stimulatory behavior will increase in response to a new person or a new environment (e.g., a testing room). A child's home or classroom may be the best setting to use for the test session as these children may be adversely affected by novel surroundings. In addition, the child's teacher, teacher assistant, or a parent may be used to administer some portions of the evaluation.

2.   Many intelligence measures will not have a large enough number of low-difficulty items to assess these significantly impaired children. Examiners should broaden their focus to assess language, gross motor, fine motor, adaptive behavior, and other skills that are at least somewhat related to cognitive development. Examiners may also need to make a dedicated attempt to describe what the child *can* do. Behavioral competencies should not be overlooked in the evaluation of the intelligence of these individuals.

3.   Attentional problems are frequently present in these children. This difficulty may result in the need for more than one test session. Ideally a second examiner or assistant should be present to record the child's responses and take notes while the examiner is testing and interacting with the child.

4.   Observe the child's teacher or parents in order to determine a method for communicating with the child. Communication methods may include pantomime, gestures, sign language, eye blinking, or any other method the child may use to signify at least a yes or no response.

5.   A physically handicapped child may require the assistance of a physical therapist, occupational therapist, or aide to be placed in position for the testing to occur. Similarly, children should have their physical assistance devices and communication devices (e.g., a computer) at their disposal.

6.   These children may require considerable rewards in order to perform up to their potential. Primary reinforcers such as food may be necessary. Similarly, it may be necessary to reinforce successive approximations to terminal behaviors in order to encourage the child to continue responding.

7.   Be observant for physical limitations, illnesses, prosthetics, or medications that may be affecting intelligence test performance. An exhaustive developmental history including medical information is central for appropriate interpretation of these children's intelligence test scores.

8.   Some of these children and adolescents will not possess even rudimentary skills such as imitation that are necessary to take tests. In this case, clinicians may work with the child's teacher in order to develop test-taking skills prior to an eventual evaluation.

Creativity is a difficult construct to define, but it does have a number of agreed-upon attributes, including the "newness" of a solution to a problem, the truthfulness or verifiability of a creative idea, and unusualness (Haensly & Torrance, 1990). Creativity tests abound. A recent tally found 225 such measures (Haensly & Torrance, 1990).

Not as clear-cut, however, is the relationship between creativity assessment and intellectual assessment when these measures are used as part of a comprehensive evaluation of a giftedness. Whether creativity, wisdom, or other constructs are separate from or central to a definition of intelligence is unclear. Constructs such as creativity, however, may be central to the assessment of giftedness, and there may be a relationship between these constructs that is similar to the intelligence/adaptive behavior relationship.

Optimal Practices

Harrison (in Kaufman, 1990) has proposed the principles listed below for the use of intelligence tests in making the diagnosis of giftedness.

1. Intelligence test scores should never be the only basis for determining gifted abilities.
2. Minimum criterion (cut) scores (e.g., IQs of 130 or 140) should not be used to exclude individuals from programs for the gifted.
3. The bands of error should be taken into account when determining if an individual has gifted abilities.
4. Intelligence test scores should be used not only for determination of gifted ability, but to plan educational, occupational, and other program plans as well. (pp. 576–577).

Profiles

Given that intellectual giftedness, as opposed to musical or other talents, is the focus of many school-based gifted programs, the above-average to high scores shown in Table 14.2 are to be expected. Similarly, there is no reason to suspect a characteristic V/P or other composite score test profile, and there is none. There is only a tendency for higher verbal/scholastic than nonverbal/performance scores. This profile is sensible given the current emphasis on academic giftedness. This profile is also virtually useless for making differential diagnoses, as was the case for the mental retardation composite score profile.

Regression Effects

Since gifted children's scores are at the tails of the ability distribution, regression effects are prominent in the assessment process, especially at the time of periodic reevaluation. There is nothing more difficult than declassifying a child as gifted based on an intelligence test score that falls just below the cut-off on reevaluation. I have seen such cases in which this has occurred, and an examiner has tried to explain to parents that despite the fact that their child is doing well in a gifted program, he or she is being removed because of a low score on reevaluation. One can imagine the consternation of parents at being told that their son or daughter has essentially become "ungifted." Such scenarios lead one to question the wisdom of periodic formal reevaluation of a gifted child with an intelligence test, especially if the child is thriving in the gifted program. This sort of mandatory reevaluation only serves to promote confusion of criterion and predictor variables. Concluding that a child has become "ungifted" (based on some slightly lower scores that are within the range to be expected by regression effects) is akin to not allowing a provisionally admitted graduate student to continue because of low GRE scores, in spite of the fact that the student is earning superior grades and favorable reviews from faculty. The predictor variable (i.e., GREs) indicates that the student cannot succeed, and these are given more credence than the criterion variable (i.e., success in graduate school).

Research Needs

While assessment of giftedness is widespread, there is a crucial need for research on the use of intelligence tests, and other tests, in this process. Hoge (1988) has concluded that the tests used in this diagnostic process are lacking validity evidence. When speaking of intelligence tests, Hoge (1988) appropriately notes, ". . . there is relatively little information available about the ability of those measures to identify gifted potential or to predict performance in gifted programs. Yet it is these latter activities that form the basis for our use of the measures" (p. 14). One could argue further that this lack of predictive validity evidence is a violation of *The*

TABLE 14.2   Mean intelligence test scores for samples of children diagnosed as intellectually gifted

Author(s)/Date	N	Composite Score	Sample Mean
WISC-R (WISC-III) STUDIES			
Wechsler (1991)	38	Verbal	128.0
		Performance	124.6
		Full Scale	128.7
Sattler & Covin (1986)	85	Verbal	126.2
		Performance	127.6
		Full Scale	130.0
Thorndike, Hagen, & Sattler (1986)	19	Verbal	117.6
		Performance	114.5
		Full Scale	117.7
Mather (1984)	46	Verbal	127.1
		Performance	123.8
		Full Scale	128.2
K-ABC STUDIES			
Mealor & Curtiss (1985)	40	Sequential	116.7
		Simultaneous	122.2
		MPC	123.1
		Achievement	122.3
Barry (1983)	50	Sequential	129.0
		Simultaneous	123.3
		MPC	130.5
		Achievement	126.5
McCallum, Karnes, & Edwards (1984)	41	Sequential	114.8
		Simultaneous	118.2
		MPC	119.2
		Achievement	120.2
Naglieri & Anderson	38	Sequential	122.4
		Simultaneous	122.8
		MPC	126.3
		Achievement	124.4
BINET-4 STUDIES			
Thorndike, Hagen, & Sattler (1986)	19	Verbal	113.5
		Abstract/Visual	109.6
		Quantitative	117.2
		Short-Term Memory	116.1
		Composite	116.3
DAS STUDIES			
Elliott (1990a)	62	Verbal	115.3
		Nonverbal	115.5
		Spatial	114.2
		GCA	118.1

Standards for Educational and Psychological Testing (Hoge, 1988). In summary, it could be said that intelligence tests have been accepted whole-heartedly as the cornerstone of many identification procedures for gifted programs with little evidence of their value. This is not to say that such tests are necessarily lacking value but rather that they should not be used as if they do possess strong research support.

HEARING IMPAIRMENTS

Definition

Deaf children cannot hear speech through the ear alone, with or without a hearing aid (Sullivan & Burley, 1990). The most common type of hearing loss encountered in the school-age child is the conductive hearing loss, in which there is an impairment of the internal or middle ear that precludes the transmission of sound (Sullivan & Burley, 1990). This type of hearing loss is commonly caused by illnesses such as otitis media (inflammation of the middle ear), commonly referred to in toddlers and preschoolers as an "ear infection." Another type of hearing impairment is the sensory-neural loss that is caused by defective inner ear structures such as auditory nerve damage or even damage to the auditory centers of the brain. A third type of hearing loss is mixed hearing loss, where there is a combination of conductive and sensory-neural problems (Sullivan & Burley, 1990).

Use of Intelligence Tests

A major impedance to assessing the intelligence of deaf children is the lack of nonverbal tests that are specifically designed for use with hearing-impaired children. Because of this lack of unique assessment technology, the most popular test for deaf children has also been the most popular test for assessing the intelligence of most children—

the WISC Performance Scale. The WISC-R remained popular for assessing deaf children because it has been adapted for this use (Ray, 1979), and it has deaf norms (Anderson & Sisco, 1977). Nevertheless, the WISC Performance Scale has significant practical limitations.

The Performance scale oral instructions given by examiners are cumbersome, especially those for the Picture Arrangement and Coding subtests. It has even been suggested that these tests be dropped (and prorating be used) if they yield dissimilar scores from the remainder of the profile (Sullivan & Burley, 1990). This suggestion, however, is highly questionable because it takes a truly insightful clinician to determine if a test yields a lower score due to administration procedures as opposed to a cognitive weakness. Probably the best advice is to administer the Performance scale along with another nonverbal measure (see Chapter 12 for a discussion of non-verbal tests of intelligence) in order to cross-validate the WISC results.

Separate Norms

A number of investigations of children with hearing impairments, many of which were conducted with children in residential settings, show remarkably little difference from the performance of the WISC-R standardization sample. Anderson and Sisco (1977) collected a national sample of hearing-impaired children consisting of 1,228 cases. This sample was compared to the WISC-R standardization sample and was found to have more male children, minority children, and children of lower parental SES. Children who participated in the norming were congenitally or prelingually deaf and had a hearing loss of at least 70 dB in their better ear. Braden (1985) also notes that the incidence of brain injury is also greater than average in hearing-impaired samples. Taking all of these caveats into account, it is striking how similar the distribution of intelligence is for the hearing-impaired and regular norming samples. The overall Performance scale mean for the hearing-impaired sample was 97 (96.89). These findings are also strengthened by those for the K-ABC Nonverbal Scale, which yielded average scores in several investigations (Reynolds & Kamphaus, 1987).

Braden (1984b) also noted few differences in subtest scores that were of practical significance. When using .33 standard deviation as a criterion of a practical significant difference, he found only Coding and Picture Arrangement to be significantly lower for hearing-impaired children. Braden (1984b) attributed these differences to a more frequent deficit in temporal sequencing among hearing-impaired children. This weakness is likely due to a greater incidence of neurological impairment among this population (Conrad & Weiskrantz, 1981).

In addition to having similar Performance scale means, the factor structure of the WISC-R for hearing-impaired children was strikingly similar to that of the WISC-R standardization sample, suggesting that nonhandicapped and hearing-impaired children's intelligence is organized in very similar ways (Braden, 1984b). In one exploratory factor analytic investigation a single factor was produced for the Performance scale for both samples. The coefficient of congruence (the correlation between the first factors yielded for the hearing-impaired and nonimpaired populations) that the single factor yielded was a remarkable .988, which suggests that the WISC-R Performance Scale showed factor analytic validity for both samples with no bias in construct validity for either group. Some researchers disagree with Braden and have suggested that the intelligence of hearing-impaired children is organized very differently from that of non–hearing-impaired children (Myklebust, 1960; Kelly & Tomlinson-Keasey, 1976).

Given that there is no evidence of construct validity bias and there are only small mean score differences between hearing-impaired and nonimpaired samples, it is necessary to question why separate norms are viewed as necessary for assessing hearing-impaired children. Braden (1985) addresses this issue directly and concludes that separate norms for hearing-impaired children for the WISC-R Performance Scale are unnecessary. He notes that in addition to the above findings, the WISC-R Performance Scale also shows similar predictive validity coefficients for hearing-impaired and nonimpaired samples. Hence, there is also no evidence of predictive validity bias.

Separate Clinicians

While separate norms for hearing-impaired children or for any other well-defined group of children may not be necessary for making diagnostic decisions, they may be useful occasionally in a supplementary role or for making *treatment decisions* (Kamphaus & Lozano, 1981). Say, for example, a clinician computes the average Performance scale standard score for hearing-impaired children at the XYZ residential program for hearing-impaired children and finds that the average Full Scale score is 83. While this substantially lower mean score is not necessarily indicative of bias and it is not useful for diagnostic purposes, it does show that the average child at this school is functioning considerably lower than the average child at other residential programs. Knowledge of this can have some benefit for making treatment decisions. Say, for example, a child enters XYZ school with a Performance scale score of 109. This score may lead the staff involved in planning this child's program to consider ways of enriching this child's course of study or placement in one of the more advanced classes. Normally a score of 109 is not considered above average, but in comparison to the *local norm* in this case it is an above average score. Again, the research to date, as summarized by the detailed review of Braden (1985), does not suggest a need for separate norms for hearing-impaired children for making *diagnostic decisions* regarding a child's level of intelligence.

While separate norms are not needed, *separate clinicians* may be in order. An examiner who is not used to evaluating hearing-impaired children may have great difficulty administering even a nonverbal scale in pantomime. This situation is akin to one in which an examiner is asked to assess a Mexican-American child without having any appreciation of the child's linguistic or cultural heritage (see Chapter 15). The examiner who is unfamiliar with hearing-impaired children and the issue of hearing impairments in general may be able to get a score, perhaps even an accurate score. The central issues, however, are *interpretation* of that score and treatment plan design. An examiner with greater expertise related to the child's referral problem will simply be able to better understand the etiology, course, and treatments. It's a matter similar to seeing a psychiatrist for heart problems. While the psychiatrist can perhaps obtain relevant EKG and other test scores, I personally would feel better in the hands of a cardiologist!

VISUAL IMPAIRMENTS

For the purposes of determining eligibility for special education services, PL 94-142 defines a visually handicapped child as someone possessing "a visual impairment which, even with correction, adversely affects a child's educational performance. The term includes both partially seeing and blind children." There is considerably less extant intelligence test research for this population. One important factor again is the lack of instruments specifically defined for this population of children.

Specific Tests

One of the few well-known tests designed for this population is the Perkins-Binet Tests of Intelligence for the Blind (Perkins-Binet). Form N of the Perkins-Binet is designed for children ages 4 through 18 with no usable vision. Form U is for children with usable vision who are ages 3 through 18. Ward and Genshaft (1983) gave the Perkins-Binet a detailed review and found it

lacking in numerous respects. Among their most relevant conclusions were:

1. The items are not stored in the test kit in their order of administration.
2. Several materials needed for administration are not included with the test kit.
3. Important scoring criteria and other parts of the manual are not easily located in the manual.
4. Some of the Vocabulary items are placed in a different order on the record form than in the test manual.

Gutterman, Ward, and Genshaft (1985) conducted a study of the intelligence of 52 "low-vision" children by administering the WISC-R Verbal Scale and the Perkins-Binet Form U. The WISC-R Verbal Scale consistently yielded lower scores than the Perkins-Binet. This finding could be due to a number of factors, including the age of the Perkins-Binet norms. This is a likely cause given that findings have been corroborated in a second study of children where 14 of them had no usable vision and 13 had vision of approximately 20/400 (Teare & Thompson, 1982). Both groups scored 2/3 of a standard deviation below the mean, similar to the Gutterman, Ward, and Genshaft (1985) study. The group with the poorer vision scored slightly lower (m = 88) than the group with slightly better vision (m = 90). These results suggest a consistent pattern of below-average intelligence test performance as measured by the WISC-R Verbal Scale. This finding suggests further that the nature of this handicapping condition produces negative consequences for intelligence test scores on the WISC-R.

Visual and Intellectual Impairments

The relationship between degree of visual impairment and intelligence test scores has also

REASEARCH REPORT

Neuropsychological assessment of children with visual impairments

Price, Mount, and Coles (1987) propose that children with visual impairments have been ignored by the assessment community. They also note that many visually impaired children suffer premorbid or secondary brain impairments. In addition to intelligence measures, the authors propose that neuropsychological measures can be invaluable for understanding the cognitive skills and integrity of children with visual impairments. Price, Mount, and Cole (1987) have identified the following neuropsychological tests as potentially useful for assessing visually impaired children.

Memory. The Wechsler Memory scale subtests of Personal and Current Information, Orientation, Mental Control, Associate Learning, and Logical Memory. Selective Reminding Memory Test. Halstead-Reitan Rhythm Test.

Sensory-Motor. Klove-Mathews Sandpaper Test, observations of gait and coordination, Benton's Test of Motor Impersistence, Halstead-Reitan Tactual Performance Test, and Smedley Hand Dynamometer.

Language. Controlled Word Association Test.

Achievement. Various tests have been made available in large print or braille forms by the American Printing House for the Blind.

---

been studied. Beck and Lindsey (1986) cite the theory of Hayes (1941) that there is a relationship between the visual acuity of the visually impaired child and the child's intelligence. Beck and Lindsey (1986) tested this hypothesis by administering the WISC-R Verbal Scale to 74 children whose corrected distance vision was 20/200 or less. The children ranged in age from 6 to 19 years. No significant relationship was found between WISC-R Verbal scores and the degree of visual impairment. Beck and Lindsey (1986) concluded that "the students with total blindness with light perception, low vision but could see close at hand, and with 20/200 vision had statistically comparable verbal intelligence quotients" (p. 52).

New Measures

A new intelligence measure for children with visual impairments was recently described by Dekker et al. (1990). This test was developed around Thurstone's theory of Primary Mental Abilities (see Chapter 2) and is designed for ages 6 to 15 years. It differs substantially from the familiar approach of using only verbal measures such as the WISC-R Verbal score by also including haptic measures. The subtests of this measure and their reliability coefficients are as follows:

1. Vocabulary (.88)
2. Digit Span (.84)
3. Learning Names (.82)
4. Verbal Analogies (.92)
5. Exclusion of Figures (.84)
6. Figural Analogies (.85)
7. Perception of Objects (.81)
8. Perception of Figures (.81)
9. Block Design (.91)
10. Rectangle Puzzles (.90)
11. Replacements of Objects on a Map and Map Questions (.92)
12. Localization on Plan and Plan Questions (.76)
13. Verbal Fluency (.84)

Haptic measures such as Block Design were accomplished by making the stimuli physically discrete. The surface of the blocks varies from smooth, to ribbed, to half smooth and half ribbed. Exploratory factor analyses using varimax rotation yielded four factors. The factors and their marker subtests are given below.

Factor 1: *Orientation.* Localization on Plan and Plan Questions, Replacement of Objects on Map and Map Questions.

Factor 2: *Reasoning.* Verbal and Figural Analogies, Exclusion of Figures, Arithmetic, and Digit Span.

Factor 3: *Spatial.* Block Design.

Factor 4: *Verbal Ability.* Vocabulary.

One interesting aspect of the Dekker et al. (1990) test is that they have provided a technology that shows promise for assessing a full range of intellectual abilities in children with visual impairments. This work is also interesting in that it points to the need to consider that intellectual skills may indeed be uniquely organized for visually impaired children.

Optimal Practices

To date there seem to have been few advances in the intellectual assessment of visually impaired children. Measures specifically created for this population have lacked the psychometric quality of tests designed for larger populations. Current research suggests that clinicians keep the following considerations in mind when assessing visually impaired children.

1.   Clinicians should be ever vigilant of children's test behavior in order to identify a previously unidentified visual impairment.

2.   Clinicians should use a low level of inference when testing the child with limited vision. For example, definitive statements about prognosis and stability of intelligence should be especially avoided in these cases.

3.   A clinician schooled in the nature of visual impairments should be called upon to conduct the intellectual evaluation of a visually impaired child. If this is not possible the evaluation could at least be supervised by such an individual or a consultant could be used to provide supervision.

4.   In many cases the verbal portions of high-quality intelligence tests may be better to use with these children than "home-grown" or experimental measures with little supportive psychometric evidence. Many verbal intelligence measures (e.g., the K-ABC Achievement scale, Verbal Reasoning scale of the Binet-4, etc.) have strong psychometric properties, including evidence of predictive validity.

CONCLUSIONS

Intelligence tests have a long history of use in special education diagnosis. They have proven invaluable for mental retardation diagnosis, and they are used with some success for populations of gifted, hearing-impaired, and visually impaired children. The limitations of intelligence test data for making diagnoses of mental retardation and giftedness, however, are now coming into clearer view. Consequently, intelligence test data are now routinely supplemented by other data such as measures of adaptive behavior and creativity. This trend toward broadening the assessment process is likely to continue. Newer research needs to focus on the relationship of domains other than intelligence to intelligence measures and how specific tests can be combined to make differential diagnoses.

CHAPTER SUMMARY

1. Most modern diagnostic systems for mental retardation are based on the criteria set by

the American Association on Mental Deficiency (AAMD)(Grossman, 1983).

2. Mental retardation is a condition marked by dual deficits in intelligence and adaptive behavior.

3. Most diagnostic systems mimic the *DSM-III-R* by defining significantly below-average intelligence as a standard score (M = 100, SD = 15 or 16) of about 70 or below.

4. Adaptive behavior scales assess the degree to which an individual meets the standards of personal independence and social responsibility expected for a child's age or cultural group (Grossman, 1983).

5. One of the oldest and most widely used measures of adaptive behavior is the Vineland Adaptive Behavior Scale (Sparrow, Balla, & Cicchetti, 1984).

6. Some of the more popular adaptive behavior scales currently available include:

Vineland Adaptive Behavior Scales: Survey, Classroom, and Expanded Forms

Adaptive Behavior Inventory for Children (ABIC)

AAMD Adaptive Behavior Scale, School Edition

Scales of Independent Behavior

7. Different levels of mental retardation are recognized by most diagnostic systems. These include:

Mild mental retardation (standard score range 50–55 to approximately 70)

Moderate mental retardation (standard score range 35–40 to 50–55)

Severe mental retardation (standard score range 20–25 to 35–40)

Profound mental retardation (standard score less than 20–25)

8. Intelligence test composite score profiles are useless for making differential diagnoses.

9. Rigid cut-off scores should not be used when making diagnoses based on intelligence test results.

10. In cases in which there are composite score differences with some scores within the mental retardation range and others outside this range, the examiner should explain why the diagnostic decision was made, whatever that decision may be.

11. Psychologists should not expect intelligence and parent-reported adaptive behavior scores to show a great deal of agreement, especially when the child is outside the mental retardation range.

12. Adaptive behavior scales are the tests of choice for differentiating between moderate, severe, and profound levels of mental retardation.

13. An intelligence test should never be used outside its age range to produce a norm-referenced score to be used in making diagnostic decisions.

14. Some researchers suggest broadening the process of gifted and talented education in order to be more inclusive (Maker & Schiever, 1989), which has resulted in less emphasis on the use of intelligence test scores in the gifted identification process.

15. Osborn (1963) makes the distinction between "critical intelligence," that which is assessed by most intelligence tests, and "creative intelligence," which has not been addressed by popular tests.

16. Harrison (1990) has proposed principles for the use of intelligence tests in making the diagnosis of giftedness.

17. Deaf children cannot hear speech through the ear alone, with or without a hearing aid.

18. The distribution of intelligence is similar for hearing-impaired and regular norming samples.

19. The factor structure of the WISC-R for hearing-impaired children is strikingly similar to that of the WISC-R standardization sample, suggesting that nonhandicapped and hearing-impaired children's intelligence is organized in very similar ways (Braden, 1984).

20. Braden (1985) concluded that separate norms for the WISC-R Performance Scale for hearing-impaired children are unnecessary.

21. An examiner who is not used to evaluating hearing-impaired children may have great difficulty administering even a nonverbal scale in pantomime.

22. In PL 94-142 a visually handicapped child is defined as someone possessing "a visual impairment which, even with correction, adversely affects a child's educational performance. The term includes both partially seeing and blind children."

23. The Perkins-Binet is an adaptation of an early version of the Binet that is designed for use with visually impaired children.

Assessing Exceptional Children: Learning Disabilities, Brain Injuries, and Emotional and Behavioral Problems

CHAPTER QUESTIONS

How are intelligence tests used in assessing learning disabilities and brain injuries?

Do particular groups of children with emotional and behavioral problems show a specific Wechsler score profile?

This chapter discusses research findings and presents issues that are associated with more controversial uses of intelligence tests with special populations. The practice of profile analysis looms particularly large in this chapter. The assessment of the intellectual/cognitive skills of children with some prevalent disorders will be discussed in this chapter, with particular emphasis on the issue of interpreting profiles versus interpretation of composite scores. In addition, considerable WISC-R research is cited, and although one would expect this research to generalize to the WISC-III, it is not a certainty.

LEARNING DISABILITIES

Definitions

The term "learning disability" is used to refer to a class of academic problems that interfere with a child's ability to acquire a particular academic skill such as reading or mathematics. Although the concept of learning disabilities has been part of the professional parlance for over a century now, this set of academic disorders still remains somewhat enigmatic, and there is considerable disagreement regarding definition of the population (Hammill, 1990; Smith, 1983) (see Box 15.1).

Hammill (1990) recently reviewed the various definitions of learning disabilities and concluded that there is increasing agreement on a definition of this set of disorders. He reviewed 11 well-known definitions of learning disabilities and identified similarities. Some of the commonalities in these definitions include (Hammill, 1990):

Box 15.1

The nature of the diagnosis of rare mild handicaps

Shepard (1989) elucidates a number of difficulties in the diagnosis of mild handicapping conditions such as learning disabilities. She concludes that misclassification in LD diagnosis will inevitably occur because we are attempting to detect a rare disorder with imperfect criteria. Using a validity coefficient of .75, the cross-tabulation table below shows that 94% of the classification decisions made were accurate—but what about the 5% of the population that were classified as LD?

   In this example over half the children labeled LD were normal. Shepard (1989) amplifies this by saying that in a group of 1,000 children classified LD, only 400 would actually have the disorder! This chapter is recommended to all who are responsible for making learning disabilities diagnostic decisions.

		True LD		
		LD	Not LD	
	LD	2%	3%	5%
Diagnostic Decision				
	Not LD	3%	92%	95%
		5%	95%	

Adapted from Shepard (1989).

1. *Academic underachievement.* Learning-disabled children do not achieve up to their intellectual potential in at least one academic area.

2. *Central nervous system dysfunction.* Several of the definitions cited by Hammill (1990) presume that the etiology of the disorder is due to some neurological dysfunction.

3. *Existence of the disorder in children and adults.* Several definitions do not limit the presence of a learning disability to childhood.

   Hammill concluded that the chances of agreeing on the definition of learning disabilities are now greatly improved. He predicts that the definition offered by the National Joint Committee on Learning Disabilities (NJCLD) is the one that is most likely to gain widespread acceptance. This definition is printed below.

Learning disabilities is a general term that refers to a heterogeneous group of disorders manifested by significant difficulties in the acquisition and use of listening, speaking, reading, writing, reasoning, or mathematical abilities. These disorders are intrinsic to the individual, presumed to be due to central nervous system dysfunction, and may occur across the life span. Problems in self-regulatory behaviors, social perception, and social interaction may exist with

RESEARCH REPORT

Cognitive deficits and acute lymphocytic leukemia (ALL)

In a recent review by Madan-Swain and Brown (in press) the research on cognitive deficits associated with acute lymphocytic leukemia (ALL) are summarized and a research agenda is outlined. ALL is the most common form of childhood cancer. The incidence is higher for males than females and the typical onset is prior to age 5. The prognosis for long-term survival of these children has improved dramatically since the 1960s. Currently, approximately 50% of ALL children achieve a normal life expectancy.

Historically, these children have been treated with radiation therapy. The use of radiation with children who have a more favorable prognosis, however, has diminished because of negative side effects. The authors cite research showing a ⅔ to 1 standard deviation decrement in intelligence scores for ⅓ of the ALL patients who were irradiated. They also noted neuropsychological impairments in visual-motor integration, psychomotor problem solving, and memory. Control groups of ALL children who were not irradiated did not show these cognitive deficits. Madan-Swain and Brown (in press) reviewed additional disturbing research that showed that young children were the ones most adversely affected cognitively by the irradiation. These deficits are also degenerative, resulting in increased risk for school difficulties including learning disabilities. The authors also note that there is some research that suggests that distractibility and inattention are associated with ALL.

Recent research suggests that the neurological effect of irradiation is destructive of white matter. White matter deterioration is associated with behavioral manifestations of inattention, poor nonverbal memory, poor mathematics calculation skills, and poor performance on nonverbal reasoning tasks. It is further suggested that the locus of the neurological insult is prominently in the right hemisphere.

Madan-Swain and Brown (in press) conclude their review by observing that there is little research that clearly shows that these cognitive deficits in ALL children are specific to ALL and not just typical of children with chronic medical problems as some research suggests. Hence, there is a need for research that identifies specific cognitive deficits in ALL children, especially those that are due to the effects of irradiation or chemotherapy.

---

learning disabilities but do not by themselves constitute a learning disability. Although learning disabilities may occur concomitantly with other handicapping conditions (for example, sensory impairment, mental retardation, serious emotional disturbance) or with extrinsic influences (such as cultural differences, insufficient or inappropriate instruction), they are not the result of those conditions or influences. (NJCLD, 1988, p. 1)

This definition is the product of a committee made up of members of several important organizations including the American Speech-Language-Hearing Association (ASHA), the Council for Learning Disabilities (CLD), the Division for Children with Communication Disorders (DCCD), the Division for Learning Disabilities (DLD), the International Reading Association (IRA), the Learning Disability Association of America (LDA), the National Association of School Psychologists (NASP), and the Orton Dyslexia Society (ODS).

Dyslexia

Perhaps the most well-known learning disability is *developmental dyslexia*, which is characterized by extraordinary difficulty acquiring basic reading skills. This disorder was first isolated in the late 1800s (Hinshelwood, 1896; Shaywitz & Waxman, 1987). There is a long history of conceptualizing this disorder as neurologically based, although documentation of flawed neurological makeup on the part of these children is only recently coming to light (Hynd & Semrud-Clikeman, 1989). To a certain degree, research in this area may now be appearing because of the availability of more sophisticated technologies of brain mapping such as magnetic resonance imaging (MRI) scanners. Prior to the existence of sophisticated noninvasive diagnostic procedures such as the MRI, the primary sources of evidence of neurological problems in learning-disabled children came from more crude diagnostic procedures such as CAT scans and autopsy studies where the pool of volunteers is small! There is evidence emerging from recent studies that some of the neurological structures of reading-disabled children may be different from those of normal readers, and that dyslexia is by no means a visual-spatial but rather a language-based disability that adversely affects the phonological coding of information (Hynd & Semrud-Clikeman, 1989). The question for this book, however, is how useful are the WISC-III and other intelligence tests for the diagnosis of learning disabilities such as dyslexia?

Ability/Achievement Discrepancies

Intelligence tests play a central role in the diagnosis of learning disabilities such as dyslexia in that they are frequently used to determine whether or not there is an ability/achievement discrepancy, with intelligence tests serving as the "ability" measure. The rationale for this practice goes something like this: If a child is inexplicably not achieving at a level that would be expected for his or her ability level, then a learning disability may be the culprit. An example of a significant discrepancy would be the case in which a child has an intelligence test composite score at the 98th percentile and a basic word reading test score at the 2nd percentile. The issue that is somewhat open to debate is the size of the difference required to denote a discrepancy as "significant" or "severe." Most state education agencies trying to implement PL 94-142 have selected a discrepancy in the range of about 1½ standard deviations (18 to 22 standard score points) as a cut-off (see Reynolds, 1984, for an overview of the various methods used for determining severe discrepancies). In other words,

if a child obtains an ability/achievement discrepancy of this magnitude or larger, then it can be considered severe. The rationale for using a discrepancy of about 1½ SD is that this would theoretically identify approximately 5% of the population as having a severe ability/achievement discrepancy.

Reynolds (1984) has identified numerous problems with many of the methods of determining a severe discrepancy. One of the common methods is to use a single cut score regardless of intelligence level. This method is referred to as the "simple standard score method" by Reynolds (1984). A criterion discrepancy of 20 points, for example, would be required whether the child had an intelligence test score of 120 or 85. This method, while simple to apply, appears to be systematically biased against children with below-average intelligence test scores. In other words, it is much easier to receive the diagnosis of LD if a child has an intelligence test score of 120 versus 85 (Shepard, 1989; Braden, 1987). One can easily imagine that it would be much more possible to obtain a reading score of less than 100 for a child with an intelligence test score of 120 than for a child with an intelligence test score of 85 to obtain a reading score of less than 65. This bias in the use of simple standard score discrepancy models is due to not taking into account the regression of achievement on intelligence (Reynolds, 1984). If the relationship of these variables is considered, then a smaller discrepancy (< 20) is required for children with low intelligence test scores and a larger discrepancy (> 20) is required for children with high intelligence test scores. Use of such a "regression" model for identifying ability/achievement discrepancies for the purposes of learning-disability diagnosis merely evens out the probabilities that a child of any intelligence level will be identified as having a severe discrepancy. The child with low intelligence test scores is equally likely as a child with high intelligence test scores to be diagnosed with a severe discrepancy.

Use of a statutorily defined cut score (ability/

achievement discrepancy) is similar to mental retardation diagnosis in that qualifying sets of scores have been specified by many regulatory agencies. In addition to specifying the size of the ability/achievement discrepancy required to make the diagnosis of LD, many state education agencies have also specified a minimal level of intelligence (or at least one may not be mentally retarded) to be eligible for the learning disability diagnosis. Usually minimum intelligence test scores must be in the below-average range or higher (e.g., > 85).

What if a severe (rare) discrepancy is found for a child? Is the child then LD? Not necessarily. The presence of a severe discrepancy merely indicates that the child has an unusual difference that may be caused by a learning disability (Reynolds, 1984). Deciding if a child is LD depends on numerous other factors, and a clinician must be schooled in the many characteristics of LD and theories regarding this set of disorders in order to make a proper diagnosis. Shepard (1989) proposes that a combination of tests and defining characteristics will eventually be required to make a proper diagnosis. At this point there is still considerable disagreement regarding how best to determine the presence of LD (Shepard, 1989).

Deciding Which Composite to Use

Another interesting issue is the case in which there is a significant difference between the composite scales. What if a child obtained a WISC-III Verbal score of 82 and Performance score of 102? Which score should be used as the criterion of intelligence for making the comparison between ability and achievement? In all likelihood the Full Scale is an average that may have little psychological meaning for the child. Some states (e.g., my home state, Georgia) have guidelines for deciding when the higher score can be used as the test of intelligence. Cut-off scores in many cases, however, are too rigid and do not encourage an in-depth understanding of the child being evaluated. A large V/P or other

composite score discrepancy often suggests that the child's cognitive skills cannot be understood in simplistic terms. One procedure for investigating a composite score discrepancy further is to administer a second intelligence measure. This can prove insightful, providing a larger sample of the child's cognitive behavior to consider. While intelligence tests correlate rather highly, they do measure distinct content, which may cause them to disagree in individual cases. Administration of a second test would also help the clinician rule out situational and other confounding factors.

If a second test results in another large discrepancy in composite scores (e.g., K-ABC Seq = 84 and Sim = 108), then the examiner remains in a diagnostic quandary even though light has been shed on the child's profile of skills. One still must choose an "ability" measure—or must one? In this case the child's profile should be evaluated for consistency and the diagnostic decision based on knowledge of the etiology, course, and prognosis for LD *disregarding any regulations or standards that foster simplistic discrepancy methods.* This is not to say that civil disobedience should be routinely practiced, but, rather, the child's needs should take precedence in making the diagnostic decision. Consider the following profile of scores.

WISC-III FS = 102, V = 82, P = 119

Binet-4 Composite = 100, V/R = 81, A/V = 117, Quant = 96, S-T M = 98

Word Reading standard score = 83

This profile could be problematic for a clinician who is advised to comply with a rigid discrepancy formula of a 20-point discrepancy between a composite intelligence test score and an academic area test score. In this case the composite scores are uninsightful, but the profile is clear. This child may suffer from a pervasive language-based learning disability that affects intelligence and academic achievement test scores. If background information supports such a diagnosis, then the intelligence composite scores are moot. As is the case with mental retardation diagnosis, *when a diagnosis deviates somewhat from the typical, then the reasoning behind the diagnosis should be explained in writing*. This also helps the clinician think through the case and clarify any biases or political considerations that may have crept into the diagnostic process.

The Search for LD Profiles

Early Profile Research

Profile analysis has encountered difficulty since the inception of the practice. Rapaport, Gill, & Schafer (1945–1946) began research on profile analysis in the 1940s shortly after the publication of the Wechsler-Bellevue scales. These authors worked at the famed Meninger Clinic with adult psychiatric populations. Their text was the product of years of research aimed at using the Wechsler-Bellevue to make differential diagnoses of conditions such as schizophrenia and depression. In their classic text, *Manual of Diagnostic Psychological Testing* (Rapaport, Gill, & Schafer, 1944–1946), which summarized their findings, the authors noted that the Wechsler scale would likely never yield characteristic profiles because of its psychometric properties. They observed:

> *An ideal test for scatter analysis should contain perfectly reliable subtests completely homogeneous and factorially simple, each of which would be as independent as possible of the others. . . . Some of the publications that have appeared in the past 20 years concerning the [Wechsler-Bellevue] and the Wechsler Adult Intelligence Scale . . . has shown how far from this ideal either of the Wechsler tests is. The standardization of the W-B left a great deal to be desired so that the average scatter-grams of normal college students, Kansas highway patrolmen . . . and applicants to the Meninger School of Psychiatry . . . all deviated from a straight line in just about the same ways. (p. 161)*

This early concern about the utility of profile analysis for diagnosing psychiatric populations demonstrates an important failure that was predictive of later research seeking profiles for LD children. Some of the impetus to find characteristic profiles for LD children was provided by the implementation of PL 94-142 and the associated "child find" effort. This law created the need to search for accurate means of identifying learning disabled children so that all of these children could receive appropriate special education services. The WISC-R was caught up in this effort, and there was an almost feverish search to find a profile, or set of profiles, that could serve as a marker for this group of children. Many researchers focused not on ability/achievement discrepancies but on finding scatter *within the WISC-R* that could signify the presence of a learning disability. To this day there is an enduring diagnostic controversy regarding the utility of using WISC-R profiles (V/P or shared subtest groupings) to diagnose the presence of a learning disability (Reynolds & Kaufman, 1990).

In the 1970s there was optimism that such a marker profile could be identified. Kaufman's (1979b) text noted some consistency in the literature regarding the ACID profile. This profile is made up of the Wechsler Arithmetic, Coding, Information, and Digit Span subtests. Kaufman (1979b) noted a tendency for samples of learning-disabled children to score more poorly on these Wechsler subtests. Similarly, the Bannatyne categorization (see Chapter 7) seemed promising for diagnosing the presence of a learning disability. Kaufman's own enthusiasm for Wechsler profiles waned, as he stated in his well-known text: ". . . the extreme similarity in the relative strengths and weaknesses of the typical profiles for mentally retarded, reading-disabled, and learning-disabled children renders differential diagnosis based primarily on WISC-R subtest patterns a veritable impossibility" (p. 206).

Kaufman (1979b) found Wechsler profiles more useful for theory building and testing than for clinical diagnosis of LD. A review of the problems associated with profile analysis, particularly regarding LD diagnosis, supports Kaufman's cautious stance regarding the distinctiveness of LD profiles.

WISC-R Profile Research for LD Samples

One of the more well-known investigations of WISC-R profiles for LD children is the meta-analysis conducted by Kavale and Forness (1984) (see Chapter 7). These researchers performed an exhaustive analysis of the ability of WISC-R profiles to differentiate samples of normal and learning-disabled children. They included an impressive number of studies, 94 to be exact, and they assessed the ability of a variety of profiles to differentiate learning-disabled from normal children. One profile investigated by these researchers was the aforementioned ACID profile. Kavale & Forness (1984) compared the performance of normal and LD children on the ACID profile for the 94 samples included in the metaanalysis. Despite the fact that the ACID profile had been proposed as being diagnostic of learning disabilities, Kavale and Forness found it to produce a very small effect size for differentiating normal from learning-disabled children. The authors found that the magnitude of the effect size of the 94 investigations produced an average scaled score equivalent for the four subtests in the ACID profile of 8.66. Given that many diagnosticians consider a significant deviation from the mean scale score of 10 to be 3 points, a deviation of 1.4 points from the average for the ACID profile hardly seems to be diagnostic of a pervasive weakness on the part of LD children.

Kavale and Forness (1984) also evaluated several possible recategorizations in addition to the ACID profile. In some cases there was a slight depression of scores for learning-disabled children, but there was nothing that would usually be considered as approaching clinical significance.

Among other findings from the Kavale and Forness (1984) investigation was the finding of no significant differences between the normal and learning disability samples on WISC-R factor scores or on Bannatyne's recategorization of the WISC (see Chapter 7). Finally, this study debunked the myth of learning-disabled children exhibiting more scatter than normal children (Reynolds & Kaufman, 1990), where scatter is defined as the difference between the child's highest and lowest WISC-R subtest score. The authors found a trend for *normal children to exhibit slightly more scatter than learning-disabled children.*

Reynolds and Kaufman (1990) echo these findings in their recent review by concluding that samples of learning-disabled children exhibit about the same amount of subtest scatter as was found for the WISC-R standardization sample—about 7 to 8 scaled score points (Anderson, Kaufman, & Kaufman, 1976; Gutkin, 1979; Naglieri, 1979; Stevenson, 1979; Tabachnik, 1979; and Thompson, 1980).

Similarly, Verbal and Performance scale differences for samples of learning-disabled children have been in the 10 to 12 point range, often with a P > V profile (Anderson, Kaufman, & Kaufman, 1976; Gutkin, 1979; Naglieri, 1979; Stevenson, 1979; and Thompson, 1980). While these V/P differences are potentially statistically reliable, they are by no means unusual in comparison to the V/P differences of the WISC-R nonhandicapped standardization sample. Differences of 10 to 12 standard score points occurred for approximately 34% to 43% of the standardization sample (Kaufman, 1979b).

The Question of Heterogeneity

Critics of nonsupportive studies of WISC-R profile analysis of learning-disabled children can always argue, however, that many of the samples used in such investigations are too heterogeneous. They may say, for example, that the learning-disabled sample was made up of children with mathematics, reading, oral expression, and other types of disabilities or perhaps children who were misdiagnosed. Of course one would not obtain a clear profile for such a diverse group!

Unfortunately, the heterogeneity argument also does not seem valid. A good example of this is a recent and well-controlled study by Semrud-Clikeman (1990). In this dissertation study, well-defined groups of normal readers, reading-disabled children, and children with attention deficit hyperactivity disorder were selected. The reading-disabled group was carefully selected from clinic cases. The sample was selected so as to have a history of reading failure, a difference of 20 standard score points between the WISC-R Full Scale standard score and a reading measure (with the WISC-R being the higher score), a Full Scale standard score > 85, and no history of seizure disorder, head injury, or other neurological history. The scores for the reading-disabled sample on the WISC-R and Woodcock Reading Mastery Tests-Revised (WRMT-R) are shown in Table 15.1. It is noteworthy how even for this homogeneous sample of reading-disabled children a V/P pattern does not emerge (they are virtually identical).

There is, however, one glaringly apparent pattern that does emerge, and that is the differ-

TABLE 15.1   WISC-R (WISC-III) mean scores for samples of children diagnosed as learning disabled

Author(s)/Date	N	Sample Type	Verbal	Performance	Full Scale
Wechsler (1991)	65	LD	92.1	97.2	93.8
Wechsler (1991)	34	RD	98.0	101.9	99.6
Vance, Fuller, & Ellis (1985)	135	LD	98.43	99.15	98.57
Smith et al. (1986)	32	LD Ref	94.45	100.81	97.23
Ipsen, McMillan, & Fallen (1983)	27	LD	100.41	98.49	99.48
Naglieri (1985)	34	LD	92.6	102.8	96.8
Phelps, Bell, & Scott (1988)	35	LD	95.36	97.16	95.60
Thorndike, Hagen, & Sattler (1986)	90	LD	85.2	92.3	87.8
Gresham & Reschly (1986)	100	Mainstreamed LD	87.64	90.13	87.59
Haddad (1986)	66	LD	89.11	95.48	91.48
Klanderman, Perney, & Kroescshell (1985)	44	LD	91.95	96.48	93.91
Obrzut (1984)	32	LD	84.71	95.28	88.59
Algozzine, Ysseldyke, & Shinn (1982)	24	LD	91.8	102.4	96.5

ence between the WISC-R and the WRMT-R. In this study the ability/achievement discrepancy is a clear marker for the LD group.

In a similarly well-controlled study, Hooper and Hynd (1985) selected a homogeneous group of reading-disabled children and compared their K-ABC and WISC-R profiles. Kaufman and Kaufman (1983b) intimated that young disabled readers may have a sequential processing weakness. The Hooper and Hynd study produced an unimpressive Sim > Seq pattern that is not characterized by rare differences between composite scores (Kamphaus & Reynolds, 1987).

Measurement Problems in Profile Analysis

McDermott, Fantuzzo, and Glutting (1990) provide a detailed review of measurement problems with profile analysis, some of which are a more sophisticated explication of the Rapaport, Gill, and Shafer (1944–45) concerns. Most importantly, McDermott, Fantuzzo, and Glutting (1990) provide some insight into the reasons why so many of the LD profiling studies have produced equivocal results. McDermott, Fantuzzo, and Glutting (1990) initially make the argument that ipsatized scores are inherently problematic. An ipsatized score is the difference score representing the difference between a child's score on a subtest and the child's mean subtest score. These are the same scores that were computed as part of the process of determining subtest strengths and weaknesses described in Chapter 7. McDermott, Fantuzzo, and Glutting (1990) cite numerous problems with these scores and conclude that "ipsative assessment has not been well researched, and there is ample evidence to militate against its current applications" (p. 292) (see Chapter 7). Composite scores such as the Verbal, Sequential, or Abstract/Visual have some evidence of factorial (construct) validity. Similarly, most of these composite scores have evidence of predictive validity, but ipsatized scores do not (McDermott, Fantuzzo, & Glutting, 1990).

Finally, by virtue of their being difference scores, ipsatized scores even lack strong evidence of reliability (McDermott, Fantuzzo, & Glutting, 1990). The unreliable and invalid nature of these scores virtually ensures that profile analysis research for LD children will fail to be diagnostically significant, as it apparently has. The McDermott, Fantuzzo, and Glutting (1990) review discusses numerous other methodological issues that should be considered by all of those engaged in profile analysis research.

The Normality of Scatter

Comparison to an adequate null hypothesis is another criticism of profile research (McDermott, Fantuzzo, & Glutting, 1990). One can crudely evaluate the utility of profiles for LD diagnosis by comparing the profiles of LD children to those of other groups, especially normal samples, to determine their distinctiveness from the null (see Table 15.2). Table 15.2 reports composite score means for several samples of learning-disabled children for a variety of intelligence tests. These results are virtually identical to those of Kavale and Forness (1984). There is a trend for LD children to score slightly below the normative mean and for them to exhibit a P > V pattern. Performance-like sub-

TABLE 15.2 Test scores for the Semrud-Clikeman reading disabled sample

WISC-R	
Full Scale	108.00
Verbal	107.00
Performance	107.70
WOODCOCK READING MASTERY TESTS-REVISED	
Word Identification	72.20
Word Attack	73.80
Word Comprehension	83.10
Passage Comprehension	75.00

tests on the K-ABC are also slightly higher than other composites. Specifically, the Simultaneous scale of the K-ABC is somewhat higher than the Sequential scale (usually less than 6 points).

The interesting aspect of the WISC-R patterns is that they are replicated for the referral samples included in Table 15.3. These samples are heterogeneous in that the referral problems included mental retardation, learning disability, emotional problems, and the like. WISC-R scores for all samples in this table are below average, and there is a mild P > V pattern. Based on intelligence test scores alone, it would be hard to differentiate the LD from a referral sample, similar to the point made by Kavale and Forness (1984).

What about nonhandicapped (normal) children? These studies are shown in Table 15.4, and they show the same P > V pattern as the LD and referral samples! The only distinctive difference for the nonhandicapped samples is that the overall score level is higher.

Implications of Profile Research

The results of LD profile analysis research suggest several implications for practice. First, the questionable and inconsistent results reiterate the necessity to deemphasize drawing shared subtest and single subtest conclusions, as was the case with the integrative approach described ear-

lier. If such conclusions are offered *it should be understood that they are offered based on the clinician's acumen and not on any sound research base.* Profile-based conclusions will be warranted in some cases, and for such purposes the requirement of having *two pieces of corroborating evidence* to draw such conclusions seems minimal, especially in the context of the typical amount of data collected in an evaluation.

Secondly, it must be concluded that intelligence test profiles remain virtually useless for diagnosing LD or its various theoretical subtypes. This is not to say, however, that intelligence tests should not be used with LD children. Profiles or subtypes may exist, but they are not likely to be found by using intelligence tests in isolation. A large discrepancy between intelligence and reading test scores, for example, may represent a profile that is a marker for reading disabilities (see Boxes 15.2 and 15.3).

Third, although profiling provides no easy answers for diagnosis, it may still be beneficial for research purposes and theory building. Profiles may be statistically significant but not clinically meaningful. A profile could be helpful for testing a theory, even though it is too indistinctive to be clinically meaningful.

Fourth, given the lack of validity and reliability evidence for profiles, one should be wary of interpreting them causally. Statements such as

TABLE 15.3   WISC-R mean scores for samples of children referred for evaluation

Author(s)/Date	N	Sample Type	Verbal	Performance	Full Scale
Vance, Hankins, & Brown (1986)	51	Referral	81.06	85.53	81.73
Reynolds & Wright (1981)	150	Referral	91.46	96.69	93.15
D'Amato, Gray, & Dean (1988)	1181	Referral for learning problems	89.37	98.22	92.95

TABLE 15.4 WISC-R mean scores for samples of children without known handicapping conditions

Author(s)/Date	N	Sample Type	Verbal	Performance	Full Scale
Gresham & Reschly (1986)	100	Regular class	109.06	111.35	111.09
Kaufman & Kaufman (1983b)	182	Regular class	115.4	114.6	116.7
Zins & Barnett (1984)	40	Regular class	114.40	116.13	117.11
Rothlisberg (1987)	32	Regular class	107.97	115.31	112.53
Wechsler (1991)	206	Not indicated	103.9	111.6	108.2
Thorndike, Hagen, & Sattler (1986)	205	Regular class	103.9	105.3	105.2

those below are at a high level of inference and therefore should be avoided.

"He has a cause-and-effect relationship problem that is causing his mathematics disability."

"His spatial processing difficulty is at the root of his reading disorder."

"Her long-term memory weakness explains her mathematics problem."

Such cause-and-effect statements made on the basis of profiles are exceedingly risky and inappropriate without overwhelming corroborating evidence. Even with corroboration the clinician is making these statements without substantial, if any, intelligence research support.

Trends

Intelligence tests are most appropriately used in a learning disability evaluation when other test data are available. In one recent investigation of the contribution of various measures to LD diagnosis, it was clear that the intelligence test

took a secondary role (Merrell & Shinn, 1990). The most important factors in making the diagnosis of LD were, first, poor reading and written language achievement and, second, teacher referral (Merrell & Shinn, 1990). With regard to the most frequent type of learning disability, reading disability (dyslexia), there is some evidence that these children will obtain lower-than-average intelligence test scores (Stanovich, Nathan, and Vala-Rossi, 1986). Stanovich, Nathan, & Vala-Rossi (1986) draw this conclusion based on their review of the learning disability research, which they summarize as follows.

In short, the vast majority of school-labeled "problem readers" are perhaps better viewed as displaying a generalized developmental lag rather than a deficit in a specific and encapsulated reading-related cognitive skill. Although this characterization does unfortunately suggest the conclusion that the cognitive problems of the poor reader are pervasive, it does have two important "positive" implications: that growth in reading ability will occur if instructional resources are expended on the child, and that these children can attain reading fluency commensurate with their other cognitive abilities. (p. 281)

Box 15.2

Advised measurement practice in learning disability assessment

One of the problems in the area of learning disability assessment is the use of basically defective data that are the product of poorly constructed tests or inappropriate tests (Reynolds, 1990). In his exhaustive review of measurement issues in learning disability assessment Reynolds provides a list of procedures for selecting and using tests that will improve the quality of the data collected for the purposes of determining the presence or absence of a learning disability. He offers 11 pieces of advice.

1. A test should meet all requirements stated for assessment devices in the rules and regulations for implementing PL 94-142.

2. Normative data should meet contemporary standards of practice and should be provided for a sufficiently large, nationally stratified random sample of children.

3. Standardization samples for tests whose scores are being compared must be the same or highly comparable.

4. For diagnostic purposes, individually administered tests should be used.

5. In the measurement of aptitude, an individually administered test of general intellectual ability should be used.

6. Age-based standard scores should be used for all measures, and all should be scaled to a common metric.

7. The measures employed should demonstrate a high level of reliability, which should be documented in the technical manual accompanying the test.

8. The validity coefficient r_{xy}, which represents the relationship between the measures of aptitude and achievement, should be based on an appropriate sample.

9. The validity of test score interpretations should be clearly established.

10. Special technical considerations should be addressed when one uses performance-based measures of achievement.

11. Bias studies on the instruments in use should be reported.

A more recent proposal is to not use intelligence tests at all in making the diagnosis of a reading disability. Siegel (1989) has concluded that intelligence tests are unnecessary for making an LD diagnosis and advises the use of reading-like processing tests in isolation. Siegel (1989) found little relationship between reading and intelligence test scores, which she maintains supports her conclusion that intelligence tests contribute little to the diagnostic process. The role that intelligence tests will play in the future of LD diagnosis is unclear given the current rate of change of LD diagnostic procedures and the numerous offerings of new proposals.

EMOTIONAL/BEHAVIORAL PROBLEMS

The most widely used nosology for the diagnosis of childhood psychopathology is the *DSM III-R*. The *DSM III-R* manual presents the defining characteristics and diagnostic criteria for child problems such as Attention Deficit Hyperactivity Disorder (ADHD), Conduct Disorder, Early Infantile Autism, and Oppositional Defiant Disorder. It is important to note that for most of these disorders, intelligence is relegated to second-class status, if any status at all. In the case of disruptive behavior disorders, such as ADHD,

Box 15.3

Severe reading disability

This psychometric summary is for a child with a severe learning disability. He was evaluated in the first grade, having been retained because of failure to read. Note the vast difference between his WISC-R scores and WRMT-R scores. All of his Wechsler composite scores were average or above, and yet his Woodcock Reading Mastery Tests scores were below average. His basic reading skill, or ability to identify words, is abysmal, with a standard score of 66. Also of interest is that his mother did not learn to read until about the sixth grade. Several neuropsychological tests were used in this evaluation.

Wechsler Intelligence Scale for Children-Revised (WISC-R)

Verbal	SS	Performance	SS
Information	9	Picture Completion	10
Similarities	12	Picture Arrangement	12
Arithmetic	9	Block Design	18
Vocabulary	9	Object Assembly	17
Comprehension	14	Coding	9
(Digit Span)	10		

Verbal Scale = 103
Performance Scale = 123
Full Scale = 113

Woodcock Reading Mastery Tests-Revised (WRMT-R)

Subtest	Percentile	SS
Visual Auditory Learning	12	82
Letter Identification	0.1	34
Word Identification	1	66
Word Attack	11	82
Word Comprehension	15	84
Passage Comprehension	2	69
Readiness Cluster	0.1	54
Basic Skills Cluster	4	73
Reading Comprehension Cluster	3	72
Total Reading	3	72

Basic Achievement Skills Individual/Screener

Subtests	Percentile	SS
Mathematics	19	87
Reading	13	83
Spelling	26	90

(continued)

Box 15.3 *(continued)*

Personality Inventory for Children (PIC)

SCALES	T-SCORES
Lie	60
Frequency	50
Defensiveness	36**
Adjustment	65
Achievement	73**
Intellectual Screening	71**
Development	59
Somatic Concerns	57
Depression	52
Family Relations	53
Delinquency	47
Withdrawal	47
Anxiety	68**
Psychosis	55
Hyperactivity	45
Social Skills	53

** Significant

SNAP Checklist

Checked Pretty Much + Very Much (Total)

	MOTHER	TEACHER
Hyperactivity	1	0
Inattention	0	0
Impulsivity	2	0

Sociometric

NOMINATIONS	
Liked Most	5
Liked Least	1
Fight the Most	0
Meanest	0
Most Shy	5

Box 15.3 *(continued)*

Children's Depression Inventory

Score = 10

Hopelessness Scale

Score = 2

Revised Children's Manifest Anxiety Scale

	PERCENTILE	T-SCORE/ SCALED SCORE
Total	27	44
I:	73	11
II:	19	7
III:	5	5
L:	94	14

Beery Test of Visual-Motor Integration (VMI)

Age Equivalent = 7–9
Percentile = 48

Benton Facial Recognition Test

Corrected Long Form Score = 37

Benton Judgement of Line Orientation, Form V

Correct: 17

Boston Naming Test

Correct: 43

Edinburg Handedness Inventory

# Left = 0
# Right = 10
LQ = 100%

(continued)

Box 15.3 *(continued)*

Grip Strength

(X of 3 trials)
Right Hand = 9.66
Left Hand = 9

Tactile Form Recognition

Right Hand = 8/8
Left Hand = 8/8
Total Time R.H. = 14″
Total Time L.H. = 29″

Trials A & B

Trials A

Total Time = 20
Errors = 0

Trials B

Total Time = 52
Errors = 0

Aphasia Screening Test

Items Failed = 14

---

no specific intellectual criteria are associated with the disorder. The crux of the ADHD diagnosis lies in the behavioral manifestations of the child, including restlessness, overactivity, impulsivity, and inattention. Since intelligence test scores are not central to making these diagnoses, they are primarily used to rule out comorbid conditions in which the role of intelligence is more central (e.g., LD and mental retardation). Because of the less central role of intelligence, there is probably much less intelligence test research available for these types of conditions than there should be. Many au-

thors of studies of these conditions do not include intelligence tests in their diagnostic protocol or in reports of their research findings. The data that are available do, however, portray a fairly clear picture (see Table 15.5).

ADHD

One of the most well-known disruptive behavior disorders is attention deficit hyperactivity disorder (ADHD). This disorder is characterized by extreme motor activity, impulsive behavior,

TABLE 15.5 WISC-R (WISC-III) mean scores for samples of children diagnosed as behaviorally/emotionally disturbed

Author(s)/Date	N	Sample Type	Verbal	Performance	Full Scale
Wechsler (1991)	68	ADHD	98.0	101.3	99.4
Shah & Holmes (1985)	18	Autistic	52	65	56
Pommer (1986)	9	SED	76.7	74.8	73.8
Paramesh (1982)	140	BD	86.38	90.41	87.20
Vance, Fuller, & Ellis (1983)	135	BD	89.85	90.06	88.84
Phelps & Rosso (1985)	60	BD	81 25	92.40	85.28
Ipsen, McMillan, & Fallen (1983)	19	ED	96.45	96.52	96.42
Semrud-Clikeman		ADHD	106.5	110.8	109.3
Goldstein, Parrell, &	44	Depressed/LD	96.02	99.52	97.46
Sanfilippo-Cohn (1985)	11	Depressed/LD IQ 70–84	80.82	81.36	79.55
	17	Depressed/LD Severely ED	98.06	108.18	103.06
	10	Depressed/LD Hyperactive	95.89	100.44	97.67
Finch et al. (1988)	56	Psychiatric population	88.9	90.2	88.4
Sinclair, Forness, &	27	"V" Codes			99
Alexson (1985)	22	ADD			99
	13	ADD & Specific Dev. Disorder			84
	21	Other Conduct Disorder			105
	18	Other Conduct Disorder & Specific Dev. Disorder			90
	10	Conduct Disorder			101
	18	Conduct Disorder & Axis 1 Disorder			93
	12	Somatic Disorder			90
	47	Affective Disorder			103
	38	Affective Disorder & Axis 1 Disorder			101
	26	Affective Disorder & Spec. Dev. Disorder			93
	35	Spec. Dev. Disorder			88
	19	Personality Disorder			101

(continued)

TABLE 15.5   *(continued)*

Author(s)/Date	N	Sample Type	Verbal	Performance	Full Scale
Sinclair, Forness, & Alexson (1985) *(continued)*	12	Psychotic Disorder			87
	19	Pervasive Dev. Disorder			76
	13	Mental Retardation			56
	36	Psychiatric Day Patient	91.3	100.2	95.0
Ackerman, Dykman, & Oglesby (1983)	24	Hyperactive Boys	107.9	105.5	107.2
	9	Hyperactive Girls	102.3	102.7	102.6
Carlson, Lahey, & Neeper (1986)	20	ADHD	85.4	95.20	90.70
	15	ADD	99.64	101.73	98.87

classroom behavior problems, and inattention. The diagnosis of ADHD remains a major controversy (Tramontana & Hooper, 1989), which contributes to difficulties in conducting intelligence test research for children with this disorder. ADHD was originally attributed to neurological problems and called Brain Damage Behavior Syndrome (Cantwell, 1986). The name was later changed to Minimal Brain Dysfunction (MBD) because of a lack of evidence of neurological problems (Cantwell & Baker, 1991). To this day, neuropsychological research on these children remains inconclusive (Tramontana & Hooper, 1990).

Regardless of etiology, intelligence tests have been used consistently in studies of this population. Mean scores for a variety of WISC-R studies are shown in Table 15.5. One can conclude from these investigations that the intelligence test scores of these children tend to be slightly below the average. Of the 10 samples of ADHD children reported in Table 15.5, only 3 have Full Scale scores above the normative mean of 100. The term "slightly," however, needs to be emphasized in conjunction with these findings. In addition to possible diagnostic confounds in these studies, SES confounds may be present. If these 10 samples are of *slightly* below-average SES, then the conclusion of a global intelligence deficit is unwarranted.

P > V Profiles

Does the familiar mild P > V profile that presents itself for nonhandicapped, referral, and LD samples also present itself for ADHD children? Yes. This finding (see Table 15.5) muddies the meaning of P > V profiles even further. This finding also supports the conclusion that a characteristic P/V profile is not going to be any more useful for diagnosing ADHD children than it is for diagnosing other disorders. This finding could also speak to the issue of the hypothesized overlap of LD and ADHD.

ADHD and LD Overlap

The *DSM III-R*, for example, postulates considerable overlap between LD and ADHD. Typical estimates are that approximately 30% of the ADHD population are also LD (Frick et al.,

1991). Any link between these two disorders, however, is speculative despite the overlap (Cantwell & Baker, 1991). Cantwell and Baker (1991) call for prospective studies of preschool children who are at risk for learning or behavior problems in order to sort out the relationship between the two disorders. For the time being, intelligence test users are best advised to treat the two syndromes as separate for diagnostic purposes.

The WISC-R Third Factor and Attention Deficits

One of the most frequent referral problems for school-age children is for attentional problems. The WISC-R third factor of Arithmetic, Coding, and Digit Span, because of its title as the distractibility factor, has been considered as potentially useful for assessing the attentional problems associated with ADHD. Kaufman (1979b) disagrees with this simplistic interpretation by highlighting the complex nature of these tests. Performance on this factor could be affected by number facility, mathematics skill and instruction, sequential processing, and short-term memory.

A recent study by Cohen, Becker, and Campbell (1990) empirically tested the relationship of the WISC-R third factor with measures of attention. This study used a sample of 135 children who were evaluated by a pediatric neurology service of a university teaching hospital. The children carried a variety of diagnoses, with learning disabilities being the most frequent referral problem. The sample was further subdivided into groups of ADHD and ADHD pervasive (showed attention deficits in multiple settings) for data analysis purposes.

The WISC-R third factor scores were correlated with other measures of attention including the Revised Behavior Problem Checklist (RBPC) and Conners' Teacher and Parent Rating Scales (Conners). Few significant correlation between behavior ratings of attention and the third factor emerged. The highest correlation of the third factor with the RBPC was .23 and with the Conners .31.

Similarly, a study of the relationship between the Continuous Performance Test (CPT, an attention measure) and the K-ABC did not show a trend for tests similar to the third factor (i.e., Sequential scale) to correlate more highly with attention measures (Gordon, Thomason, & Cooper, 1990). In this investigation the Sequential scale did not correlate more highly with the CPT than any other of the K-ABC scales.

In a recent treatise on this issue, the well-known ADHD researcher Russell Barkley (1988) also questioned the use of the third factor as a measure of attention. He reiterates Kaufman's (1979b) point of view that these are complex tasks and performance on them is multi-determined. Interpretation of a third factor weakness as being due to inattention is fraught with problems and is probably an oversimplification (Ownby & Matthews, 1985). The reigning opinion is that multiple methods and multiple sources should be utilized to diagnose ADHD (Guervremont, DuPaul, & Barkley, 1990). Guervremont, DuPaul, and Barkley (1990) advise diverse methods, including parent and teacher ratings and child, parent, and teacher interviews, to capture enough information to make an ADHD diagnosis. Guervremont, DuPaul, and Barkley (1990) advise that the ADHD diagnosis can only be made if (1) developmental deviance is evident from the results of well-constructed behavior rating scales, (2) symptoms last at least 12 months, (3) onset is prior to age 6, (4) symptoms are exhibited across settings, and (5) mental retardation is ruled out. In the context of such guidelines for making an ADHD diagnosis, the use of the WISC-R third factor or other similar measure to make the diagnosis seems to be less-than-adequate professional practice.

Medication Effects

A reasonable assumption is that anywhere from 1% to 2% of school-age children are prescribed stimulant medication (Brown & Borden, 1989).

A "psychostimulant" is a drug that produces excitation of the nervous system. The most frequent ones prescribed are dextroamphetamines, methylphenidate, and pemoline (Brown & Borden, 1989). These stimulant medications have a variety of therapeutic and nontherapeutic effects on children. Some undesirable effects of these medications include difficulty falling asleep and slight elevation of blood pressure and heart rate (Brown & Borden, 1989). These medications may also provide at least short-term beneficial effects for attention *and* intelligence test performance. Beneficial cognitive effects that may be attributable to psychostimulants include improved rote learning skills, attention and vigilance, memory, and concept formation (Brown & Borden, 1990).

A former student of mine encountered an interesting and dramatic case of medication effects (see Box 15.4). The child was so inattentive during the initial evaluation that the psychologists involved in the case felt that the scores were suspect and appropriately did not report them. They described them as "below average" (80–90). The score difference with the child on medication was nothing short of remarkable, as the child obtained scores in the "above average" range. This case example should caution psychologists who evaluate ADHD children that medication, or lack of it, can confound Wechsler and likely other intelligence test scores.

Autism and Schizophrenia

Autism and schizophrenia are sometimes referred to as "severe emotional disturbance" (SED) because of the flagrant nature of the symptomatology (see Table 15.6). While both disorders are associated with disturbed relationships with peers and adults alike, the differential criteria shown in Table 15.6 suggest the more chronic and devastating nature of autism. In the case of autism, interpersonal relationships are grossly impaired. This disturbance is characterized by poor relationships, communication, and language skills, and there are numerous signs of neurological dysfunction (Tramontana & Hooper, 1989). These children make few interpersonal overtures, often overtly eschewing social contact. Communication skills may be extremely impaired, and the child may not speak or imitate adequately to be administered an intelligence test in standardized fashion. The language deficiencies of these children are most striking, making it difficult for them to adapt to situational demands. Some have theorized that severe language impairment is central to the etiology of the disorder (Rutter, 1978). These characteristics result in low intelligence test scores for autistic children, often in the mental retardation range (see Table 15.6).

The frequently low scores for autistic children make the differential diagnosis of autism and mental retardation difficult. Both populations are beset by physical limitations, neurological difficulties, and intellectual impairment. This constellation of symptoms makes differential diagnosis impossible based solely on intelligence measures. Rating scales and other measures of autistic symptomatology are needed to differentiate these groups with confidence.

The autistic or childhood schizophrenic child also presents symptoms that make intellectual assessment difficult. Behaviors such as head banging, head rolling, rocking, echolalia, and hallucinatory behavior make valid testing difficult (Sullivan & Burley, 1990). For the childhood schizophrenic who is hallucinating, timing may be of the essence. The examiner may wish to wait until the child is in remission in order to conduct an intellectual evaluation. Some autistic children may have to first be taught to imitate in order to later conduct formal testing (see additional suggestions in Chapter 13). The examiner who tests SED children for the first time will require some supervision in order to carry out an accurate and relevant evaluation.

Box 15.4 •

Confounding effects of hyperactivity

The two evaluations that follow show dramatic medication effects, hyperactivity, and intelligence test scores. In the first evaluation (off medication), the child scored in the 80s on the WISC-R, and in the second evaluation (on medication) his scores were consistently above 110.

Psychological evaluation (off Ritalin therapy)

Child's Name: Ben   Child's Grade: Second
Age: 7 years, 9 months   History Given By: Biological Mother

General Observations

Ben is a 7-year-old white male. He was described by all examiners as being extremely talkative and distractible and having a very short attention span. Because of these behaviors, Ben was very difficult to test and had to be constantly redirected in tasks. Also, Ben was described as being very active and fidgety and he was not able to stay in his seat even for very short periods of time. With constant redirection to the task at hand and with a very structured environment, Ben was able to complete most tasks and was pleasant with all examiners.

Background Information

Ben lives with his biological mother, who has a bachelor's degree and is currently employed. Ben is an only child. His mother and father are currently separated and by maternal report are planning to get divorced. However, Ben has frequent contact with his biological father, who lives nearby. According to maternal report there is a history of marital instability over the last several years. The primary reason given for the instability is the father's alcoholism.

Ben is currently in the second grade at a public elementary school. According to maternal report, Ben has consistently performed well in school, making all A's each report card. He has never been placed in any special classes at school.

Psychiatric History

Ben was seen at this clinic at age 4 for behavior problems that he was exhibiting at home. At this time he was diagnosed as having Attention Deficit Disorder with Hyperactivity.

Ben and his parents were seen for 6 months to develop behavioral management strategies targeting the problems associated with ADHD. He was also referred to a pediatrician, who placed him on Ritalin (5 mg. T.I.D.). Throughout the past year Ben has continued on Ritalin (20 mg. time release) according to maternal report, although he was taken off medication on the day of the testing.

Medical History

Ben was a product of a vaginal delivery during which forceps were used. Ben weighed 8 pounds 2 ounces at birth and maternal age at the time of his birth was 27 years. Maternal report indicates a relatively uneventful pregnancy with extreme nausea, for which the medicine Bendectin was taken, being the only reported problem. It was reported that during infancy, Ben reached all developmental milestones within normal limits.

Maternal report indicates that Ben has experienced throughout childhood various allergies including allergies to dust, various foods, and penicillin. It was also reported that Ben has had ear tube surgery as well as surgery to remove his tonsils and adenoids. And, finally, maternal report indicates that Ben has had many minor injuries from household accidents throughout his childhood, with the worst incident occurring at age 5 when he required stitches for a cut on his forehead.

(continued)

Box 15.4 *(continued)*

Test Results

Wechsler Intelligence Scale for Children-Revised

Ben was administered a WISC-R as part of the evaluation and the results are discussed in the diagnostic summary. The specific scores are not reported in this section because it is felt that Ben's extreme inattention and overactivity prevented a valid assessment of his intellectual functioning.

Basic Achievement Skills Individual Screener

	GRADE LEVEL	SCORE	RANK
Reading	3.2	135	99
Arithmetic	1.8	91	28

Revised Behavior Problem Checklist (factor raw scores) (mother's ratings)

Conduct Disorder	26 — extreme
Socialized Aggression	0
Attention Problems-Immaturity	17 — extreme
Anxiety-Withdrawal	6
Psychotic Behavior	2 — moderate
Motor Excess	7 — extreme

Child Behavior Rating Scale (mean factor rating) (teacher's ratings)

Inattentive-Disorganized	1.75
Language-Information Processing Deficits	1.38
Conduct Disorder	1.07
Hyperactivity	2.00
Anxiety-Depression	2.07
Sluggish-Drowsy	2.20
Social Competence	3.66

Sociometric

1. Like Most	0
2. Like Least	2
3. Fight the Most	0
4. Meanest	3
5. Most Shy	3

Diagnostic Summary of Child

Ben was given a WISC-R as part of the psychological evaluation. Throughout the WISC-R administration, Ben was extremely inattentive and overactive. As a result of these behaviors, it is quite possible that the scores obtained

Box 15.4 *(continued)*

on the WISC-R are not a valid representation of his ability. On the WISC-R, he obtained a Full Scale IQ in the below-average range with no significant differences being obtained between his Verbal or Performance IQ and both being in the *below-average range*. Because it is not clear to what extent Ben's behavior during testing affected his performance, it is important to retest Ben on medication, which will reduce the off-task behavior and may give a different assessment of his intellectual functioning.

On the BASIS, Ben obtained a mathematics age standard score of 91, placing him in the average range at the 28th percentile. On the reading subtest, Ben obtained an age standard score of 135, placing him in the superior range at the 99th percentile. Ben's variable level of performance may reflect differential achievement in the two subject areas tested, although it is also possible that Ben's behavioral problems are contributing to the variability in performance. However, the very high level of performance on the reading section calls into question the validity of the below-average scores obtained on the WISC-R.

Based on structured interviews conducted with Ben's mother, teacher, and Ben himself, and based on mother- and teacher-completed behavior rating scales, it is clear that Ben meets *DSM-III-R* criteria for Attention Deficit-Hyperactivity Disorder (ADHD). All informants reported problems associated with inattention, such as having trouble sustaining attention, often not seeming to listen, having trouble finishing tasks, and being very distractible. Problems associated with impulsivity were also reported and include being messy and disorganized, needing constant supervision, doing things without thinking of the consequences, and having trouble waiting his turn in group activities. Finally, problems of overactivity were reported, which include being excessively restless and fidgety, running around a lot more than other boys his age, and having a hard time sitting still.

It was clear from the maternal report that Ben has been exhibiting the problems of inattention, impulsivity, and overactivity since the age of 3. These problems associated with ADHD are supported by behavioral observations during testing, which indicates a marked degree of inattention, overactivity, and impulsivity throughout the evaluation. While teacher report indicated that these problems are noticeable in the classroom, they do not appear to be as problematic for Ben at school. It is possible that this pattern of fewer problems being exhibited in school is a function of the effectiveness of the Ritalin that he takes each day at school.

Also, from the structured interviews and behavior rating scales there were reports of a number of oppositional behaviors, such as often refusing to do what he is told, having temper tantrums, being easily annoyed, and often seeming to be angry. While this pattern of behavior is not severe enough to meet the *DSM-III-R* criteria for Oppositional-Defiant Disorder, it does show a pattern of oppositional behavior that is causing problems for Ben and his mother. Like the ADHD behaviors, the oppositional behaviors seem to be more severe at home than at school and they may be helped by Ritalin at school. It is also possible that some of the conflict between Ben's parents associated with the impending divorce may be exacerbating some of the behavior problems at home and these stressful circumstances may be preventing appropriate consistent discipline from being instituted in the home.

It was also consistent across all informants that Ben meets *DSM-III-R* criteria for Overanxious Disorder. It was reported that Ben worries a lot about things before they happen, needs frequent reassurance from adults, often worries about his social competence, and often feels tense and cannot relax. While it is clear that Ben experiences a number of worries and that this has been characteristic of him since age 5, it is also clear that this anxiety diagnosis is secondary to the ADHD, and it is possible that some of Ben's motor overactivity may be interpreted as nervousness.

Diagnosis

(From the *Diagnostic and Statistical Manual of Mental Disorders*-Third Edition-Revised)

1. Attention Deficit-Hyperactivity Disorder 314.01
2. Overanxious Disorder 313.00

(continued)

Box 15.4 *(continued)*

Recommendations

1.   Because of the severe symptomatology of ADHD and because of its effectiveness in controlling much of Ben's problematic behavior in the classroom, it seems that continued prescription of Ritalin by a pediatrician is warranted. Because of the severity of the problems in the home, the possibility of prescribing the medication during times when Ben is not in school should also be considered.

2.   Behavioral interventions should also be instituted through consultation with a child psychologist in conjunction with the medication, which would target ways of helping Ben cope with the problems of ADHD and help his mother institute an appropriate system of discipline to prevent further worsening of the oppositional behavior. This consultation with a child psychologist would include monitoring the effects of medication and would also include further assessment of Ben's anxious behavior and intervention for these behaviors as necessary.

3.   Finally, Ben should be retested on both intelligence and achievement tests while on medication in order to get a more accurate indication of his intellectual and academic functioning.

Psychological Evaluation (on ritalin therapy)

Name: Ben
Age: 7 years, 9 months
Grade: Second

Tests Administered

> Wechsler Intelligence Scale for Children-Revised
>
> Basic Achievement Skills Individual Screener
>
> Kaufman Assessment Battery for Children

Referral Reason

Recently Ben was given a comprehensive psychological evaluation by the staff of the clinic. As part of this assessment, Ben was given a WISC-R, on which he obtained a Full Scale IQ in the below-average range. It was reported in this evaluation that Ben was tested after being off stimulant medication for several days and his extreme inattentive and overactive behavior during testing called into question the accuracy of the IQ score as an indication of Ben's intellectual functioning. Therefore, it was recommended that Ben be retested on medication.

Behavioral Observations

Ben was tested on two separate dates. On the first date, Ben was retested with the WISC-R and BASIS and on the second date he was given the K-ABC. Prior to the first testing date, Ben had been placed on Ritalin again by his pediatrician for 2 weeks. His dosage was reported as being 20 mg B.I.D., with 10 mg taken in the morning and 10 mg taken at lunch. Both testings took place at 2:00 P.M.

   Throughout both testing sessions there was a marked difference in Ben's behavior relative to that reported in the previous evaluation. It was observed that Ben had no trouble maintaining his attention, he remained in his seat, he seemed to try hard on all tasks, and he was cooperative with the examiner. At times it was noticed that Ben would answer quickly and impulsively. He also seemed curious about the tests administered, often asking what comes next and how he was performing on the tests.

Test Results and Conclusions

On the WISC-R, Ben obtained a Full Scale IQ in the above-average range with there being a 90% probability that his true score is in the range of scores of 110 to 120. The following are the age standard score ranges and percentile rank ranges obtained by Ben.

Box 15.4 (*continued*)

	STANDARD SCORE RANGE	PERCENTILE RANK RANGE
Verbal IQ	107–119	68–90
Performance IQ	106–122	66–93
Full Scale IQ	110–120	75–91

As can be seen from these scores, Ben performed equally well on the verbal and the nonverbal sections of the test. This indicates that Ben's above-average Full Scale IQ is an appropriate summary score for his intellectual functioning. Within the subtests of the WISC-R, Ben had a relative strength in subtests requiring verbal concept formation but had a relative weakness on a subtest requiring him to answer orally administered arithmetic questions.

All of Ben's WISC-R scores must be interpreted cautiously because of a recent previous administration of the test that may have influenced his scores through a practice effect. Therefore, the K-ABC was also given as a second measure of Ben's intellectual functioning.

On the K-ABC, Ben obtained a Mental Processing Composite (MPC) in the above-average range, with there being a 90% probability that his true score falls within the range of scores of 106 to 120 and placing him at approximately the 81st percentile for his age. Ben's MPC on the K-ABC is equivalent to his Full Scale IQ on the WISC-R and lends support to the hypothesis that Ben's intellectual functioning is in the above-average range. It should also be noted that there was no significant difference in performance on the K-ABC on tasks requiring step-by-step sequential processing in comparison to tasks requiring him to integrate parts into a whole, or simultaneous processing.

On the BASIS, Ben's reading achievement was in the well-above-average range, his mathematics achievement in the average range, and spelling in the above-average range. The following are Ben's age standard scores and age percentile ranks.

	AGE STANDARD SCORE	AGE PERCENTILE SCORE
Mathematics	98	44
Reading	126	96
Spelling	116	86

Test Results and Conclusions

In summary, both tests of intellectual functioning indicate functioning in the above-average range for Ben. This suggests that his earlier scores that placed him in the below-average range were a function of his being off medication and engaging in a number of off-task behaviors. His WISC-R subtest scores combined with his academic achievement scores on the BASIS indicate a relative strength for Ben in verbal concept formation and reading and a relative weakness in arithmetic. While Ben's above-average intellectual functioning would predict adequate school performance, his behavior problems associated with Attention Deficit-Hyperactivity Disorder described in the previous evaluation and his weakness in arithmetic should all be taken into account in planning an academic program appropriate for him.

TABLE 15.6   Diagnostic distinctions between early infantile autism and childhood schizophrenia

Characteristic or Symptom	Autism	Schizophrenia
Onset	Before 2½ years	Later than 7 years
Gender frequency	Male	None
Family history	Usually not	Sometimes
Course	Usually stable	Often relapsing, remitting
Delusions or hallucinations	Rare	Frequent
Intellectual deficiency	Usual	Uncommon
Seizures	Not uncommon	Rare
Pre- or perinatal difficulties	Frequent	Infrequent
Nonrighthandedness	Frequent	Infrequent

Adapted from Herskowitz and Rosman (1982).

Intelligence Tests and Behavioral/Emotional Disorders

There are several reasons for including intelligence tests as part of a test battery for the evaluation of children who are referred for emotional/behavioral problems. Intelligence tests can be helpful for ruling out mental retardation, identifying intellectual giftedness, and for ruling out a comorbid learning disability. Since child behavior is complex and at-risk children frequently have problems in multiple domains (e.g., children with ADHD are often referred because of school problems), intelligence tests can play an important *supplementary* role in the diagnostic process, even for children who are not referred because of intellectual problems.

BRAIN INJURIES

Perhaps one of the more interesting areas for the use of intelligence tests is the assessment of brain/behavior relationships in children and adolescents. This work began in earnest in the 1800s with some detailed analyses of brain-behavior relationships by Flourens, Broca, and Lashley (Puente, 1989) (see Chapter 2). Halstead (1947) and Reitan (1964) spearheaded modern methods of neuropsychological assessment. More recently the work of the eminent Russian neuropsychologist A. R. Luria (1970) has had a profound impact on the field. According to Luria (cited in Puente, 1989) the two primary functions of neuropsychology are to localize brain dysfunction and to analyze the various activities associated with brain function. This section focuses more on the latter by trying to relate intelligence test findings to processes and functions of the brain.

Intelligence and Neuropsychological Tests

Intelligence tests are not comprehensive measures of the various functions commonly assessed by a neuropsychologist. The WISC-R, for example, is particularly lacking in the area of memory assessment (Bigler, 1989) (see Table 15.7 for a description of many of the functions

TABLE 15.7 Skills assessed in a neuropsychological evaluation

I. Cognitive functions
A. General ability
B. Verbal functions
  1. Language
    a. Receptive
    b. Expressive
    c. Fund of knowledge
  2. Abstract reasoning
    a. Concept formation
    b. Symbolic manipulation
  3. Memory/learning
    a. Registration of information
    b. Immediate (short-term) memory
    c. Long-term (intermediate) memory
    d. Memory for remote events
    e. Acquisition rate
  4. Integrative functions
    a. Visual-verbal
    b. Auditory-verbal
    c. Motor-verbal
  5. Numerical ability
    a. Receptive
    b. Expressive
    c. Knowledge base
C. Nonverbal functions
  1. Perceptual organization
    a. Receptive
    b. Expressive
  2. Abstract reasoning
    a. Concept formation
    b. Spatial manipulation
  3. Memory
    a. Registration of information
    b. Immediate (short-term) memory
    c. Long-term (intermediate) memory
    d. Memory for remote events
    e. Rate of acquisition
  4. Integrative functions
    a. Visual-motor
    b. Auditory-motor
    c. Tactile-motor
  5. Construction
II. Perception
A. Visual
  1. Acuity
  2. Ocular dominance

(continued)

TABLE 15.7 *(continued)*

  3. Fields of vision
B. Auditory
  1. Acuity
  2. Discrimination
    a. Verbal
    b. Nonverbal
  3. Lateralization of ability
C. Tactile-kinesthetic
  1. Acuity
  2. Discrimination
  3. Lateralization of ability
III. Motor functions
A. Strength
B. Speed of performance
C. Perceptual-motor speed
D. Coordination
E. Dexterity
F. Lateral preference
IV. Emotional/control functions
A. Attention
B. Concentration
C. Frustration tolerance
D. Interpersonal/social skills
E. Flexibility
F. Emotional functioning
G. Personality

Adapted from Dean and Gray (1990).

typically assessed in a neuropsychological evaluation). Neuropsychological test batteries possess considerable breadth, assessing intelligence-like skills as well as measures of speech, motor, haptic, and other functions. Intelligence tests, then, are interpreted as one piece of data in a large collection.

Approaches to Interpretation

Nussbaum and Bigler (1989) provide a detailed description of common neuropsychological assessment procedures and interpretive methods. Some of the typical interpretive approaches include those discussed below, as indicated by Nussbaum and Bigler (1989).

Normative Comparisons

Psychologists may interpret subtest scores from tests such as the Halstead-Reitan Neuropsychological Test Battery. This aspect of neuropsychological test performance is the same approach that is used with other popular tests such as intelligence and academic achievement measures. If, for example, a child obtains a score that is 2 standard deviations below the mean on a tactile finger localization test, then the clinician may infer that the child has impaired tactile perception/localization skills. Nussbaum and Bigler (1989) also point out caveats with this approach to interpretation, including "nonintellective" factors such as attention and motivation and the poor psychometric properties of some neuropsychological tests. Some tests have standard deviations larger than their means (Nussbaum & Bigler, 1989).

Shared Subtest Approach

In the same manner as has been used in intellectual assessment since the 1930s, one neuropsychological approach to interpretation is to evaluate "patterns of performance" across subtests (Nussbaum & Bigler, 1989).

Pathognomonic Signs

This deviant sign methodology comes into play when a child exhibits a behavior, symptom, or "sign" that is extremely rare in the normal population. One of the difficulties with this approach is deciding how unusual a behavior is when there is so much variability in the normal population. Another problem is the tendency of this approach to produce so many false negatives (Nussbaum & Bigler, 1989). A false negative is a case in which a child has a history of significant brain injury but is not diagnosed as such by a deviant signs methodology.

Comparison of Right and Left Body Sides

This approach compares the performance of one side of the body to the other on sensory and motor measures of neuropsychological test batteries. Such an interpretation may implicate hemispheric dysfunction, although this approach has problems, especially with younger children where laterality may not be well established (Nussbaum & Bigler, 1989).

Multiple Approaches

Nussbaum and Bigler (1989) also note that now there are integrative approaches to interpretation that combine all of the methods just mentioned. These methods are known variously as "multiple inferential" or "rules approaches" to interpretation that attempt to compensate for the various weaknesses of the individual approaches described earlier. Because of the large realm of possible neurological disorders and sequelae associated with pediatric medical problems, it is also important in neuropsychological test interpretation to have extensive experience with clinical cases. The application of the various rules described earlier is fraught with problems in the hands of the inexpert.

Brain Injury and Global Deficits

Wechsler (1958) hypothesized that there is generally little correspondence between WISC-R performance and specific loci of injury. He concluded that intelligence is a complex phenomenon, measuring numerous interactions of various brain systems (refer to Chapter 2 for a review of some of the basics of neuropsychological theory). This conclusion of Wechsler from long ago is consistent with current findings suggesting that characteristic profiles for groups of brain-injured children have not been found, not even a V/P pattern of note. In this regard, Tramontana and Hooper (1988) concluded that, "[f]or example, differences between Wechsler Verbal IQ and Performance IQ do not provide a valid means of lateralizing brain damage to either the left or right hemisphere in children with early lesions . . ." (p. 11).

The most important finding for children with

neurological problems of consequence is that there is significant global cognitive impairment, as is shown by below-average WISC-R scores (see Table 15.8). In comparison to the average WISC-R scores for the learning disability and emotional problem samples described in Tables 15.2 and 15.5, the brain-injured groups show significantly more impairment. With this in mind, one of the indicators of the effects of brain insult on intelligence that is particularly important is premorbid status. Marked decrements from the child's previous record of academic achievement or intelligence test scores raise the specter that the injury was consequential and requires further assessment by a neuropsychologist and/or neurologist. The Chadwick et al. (1981) study is also of interest in that it shows considerable recovery of function in mild and severe brain-injured samples. These results indicate that strong evidence of the effect of neurological impairment on WISC-R scores may become more elusive the further they are removed in time from the point of injury.

One impressive finding is that the WISC-R Full Scale score has been shown to be more sensitive to brain impairment than some neuropsychological tests. The WISC-R has been compared to the Halstead Impairment Index of the Halstead-Reitan Neuropsychological Test Battery. The Halstead Impairment Index consists of the proportion of the most impairment-sensitive tests with scores in the impairment range (Dean & Gray, 1990). Studies of the ability of the WISC-R and Halstead Impairment Index to diagnose brain injury have shown that the WISC-R Full Scale is more sensitive to brain injury than the Halstead Index (Dean & Gray, 1990). Thus, the composite score from an intelligence test may be the best measure available for determining the presence or absence of cognitive impairment post brain injury.

Epilepsy

Epilepsy is a common neurological problem that afflicts 8 out of 1,000 children at some point in their development and 5 out of 1,000 adults.

One of the most common classifications of seizures identifies three types: generalized tonic-clonic, partial complex, and absence (Hartlage & Hartlage, 1989). These three classifications of seizures are also differentially associated with level of cognitive impairment (Bennett & Krein, 1989).

Etiology

A rather clear trend in the literature is for children with ideopathic (unknown etiology) seizures to score 4 to 11 points higher than children with known neural pathology (i.e., seizures due to tumor, traumatic injury, etc.)(Bennett & Krein, 1989).

Seizure Type

Greater cognitive impairment and thus lower intelligence test scores are associated with seizures with more dramatic symptomatology (e.g., gross motor or tonic-clonic type). Seizures with less obvious symptoms such as absence seizures tend to be associated with less severe cognitive impairment (Bennett & Krein, 1989). Children with mild seizure activity may score 10 to 14 standard score points higher than children with generalized motor seizures (Bennett & Krein, 1989).

Seizure Frequency

There is an inverse relationship between seizure frequency and intelligence test scores. As seizure frequency increases, intelligence test scores decrease (Bennett & Krein, 1989). This finding is associated with the notion of severity since the more severe the condition, the more likelihood of frequent seizures.

Age at Onset

Early onset, particularly of major motor seizures, is associated with greater cognitive impairment (Bennett & Krein, 1989). Early onset in many studies is defined as the preschool years.

TABLE 15.8   WISC-R mean scores for samples of children diagnosed as brain injured

Author(s)/Date	N	Sample Type	Verbal	Performance	Full Scale
Levine et al. (1987)*	20	Hemiplegics categorized by lesion size where 0 = small & 3 = large			
		0 (small)	100	95–100	
		1		80–90	80–90
		2		80–90	70–80
		3 (large)	70–80	70–80	
Dennis (1985a,b)**	13	Onset age, congenital malformation, tumor	94.38	76.08	84.15
	20	Internal hydrocephalus, external hydrocephalus, left or right lateralization	99.50	91.75	95.20
	8	Congenital malformation	84.00	81.17	81.38
	18	Onset age, tumor	93.89	83.83	88.28
	11	Onset age, left lateralization	80.64	93.64	85.73
	35	Head injury	92.26	88.91	89.77
	20	Pathology	94.10	91.55	92.00
	34	Tumor	94.44	89.59	91.35
	53	Seizure	91.64	93.06	91.87
	26	Seizure, right lateralization	86.62	81.15	82.73
	16	Internal hydrocephalus, congenital malformation	97.06	82.06	88.81
	13	Seizure, early syndrome, left lateralization	88.23	82.77	85.00
	24	Onset age	100.79	89.08	94.63
	16	Internal hydrocephalus, congenital malformation	91.63	81.94	85.64
	22	External hydrocephalus	92.77	84.86	88.09
	56	No characteristic pattern	96.27	89.34	92.39
	22	Chiasm tumor	97.45	84.95	90.41
Chadwick, Rutter, Brown, Shaffer, & Traub (1981)	29	Mild head injuries-initial	98.4		
		1-yr. follow-up	103.8		
		2½-yr. follow-up	107.0		
	25	Severe head injuries-initial	76.8		
		1-yr. follow-up	102.3		
		2½-yr. follow-up	104.4		

*This study only reports approximate or ranges of WISC-R scores.

**These groups were formed by cluster analysis. The sample descriptors were the major descriptors of children in these groups.

Box 15.5

Neurological soft signs

Developmental Soft Signs

These signs are called developmental because they exist normally in younger children; they are only considered abnormal when they exist in older children.

Associated movements (overflow or mirror movements)

Difficulty building with blocks

Immature grasp of pencil

Inability to catch a ball

Late achievement of developmental milestones (e.g., standing, talking, walking)

Late suppression of primitive signs (e.g., Babinski, tonic neck reflexes)

Clumsiness for age

Motor impersistence

Poor gait, posture, stance

Slowness of gait, hand movements, opposing the fingers to the thumb, tapping

Speech articulation problems

Tactile extinction on double simultaneous stimulation

Abnormal Soft Signs

These signs are considered abnormal at any age.

Asterognosis

Asymmetries of associated movements

Auditory-visual integration difficulties

Choreiform movements

Dysarthria

Dysdiadochokinesis

Dysgraphesthesia

Hypokinesis

Labile affect

Nystagmus

Oromotor apraxia, drooling, active jaw jerk

Posturing of hands while walking

Tremors

Word-finding difficulty

Adapted from Tupper (1986).

Box 15.6

An interview with George W. Hynd (Research Professor, Departments of Special Education and Psychology; University of Georgia, Department of Neurology; Medical College of Georgia)

How does neuropsychological research help us understand the construct of intelligence better?

I think that to answer this question appropriately, it is necessary that one have some idea as to how the neurological basis of intelligence has historically been conceptualized. In my mind, there is still no more astute observation regarding the interface between neurological processes and intelligence than that offered by Wechsler in 1958. As he suggested:

> . . . one cannot expect anything like fixed centers of intelligence for purely logical reasons. Intelligence deals not with mental representations but with relations that may exist between them, and the relations cannot be localized. . . . For effective functioning intelligence may depend more upon the intactness of some rather than other portions of the brain, but in no sense can it be said to be mediated by any single part of it. Intelligence has no locus. (p. 20)

If one were to take this idea at face value, then any hope of more clearly articulating the neurological basis of intelligence would not seem reasonable. However, one of the most profound effects of closed head trauma is that intelligence is often seriously affected. In fact, if one examines data originally provided by Boll (1974), it can be seen that of the 10 most discriminating measures between adolescents with and without head injury, 7 are measures of intelligence. More recent reports confirm the fact that it is general intellectual ability that is often most seriously affected in head trauma (Seinberg, Giordani, Berent, & Boll, 1983).

It must be concluded then that intelligence clearly does have a neurological basis; but the important point is that generalized head trauma most often produces general deficits in intelligence. Thus, a generalized disruption of neurological systems produces deficits in the ability to perceive relations, or as Spearman and Jones (1950) suggested, the ability to engage in the *"education of correlates."*

Neuropsychology will contribute little to the understanding of the locus of intelligence, of *g*. However, neuropsychological research may contribute significantly to our understanding of the correlates or components associated with intellectual reasoning. In this sense, neuropsychological research in the next few decades may indeed assist us in disentangling of the neurological correlates of subprocesses and subcomponents of perceptual and associative abilities which underly the ability to perceive relations among and between mental representations.

Luria's (1980) conceptualization of brain-behavior relations is most frequently discussed in terms of how basic perceptual and associative processes interrelate at a neurological level (e.g., Hynd & Willis, 1985). Based on the clinical evidence he provides and on validating evidence, it might be concluded that we now have a reasonably good understanding of how basic perceptual and associative processes may be organized; at least as reflected in the disordered brain. Considerably less is known about how the normal brain processes information or, perhaps more relevant to the focus of this book, how the brains of children with developmental disabilities (e.g., mental retardation, learning disabilities, attention-deficit hyperactivity disorder, etc.) are organized.

Until recently, our ability to understand brain-behavior relations has depended on traumatic modifications of brain structure which has allowed us to study the resulting cognitive and behavioral pathology. More recently, neuroimaging procedures have provided a means by which both brain morphology and brain metabolic processes can be visualized in a relatively non-invasive manner. Computed tomography (CT) and magnetic resonance imaging (MRI) allow us to examine in relatively minute detail very specific brain structures. Neurometric procedures assist in quantifying morphology of selected regions of interest which can then be employed in examining cognitive or behavioral correlates (Filipek, Kennedy, Caviness, Rossnick, Spraggins, & Starewicz, 1989) in both normal and pathological populations.

By employing such procedures, normal variation in brain morphology can be documented and significant deviations in brain morphology can be correlated with the unique cognitive profiles of various clinical populations. For example, we have found that the length of the left planum temporal (most posterior regions in the superior

Box 15.6 *(continued)*

temporal region) is significantly shorter in dyslexics when compared to clinic control children with diagnosed hyperactivity and normal control children (Hynd, Semrud-Clikeman, Lorys, Novey, & Eliopulos, 1990). Furthermore, when one examines performance on phonological coding measures, significant relationships emerge with asymmetries in selected brain regions as revealed on MRI scans of the brains of children with dyslexia (Semrud-Clikeman, Hynd, Novey, & Eliopulos, 1990). Consistent with Wechsler's (1958) notions, however, there exist no significant correlations between performance on measures of intelligence and empirical measures of brain morphology (Hynd, et al., 1990).

What these results should suggest than, is that there may exist very discrete relationships between select measures of neurolinguistic functioning and deviations in brain morphology. The clinical literature has, of course, suggested this for well over a century (Hynd, 1988). However, these potential relations only involve structure-function relations, not structure function-neurometabolic interactions. Within the next few decades we should see more interactive research among scholars in cognitive psychology, experimental psychology, neurology, and neuroradiology in integrative research that examines functional, structural, and neurometabolic brain interactions.

Neurometabolic imaging couples with MRI or CT in normals or clinical groups may assist in disentangling more complex relations between neural systems and components of ability that underlie intelligence. Positron emission tomography (PET) allows one to image brain metabolic activity during the performance of very specific cognitive or perceptual tasks (Posner, Petersen, Fox, & Raichle, 1988). There exist procedures to superimpose these images of functional brain activity with images of the actual structure of the brain thus enhancing our ability to correlate more specifically the locus of subprocesses and subcomponents of intelligence (Duara, Apicella, Smith, Chang, Barker, & Yoshii, 1988).

What these kinds of studies are revealing in terms of the functional localization of components of intelligence is that there is no simple locus for each ability. While there may be regions important in perceptual processing or in the regulation of attention, there exists significant intraindividual variation in locus of function depending on the interaction of simultaneous processes (Posner, et al., 1988). Thus, while the primary visual cortex may be vital in word perception, factors such as prior knowledge, type of words (highly semantic associative or visually associative, target or non-target), or method of presentation may all contribute to the involvement of divergent neurometabolic or structural systems.

So, how can neuropsychological research contribute to our understanding of the construct of intelligence? Our understanding of intelligence will be furthered by developing a better understanding of not only the sub-components of intelligence (to which multivariate procedures have contributed so much), but how these sub-components interact in a synergistic manner neurologically involving multiple systems and structures (processors). In the past several decades, psychometric procedures such as found in popular neuropsychological assessment batteries have been useful in exploring these possible relations. But, these procedures are severely limited in correlating specific abilities (as opposed to *dis*abilities) to specific neurological structures and systems. Complex cognitive models of components of intellectual ability (e.g., Guilford, 1985; Sternberg, 1985) may eventually be linked in a meaningful fashion to associated neurological structures and systems identified as important using data provided through studies of brain pathology in clinically involved populations as well as studies employing neuroimaging procedures (Hynd & Semrud-Clikeman, 1989). Perhaps in this fashion, we will develop a better understanding of the neurological hardware that serves as the foundation for our dynamic and evolving "intelligence."

What will neuropsychological tests of the next decade look like?

In my mind, the history of neuropsychological testing was profoundly influenced by the early work of Halstead (1947) and later by Reitan (1955) and his colleagues over the past several decades. It was their original intent to chart the effects of localized brain damage on various components of cognitive ability. More recently, Luria's (1980) conceptualization of brain-behavior relations led to a more process oriented approach to neuropsychological assessment (Christensen, 1979).

(continued)

Box 15.6 *(continued)*

However, each of these approaches is accompanied by serious conceptual and methodological problems (Hynd & Semrud-Clikeman, 1990). The Halstead-Reitan batteries have been criticized for reflecting an atheoretical, unidimensional, and static view of brain-behavior relations (Luria & Majovski, 1977). The assessment procedures based on Luria's conceptualization have for the most part not been validated nor have norms been provided such that these procedures can be employed with confidence with children. Other neuropsychological batteries such as the Luria Nebraska Neuropsychological Battery-Children's Revision have been criticized for not assessing more basic perceptual abilities and neuropsychological functions (Hynd, 1988). Consequently, while these batteries are frequently employed in the neuropsychological assessment of children, it would appear that there is significant room for improvement in devising measures that more accurately reflect brain-behavior relations in children.

I do not think that new or forthcoming intelligence or cognitive ability tests will provide psychologists with much more new information than is presently provided on more traditional intelligence tests. This may be especially true in terms of the assessment of young children's cognitive abilities where intelligence tests are used primarily for determining eligibility for special class placement. In fact, Lezak (1988) has urged neuropsychologists to forgo such a rigid adherence to tests of intelligence to determine the intactness of neurological integrity.

What the future may indeed bring is an exponential increase in tests designed to measure more discrete neuropsychological processes, perhaps as represented by Benton's tests (Benton, Hamsher, Varney, & Spreen, 1983). Neuropsychological studies have revealed that processes associated with neuropsychological functioning are so complex and diverse, and have such age-related manifestations particularly in clinical populations (e.g., Morris, Blashfield, & Satz, 1986), that it is only reasonable to expect a proliferation of tests assessing more and more discrete subcomponents of higher cognitive functions. Thus, in the future, it might be an expectation that in the next decade a book such as this one will necessarily double in its coverage of better validated and normed neuropsychological tests appropriate for children. This fact alone will ensure that increasingly higher levels of training and continuing education will be necessary for psychologists whose responsibilities include assessment of children's abilities.

Antileptic Drugs

Medication intended to control seizure activity has also been associated with some detrimental intellectual effects. These medications may have an additive effect that may interact with the seizure disorder to impair intellectual development (Bennett & Krein, 1989). A review by Bennett and Krein (1989) implicates four medications as potentially iatrogenic to intelligence:

Phenobarbital (Luminal)—impairs short-term memory and concentration.

Phenytoin (Dilantin)—impairs attention and concentration, problem-solving, and visual-motor performance.

Ethosuximide (Zarontin)—Impairs attention.

Carbamazepine (Tegretol)—Impairs motor performance.

Given the relatively high incidence of seizure disorders, it is important for clinicians to consider how this disorder may affect the interpretation of intelligence test performance. Clinicians, however, also have to be keenly aware of the symptoms of this disorder, as they will sometimes be in a position to identify the disorder before a physician does. Sometimes the "blank stare" of an absence seizure disorder is interpreted by teachers as disinterest or daydreaming and by parents as inattention. The astute clinician will consider a number of hypotheses for this problem, including neurological dysfunction. The intelligence exam provides a unique opportunity to observe a child under controlled circumstances that may reveal epilepsy and substantiate the need for medical evaluation.

CONCLUSIONS

This chapter reviewed research on the use of intelligence tests, particularly the WISC-R, with children presenting frequent referral problems. There are some trends in the data to suggest that learning-disabled children have a mild global cognitive deficit in comparison to nonhandicapped children. Children with disruptive behavior disorders (not including autism), on the other hand, show little evidence of significant cognitive problems. Brain-injured children are most likely to show global rather than specific deficits (Dean & Gray, 1990).

The utility of intelligence tests for learning disability diagnosis appears to be overrated. New methods for diagnosing learning disabilities are evolving, and the role of intelligence tests in this diagnostic process may change dramatically.

CHAPTER SUMMARY

1. The term "learning disability" is used to refer to a class of academic problems that interfere with a child's ability to acquire a particular academic skill.

2. Developmental dyslexia, which is characterized by extraordinary difficulty acquiring basic reading skills, was first isolated in the late 1800s.

3. Intelligence tests play a central role in the diagnosis of learning disabilities, where they are used to determine whether or not there is an ability/achievement discrepancy.

4. A simple standard score discrepancy method of LD diagnosis may use a criterion discrepancy of 20 points, for example, as an indication of a significant ability/achievement discrepancy.

5. Cut-off scores in many cases, however, are too rigid and do not encourage an in-depth understanding of the child being evaluated.

6. Profile analysis has encountered difficulty since the inception of the practice.

7. Kaufman (1979b) found Wechsler profiles more useful for theory building and testing than for clinical diagnosis of LD.

8. Kavale and Forness found the ACID profile to produce a very small effect size for differentiating normal from learning-disabled children.

9. Reynolds and Kaufman (1990) concluded that samples of learning-disabled children exhibit about the same amount of subtest scatter as was found for the WISC-R standardization sample—about 7 to 8 scaled score points.

10. McDermott, Fantuzzo, and Glutting (1990) provide a detailed review of measurement problems with profile analysis, some of which are a more sophisticated explication of the Rapaport et al. (1944–45) concerns.

11. Many samples of nonhandicapped ("normal") children show a mild P > V pattern similar to those found for LD and referral samples.

12. When conclusions are drawn based on profiles, clinicians must understand that these conclusions are based on the clinician's acumen and not on a sound research base.

13. The most widely used nosology for the diagnosis of childhood psychopathology is the *DSM III-R.*

14. Early infantile autism is characterized by poor relationships, communication, and language skills and there are numerous signs of neurological dysfunction (Tramontana & Hooper, 1989).

15. The frequently low intelligence test scores for autistic children make the differential diagnosis of autism and mental retardation difficult.

16. Attention deficit hyperactivity disorder (ADHD) is characterized by extreme motor activity, impulsive behavior, classroom be-

havior problems, and inattention (Cantwell & Baker, 1990).

17. In a recent treatise on the issue, the well-known ADHD researcher Russell Barkley (1988) questioned the use of the WISC-R third factor as a measure of attention.

18. Psychostimulant medications may provide short-term beneficial effects for attention *and* intelligence test performance.

19. Since child behavior is complex and at-risk children frequently have problems in multiple domains (e.g., children with ADHD are often referred because of school problems), intelligence tests can play an important *supplementary* role in the diagnostic process, even for children who are not referred because of intellectual problems.

20. Intelligence tests are not comprehensive measures of the various functions commonly assessed by a neuropsychologist.

21. Tramontana and Hooper (1989) concluded that "for example, differences between Wechsler Verbal IQ and Performance IQ do not provide a valid means of lateralizing brain damage to either the left or right hemisphere in children with early lesions . . ." (p. 11).

22. The three classifications of epilepsy are also differentially associated with level of cognitive impairment (Bennett & Krein, 1989).

23. Medication intended to control seizure activity has also been associated with some detrimental intellectual effects.

24. New methods for diagnosing learning disabilities are evolving, and the role of intelligence tests in this diagnostic process may change dramatically.

Multicultural Assessment and Bias

CHAPTER QUESTIONS

Why were intelligence tests and special education the subject of so much litigation in the 1970s?

How would one assess the intelligence of a non–English-speaking child when only English language tests are available?

Several issues have led to concern about the use of intelligence tests with children from cultures different from that of the test developers. The traditions of Galton, Binet, Wechsler, Cattell, and others underlie all modern tests of intelligence. These tests emanated from French, British, German, North American, and other similarly European cultures. Intelligence testing, however, became unusually popular in the United States, a society that is perhaps unusually multicultural, being characterized by diverse values, languages, and religious beliefs.

The utility of intelligence tests for children of non-European descent or non–English-speaking background has been questioned since the early days of intelligence testing (French & Hale, 1990). Since intelligence tests have resembled academic achievement tests, their content has always been easily criticized as being culturally specific. The essential question is, can an intelligence test serve the same purpose as measures from the physical sciences? Can an intelligence measure serve the same purpose as a mammogram, for example, which is used successfully cross-culturally?

Intelligence tests came under greater scrutiny because of their *use* more than because of their characteristics. The involvement of intelligence tests in special education diagnosis has brought additional controversy to these measures. The seemingly arbitrary and capricious nature of special education diagnosis brought the use of intelligence measures to the attention of the courts in the 1970s.

RESEARCH REPORT

Different intelligences for different societies

Dasen (1984) proposes that while all cultures have terms roughly similar to the term "intelligence" (see Chapter 2), their emphasis on the component skills or abilities of this construct vary substantially. His expectation regarding the study of the Baoulé, an African culture, was that this illiterate cultural group would have a term corresponding to the Western term "intelligence" but that its connotations would differ substantially. His study found that the Baoulé do have a comparable term for intelligence that is called *n'glouêlê*. Dasen found several aspects of this term that differ from Western notions of intelligence. He found that among the adult Baoulé who were interviewed regarding the use of this term and its meaning the characteristic identified by most of the group members was that an individual with n'glouêlê displayed a "readiness to carry out tasks in the service of the family and the community." This emphasis on social aspects of intelligence is characteristic of other research findings regarding African cultures. It is also interesting that the Baoulé refer to n'glouêlê primarily in the future tense. He notes that they are reluctant to assess children in the present, feeling that this particular characteristic is relatively malleable and may change through a variety of interventions. Similar to Western societies, however, they are willing to use current behavior as something of a predictor of future behavior. The various descriptors of n'glouêlê that were given by the adults interviewed include the following:

Serviceableness and responsibility

Politeness, obedience, and respect

To retell a story with precision; verbal memory

To speak in a socially appropriate way

To act like an adult

Reflection, responsibility, and memory

Observation, attention, fast learning, and memory

Literacy, school intelligence

To be lucky, to bring luck

Manual dexterity, writing, and drawing

Dasen notes that there is some distinction in these descriptors of intelligent behavior between the social and the academic. Among this particular culture, the academic is deemed relatively useless unless it is applied to enhance the social well-being of the cultural group. Dasen (1984) thinks that it is this integration of the social and cognitive intelligences that makes this culture's view of intelligent behavior unique from that of Western societies.

The next part of the investigation was to test these adult conceptualizations of child intelligence by determining the extent to which Baoulé children show knowledge of concrete operations. Another interesting observation regarding cultural differences was that Dasen and his colleagues could not praise children as they performed the tasks as is typical of Piaget's clinical method. In this particular culture, praising a child may bring bad luck. After assessing the concrete operation skills of a sample of Baoulé children, the authors then had parents rate the children on the extent to which they possess n'glouêlê (intelligence). These ratings were then correlated with performance on the Piaget concrete operation tasks. The correlations between three Piagetian tasks of space, conservation, and elementary logic yielded small and frequently negative correlations with the parents' ratings of n'glouêlê. School intelligence, for example, correlated -.74 with parent ratings of n'glouêlê. The only consistent positive correlation between parent ratings of n'glouêlê were with regard to *otikpa* (serviceableness). These correlations ranged from .03 to .23. The logical conclusion from these results was that parent ratings of n'glouêlê value social intelligence to a greater extent, resulting in low and frequently negative correlations between parent

RESEARCH REPORT *(continued)*

ratings and Piagetian cognitive task performance. Further analyses of the data showed that parents were generally not concerned about a child's school marks and that spatial skills were not prized.

While the results showed that certain cognitive skills were valued in the culture, they were only valued if they were put into the service of the culture group. Dasen (1984) made the following comments on cultural differences in intelligence based on these results.

> *But are these implications valid only for African cultures? Could we, in the over-industrialized west, not learn something from the African definition of intelligence? . . . Our society values mainly intellectual skills, and uses these selfishly, in particular for developing more deadly weapons, over-exploiting non-renewable sources, and increasing its wealth at the expense of the third world. Wouldn't these skills be more useful if they were more integrated with social skills, in the service of the world as a community? (p. 431)*

TEST BIAS AND THE COURTS

History

Psychologists learned a great deal about intelligence test bias in the 1970s and 1980s. The premier reason for this was the litigation of the 1970s. Court cases forced organized psychology to study test bias issues with greater urgency. Research in this area was substantial in the late 1970s and early 1980s so that today we know a great deal about the statistical properties of intelligence tests for various cultural groups.

More importantly, the issues regarding intelligence test misuse have been clarified. This has led to numerous publications advising clinicians how to use intelligence, and other, tests appropriately in multicultural settings (Sandoval & Irvin, 1990).

Court Cases

One can imagine how these court cases came about. Put yourself in the shoes of a parent for a moment. Imagine receiving a letter from your child's school saying that your child has been evaluated and you need to come to school for a meeting to decide what to do with your child.

You arrive at school and are ushered into a room with a half-dozen school personnel, some of whom you may not know, including the principal, your child's teacher, a school psychologist, a social worker, a guidance counselor, and a special education teacher. Is it not clear to you at this point that you are going to hear some *very bad news*? These people are not gathered here to give you some parenting award! Then they tell you that your 12-year-old son has some school problems, which, by the way, is not news to you. You were already aware that his achievement motivation has become worse from year to year, and you have tried your best but not solved the problem. Now they tell you that your child was given "some tests" and that these showed that his ability was poor, to the point that he qualified as "mildly mentally handicapped," which you know means that they are calling him "retarded." Note that it is easier for the professionals to emphasize the test's role rather than their own. It is easier to say, "The test indicates . . ." than "I think . . .". You may now have several thoughts running through your mind, such as, "I know he can do better," "Why didn't they tell me about it in grade school—how can he suddenly be retarded?", "Is it my fault?", and, finally, "What are these intelligence tests? I know that he can figure things out at

RESEARCH REPORT

Problems in constructing equivalent tests

A fascinating and detailed study by Valencia and Rankin (1985) highlights the difficulty involved in creating equivalent instruments in different cultural and linguistic groups. The authors conducted a study of the standard English version of the McCarthy Scales of Children's Abilities and a Spanish translation of the McCarthy. The subjects of their study were 304 children with a mean age of 4½ years. All of these were Head Start children or children from public school–sponsored preschool programs. The Hollingshead two-factor index of social position was used to determine socioeconomic status. The majority of the children were from working class backgrounds and their socioeconomic status was determined to be very low by the Hollingshead.

The language status of the children was evaluated using teacher judgment, knowledge of parental language, language spoken to the child by the parents, examiner judgment as determined by conversation repertoire established the day before testing, and child preference. For a child to be classified as either English or Spanish speaking, there had to be total agreement for these five sources of information. In addition, the verbal subtest protocols of the McCarthy were evaluated to determine if there was any language switching on individual items. An extremely small number of children were judged to be bilingual based upon this review and were eliminated from the study. The resulting sample included 142 children who were classified as English language dominant and 162 children who were classified as Spanish dominant.

The English-language children were administered the standard McCarthy scale. The Spanish-language children were administered a translated version of the McCarthy that was developed for research purposes. This Spanish-language McCarthy was developed by researchers with the assistance of bilingual preschool teachers and a Spanish professor. The goal was to develop a Spanish-language version that was as close as possible to the English-language McCarthy. The examiners were bilingual Mexican-American women. The motor tasks were not administered to either group.

An item by-group partial correlation was used to determine item bias. This method basically determines the proportion of variance of any individual item that is due to language differences because total score (ability), age, and gender are partialed out. This method seems to do a good job for controlling for overall ability level.

The results reveal that 6 of the 16 McCarthy subtests showed some evidence of bias. Bias is indicated by a significant partial correlation between language and subtest score. The two drawing tests of the McCarthy showed a mild bias effect in favor of the Spanish-speaking children. Four of the tests showed more substantial and consistent bias in favor of English-speaking children. In particular, the Numerical Memory I test had 16% of its variance attributed to the language the child speaks ($r = .40$). In order to explore the nature of the observed bias in greater detail, the authors investigated item bias on the McCarthy. Of the 157 McCarthy items, they identified 23 that were biased. Of these, 6 were biased against the English-language group and 17 were biased against the Spanish-language group. Notably, the 6 items biased against the English-language group were spread across a variety of subtests, suggesting a more random effect. The bias against the Spanish-language children was centralized on two measures of Serial Order Short-term Memory; Verbal Memory I and Numerical Memory I.

The authors reviewed research on variables affecting memory performance in order to explain this significant bias. They cite two effects, the "word length effect" and the "acoustic similarity effect," as explanations for this difference. The word length effect states that words with more syllables increase the short-term memory load and thus reduce the number of words that can be recalled. They tested for the presence of this effect by reviewing the number of syllables involved in the English and Spanish words included on these two subtests. They cite the well-known phenomenon that Spanish words typically contain more syllables than their English equivalents. The number of English syllables in Verbal Memory I items was 44 for the English- and 73 for the Spanish-language version. Similarly, on Numerical Memory I, the English version included 28 syllables and the Spanish version 48 syllables. These results indicate that the word length effect may be a plausible explanation for the poor performance of the Spanish-speaking children on these two subtests.

The acoustic similarity effect maintains that when words sound similar, they create confusion on the part of the examinee. This lack of distinctiveness between stimuli on a memory task makes the task more difficult. The authors note that the Spanish language is less complex, involving only a 5-vowel system. On the other hand, the English language is considerably more complex, including an 11-vowel system. The authors made a count of the number of phonemes on Verbal Memory I and found that 23 Spanish phonemes were represented 160 times on this test, whereas the 36 English phonemes were represented only 117 times. Again, there is evidence for the acoustic similarity effect in that the Spanish-speaking child heard more phonemes repeated, thus decreasing the distinctiveness of the memory items.

The authors conclude by saying that Spanish versions of popular intelligence measures are likely to be developed and used. They also maintain that "it is critical that these tests meet the minimal psychometric properties of reliability and validity and are free of bias" (p. 206). Evidently, considerable care and sophisticated research and development will be necessary to construct equivalent forms of tests that are administered in different languages.

---

home if he wants to—he handles his own paper route."

The foregoing vignette provides a concrete example of the frustration and tension surrounding special education placement decisions. The consternation of parents and others came to a boiling point in the late 1960s when a number of well-known court cases were filed in order to deal with the very thorny special education placement issue. More specifically, special education aimed at mentally retarded children was the focus of numerous court cases.

The folk definition of intelligence is that it is an innate capacity (see Chapter 2). Hence there is an extraordinary stigma associated with low scores on intelligence measures. This stigmatization is even more clear-cut and abhorrent to many individuals when the term "mentally retarded" is used. It is the diagnosis of mental retardation and the associated educational placement of children in classes for the mentally retarded that has created a search for an alternative or remedy to what has been viewed by many as a stigmatizing and ineffective enterprise.

Hobson v. Hanson

One of the first cases to question the use of so-called "ability tests" to make special education decisions for mental retardation placement

(the oft-used term is "EMR," "educable mentally retarded") was the case of *Hobson v. Hansen* (1967). This decision resulted in the dissolution of a tracking system in the Washington, DC public schools that depended on the use of group-administered achievement tests. It was determined that as a result of the tracking system, many African-American children were placed in the lower tracks in a proportion that exceeded the proportion of African-American children in the total school population. Some 90% of the school population was black, but black children accounted for approximately 95% of the children in the "mental retardation" track (Elliott, 1987). Judge Wright in this case was concerned that in addition to the use of tests that were not true measures of innate ability, the tracking system resulted in children being placed in tracks that provided a lower-quality educational experience. These tracks also had the potential to be stigmatizing and produce expectations on the part of teachers and students alike for low academic achievement. One of Judge Wright's concerns was that this self-fulfilling prophecy would lead to children staying in this track for the remainder of their school career.

Diana

A second case filed in 1970 in northern California was the case of *Diana v. State Board of Educa-*

tion (1970). There were nine plaintiffs in this particular case, all of Latino descent. These nine children were placed in an EMR (educable mentally retarded) class based upon individually administered intelligence test results. Upon retesting, however, eight of the nine children scored outside the EMR range. The case of *Diana* resulted in consent decrees that served to clarify the appropriate and inappropriate uses of intelligence measures and special education assessment procedures in general with children for whom English was not their primary language. Some of the decrees of this case are strikingly similar to the regulations later included in Public Law 94-142. Some important practices that were to be implemented as a result of this case included using more than one assessment device to make the diagnosis of mental retardation. Related to this was a stipulation that adaptive behavior scores should also be used in the mental retardation diagnostic process. Although it had long been standard practice to diagnose mental retardation on the basis of concurrent deficits in intelligence and adaptive behavior (see Chapter 13), apparently this standard practice was not routine practice for the school system involved in this particular case. Hence, by emphasizing multiple measures and the use of adaptive behavior scales, the consent decree was reiterating long-standing practices of sound psychological assessment and diagnosis. The *Diana* decision also required the periodic reevaluation of the EMR students in order to allow for their passage out of the EMR program should improvements obtain.

Another result of the *Diana* case was to clearly identify the criterion of 2 standard deviations below the mean as the cut-off for mental retardation special education placement. This decision resulted in a reduction in the total number of EMR enrollment in California schools from a high of 57,148 in 1968–1969 to 38,208 in 1971–1972 after the *Diana* decision (Elliott, 1987). This reduction of EMR enrollment because of the new standard, however, did not solve the continuing problem of overrepresenta-

tion of minority, especially African-American, children in proportion to the total population. In 1968 and 1969, African-Americans constituted 25.5% of the EMR enrollment, and in 1971–72, they constituted 26.7% of the EMR enrollment. Even as late as 1976–77 when EMR enrollment was only about 19,000 students, 25% of these students were African-American (Elliott, 1987).

After *Hobsen v. Hansen* and the case of *Diana*, section 504 of the Rehabilitation Act of 1973 and PL 94-142, the Education for all Handicapped Children Act of 1975, clarified some of the standards of nondiscriminatory assessment and, more importantly, specified criteria for the selection and use of measures such as intelligence tests. These regulations essentially borrowed the principles that were discovered as part of litigation over employment testing of a decade earlier. As a consequence of this litigation, the Equal Employment Opportunity Commission (EEOC) developed guidelines and regulations that a test must be specifically validated for the purpose for which it is being used (Anastasi, 1988). This is the standard to which intelligence tests would be held in later cases. In the case of employment testing, it was necessary for every employer to show that a particular selection test was appropriate for the particular job classification.

Larry P.

The *Larry P. v. Riles* case began in 1971 when the plaintiffs, representing black children who were overrepresented in classes for the mentally retarded, asked for an injunction against the use of intelligence tests in the San Francisco public schools. The injunction was granted by Judge Peckham in June of 1972 (Elliott, 1987). The injunction insinuated that before the trial began, there was the presumption that the intelligence tests were culturally biased. The trial did not actually occur until 1977 and 1978. Many well-known psychologists testified at the hearing. Dr. Leon Kamin, the author of the book *The Science and Politics of IQ* (1974), provided some compelling testimony about the history of intelligence testing. He provided quotations from such luminaries as Lewis Terman, Henry Goddard, and Robert Yerkes that revealed clearly racist viewpoints. These viewpoints were so strident that they could not be differentiated from the viewpoints of modern groups such as the Klu Klux Klan (Elliott, 1987). This sort of testimony certainly created concern about the intentions of early intelligence test developers. Additional damaging evidence against the use of the WISC-R was provided by Dr. Jane Mercer of the University of California at Riverside. She suggested that intelligence tests were unable to predict school grades, especially those of minority children. This belief is reflected in the development of her own SOMPA (as is discussed later in this chapter). She proposed that minority group children should routinely have their scores adjusted in order to preclude placement in classes for the mentally retarded (the adjusted score is called an "ELP," "estimated learning potential," score). In a sense the use of the ELP is similar to a veteran's preference (Elliott, 1987).

Many noted psychologists also provided testimony supporting the use of intelligence tests. Well-known measurement experts such as Dr. Lloyd Humphries, Dr. Robert Thorndike, and Dr. Jerome Doppelt testified in the case. Measurement experts provided considerable evidence that the WISC-R was not biased. Dr. Nadine Lambert of the University of California at Berkeley testified in support of the use of intelligence tests, suggesting that teachers were the most important variable in making placement decisions and that because of the high teacher referral rate of minority group children there was overrepresentation in classes for the mentally retarded.

Data in support of teacher referral as a biasing factor were collected by Ashurst and Meyers (1973) (as cited in Elliott, 1987). These data from the Riverside, California school system showed that the population of the school system at the time was 80% white, 8% black, and 11% Latino. Of the 257 children referred and studied in the investigation, 48% were Anglo, 20% were black, and 31% were Latino. The percentage of different ethnic groups actually placed in special education classes were 41% white, 20% black, and 30% Latino. These results support Lambert's argument that teacher referral is the major arbiter in the special education decision for the mental retardation placement.

PASE

The 1980 *PASE* case came to the opposite conclusion of the *Larry P.* case, although much of the testimony was the same. The acronym PASE stands for Parents in Action on Special Education. Most of the individuals involved in the lawsuit were Latino. The organizer of the case, Dan Merquez, was a student interning in an EMR classroom in a heavily Latino area of the city. He thought that many of the students were inappropriately placed in the class because of linguistic differences (Elliott, 1987). Elliott (1987) provides interesting information on the social milieu of the *PASE* case and its differences from that of the *Larry P.* case. For example, by the time of the filing of the *PASE* case, most of the central office administration of the Chicago Public Schools were minority group members. In addition, the vast proportion of students in the Chicago public schools were minorities.

One of the more famous incidents in the *PASE* case was Judge Grady's emphasis on item bias. He was very interested in obtaining data on the individual Wechsler items, and his interest was clearly piqued by the controversy over the famous WISC-R "fight" item. This comprehension item asked what a boy or girl should do if a child much smaller than himself or herself should start to pick a fight. This item was identified in the *Larry P.* case as an inappropriate item for black children from a ghetto, because these children would customarily get the item wrong because the most adaptive response in their harsh environment would be to fight back. Judge Grady was very impressed by the research on this item. Contrary to the testimony in the *Larry P.* case, the item was found to be easier for African-American than for Anglo children (Elliott, 1987). Judge Grady apparently expended considerable time on his own study of Wechsler and Stanford-Binet items and identified some as potentially biased. Regardless, Judge Grady decided in favor of the Chicago Board of Education, indicating that the bias identified in the Wechsler and Binet items was not substantial.

The issue of overrepresentation can also be overstated by the use of statistics. For example, if 10% of the population in a particular school system might be black, it sounds like a gross overrepresentation to have 20% of the children in EMR classes to be black. However, when one looks at the absolute numbers, this is still a relatively small proportion of African-American children. Consider the hypothetical example where 90% of the children are Anglo and 10% are minority, and 100 of the children in the school district were placed in EMR classes in a given year. If black children were 100% overrepresented, then the makeup of the class of mentally retarded children would be 20% black children and 80% white children. If there were 10,000 students in the entire school system, of the 1,000 black children in the school system (10% of the 10,000 children), 20 are in classes for the mentally retarded. The 20 children represent 2% of the entire black population. When the statistics are presented in this fashion, the rate of special education placement whereby black children are 100% overrepresented in classes for the mildly retarded does not sound nearly as aberrant. Because of such caveats the statistics offered in these court cases had to be considered very carefully, since only a small proportion of the school-age population is identified as suffering from mental retardation.

Marshall v. Georgia

A more recent case along these lines is the *Marshall v. Georgia* (1984) case. This case was brought against rural school districts in the state of Georgia by the NAACP. It argued that instructional grouping and placement practices were discriminatory. The *Marshall* case heard considerable testimony by numerous experts in testing mental retardation and intellectual development. As was the case with Judge Grady, the grouping and placement practices were upheld.

Elliott (1987), in his extensive and thoughtful review of these and other court cases, draws the conclusion that court decisions regarding the use of tests (other than those rendering judgments in favor of the test or opposed to the test) have not substantially helped minority group children. He suggests that what is needed is strong leadership, patience, and the expenditure of large sums of money to help disadvantaged children of all ethnic groups.

Effects of Court Decisions

The effects of these cases are not widely discussed. Certainly one of the most important impacts of these cases has been an increase in research on test bias issues. Judge Grady's consternation at a lack of item bias data for the WISC-R (Elliott, 1987) was one factor that undoubtedly spawned a number of studies on item bias. Now, in the 1990s, it is ordinary and customary practice for new tests of intelligence to have investigated bias judgmentally and statistically before publication. Furthermore, it is increasingly likely that new tests will assess construct validity bias prior to publication. Examples of the consideration of bias in the development of item pools are given in the K-ABC and DAS manuals.

There has for many years been a hesitancy to place minority group children in classes for the mentally retarded. This reluctance was reinforced by the attention that intelligence testing received in the courts in the 1970s. This in turn may be one of the factors that has decreased placement rates in classes for the mildly retarded. Potentially another factor is a lack of convincing effectiveness research for special education of the mildly retarded. EMR enrollment in California went from an all-time high of 58,000 children in EMR classrooms for the years 1968–69 to only 12,000–13,000 in 1984 (Elliott, 1987). This prevalence rate for EMR children is lower than the rate for moderately mentally retarded children. Elliott (1987) has argued that many of these children have been picked up for services in the less stigmatizing learning disabilities program or other remedial programs.

These court cases also spawned a search for new assessment approaches. One of the most favored assessment approaches to come from this era was the SOMPA (described in the next section). These trials also increased interest in test-teach-test assessment paradigms. The most popular such paradigm of the 1970s was Feuerstein's Learning Potential Assessment Device (LPAD) (described in Chapter 12). The dynamic assessment model of Feuerstein emphasizes the malleability of intelligence. This paradigm emphasizes an initial assessment, then the application of the intervention program, and a subsequent posttesting.

Another popular adaptation of intelligence tests that could potentially be related to the litigation of the 1970s is the increasing availability of nonverbal scales. Nonverbal scales presumably allow the scores to be less influenced by cultural and linguistic differences. There has been a burst of new entries in the nonverbal intelligence market (see Chapter 12).

The SOMPA Alternative

One proposed solution to the issues posed by the *Larry P.* case was the *System of Multicultural Pluralistic Assessment (SOMPA)* (Mercer, 1979). The SOMPA, created by Dr. Jane Mercer, had several aims for attacking the overrepresentation problem, including: (1) adjusting IQ scores based on social and cultural differences in order to prevent overrepresentation, (2) offering a variety of domains of assessment to consider when making special education decisions, and (3) using Spanish-language materials for the assessment of Latino children and their families.

To fulfill these goals the SOMPA had to be comprehensive, including medical, social, and pluralistic components. These components included:

Medical

1. Physical Dexterity Tasks
2. Bender-Gestalt Test
3. Visual Acuity
4. Auditory Acuity
5. Health History Inventory

Social

1. Adaptive Behavior Inventory for Children (ABIC) (a parent report adaptive behavior scale)
2. Wechsler Intelligence Scale for Children—Revised (WISC-R)

Pluralistic

1. *Sociocultural scales* These assess the degree to which a child's culture differs from the dominant Anglo culture.
2. *Estimated learning potential* This score is computed based on multiple regression techniques that use the sociocultural scales to "adjust" the child's WISC-R IQ's according to his or her own culture (Anglo, Latino, African-American). This score is intended to project how a child may perform if all impediments to learning, such as language differences, were removed.

The SOMPA was normed in the early 1970s on a California sample of 2,100 public school children aged 5 to 11 years. There were 700

Latinos, 700 African-Americans, and 700 Anglos. Parent interviews were conducted by fluent bilingual examiners, and child testing was completed by qualified examiners.

While the SOMPA originally seemed like a reasonable approach, my impression is that it has fallen into disuse. Why is this? The predictive validity of the ELP score is the primary culprit. For example, say a child obtains a Full Scale IQ score of 78 and an ELP of 94. What does this mean? Many psychologists had trouble grappling with this issue because they knew that the child was referred because of academic problems and that the Full Scale was fairly predictive of school achievement. How could the more optimistic prediction of the ELP be fulfilled? This question and others did not have clear answers. There are, however, clear answers to the predictive validity question regarding the ELP score.

The most impressive study in this area was conducted by Figueroa and Sassenrath (1989). These researchers were able to find 1,184 of the original SOMPA standardization participants and retest them approximately a decade later in 1981-83. At this point the children were all in high school. This sample does have some problems, however, since it only includes children that were still in school. Certainly this is a skewed sample since the dropout rates, especially for impoverished children, are distressingly high. The original Full Scale and ELP scores were correlated with students' reading and mathematics scores from the Stanford Achievement Test and various GPAs.

The results are generally congruent with clinicians' impressions that the ELP score would not show better predictive validity than the regular Wechsler IQs. Predictive validities for the IQs and ELPs were consistently in the .40s and .50s. There were no differences across ethnic group or level of SES, with one exception. For the African-American children at the lowest level of SES there was some slight superiority for the predictive validity of the ELP. This finding, however, could be explained by sampling

error. Since these were impoverished children who did not drop out of school, they may have some special characteristics that allowed them to "beat the odds." Figueroa and Sassenrath (1989) concluded: "For all three ethnic groups, VIQ correlated slightly but consistently higher with all the achievement measures than did VIQ-ELP. . . . Consequently, VIQ rather than VIQ-ELP generally appears to be the more sensitive predictor of school achievement" (p. 17).

It is also possible that the ELP is a viable construct but was simply poorly executed (Figueroa & Sassenrath, 1989). It could also be that the value of the ELP does not rest with prediction but with focusing treatment goals. Both the Wechsler Full Scale and ELP long-term predictive validity coefficient found in the Figueroa and Sassenrath (1989) investigation are low to moderate. Although it sounds axiomatic, these results show that there are factors above and beyond the Wechsler scores that are important to consider when gauging a child's needs in order to provide educational/cognitive intervention.

A. R. van den Berg (1986) proposes a score similar to an ELP but offers it for very different uses. He essentially advocates computing a "range of reaction" for each child tested. He first computes an SEDIQ (socioeconomically deprived IQ). This is the norm-referenced score for the low-SES child living in an English-dominant society. This score is depressed in these cases because of the known relationship between environmental factors and intelligence scores. Van den Berg (1986) cites the environmental factors identified by Thorndike and Hagen (1977) as the causative agents for this low score. These factors include:

1. A home language other than "standard" English

2. Home values that do not emphasize school learning

3. Home, social, and economic factors that may interfere with development

4. Undereducated parents who cannot function as teachers for their children

5. A feeling of separation and alienation from the dominant culture

The next score derived by van de Berg is the PROIQ (projected IQ). This score is like an ELP. It is an SEDIQ (obtained IQ) that is adjusted by a measure of the child's difference from the norm based on the socioeconomic factors identified by Thorndike and Hagen (1977) above. Van den Berg (1986), however, departs from Mercer's notion of the ELP. He states:

I am not in favour of the notion that the IQ score of a socioeconomically deprived testee should be adjusted routinely in the hope that this will compensate for his handicap. This kind of "compensation" is simply an illusion because it can make no real change in the testee's ability to solve intellectual problems in the scientifically and technologically based culture. (p. 20)

He continues by describing the PROIQ, saying: "The PROIQ index estimates the IQ that could be expected for the deprived pre-adolescent if intensive long-term remedial treatment, which would include improving his environment but exclude direct training in answering IQ tests, were given to him" (p. 21).

If this sounds familiar, it should. Van den Berg is advocating "peeling" the phenotype, just as Haywood proposed in his transactional theory (see Chapter 2). Van den Berg (1986) also maintains that successful achievement of the PROIQ is rare in reality because interventions are not strong or lengthy enough. Preschool interventions, for example, often are undermined when the child goes home after school to an environment that still has one of the risk factors identified above. Environments work two ways, both to gradually foster or hamper intellectual development (van den Berg, 1986). Unfortunately, we still await the model intervention that can reliably peel the phenotype and help us understand which children respond best to various types of intervention.

DEFINING THE ISSUES

In addition to suggesting new methodologies for assessing intelligence, court cases have served to define the issues of intelligence test use more clearly. Test bias has always been a difficult issue to discuss because it is so imbedded in other issues. Hence, in order to consider issues of test bias one must first define the issues involved. One source of confusion is the nature-nurture debate (see Chapters 2 and 3). The public, and some professionals, seem to take the news that one cultural group has a higher mean score than another cultural group as evidence of either genetic inferiority or superiority. As is apparent, the conclusion of genetic differences has nothing to do with the issue of whether or not a test is biased (Reynolds & Kaiser, 1990).

Another common source of confusion is the relationship between special education and test bias. If one cultural group scores lower than others, then more members of this group would be diagnosed as mildly retarded—a label considered abhorrent by many parents, including myself. Not only is the label stigmatizing, but as a parent I would be concerned that my child might be "warehoused" and not receive a quality instructional program. Here the issue of the effectiveness of special education becomes intertwined with intelligence test bias. This confusion highlights the relationship between test bias and differential impact. It is this latter issue that has led to many of the court cases regarding the use of intelligence tests.

Unfortunately, most of the research on intelligence tests does not directly address these "larger" issues. The wealth of data available focuses on the properties of tests per se, rather than on some equally interesting issues such as the reasons for referring more children from one cultural group for a psychological evaluation than others, the effectiveness of special education, stigmatization associated with being diagnosed as mentally retarded, and the relationship between stigmatization and a child's achievement motivation.

The point of this prelude is to emphasize that there is *much more to the test bias issue than the research on bias in intelligence tests*. This is why the next chapter focuses on test *use*. Test use is an equally, if not more, important issue, just as it is in medical diagnosis. For example, X-rays have proven their value for diagnosing a host of disorders. Recently, however, there has been concern expressed about their overuse because of research showing that exposure to X-rays may increase the risk of some cancers. Similarly, there is concern about the overuse of intelligence tests by less qualified individuals who may misuse the results or let tests rather than the professional make the decisions (Kaufman, 1990).

Even a moratorium on the use of intelligence tests would likely not eliminate injustice and poor instruction of children. Unfortunately, such assaults on children predate the invention of intelligence tests. Jensen (1980) explains why the elimination of tests will not solve problems:

> The answers to questions about test bias surely need not await a scientific consensus on the so-called nature-nurture question. A proper assessment of test bias, on the other hand, is an essential step towards a scientific understanding of the observed differences in all the important educational, occupational, and social correlates of test scores. Test scores themselves are merely correlates, predictors, and indicators, of other socially important variables, which would not be altered in the least if tests did not exist. The problem of individual differences and group differences would not be made to disappear by abolishing tests. One cannot treat a fever by throwing away a thermometer. (p. xi)

Scientific Studies of Bias

Mean Score Differences

One of the conventional pieces of wisdom regarding test bias is that if two cultural groups, linguistic groups, or racial groups obtain mean score differences on a test, then the test is biased against one group or another. It is difficult to determine how this logic became applied to intelligence tests, but this has been this case. This view has distorted somewhat the issue of intelligence test bias because essentially the issue of mean scores differences between cultural groups is irrelevant (Reynolds & Kaiser, 1990; Thorndike, 1971). If intelligence tests did not produce mean score differences between groups such as younger children and older children, they would be worthless. The essence of any type of psychological or physical test is for the measure to be able to discriminate among individuals and groups of individuals. In almost all other types of measures, mean score differences between cultural groups exist. For example, it is well documented that certain groups of children are on average shorter than others. Similarly, men are consistently taller than women as indicated by tests of height. In all these incidences, we do not say that the test is biased, because it measures height, medical condition, or whatever. However, when it comes to intelligence and academic achievement testing, the lay public is much more willing to consider mean score differences as evidence of bias in the test.

The Psychometric Approach

Psychometric studies of test bias do not even consider the issue of mean score differences as a meaningful test of bias. Hence, when professionals talk of test bias, they may be talking about vastly different issues than lay individuals or others who are unfamiliar with the science of measurement. The psychometrician is assessing the validity of an intelligence test across groups as opposed to evaluating mean score differences. In this approach to bias there would have to be evidence that the *construct validity* for an intelligence test differs across groups. Numerous studies have addressed these technical issues. For the purpose of this chapter, the definition of test bias offered by Reynolds and Kaiser (1990) is most appropriate.

"Test bias" refers in a global sense to systematic error in the estimation of some "true" value for a group of individuals. The key word here is "systematic"; all measures contain error, but this error is assumed to be random unless shown to be otherwise. Bias investigation is a statistical inquiry that does not concern itself with culture loading, labeling effects, or test use/test fairness. (p. 624)

Hence, the latter part of this chapter will discuss the uses and abuses of intelligence tests. The use of intelligence tests should be considered as a separate issue from that of internal evidence of bias in the test. It is possible that an unbiased test can be used unfairly and do harm, and, similarly, biased tests can potentially be used fairly (Jensen, 1980).

Content Validity Bias

Bias in content validity was one of the first areas of investigation of intelligence test bias. This is highly understandable given that the scoring criteria for many intelligence test items seem arbitrary and were devised primarily by Anglo males and females. WISC-R comprehension items are especially prone to arguments of inappropriate content or bias. Again, a helpful definition of content validity bias may be taken from Reynolds & Kaiser (1990).

An item or subscale of a test is considered to be biased in content when it is demonstrated to be relatively more difficult for members of one group than for members of another in a situation where the general ability level of the groups being compared is held constant and no reasonable theoretical rationale exist to explain group differences on the item (or subscale) in question. (p. 625)

Numerous procedures have been proposed for assessing bias in individual items, but the logic behind item bias detection techniques is fairly simple. The central aspect of most statistical methods that assess for bias across cultural or gender groups is at the first step in the procedure, which is to match the groups on overall score (ability) level. If, for example, one was looking for gender bias in a pool of intelligence test items, one would first match boys and girls on their overall intelligence test score, be it standard or raw score. So if one wanted to evaluate biased items in the Differential Ability Scales, for example, one would first statistically group the cases with perhaps all of the boys and girls with composite standard scores above 150 as one group, those between 140 and 149 as another group, those between 130 and 139 as another group, and so on (it should be understood that this is not the exact procedure used by most item bias techniques but an oversimplification of such procedures). Then some statistical test of significance is applied to see if within these various ability groups there are still significant differences in difficulty for the items for one gender group or another. An approach similar to this was used in the development of the K-ABC. Most of these items thus identified as biased were removed from the K-ABC; however, some were retained (Kamphaus & Reynolds, 1987). For example, item 15 of Gestalt Closure was biased against boys at age 7 only, and item 37 of the Arithmetic subtest was biased against girls only at age 11. These items were likely retained because although they were biased, it was only at a particular age group. Item 15 on Gestalt Closure is a crown, and item 37 on Arithmetic requires the child to round a four-digit number.

As is obvious from these examples, it is often difficult to interpret the results of the statistical analysis of item bias on a particular test. Why would the crown item be biased against boys, and only 7-year old boys, and why is only one Arithmetic rounding item, the second-most difficult on the test, biased only against girls who are age 11? Why not 10-year-old or 12-year-old girls? It appears that it would require a rather rich imagination on the part of the test developer to determine why some of these items are biased against one gender or cultural group.

This discussion relates to another popular

item bias technique, that of using judgmental bias reviews. The procedure used by many publishers is to have groups of individuals review the items carefully. This procedure ensures that members of a number of cultural groups review the items to determine not only potential bias but also items that may be insulting or inappropriate for various cultural groups. Many tests in the past, such as the K-ABC, used Anglo male and female reviewers, African-American reviewers, and Latino item reviewers. This procedure resulted in a few items being removed from the K-ABC (Kamphaus & Reynolds, 1987). One of these items so removed was a vacuum cleaner from the Gestalt Closure subtest. One of the Latino reviewers remarked that in the inner-city environment where she worked, many Latino children lived in apartments where brooms were used in lieu of vacuum cleaners. There is, however, much disagreement between judgmental reviews of items and statistical analyses of bias. It appears that statistical analyses of bias are more reliable (Reynolds & Kaiser, 1990). In another investigation of judgmental bias reviews, Sandoval and Mille (1979) compared the ratings of 45 WISC-R items by 38 African-American, 22 Mexican-American, and 40 undergraduate students. This study found that minority and nonminority judges did not differ in their ability to identify culturally biased items. The conclusions of Sandoval and Mille (1979) were that "(1) judges are not able to detect items which are more difficult for a minority child than for an Anglo child, and (2) the ethnic background of the judges makes no difference in accuracy of item selection for minority children" (p. 6). It should also be noted that in the Sandoval and Mille investigation, the most biased items were used from the WISC-R to try to make it easier for the judges to select biased items.

The most important question regarding this line of research is not technical issues but whether or not very popular tests of intelligence such as the WISC-R are riddled with biased items for cultural groups, gender, geographic region, or whatever. Results suggest that this is not the case. Numerous studies (Jensen, 1976; Sandoval, 1979; Mille, 1979) have found that anywhere from 2% to 5% of the variance in the WISC-R is due to biased items. Also, it is important to note that the biased items in the WISC-R items seem to work in various directions: against boys, in favor of boys, against Anglos, in favor of Anglos, and so on.

Construct Validity Bias

A workable definition of construct validity bias by Reynolds and Kaiser (1990) suggests that

> *Bias exists in regard to construct validity when a test is shown to measure different hypothetical traits (psychological constructs) for one group or another, or to measure the same trait but with differing degrees of accuracy (p. 632).*

The most popular method used for the study of construct validity bias is factor analysis. Numerous researchers have used similar procedures. The central characteristic of these procedures is to conduct factor analyses separately for various cultural and gender groups. Since the WISC-R was the target of early court cases in the 1970s, it was the recipient of the largest number of factor analytic investigations. Reschly (1978) compared the factor structure of the WISC-R for groups of Anglo, African-American, Mexican-American, and Native American children. All of these children were from the southwestern United States. Reschly compared two factor solutions across the various cultural groups and found substantially high correlations among the factor solutions across group. The most popular procedure used for assessing the agreement between the factor structures across groups is a coefficient of congruence, which is interpreted similarly to a correlation coefficient. Reschly found coefficients of congruence across groups to range from .97 to .99 — in other words, near perfect congruence of factors across these four cultural groups for the WISC-R. These findings suggest that in terms of factor structure, the WISC-R is virtually identical across these four groups and no evidence of bias is present. Other studies have come to the identical conclusions (Wherry & Wherry, 1969; Vance & Walbrown, 1978). Oakland and Feigenbaum (1979) factor analyzed the WISC-R separately for samples of nonhandicapped African-American, Anglo, and Mexican-American children from an urban area in the southwestern United States. Pearson coefficients were used to assess the similarity of factors for each group. The first unrotated "g" factor showed an Anglo/African-American correlation of .95 and a Mexican American/Anglo correlation of .97. The lowest correlation among factors found in this investigation was still high at .94. The authors concluded that there is no evidence of construct validity bias for the WISC-R. Gutkin and Reynolds (1980, 1981) conducted two large-scale investigations of construct validity bias for the WISC-R. The first investigation (1980) involved comparing the factor structure of the WISC-R for samples of referred children including Anglo-American and Mexican-American children. Coefficients of congruence for this investigation ranged from .91 to .99. Similarly, the second investigation (Gutkin and Reynolds, 1981) of the WISC-R standardization sample comparing African-American and Anglo-American children produced coefficients of congruence in the .90s. Similar studies of construct validity bias have been conducted for the McCarthy scales (Kaufman & DiCuio, 1975), the WPPSI (Kaufman and Hollenbeck, 1974), and the K-ABC (Reynolds, Willson, & Chatman, 1985). There is also a factor analytic study of the K-ABC for separate groups of boys and girls (Kamphaus & Kaufman, 1986). All of these investigations have resulted in similar findings—a great deal of similarity of factor structure across ethnic and gender groups. These results, then, mimic the findings for content validity bias in that evidence of bias is difficult to find and erratic when it does occur. The final type of bias that has received a great deal of attention in the adult personnel selection literature is bias in predictive validity.

Predictive Validity Bias

A working definition of predictive validity bias as adapted from Cleary et al. (1975) by Reynolds and Kaiser (1990) is: "A test is considered biased with respect to predictive validity if the inference drawn from the test score is not made with the smallest feasible random error or if there is constant error in an inference for prediction as a function of membership in a particular group" (p. 638).

The issue regarding predictive or criterion-related validity is that these coefficients (see Chapter 5) should not differ significantly across cultural or gender group. One of the typical procedures in this research literature is to compare the predictive validity coefficients across groups. A study by Glutting (1986) is an excellent example of such an investigation. This investigation studied the predictive validity of the K-ABC for 146 Anglo, African-American, and Puerto Rican children from the New York City metropolitan area. In addition, the Puerto Rican sample was subdivided into English-dominant children and Spanish-dominant children. The predictive validity coefficients found for this investigation were strikingly similar across ethnic and linguistic groups. That is, the magnitude of the coefficients were very similar. Comparing the magnitude of the coefficients as Glutting did by collecting a sample, administering an intelligence test, and administering a criterion test such as an achievement test at some subsequent date is a common procedure. If Glutting had found, for example, that the predictive validity coefficient for the K-ABC for the Anglo group was .90 and for the other groups it was .30, this would be evidence of significant predictive validity bias and that the test is more predictive for the Anglo than for the other groups. This result, however, did not occur in this investigation. If this type of bias (different predictive validity coefficients) were to occur, it would be called "slope bias." In order to understand the concept of slope bias, it is helpful to recollect how correlation coefficients are learned in introductory statistics courses. Such procedures are typically taught by having the students collect data on two variables and plotting the scores of a group of individuals on these two variables. This plot results in a scatter plot (see Chapter 5). Then students compute a correlation coefficient and draw a line of best fit through the scatter plot. This line of best fit is a visual representation of the slope (see Chapter 5). A correlation coefficient (predictive validity coefficient) of .90 would produce a very different slope than a correlation coefficient of .30. This is why this type of bias in predictive validity is referred to as slope bias. Studies of the WISC-R have produced little evidence of slope bias.

Reynolds and Hartlage (1979) conducted a study of the predictive validity of the Full Scale standard scores from the WISC-R for African-American and Anglo children who were referred for psychological services. In addition, they used the Potthoff (1966) technique to test for identity of the slopes or regression lines for the two groups for predicting reading and mathematics achievement. This study did not yield significant evidence of bias for the two groups. In a series of studies, Reynolds and Gutkin (1980) conducted a predictive validity study of bias for Anglo and Mexican-American children from the southwestern United States and found no evidence of bias. In another study by Reynolds and colleagues (1979), no evidence of predictive validity bias was found for groups of boys and girls on the WISC-R.

One study is something of an outlier as far as predictive validity bias goes, and this is a study by Goldman and Hartig (1976). This study used the 1949 WISC-R and compared predictive validity coefficients for African-American, Mexican-American, and Anglo children. It found adequate predictive validity coefficients for the Anglo children, but coefficients were not adequate for African-American and Mexican-American children. This is the only study to

show such substantial evidence of predictive validity or slope bias. But it has been criticized on methodological grounds (Reynolds & Kaiser, 1990). The study is one of a very few to use academic GPA, or school grades, as a criterion measure of academic achievement. There were significant differences in the variances or range of scores between the Anglo children and the two other groups. This fact alone could account for the difference in predictive validity coefficients (see the discussion in Chapter 5 of restriction of range and how this may deflate correlation coefficients). In addition, however, Reynolds and Kaiser suggest that the study may also be an outlier because of the use of GPA, a questionable and frequently unreliable measure of performance. They point out that academic GPA in this particular study also included grades in music, health, art, and physical education and that in these particular courses it looked as if the students received exceedingly high grades, producing little variability. These studies of slope bias are strikingly similar to the studies of content validity and construct validity bias. Evidence of predictive validity bias is infrequent. When it does occur, it is often counterintuitive and inexplicable, as in the case of the Glutting analysis of the K-ABC. Thus, the wealth of findings suggest that as far as most major tests of intelligence go, evidence of internal test bias is exceedingly difficult to document.

Summary Comments on Bias

The results of bias studies, many of which were conducted from the mid-1970s to the mid-1980s as a consequence of the numerous court cases in the 1970s, have turned up little substantial evidence of bias in modern tests of intelligence. This evidence suggests that intelligence tests are measures very similar to medical tests that have shown significant group differences. Group differences between intelligence test scores are likely real, but what do they mean and what are the implications of this finding?

In the same way that the SAT and other

achievement test scores have sounded an alarm and caused considerable concern about the state of American education, so, too, intelligence test scores should sound an alarm. This alarm is concern for the cognitive development of children. If intelligence test scores continue to be somewhat lower for some groups of children into the 1990s, then this is a cause for concern. And the various factors that are discussed in Chapter 3 should be considered in trying to explain the reasons for this. Such factors might include high-risk pregnancies such as those of teenagers, the effects of teratogens during pregnancy, poor quality of preschool and school programs, poverty, and other factors that may differ across cultural groups. Just as differences in the occurrence of breast cancer, blood pressure, diabetes, and achievement test scores raise alarms as they afflict cultural groups differentially, so, too, intelligence test scores that may differ across cultural groups should be a call to arms for those individuals concerned about the welfare of children. As van den Berg (1986) states aptly: "Inappropriate acceptance of the test bias hypothesis could therefore inadvertently maintain the poverty cycle; inadvertently for those who wish to break the cycle but perhaps advertently for those who might wish to maintain it" (p. 16).

CULTURAL DIVERSITY AND ASSESSMENT PRACTICE[1]

The creation of new tests (e.g., SOMPA and nonverbal measures) has not proved sufficient to meet the assessment needs of a diverse society because new tests cannot preclude poor interpretation. In too many cases, clinicians choose the wrong test and make inappropriate interpretations of the data (Shepard, 1989). Interpretations have often been simplistic and culturally bound, showing a lack of appreciation for cultural and linguistic differences and traditions. Clinicians can do a better job assessing diverse groups of children by improving their knowledge of the effects of culture and language on children's test performance.

No gains have been made in devising specific tests for specific populations. Again, proper interpretation of well-constructed intelligence tests appears to be the key. As Figueroa (1990) observes:

> *Currently, bilingual testing is an art form. The tester must infer and estimate the impact of language, culture, and schooling in the English versions of intelligence tests, and then do the same with even more marginal tests in another language (p. 687).*

Inappropriate interpretations are more likely when a clinician is unfamiliar with important aspects of a child's culture. An examiner may conclude, for example, that a 13-year-old girl of Asian heritage is socially introverted, and perhaps in need of assertiveness training because of her behavior during an interview with a male clinician. She may have engaged in little conversation and made no eye contact. The examiner may even draw such a conclusion despite the fact that she appeared friendly and outgoing when she was observed on the school playground and seemed to interact more openly with her family members. This client may not in fact be pathologically shy; rather, she may be adhering to a prohibition against making eye contact with a male because of her cultural values, which suggest that this is a highly seductive behavior (or an indication of a lack of respect) that is deemed inappropriate for her (Hasegawa, 1989).

Another example of the importance of multicultural knowledge may help clarify the need for such expertise. Perhaps a clinician is working in a neighborhood where most of the inhabitants are children of African and Indian/Pakistani descent and Italian-American children are in the minority. Yet the Italian immigrant children are making up a large percentage of the referrals for

[1]This section is an adaptation of an article by Kamphaus (1991).

mental health services, much larger than would be expected based on their proportions in the neighborhood. A clinician may conclude that there is something awry with the Italian-American family, physical constitution, or whatever. If, however, the clinician is familiar with multicultural issues, he or she may more appropriately conclude that community/preventive interventions may be most appropriate since research shows that *minority status itself is a stressor* for any cultural group. Mintz and Schwartz (1964, cited in Gibbs & Huang, 1989), for example, found that whites living in black areas had an incidence of psychosis about 313% higher than whites who lived in communities where they were the majority.

Within cultural groups, variability can also be substantial (Zuckerman, 1990). It may be assumed by some that Vietnamese and Chinese children have similar values due to earlier Chinese domination and inculcation with the Confucian ethic. There have also been other influences on this culture that may affect a child's behavior, including European Roman Catholicism brought by the French conquest of 1958, the influence of American culture from the Vietnam War, and Buddhist influences from neighboring Cambodia (Huang, 1990). Classifying children by race, culture, or language background is an appealing approach for researchers and clinicians alike that is fraught with errors, primarily due to the tendency to overgeneralize about a particular group of people (Zuckerman, 1990). Thus, the potential for stereotyping looms large. Zuckerman (1990) suggests that the heterogeneity within cultural groups makes conclusions about any cultural group highly suspect.

Intelligence test users have to develop an enlarged knowledge base in order to deal effectively with their referral population. Just as clinicians have to have knowledge of behavioral principles, psychometrics, child development, child psychopathology, and physiological psychology to conduct an evaluation competently, it is increasingly clear that they must know the history, culture, and language of their community extremely well in order not to use intelligence tests inappropriately and make naive interpretations.

Assessing Multilingual Children

One advised alternative for the assessment of children for whom English is not the primary language is to use a translation of a popular intelligence test. This practice, however, is beset with problems, because once a test is translated its psychometric properties are unknown (Figueroa, 1989). The Test Standards (see Chapter 17) suggest that if the DAS were to be used with a Spanish-speaking population, for example, it would have to be created anew. In fact, problems of translation can occur even if minor changes are made in an item. I was reminded of this when I recently attended a conference in Canada where the metric system is used. There was concern expressed about an Arithmetic item on an intelligence test that involved calculating miles per hour from the miles driven in a specified time period. Would this item remain in the same difficulty order on the test if the metric were changed to kilometers? At any rate, if there are difficulties with changes within the English language, one can imagine the potential problems when an entire test is translated from one language to another.

A second method for assessing a limited English proficient child is to use a nonverbal intelligence test. This practice, however, is not advised since these measures are less predictive of future academic achievement (Figueroa, 1990). In other words, they possess questionable predictive validity.

A third method of assessing limited English proficient children is to administer an English language test via a translator. As one can imagine, this introduces further complications into the interpretation of the results. As Figueroa (1989) states:

> When a psychologist uses an interpreter, the child is at risk and the psychologist is at risk. There is no empirically validated model for training or using an

interpreter. There is no data indicating the operative conditions necessary to insure that the one-on-one experience of an English-speaking child is comparable to the one-on-one experience of an LEP [limited English proficient] child with her/his psychologist and interpreter. There is no information on which tests to use in this process, though some have argued that only with psychometrically valid tests in the child's primary language can an interpreter be used. There is no cross-cultural data on how children from different cultures and languages respond to two unknown adults asking decontextualized questions and presenting progressively more complex problems. Finally, there is no recognition of the legal distinctions that can be raised about which linguistic groups may have to be tested with an interpreter. (p. 19)

So what is an intelligence test user to do when cultural and/or linguistic factors may confound results? If possible (unfortunately, it usually is not) it would be best to refer the case to an examiner who shares some linguistic similarity with the child. Frequently linguistic differences are associated with cultural differences, and a clinician may unwittingly behave in a way that is insulting or intimidating to a child from a different culture. It is also overly simplistic to give general guidelines for assessing children from diverse groups such as Latino, African-American, Asian, and other cultural groups. These groups are not monoliths (Zuckerman, 1990). In constructing prediction equations for academic achievement for Asian-American children, Sue and Abe (1988) found significant differences among Asian groups including Chinese, Japanese, Koreans, Filipinos, and East Indians/Pakistanis. A comparable American example would be the various Native American tribes and their languages and cultures. For these reasons, clinicians cannot expect to memorize a few simple rules about cultural values. Assessment situations will have to be individualized and perhaps improvised by the savvy clinician.

Some suggestions for dealing with linguistic differences in the intellectual assessment process follow.

Collect detailed background information on each case. Clinicians already typically collect various types of developmental, medical, and social history information. The diversity of children's backgrounds requires the collection of information that may not be part of traditional developmental history questionnaires. Castaneda (1976) gives an example of additional information that would be desirable for proper interpretation of the assessment data for a Mexican-American child. He proposes that the following factors affect the acculturation and behavior of Mexican-American students.

Length of residence in the United States

Distance from the Mexican border

Degree of urbanization

Degree of economic and political strength of Mexican-Americans in the community

Identity with Mexican and/or Mexican-American history

Degree of prejudice toward Mexican-Americans in the community

Attempt to refer the child to a clinician who speaks the child's native tongue. This examiner could use tests designed specifically for the child's linguistic group (e.g., there could be some from the child's homeland, although often there will not be any) or administer nonverbal measures.

If a referral is not possible, the examiner could consult with a community resource about the child's language and culture before proceeding with the evaluation. There are usually others in the community who speak the same language. Potential resources could include a parent, shopkeeper, bilingual educator, or minister. These individuals could give advice as to how to interact with the child. They may also be willing to join the test session, much as parents will sometimes join a session, to help make the child feel more at ease. The examiner could then use one or several less verbal (nonverbal) measures of intelligence.

In these circumstances, however, the results may still be speculative. Hence, psychologists should make greater use of "therapeutic testing" with children who speak a language other than English (Kamphaus, 1991). Many of us remember visits to the physician when the doctor told us to take an over-the-counter medication and get bed rest. In most cases we get better soon after. This is one type of therapeutic testing, where the physician takes an educated guess that we are suffering from the common cold, prescribes treatment, and tells us to call back if we don't get better. If the therapy works, then the diagnosis must have been correct—hence the term "therapeutic testing." If the bilingual child scores extremely well on the intelligence test, we may want to have him or her try some enrichment classes to mitigate against boredom. If the child scores poorly, remedial work or tutoring could be advised. Regardless, these should be *tentative, short-term, therapeutic tests* that should be reevaluated by consulting with teachers and parents in an ongoing fashion (probably at least once a week) to make modifications in the "treatment" as necessary. This process will also allow the psychologist to collect more long-term data on the child and assess the trajectory of his or her cognitive development. In this paradigm the administration and scoring of the intelligence test are the *beginning of the assessment process, not the end result*. Actually, all children would likely benefit from such careful case management, but particularly those children for whom the clinician feels less certain of the results.

Conclusions

Much progress has been made in exploring the issue of test bias. Litigation regarding assessment practices and intelligence testing specifically has created needed motivation to carefully consider the nature and use of such tests with children from diverse backgrounds. While bias internal to intelligence tests is rare, test overuse, misuse, misinterpretation, and differential impact remains problematic. The increasing consideration of misuse and human diversity issues and hypotheses will hopefully mitigate against such use problems.

Chapter Summary

1. The utility of intelligence tests for children of non-European descent or non–English speaking background has been questioned since the early days of intelligence testing (French & Hale, 1990).

2. Psychologists learned a great deal about intelligence test bias in the decades of the 1970s and 1980s.

3. One of the first cases to question the use of so-called "ability tests" to make special education decisions for mental retardation placement was the case of *Hobson v. Hansen* (1967).

4. One result of the *Diana* case was to clearly identify the criterion of 2 standard deviations below the mean as the cut-off for mental retardation special education placement.

5. The *Larry P. v. Riles* case began in 1971 when the plaintiffs representing black children who were overrepresented in classes for the mentally retarded asked for an injunction against the use of intelligence tests in the San Francisco public schools.

6. The 1980 *PASE* case came to the opposite conclusion of the *Larry P.* case, although much of the testimony was the same.

7. The statistics offered in these court cases had to be considered very carefully since only a small proportion of the school-age population is identified as suffering from mental retardation.

8. One proposed solution to the issues posed

by the *Larry P.* case was the System of Multicultural Pluralistic Assessment (SOMPA).

9. The ELP score does not show better predictive validity than the regular Wechsler scores.

10. If intelligence tests did not produce mean score differences between groups such as younger children and older children, they would be worthless. Psychometric studies of test bias do not consider the issue of mean score differences as a meaningful test of bias.

11. The central aspect of most statistical methods that assess for bias across cultural or gender groups is that the first step in the procedure is to match the groups on overall score (ability) level.

12. There is much disagreement between judgmental reviews of items and statistical analyses of bias. It appears that statistical analyses of bias are more reliable.

13. Numerous studies have found that anywhere from 2% to 5% of the variance in the WISC-R is due to biased items. Biased items in the WISC-R seem to work in various directions: against boys, in favor of boys, against Anglos, in favor of Anglos, and so on.

14. The most popular method used for the study of construct validity bias is factor analysis.

15. Content validity bias is difficult to find and erratic when it does occur.

16. The results of bias studies, many of which were conducted from the mid-1970s to the mid-1980s as a consequence of the numerous court cases in the 1970s, have turned up little substantial evidence of bias in modern tests of intelligence.

17. Translation of a popular intelligence test such as the WISC-III for children for whom English is not the primary language is fraught with problems, including the fact that once the test is translated its psychometric properties are unknown.

Ethics and Standards of Practice

CHAPTER QUESTIONS

Is it permissible to demonstrate the use of an intelligence test to a group of parents at a PTA meeting?

What are the major types of validity defined by the *Standards for Educational and Psychological Tests?*

This chapter addresses three important areas of practice: test standards, ethics, and test selection. The first two topics are routinely considered in assessment texts, but often not in a separate chapter giving them substantial emphasis. The issue of test selection is often ignored. Intelligence tests are becoming available in numerous shapes, sizes, and varieties. The last section of this chapter suggests to the clinician a framework for selecting a test in order to maximize the effectiveness of the evaluation.

These last issues are considered "advanced" in that they require the previous chapters as a knowledge base. Such topics are also advanced in that they require a conscientious and dedicated clinician who exercises considerable forethought in the assessment process.

PSYCHOMETRIC STANDARDS

The practicing clinician will be assaulted with new intelligence tests promising phenomenal results or features (Buros, 1961). Clinicians will have to know psychometric principles well in order to judge the quality of new methods. As Buros (1961) laments, clinicians are left to their own devices when judging the qualities of new measures (see Box 17.1), as publishers and test authors will sometimes make exaggerated claims that may dupe the clinician.

In order to make an informed decision about the purchase and use of a particular instrument, a standard is needed. Fortunately, considerable

462

Box 17.1

Buros's lament

This is a rather unusual research report in that it is not a study per se but a statement by O. K. Buros on the relationship (or lack of it) between psychometric quality and test popularity. The amazing thing about this quote is its timeless nature. The same problems persist today so test users should consider themselves forewarned.

At present, no matter how poor a test may be, if it is nicely packaged and if it promises to do all sorts of things which no test can do, the test will find many gullible buyers. When we initiated critical test reviewing (1938) we had no idea how difficult it would be to discourage the use of poorly constructed tests of unknown validity. Even the better informed test users who finally become convinced that a widely used test has no validity after all are likely to rush to use a new instrument which promises far more than any good test can possibly deliver. Counselors, personnel directors, psychologists, and school administrators seem to have an unshakable will to believe the exaggerated claims of test authors and publishers. If these users were better informed regarding the merits and limitations of their testing instruments, they would probably be less happy and less successful in their work. The test user who has faith—however unjustified—can speak with confidence in interpreting test results and in making recommendations. The well informed test user cannot do this; he knows that the best of our tests are still highly fallible instruments which are extremely difficult to interpret with assurance in individual cases. Consequently, he must interpret test results cautiously and with so many reservations that others wonder whether he really knows what he is talking about. Children, parents, teachers, and school administrators are likely to have a greater respect and admiration for a school counselor who interprets test results with confidence even though his interpretations have no scientific justification. The same applies to psychologists and personnel directors. Highly trained psychologists appear to be as gullible as the less well trained school counselor. It pays to know only a little about testing; furthermore, it is much more fun for everyone concerned—the examiner, examinee, and the examiner's employer.

It is difficult to allocate the blame for the lack of greater progress. We think, however, that the major blame rests with test users. The better test publishers would like to make more moderate claims for their tests. Unfortunately, test buyers don't want tests which make only moderate claims. Consequently, even the best test publishers find themselves forced by competition to offer test users what they want. Bad usage of tests is probably more common than good usage. Must it always be this way? We are afraid so.

From O. K. Buros (1961), *Tests in print: A comprehensive bibliography of tests for use in education, psychology and industry* (Highland Park, NJ: Gryphon Press). Reprinted with permission of the Buros Institute, University of Nebraska, Lincoln, NE.

attention has been directed of late to setting standards for intelligence and other measures. The next section highlights the application of some standards to test selection and use.

Test Standards

The *Standards for Educational and Psychological Tests* (APA, 1985) discuss three primary types of validity evidence that should be provided for tests. These types are content-related, criterion-related, and construct-related evidence of validity. One of the important points presented by the test standards is that *it is incorrect to use the phrase "the validity of the test"* because it cannot be concluded that a particular test is valid for all children under all assessment situations (APA, 1985). The validity of an intelligence test should be gauged properly in relation to every assessment situation where it may be put to use. Clinicians who assess children's intelligence must, therefore, learn how to use more than one intelligence test well in order to validly assess chil-

Box 17.2

Questions to consider when evaluating a new intelligence test

New intelligence assessment measures are constantly being released, and clinicians have to be savvy consumers. Here are some questions that the clinician may ask in order help make a purchase decision.

1. Is the premise of the test reasonable? Is its theory based on some supportive citations of previous research?
2. Are the test development goals clearly delineated?
3. Are the manuals complete, including topics ranging from theory to interpretation of the results?
4. Are administration and scoring guidelines complete and easy to follow?
5. Are the test materials attractive to children? Are they sturdy and practical?
6. Are all of the items derivatives of those on other tests? Are some of them new?
7. Were the items subjected to judgmental bias reviews so as to not be offensive to test users or takers?
8. Is the test easy to administer so that the examiner can focus on the child's behavior during testing?
9. Is there evidence of content validity? Were cognitive science experts consulted? Does the item content seem consistent with the theory?
10. Were statistical item bias studies undertaken?
11. Was the test norming sample collected recently?
12. Does the norming sample closely match the stratification statistics selected? Was there some measure of SES used for stratification?
13. Are the internal consistency and stability coefficients high—above .90 for the composite?
14. Is there evidence of good factorial, predictive, and concurrent validity?
15. Are several derived scores offered, such as standard scores and percentile ranks, in order to enhance interpretation?
16. Are interpretive tables for determining intraindividual strengths and weaknesses offered?
17. Are the scaling methods (i.e., norm development procedures) described in detail?
18. Have early reviews been either favorable or optimistic?
19. Is the test appropriate for the population of children that I serve? For example, does it have extended norms for a severely mentally handicapped population?

---

dren from a number of different backgrounds and circumstances. Some of the important aspects of validation of intelligence tests are given in the following excerpts from the Standards (APA, 1985).

  1. *Evidence of validity should be presented for the major types of interpretations for which a test is recommended.*

      Comment. If, for example, an intelligence test is used as part of the evidence in making the diagnosis of giftedness, then specific validation of

the test for this purpose should be included in a test manual or technical manual. If this type of validity evidence is not presented, the manual should discuss why it is not presented and caution the user about using the test for this purpose. This type of validity evidence favors existing tests that have accumulated considerable validity studies. Another implication of this standard is that new tests must have considerable validity evidence reported in their manuals. Gone are the days when a test can be published with only evidence of reliability and factorial validity. New intelligence tests will have to possess thorough manuals like those for the DAS and K-ABC if the tests are going to be immediately usable. Otherwise, the test should lie dormant until some evidence is gathered.

2. *When the interpretation of subtest profiles is encouraged by a test manual, the validity evidence for this type of interpretation should be presented. If this type of evidence is not presented, the user should be warned that validity evidence for this type of interpretation is not available.*

   Comment. The specter of improper profile analysis is also present in the *Test Standards*. Test manuals such as those for the Binet-4 (Delaney & Hopkins, 1987), WISC-III, DAS, and the K-ABC provide tables for conducting profile analysis. These standards and the recent research on the issue of profile analysis (see Chapter 7) are thus consistent. Examiners must be cautious in using such interpretive systems without prior validity evidence.

3. *Test manuals should give detailed descriptions of the nature of the samples used in reliability and validity studies that allow the test user to gauge accurately the strength or weakness of the evidence presented.*

   Comment. Such detailed information might include number of participants, age/grade range of the sample, gender and ethnic group composition, language background, whether or not subjects were considered handicapped, and dates of data collection. Sampling information is crucial for determining the generalizability of the research findings.

4. *Internal consistency coefficients should not be presented in the manual as substitutes for stability or test/retest coefficients.*

   Comment. This guideline is self-explanatory. It is relatively rare for stability coefficients to differ substantially from internal consistency coefficients, but it does happen. The Gestalt Closure subtest of the K-ABC, for example, produced a mean internal consistency coefficient at the school-age level of .71, whereas its test-retest coefficient at ages 5 through 8 was .84 (Kaufman & Kaufman, 1983). All new tests must include evidence of test-retest reliability.

Standards for Interpretation

The standards are demanding of the test developer, the publisher, and of the clinician as well. One implication of these standards is that *every test interpretation made by a clinician must be supported by some type of evidence* (see Chapter 7). Can all clinicians make this claim for every situation where they have made an interpretation? I doubt it, but this is a laudable goal to strive for in order to meet current test standards.

Let us consider an example of applying the *Test Standards* (every clinician should read the full standards, not just the excerpts given in this chapter). A psychologist wishes to begin using the Differential Ability Scales (DAS) for the diagnosis of intellectual problems of children who are suspected of moderate to severe levels of mental retardation. Standard number 1 above suggests that the DAS manual or *Handbook* (Elliott, 1990a) or an independent research study should provide evidence for the utility of the DAS in making such a diagnosis. This seems like a high standard, especially in light of the fact that the DAS *Handbook* includes an impressive array of prepublication research with special populations of children. This also seems like a high standard since the DAS has an extended score scale that would seem ideal for use with such a population (see Chapter 11). If, however, an independent study of the use of the DAS with this population cannot be found, the use of the DAS for making the diagnosis of moderate and severe mental retardation could be construed as

RESEARCH REPORT

Individual assessment accuracy

Lawrence Rudner (1983) conducted an interesting simulation study where he compared nine statistics that assess individual assessment accuracy. These statistics are generally unheard of in the realms of clinical assessment practice. This is an oversimplification, but basically these statistics assess the degree to which a child's item responses on a test compare to those of the standardization sample. Essentially, "high ability examinees are expected to get few easy items wrong, low ability examinees are expected to get few difficult items right" (p. 207).

In order to test the accuracy of nine statistical methods, Rudner created two data sets through computer-simulation methods. The first data set was based on 80 verbal items from the Scholastic Aptitude Test (SAT). The second data set consisted of 45 items from a general biology test. Rudner then generated large samples of examinees, over 2,000, for each of these tests. In order to test the comparative accuracy of the nine statistics, however, he created several subsamples of 100 cases each. These various hypothetical subsamples consisted of groups that received inordinately high scores or low scores on the two tests. In this way, the relative accuracy of each of the nine measures to identify spuriously high and low scores could be directly tested.

The nine statistics that were used for assessing individual accuracy included a variety of procedures. Among them were Rasch model approaches, Birnbaum model approaches, correlational approaches, and sequence approaches. The least complicated approaches are the correlational methods. One method utilized a personal point-biserial correlation statistic. This is a correlation between a child's correct and incorrect responses on a set of items and the item difficulty indices (p-values) for the norming population for the same test.

The results of the study showed that all of the nine approaches were able to identify irregular item response sets at a statistically significant level. However, some of the approaches were more suited to the longer SAT examination and some were better suited to the shorter examination. The Rasch model statistic, for example, tended to work better on the shorter test. The various point-biserial correlational methods also seemed to work better on the shorter examination.

Rudner (1983) concluded that while all nine approaches were relatively effective, their accuracy was not startlingly different. There remained a number of spuriously high and low scores that were not detected by these various methods. He concluded that these techniques would not be valid for developing a particularly useful cut score that would be indicative of a flawed response pattern. He stated, rather, "Professional judgement must be used in selecting an approach, determining critical values, and in using the statistics" (p. 217).

Many an examiner has scratched his or her head in puzzlement when viewing the subtest performance of a child who gets easy items incorrect and difficult items correct, and vice versa. The techniques described by Rudner allow the clinician to obtain a quantitative index of the irregularity of a specific response pattern. This could be useful for a number of purposes, including determining when a second measure of intelligence should be administered and whether or not a child from another culture may not be understanding the directions of a test. The statistics, however, are relatively complex and will likely be most useful when intelligence tests of the future become computer-based.

---

a violation of the *Test Standards* if a strict interpretation of the standards were applied. I have not a clue as to how the standards would be applied in such a situation. This is an issue for others to decide.

Even if the *Test Standards* were not rigidly enforced in this scenario, it is important for the clinician to know that he or she is making an interpretation that is not specifically supported

by research. This interpretation is supported by related research (such as that for mildly retarded children) and reasonable educated supposition. This is a crucial distinction that clinicians should consider when making their interpretations of intelligence tests—that is, the source of support for their interpretation. Clinicians should ask themselves questions such as, "Am I basing this interpretation on my experience, something a

RESEARCH REPORT

The Case Against Intelligence Testing

Asa Hilliard, a well-known critic of the use of intelligence tests, particularly in the schools, questions the use of intelligence measures in a recent article (Hilliard, 1989). Hilliard's critique focuses primarily on the use of such measures for intervention planning in the schools. In commenting on the question of bias Hilliard remarks, "Unfortunately, the bias and fairness debate obscures the more fundamental issue of the pedagogical utility of the IQ test, not just for minority cultural groups, but for everyone" (p. 125). Hilliard's concern about the relevance of IQ testing to designing instructional interventions is expressed clearly in the following quote.

> *There is little, if any, evidence that test designers, producers, and administrators are any more pedagogically prepared today. To the extent that professional educators were skilled and insightful, the record does not show that they were a part of the design of diagnostic instruments that were to be used for their benefit. In fact, one clear thing stands out in the abundant effective teacher and effective schools research literature.* In no studies of successful teachers and successful schools is there ever any mention of reliance on IQ measures. *In other words, IQ is irrelevent to successful instruction.* (p. 129)

Hilliard's comments are not isolated. Objections to the widespread use of intelligence tests for "placement" purposes in public schools have been expressed since the time of Terman's original work (see Chapter 1). Hilliard's remarks, and those of others, should caution all clinicians to evaluate carefully the situations in which tests are used.

---

colleague told me, the advice of my supervisor, or my reading of a relevant research finding?" Some users may be surprised to discover that much of their interpretive practice is not based on current research findings. While in some cases it may be necessary to make an unsupported interpretation (since research is not available on every topic), the clinician should make this distinction in his or her own mind. As clinicians are asked more frequently to defend their decisions to regulatory agencies and the courts, they will be asked more frequently to produce citations for their interpretations (Matarazzo, 1990).

The APA *Test Standards* are likely *optimal* practices. They do, however, provide an important benchmark for everyday practice. Clinicians who strive for these standards will be serving their clients well. Similarly, intelligence tests that meet or approximate these standards should be preferred. The standards do suggest that new tests must be accompanied by considerable psychometric evidence. Gone are the days when tests could be published with minimal reliabil-

ity and validity evidence. This void was then to be filled by graduate student theses and researchers.

Code of Fair Testing Practices in Education

Another helpful document that encourages proper use of children's intelligence tests is the *Code of Fair Testing Practices in Education*, which was published in 1988 by the Joint Committee on Testing Practices. This work is an extension of the earlier test standards in that it was also produced by a joint committee of the American Educational Research Association, the American Psychological Association, and the National Council on Measurement in Education. This document is divided into four sections: Developing/Selecting Appropriate Tests, Interpreting Scores, Striving for Fairness, and Informing Test Takers. Some of the more helpful guidelines from the Code are given in Table 17.1.

TABLE 17.1 Excerpts from the *Code of Fair Testing Practices in Education*

DEVELOPING/SELECTING APPROPRIATE TESTS

1. First define the purpose for testing in the population to be tested. Then, select a test for that purpose and that population based on a thorough review of the available information.

2. Investigate potential useful sources of information, in addition to test scores, to corroborate the information provided by tests.

3. Read the materials provided by test developers and avoid using tests for which unclear or incomplete information is provided.

4. Become familiar with how and when the test was developed and tried out.

5. Read independent evaluations of a test and, if possible, alternative measures. Look for evidence to support the claims of test developers.

6. Select and use only those tests for which the skills needed to administer the test and interpret scores correctly are available.

INTERPRETATION OF TEST SCORES

1. Obtain information about the scale used for reporting scores, the characteristics of any norms or comparison group(s), and the limitation of these scores.

2. Interpret scores taking into account any major differences between the norms or comparison groups and the actual test takers. Also take into account any differences in test administration practices or familiarity with specific questions in the test.

3. Avoid using tests for purposes not specifically recommended by the test developer unless evidence is obtained to support the intended use.

4. Explain how any passing scores were set and gather evidence to support the appropriateness of the scores.

5. Obtain evidence to show the test is meeting its intended purpose(s).

STRIVING FOR FAIRNESS

1. Evaluate the procedures used by test developers to avoid potentially insensitive content or language.

2. Review the performance of test takers of different races, gender, ethnic backgrounds when samples of sufficient size are available. Evaluate the extent to which performance differences may have been caused by inappropriate characteristics of the test.

3. When necessary and feasible, use appropriately modified forms of tests or administration procedures for test takers with handicapping conditions. Interpret standard norms with care in the light of the modifications that were made.

INFORMING EXAMINEES

1. When a test is optional, provide test takers or their parents/ guardians with information to help them judge whether the test

TABLE 17.1 *(continued)*

should be taken, or if an available alternative to the test should be used.

2. Provide test takers the information they need to be familiar with the coverage of the test, the types of question formats, the directions, and appropriate test taking strategies. Strive to make such information equally available to all test takers.

3. Provide test takers or their parents/guardians with information with rights test takers may have to obtain copies of test and completed answer sheets, re-take tests, have tests rescored, or cancel scores.

4. Tell test takers or their parents/guardians how long scores will be kept on file and indicate to whom and under what circumstances test scores will or will not be released.

5. Describe the procedures that test takers or their parents/guardians may use to register complaints and have problems resolved.

SOURCE: Reprinted from the *Code of Fair Testing Practices in Education.*

While many aspects of the *Code* are redundant with those of the *Test Standards*, some are new. The *Code* also emphasizes educational testing, resulting in some of the guidelines being less than applicable to intelligence assessment. The guidelines for informing examinees, however, are especially helpful.

Informing Examinees

PRINCIPLE 2. This guideline, which involves preparing children for the testing, is too easily ignored. Often the parents of school children have given written consent for their child to be tested but they may not have been made aware of the specific day or time of day of the assessment. This may result in the child being completely unprepared for the testing. One of my students had a case recently where the 14-year-old adolescent girl being assessed was informed about 30 minutes before the test session that she was pregnant, and she was facing the prospect of informing her parents that evening during visiting hours at the hospital. She was obviously distracted by the prospect. Fortunately, my student was informed of this situation before be-

ginning the testing. The student astutely discussed the pregnancy issue at length, which served to put the adolescent at ease. The examinee then seemed to complete the testing with little distraction.

Test developers have become more sensitive to preparing examinees for taking an intelligence test, building sample items into the tests. The K-ABC made large-scale use of sample items and the Binet-4, W-J, WISC-III, and DAS followed suit. These efforts help familiarize students with item content prior to the actual scoring of items.

Efforts to prepare examinees need to be made, however, *before the test session.* Parents should be informed in advance of intelligence testing that is being done at school, including the exact date of the testing. This will help the parents prepare the child for the testing by seeing that the child obtains adequate sleep the evening before the testing and enough nourishment to sustain stamina during the test session.

A child may also not be "prepared" for a test session because of illness. Examiners need to be prepared to cancel and reschedule test sessions in order to ensure optimal performance on the child's part. This is a great inconvenience to the examiner, but the examiner's needs are clearly secondary in this situation.

Examiners should also introduce themselves to the child prior to the testing. This procedure will be particularly helpful in "preparing" young children, many of whom do not respond well to "strangers" (see Chapter 4). An early introduction may not only put the young child at ease, but it also allows the examiner to gauge whether or not he or she can adequately assess the intellectual status of a child because of language/cultural differences or other factors.

PRINCIPLE 4.   This tenet regarding the future of the test report is also easily ignored, especially in school settings. In contrast to the private practitioner's office, where the clinician may be the only one to see the child's test results, school files are more difficult to secure. All of a child's teachers may have access to a child's test results, as well as building-level administrators.

Clinicians should customarily make efforts to explain how test results will be used and how they may be released to others. This is a difficult process to explain given ever changing legal guidelines. Consumers of psychological services are less likely to be aware of such issues and cannot be expected to be knowledgeable of such matters.

Code Availability

The *Code* is not copyrighted and is printed in a format that lends itself to wide distribution. Clinicians might benefit from having a copy of it available in their office for periodic reference.

Assessment Ethics

In addition to the *Test Standards* and the *Code*, sets of ethical principles regarding the use of educational and psychological tests have been developed by a variety of professional organizations. Many of the users of intelligence tests are members of the American Psychological Association and are, therefore, responsible for following the *APA Ethical Guidelines* (APA,

1981). (Copies of the APA Ethical Standards, the Test Standards, and the Code of Fair Testing Practices in Education, can be ordered from the American Psychological Association, 750 First Street, NE, Washington, D.C. 20002-4242.)

The *APA Ethical Guidelines* are somewhat cursory, but they at least provide a starting point for the beginning user of intelligence tests in the proper use of assessment techniques. These *Guidelines* build on the foundation of the *Test Standards* and the *Code* by providing additional issues for the clinician to consider in the use of intelligence tests. Some of the Guidelines are discussed below.

Principle 8a

In using assessment techniques, psychologists respect the right of clients to have full explanations of the nature and purpose of the techniques in language the clients can understand, unless an explicit exception to this right has been agreed upon in advance. When the explanations are to be provided by others, psychologists establish procedures for ensuring the adequacy of these explanations.

It is important to be clear and honest in communicating with clients, including children and their parents, about the nature of the use of intelligence tests for an evaluation. The *Guidelines* make it clear that the burden of the accuracy of communication with clients is on the psychologist. The clinician may have to enlist the help of others, such as translators, if necessary, to communicate clearly with clients, parents, and others involved in an evaluation. This emphasis on accurate and clear communication also applies to any reservations the psychologist may have about the test results.

Principle 8c

In reporting assessment results, psychologists indicate any reservations that exist regarding validity or reliability because of the circumstances of the assessment or the inappropriateness of the norms for the person tested. Psychologists strive to ensure that the results of assessments and their interpretations are not misused by others.

According to the *Guidelines*, clinicians should also be honest about their perception of the reliability and the validity of the obtained scores for an individual child. There may also be degrees of "invalidity" for a given set of results. A clinician may note some minor attention problems during the evaluation, or a child may have refused to complete 20% of the items on an intelligence test. These situations may warrant different means of communicating concern about the validity of the obtained results. In the first scenario the clinician may place a sentence or two of caution in the written report. In the latter circumstance the psychologist may go so far as to not compute scores and call for a reevaluation. Clinicians have to be willing to consider a variety of ways of communicating concerns about validity as each assessment situation places new demands.

Principle 8f

Psychologists do not encourage or promote the use of psychological assessment techniques by inappropriately trained or otherwise unqualified persons through teaching, sponsorship, or supervision.

This guideline warrants special mention since it is not addressed as directly in either the *Code* or the *Test Standards*. On the one hand, this guideline sounds elitist and guild-serving. On the other hand, there is justifiable cause for concern about the improper use of assessment techniques—intelligence tests in particular. Experts on psychological assessment are well aware of the misuses to which even technically superior tests may be put (Matarazzo, 1990; Thorndike, 1990; Jensen, 1980). This volume makes clear the high level of expertise required to interpret intelligence tests properly. But this text still does not provide adequate expertise to use intelligence tests. One must remember that Chapters 2, 3, and 5 in particular are merely proxies for major content areas. This volume cannot cover all of the content necessary to use intelligence tests properly, including separate graduate-level coursework in physiological psychology, mea-

surement theory, statistics, developmental psychology, and cognitive psychology, to name but a few important content areas. Principle F suggests that clinicians have an appreciation for the fact that assessment practice, particularly the use of intelligence tests, requires an extraordinary level of expertise in the science of human behavior and its measurement.

TEST SELECTION

The premise underlying this chapter is consistent with the premise underlying the *Test Standards*—not all intelligence tests are valid for all children all of the time (Wesman, 1968). This section assumes that intelligence tests have accumulated various types of validity evidence that makes them useful for particular purposes. It is also not likely that a single intelligence test will prove useful for all assessment purposes. This last section builds on the assumption of a lack of universal validity for an intelligence test by giving guidance to test selection. Having considered this issue the clinician will be able to choose an intelligence test more wisely in the future. There are a number of variables that may influence test selection for an individual case. Among the variables that clinicians should consider are the following.

Purpose of the Assessment

Is the purpose screening or diagnosis? A screening measure would require only a few subtests from a major test of intelligence, with the focus of the assessment on deriving a global estimate of intellectual functioning. Screeners such as the Kaufman Brief Intelligence Test (K-BIT) (Kaufman & Kaufman, 1990) or the Vocabulary and Pattern Analysis subtests of the Binet-4 might suffice if intelligence screening is all that is needed.

An assessment that is aimed at diagnostic decision making, by contrast, calls for an in-depth evaluation that measures multiple domains of intelligence. Cognitive domains of interest might include verbal, spatial, or short-term memory skills.

The diagnostic assessment of intelligence also requires a measure of intelligence that is highly reliable and valid. Screening measures are less reliable because of their brevity. A diagnostic decision should never be based on a measure with low reliability. Diagnostic decision making requires that a measure have reliability estimates in the .90 and above range.

The screening versus diagnosis test selection decision, then, requires the clinician to weigh the need for a highly reliable estimate of intelligence that considers multiple intelligence domains versus a global estimate of intelligence with lower reliability. A third possibility is to assess only global capacity with an intelligence measure that has strong reliability estimates. The Binet-4 subtests, for example, are rather long, and combining two of them in many cases will result in reliability estimates that approach or exceed .90.

There are several reasons for choosing screeners over a longer examination. One reason is triage. All children who are evaluated by the psychologist may receive a screener in order to assess the need for administration of a diagnostic measure. One colleague of mine always uses the Draw-a-Person (DAP) and the Peabody Picture Vocabulary Test-Revised (PPVT-R) as screeners for children referred for school problems. The PPVT-R serves as a screener for verbal skills and the DAP for spatial/visual-motor skills. Although the DAP in particular is a fairly poor correlate of comprehensive measures (see Chapter 12), my colleague has found this set of measures helpful for planning the remainder of the evaluation. This psychologist found these screeners to be extremely powerful in one case. In this case she had a boy referred for school problems who drew a sexually explicit DAP.

When asked how he had learned to draw like this, he indicated that the girl seated next to him in class had taught him. Further investigation revealed the girl *seated next to him* was being sexually abused at home. This is an unusually powerful result for a screener. The screeners served a triage function in this case by helping decide which child needed the most immediate attention.

Screeners may also be used when abundant information about intelligence is already available for the child. A child may have received the DAS on two separate occasions in the past year and received similar scores both times. If the child were evaluated a third time, a shorter form may be adequate.

Screeners may also be useful when intelligence is not central to the referral problem. If, for example, a child were referred for depression but was obtaining good grades in school, the focus of the evaluation would likely be on the referral problem. A screener for intelligence may be administered just to ensure that there are no unidentified problems in the cognitive realm. If screener results are suspicious, then a more comprehensive measure would be in order.

Age/Score Range

For some assessment purposes an extended score range is necessary. An example would be differentiation among levels of mental retardation—mild, moderate, severe, and profound (see Chapter 14). Many tests simply do not have the score range necessary for such differential diagnoses. In fact, some intelligence measures do not possess a wide enough range of scores to differentiate mental retardation from below-average intelligence or giftedness from above-average intelligence (see Table 17.2).

Tests are most likely to pose floor and ceiling problems near the "tails" of their age range. Hence, age is merely a proxy variable for score range. The low score ranges of particular tests

TABLE 17.2 Lowest possible composite scores for a variety of intelligence tests

Test	Age in Years and Months*								
	1–6	2–0	2–6	3–0	6–0	8–0	12–0	16–0	22–0
Battelle		65	65	65					
Bayley		50	50						
Binet-4		95	87	73					
DAS			64	53					
K-ABC			88	77					
McCarthy			89	74	69	<50			
WAIS-R								50	46
WISC-III					52	40			
WIPPSI-R				68	42				

*These scores were based on the premise that a child obtained a raw score of 1 on each subtest.

are shown in Table 17.2. This table is very informative in that it shows the range of scaled scores possible on various instruments at several age levels. It appears that test developers have become sensitized to the need for extended score ranges, as some of the newer tests have impressive ranges (e.g., the DAS).

Clinicians are not adequately assessing a child when the child obtains too many raw scores of zero or too many perfect scores (or fails to obtain a ceiling) on a test. Table 17.2 is intended to help the clinician avoid floor problems, particularly at age levels where several different tests are available.

Practicality

To some the practicality issue seems trite, but this is a central issue with infants and preschoolers, especially those who exhibit behavior problems. Practicality can include several components. One component is interest level to children (see Tables 17.3 to 17.10). Interest level may not only be important for the practicality of administration but also because a high level of

interest may enhance validity. Children who are highly motivated will presumably put forth their best effort for the examiner. While interest level is somewhat of an intangible, there is accumulated clinical experience to suggest that some instruments are more child-like and inherently more interesting to young children than others. The McCarthy and K-ABC appear to be more attractive, for example, than the WPPSI-R (Child Assessment News, 1991). Realistically, clinicians will have to decide which tests are more interesting and attractive to their clientele, especially in light of multicultural issues. Although the K-ABC is attractive to many children, some items may be offensive or inappropriate for children from some cultural groups. An attendee at a workshop that I once presented suggested that the "clapping hands" item on the Reading Understanding subtest was inappropriate for some of the Soviet immigrant children with whom she was working because they were members of a religious sect that did not allow hand clapping.

Another aspect of practicality is ease of administration. If a child is exhibiting substantial behavior problems, administration of a complex

TABLE 17.3   Summary evaluation of Wechsler Intelligence Scale for Children-III

Category	Rating*	Comments
Materials packaging	Good	
Materials quality	Good	
Interest to children	Fair	Although the structure of the test is unchanged, the stimuli have been made more age-appropriate and color has been used extensively.
Ease of administration	Fair	Administration has been eased (e.g., putting Verbal subtest scoring keys adjacent to the item). The difficult multipoint scoring procedure has been retained for Verbal tests, and a stopwatch is still required.
Ease of scoring	Fair	See above.
Record form design	Good	Had more space to record responses than previous edition.
Computer software	IE	Software is forthcoming.
Norming sample	Excellent	
Primary norms	Excellent	
Adequate floor (easy items)	Excellent	Floor and ceiling have been improved.
Adequate ceiling (difficult items)	Excellent	
Reliability	Good	
Supplementary norms/scales	IE	
Content validity	Poor	No explicit ties between item development and theory have been offered.
Factorial validity	Fair/ Excellent	This is confusing because the featured scales are not fully supported by factor analysis, yet the factor structure offered for optional interpretation seems clear.
Age differentiation	Excellent	
Concurrent validity	Excellent	
Predictive validity	Good	
Convergent/Discriminant validity	IE	

Other comments: The WISC-III is a substantial improvement over the WISC-R, yet it retains much of the original structure and the associated weaknesses inherent in that structure.

*Scale is Poor, Fair, Good, Excellent, and IE (inadequate evidence).

TABLE 17.4   Summary evaluation of Differential Ability Scales

Category	Rating*	Comments
Test kit weight and materials packaging	Fair	Heavier than most competitors. There is a dizzying number of components in the test kit.
Materials quality	Excellent	
Interest to children	IE	
Ease of administration	Fair	
Ease of scoring	Fair to Good	
Record form design	Good	The amount of information provided takes some getting used to.
Computer software	IE	The availability of software is not known.
Norming sample	Excellent	
Primary norms	Excellent	
Adequate floor (easy items)	Excellent	
Adequate ceiling (difficult items)	Excellent	
Reliability	Good	Comparable to other scales.
Content validity	Poor	Content was not selected based on an apriori theoretical model.
Factorial validity	Good	Composites are well supported by factor analytic evidence. More analysis is needed to test the robustness of the factors.
Age differentiation validity	Excellent	
Concurrent validity	Excellent	
Predictive validity	Good	More evidence is needed.
Convergent/Discriminant validity	IE	

*Scale is Poor, Fair, Good, Excellent, and IE (inadequate evidence).

instrument may be difficult. The extensive follow-up questioning required on the Vocabulary, Similarities, and Comprehension subtests of the WISC-III, for example, may be interpreted by some children as an unnecessary inquisition. Some obstreperous children may respond to this administration format by refusing to complete the test. Similarly, a test with complex instructions may not be welcomed by the impatient child with attention difficulties.

There are many aspects of practicality, ranging from the size of the test kit, to administration time, to cost, to ease of scoring. One would not think that ease of scoring could be a factor, but it can be. The W-J Cognitive, for example, is a poor choice for emergency work because it is

TABLE 17.5   Summary evaluation of Woodcock-Johnson Test of Cognitive Ability

Category	Rating*	Comments
Test kit weight and materials packaging	Excellent	The small number of manipulatives makes the test materials portable. They can easily be placed in a briefcase or data case with other tests.
Materials quality	Excellent	
Interest to children	Fair	Lacks manipulatives for preschoolers.
Ease of administration	Excellent	The requirement for a tape recorder is troublesome if a clinician typically does not use one.
Ease of scoring	Poor	Difficult to score by hand.
Record form design	Good	
Computer software	Excellent	Obviates the need for hand scoring.
Norming sample	Good	
Adequate floor (easy items)	Good	
Adequate ceiling (difficult items)	Excellent	
Reliability	Good	Comparable to other scales.
Content validity	Good	No specific evidence is given, although the development was theory driven.
Factorial validity	Good	Independent cross-validation studies are needed to bolster interpretive confidence.
Age differentiation	Excellent	
Concurrent validity	Fair	Lower correlations with other intelligence tests than previous research suggests.
Predictive validity	IE	
Convergent/Discriminant validity	IE	

*Scale is Poor, Fair, Good, Excellent, and IE (inadequate evidence).

so complex to score that many people prefer using computer scoring routinely. This makes the W-J less desirable for emergency cases in a hospital or other setting where the psychologist needs to score all tests immediately and does not have access to the software scoring back at the office.

Even administration time may become important in some assessment situations. The Battelle, for instance, possesses numerous strengths

TABLE 17.6 Summary evaluation of Kaufman Assessment Battery for Children (K-ABC)

Category	Rating*	Comments
Test kit weight	Poor/ Good	The kit has been redesigned to make it lighter and more portable.
Materials packaging	Good	
Materials quality	Good	
Interest to children	Excellent	
Ease of administration	Good	The lack of need for a stopwatch and examiner oral directions eases administration.
Ease of scoring	Excellent	
Record form design	Fair	Small page size is difficult to work with.
Computer software	Poor	The content and algorithms are good, but the slow speed makes the program virtually useless.
Norming sample	Good	An excellent sample, but it is now a decade old.
Adequate floor (easy items)	Fair	At younger ages.
Adequate ceiling (difficult items)	Fair	At ages 10 and above
Reliability	Good	
Supplementary norms/scales	Good	The Nonverbal scale seems useful. Sociocultural norms are available.
Content validity	Good	Used an apriori theory to develop items and scales.
Factorial validity	Excellent	
Age differentiation	Fair	Because of floor and ceiling effects.
Concurrent validity	Excellent	
Predictive validity	Good	
Convergent/Discriminant validity	Good	One of the few manuals that includes such evidence.

Other comments: The K-ABC manuals are unusually comprehensive and informative.

*Scale is Poor, Fair, Good, Excellent, and IE (inadequate evidence).

TABLE 17.7   Summary evaluation of McCarthy Scales of Children's Abilities

Category	Rating*	Comments
Test kit weight	Good	
Materials packaging	Good	
Materials quality	Excellent	
Interest to children	Excellent	Many of the tasks resemble children's toys and games.
Ease of administration	Good	After some examiner practice.
Ease of scoring	Good	
Record form design	Good	
Computer software	IE	
Norming sample	Poor	While it was excellent at the time, it is now two decades out of date.
Adequate (floor (easy items)	Fair	
Adequate ceiling (difficult items)	Fair	
Reliability	Good	
Supplementary norms/scales	IE	
Content validity	Poor	
Factorial validity	Fair	The factor structure does not resemble closely the score structure.
Age differentiation	Fair	
Concurrent validity	Fair	There is a tendency for the McCarthy to yield lower scores than some popular measures, notably the WISC-R.
Predictive validity	Good	
Convergent/Discriminant validity	IE	

Other Comments: The small range of the McCarthy limits its range of applicability, particularly in longitudinal applications.

*Scale is Poor, Fair, Good, Excellent, and IE (inadequate evidence).

including a broad sampling of infant behavior. The Bayley takes a narrower swath, but it provides an estimate of cognitive development in a more time-efficient manner when time is at a premium. Time may be crucial when intelligence is being assessed in a neonatal (perhaps intensive) care unit.

Examiners will have to gauge the practicality of individual tests in light of the clientele they serve. Although frequently neglected, these can be crucial issues to the practitioner.

Clinicians, however, have to balance the needs for practicality against the need to enhance the validity of the results. Clinicians could be encouraged by administrators to emphasize issues such as cost and time that may hinder the

TABLE 17.8 Summary evaluation of Battelle Developmental Inventory (BDI)

Category	Rating*	Comments
Test kit weight	Good	
Materials packaging	Good	Supplementary materials required. Some materials are provided by the examiners.
Materials quality	Good	
Interest to children	Good	
Ease of administration	Poor	Administration can be lengthy. Samples domains in addition to cognitive development.
Ease of scoring	Fair	Scoring can be lengthy.
Record form design	Good	
Computer software	IE	
Norming sample	Fair	Failed to control for SES.
Primary norms	Poor	DQs below 65 are not lawful.
Adequate floor (easy items)	Good	
Adequate ceiling (difficult items)	Good	
Reliability	Good	
Supplementary norms/scales	IE	
Content validity	Good	Began with large item pool.
Factorial validity	Good	
Age differentiation	Good	
Concurrent validity	Fair	Good with Bayley, mediocre with WISC-R, Binet.
Predictive validity	Good	
Convergent/Discriminant validity	IE	
Other comments: Has a large age range.		

*Scale is Poor, Fair, Good, Excellent, and IE (inadequate evidence).

ability of the clinician to do a thorough job (see Box 17.1). Clinicians should never sacrifice validity for practicality.

Revisions versus Old Editions

Often clinicians debate whether or not to switch from an old edition of a test to a revision. The WISC-III versus the WISC-R is an excellent example. The *Test Standards* would lead the clinician to *always use tests with the strongest validity evidence*. If a revision has better evidence of validity, then it should be adopted. This scenario is the most frequent one.

In the case of the WISC-III there is considerable evidence that the new edition is as valid as the old one. In addition, there is strong evidence that the WISC-R norms are inadequate (see

TABLE 17.9   Summary evaluation of Bayley Scales of Infant Development (Bayley)

Category	Rating*	Comments
Test kit weight	Good	
Materials packaging	Good	The manipulatives can be hard to find in the test kit.
Materials quality	Good	
Interest to children	Excellent	
Ease of administration	Fair	
Ease of scoring	Good	Few derived scores are offered, making scoring easy.
Record form design	Good	
Computer software	IE	Not available.
Norming sample	Poor	Sample is two decades old.
Adequate floor (easy items)	Good	
Adequate ceiling (difficult items)	Good	
Reliability	Good	
Supplementary norms/scales	IE	
Content validity	Poor	
Factorial validity	IE	Few studies have been conducted.
Age differentiation	Excellent	
Concurrent validity	Good	There are few alternative measures at the Bayley age range.
Predictive validity	Good	These are not as high as for older ages because of the nature of change in preschoolers.
Convergent/Discriminant validity	IE	
Other comments: Has a large age range.		

*Scale is Poor, Fair, Good, Excellent, and IE (inadequate evidence).

Chapter 5). In most cases the new edition of a test does possess strengths over the old one.

In some cases, however, the issue of whether or not to use a new edition of a test clouds the essential issue of choosing the best test for the assessment situation. For example, a clinician may wish that the old Stanford-Binet Form L-M were still available for assessing young children with developmental problems. There may be another option here that is less obvious, and that is the DAS. The DAS has some Binet-LM item types, and it has more floor than either the Binet-LM or the Binet-4. In other words, in some cases the clinician may feel that the only choice is between a new or old edition when, in fact, an entirely new measure should be considered. The days of the Wechsler-Binet monopoly are gone. There are now many good measures that meet a greater variety of assessment needs.

TABLE 17.10 Summary evaluation of Stanford-Binet Intelligence Scale-Fourth Edition

Category	Rating*	Comments
Materials packaging	Good	
Materials quality	Good	The print on the Pattern Analysis blocks fades too quickly.
Interest to children	Fair to Good	
Ease of administration	Fair	Administration has been eased by using easels and having fewer manipulatives. Finding one's place and working backwards in easels is difficult. The change of item types within subtests is cumbersome.
Ease of scoring	Good	Dichotomous scoring is used throughout.
Record form design	Good	Has more space to record responses than previous edition.
Computer software	Excellent	Fast and easy.
Norming sample	Excellent	
Primary norms	Excellent	
Adequate floor (easy items)	Excellent	
Adequate ceiling (difficult items)	Fair	Many adolescents get perfect or near perfect scores on Pattern Analysis. Gifted adolescents often obtain more than one perfect score.
Reliability	Excellent	
Supplementary Norms/scales	IE	
Content validity	Fair	Some ties between item development and theory have been offered.
Factorial validity	Fair/ Good	Strong "g" factor. Good support for Abstract/Visual and Verbal Reasoning areas. Quantitative and Short-Term Memory scores are problematic.
Age differentiation	Excellent	
Concurrent validity	Excellent	
Predictive validity	Good	
Convergent/Discriminant validity	IE	

Other comments: The Binet-4 is psychometrically stronger than the Stanford-Binet Form L-M.

*Scale is Poor, Fair, Good, Excellent, and IE (inadequate evidence).

Domains Assessed

Assessment domain is becoming a more crucial variable as new intelligence tests are offered that include an enlarged sampling of children's cognitive performance. The clinician needs to gauge beforehand which domains of intelligence require assessment and select the test(s) that best assesses these domains. A sample case would be a child who is referred for a short-term memory deficit. In this case the current status of the deficit is important to assess. In this situation the clinician would likely choose to use the Binet-4, DAS, K-ABC, or W-J, all of which possess more short-term memory subtests. If, on the other hand, a child is referred for a possible processing speed problem, then the WISC-III, DAS, or W-J would likely serve this purpose best.

Someone may query, however, what would happen if a clinician assesses weaknesses and this serves to lower the child's composite score and qualify a child for mental retardation placement when this would be inappropriate? *This is why intelligence test scores should never "qualify" any child for placement. Professional judgement and consultation should be the only vehicles used to decide what services a child may need.* I refer back to my previous example of a physician only being allowed to prescribe a medication for high blood pressure if a person's systolic pressure is beyond a certain level. This latter scenario is an example of uninspired medicine, just as the former scenario is a example of poor psychological assessment practice.

Intelligence tests may also be selected so as to assess for the presence of cognitive strengths. If a child were referred for an evaluation for giftedness and is reported to have strong quantitative skills, the Binet-4 may be the test of choice because of its Quantitative Reasoning scale. The clarification of this strength may be helpful for emphasizing its presence so that it could be capitalized on in curriculum planning.

Test Strengths and Weaknesses

The strong and weak points of individual tests are crucial elements in the test selection process.

It is for this reason that Tables 17.3 through 17.10 were developed. These tables are obviously oversimplifications, but they do serve as efficient reminders of some of the major assets and liabilities of several important tests. An example will highlight the use of these tables.

Table 17.7 reveals that the McCarthy possesses a number of positive attributes. This test, however, is also aging. Specifically, the norming sample is nearing 20 years of age. This fact leads one to hypothesize that the norms for the McCarthy will result in scores that differ somewhat from other major tests (see Chapters 5 and 13). This weakness of the McCarthy will mitigate against its use in some cases. Other examples of the use of Tables 17.3 through 17.10 are given in the next section.

SAMPLE CASES OF TEST SELECTION

Some scenarios for test selection are discussed next. These scenarios will derive their logic from the summary tables of strengths and weaknesses (see Tables 17.3 through 17.10), and from previous chapters on these various tests.

Case 1

Referral/Background

Alexandra is a 6-year-old who is referred for attention deficit. She is also suspected of below-average intelligence.

Test Selection Considerations

Such a referral would require a high-interest test that is not too lengthy. Tests lacking considerable appeal for young children would be ruled out, including the Binet-4, DAS, W-J, and WPPSI-R. High-appeal tests available for this age group would include the K-ABC and McCarthy. While the K-ABC is appealing, this is a "crossover" age for the scale in that a number of new tests begin at ages 5 and 6 (e.g., Matrix Analogies, Photo Series, and Reading/Decoding). Where new tests begin for an age group they may be difficult. Since Alexandra is suspected of below-average intelligence, some of the K-ABC subtests may prove too difficult for her, resulting in too many raw scores of zero. In this case the McCarthy would be a good test to attempt with Alexandra because it should have enough easy items, administration time is reasonable, and the test provides built-in "breaks" (i.e., the Motor scale) for children with limited attention spans.

Case 2

Referral/Background

Alai is an 11-year-old boy who is referred for reading problems. He has a history of above-average grades in all school subjects except for reading and spelling.

Test Selection Considerations

The K-ABC would be ruled out quickly in this case because of a lack of difficult items for this age group. The WISC-III, Binet-4, DAS, and W-J may all be useful in this case.

Case 3

Referral/Background

Janine is a 16-year-old who is seeking assistance in choosing a college. She has always been in gifted classes and she is attending an elite boarding school for high school.

Test Selection Considerations

The WISC-III would be a poor choice here because of a lack of difficulty. The Binet-4 also lacks some difficulty at this age. The DAS, W-J, and WAIS-R may be reasonable options.

Case 4

Referral/Background

Pablo is an 8-year-old who is referred for poor academic performance. His performance began to deteriorate about a year ago subsequent to a head injury incurred in an automobile accident. His family speaks Spanish at home. Pablo speaks English most of the time.

Test Selection Considerations

The English-language demands of the WISC-III, Binet-4, DAS, and W-J may be an impediment here. The brief oral instructions of the K-ABC may help ensure that Pablo understands what is expected of him in the test session.

Caveat

It is important to understand that these test selection examples are based on the examiner's predictions that have emanated from extensive knowledge of numerous test instruments. As a result, these predictions will occasionally be flawed. The word "occasionally" is the operative term here. Regardless of the "hit rate," the importance of examiner foresight in test selection cannot be emphasized too much. There is no substantial evidence right now that any intelligence test works well with all children all of the time.

CONCLUSIONS

As is eminently clear from reading excerpts from the *Test Standards*, the ethical *Guidelines*, and the *Code*, the modern-day user of children's intelligence tests has to aspire to an entirely new level of practice in comparison to previous generations of clinicians. As much as anything else, users of modern intelligence tests have to be extremely well informed about the tests they use and about appropriate practices for their use. It is likely that should there be a problem with the use of a child's intelligence test results, the clinician will be held accountable for compliance to relevant standards and guidelines. Readers of this text would be well advised to discuss the implications of various standards and guidelines in order to ensure that they are using children's intelligence tests appropriately.

CHAPTER SUMMARY

1. Clinicians have to know psychometric principles well in order to judge the quality of new methods.

2. The *Standards for Educational and Psychological Tests* discuss three primary types of validity evidence: content-related, criterion-related, and construct-related evidence of validity.

3. Relevant *Test Standards* include the following.

    A. Evidence of validity should be presented for the major types of interpretations for which a test is recommended.

    B. When the interpretation of subtest profiles is encouraged by a test manual, the validity evidence for this type of interpretation should be presented. If this type of evidence is not presented, the user should be warned that validity evidence for this type of interpretation is not available.

    C. Test manuals should give detailed descriptions of the nature of the samples used in reliability and validity studies that allow the test user to gauge accurately the strength or weakness of the evidence presented.

    D. Internal consistency coefficients should not be presented in the manual as substitutes for stability or test-retest coefficients.

4. It is important for the clinician to know that he or she is making an interpretation that is not specifically supported by research.

5. The *Test Standards* suggest that new tests must be accompanied by considerable psychometric evidence.

6. The *Code of Fair Testing Practices in Education* was published in 1988 by the Joint Committee on Testing Practices.

7. According to the *Code*, efforts to prepare examinees need to be made prior to the test session.

8. Clinicians should customarily make efforts to explain how test results will be used and how they may be released to others.

9. Experts on psychological assessment are well aware of the misuses to which even technically superior tests may be put.

10. Not all intelligence tests are valid for all children all of the time.

11. An assessment that is aimed at diagnostic decision making, as opposed to screening, requires an in-depth evaluation that measures multiple domains of intelligence.

12. Screening measures may be preferred for uses such as triage, in situations when abundant information about intelligence is already available for the child, and when intelligence is not central to the child's referral problem(s).

13. An extended score range is necessary for differentiating among levels of mental retardation—mild, moderate, severe, and profound.

14. The practicality of an intelligence test can include several components, such as interest level to children, administration time, and ease of administration and scoring.

15. Another factor to consider in test selection is assessment domain, which is becoming a more crucial variable as new intelligence tests are offered that include an enlarged sampling of children's cognitive performance.

References

Abram, D. M., Ebelman, B. L., Rose, D. F., & Whitaker, H. A. (1985). Verbal and cognitive sequelae following unilateral lesions acquired in early childhood. *Journal of Clinical and Experimental Neuropsychology, 7*(5), 55–78.

Ackerman, P. T., Dykman, R. A., & Oglesby, D. M. (1983). Sex and group differences in reading and attention disordered children with and without hyperkinesis. *Journal of Learning Disabilities, 16*(7), 407–415.

Ackerman, P. T., Dykman, R. A., & Peters, J. E. (1976). Hierarchal factor patterns on the WISC as related to areas of processing deficit. *Perceptual and Motor Skills, 42,* 381–386.

Alexander, H. B. (1922). A comparison of ranks of American states in Army Alpha and in social-economic status. *School and Society, 16,* 388–392.

Algozzine, B., Ysseldyke, J., & Shinn, M, (1982). Identifying children with learning disabilities: When is a discrepancy severe? *Journal of School Psychology, 20,* 299–305.

American Educational Research Association, American Psychological Association, and National Council on Measurement in Education (1985). *Standards for educational and psychological testing.* Washington, DC: American Psychological Association.

American Psychological Association (1981). *Ethical principles of psychologists.* Washington, DC: APA.

American Psychological Association (1985). *Standards for educational and psychological testing.* Washington, DC: APA.

American Psychological Association Committee on Professional Standards and Committee on Psychological Tests and Assessment. (1986). *Guidelines for computer-based tests and interpretations.* Washington, DC: APA.

Anastasi, A. (1982). *Psychological testing* (5th ed.). New York: Macmillan.

Anastasi, A. (1983). *Review of the Kaufman Assessment Battery for Children.* [Machine-readable data file]. Latham, NY: Buros Review Service.

Anastasi, A. (1984). The K-ABC in historical and contemporary perspective. *Journal of Special Education, 18,* 357–366.

Anastasi, A. (1985). Testing the test: Interpreting the scores from multiscore batteries. *Journal of Counseling and Development, 64,* 84–86.

Anastasi, A. (1986). Intelligence as a quality of behavior. In R. J. Sternberg & D. K. Detterman (Eds.), *What is intelligence: Contemporary viewpoints on its nature and definition.* Norwood, NJ: Ablex.

Anastasi, A. (1988). *Psychological testing* (6th ed.). New York: Macmillan.

Anastasi, A. (1989). [Review of the Stanford-Binet Intelligence Scales: Fourth Edition]. *Tenth Mental Measurements Yearbook.* Lincoln, NE: Buros Institute.

Anderson, R. J., & Sisco, F. H. (1977). *Standardization of the WISC-R Performance Scale for deaf children.* Washington, DC: Gallaudet University, Office of Demographic Studies.

Angoff, W. H. (1988). The nature-nurture debate, aptitudes, and group differences. *American Psychologist, 43,* 713–720.

Applegate, B., & Kaufman, A. S. (1988). Short form estimates of K-ABC sequential and simultaneous processing for research and screening purposes. Manuscript submitted for publication.

Arthur, G. A. (1947). *Point Scale of Performance Tests: Form II* (rev.). New York: The Psychological Corporation.

Arthur, G. (1950). *The Arthur Adaptation of the Leiter International Performance Scale.* Chicago: Stoelting.

Atkinson, R. C., & Shriffrin, R. M. (1971). The control of short-term memory. *Scientific American, 225,* 82–90.

Avery, R. O., Slate, J. R., & Chovan, W. (1989). A longitudinal study of WISC-R and WAIS-R scores with students who are educable mentally handicapped. *Education and Training of the Mentally Retarded, 24*(1), 28–31.

Aylward, G. P., & MacGruder, R. W. (1986). *Test Behavior Checklist (TBC).* Clinical Psychology Publishing.

Ayres, R. R., Cooley, E. J., & Severson, H. H. (1988). Educational translation of the Kaufman Assessment Battery for Children: A construct validity study. *School Psychology Review, 17*(1), 113–124.

Bagnato, S. J., & Neisworth, J. T. (1989). *System to plan early childhood services.* Circle Pines, MN: American Guidance Service.

Bailey, D. B., Jr., Vandiviere, P., Dellinger, J., & Munn, D. (1987). The Battelle Developmental Inventory: Teacher perceptions and implementation data. *Journal of Psychoeducational Assessment, 3,* 217–226.

Baltes, P. B. (1986). Notes on the concept of intelligence. In R. J. Sternberg & D. K. Detterman (Eds.), *What is intelligence? Contemporary viewpoints on its nature and definition.* Norwood, NJ: Ablex.

Bannatyne, A. (1974). Diagnosis: A note on recategorization of the WISC scale scores. *Journal of Learning Disabilities, 7,* 272–274.

Barber, T. X. (1973). Pitfalls in research: Vine investigator and experimenter effects. In R. M. W. Travers (Ed.), *Second handbook of research on teaching* (pp. 382–404). Chicago: Rand McNally.

Bardos, A. N., Softas, B. C., & Petrogiannis, R. K. (1989). Comparison of the Goodenough-Harris and Naglieri's Draw-a-Person scoring systems for Greek children. *School Psychology International, 10,* 205–209.

Barkley, R. A. (1989). Attention deficit-hyperactivity disorder. In E. J. Mash & R. A. Barkley (Eds.), *Treatment of childhood disorders* (pp. 39–72). New York: Guilford.

Barnes, T., & Forness, S. (1982). Learning characteristics of children and adolescents with various psychiatric diagnoses. In R. Rutherford (Ed.), *Severe behavior disorders of children and youth* (Vol. 5) (pp. 32–41). Austin, TX Pro-Ed.

Barry, B. J. (1983). Validity study of the Kaufman Assessment Battery for Children compared to the Stanford-Binet, Form L-M, in the identification of gifted nine- and ten-year-olds. Unpublished master's thesis, National College of Education, Chicago.

Barry, B., Klanderman, J., & Stipe, D. (1983). Study number one. In A. S. Kaufman & N. L. Kaufman (Eds.), *Kaufman Assessment Battery for Children: Interpretive manual* (p. 94). Circle Pines, MN: American Guidance Service.

Bauer, J. J., & Smith, D. K. (1988, April). Stability of the K-ABC and the S-B:4 with preschool children. Paper presented at the meeting of the National Association of School Psychologists, Chicago.

Bayley, N. (1969). *Bayley scales of infant development.* New York: The Psychological Corporation.

Beitchman, J. H., Patterson, P., Gelfand, B., & Minty, G. (1982). IQ and child psychiatric disorder. *Canadian Journal of Psychiatry, 27,* 23–28.

Belmont, J. M. (1989). Cognitive strategies and strategic learning: The socio-instructional approach. *American Psychologist, 44,* 142–148.

Bennett, T. L., & Krein, L. K. (1989). The neuropsychology of epilepsy: Psychological and social impact. In C. R. Reynolds and E. Fletcher-Janzen (Eds.), *Handbook of clinical child neuropsychology.* New York: Plenum.

Benton, A. L. (1980). The neuropsychology of facial recognition. *American Psychologist, 35,* 176–186.

Benton, A. L., Hamsher, K., Varney, N. R., & Spreen, O. (1983). *Contributions to neuropsychological assessment: A clinical manual.* New York: Oxford University Press.

Berk, R. A. (1982). *Handbook of methods for detecting test bias.* Baltimore, MD: Johns Hopkins University Press.

Bever, T. G. (1975). Cerebral asymmetries in humans are due to the differentiation of two incompatible processes: Holistic and analytic. In D. Aaronson & R. Rieber (Eds.), *Developmental psycholinguistics and communication disorders.* New York: New York Academy of Sciences.

Binet, A., & Simon, T. (1905). New methods for the diagnosis of the intellectual level of subnormals. *L'année Psychologique, 11,* 191–244.

Binet, A., & Simon, T. (1908). The development of intelligence in the child. *L'année Psychologique, 14,* 1–90.

Bing, S., & Bing, J. (1984, April). *Relationship between the K-ABC and PPVT-R for preschoolers.* Paper presented at the meeting of the National Association of School Psychologists, Philadelphia.

Bing, S. B., & Bing, J. R. (1985, February). *Comparison of the Kaufman Assessment Battery for Children and the Stanford Early School Achievement Test for non-referred kindergarten children.* Paper presented at the meeting of the Eastern Educational Research Association, Virginia Beach, VA.

Bjorklund, D. F. (1989). *Children's thinking: Developmental function and individual differences*. Pacific Grove, CA: Brooks/Cole.

Bloom, A. S., Allard, A. M., Zelks, A. J., Brill, W. J., Epinka, C. W., & Pfohl, W. (1988). Differential validity of the K-ABC for lower functioning preschoolers versus those of high ability. *American Journal of Mental Deficiency, 93*, 273–277.

Bloom, B. S. (1964). *Stability and change in human characteristics*. New York: Wiley.

Bogen, J. E. (1969). The other side of the brain: Parts I, II, and III. *Bulletin of the Los Angeles Neurological Society, 34*, 73–105, 135–162, 191–203.

Bogen, J. E., Dezure, R., Tenouten, W., & Marsh, J. (1972). The other side of the brain: Part IV. *Bulletin of the Los Angeles Neurological Society, 37*, 49–61.

Boll, T. J. (1974). Behavioral correlates of cerebral damage in children aged 9 through 14. In R. M. Reitan & L. A. Davison (Eds.), *Clinical neuropsychology: Current status and applications* (pp. 91–120). Wsahington, DC: Winston.

Bolton, B. (1978). Differential ability structure in deaf and hearing children. *Applied Psychological Measurement, 2*, 147–149.

Boring, E. G. (1929). *A history of experimental psychology*. New York: Century.

Borkowski, J. G. (1985). Signs of intelligence: Strategy generalization and metacognition. In S. R. Yussen (Ed.), *The growth of reflection in children*. New York: Academic Press.

Bouchard, T. J., & McGue, M. (1981). Familial studies of intelligence: A review. *Science, 212*, 1055–1059.

Bouchard, T. J., Jr., & Segal, N. L. (1985). Environment and IQ. In B. B. Wolman (Ed.), *Handbook of intelligence: Theories, measurements, and applications* (pp. 391–464). New York: Wiley.

Boyle, G. J. (1989). Confirmation of the structural dimensionality of the Stanford-Binet Intelligence Scale (4th ed.). *Personal and Individual Differences, 10*, 709–715.

Bracken, B. A. (1985). A critical review of the Kaufman Assessment Battery for Children (K-ABC). *School Psychology Review, 14*, 21–36.

Bracken, B. A. (1987). Limitations of preschool instruments and standards for minimal levels of technical adequacy. *Journal of Psychoeducational Assessment, 5*, 313–326.

Bracken, B. A., & Delugach, R. R. (1990, October). Changes improve test. *Communique*, 21.

Bracken, B. A., & Fagan, T. K. (1988). Abilities assessed by the K-ABC Mental Processing subtests: The perceptions of practitioners with varying degrees of experience. *Psychology in the Schools, 25*(1), 22–34.

Bracken, B. A., Prasse, D. P., & McCallum, R. S. (1984). Peabody Picture Vocabulary Test-Revised: An appraisal and review. *School Psychology Review, 13*, 49–60.

Braden, J. P. (1984). The factorial similarity of the WISC-R Performance Scale in deaf and hearing samples. *Personal and Individual Differences, 5*(4), 403–409.

Braden, J. P. (1985a). The structure of nonverbal intelligence in deaf and hearing subjects. *American Annals of the Deaf, 130*, 496–501.

Braden, J. P. (1985b). WISC-R deaf norms reconsidered. *Journal of School Psychology, 23*, 375–382.

Braden, J. P. (1987). A comparison of regression and standard score discrepancy methods for learning disabilities identification: On racial representation. *Journal of School Psychology, 25*, 23–29.

Brandt, H. M., & Giebink, J. W. (1968). Concreteness and congruence in psychologists' reports to teachers. *Psychology in the Schools, 5*, 87–89.

Brody, N. (1985). The validity of tests of intelligence. In B. B. Wolman (Ed.), *Handbook of intelligence* (pp. 353–389). New York: Wiley.

Brown, A. L., & French, L. A. (1979). *The zone of potential development: Implications for intelligence testing in the year 2000* (Report No. 128). University of Illinois at Urbana-Champaign.

Brown, J. W., & Hecaen, H. (1976). Lateralization and language presentation. *Neurology, 26*, 183–189.

Brown, R. T., & Bordon, K. A. (1989). Neuropsychological effects of stimulant medication on children's learning and behavior. In C. R. Reynolds & E. Fletcher-Janzen (Eds.), *Handbook of clinical child neuropsychology*. New York: Plenum.

Brown, R. T., Coles, C. D., Smith, I. E., Platzman, K. A., Silverstein, J., Erickson, S., & Falek, A. (in press). Effects of prenatal alcohol exposure at school age: Attention and behavior. *Neurotoxicology and Teratology*.

Bruininks, R. H., Woodcock, R. W., Weatherman, R. F., & Hill, B. K. (1984). *Scales of Independent Behavior: Woodcock-Johnson Psycho-Educational Battery: Part IV*. Allen, TX: DLM Teaching Resources.

Brumbach, R. A., Staton, R. D., Wilson, H. (1980). Neuropsychological study of children during and after remission of endogenous depressive episodes. *Perceptual and Motor Skills, 50*, 1163–1167.

Bruner, J. S., Olver, R. R., & Greenfield, P. M. (Eds.) (1966). *Studies in cognitive growth*. New York: Wiley.

Budoff, M. (1975). *Learning potential test using Raven Progressive Matrices*. Cambridge, MA: Research Institute for Educational Problems.

Budoff, M. (1987). The validity of learning potential assessment. In C. S. Lidz (Ed.), *Dynamic assessment: An interactional approach to evaluating learning potential*. New York: Guilford.

Burgmeister, B., Blum, L. H., & Lorge, I. (1972). *Columbia Mental Maturity Scale*. New York: Harcourt Brace Jovanovich.

Burt, C. L. (1950). *The backward child.* London: University of London.

Buss, A. R., & Poley, W. (1976). *Individual differences: Traits and factors.* New York: Halsted Press.

Caldwell, B. M., & Bradley, R. H. (1978). *Home observation for measurement of the environment.* Little Rock: University of Arkansas Press.

Campbell, F. A., & Ramey, C. T. (1990). The relationship between Piagetian cognitive development, mental test performance, and academic achievement in high-risk students with and without early educational experience. *Intelligence, 14,* 293–308.

Campione, J. C., & Brown, A. L. (1978). Toward a theory of intelligence: Contributions from research with retarded children. *Intelligence, 2,* 279–304.

Carlson, L., Reynolds, C. R., & Gutkin, T. B. (1983). Consistency of the factorial validity of the WISC-R for upper and lower SES groups. *Journal of School Psychology, 21,* 319–326.

Carroll, J. B., Kohlberg, L., & DeVries, R. (1984). Psychometric and Piagetian intelligences: Toward resolution of controversy. *Intelligence, 8,* 67–91.

Carter, B. D., Zelko, F. A. J., Oas, P. T., & Waltonen, S. (1990). A comparison of ADD/H children and clinical controls on the Kaufman Assessment Battery for Children (K-ABC). *Journal of Psychoeducational Assessment, 8,* 155–164.

Carvajal, H., Gerber, J., Hewes, P., & Weaver, K. A. (1987). Correlations between scores on Stanford-Binet IV and Wechsler Adult Intelligence Scale-Revised. *Psychological Reports, 61,* 83–86.

Carvajal, H., & Weyand, K. (1986). Relationships between scores on Stanford-Binet IV and Wechsler Intelligence Scale for Children-Revised. *Psychological Reports, 59,* 963–966.

Castaneda, A. (1976). Cultural democracy and the educational needs of Mexican American children. In R. L. Jones (Ed.), Mainstreaming and the minority child. Reston, VA: Council for Exceptional Children. Cited in C. J. Maker & S. W. Schiever (Eds.), *Defensible programs for cultural and ethical minorities* (vol. 2). Austin, TX: Pro-Ed.

Catron, D. W., & Catron, S. S. (1977). WISC-R vs. WISC: A comparison with educable mentally retarded children. *Journal of School Psychology, 15*(3), 264–266.

Cattell, R. B. (1940). A culture-free intelligence test. *Journal of Educational Psychology, 31,* 161–179.

Cattell, R. B. (1971). *Abilities: Their structure, growth, and action.* Boston: Houghton Mifflin.

Cattell, R. B. (1979). Are culture fair intelligence tests possible and necessary? *Journal of Research and Development in Education, 12*(2), 3–13.

Chadwick, O., Rutter, M., Brown, E., Shaffer, D., & Traub, M. (1981). A prospective study of children with head injuries. II Cognitive sequelae. *Psychological Medicine, 11,* 49–61.

Childers, J. S., Durham, T. W., Bolen, L. M., & Taylor, L. H. (1985). A predictive validity study of the Kaufman Assessment Battery for Children with the California Achievement Test. *Psychology in the Schools, 22,* 29–33.

Christensen, A. L. (1979). *Luria's neuropsychological investigation.* Copenhagen: Munksgaard.

Clark, R. (1984, April). *Research with the K-ABC and an Appalachian sample.* Paper presented at the meeting of the National Association of School Psychologists, Philadelphia.

Cohen, J. (1959). The factorial structure of the WISC at ages 7-6, 10-6, and 13-6. *Journal of Consulting Psychology, 23,* 285–299.

Cohen, M., Becker, M., & Campbell, R. (1990). Relationships among four methods of assessment of children with attention deficit-hyperactivity disorder. *Journal of School Psychology, 28,* 189–202.

Code of fair testing practices in education (1988). Washington, DC: Joint Committee on Testing Practices.

Cole, M., Gay, J., Glick, J., & Sharp, D. W. (1971). *The cultural context of learning and thinking.* New York: Basic Books.

Coleman, J. S., Campbell, E. Q., Hobson, C. J., McPartland, J., Mood, A. M., Winfield, F. D., & Work, R. L. (1966). *Equality of educational opportunity.* Washington, DC: U.S. Office of Education, OE 38001.

Coles, C. D., Brown, R. T., Smith, I. E., Platzman, K. A., Erickson, S., & Falek, A. (in press). Effects of prenatal alcohol exposure at school age: Physical and cognitive development. *Neurotoxicology and Teratology.*

Conoley, J. C. (1990). Review of the K-ABC: Reflecting the unobservable. *Journal of Psychoeducational Assessment, 8,* 369–375.

Conrad, R., & Weiskrantz, B. C. (1981). On the cognitive ability of deaf children with deaf parents. *American Annals of the Deaf, 126,* 995–1003.

Cox, T. (1983). Cumulative deficit in culturally disadvantaged children. *British Journal of Educational Psychology, 53,* 317–326.

Cronbach, L. J. (1975). Five decades of public controversy over mental testing. *American Psychologist, 30,* 1–14.

Curtis, M. E., & Glaser, R. (1984). Intelligence testing, cognition, and instruction. *International Journal of Psychology, 19,* 475–497.

Cummins, J., & Das, J. P. (1977). Cognitive processing and reading difficulties: A framework for research. *Alberta Journal of Educational Research, 23,* 245–256.

Cummins, J. P., & Das, J. P. (1980). Cognitive processing, academic achievement, and WISC-R performance in EMR children. *Journal of Consulting and Clinical Psychology, 48,* 777–779.

D'Amato, R. C., Gray, J. W., & Dean, R. S. (1988). A

comparison between intelligence and neuropsychological functioning. *Journal of School Psychology, 26,* 283–292.

Damarin, F. (1978). [Review of Bayley Scales of Infant Development]. *Eighth Mental Measurements Yearbook.* Highland Park, NJ: Gryphon Press.

Davis, F. B. (1964). *Educational measurements and their interpretation.* Belmont, CA: Wadsworth.

Das, J. P. (1984a). Review of the Kaufman Assessment Battery for Children [K-ABC]. *Journal of Psychoeducational Assessment, 2,* 83–88.

Das, J. P. (1984b). Simultaneous and successive processes and K-ABC. *Journal of Special Education, 18,* 229–238.

Das, J. P., Kirby, J. R., & Jarman, R. F. (1975). Simultaneous and successive synthesis: An alternative model for cognitive abilities. *Psychological Bulletin, 82,* 87–103.

Das, J. P., Kirby, J. R., & Jarman, R. F. (1979a). *Sequential and simultaneous cognitive processes.* New York: Academic Press.

Das, J. P., Kirby, J. R., & Jarman, R. F. (1979b). *Simultaneous and successive cognitive processes.* New York: Academic Press.

Das, J. P., & Naglieri, J. A. (1987). Construct and criterion-related validity of planning, simultaneous, and successive cognitive processing tasks. *Journal of Psychoeducational Assessment, 4,* 353–363.

Dasen, P. R. (1984). The cross-cultural study of intelligence: Piaget and the Baoule. *International Journal of Psychology, 19,* 407–434.

Dean, R. S. (1984). Functional lateralization of the brain. *Journal of Special Education, 8,* 239–256.

Dean, R. S., & Gray, J. W. (1990). Traditional approaches to neuropsychological assessment. Psychological assessment. In C. R. Reynolds & R. W. Kamphaus (Eds.), *Handbook of psychological and educational assessment of children* (pp. 371–388). New York: Guilford.

DeFries, J. C., Vandenberg, S. G., McClearn, G. E., Kuse, A. R., Wilson, J. R., Ashton, G. C., & Johnson, R. C. (1974). Near identity of cognitive structure in two ethnic groups. *Science, 183,* 338–339.

Delaney, E. A., & Hopkins, T. F. (1987). *The Stanford-Binet Intelligence Scale Fourth Edition: Examiner's handbook.* Chicago: Riverside.

Denckla, M. B. (1979). Childhood learning disabilities. In K. M. Heilman & E. Valenstein (Eds.), *Clinical neuropsychology.* New York: Oxford University Press.

Dennis, M. (1985). Intelligence after early brain injury I: Predicting IQ scores from medical variables. *Journal of Clinical and Experimental Neuropsychology, 7(5),* 526–554.

Dennis, M. (1985). Intelligence after early brain injury II: Predicting IQ scores from medical variables. *Journal of Clinical and Experimental Neuropsychology, 7(5),* 555–576.

Destefano, L., & Thompson, D. S. (1990). Adaptive behavior: The construct and its measurement. In C. R. Reynolds & R. W. Kamphaus (Eds.), *Handbook of psychological and educational assessment of children: Vol. 2. Personality, behavior, and context.* New York: Guilford.

Detterman, D. K. (1985). Review of Wechsler Intelligence Scale of Children-Revised. In J. V. Mitchell (Ed.), *The ninth mental measurement yearbook* (vol. 2) (pp. 1715–1716). Lincoln, NE: Buros Institute of Mental Measurements.

Detterman, D. K. (1986). Human intelligence is a complex system of separate processes. In R. J. Sternberg & D. K. Detterman (Eds.), *What is intelligence? Contemporary viewpoints on its nature and definition.* Norwood, NJ: Ablex.

Detterman, D. K. (1987). Theoretical notions of intelligence and mental retardation. *American Journal of Mental Deficiencies, 92,* 2–11.

Diana v. State Board of Education, C. A. No. C-70-37 (N. D. Cal. 1970).

Dietzen, S. R. (1986). Hemispheric specialization for verbal sequential and non-verbal simultaneous information processing styles of low income 3 to 5 year olds. Doctoral dissertation, Washington State University.

Dirks, J., Bushkuhl, J., & Marzano, P. (1983). Parents' reactions to finding out that their children have average or above average IQ scores. *Journal of School Psychology, 21,* 23–30.

Dixon, R. A., Kramer, D. A., & Baltes, P. B. (1985). Intelligence: A life-span developmental perspective. In B. B. Wolman (Ed.), *Handbook of intelligence: Theories, measurements, and applications* (pp. 301–350). New York: Wiley.

Doll, E. A. (1953). *Measurement of social competence.* Circle Pines, MN: American Guidance Service.

Doppelt, J. E., & Kaufman, A. S. (1977). Estimation of the differences between WISC-R and WISC IQs. *Educational and Psychological Measurement, 37,* 417–424.

Douglas, V. I. (1983). Attentional and cognitive problems. In M. Rutter (Eds.), *Developmental neuropsychiatry* (pp. 280–329). New York: Guilford.

Douglas, V. I., & Peters, K. G. (1979). Toward a clearer definition of the attentional deficit of hyperactive children. In G. A. Hale & M. Lewis (Eds.), *Attention and the development of cognitive skills* (pp. 173–247). New York: Plenum.

Downs, M. P. (1976). The handicap of deafness. In J. L. Northern (Ed.), *Hearing disorders* (pp. 195–206). Boston: Little, Brown.

Duara, R., Apicella, A., Smith, D. W., Chang, J. Y., Barker, W., & Yoshii, D. W. (1988). Anatomical definition in PET using superimposed MR images. *Journal of Mind and Behavior, 9,* 299–310.

Dubois, P. H. (1970). *A history of psychological testing.* Boston: Allyn and Bacon.

Dunn, L. M. (1959). *Peabody Picture Vocabulary Test.* Circle Pines, MN: American Guidance Service.

Dunn, L. M., & Dunn, L. (1981). *Peabody Picture Vocabulary Test-Revised.* Circle Pines, MN: American Guidance Service.

Ebel, R. L. (1979). Intelligence, a skeptical view. *Journal of Research and Development in Education, 12,* 14–21.

Education for All Handicapped Children Act of 1975 (Public Law 94-142). 34 C.F.R. 300 (1975). APA, p. 115.

Elliott, C. D., Murray, D. J., & Pearson, L. S. (1979). *British Ability Scales.* Windsor, England: National Foundation for Educational Research.

Elliott, C. D. (1990a). *Differential ability scales: Introductory and technical handbook.* New York: The Psychological Corporation.

Elliott, C. D. (1990b). The nature and structure of children's abilities: Evidence from the Differential Ability Scales. *Journal of Psychoeducational Assessment, 8,* 376–390.

Elliott, C. D., Daniel, M. H., & Guiton, G. W. (1990). Preschool cognitive assessment with the Differential Ability Scales. In B. A. Bracken (Ed.), *The psychoeducational assessment of preschool children.* Needham Heights, MA: Allyn and Bacon.

Elliott, R. (1987). *Litigating intelligence: IQ tests, special education, and social science in the courtroom.* Dover, MA: Auburn House.

Epps, E. G. (1974). Situational effects in testing. In L. P. Miller (Ed.), *The testing of black students* (pp. 41–51). Englewood Cliffs, NJ: Prentice-Hall.

Eysenck, H. J. (1988). The concept of 'intelligence': Useful or useless? *Intelligence, 12,* 1–16.

Eysenck, H. J., & Kamin, L. (1981). *The intelligence controversy.* New York: Wiley.

Fagan, J. F. (1984). The intelligent infant: Theoretical implications. *Intelligence, 8,* 1–9.

Fagan, J. F., III (1984). The relationship of novelty preferences during infancy to later intelligence and later recognition memory. *Intelligence, 8,* 339–346.

Fagan, J. F., Singer, L. T., Montie, J. E., et al. (1986). Selective screening device for the early detection of normal or delayed cognitive development in infants at risk for later mental retardation. *Pediatrics, 78,* 1021–1026.

Felton, R. H., Wood, F. B., Brown, I. S., Campbell, S. K., & Harter, R. (1987). Separate verbal memory and naming deficits in attention deficit disorder and reading disability. *Brain and Language, 31,* 171–184.

Feuerstein, R. (1979). *The dynamic assessment of retarded persons.* Baltimore, MD: University Park Press.

Feuerstein, R., Rand, Y., & Hoffman, M. B. (1979). *The dynamic assessment of retarded performers: The learning potential assessment device, theory, instruments, and techniques.* Baltimore, MD: University Park Press.

Field, D., Schaie, K. W., & Leino, E. Z. (1988). Continuity in intellectual functioning: The role of self-reported health. *Psychology and Aging, 3,* 385–392.

Figueroa, R. A. (1989, May). Using interpreters in assessments. *National Association of School Psychologists Communique,* p. 19.

Figueroa, R. A. (1990). Assessment of linguistic minority group children. In C. R. Reynolds & R. W. Kamphaus (Eds.), *Handbook of psychological and educational assessment of children: Vol. 1. Intelligence and achievement.* New York: Guilford.

Figueroa, R. A., & Sassenrath, J. M. (1989). A longitudinal study of the predictive validity of the System of Multicultural Pluralistic Assessment (SOMPA). *Psychology in the Schools, 26,* 1–19.

Filipek, P. A., Kennedy, D. N., Caviness, V. S., Rossnick, S. L., Spraggins, T. A., & Starewicz, P. M. (1989). Magnetic resonance imaging-based brain morphometry: Development and application to normal subjects. *Annals of Neurology, 25,* 61–67.

Finch, A. J., Jr., Blount, R. L., Saylor, C. F., Wolfe, V. V., Pallmeyer, T. P., McIntosh, J. A., Griffin, J. M., & Careh, D. J. (1988). Intelligence and emotional/behavioral factors as correlates of achievement in child psychiatric inpatients. *Psychological Reports, 63,* 163–170.

Finegan, J. K., Zucher, K. J., Bradley, S. J., & Doering, R. W. (1982). Pattern of intellectual functioning and spatial ability in boys with gender identity disorder. *Canadian Journal Psychiatry, 27,* 135–139.

Fish, J. M. (1988). Reinforcement in testing: Research with children and adolescents. *Professional School Psychology, 3,* 203–218.

Fish, J. M. (1990). IQ terminology: Modification of current schemes. *Journal of Psychoeducational Assessment, 8,* 527–530.

Flaugher, R. L. (1974). Some points of confusion in discussing the testing of black students. In L. P. Miller (Ed.), *The testing of black students: A symposium.* New York: Prentice-Hall.

Flavell, J. H., & Wellman, H. M. (1977). Metamemory. In R. V. Kail, Jr. & J. W. Hagen (Eds.), *Perspectives on the development of memory and cognition.* Hillsdale, NJ: Erlbaum.

Flynn, J. R. (1984). The mean IQ of Americans: Massive gains 1932 to 1978. *Psychological Bulletin, 95,* 29–51.

Flynn, J. R. (1985). Wechsler intelligence tests: Do we really have a criterion of mental retardation? *American Journal of Mental Deficiency, 90,* 236–244.

Flynn, J. R. (1987). Massive IQ gains in 14 nations: What IQ tests really measure. *Psychological Bulletin, 101,* 171–191.

Fourqurean, J. M. (1987). A K-ABC and WISC-R comparison for Latino learning-disabled children of limited English proficiency. *Journal of School Psychology, 25,* 15–21.

Frederiksen, N. (1986). Toward a broader conception of human intelligence. *American Psychologist, 41*, 445–452.

Freeman, B. J., Lucas, J. C., Forness, S. R., & Ritvo, E. R. (1985). Cognition processing of high-functioning autistic children: Comparing the K-ABC and the WISC-R. *Journal of Psychoeducational Assessment, 3*, 357–362.

French, J. L. (1964). *Pictorial Test of Intelligence.* Boston: Houghton-Mifflin.

French, J. L., & Hale, R. L. (1990). A history of the development of psychological and educational testing. In C. R. Reynolds & R. W. Kamphaus (Eds.), *Handbook of psychological and educational assessment of children* (pp. 3–28). New York: Guilford.

Frick, P. J., Kamphaus, R. W., Lahey, B. B., Loeber, R., Christ, M. G., Hart, E. L., & Tannenbaum, L. E. (1991). Academic underachievement and the disruptive behavior disorders. *Journal of Consulting and Clinical Psychology, 59*, 289–294.

Fuller, G. B., & Goh, D. S. (1981). Intelligence, achievement, and visual-motor performance among learning disabled and emotionally impaired children. *Psychology in the Schools, 18*, 261–268.

Gaddes, W. H. (1981). An examination of the validity of neuropsychological knowledge in educational diagnosis and remediation. In G. W. Hynd & J. E. Obrzut (Eds.), *Neuropsychological assessment of the school-aged child: Issues and procedures.* New York: Grune & Stratton.

Galton, F. (1883). *Inquiries into human faculty and its development.* London: Macmillan.

Galton, F. (1952). *Hereditary genius: An inquiry into its laws and consequences.* New York: Horizon Press.

Galton, F. H. (1978). *Hereditary genius.* New York: St. Martin's. (Originally published in 1869).

Garrett, H. E. (1961). A developmental theory of intelligence. In J. J. Jenkins & D. G. Paterson (Eds.), *Studies in individual differences: The search for intelligence* (pp. 572–581). New York: Appleton-Century-Crofts. (Reprinted from *The American Psychologist*, 1946, *1*, 372–378.

Gazzaniga, M. S. (1970). *The bisected brain.* New York: Appleton-Century-Crofts, 1970.

Gazzaniga, M. S. (1974). Cerebral dominance viewed as a decision system. In S. Dimond & J. Beaumont (Eds.), *Hemispheric functions in the human brain.* London: Halstead Press.

Gazzaniga, M. S. (1975). Recent research on hemispheric lateralization of the human brain: Review of the split brain. *UCLA Educator, 17*, 9–12.

Gellis, S., & Kagan, B. (1976). *Current pediatric therapy,* Philadelphia: Saunders.

Gerken, K. C. (1978). Performance of Mexican American children on intelligence tests. *Exceptional Children, 44*, 438–443.

Gibbins, S., Ulissi, S. M., & Brice, P. (in press). The use of the Kaufman Assessment Battery for Children with the hearing impaired. *American Annals of the Deaf.*

Gibbs, J. T., & Huang, L. N. (1989). *Children of color.* San Francisco: Jossey-Bass.

Glasser, A. J., & Zimmerman, I. L. (1967). *Clinical interpretation of the Wechsler Intelligence Scale for Children.* New York: Grune & Stratton.

Glaub, V. E., & Kamphaus, R. W. (1991). Construction of a nonverbal adaptation of the Standford-Binet: Fourth Edition. *Educational and Psychological Measurement, 51*, 231–241.

Glutting, J. J. (1986). Potthoff bias analysis of K-ABC MPC and non-verbal scale IQ's among Anglo, black, and Puerto Rican kindergarten children. *Professional School Psychology, 4*, 225–234.

Glutting, J. J., & Kaplan, D. (1990). Stanford-Binet Intelligence Scale: Fourth Edition: Making the case for reasonable interpretations. In C. R. Reynolds & R. W. Kamphaus (Eds.), *Handbook of psychological and educational assessment of children.* New York: Guilford.

Glutting, J. J., & McDermott, P. A. (1990). Principles and problems in learning potential. In C. R. Reynolds & R. W. Kamphaus (Eds.), *Handbook of psychological and educational assessment of children.* New York: Guilford.

Glutting, J. J., Oakland, T., & McDermott, P. A. (1989). Observing child behavior during testing: Constructs, validity, and situational generality. *Journal of School Psychology, 27*, 155–164.

Goddard, H. H. (1912). Echelle metrique de l'intelligence de Binet-Simon. *L'année psychologique, 18*, 288–326.

Golden, C. J. (1981). The Luria-Nebraska Children's Battery: Theory and initial formulation. In G. Hynd & S. Obrzut (Eds.), *Neuropsychological assessment and the school age child: Issues and procedures.* New York: Grune & Stratton.

Goldman, J., Stein, C. L., & Querry, S. (1983). *Psychological methods of child assessment.* New York: Brunner/Mazel.

Goldstein, D., Parell, G. G., & Sanfilippo-Cohn, S. (1985). Depression and achievement in subgroups of children with learning disabilities. *Journal of Allied Development Psychology, 6*, 263–275.

Goldstein, S., & Goldstein, M. (1990). *Managing attention disorders in children: A guide for practitioners.* New York: Wiley.

Goodenough, F. L. (1926). *Measurement of intelligence by drawings.* New York: Harcourt Brace Jovanovich.

Goodman, J. F. (1990). Infant intelligence: Do we, can we, should we assess it? In C. R. Reynolds & R. W. Kamphaus (Eds.), *Handbook of psychological and educational assessment of children* (pp. 183–208). New York: Guilford.

Gordon, M., Thomason, D., & Cooper, S. (1990). To what extent does attention affect K-ABC scores? *Psychology in the Schools, 27*, 144–147.

Gorsuch, R. L. (1988). *Factor analysis* (3rd ed.). Hillsdale, NJ: Erlbaum.

Gottfried, A. W. (1973). Intellectual consequences of perinatal anoxia. *Psychological Bulletin, 80*, 231–242.

Gottling, S. (1985). Comparison of the reliability of the Goodenough-Harris Draw-a-Man Test with the Naglieri Draw-a-Person: A Quantitative System. Unpublished master's thesis, Ohio State University.

Grace, W. C. (1986). Equivalence of the WISC-R and WAIS-R in delinquent males. *Journal of Psychoeducational Assessment, 4*, 155–162.

Grady, J. (1980). Opinion. *PASE v. Hannon. Federal Supplement 506*, 831–883.

Greene, A. C., Sapp. G. L., & Chisson, B. (1990). Validation of the Stanford-Binet Intelligence Scale Fourth Edition with exceptional black male students. *Psychology in the Schools, 27*(1), 35–41.

Gresham, F. M., & Reschly, D. J. (1986). Social skills deficits and low peer acceptance of mainstreamed learning disabled children. *Learning Disability Quarterly, 9*, 23–31.

Gribbin, K., Schaie, K. W., & Parham, I. A. (1975). *Cognitive complexity and maintenance of intellectual abilites.* Paper presented at the Tenth International Congress of Gerontology, Jerusalem, Israel.

Griggs v. Duke Power Co., 401 U. S. 424 (1971).

Grossman, H. J. (1983). *Classification in mental retardation.* Washington, DC: American Association of Mental Deficiency.

Guidubaldi, J., & Perry, J. D. (1984). Concurrent and predictive validity of the Battelle Development Inventory at the first grade level. *Educational and Psychological Measurement, 44*, 977–985.

Guilford, J. P. (1967). *The nature of human intelligence.* New York: McGraw-Hill.

Guilford, J. P. (1979). Intelligence isn't what it used to be: What to do about it. *Journal of Research and Development in Education, 12*(2), 33–46.

Guilford, J. P. (1985). The structure-of-intellect model. In B. B. Wolman (Ed.), *Handbook of intelligence* (pp. 225–266). New York: Wiley.

Gunderson, V. M., Grant-Webster, K. S., & Fagan, J. F., III. (1987). Visual recognition memory in high- and low-risk infant pigtailed macaques *(Macaca nemestrina). Developmental Psychology, 23*, 671–675.

Gunderson, V. M., Grant-Webster, K. S., & Sackett, G. P. (1989). Deficits in visual recognition in low birth weight infant pigtailed monkeys *(Macaca nemestrina). Child Development, 60*, 119–127.

Gutkin, T. B. (1978). Some useful statistics for the interpretation of the WISC-R. *Journal of Consulting and Clinical Psychology, 46*, 1561–1563.

Gutkin, T. B. (1979). The WISC-R verbal comprehension, perceptual organization, and freedom from distractibility deviation quotients: Data for practitioners. *Psychology in the Schools, 16*, 359–360.

Gutkin, T. B. (1982). WISC-R deviation quotients vs. traditional IQs: An examination of the standardization sample and some implications for scores interpretation. *Journal of Clinical Psychology, 38*, 179–182.

Gutkin, T. B., & Reynolds, C. R. (1980). Factorial similarity of the WISC-R for Anglos and Chicanos referred for psychological services. *Journal of School Psychology, 18*, 34–39.

Gutkin, T. B., & Reynolds, C. R. (1981). Factorial similarity of the WISC-R for white and black children from the standardization sample. *Journal of Educational Psychology, 73*, 227–231.

Gutterman, J. E., Ward, M., & Genshaft, J. (1985). Correlations of scores of low vision children on the Perkins-Binet Tests of Intelligence for the Blind, the WISC-R and the WRAT. *Journal of Visual Impairment & Blindness, 79*, 55–58.

Gyurke, J. S. (1991). The assessment of preschool children with the Wechsler Preschool Primary Scale of Intelligence-Revised. In B. A. Bracken (Ed.), *The psychoeducational assessment of preschool children* (2nd ed.). Needham Heights, MA: Allyn and Bacon.

Haddad, F. A. (1986). Concurrent validity of the test of nonverbal intelligence with learning disabled children. *Psychology in the Schools, 23*, 361–364.

Haensly, P. A., & Torrance, E. P. (1990). Assessment of creativity in children and adolescents. In C. R. Reynolds & R. W. Kamphaus (Eds.), *Handbook of psychological and educational assessment.* New York: Guilford.

Hales, R. L. (1983). Intellectual assessment. In M. Hersen, A. Kazdin, & A. Bellack (Eds.), *The clinical psychology handbook* (pp. 345–376). New York: Pergamon Press.

Hales, R. L., & Landino, S. A. (1981). Utility of WISC-R subtest analysis in discriminating among groups of conduct-problem, withdrawn, mixed and nonproblem boys. *Journal of Consulting and Clinical Psychology, 49*, 91–95.

Halstead, W. C. (1947). *Brain and intelligence: A quantitative study of the frontal lobes.* Chicago: University of Chicago Press.

Ham, S. J. (1985). *A validity study of recent intelligence tests on a deaf population.* (Available from Sandra J. Ham, School Psychologist, North Dakota School for the Deaf, Devils Lake, ND 58301.)

Hammill, D. D. (1990). On defining learning disabilities: An emerging consensus. *Journal of Learning Disabilities, 23*, 74–84.

Hanson, R. A. (1975). Consistency and stability of home environmental measures related to IQ. *Child Development, 46,* 470–480.

Harnad, S., Doty, R. W., Goldstein, L., Jaynes, J., & Krauthamer, G. (Eds.) (1977). *Lateralization in the nervous system.* New York: Academic Press.

Harnqvist, K. (1968). Relative changes in intelligence from 13 to 18. *Scandinavian Journal of Psychology, 9,* 50–64.

Harrison, P. L., & Kamphaus, R. W. (1984, April). *Comparison between the K-ABC and Vineland Adaptive Behavior Scales.* Paper presented at the meeting of the National Association of School Psychologists, Philadelphia.

Hartlage, L. C., & Hartlage, P. L. (1989). Neuropsychological aspects of epilepsy: Introduction and overview. In C. R. Reynolds & E. Fletcher-Janzen (Eds.), *Handbook of clinical child neuropsychology.* New York: Plenum.

Hartlage, L. C., & Telzrow, C. F. (1983). The neuropsychological basis of educational intervention. *Journal of Learning Disabilities, 16,* 521–528.

Hartwig, S. S., Sapp, G. L., & Clayton, G. A. (1987). Comparison of the Stanford-Binet Intelligence Scale: Form L-M and the Stanford-Binet Intelligence Scale Fourth Edition. *Psychological Reports, 60,* 1215–1218.

Harvey, V. S. (1989, March). Eschew obfuscation: Support of clear writing. *Communique,* p. 12.

Hasegawa, C. (1989). The unmentioned minority. In C. J. Maker & S. W. Schiever (Eds.), *Defensive programs for cultural and ethnic minorities* (vol. 2). Austin, TX: Pro-Ed.

Haskins, R. (1989). Beyond metaphor: The efficacy of early childhood education. *American Psychologist, 44,* 274–282.

Haynes, J. P., & Bensch, M. (1981). The P > V sign on the WISC-R and recidivism in delinquents. *Journal of Consulting and Clinical Psychology, 49,* 480–481.

Hays, J. R., & Smith, A. L. (1980). Comparison of the WISC-R and culture-fair intelligence tests for three ethnic groups of juvenile delinquents. *Psychological Reports, 46,* 931–934.

Haywood, H. C. (1986). A transactional approach to intellectual and cognitive development. Prepared for presentation at Université de Provence, Aix-en-Provence, France, Conference on Cognitive Development.

Haywood, H. C., & Switzky, H. N. (1986). The malleability of intelligence: Cognitive processes as a function of polygenic-experiential interaction. *School Psychology Review, 15,* 245–255.

Hayden, D. C., Furlong, M. J., & Linnemeyer, S. (1988). A comparison of the Kaufman Assessment Battery for Children and the Stanford-Binet IV for the assessment of gifted children. *Psychology in the Schools, 22,* 133–141.

Hebb, D. O. (1949). *The organization of behavior.* New York: Wiley.

Heber, R. (1961). A manual on terminology and classification in mental retardation (rev. ed.). *American Journal of Mental Deficiency,* Monograph (Supp. 64).

Herskowitz, J., & Rosman, N. P. (1982). *Pediatrics, neurology, and psychiatry—common ground.* New York: Macmillan.

Hertzog, C., Schaie, K. W., & Gribbin, K. (1978). Cardiovascular disease and changes in intellectual functioning from middle to old age. *Journal of Gerontology, 33,* 872–883.

Hickman, J. A., & Stark, K. D. (1987, April). *Relationship between cognitive impulsivity and information processing abilities in children: Implications for training programs.* Paper presented at the meeting of the National Association of School Psychologists, New Orleans, LA.

Hinshelwood, J. (1986). A case of dyslexia: A peculiar form of word blindness. *Lancet, 2,* 1451.

Hiskey, M. S. (1966). *Hiskey-Nebraska test of learning aptitude,* Lincoln, NE: Union College Press.

Hofmann, R. (May, 1988). Comparability of Binet (4th) Full Scale and abbreviated IQs. *National Association of School Psychologists: Communique, 27.*

Hobson v. Hansen, 269 F. Supp. 401 (D. C. 1967).

Hollenbeck, G. P., & Kaufman, A. S. (1973). Factor analysis of the Wechsler Preschool and Primary Scale of Intelligence (WPPSI). *Journal of Clinical Psychology, 29,* 41–45.

Honzik, M. P., Macfarlane, J. W., & Allen, L. (1948). The stability of mental test performance between two and eighteen years. *Journal of Experimental Psychology, 17,* 309–324.

Hopkins, K. D., & Glass, G. V. (1978). *Basic statistics for the behavioral sciences.* Englewood Cliffs, NJ: Prentice-Hall.

Hooper, S. R., & Hynd, G. W. (1985). Differential diagnosis of subtypes of developmental dyslexia with the Kaufman Assessment Battery for Children (K-ABC). *Journal of Clinical child Psychology, 14,* 145–152.

Horn, J. L. (1979). The rise and fall of human abilities. *Journal of Research amd Development in Education, 12*(2), 59–78.

Horney, K. (1939). *New ways in psychoanalysis.* New York: Norton.

Horowitz, F. D., & O'Brien, M. (1989). A reflective essay on the state of our knowledge and the challenges before us. *American Psychologist, 44,* 441–445.

Hubble, L. M., & Groff, M. (1981). Magnitude and direction of WISC-R Verbal-Performance IQ discrepancies among adjudicated male delinquents. *Journal of Youth and Adolescence, 10,* 179–184.

Humphreys, L. G., & Parsons, C. K. (1979). Piagetian tasks measure intelligence and intelligence tests assess cognitive development: A reanalysis. *Intelligence, 3,* 369–382.

Hunt, J. M. (1961). *Intelligence and experience.* New York: Ronald Press.

Hunter, J. E., & Schmidt, F. L. (1976). Critical analysis of the statistical and ethical implications of various definitions of test bias. *Psychological Bulletin, 83,* 1053–1071.

Hunter, J. E., Schmidt, F. L., & Rauschenberger, J. (1984). Methodological, statistical, and ethical issues in the study of bias in psychological tests. In C. R. Reynolds & R. T. Brown (Eds.)., *Perspectives on bias in mental testing.* New York: Plenum.

Hutchens, T., & Thomas, M. G. (1990). The effects of vocal intonation in digit span testing. *Journal of Psychoeducational Assessment, 8,* 150–154.

Hynd, G. W. (1988). *Neuropsychological assessment in clinical child psychology.* Newbury Park, CA: Sage.

Hynd, G. W., & Semrud-Clikeman, M. (1989). Dyslexia and brain morphology. *Psychological Bulletin, 106,* 447–482.

Hynd, G. W., & Semrud-Clikeman, M. (1990). Neuropsychological assessment: Introduction and overview. In A. S. Kaufman (Ed.), *Assessing adolescent and adult IQ.* Needham Heights, MA: Allyn and Bacon, in press.

Hynd, G. W., Semrud-Clikeman, M., Lorys, A. R., Novey, E. S., & Eliopulos, D. (1990). Brain morphology in developmental dyslexia and attention deficit disorder/hyperactivity. *Archives of Neurology,* in press.

Hynd, G. W., & Willis, W. G. (1985). Neurological foundations of intelligence. In B. B. Wolman (Ed.), *Handbook of intelligence* (pp. 119–158). New York: Wiley.

Hynd, G. W., & Willis, W. G. (1988). *Pediatric neuropsychology.* Orlando, FL: Grune & Stratton.

Inclan, J. E., & Herron, D. G. (1989). Puerto Rican adolescents. In G. T. Gibbs & L. N. Huang (Eds.), *Children of color.* San Francisco: Jossey-Bass.

Ingram, G., & Hakari, L. (1985). Validity of the Woodcock-Johnson Test of Cognitive Ability for gifted children: A comparison with the WISC-R. *Journal for the Education of the Gifted, 9,* 11–23.

Ipsen, S. M., McMillan, J. H., & Fallen, N. H. (1983). An investigation of the reported discrepancy between the Woodcock-Johnson Tests of Cognitive Ability and the Wechsler Intelligence Scale for Children-Revised. *Diagnostique, 9,* 32–44.

Jacklin, C. N. (1989). Female and male: Issues of gender. *American Psychologist, 44,* 127–133.

Jacob, S., & Brantley, J. C. (1987). Ethical-legal problems with computer use and suggestions for best practices: A national survey. *School Psychology Review, 16,* 69–77.

Jastrow, J. (1901). Some currents and undercurrents in psychology. *Psychological Review, 8,* 1–26.

Jenkins, J. J., & Paterson, D. G. (Eds.) (1961). *Studies in individual differences.* New York: Appleton-Century-Crofts.

Jensen, A. R. (1969). How much can we boost IQ and scholastic achievement? *Harvard Educational Review, 39,* 1–123.

Jensen, A. R. (1974). Cumulative deficit: A testable hypothesis. *Developmental Psychology, 10,* 996–1019.

Jensen, A. R. (1976). Test bias and construct validity. *Phi Delta Kappan, 58,* 340–346.

Jensen, A. R. (1977). Cumulative deficit in IQ of blacks in the rural south. *Developmental Psychology, 13,* 184–191.

Jensen, A. R. (1980). *Bias in mental testing.* New York: The Free Press.

Jensen, A. R. (1982). Reaction time and psychometric g. In R. J. Sternberg (Ed.), *A model for intelligence* (pp. 93–132). Heidelberg, Germany: Springer-Verlag.

Jensen, A. R. (1984). The black-white difference on the K-ABC: Implications for future tests. *Journal of Special Education, 18,* 377–408.

Jensen, A. R. (1986). g: Artifact or reality. *Journal of Vocational Behavior, 29,* 301–331.

Jensen, A. R. (1987). Intelligence as a fact of nature. *Zeitschrift fur Padagogische Psychologie, 3,* 157–169.

Joreskog, K. G., & Sorbom, D. (1984). *LISREL VI: Analysis of linear structural relaitonships by the method of maximum likelihood: User's guide.* Mooresville, IN: Scientific Software.

Joreskog, K. G., & Sorbom, D. (1987). *LISREL 6.13: User's reference guide.* Chicago: Scientific Software.

Juliano, J. M., Haddad, F. A., & Carroll, J. L. (1988). Three year stability of the WISC-R factor scores for black and white, female and male children classified as learning disabled. *Journal of School Psychology, 26,* 317–325.

Kagan, J., & Klein, R. E. (1973). Cross-cultural perspectives on early development. *American Psychologist, 28,* 947–961.

Kagan, J., & Salkind, N. J. (1965). *Matching Familiar Figures Test.* (Available from Jerome Kagan, Harvard University, 33 Kirkland Street, 1510 William James Hall, Cambridge, MA 02138.)

Kagan, V. E. (1981). Nonprocess autism in children: A comparative etiopathogenic study. *Soviet Neurology and Psychiatry, 14,* 25–30.

Kamin, L. J. (1974). *The science and politics of IQ.* Potomac, MD: Erlbaum.

Kamphaus, R. W. (1983, August). *The relationship of the Kaufman Assessment Battery for Children (K-ABC) to diagnostic measures of academic achievement.* Paper presented at the meeting of the American Psychological Association, Anaheim, CA.

Kamphaus, R. W. (1987). Conceptual and psychometric issues in the assessment of adaptive behavior. *Journal of Special Education, 21,* 27–36.

Kamphaus, R. W. (1990). K-ABC theory in historical and current contexts. Journal of Psychoeducational Assessment, 8, 356–368.

Kamphaus, R. W. (1991, October). Multicultural expertise. *Child Assessment News*, pp. 1, 8–10.

Kamphaus, R. W., Dresden, J., & Kaufman, A. S. (in press). Clinical and psychometric considerations in the assessment of preschool children. In D. J. Willis & J. L. Culbertson (Eds.), *Testing young children*. Austin, TX: Pro Ed. Allyn and Bacon.

Kamphaus, R. W., & Kaufman, A. S. (1986). Factor analysis of the Kaufman Assessment Battery for Children (K-ABC) for separate groups of boys and girls. *Journal of Clinical Child Psychology, 3*, 210–213.

Kamphaus, R. W., Kaufman, A. S., & Kaufman, N. L. (1982, August). *A cross-validation study of sequential-simultaneous processing at 2 ½ to 12 ½ using the Kaufman Assessment Battery for Children*. Paper presented at the meeting of the American Psychological Association, Washington, DC.

Kamphaus, R. W., & Lozano, R. (1981). Developing local norms for individually administered tests. *School Psychology Review, 13*, 491–498.

Kamphaus, R. W., & Pleiss, K. (1991). Draw-a-person techniques: Tests in search of a construct. *Journal of School Psychology, 29*, 395–401.

Kamphaus, R. W., & Reynolds, C. R. (1984). Development and structure of the Kaufman Assessment Battery for Children. *Journal of Special Education, 18* (3), 213–228.

Kamphaus, R. W., & Reynolds, C. R. (1987). *Clinical and research applications of the K-ABC*. Circle Pines, MN: American Guidance Service.

Kamphaus, R. W., & Stanton, H. (1988, August). *Reliability of the parent rating scale of the Behavior Assessment System for Children (BASC)*. Paper presented at the meeting of the American Psychological Association, Atlanta, GA.

Kaplan, R. J., & Klanderman, J. W. (1984, April). *Neuropsychological profile of T.M.H. youngsters assessed with the K-ABC*. Paper presented at the meeting of the National Association of School Psychologists, Philadelphia.

Karnes, F. A., Edwards, R. P., & McCallum, R. S. (1986). Normative achievement assessment of gifted children: Comparing the K-ABC, WRAT, and CAT. *Psychology in the Schools, 23*, 361–364.

Kaufman, A. S. (May, 1972). *Restriction of range: Questions and answers* (Test Service Bulletin No. 59). San Antonio, TX: The Psychological Corporation.

Kaufman, A. S. (1975a). Factor analysis of the WISC-R at 11 age levels between 6 ½ and 16 ½ years. *Journal of Consulting and Clinical Psychology, 43*, 135–147.

Kaufman, A. S. (1975b). Factor structure of the McCarthy Scales at five age levels between 2-½ and 8-½. *Educational and Psychological Measurement, 35*, 641–656.

Kaufman, A. S. (1976a). A four-test short form of the WISC-R. *Contemporary Educational Psychology, 1*, 180–196.

Kaufman, A. S. (1976b). Verbal-Performance IQ discrepancies on the WISC-R. *Journal of Consulting and Clinical Psychology, 44*, 739–744.

Kaufman, A. S. (1977). A McCarthy short form for rapid screening of preschool, kindergarten, and first-grade children. *Contemporary Educational Psychology, 2*, 149–157.

Kaufman, A. S. (1978). The importance of basic concepts in the individual assessment of preschool children. *Journal of School Psychology, 16*, 207–211.

Kaufman, A. S. (1979a). Cerebral specialization and intelligence testing. *Journal of Research and Development in Education, 12*, 96–107.

Kaufman, A. S. (1979b). *Intelligent testing with the WISC-R*. New York: Wiley-Interscience.

Kaufman, A. S. (1979c). Role of speed on WISC-R performance across the age range. *Journal of Consulting and Clinical Psychology, 47*, 595–597.

Kaufman, A. S. (1982). An integrated review of almost a decade of research of the McCarthy Scales. In T. R. Kratochwill (Ed.), *Advances in school psychology* (vol. 2) (pp. 119–169). Hillsdale, NJ: Erlbaum.

Kaufman, A. S. (1983). Some questions and answers about the Kaufman Assessment Battery for Children (K-ABC). *Journal of Psychoeducational Assessment, 1*, 205–218.

Kaufman, A. S. (1984). K-ABC and controversy. *Journal of Special Education, 18*, 409–444.

Kaufman, A. S. (1990). *Assessing adolescent and adult intelligence*. Needham, MA: Allyn and Bacon.

Kaufman, A. S., & Applegate, B. (1988). Short forms of the K-ABC Mental Processing and Achievement scales at ages 4 to 12-½ years for clinical and screening purposes. *Journal of Clinical Child Psychology, 17*, 359–369.

Kaufman, A. S., & DiCuio, R. F. (1975). Separate factor analysis of the McCarthy Scales for groups of black and white children. *Journal of School Psychology, 13*, 10–17.

Kaufman, A. S., & Doppelt, J. E. (1976). Analysis of WISC-R standardization data in terms of the stratification variables. *Child Development, 47*, 165–171.

Kaufman, A. S., & Hollenbeck, G. P. (1973). Factor analysis of the standardization edition of the McCarthy Scales. *Journal of Clinical Psychology, 29*, 358–362.

Kaufman, A. S., & Hollenbeck, G. P. (1974). Comparative structure of the WPPSI for blacks and whites. *Journal of Clinical Psychology, 13*, 10–18.

Kaufman, A. S., & Kamphaus, R. W. (1984). Factor analysis of the Kaufman Assessment Battery for Children (K-ABC) for ages 2 ½ through 12 ½ years. *Journal of Educational Psychology, 76*(4), 623–637.

Kaufman, A. S., Kamphaus, R. W., & Kaufman, N. L. (1985). The Kaufman Assessment Battery for Children (K-

ABC). In C. S. Newmark (Ed.), *Major psychological assessment instruments*. Newton, MA: Allyn and Bacon.

Kaufman, A. S., & Kaufman, N. L. (1977). *Clinical evaluation of young children with the McCarthy Scales*. New York: Grune & Stratton.

Kaufman, A. S., & Kaufman, N. L. (1983a). *Administration and scoring manual for the Kaufman Assessment Battery for Children*. Circle Pines, MN: American Guidance Service.

Kaufman, A. S., & Kaufman, N. L. (1983b). *Interpretive manual for the Kaufman Assessment Battery for Children*. Circle Pines, Minnesota: American Guidance Service.

Kaufman, A. S., Kaufman, N. L., Kamphaus, R. W., & Naglieri, J. A. (1982). Sequential and simultaneous factors at ages 3–12 ½: Developmental changes in neuropsychological dimensions. *Clinical Neuropsychology, 4,* 74–81.

Kaufman, A. S., and McLean, J. E. (1986). K-ABC/WISC-R factor analysis for a learning disabled population. *Journal of Learning Disabilities, 19,* 145–153.

Kaufman, A. S., & McLean, J. E. (1987). Joint factor analysis of the K-ABC and WISC-R with normal children. *Journal of School Psychology, 25* (2), 105–118.

Kaufman, A. S., O'Neal, M. R., Avant, A. H., & Long, S. W. (1987). Introduction to the Kaufman Assessment Battery for Children (K-ABC) for pediatric neuroclinicians. *Journal of Child Neurology, 2,* 3–16.

Kaufman, A. S., Reynolds, C. R., & McLean, J. E. (1989). Age and WAIS-R intelligence in a national sample of adults in the 20- to 74-year range: A cross-sectional analysis with education level controlled. *Intelligence, 13,* 235–253.

Kavale, K. A., & Forness, S. R. (1984). A meta-analysis of the validity of Wechsler Scale profiles and recategorizations: Patterns or parities. *Learning Disabilities Quarterly, 7,* 136–156.

Keith, T. Z. (1985). Questioning the K-ABC: What does it measure? *School Psychology Review, 14,* 9–20.

Keith, T. Z. (1990). Confirmatory and hierarchical confirmatory analysis of the Differential Ability Scales. *Journal of Psychoeducational Assessment, 8,* 391–405.

Keith, T. Z., & Bolen, L. M. (1980). Factor structure of the McCarthy Scales for children experiencing problems in school. *Psychology in the Schools, 17,* 320–326.

Keith, T. Z., Cool, V. A., Novak, C. G., White, L. J., & Pottebaum, S. M. (1988). Confirmatory factor analysis of the Stanford-Binet Fourth Edition: Testing the theory-test match. *Journal of School Psychology, 26,* 253–274.

Keith, T. Z., & Dunbar, S. B. (1984). Hierarchical factor analysis of the K-ABC: Testing alternate models. *Journal of Special Education, 18*(3), 367–375.

Keith, T. Z, Fehrmann, P. G., Harrison, P. L., & Pottebaum, S. M. (1986). The relation between adaptive behavior

and intelligence: Testing alternative explanations. *Journal of School Psychologists, 25,* 31–43.

Keith, T. Z., Hood, C., Eberhart, S., & Pottebaum, S. M. (1985, April). *Factor structure of the K-ABC for referred school children*. Paper presented at the meeting of the National Association of School Psychologists, Las Vegas, NV.

Kellerman, H., & Burry, A. (1981). *Handbook of psychodiagnostic testing*. New York: Grune & Stratton.

Kelly R. R., & Tomlinson-Keasey, C. (1976). Information processing of visually presented picture and word simulation by young hearing-impaired children. *Journal of Speech and Hearing Resources, 19,* 628–638.

Kennedy, M. H., & Hiltonsmith, R. W. (1988). Relationship among the K-ABC Nonverbal Scale, the Pictorial Test of Intelligence, and the Hiskey-Nebraska Test of Learning Aptitude for speech- and language-disabled preschool children. *Journal of Psychoeducational Assessment, 6,* 49–54.

Kinsbourne, M. (1975). Cerebral dominance and learning. In H. R. Myklebust (Ed.), *Progress in learning disabilities*. New York: Grune & Stratton.

Kinsbourne, M. (1978). Biological determinants of functional bisymmetry and asymmetry. In M. Kinsbourne (Ed.), *Asymmetrical function of the brain*. London: Cambridge University Press.

Klanderman, J. W., Perney, J., & Kroeschell, Z. B. (1984, April). *Comparisons of the K-ABC and WISC-R for LD children*. Paper presented at the meeting of the National Association of School Psychologists, Philadelphia.

Klanderman, J. W., Perney, J., & Kroeschell, Z. B. (1985). Comparisons of the K-ABC and WISC-R for LD children. *Journal of Learning Disabilities, 18*(9), 524–527.

Kline, R. B. (1989). Is the Fourth Edition Stanford-Binet a four-factor test? Confirmatory analysis of alternative models for ages 2 through 23. *Journal of Psychoeducational Assessment, 7,* 4–13.

Kline, R. B. (in press). Latent variable path analysis in clinical research: A beginner's tour guide. *Journal of Clinical Psychology.*

Knight, R. M., & Bakker, D. J. (1980). *Treatment of hyperactive and learning disordered children: Current research*. Baltimore, MD: University Park Press.

Kohs, S. C. (1923). *Intelligence measurement: A psychological and statistical study based upon the Block-Design Test*. New York: Macmillan.

Kohs, S. C. (1927). *Intelligence measurement*. New York: Macmillan.

Kolb, B., & Whishaw, I. Q. (1985). *Fundamentals of human neuropsychology* (2nd ed.). San Francisco: Freeman.

Koppitz, E. M. (1963). *Psychological evaluation of children's human figure drawings*. New York: Grune & Stratton.

Kyllonen, P., & Alluisi, E. (1987). Learning and forgetting facts and skills. In G. Salvendy (Ed.), *Handbook of human factors.* New York: Wiley.

LaBuda, M. C., DeFries, J. C., Plomin, R., & Fulker, D. W. (1986). Longitudinal stability of cognitive ability from infancy to early childhood: Genetic and environmental etiologies. *Child Development, 57,* 1142–1150.

Lambert, N. M. (1981). Psychological evidence in *Larry P. v. Wilson Riles:* An evaluation by a witness for the defense. *American Psychologist, 36,* 937–952.

Lambert, N. M. (1990). Consideration of the DAS-Naglieri Cognitive Assessment System. *Journal of Psychoeducational Assessment, 8,* 338–343.

Landers, S. (1986, December). Judge reiterates I.Q. test ban. *Monitor.* Washington, DC: American Psychological Association.

Larry P. v. Riles, 495 F. Supp. 926 (N. D. Cal. 1979).

Larry P. et al v. Riles. (1979, October). United States District Court for the Northern District of California, C-71-2270 RFP.

Larry P. v. Riles. (1986). United States District Court for the Northern District of California, C-71-2270 RFP. Order Modifying Judgement.

Lampley, D. A., & Rust, J. O. (1986). Validation of the Kaufman Assessment Battery for Children with a sample of preschool children. *Psychology in the Schools, 23,* 131–137.

Leark, R. A., Snyder, T., Grove, T., & Golden, C. J. (1983, August). *Comparison of the K-ABC to standardized neuropsychological batteries: Preliminary results.* Paper presented at the meeting of the American Psychological Association, Anaheim, CA.

Leiter, R. G. (1979). *Leiter international performance scale: Instruction manual.* Chicago: Stoelting.

Leiter, R. G., & Arthur, G. (1948). *Leiter International Performance Scale.* Chicago: Stoelting.

Lennon, R. T. (1985). Group tests of intelligence. In B. B. Wolman (Ed.), *Handbook of intelligence: Theories, measurements, and applications* (pp. 825–845). New York: Wiley.

Levine, A. J., & Marks, L. (1928). *Testing intelligence and achievement.* New York: Macmillan.

Levine, E. S. (1974). Psychological tests and practices with the deaf: A survey of the state of the art. *Volta Review, 76,* 298–319.

Levine, M. D., Busch, B., & Aufsuser, C. (1982). The dimension of inattention among children with school problems. *Pediatrics, 70,* 387–395.

Levine, S. C., Huttenlock, P., Banich, M. T. & Duda, C. (1987). Factors affecting cognitive functioning in hemiplegic children. *Developmental Medicine and Child Neurology, 29,* 27–35.

Levy, J. (1974). Psychobiological implications of bilateral asymmetry. In S. Dimond & G. Beaumont (Eds.), *Hemispheric functioning in the human brain.* New York: Halsted Press.

Lewandowski, L. J., & de Rienzo, P. J. (1985). WISC-R and K-ABC performances of hemiplegic children. *Journal of Psychoeducational Assessment, 3*(3), 215–221.

Lidz, C. S. (1983). Issues in assessing preschool children. In K. D. Paget & B. A. Bracken (Eds.), *The psychoeducational assessment of preschool children* (pp. 17–27). New York: Grune & Stratton.

Lidz, C. S., & Mearig, J. S. (1989). A response to Reynolds. *Journal of School Psychology, 27,* 81–86.

Linn, R. L. (1983). Pearson selection formulas: Implications for studies of predictive bias and estimates of educational effects in selected samples. *Journal of Educational Measurement, 20,* 1–15.

Little, S. G. (1991, October). Is the WISC-III factor structure valid? (Letter to the editor). *Communique,* p. 24.

Locurto, C. (1990). The malleability of IQ as judged from adoption studies. *Intelligence, 14,* 275–292.

Lufi, D., Cohen, A., & Parish-Plass, J. (1990). Identifying attention deficit hyperactivity disorder with the WISC-R and the Stroop Color and Word Test. *Psychology in the Schools, 27*(1), 28–34.

Lukens, J. (1988). Comparison of the Fourth Edition and the L-M Edition of the Stanford-Binet used with mentally retarded persons. *Journal of School Psychology, 26,* 87–89.

Luria, A. R. (1966a). *Higher cortical functions in man.* New York: Basic Books.

Luria, A. R. (1966b). *Human brain and psychological processes.* New York: Harper & Row.

Luria, A. R. (1970). The functional organization of the brain. *Scientific American, 222,* 66–78.

Luria, A. R. (1980). *Higher cortical functions in man* (2nd ed.). New York: Basic Books.

Luria, A. R., & Majovski, L. V. (1977). Basic approaches used in American and Soviet clinical neuropsychology. *American Psychologist, 32,* 959–968.

Lyman, H. (1963). *Test scores and what they mean.* Englewood Cliffs, NJ: Prentice-Hall.

Lynn, R. (1977). The intelligence of the Japanese. *Bulletin of the British Psychological Society, 30,* 69–72.

Lyon, M. A., & Smith, D. K. (1986). A comparison of at-risk preschool children's performance on the K-ABC, McCarthy Scales, and Stanford-Binet. *Journal of Psychoeducational Assessment, 4,* 35–43.

Majovski, L. V. (1984). The K-ABC: Theory and applications for child neuropsychological assessment and research. *Journal of Special Education, 18,* 266–268.

Markwardt, F. C. (1991). *Peabody Individual Achievement Test-Revised.* Circle Pines, MN: American Guidance Service.

Martin, R. P. (1988). *The Temperament Assessment Battery for Children.* Brandon, VT: Clinical Psychology Publishing.

Matarazzo, J. D. (1972). *Wechsler's measurement and appraisal of adult intelligence.* Baltimore, MD: Williams & Wilkins.

Matarazzo, J. D. (1990). Psychological assessment versus psychological testing? Validation from Binet to the school, clinic, and courtroom. *American Psychologists, 45*(9), 999–1017.

Mather, N. (1984). Performance of learning disability subjects and gifted subjects on the Woodcock-Johnson Psycho-Educational Battery and the Wechsler Intelligence Scale for Children-Revised. Unpublished doctoral dissertation, University of Arizona, Tucson.

Matheson, D. W., Mueller, H. H., & Short, R. H. (1984). The validity of Bannatyne's acquired knowledge category as a separate construct. *Journal of Psychoeducational Assessment, 2,* 279–291.

McCall, R. B. (1983). A conceptual approach to early mental development. In M. Lewis (Ed.), *Origins of intelligence* (2nd ed.). New York: Plenum.

McCallum, R. S., Karnes, F. A., & Edwards, R. P. (1984). The test of choice for assessment of gifted children: A comparison of the K-ABC, WISC-R, and Stanford-Binet. *Journal of Psychoeducational Assessment, 2,* 57–63.

McCarthy, D. (1972). *McCarthy scales of children's abilities.* New York: The Psychological Corporation.

McDermott, P. A., Fantuzzo, J. W., & Glutting, J. J. (1990). Just say no to subtest analysis: A critique on Wechsler theory and practice. *Journal of Psychoeducational Assessment, 8,* 290–302.

McDermott, P. A., Glutting, J. J., Jones, J. N., Watkins, M. W., & Kush, J. (1989). Core profile types in the WISC-R national sample: Structure, membership, and applications. *Psychological Assessment, 1,* 292–299.

McGrew, K. S., & Pehl, J. (1988). Prediction of future achievement by the Woodcock-Johnson Psycho-Educational Battery and the WISC-R. *Journal of School Psychology, 26,* 275–281.

McKay, H., Sinisterra, L., McKay, A., Gomez, H., & Lloreda, P. (1978). Improving cognitive ability in chronically deprived children. *Science, 200,* 270–278.

Mclean, M., McCormick, K., Baird, S., & Mayfield, P. (1987). Concurrent validity of the Battelle Developmental Inventory Screening Test. *Diagnostique, 13,* 10–20.

McLinden, S. E. (1989). An evaluation of the Battelle Developmental Inventory for determining special education eligibility. *Journal of Psychoeducational Assessment, 7,* 66–73.

McLoughlin, C. S., & Ellison, C. L. (1984, April). *Comparison of scores for normal preschool children on the Peabody Picture Vocabulary Test-Revised and the Achievement Scale of the Kaufman Assessment Battery for Children.* Paper presented at the meeting of the National Association of School Psychologists, Philadelphia.

McManis, D. L., Figley, C., Richert, M., & Fabre, T. (1978). Memory for Designs, Bender Gestalt, Trailmaking Test, and WISC-R performance of retarded inadequate readers. *Perceptual and Motor Skills, 46,* 443–450.

Mealor, D., Livesay, K. K., & Finn, M. H. (1983). Study Number 27. In A. S. Kaufman & N. L. Kaufman (Eds.), *Kaufman assessment battery for children: Interpretive manual* (p. 97). Circle Pines, MN: American Guidance Service.

Mercer, J. R. (1979). *The system of multicultural pluralistic assessment: Conceptual and technical manual.* New York: The Psychological Corporation.

Mercer, J. R., & Lewis, J. E. (1978). *Adaptive behavior inventory for children.* New York: The Psychological Corporation.

Merrill, K. W., & Shinn, M. R. (1990). Critical variables in the learning disabilities identification process. *School Psychology Review, 19*(1), 74–82.

Mille, F. (1979). Cultural bias in the WISC. *Intelligence, 3,* 149–164.

Miller, L. J. (1982). *Miller assessment for preschoolers.* Littleton, CO: Foundation for Knowledge and Development.

Miller, T. L., & Reynolds, C. R. (1984). Special issue . . . The K-ABC. *Journal of Special Education, 18*(3), 207–448.

Minton, H. L., & Schneider, F. W. (1980). *Differential psychology.* Monterey, CA: Brooks/Cole.

Misra, G. (1983). Deprivation and development: A review of Indian studies. *Indian Educational Review,* 12–32.

Moores, D. F. (1987). *Educating the deaf: Psychology, principles, and practices* (3rd ed.). Boston: Houghton Mifflin.

Morris, J. D., Evans, J. G., & Pearson, D. D. (1978). The WISC-R subtest profile of a sample of severely emotionally disturbed children. *Psychological Reports, 42,* 319–325.

Morris, J. M., & Bigler, E. (1985, January). *An investigation of the Kaufman Assessment Battery for Children (K-ABC) with neurologically impaired children.* Paper presented at the meeting of the International Neuropsychological Society, San Diego, CA.

Morris, R., Blashfield, R., & Satz, P. (1986). Developmental classification of reading-disabled children. *Journal of Clinical and Experimental Neuropsychology, 8,* 371–392.

Mott, S. E. (1987). Concurrent validity of the Battelle Developmental Inventory for speech and language disordered children. *Psychology in the Schools, 24,* 215–220.

Murray, A., & Bracken, B. A. (1984). Eleven-month predictive validity of the Kaufman Assessment Battery for Children. *Journal of Psychoeducational Assessment, 2,* 225–232.

Mussman, M. C. (1964). Teacher's evaluations of psychological reports. *Journal of School Psychology, 3,* 35–37.

Myklebust H. R. (1960). *The psychology of deafness: Sensory deprivation, learning, and adjustment.* New York: Grune & Stratton.

Naeye, R. L., Diener, M. M., Dellinger, W. S., & Blanc, W. A. (1969). Urban poverty: Effect on prenatal nutrition. *Science, 166,* 1026.

Nagle, R. J. (1979). The McCarthy Scale of Children's Abilities: Research implications for the assessment of young children. *School Psychology Review, 8,* 319–326.

Naglieri, J. A. (1981a). Extrapolated developmental indices for the Bayley Scales of Infant Development. *American Journal of Mental Deficiencies, 85,* 548–550.

Naglieri, J. A. (1981b). Factor structure of the WISC-R for children identified as learning disabled. *Psychological Reports, 49,* 891–895.

Naglieri, J. A. (1984). Concurrent and predictive validity of the Kaufman Assessment Battery for Children with a Navajo sample. *Journal of School Psychology, 22,* 373–380.

Naglieri, J. A. (1985a). Assessment of mentally retarded children with the Kaufman Assessment Battery for Children. *American Journal of Mental Deficiency, 89,* 367–371.

Naglieri, J. A. (1985b). Normal children's performance on the McCarthy Scales, Kaufman Assessment Battery, and Peabody Individual Achievement Test. *Journal of Psychoeducational Assessment, 3,* 123–129.

Naglieri, J. A. (1985c). Use of the WISC-R and K-ABC with learning disabled, borderline mentally retarded, and normal children. *Psychology in the Schools, 22,* 133–141.

Naglieri, J. A. (1986). WISC-R and K-ABC comparison for matched samples of black and white children. *Journal of School Psychology, 24,* 81–88.

Naglieri, J. A. (1988a). Interpreting area score variation on the Fourth Edition of the Stanford-Binet Scale of Intelligence. *Journal of Clinical Child Psychology, 17,* 224–228.

Naglieri, J. A. (1988b). *Draw-a-Person: A Quantitative System.* New York: The Psychological Corporation.

Naglieri, J. A. (1988c). Interpreting the subtest profile on the Fourth Edition of the Stanford-Binet Scale of Intelligence. *Journal of Clinical Child Psychology, 17,* 62–65.

Naglieri, J. A., & Anderson, D. F. (1985). Comparison of the WISC-R and K-ABC with gifted students. *Journal of Psychoeducational Assessment, 3,* 175–179.

Naglieri, J. A., & Bardos, A. N. (1987). *Draw-A-Person and Matrix Analogies Test cross-culture validity.* Paper presented at the annual meeting of the National Association of School Psychologists, New Orleans, LA.

Naglieri, J. A., & Bardos, A. N. (1988). Canadian children's performance on the Matrix Analogies Test. *School Psychology International, 9,* 309–313.

Naglieri, J. A., & Das, J. P. (1988). Planning-arousal-simultaneous-successive (PASS); A model for assessment. *Journal of School Psychology, 26,* 35–48.

Naglieri, J. A., & Das, J. P. (1990). Planning, attention, simultaneous, and successive (PASS) cognitive processes as a model for intelligence. *Journal of Psychoeducational Assessment, 8,* 303–337.

Naglieri, J. A., & Haddad, F. (1984). Learning disabled children's performance on the Kaufman Assessment Battery for Children: A concurrent validity study. *Journal of Psychoeducational Assessment, 2,* 49–56.

Naglieri, J. A., & Jensen, A. R. (1987). Comparison of black-white differences on the WISC-R and the K-ABC: Spearman's hypothesis. *Intelligence, 11,* 21–43.

Naglieri, J. A., Kamphaus, R. W., & Kaufman, A. S. (1983). The Luria-Das simultaneous-successive model applied to the WISC-R. *Journal of Psychoeducational Assessment, 1,* 25–34.

Naglieri, J. A., & Kamphaus, R. W. (in press). Interpreting the subtest profile on the Kaufman Assessment Battery for Children. *Clinical Neuropsychology.*

Naglieri, J. A., Kaufman, A. S., Kaufman, N. L., & Kamphaus, R. W. (1981). Cross-validation of Das' simultaneous and successive processes with novel tasks. *Alberta Journal of Educational Research, 27,* 264–271.

Naglieri, J. A., & Prewett, P. N. (1990). Nonverbal intelligence measures: A selected review of instruments and their use. In C. R. Reynolds & R. W. Kamphaus (Eds.), *Handbook of psychological and educational assessment of children: Intelligence and achievement* (pp. 348–370). New York: Guilford.

Naglieri, J. A., & Wisniewski, J. J. (1988). Clinical use of the WISC-R, MAT-EF, and PPVT-R. *Journal of Psychoeducational Assessment, 6,* 390–395.

Narrett, C. M. (in press). Review of the Kaufman Assessment Battery for Children (K-ABC). *Reading Teacher.*

Nass, R., Peterson, H. D., & Koch, D. (1989). Differential effects of congenital left and right brain injury on intelligence. *Brain and Cognition, 9,* 258–266.

National Association of School Psychologists (1985). *Principles for professional ethics.* Silver Springs, MD: NASP.

Nebes, R. D. (1974). Hemispheric specialization in commisurotomized man. *Psychological Bulletin, 81,* 1–14.

Neisser, U. (1967). *Cognitive psychology.* New York: Appleton-Century-Crofts.

Neisser, U. (1979). The concept of intelligence. *Intelligence, 3,* 217–227.

Neisworth, J. T., & Butler, R. J. (1990). [Review of the Draw A Person: A Quantitative Scoring System]. *Journal of Psychoeducational Assessment, 8,* 190–194.

Nelson, R. B., Obrzut, A., & Cummings, J. (1984). *Construct *and predictive validity of the K-ABC with EMR children.* (Available from R. Brett Nelson, Weld County School District #6, Greeley, CO 80631.)

Newborg, J., Stock, J. R., Wnek, L., Guidubaldi, J., & Svinicki, J. (1984). *Battelle developmental inventory.* Allen, TX: DLM Teaching Resources.

Newman, I., & Guidubaldi, J. (1989, April). *Factor validity estimate of the Battelle Developmental Inventory for three age groupings.* Paper presented at the meeting of the National Association of School Psychologists, Houston, TX.

Nihira, K., Foster, R., Shellhaas, M., Leland, H., Lambert, N., & Windmiller, M. (1981). *AAMD adaptive behavior scale, school edition.* Monterey, CA: Publisher's Test Service.

Nitko, A. (1983). *Educational tests and measurement: An introduction.* New York: Harcourt Brace Jovanovich.

Nussbaum, N. L., & Bigler, E. D. (1989). Halstead-Reitan Neuropsychological Test Batteries for Children. In C. R. Reynolds & E. Fletcher-Janzen (Eds.), *Handbook of clinical child neuropsychology.* New York: Plenum.

Oakland, T. (1979). Research on the Adaptive Behavior Inventory for Children and the Estimated Learning Potential. *School Psychology Digest, 8,* 63–70.

Oakland, T. (1983). Joint use of adaptive behavior and IQ to predict achievement. *Journal of Consulting and Clinical Psychology, 51,* 298–301.

Oakland, T., & Dowling, L. (1983). The Draw-a-Person Test: Validity properties for nonbiased assessment. *Learning Disability Quarterly, 6,* 526–534.

Oakland, T., & Feigenbaum, D. (1979). Multiple sources of test bias on the WISC-R and the Bender-Gestalt Test. *Journal of Consulting and Clinical Psychology, 47,* 968–974.

Oakman, S., & Wilson, B. (1988). Stability of WISC-R intelligence scores: Implication for 3-year reevaluations of learning disabled students. *Psychology in the Schools, 25*(2), 118–120.

Obringer, S. J. (1988, November). *A survey of perceptions by school psychologists of the Stanford-Binet IV.* Paper presented at the meeting of the Mid-South Educational Research Association, Louisville, KY.

Obrzut, A., Nelson, R. B., & Obrzut, J. E. (in press). Construct validity of the K-ABC with mildly mentally retarded students. *American Journal of Mental Deficiency.*

Obrzut, A., Obrzut, J., & Shaw, D. (1984). Construct validity of the Kaufman Assessment Battery for Children with learning disabled and mentally retarded. *Psychology in the Schools, 4,* 417–424.

Oehler-Stinnett, J. (1989). Review of the Battelle Developmental Inventory. In J. C. Conoley & J. J. Kramer (Eds.). *The tenth mental measurements yearbook.* Lincoln: Univ. of Nebraska Press.

Ornstein, R., Johnstone, J., Herron, J., & Swencionis, C.

(1980). Differential right hemisphere engagement in visuo-spatial tasks. *Neuropsychologia, 18,* 49–64.

Osborne, A. F. (1963). *Applied imagination* (3rd ed.). New York: Scribner.

Osborne, R. T. (1980). *Twins, black and white.* Athens, GA: Foundation for Human Understanding.

Ownby, R. L., & Carmin, C. N. (1988). Confirmatory factor analysis of the Stanford-Binet Intelligence Scale, Fourth Edition. *Journal of Psychoeducational Assessment, 6,* 331–340.

Ownby, R. L., & Wallbrown, F. (1986). Improving report writing in school psychology. In T. R. Kratochwill (Ed.), *Advances in school psychology* (vol. 5). Hillsdale, NJ: Erlbaum.

Paget, K. D. (1983). The individual examining situation: Basic considerations for preschool children. In K. D. Paget & B. A. Bracken (Eds.), *The psychoeducational assessment of preschool children* (pp. 51–61). New York: Grune & Stratton.

Paget, K. D. (1989). Review of the Battelle Developmental Inventory. In J. C. Conoley & J. J. Kramer (Eds.), *The tenth mental measurements yearbook.* Lincoln: Univ. of Nebraska Press.

Paramesh, C. R. (1982). Relationship between Quick Test and WISC-R and reading ability as used in a juvenile setting. *Perceptual and Motor Skills, 55,* 881–882.

PASE: Parents in Action on Special Education et al, v. Hannon et al. (1980, July). United States District Court for the Northern District of Illinois, Eastern Division, C-74-3586RFP, slip opinion.

Payne, J. S., & Patton, J. R. (1981). *Mental retardation.* Columbus, OH: Merrill.

Pearson, K. (1901). On lines and planes of closest fit to systems of points in space. *Philosophical Magazine (Series 6), 2,* 559–572.

Peckham, R. F. (1972). Opinion, *Larry P. v. Riles. Federal Supplement 343,* 1306–1315.

Peckham, R. F. (1979). Opinion, *Larry P. v. Riles. Federal Supplement 495,* 926–992.

Pellegrino, J. W. (1986). Intelligence: The interaction of culture and cognitive processes. In R. J. Sternberg & D. K. Detterman (Eds.), *What is intelligence? Contemporary viewpoints on its nature and definition.* Norwood, NJ: Ablex.

Perrine, J. (1989). Situational identification of gifted Hispanic students. In C. J. Maker & S. W. Schiever (Eds.), *Critical issues in gifted education* (vol. 2), Defensible programs of cultural and ethnic minorities. Austin, TX: Pro-Ed.

Petersen, N. S., Kolen, M. J., & Hoover, H. D. (1989). Scaling, norming, and equating. In R. L. Linn (Ed.), *Educational measurement* (3rd ed.). New York: Macmillan.

Phelps, L., & Branyan, L. T. (1988). Correlations among the Hiskey, K-ABC Nonverbal Scale, Leiter, and WISC-R Performance Scale with public school deaf children. *Journal of Psychoeducational Assessment, 6,* 354–358.

Phelps, L., & Rosso, M. (1985). Validity assessment of the Woodcock-Johnson Broad Cognitive Ability and scholastic ability cluster scores for behavior-disordered adolescents. *Psychology in the Schools, 22,* 398–403.

Phelps, L., Bell, M. C., & Scott, M. J. (1988). Correlations between the Stanford-Binet: Fourth Edition and the WISC-R with a learning disabled population. *Psychology in the Schools, 25,* 380–382.

Phelps, L., Rosso, M., & Falasco, S. L. (1985). Multiple regression data using the WISC-R and the Woodcock-Johnson Tests of Cognitive Ability. *Psychology in the Schools, 22,* 46–49.

Pintner, R. (1923). *Intelligence testing.* New York: Holt, Rinehart & Winston.

Plomin, R. (1988). The nature and nurture of conitive abilities. In R. J. Sternberg (Ed.), *Advances in the psychology of human intelligence* (vol. 4) (pp. 1–33). Hillsdale, NJ: Erlbaum.

Plomin, R. (1989). Environment and genes: Determinants of behavior. *American Psychologist, 44,* 105–111.

Plotkin, L. (1974). Research, education, and public policy: Heredity v. environment in Negro intelligence. In L. P. Miller (Ed.), *The testing of black students: A symposium.* New York: Prentice-Hall.

Pommer, L. T. (1986). Seriously emotionally disturbed children's performance on the Kaufman Assessment Battery for Children: A concurrent validity study. *Journal of Psychoeducational Assessment, 4,* 155–162.

Porter, L. J., & Kirby, E. A. (1986). Effects of two instructional sets on the validity of the Kaufman Assessment Battery for Children-Nonverbal scale with a group of severely hearing impaired children. *Psychology in the Schools, 23,* 1–6.

Posner, M. I., Petersen, S. E., Fox, P. T., & Raichle, M. E. (1988). Localization of cognitive operations in the human brain. *Science, 240,* 1627–1631.

Potthoff, R. F. (1966). *Statistical aspects of the problem of biases in psychological tests.* (Institute of Statistics Mimeo Series No. 479). Chapel Hill: University of North Carolina, Department of Statistics.

Prewett, P. N., Bardos, A. N., & Naglieri, J. A. (1989). Assessment of mentally retarded children with the Matrix Analogies Test-Short Form, Draw A Person: A Quantitative Scoring System, and the Kaufman Test of Educational Achievement. *Psychology in the Schools, 26,* 254–260.

Pribram, K. (1971). *Language of the brain.* Englewood Cliffs, NJ: Prentice-Hall.

Psychological Corporation (1978). *The McCarthy screening test.* San Antonio, TX: The Psychological Corporation.

Puente, A. E. (1989). Historical perspectives in the development of neuropsychology as a professional psychological specialty. In C. R. Reynolds & E. Fletcher-Janzen (Eds.), *Handbook of clinical child neuropsychology.* New York: Plenum.

Quereshi, M. Y., & McIntire, D. H. (1984). The comparability of the WISC, WISC-R, and WPPSI. *Journal of Clinical Psychology, 40*(4), 1036–1043.

Rafferty, Y., & Shinn, M. (1991). The impact of homelessness on children. *American Psychologist, 46,* 1170–1179.

Rapaport, D., Gill, M., & Schafer, R. (1945–1946). *Diagnostic psychological testing* (2 vols.). Chicago: Year Book.

Ratcliffe, K. J., & Ratcliffe, M. W. (1979). The Leiter Scales: A review of validity findings. *American Annals of the Deaf, 124,* 38–45.

Raven, J. C. (1947a). *Standard progressive matrices.* London: Lewis.

Raven, J. C. (1947b). *Coloured progressive matrices.* London: Lewis.

Raven, J. (1948). *Progressive matrices.* New York: The Psychological Corporation.

Raven, J. C. (1965). *Raven's progressive matrices.* New York: The Psychological Corporation.

Raven, J. C. (1986). A compendium of North American normative and validity studies. New York: The Psychological Corporation.

Ray, S. (1979). *Wechsler's intelligence scales for children-revised: For the deaf.* LA: State University of Louisiana. OK: Ray.

Reilly, T. P., Drudge, O. W., Rosen, J. C., Loew, D. E., & Fischer, M. (1985). Concurrent and predictive validity of the WISC-R, McCarthy Scales, Woodcock-Johnson, and academic achievement. *Psychology in the Schools, 22,* 380–382.

Reitan, R. M. (1955). Certain differential effects of left and right cerebral lesions in human adults. *Journal of Comparative and Physiological Psychology, 48,* 474–477.

Reitan, R. M. (1981). *Halstead-Reitan neuropsychological test battery.* Tucson, AZ: Reitan Neuropsychological Laboratories.

Reitan, R. M., & Davison, L. A. (1974). *Clinical neuropsychology: Current status and applications.* Washington, DC: Winston.

Reschly, D. J. (1978). WISC-R factor structures among Anglos, blacks, Chicanos, and Native-American Papagos. *Journal of Consulting and Clinical Psychology, 46,* 417–422.

Reschly, D. J. (1980). Psychological evidence in the *Larry P.* opinion: A case of right problem—wrong solution? *School Psychology Review, 9,* 123–135.

Reschly, D. J. (1987). *Marshall v. Georgia.* In C. R. Reynolds & L. Mann (Eds.), *Encyclopedia of special education* (vol. 2). New York: Wiley-Interscience.

Reschly, D. J. (1990). Found: Our intelligences: What do they mean? *Journal of Psychoeducational Assessment, 8,* 259–267.

Reschly, D. J., & Saber, D. L. (1979). Analysis of test bias in four groups with the regression definition. *Journal of Educational Measurement, 16,* 1–9.

Rethazi, M., & Wilson, A. K. (1988). The Kaufman Assessment Battery for Children (K-ABC) in the assessment of learning disabled children. *Psychology in the Schools, 25*(4), 131–137.

Reynolds, C. R. (1981). Neuropsychological assessment and the habilitation of learning: Considerations in the search for the aptitude × treatment interaction. *School Psychology Review, 10,* 343–349.

Reynolds, C. R. (1982a). The importance of norms and other psychometric concepts to assessment in clinical neuropsychological. In R. N. Malatesha & L. C. Hartlage (Eds.), *Neuropsychology and cognition* (vol.2) (pp. 55–76). The Hague, Netherlands: Martinus Nijhoff.

Reynolds, C. R. (1982b). The problem of bias in psychological assessment. In C. R. Reynolds & T. B. Gutkin (Eds.), *The handbook of school psychology.* New York: Wiley.

Reynolds, C. R. (1984a). Critical measurement issues in learning disabilities. *Journal of Special Education, 18,* 451–476.

Reynolds, C. R. (1984b). K-ABC. Special issue of *Journal of Special Education, 18*(3).

Reynolds, C. R. (1986). Transactional models of intellectual development, yes. Deficit models of process remediation, no. *School Psychology Review, 15,* 256–260.

Reynolds, C. R. (1987). Playing IQ roulette with the Stanford-Binet, 4th Edition. *Measurement and Evaluation in Counseling and Development, 20,* 139–141.

Reynolds, C. R. (1990). Conceptual and teaching problems in learning disability diagnosis. In C. R. Reynolds & R. W. Kamphaus (Eds.), *Handbook of psychological and educational assessment of children.* New York: Guilford.

Reynolds, C. R., & Clark, J. H. (1985). Profile analysis of standardized intelligence test performance of very low functioning individuals. *Journal of School Psychology, 23,* 277–283.

Reynolds, C. R., & Clark, J. H. (Eds.) (1983). *Assessment and programming for children with low incidence handicaps.* New York: Plenum.

Reynolds, C. R., & Clark, J. H. (1984, November). *Profile analysis of standardized intelligence test performance of high IQ children.* Paper presented to the annual meeting of the National Association for Gifted Children, St. Louis, MO.

Reynolds, C. R., & Clark, J. H. (1986). Profile analysis of standardized intelligence test performance of very high IQ children. *Psychology in the Schools, 23,* 5–12.

Reynolds, C. R., & Gutkin, T. B. (1980a). A regression analysis of test bias on the WISC-R for Anglos and Chicanos referred to psychological services. *Journal of Abnormal Child Psychology, 8,* 237–243.

Reynolds, C. R., & Gutkin, T. B. (1980b). Stability of the WISC-R factor structure across sex at two age levels. *Journal of Clinical Psychology, 36,* 775–777.

Reynolds, C. R., & Gutkin, T. B. (1980c, September). *WISC-R performance of blacks and whites matched on four demographic variables.* Paper presented at the annual meeting of the American Psychological Association, Montreal.

Reynolds, C. R., Gutkin, T. B., Dappen, L., & Wright, D. (1979). Differential validity of the WISC-R for boys and girls referred for psychological services. *Perceptual and Motor Skills, 48,* 868–879.

Reynolds, C. R., Kamphaus, R. W., & Rosenthal, B. (1988). Factor analysis of the Stanford-Binet Fourth Edition for ages 2 through 23. *Measurement and Evaluation in Counseling and Development, 21,* 52–63.

Reynolds, C. R., & Kaufman, A. S. (1990). Assessment of children's intelligence with the Weschsler Intelligence Scale for children-Revised (WISC-R). In C. R. Reynolds & R. W. Kamphaus (Eds.), *Handbook of psychological and educational assessment of children: Intelligence and achievement* (pp. 127–165). New York: Guilford.

Reynolds, C. R., Willson, V. L., & Chatman, S. P. (1985). Regression analyses of bias on the Kaufman Assessment Battery for Children. *Journal of School Psychology, 23,* 195–204.

Reynolds, C. R., & Wright, D. (1981). A comparison of the criterion-related validity (academic achievement of the WPPSI and the WISC-R). *Psychology in the Schools, 18,* 20–23.

Reynolds, C. R., & Willson, V. L. (1984, April). *Factorial consistency of simultaneous and sequential cognitive processing for whites and blacks ages 3 to 12 ½.* Paper presented at the meeting of the National Council on Measurement in Education, New Orleans, LA.

Reynolds, C. R., Willson, V. L., and Chatman, S. P. (1983, March). *Relationships between age and raw score increases on the Kaufman Assessment Battery for Children.* Paper presented at the meeting of the National Association of School Psychologists, Detroit, MI.

Reynolds, C. R., Willson, V. L., and Chatman, S. P. (1984). Relationships between age and raw score increases on the Kaufman Assessment Battery for Children. *Psychology in the Schools, 21,* 19–24.

Reynolds, C. R., Willson, V. L., & Chatman, S. P. (1985). Regression analyses of bias on the Kaufman Assessment Battery for Children. *Journal of School Psychology, 23,* 195–204.

Richardson, K., & Bynner, J. M. (1984). Intelligence: Past and future. *International Journal of Psychology, 19,* 499–526.

Roid, G. H. (1986). Computer technology in testing. In B. S. Plake, J. C. Witt, & J. V. Mitchell, Jr. (Eds.), *The future of testing: Buros-Nebraska Symposium on Measurement and Testing.* Hillsdale, NJ: Erlbaum.

Roid, G. H. (1990, August). Historical continuity in intelligence assessment: Goals of the WISC-III standardization. In *Development of the Wechsler Intelligence Scale for Children* (3rd ed.). Symposium conducted at the meeting of the American Psychological Association, Boston.

Roid, G. H., & Gorsuch, R. L. (1984). Development and clinical use of test interpretive programs on microcomputers. In M. D. Schwartz (Ed.), *Using computers in clinical practice: Psychotherapy and mental health applications.* New York: Haworth Press.

Rosenthal, B. L., & Kamphaus, R. W. (1988). Interpretive tables for test scatter on the Stanford-Binet Intelligence Scale: Fourth Edition. *Journal of Psychoeducational Assessment, 6,* 359–370.

Ross, G. R. (1989). Some thoughts on the value of infant tests for assessing and predicting mental ability. *Journal of Developmental and Behavioral Pediatrics, 10,* 44–47.

Rothlisberg, B. A. (1987). Comparing the Stanford-Binet, Fourth Edition to the WISC-R: A concurrent validity study. *Journal of School Psychology, 25,* 193–196.

Rothlisberg, B. A., & McIntosh, D. E. (1991). Performance of a referred sample on the Stanford-Binet IV and the K-ABC. *Journal of School Psychology, 29,* 367–370.

Ruchala, E., Schalt, E., & Bogel, F. (1985). Relations between mental performance and reaction time: New aspects of an old problem. *Intelligence, 9,* 189–205.

Rucker, C. N. (1967). Technical language in the school psychologists' report. *Psychology in the Schools, 4,* 146–150.

Rudner, L. M. (1983). Individual assessment accuracy. *Journal of Educational Measurement, 20,* 207–219.

Rules and Regulations for Implementing Education for All Handicapped Children Act of 1975, P.L. 94-142, 42 Fed. Reg. 42474 (1977).

Rutter, M. (1978). Diagnosis and definition of childhood autism. *Journal of Autism and Childhood Schizophrenia, 8,* 139–161.

Rutter, M., Chadwick, O., & Shaffer, D. (1983). Head injury. In M. Rutter (Ed.), *Developmental neuropsychiatry.* New York: Guilford.

Saco-Pollitt, C., Pollitt, E., & Greenfield, D. (1985). The cumulative deficit hypothesis in the light of cross-cultural evidence. *International Journal of Behavioral Development, 8,* 75–97.

Salvia, J., & Hritcko, T. (1984). The K-ABC and ability training. *Journal of Special Education, 18*(3), 345–356.

Sandoval, J. (1979). The WISC-R and internal evidence of test bias with minority groups. *Journal of Consulting and Clinical Psychology, 47*(5), 919–927.

Sandoval, J., & Irvin, M. G. (1990). Legal and ethical issues

in the assessment of children. In C. R. Reynolds & R. W. Kamphaus (Eds.), *Handbook of psychological and educational assessment of children: Intelligence and achievement.* New York: Guilford.

Sandoval, J., & Mille, M. (1979, September). *Accuracy judgments of WISC-R item difficulty for minority groups.* Paper presented at the annual meeting of the American Psychological Association, New York.

Sarasan, S. B. (1954). *The clinical interaction.* New York: Harper & Row.

Sattler, J. M. (1988). *Assessment of children* (3rd ed.). San Diego, CA: Sattler.

Sattler, J. M., & Covin, T. M. (1986). Comparison of the Slosson Intelligence Test, Revised Norms and WISC-R for children with learning problems and for gifted children. *Psychology in the Schools, 23,* 259–264.

Scarr, S. (1981). *Social class, race and individual differences in intelligence.* New York: Plenum.

Scarr, S., & Weinberg, R. A. (1976). IQ test performance of black children adopted by white families. *American Psychologist, 31,* 726–739.

Scarr, S., & Weinberg, R. A. (1978). The influence of "family background" on intellectual attainment. *American Sociological Review, 43,* 674–692.

Schaie, K. W., & Hertzog, C. (1983). Fourteen-year cohort-sequential analyses of adult intellectual development. *Developmental Psychology, 32,* 1118–1120.

Schaughency, E. A., Lahey, B. B., Hynd, G. W., Stone, P. A., Piacentini, J. C., & Frick, P. J. (1989). Neuropsychological test performance and the attention deficit disorders: Clinical utility of the Luria-Nebraska Neuropsychological Battery-Children's Revision. *Journal of Consulting and Clinical Psychology, 57*(1), 112–116.

Schorr, D., Bower, G. H., & Kiernan, R. (1982). Stimulus variables in the block design task. *Journal of Consulting and Clinical Psychology, 50,* 479–487.

Schuerger, J. M., & Witt, A. C. (1989). The temporal stability of individually tested intelligence. *Journal of Clinical Psychology, 45,* 294–302.

Schwartz, G. E., Davidson, R. J., & Mear, F. (1975). Right hemisphere lateralization for emotion in the human brain: Interactions with cognition. *Science, 190,* 286–288.

Seashore, H. G. (1951). Differences between verbal and performance IQ's on the WISC. *Journal of Consulting Psychology, 15,* 62–67.

Sechenov, I. (1965). *Reflexes of the brain.* Cambridge, MA: MIT Press. (Originally published in 1863.)

Segalowitz, S. J., & Gruber, F. A. (Eds.) (1977). *Language development and neurological theory.* New York: Academic Press.

Seidenberg, M., Giordani, B., Berent, S., & Boll, T. J.

(1983). IQ level and performance on the Halstead-Reitan Neuropsychological Test Battery for older children. *Journal of Consulting and Clinical Psychology, 51,* 406–413.

Semrud-Clikeman, M. (1990). Dyslexia and brain morphology: Contributions to disturbances in phonological coding, naming, and reading. Unpublished doctoral dissertation, University of Georgia, Athens.

Sexton, D., McLean, M., Boyd, R. D., Thompson, B., & McCormick, K. (1988). Criterion-related validity of a new standardized developmental measure for use with infants who are handicapped. *Measurement and Evaluation in Counseling and Development, 21,* 16–24.

Shah, A., & Holmes, N. (1985). Brief report: The use of the Leiter International Performance Scale with autistic children. *Journal of Autism and Developmental Disorders, 15*(2), 195–203.

Shapiro, E. G., & Dotan, N. (1985, October). *Neurological findings and the Kaufman Assessment Battery for Children.* Paper presented at the National Association of Neuropsychologists, Philadelphia.

Shapiro, E. G., & Dotan, N. (1986). Neurological findings and the Kaufman Assessment Battery for Children. *Developmental Neuropsychology, 2*(1), 51–64.

Shaywitz, S. E., Shaywitz, B. A., Fletcher, J., & Shupack, H. (1986). Evaluation of school performance: Dyslexia and attention deficit disorder. *Pediatrician, 13,* 96–107.

Shaywitz, B. A., & Waxman, S. G. (1987). Dyslexia. *New England Journal of Medicine, 316,* 1268–1270.

Shellenberger, S., & Lachterman, T. (1976, March). *Usability of the McCarthy Scales of Children's Abilities in the intellectual assessment of the Puerto Rican child.* Paper presented at the meeting of the Naitonal Association of School Psychologists, Kansas City, MO.

Shephard, L. A. (1989). Identification of mild handicaps. In R. L. Linn (Ed.), *Educational measurement* (3rd ed.). New York: Macmillan.

Shephard, L. A., Smith, M. L., & Vojir, C. P. (1983). Characteristics of pupils identified as learning disabled. *American Educational Research Journal, 20,* 309–331.

Sherman, M., & Key, C. V. (1932). The intelligence scores of isolated mountain children. *Child Development, 3,* 279–290.

Shure, G. H., & Halstead, W. C. (1959). Cerebral lateralization of individual processes. *Psychological Monographs: General and Applied, 72,*(12).

Siegel, L. S. (1979). Infant perceptual, cognitive, and motor behaviors as predictors of subsequent cognitive and language development. *Canadian Journal of Psychology, 33,* 382–395.

Siegel, L. S. (1988). Evidence that IQ scores are irrelevant to the definition and analysis of reading disability. *Canadian Journal of Psychology, 42,* 201–215.

Siegel, L. S. (1990). IQ and learning disabilities: R.I.P. In H. L. Swanson & B. Keogh (Eds.), *Learning disabilities: Theoretical and research issues.* Hillsdale, NJ: Erlbaum.

Silverstein, A. B. (1974). A short-short form of the WISC-R for screening purposes. *Psychological Reports, 35,* 817–818.

Silverstein, A. B. (1976). Comparison of two criteria for determining the number of factors. *Psychological Reports, 41,* 387–390.

Silverstein, A. B. (1980). Cluster analysis of the Wechsler Intelligence Scale for Children-Revised. *Educational and Psychological Measurement, 40,* 51–54.

Silverstein, A. B. (1981). Reliability and abnormality of test score differences. *Journal of Clinical Psychology, 37*(2), 392–394.

Silverstein, A. B. (1982a). Alternative multiple-group solutions for the WISC and the WISC-R. *Journal of Clinical Psychology, 38,* 166–168.

Silverstein, A. B. (1982b). Pattern analysis as simultaneous statistical inference. *Journal of Consulting and Clinical Psychology, 50,* 234–240.

Silverstein, A. B. (1983a). Full Scale IQ equivalents for a two-subtest short form of the Wechsler Preschool and Primary Scale of Intelligence and the Wechsler Intelligence Scale for Children-Revised. *Psychological Reports, 53,* 16–18.

Silverstein, A. B. (1983b). Validity of random short forms: III. Wechsler's intelligence scales. *Perceptual and Motor Skills, 56,* 572–574.

Silverstein, A. B., & Legutki, G. (1982). Direct comparisons of the factor structures of the WISC and the WISC-R. *Psychology in the Schools, 19,* 5–7.

Sinclair, E., Forness, S. R., & Alexson, J. (1985). Psychiatric diagnosis: A study of its relationship to school needs. *Journal of Special Education, 19*(3), 333–344.

Siskind, G. (1967). Fifteen years later: A replication of "a semantic study of concepts of clinical psychologists and psychiatrists." *The Journal of Psychology, 65,* 3–7.

Slate, J. R., & Chick, D. (1989). WISC-R examiner errors: Cause for concern. *Psychology in the Schools, 26,* 78–83.

Slate, J. R., & Saddler, C. D. (1990, October). Improved but not perfect. *NASP Communique,* p. 20.

Slosson, R. L. (1981). *Slosson Intelligence Test.* East Aurora, NY: Slosson Educational Publications.

Smith, C. R. (1983). *Learning disabilities: The interaction of learner, task, and setting.* Boston: Little, Brown.

Smith, D. K., Lyon, M. A., Hunter, E., & Boyd, R. (1986, April). Relationship between the K-ABC and WISC-R for students referred for severe learning disabilities. *Journal of Learning Disabilities, 21*(8), 509–513.

Snyder, T. J., Leark, R. A., Golden, C. J., Grove, T., & Allison, R. (1983, March). *Correlations of the K-ABC, WISC-*

R, and Luria-Nebraska Children's Battery for exceptional children. Paper presented at the meeting of the National Association of School Psychologists, Detroit, MI.

Snyderman, M., & Rothman, S. (1986). Science, politics and the IQ controversy. *Public Interest, 83,* 79–97.

Snyderman, M., & Rothman, S. (1987). Survey of expert opinion on intelligence and aptitude testing. *American Psychologist, 42,* 137–144.

Sparrow, S. S., Balla, D. A., & Cicchetti, D. V. (1984). *Vineland adaptive behavior scales.* Circle Pines, MN: American Guidance Service.

Spearman, C. (1927). *The abilities of man.* New York: Macmillan.

Spearman, C., & Jones, L. (1950). *Human abilities.* London: Macmillan.

Sperry, R. W. (1968). Hemisphere deconnection and unity in conscious awareness. *American Psychologist, 23,* 723–733.

Sperry, R. W. (1970). Cerebral dominance in perception. In F. A. Young & D. B. Lindsley (Eds.), *Early experience and visual information processing in perceptual and reading disorders* (pp. 167–178). Washington, DC: National Academy of Sciences.

Sperry, R. W. (1974). Lateral specialization in the surgically separated hemispheres. In F. O. Schmitt & F. G. Worden (Eds.), *The neurosciences: Third study program.* Cambridge, MA: MIT Press.

Sperry, R. W., Gazzaniga, M. S., & Bogan, J. E. (1969). Interhemispheric relationships: The neocortical commissures: Syndromes of hemispheric disconnection. In P. Vinken & G. W. Bruyn (Eds.), *Handbook of clinical neurology.* New York: Wiley-Interscience.

Spitz, H. H. (1983). Intratest and interest reliability and stability of the WISC, WISC-R, and WAIS full scale IQs in a mentally retarded population. *Journal of Special Education, 17,* 69–80.

Spitz, H. H. (1986a). Disparities in mentally retarded persons' IQs derived from different intelligence tests. *American Journal of Mental Deficiency, 90,* 588–591.

Spitz, H. H. (1986b). *The raising of intelligence.* Hillsdale, NJ: Erlbaum.

Spitz, H. H. (1988). Inverse relationship between the WISC-R/WAIS-R score disparity and IQ level in the lower range of intelligence. *American Journal of Mental Deficiency, 92,* 376–378.

Springer, S. P., & Deutsch, G. (1981). *Left brain, right brain.* San Francisco: Freeman.

Spruill, J. (1988). Two types of tables for use with the Stanford-Binet Intelligence Scale: Fourth Edition. *Journal of Psychoeducational Assessment, 6,* 78–86.

Stanovich, K. E. (1986). Cognitive processes and the reading problems of learning disabled children: Evaluating the assumption of specificity. In J. Torgesen & B. Wong (Eds.), *Psychological and educational perspectives on learning disabilities.* New York: Academic Press.

Starr, R. W. (1983). Split-brain IQ test. *Omni, 5*(10), 35.

Staton, R. D., Wilson, H., & Brumback, R. A. (1981). Cognitive improvement associated with tricyclic antidepressant treatment of childhood major depressive illness. *Perceptual and Motor Skills, 53,* 219–234.

Stern, W. (1914). *The psychological methods for testing intelligence.* Baltimore, MD: Warwick & York.

Sternberg, R. J. (1984). The Kaufman Assessment Battery for Children: An information-processing analysis and critique. *Journal of Special Education, 18,* 269–279.

Sternberg, R. (1985). Cognitive approaches to intelligence. In B. B. Wolman (Ed.), *Handbook of intelligence* (pp. 59–117). New York: Wiley.

Sternberg, R. J. (1985). *Beyond IQ: A triarchic theory of intelligence.* London: Cambridge University Press.

Sternberg, R. J. (1987). Synopsis of a triarchic theory of human intelligence. In S. H. Irvine & S. E. Newstead (Eds.), *Intelligence and cognition: Contemporary frames of reference* (pp. 141–175). Boston: Martinus Nijhoff.

Sternberg, R. J., & Detterman, D. K. (1986). *What is intelligence? Contemporary viewpoints on its nature and definition.* Norwood, NJ: Ablex.

Stevenson, H. W., Stigler, J. W., Lee, S., Lucker, G. W., Kitamura, S., & Hsu, C. (1985). Cognitive performance and academic achievement of Japanese, Chinese, and American children. *Child Development, 56,* 718–734.

Street, R. F. (1931). A gestalt completion test. *Contributions to Education.* New York: Bureau of Publications, Teachers College, Columbia University.

Stutsman, R. (1931). *Merrill-Palmer scale of mental tests.* Chicago: Stoelting.

Sue, S., & Abe, J. (1988). *Predictors of academic achievement among Asian American and white students* (Report No. 88-11). New York: College Entrance Examination Board.

Sue, S., & Okazaki, S. (1990). Asian-American educational achievements: A phenomenon in search of an explanation. *American Psychologist, 45,* 913–920.

Sullivan, P. M., & Burley, S. K. (1990). Mental testing of the hearing-impaired child. In C. R. Reynolds & R. W. Kamphaus (Eds.), *Handbook of psychological and educational assessment of children.* New York: Guilford.

Swanson, H. L., Brandenbury-Ayers, S., & Wallace, S. (1989). Construct validity of the K-ABC with gifted children. *Journal of Special Education, 23*(10), 342–352.

Szatmari, P., Offord, D. R., & Boyle, M. H. (1989). Ontario child health study: Prevalence of attention deficit disorder with hyperactivity. *Journal of Child Psychology and Psychiatry, 2,* 219–230.

Tabachnick, B. G. (1979). Test scatter on the WISC-R. *Journal of Learning Disabilities, 12,* 626–628.

Tallent, N. (1988). *Psychological report writing* (3rd ed.). Englewood Cliffs, NJ: Prentice-Hall.

Tarnopol, L., & Tarnopol, M. (1977). Introduction to neuropsychology. In L. Tarnopol & M. Tarnopol (Eds.), *Brain function and reading disabilities.* Baltimore, MD: University Park Press.

Taylor, R. L., Slocumb, P. R., & O'Neill, J. (1979). A short form of the McCarthy Scales of Children's Abilities: Methodological and clinical applications. *Psychology in the Schools, 16,* 347–350.

Teare, J. F., & Thompson, R. W. (1982). Concurrent validity of the Perkins-Binet Tests of Intelligence for the Blind. *Journal of Visual Impairment and Blindness, 76,* 279–280.

Teeter, P. A. (1984). Cross validation of the factor structure of the McCarthy Scales for kindergarten children. *Psychology in the Schools, 21,* 158–164.

Teglasi, H. (1983). Report of a psychological assessment in a school setting. *Psychology in the Schools, 20,* 466–479.

Telzrow, C. F. (1990). Does PASS pass the test? A critique of the DAS-Naglieri Cognitive Assessment System. *Journal of Psychoeducational Assessment, 8,* 344–355.

Telzrow, C. F., Century, E., Harris, B., & Redmond, C. (1985, April). *Relationship between neuropsychological processing models and dyslexia subtypes.* Paper presented at the National Association of School Psychologists, Las Vegas, NV.

Telzrow, C. F., Redmond, C., & Zimmerman, B. (1984, October). *Dyslexic subtypes: A comparison of the Bannatyne, Boder, and Kaufman models.* Paper presented at the meeting of the National Academy of Neuropsychologists, San Diego, CA.

Terman, L. M. (1916). *The measurement of intelligence.* Cambridge, MA: Riverside Press.

Terman, L. M., & Merrill, M. A. (1960). *Stanford-Binet intelligence scale.* Boston: Houghton Mifflin.

Terman, L., & Merrill, M. (1973). *Technical manual for the Stanford-Binet Intelligence Scale: 1972 norms edition.* Boston: Houghton Mifflin.

Thorndike, E. L., Bregman, E. O., Cobb, M. V., Woodyard, E. (1927). *The measurement of intelligence.* New York: Columbia University, Teachers College.

Thorndike, R. L. (1971). Concepts of culture-fairness. *Journal of Educational Measurement, 8,* 63–70.

Thorndike, R. L., & Hagen, E. P. (1977). *Measurement and evaluation in psychology and education* (4th ed.). New York: Wiley.

Thorndike, R. L., Hagen, E. P., & Sattler, J. M. (1986).

Technical manual for the Stanford-Binet Intelligence Scale: Fourth Edition. Chicago: Riverside.

Thorndike, R. M. (1990). Would the real factors of the Stanford-Binet Fourth Edition please come forward? *Journal of Psychoeducational Assessment, 8,* 412–435.

Thorndike, R. M., & Lohman, D. F. (1990). *A century of ability testing.* Chicago: Riverside.

Thurstone, L. L. (1938). *Primary mental abilities.* Chicago: Chicago University Press.

Thurstone, T. W. (1951). Primary mental abilities of children. In J. J. Jenkins & D. G. Paterson (Eds.), *Studies in individual differences: The search for intelligence* (pp. 527–533). New York: Appleton-Century-Crofts. (Reprinted from *Educational and Psychological Measurement,* 1941, *1,* 105–116.)

Thurstone, L. L., & Thurstone, T. (1941). *The Chicago tests of primary mental abilities.* Chicago: Science Research Associates.

Tomlinson-Keasey, C., & Clarkson-Smith, L. (1980, February). *What develops in hemispheric specialization?* Paper presented at the meeting of the International Neuropsychological Society, San Francisco.

Torrance, E. P. (1965). *Rewarding creative behavior.* Englewood Cliffs, NJ: Prentice-Hall.

Tramontana, M. G., & Hooper, S. R. (1989). Neuropsychology of child psychopathology. In C. R. Reynolds & E. Fletcher-Janzen (Eds.), *Handbook of clinical child neuropsychology.* New York: Plenum.

Tuma, J. M., & Elbert, J. C. (1990). Critical issues and current practice in personality assessment of children. In C. R. Reynolds & R. W. Kamphaus (Eds.), *Handbook of psychological and educational assessment of children: Personality, behavior, and context.* New York: Guilford.

Tupper, D. E. (1986). Neuropsychological screening and soft signs. In J. E. Obrzut & G. W. Hynd (Eds.), *Child neuropsychology, Volume 2, Clinical practice.* Orlando, FL: Academic Press.

Ulissi, S. M., Brice, P. J., & Gibbons, S. (1985, April). *The use of the Kaufman Assessment Battery for Children with the hearing impaired.* Paper presented at the meeting of the National Association of School Psychologists, Las Vegas, NV.

Uzgiris, I. C., & Hunt, J. McV. (1989). *Assessment in infancy: Ordinal scales of psychological development.* Urbana: University of Illinois Press.

Valencia, R. R. (1985). Concurrent validity of the Kaufman Assessment Battery for Children in a sample of Mexican-American children. *Educational and Psychological Measurement, 44,* 365–372.

Valencia, R. R. (1990). Clinical assessment of young children with the McCarthy Scales of Children's Abilities. In C. R. Reynolds & R. W. Kamphaus (Eds.), *Handbook of psychological and educational assessment of children: Intelligence and achievement.* New York: Guilford.

Valencia, R. R., & Rankin, R. (1986). Factor analysis of the K-ABC for groups of Anglo and Mexican-American children. *Journal of Educational Measurement, 23,* 209–219.

Valsiner, J. (1984). Conceptualizing intelligence: From an internal static attribution to the study of the process structure of organism-environment relationships. *International Journal of Psychology, 19,* 363–389.

Vance, H. B., & Wallbrown, F. H. (1978). The structure of intelligence for black children: A hierarchical approach. *Psychological Record, 28,* 31–39.

Vance, H. B., Fuller, G. B., & Ellis, R. (1983). Discriminant function analysis of LD/BD children scores on the WISC-R. *Journal of Clinical Psychology, 39*(5), 749–753.

Vance, B., Hankins, N., & Brown, N. (1986). The relationship among the Test of Nonverbal Intelligence, Ammons' Quick Test, and Wechsler Intelligence Scale for Children-Revised. *Diagnostique, 12*(1), 47–52.

Vance, B., Kitson, D., & Singer, M. (1983). Further investigation of comparability of the WISC-R and PPVT-R for children and youth referred for psychological services. *Psychology in the Schools, 20,* 307–310.

Van den Berg, A. R. (1986). *The problems of measuring intelligence in a heterogeneous society and possible solutions to some of these problems.* Pretoria, IL: Institute for Psychological and Edumetric Research, Human Sciences Research Council.

Vandenberg, S. G., & Vogler, G. P. (1985). Genetic determinants of intelligence. In B. B. Wolman (Ed.), *Handbook of intelligence: Theories, research and applications.* New York: Wiley.

Vernon, P. A. (1985). Individual differences in general cognitive ability. In L. C. Hartlage & C. F. Telzrow (Eds.), *The neuropsychology of individual differences.* New York: Plenum.

Vernon, P. E. (1950). *The structure of human abilities.* New York: Wiley.

Vernon, P. E. (1979). *Intelligence: Heredity and environment.* San Francisco: Freeman.

Vernon, P. E. (1984). Intelligence, cognitive styles, and brain lateralization. *International Journal of Psychology, 19,* 435–455.

Vygotsky, L. S. (1978). *Mind in society* (M. Cole, V. John-Steiner, S. Scribner, & E. Souberman, Eds.). Cambridge, MA: Harvard University Press.

Wada, J., Clarke, R., & Hamm, A. (1975). Cerebral hemisphere asymmetry in humans. *Archives of Neurology, 37,* 234–246.

Wallbrown, F. H., Blaha, J., & Wherry, R. J. (1973). The hierarchical factor structure of the Wechsler Preschool and Primary Scale of Intelligence. *Journal of Consulting and Clinical Psychology, 41,* 356–362.

Wallbrown, F., Blaha, J., Wallbrown, J., & Engin, A. (1975). The hierarchical factor structure of the Wechsler Intelligence Scale for Children-Revised. *Journal of Psychology, 89,* 223–235.

Watson, B. U. (1983). Test-retest stability of the Hiskey-Nebraska Test of Learning Aptitude in a sample of hearing-impaired children and adolescents. *Journal of Speech and Hearing Disorders, 48,* 145–149.

Watson, B. U., & Goldgar, D. E. (1985). A note on the use of the Hiskey-Nebraska Test of Learning Aptitude with deaf children. *Language, Speech, and Hearing Services in Schools, 16,* 53–57.

Wechsler, D. (1952). *The range of human capacities.* Baltimore, MD: Williams & Wilkins.

Wechsler, D. (1958). *The measurement and appraisal of adult intelligence* (4th ed.). Baltimore, MD: Williams & Wilkins.

Wechsler, D. (1974). *Manual for the Wechsler Intelligence Scale for Children-Revised (WISC-R).* New York. The Psychological Corporation.

Wechsler, D. (1981). *Manual for the Wechsler Adult Intelligence Scale-Revised (WAIS-R).* New York: The Psychological Corporation.

Wechsler, D. (1991). *Wechler intelligence scale for children-Third edition: Manual.* New York: The Psychological Corporation.

Weinberg, R. A. (1989). Intelligence and IQ: Landmark issues and great debates. *American Psychologist, 44*(2), 98–104.

Weiner, P. S. (1971). Stability and validity of two measures of intelligence used with children whose language development is delayed. *Journal of Speech and Hearing Research, 14,* 254–261.

Weiss, B., & Weisz, J. R. (1986). General cognitive deficits: Mental retardation. In R. T. Brown & C. R. Reynolds (Eds.), *Psychological perspectives on childhood exceptionality.* New York: Wiley.

Weiss, L. G. (1991, December). WISC-III: The revision of the WISC-R. *Child Assessment News,* pp. 1, 9.

Wesman, A. G. (1968). Intelligent testing. *American Psychologist, 23,* 267–274.

West, S. (1982). A smarter test for intelligence? *Science, 82,* 3(9), 14.

Wherry, R. J., & Wherry, R. J., Jr. (1969). WHEWH program. In R. J. Wherry (Ed.), *Psychology department computer programs.* Columbus: Ohio State University, Department of Psychology.

Whitworth, R. H., & Chrisman, S. B. (1987). Validation of the Kaufman Assessment Battery for Children comparing Anglo and Mexican-American preschoolers. *Educational and Psychological Measurement, 47,* 695–702.

Wiener, J. (1985). Teachers' comprehension of psychological reports. *Psychology in the Schools, 22,* 60–64.

Wiener, J., & Kohler, S. (1986). Parents' comprehension of psychological reports. *Psychology in the Schools, 23,* 265–270.

Willson, V. L., & Reynolds, C. R. (1984). Regression effects on part scores based on whole-score selected samples. *Educational and Psychological Measurement, 44,* 95–99.

Willson, V. L., Reynolds, C. R., Chatman, S. P., & Kaufman, A. S. (1985). Confirmatory analysis of simultaneous, sequential, and achievement factors on the K-ABC at 11 age levels ranging from 2½ to 12½ years. *Journal of School Psychology, 23,* 261–269.

Winick, M., Meyer, K., & Harris, R. C. (1975). Malnutrition and environmental enrichment by early adoption. *Science, 190,* 1173–1175.

Wisniewski, J. J., & Naglieri, J. A. (1989). Validity of the Draw A Person: A Quantitative Scoring System with the WISC-R. *Journal of Psychoeducational Assessment, 7,* 346–351.

Wissler, C. (1901). The correlation of mental and physical tests. *Psychological Review Monograph Supplement, 3,* No. 6.

Witmer, L. (1911). *The special class for backward children.* Philadelphia: The Psychological Clinic Press.

Wittrock, M. C. (1980). *The brain and psychology.* New York: Academic Press.

Witt, J. C., & Gresham, F. M. (1985). Review of Wechsler Intelligence Scale of Children-Revised. In J. V. Mitchell (Ed.), *The ninth mental measurement yearbook* (vol. 2) (pp. 1715–1716). Lincoln, NE: Buros Institute of Mental Measurements.

Wolf, T. H. (1961). An individual who made a difference. *American Psychologist, 16,* 245–248.

Wolf, T. H. (1964). Alfred Binet: A time of crisis. *American Psychologist, 19,* 762–771.

Wolf, T. H. (1966). Intuition and experiment: Alfred Binet's first efforts in child psychology. *Journal of History of Behavioral Sciences, 2,* 233–239.

Wolman, B. (1985). *Handbook of intelligence.* New York: Wiley-Interscience.

Woodcock, R. W. (1984). A response to some questions raised about the Woodcock-Johnson 1. The mean score discrepancy issue. *School Psychology Review, 13*(3), 342–354.

Woodcock, R. W. (1990). Theoretical foundations of the WJ-R Measures of Cognitive Ability. *Journal of Psychoeducational Assessment, 8,* 231–258.

Woodcock, R. W., & Johnson, M. B. (1977). *Woodcock-Johnson psychoeducational battery.* Allen, TX: DLM Teaching Resources.

Woodcock, R. W., & Johnson, M. B. (1989). *Woodcock-Johnson psycho-educational battery-revised.* Allen, TX: DLM Teaching Resources.

Woodcock, R. W., & Mather, N. (1989). WJ-R Tests of Cognitive Ability-Standard and Supplemental Batteries: Examiner's manual. In R. W. Woodcock & M. B. Johnson, *Woodcock-Johnson psycho-educational battery-revised.* Allen, TX: DLM Teaching Resources.

WPPSI-R poll results. (1991, October). *Child Assessment News,* p. 11.

Wright, J. S. (1967). Opinion, *Hobson v. Hansen. Federal Supplement 269,* 401–510.

Ysseldyke, J, E. (1990). Goodness of fit of the Woodcock-Johnson Psycho-Educational Battery-Revised to the Horn-Cattell Gf-Gc theory. *Journal of Psychoeducational Assessment, 8,* 268–275.

Zajonc, R. B., & Marcus, G. B. (1975). Birth order and intellectual development. *Psychological Review, 82,* 74–88.

Zimmerman, I. L., & Woo-Sam, J. M. (1967). Reporting results. In A. J. Glasser & I. L. Zimmerman (Eds.), *Clinical interpretation of the Wechsler Intelligence Scale for Children (WISC).* New York: Grune & Stratton.

Zimmerman, I. L., & Woo-Sam, J. M. (1985). Clinical applications. In B. B. Wolman (Ed.), *Handbook of intelligence: Theories, measurements, and applications* (pp. 873–898). New York: Wiley.

Zins, J. E., & Barnett, D. W. (1983). The Kaufman Assessment Battery for Children and school achievement: A validity study. *Journal of Psychoeducational Assessment, 1,* 235–241.

Zins, J. E., & Barnett, D. W. (1984). A validity study of the K-ABC, the WISC-R, and the Stanford-Binet with non-referred children. *Journal of School Psychology, 22,* 369–371.

Zuckerman, M. (1990). Some dubious premises in research and theory on racial differences: Scientific, social, and ethical issues. *American Psychologist, 45,* 1297–1303.

Author Index